A LILY AMONG THE THORNS

JB JOSSEY-BASS

A LILY AMONG THE THORNS

Imagining a New Christian Sexuality

Miguel A. De La Torre

John Wiley & Sons, Inc.

Published by Jossey-Bass
A Wiley Imprint
989 Market Street, San Francisco, CA 94103-1741 www.josseybass.com

Jossey-Bass books and products are available through most bookstores. To contact Jossey-Bass directly call our Customer Care Department within the U.S. at 800-956-7739, outside the U.S. at 317-572-3986, or fax 317-572-4002.

Jossey-Bass also publishes its books in a variety of electronic formats. Some content that appears in print may not be available in electronic books.

Library of Congress Cataloging-in-Publication Data

De La Torre, Miguel A.
A lily among the thorns : imagining a new Christian sexuality/Miguel A. De La Torre.
    p. cm.
Includes bibliographical references (p.) and index.
  ISBN-13: 978-0-7879-8146-4 (cloth)
  ISBN-10: 0-7879-8146-X (cloth)
  1. Sex–Religious aspects–Christianity. 2. Sex–Biblical teaching. I. Title
  BT708.D45 2007
  241'.66–dc22   2006036607

Printed in the United States of America
FIRST EDITION
HB Printing   10 9 8 7 6 5 4 3 2 1

To My Beloved
As a lily among thorns,
so is my lover among other women.
(Song of Songs 2:2)

CONTENTS

A NOTE OF THANKS

This book is the product of more than one person, as many have joined me in this dialogue, raising questions and contributing comments. I specifically wish to thank the fifteen students who took an upper-class course I taught at my previous academic institution, titled "The Exotic Bible." Many of the concepts and ideas that appear in this book were first discussed during our Tuesday and Thursday seminar. I am also grateful to the six graduate students at my present institution who enrolled in a summer seminar in which portions of this manuscript were read and debated. I am deeply grateful to Catherine Craddock of Jossey-Bass, who read the entire first draft of this book and provided invaluable editorial suggestions. And special thanks are due to the publishing house editor, Sheryl Fullerton, for her support during the process of taking the book from concept to finished manuscript. Finally, I am grateful to my beloved, who read this text as it was being written, constantly challenging me to rethink and more deeply explore the issue of sexuality.

PREFACE

DURING POLITICAL CAMPAIGNS, politicians can make the most outrageous promises to potential voters—everything from filling all the street potholes, to ending poverty, to putting "a chicken in every pot and a car in every garage." But it was Italy's Prime Minister Silvio Berlusconi, age sixty-nine, who made what must be one of the most interesting campaign promises in recent memory. Trailing in the polls in his 2006 reelection campaign, the prime minister, who had been married for sixteen years, publicly announced a vow he made to a priest. At a political rally he proclaimed: "I promise you two and a half months of complete sexual abstinence until April 9 [election day] . . . I'll try not to let you down." For Berlusconi's self-sacrifice, Rev. Pusceddu anointed him as the only defender of family values in Italy.[1] Unfortunately for Berlusconi, abstinence was not enough for him to win his reelection. Nevertheless, this unique campaign promise, and the minister's response, reveal a disturbing undercurrent in Western Christianity's understanding of sexuality.

Why is sexual abstinence linked to family values? The prevalent ascetic tradition within Christianity has taught us to associate sexual abstinence with purity and holiness. Many Christians, believing that there is a moral degradation of our society and that it is the result of excessive sexual promiscuity, recoil at the concept of sacred sexuality or the possibility of an ethics based on sex. These Christians see sexual desire as both powerful and dangerous, and they believe that lack of sexual control has led to the present crises of skyrocketing divorce rates and broken families.

In its campaign against sexual immorality, the U.S. Religious Right reduces sex to an act involving nothing more than the genitals, with emphasis placed on who you have sex with and the sexual act itself, rather than defining relationships in which sex can and should occur. This prevailing attitude makes it difficult for committed Christians to openly discuss and explore sexual issues without appearing "dirty." What discussions exist are usually fear-driven: have sex, it is said, and you'll die of AIDS, your life will be over because you'll get pregnant, you'll catch some sexually transmitted disease that will ruin the rest of your life; if you are female, you'll become a whore, never be able to attract the love of a godly man, and suffer being shamed and shunned by your friends, family, church, and community.

Generally speaking, many conservatives view sexual desire as dangerous. To further their crusade for the reining in of sex, they preach sermons, host rallies, and enact legislation against sexual education in our public schools and "sexual perversions" like homosexuality. Their answer for all sexual issues is celibacy when single and monogamous heterosexual sex in marriage. Several conservative organizations believe that public policies and legislation are imperative to protect society from the destructive nature of an unchecked sexuality.

Many liberals, on the other hand, seek to privatize sexuality by reducing it to something personal, kept in the seclusion of the bedroom. What occurs between two or more consenting adults is no one else's concern, they say; after all, sex is simply a biological function, one that is shared with other animals. As a bodily function like eating, sexuality, they argue, should require few, if any, moral considerations as long as the participants are consenting adults. The biblical text becomes an ancient document with little or no influence. On matters of sexuality, one's reason and experiences, rather than the Bible, become guides toward a utilitarian-type approach. Live and let live. If no one is hurt, and pleasure can be derived and maximized, then go ahead and participate in whatever sexual encounter you desire.

Toward a New Sexual Ethos

Neither the conservative nor the liberal view toward sex in the United States is adequate. Both are rooted in the dominant hyperindividualist U.S. culture, and as such, they share common assumptions and presuppositions about sexuality. For example, both conservatives and liberals tend to reduce the Christian faith to a personal piety that dictates which acts are and are not permissible for the individual. Accordingly, sex falls under the private rather than the communal. But although sex may indeed be private, it does have public, social, and cultural ramifications that cannot be ignored. We need a new way of approaching Christian sexuality. But how does one construct a sexual ethic within a conservative religious atmosphere that usually equates sex with sin and a liberal secularized society in which sexual images are ubiquitous in film and television, on our advertising billboards, and on the Internet?

In this book I will search the Christian Scripture, in spite of their patriarchal tendencies, to find biblically based guidelines and principles for developing an ethical sexual lifestyle that is aware of how sexism, homophobia, and even racism and classism have influenced past and current conversations on sexual ethics. Avoiding either a conservative or a liberal approach to sexual ethics, this book will attempt a *liberative* methodology; that is, sexual ethics influenced by the viewpoint of those who reside on the margins of power and privilege. To use a liberative methodology means to explore sexual ethics by (1) listening to the stories of those voices that are usually ignored, the voices of those abused by the prevailing sexual norms; (2) paying close attention to who benefits, either through power or privilege, from the present normative sexual practices of society; and (3) challenging sexual norms that prevent individuals from living the abundant life promised to them by Christ (John 10:10). I believe that social injustices pervert human relationships and distort any definition or concept of love. Because justice-making (the fostering of nonoppressive structures) is an action done in obedience to unconditional love (loving the other as yourself), any sexual ethic that ignores the communal ramification of healthy sexual relationships will fall short of offering an alternative to either the Religious Right's stringent purity code or the hyperliberal view of "anything goes." For sex to be liberating, sexuality must be understood as an issue of justice. Great lovemaking is needed for justice-making to take place, and vice versa.

From Divisiveness to Liberation

Postmodern philosopher Michel Foucault (1926–84) asserts that for our present culture, sex has become "more important than our souls, more important almost than our life."[2] Although Moses, the prophets, Jesus, and Paul did not make sexuality the focal point of their teachings, issues involving sexuality are currently tearing apart Christian denominations and individual churches. Believers are no longer divided over issues of doctrine, but rather over issues concerning sex. Once upon a time, questions about such issues as transubstantiation (Christ present within the Eucharist) tore the church apart, spawning new denominations. Today, such doctrinal issues have been replaced by questions concerning women's autonomy and the type of sex one can engage in. Few sitting in the pews properly know their denomination's Christological doctrines, but they do know where their church stands on premarital sex, homosexuality, and ordination of women.

Sidetracked by these divisive issues and afraid to tackle the topic of sexual ethics head-on, Christians have failed to seriously and openly discuss sexuality as an integral part of our humanity. Quite simply, they run the risk of making their perspective on the topic irrelevant. This need not be the case. Christians can be at the forefront of this discussion. The Bible can provide guidance for human sexuality and the multiple social and political issues associated with sexual practices. After all, if God is love, what can teach us humans more about the nature of God than human love?

Sexuality is part of our shared experience as a community, contributing to its ethos and literally to its continued survival. Sex is an important issue that everyone must face and about which the Bible has something exceptionally important to say. This book's focus will be on developing frameworks for healthy models that foster intimacy and vulnerability for a disjointed and at times oppressive society. The church's traditionally negative attitudes toward sex in general—and, by extension, toward women, people of color, and gays in particular—have made it difficult, if not impossible, to create biblically based and just sexual ethics. But when the biblical text is read from the viewpoint of the marginalized in society, specifically those who are normally oppressed due to their gender or sexual orientation, preconceived notions about Christianity and sex get turned on their heads. Reading from these margins of power forces the reader to move beyond a biblical interpretation that merely reflects their own opinions about sexuality. To read from the margins provides a liberating approach to dealing with issues of sexuality.

An Autobiographical Note

A word about my social location as the author of this book is needed from the outset. The contribution being made by ethicists from marginalized communities include autobiographical elements so as to avoid creating a lifeless ethical framework. The methodological inclusion of one's story powerfully connects ethical theory with reality. Yet for some scholars, considering the interpreter's identity or social location somewhat adulterates the intended meaning of scholarship. They insist that revealing a person's identity interferes with the job of ascertaining a so-called "objective" rendering. I maintain that there is no such thing as objectivity. All ethical reflections are subjective. Only the subjective ethical reflections of those within the dominant culture are labeled *objective*. The approach employed in this book challenges the assumption that ethics—in this case, sexual ethics—can be understood apart from what the interpreter brings to the analysis. Hence, the analysis conducted in this book is autobiographically influenced, even though academia at times considers the hermeneutics of the self as unscholarly. I approach the task of understanding sexual ethics via my own sexual experiences, specifically as a heterosexual Latino man who has been married for nineteen years and is blessed with children. I also write as a committed Christian who takes Scripture seriously, yet remains keenly aware of how oppressive ideologies have been fused and confused with the Christian faith.

When I first thought of writing this book, I deeply considered who would be my audience. The book will address conservative Christians in the hopes of presenting a more liberative sexual ethics rooted within the biblical text. I also address liberal Christians, hoping to elucidate the biblical and historical roots of the conservative Christian's world view on sexuality. The result, I hope, will be to provide a better framework from which diverse views on sexual ethics can engage in conversation. I have also attempted to develop a new way to discuss the important issues of sexuality with our youth. As I wrote, I had my two teenage children in mind, hoping to share with them the biblical principles their mother and I have employed to develop a deep familial relationship. Obviously, not all readers will be a part of this audience, or want to be. And that is fine. But I must remain faithful to my chosen audience, and it is to them, as personified by my own children, that I write this book.

INTRODUCTION

DURING CREATION, God formed humans with the capacity to engage in sexual activity. Not only was this among the first gifts given to humans by God, it was a gift God declared "good" (Genesis 1:31). But to say that sex is good is an understatement. Sex is great! It is great because it fosters intimacy within relationships that serve as the bases for healthy and just communities. As such, the first words God addresses to humans, the very first instructions given—before even forbidding them to eat the fruit from the tree of the knowledge of good and evil—were to engage in sexual relationships. God instructs this new human creation to "be fruitful and multiply" (Genesis 1:28), a goal that can only be achieved through copulation. This is not to conclude that reproduction is sex's ultimate purpose, for although sex is the source for future generations, it is also the source of extreme pleasure. The task before us is to forge a biblical sexual ethics that captures the pleasures of sex.

Reading the Bible Through Which Lens?

Any discourse on Christian sexual ethics is also a debate over biblical revelation and inspiration; specifically, how scriptural interpretations are formulated and used. Although there are many theories, the basic question is whether the Bible consists of God's actual words as dictated to human secretaries or the testimony of believers who witnessed God's movement in their specific time and place. If the latter is true, could God's revelation be misconstrued due to the prevalent existing social structures of the time—social structures that accepted polygamy, genocide, or slavery without any qualms? The question we must wrestle with is whether the Bible itself supports patriarchy, or rather that the authors of the text, as members of an unquestioning male-centered social order, simply presumed their own gender-based social structures as normative?

Those with a sense of how the Bible has historically been used to foster oppressive structures voice concern about returning to some romanticized pristine illusion of biblical times. There is a keen awareness of how the Bible has been and continues to be used to justify all forms of oppressive structures. Following God's biblical call to evangelize the heathens and fulfill the United States' "manifest destiny," European settlers decimated the indigenous people. Based on the Word of God, the townspeople of Salem, Massachusetts, charged independent-thinking women as witches and burned them alive. Following God's ordained order for the universe as laid out in the Bible, European colonists kidnapped, raped, enslaved, and murdered Africans. Even now Americans in predominately white suburbia offer thanksgiving to God for how they are blessed, continuing to ignore how their riches are maintained at the expense of the black and brown urban centers they surround. Maintaining God's scriptural command that men are to rule over women, men denied them the right to vote, and even today women are paid a fraction on the dollar for the same work done by men. And when the Reverend Martin Luther King Jr. voiced the call for freedom and liberation to flow like living water, most white churches stood against someone who was seen at the time as an outside agitator, because the desegregation he advocated contradicted how they had been taught to read the Bible.

I do not question the good intentions of those wishing to return to a more traditional and literal interpretation of the biblical text, but I do wonder if they realize the full ramifications. Furthermore, as the spiritual heirs of those who have historically used the Bible to sustain and justify oppressive structures, they continue to be responsible for much of the misery suffered on the margins of society today, despite their good intentions.

Though we do not want to admit it, we all read biblical texts selectively. All of us come to the Bible with a specific life story and read our personal biases into the text. Our social location influences how we interpret Scripture, and the biblical interpretations we construct—which usually justify lifestyles beneficial to us—can contradict the very essence of the Gospel message. As we all well know, the Bible has historically been used to justify atrocities like genocide, slavery, war, crusades, colonialism, economic plunder, and, of course, gender oppression. Bible verses have been quoted, sermons preached from pulpits, and theses written in theological academies to justify barbaric acts in the name of Jesus.

When it comes to sex, Christians are usually taught to begin with the Bible. Based on how the Bible is read, we arrive at a truth concerning sex—a truth that serves as the basis for establishing doctrine, which in turn creates church traditions. Once we articulate this truth, we derive moral actions in accordance with said truth. But what happens if the determined truth is based on an erroneous sexist premise? Usually, men who are accustomed to the privileges bestowed upon them by patriarchy read their sexist biases into the text. Likewise, the original writers of the text—rooted in the social customs, traditions, and laws of their time—recounted God's revelation to humanity from the patriarchal framework in which they were embedded. The truth is thus tainted. What is determined to be the revelatory biblical mandate merges with the customs of the dominant male-centric culture. All too often we assume the prevalent existing patriarchy of the original text writers' times as God's will, or we read into the biblical text the prevalent sexism of our own culture, finding verses that justify the prevailing social power structures. Those who read the Bible from the position of authority must guard against misinterpreting scripture, consciously or unconsciously, as a way to protect their power and privilege. Passages that foster either sexism or patriarchy must be reinterpreted from the perspective of those marginalized by the text, or rejected in the same way we Christians today reject passages that foster genocide (Exodus 23:23), slavery (Numbers 31:25–47), wars of conquest (Joshua 1:10–18), and ethnic cleansing (Deuteronomy 19:1; 31:3–5). In addition to these passages, there are those establishing dietary, sacrificial, and cleansing laws that are no longer practiced or followed by today's modern (or postmodern) Christians. We no longer consider such passages authoritative, nor should we. Similarly, the biblical text can prove to be unreliable for establishing sexual ethics if we solely and uncritically begin (and end) with the text.

What if the reflections on the Bible conducted by American Christians in their search for truth were grounded in the experiences of those who are negatively impacted by the prevailing sexual mores? What if we were to use a lens for reading and interpreting the biblical text other than the one used by those in power? By consciously reading the text from the perspective of those who are oppressed by the present sexual mores, we can liberate the Bible from the patriarchal culture in which it is entrenched. Crucial, then, to any understanding of sexual ethics are the voices of those whom society seldom listens to—specifically women, people of color, and gays. By reading the Bible from the margins, we gain an opportunity to better grasp the scriptural message from those who not only know what it means to live in a hierarchical society, but also know what it means to live subject to those power structures.

How then can we read the biblical text as a source of liberation from oppressive structures? Jesus Christ said, "I came that they may have life, and have it abundantly" (John 10:10). (The reader should note that all scriptural quotations are the translation of the author from the original Hebrew or Greek.) The mission and purpose of Christ's coming was to abundantly provide life, both temporal and eternal. It is through this lens, rather than the lens of patriarchy so often used, that we must read and interpret the entire biblical text. In short, if a biblical interpretation prevents life from being lived abundantly by a segment of the population—or worse, if it brings death—then it is anti-Gospel. When a reading of the Bible relegates women to second-class status, reducing them from persons to sexual objects, then such interpretations cease to be biblically based. Only those interpretations that continue Christ's mission of empowering all elements of humanity—offering abundant life in the here and now, as opposed to just the hereafter—are biblically sound.

For example, during the antebellum period, white masters read the Bible through the lens that justified slavery and, by extension, their economic and race privilege. Thus, they focused on passages like "Slaves, obey your masters" (Ephesians 6:5) or the epistle to Philemon in which Paul returns a runaway slave to his master. To read the Bible from the margins is to read the Bible from the experience of slaves, who would have instead emphasized the Gospel message that the "truth has set us free" (John 8:32) or the Exodus story of a God who enters history so as to lead God's enslaved people to freedom. (For further information on how to read the biblical text from the perspective of the disenfranchised, see my *Reading the Bible from the Margins* [Maryknoll, NY: Orbis Books, 2002].)

Family Ties

God created sex, and it was a gift God declared to be good, but that doesn't mean that all forms of sex are holy or ethical. We will explore different types of sexual unions in Part Two, but for now I want to introduce a term that I will use throughout this book to describe the type of sexual union that best reflects the spiritual union one can expect to have with and in God. It is a union based on the biblical concept of the *familial*. Familial—that is, that which is of or common to a family—means relation-centered. As a corrective measure to the hyperindividuality salient in Euro-American western culture, the familial reinforces the family, not the individual, as the basic social unit of society.

Familial relationships are not limited to two individuals forming a marriage bond; they also encompass children, siblings, elders, and all others whom we term *extended family*. Thus, of course, not all familial relationships are sexual, nor should they be. For purposes of our discussion, however, we will solely focus on the particular familial relationship that constitutes a union of two adult individuals engaged in mutual sexual activity. In such unions, sex can be a binding part of that relationship, but it certainly is not, nor should it be, the central act of or purpose for the relationship. Still, when the familial relationship is consummated with sex, it does have the potential of becoming more potent than any type of platonic relationship based on friendship or comradeship. When two choose to become one flesh within a familial-based relationship, there is the opportunity to create intimacy, in which mutual sexual pleasure can be epitomized. This sexual pleasure is not only abundantly satisfying, but it also opens us up to the possibility of communing with God, a concept to be explored in greater detail in the third chapter of this book. At its best, sex creates a feeling of security, fulfillment, and ultimate love due to the process of two becoming one mind, one flesh, and one spirit.

Establishing a familial relationship does not necessarily signify marriage. Although church weddings are religious rituals and celebrations that publicly proclaim the existence of a familial relationship, these events do not create family—people do. Church weddings serve to bless a relationship. If a sexual relationship fails to meet the deepest physical, emotional, spiritual, and intellectual needs of both partners, there may be a marriage because a ritual occurred in a church building, but it is no family.

At its core, a familial relationship is based on mutual commitment. Recognizing this, one should be cautious in describing the markings of familial relationships in specific detail. There are no hard and fast rules with clear parameters; rather, a familial-based relationship is a fluid state, based on the reality and circumstances of those entering into the relationship.

Some may wonder why I shy away from the term *covenant*. Covenant is presented in the biblical text as an agreement between two entities, usually between two strangers. I am struck by the fact that covenants became necessary after sin entered the world (the Fall). The creation of Adam and Eve was to establish not a covenant, but a relationship, a family. Even though the concept of covenant, with its stipulations, blessings, and curses, is usually posed as an alternative to a contract, still, its biblical link to treaties continues to carry a sense of establishing a contractual relationships. Perhaps covenants are a necessity of a fallen world, but if we are striving to return to the wholeness of God's perfect will—as expressed in the Garden of Eden prior to the Fall—then seeing the union of two individuals as familial better captures the ideal relationship. Therefore, because familial relationships are not covenant agreements, we should hesitate to specifically spell out what its necessary terms are, recognizing that real life is seldom so clear-cut. That being said, we can still attempt to describe and better understand familial relationships by exploring their leading characteristics, which are mutual giving and vulnerability. Only by giving fully of oneself can there be hope of fully possessing another. And only by becoming totally vulnerable can one hope to gain full security.

Mutual Giving

The lovers exclaim, "My beloved is mine and I am my beloved's" (Song of Songs 2:16). A guiding principle of the Scripture is the placing of others first. Paul, in his letter to the Ephesians, writes, "Be subject to one another in the fear of the Lord" (Ephesians 5:21). Jesus is more direct, stating: "For whosoever among you would become great, let them be a servant to you. And whosoever among you desires to be first, let them be a slave to you, for even the Son of Humanity did not come to be served, but to serve" (Matthew 20:26–27). This principle is advocated even in a marriage relationship. Placing the spouse's needs before one's own is clearly spelled out in Paul's instructions to the Corinthians: "The wife is due kindness from her husband; likewise the wife to the husband. The wife does not have authority of her body but the husband does; likewise the husband does not have authority of his body but the wife does" (1 Corinthians 7:2–3). Of course, down through time most Christian men have skipped the last phrase of these verses, concentrating only on men having authority over women's bodies.

Does mutual giving mean forfeiting personal autonomy? One can give of oneself only if one has authority over one's own personhood. One cannot give that which one has no authority over. Mutual giving (rather than taking) presupposes autonomy. When a father gives his daughter to another man to marry, regardless of his daughter's wishes, he denies her the moral right to choose with whom she wishes to share her life, soul, spirit, and body. The newlyweds may be legally married, but because they lack a familial relationship in which both spouses have given freely of themselves, they are truly "living in sin." Only when the daughter and her beloved mutually and willingly give themselves to each other can they subvert the inherent patriarchy rooted in our culture and in common interpretations of the Bible and live in a sexual union that God truly desires for us—in other words, the gift of great sex that God gave us as our birthright.

If we are to dismantle patriarchal structures within relationships, then each partner must learn to give him- or herself freely to the other. By placing the needs of the other first, neither can be the head or Lord. Of course, such a mutual giving can be ripe for abuse by either party, more commonly by men. Thus, mutual giving can never mean the obliteration of the self. Autonomy must always be respected. And if self-giving leads to one's harm or destruction, then the relationship should be dissolved.

Total surrender, each to the other, cannot be achieved as long as one of the two parties is holding onto power over the partner. Herein lies the paradox that prevents so many from experiencing great sex. Our modern

Western concept of the superiority of reason (which has superseded the spirit) forces us to constantly remain in control, lest the passions of life conquer the supremacy of the mind. "How delicious is your love, more delicious than wine!" (4:10) is how the lovers of the Song of Songs describe it, for both great sex and fine wine are sweet to the taste but intoxicating in their effects. They go on to say, "Let us be drunk with love" (5:1). For them, to love is to be drunk with delicious wine, in which control is surrendered to passion. Like the lovers in the Song of Songs, we desire to love and be loved beyond our wildest dreams, but unlike them, we fear intoxication. Hence, the paradox of wanting to lose oneself in the beloved, yet not being able to do it fully due to the fear of losing oneself. Abandonment to love occurs in the messiness of real life, thus it should take place only in a safe environment, in which the fear of abuse and domination can be eliminated. This giving of oneself to the drunkenness of love can occur only if it is mutual, and a mutual giving in to the joys of mind-blowing, toe-curling passion is possible only when both parties feel the kind of safety and stability in the relationship that allows them to become totally vulnerable.

Vulnerability

And God said to the woman, "Your desire shall be for your husband, and he shall rule over you" (Genesis 3:16). So many men give a resounding "amen" after proclaiming this verse to be the word of the Lord. Right? As a man, I confess that early in my marriage I too was tempted by this verse, fantasizing about reciting it to my wife every morning. "Woman, you will desire me and I will rule, dominate, and be a master over you!" This verse justifies patriarchy, my supposed divine right as a man to be in authority over my woman or women. God, so the logic goes, ordained the proper arrangement in marriage to be one of domination and submission, with the man on top and the woman on the bottom, literally. And as long as I refuse to situate this verse within the overall story of creation, I could continue to use the biblical text to justify my sexism.

But what happens if we read the biblical text through a liberative lens—that is, as a text that calls for the dismantling of oppressive social structures so that all can participate in the abundant life offered by Christ? Then verses like these, misquoted for the sole purpose of maintaining male superiority, can lose their grip on our churches and culture. Genesis 3:16 is not God's will for familial relationships, but rather the first consequence of sin. God pronounced these words after the Fall, after sin entered the world and perverted all relationships. The great error and continued danger in interpreting Scripture through the lens of patriarchy is that we read the consequence of sin as if it were God's will and the divine norm for humanity. We must then ask, what was God's ordained model for relationships *prior* to the introduction of sin?

To answer this, we must turn our attention to the relationship between Adam and Eve prior to the Fall and to how it was described. We are told that "the man and woman were both naked, yet felt no shame" (Genesis 2:25). To the ancient Hebrew mind, *nakedness* was a metaphor for vulnerability. Picture this if you will: both the man and woman were standing stark naked before each other, totally vulnerable, yet they were not ashamed of their bodies.

Now, when I was a younger man in my twenties, trim and well-built, I too was not ashamed of my body. In fact, at the beach I would flaunt my physique by wearing a Speedo. However, as I approach a half-century of life, I am a bit more modest about my body. Gravity and too many second helpings of dessert make me so self-conscious that I have at times refused to remove my shirt at the beach. Yet when I am with my wife in the privacy of our home, I can stand before her, naked, and feel no shame whatsoever. Even though I cannot hide my sagging excess weight, stretch marks, wrinkles, and grayness, I can stand totally vulnerable and exposed to her gaze without fear of ridicule or abandonment. I stand before her not just physically naked, but also emotionally, intellectually, and psychologically naked. And the good news is that she can do likewise. We are able to stand fully transparent before each other, because for years, during good times and bad, we have created a familial relationship based on vulnerability. For only when two are totally vulnerable to each other and are able to stand naked—warts and all—are they truly free to fully share themselves with each other in body, spirit, and soul.

When sin entered the world, God proclaimed not what God's ultimate purpose for human relationships was, but *the result of what humans had done*. When declaring to the woman, "Your desire shall be for your husband, and he shall rule over you" (Genesis 3:16), God was explaining the consequence of sin—the establishment of oppressive power structures. Sin now existed, so the idea of being naked and feeling no shame was perverted by the establishment of male superiority. The original familial relationship established by God was replaced by the curse of patriarchal relationships. The curse led to the concept of and need for covenant.

To return to Eden for the purpose of implementing the type of vulnerability described in Genesis 2:25, we must turn away from the patriarchy established as sin's consequence. We must reject the curse of patriarchy that declares man as the head of the household. Familial relationships are an attempt to move beyond marriage as covenant toward creating a family-based relationship founded upon mutuality and vulnerability. This vision of sexual union becomes possible as we conform to the model provided for us in the familial relationship existing within the doctrine of the Trinity.

Trinity as a Model for Love

The model upon which the familial relationship is based is found within the theological concept of the Trinity. For many within the Euro-American culture, the concept of Trinity is an enigma, a cosmic puzzle to be solved. Trinity is a doctrine that points to the mystery that we call God—a mystery that, although beyond the comprehension of mere mortals like us, is crucial for defining the nature and essence of the Deity. In short, God is understood as one being in three, a mathematically contradictory assertion that many theologians have attempted to convince us is not really contradictory.

All too often, when we think of the Trinity we impose a hierarchal structure on the relationship within the Trinity. Many of us today conceive of the Father as reigning supreme, followed by the Son and trailed by the Holy Ghost. Yet Christian theologians agree almost unanimously that the Father, Son, and Spirit do not exist in a hierarchical relationship; rather, all three share equally in substance, power, and importance. Although historically many theologians from the dominant Eurocentric culture attempted to solve this mystery of how three can be one, several theologians of color, specifically from the Latino community, see the Trinity concept as a pattern for humanity to emulate. Rather than attempting to decipher the baffling concept of Trinity, theologians from the margins of society—specifically, early theologians of liberation—have contributed to the understanding of the Trinity symbol by focusing on the existing relationships among the Father, Son, and Holy Ghost.

"By understanding the Trinity in terms of communal relationships, those living at the margins of society cannot only find parallels with their experience, but can discover a sense of belonging as part of God's community," contemporary theologian Luis Pedraja reminds us. "To speak of the Trinity in terms of community means that we understand God as being relational in nature."[1] The Trinity reveals the character of God—a character based on the act of sharing, in which the internal relationship of the Deity is understood as being coequal in authority and power, because of the unconditional love—agape—which makes this sharing possible. God as *being in relationship* becomes a paradigm for sharing. This communal familial relationship within the Deity becomes the pattern for the relationships among humans, as well as between God and humans.

The concept of mutual sharing and vulnerability is not limited to the intra-relationship within the Trinity. We humans are also invited to share in this Divine relationship, becoming ". . . heirs with God and co-heirs with Christ" (Romans 8:17). Jesus explicitly invites us to become one with him as he is one with the Father (John 17:21–23). But to continue insisting on a Christian tradition in which God is perceived as some sort of dominator with full autonomy over humans not only nullifies the concept of free will, but also creates a pattern for human relationships in which men reserve for themselves the right to play such a god within their own marriages. Familial relationships that follow the Trinitarian model of sharing become hierarchy-free associations in which one does not stand superior to another. In its purest form, the familial relationship is a return to Eden, in which God's perfect will for how humans are to relate to each other existed. And how was this relationship described? It was a relationship in which both were naked but felt no shame (Genesis 2:25).

Returning to Eden, to the familial relationship that existed prior to the Fall, is a major focus of this book. In the chapters that follow, we will challenge a sexual ethics legitimized by those with power, a sexual ethics that has brought much oppression and misery to so many throughout history, specifically women. In a very real sense, the liberative sexual ethics this book introduces is the imagery of the "lily" referred to in the book's title. The "thorns" are the oppressive patriarchal structures that have emerged over the past two centuries of Christian thought. So with one eye on the Bible and the other on the experiences of those who have suffered due to sexual repression, I attempt to create a sexual ethics that is both faithful to the biblical mandate for justice and liberating for those trapped in relationships that suffocate and destroy sex that was originally designed to be great.

PART ONE

RESTORING GREAT SEX

I

LIBERATING THE FEMALE BODY

Every woman should be filled with shame by the thought that she is a woman.[1]

—Clement of Alexandria (c. 150–215)

God created man with a broad chest, not broad hips, so that in that part of him he can be wise; but that part out of which filth comes is small. In a woman, this is reversed. That is why she has much filth and little wisdom.[2]

—Martin Luther (1483–1546)

I listen to feminists and all these radical gals—most of them are failures. They've blown it. Some of them have been married, but they married some Casper Milquetoast who asked permission to go to the bathroom. These women just need a man in the house. That's all they need. Most of the feminists need a man to tell them what time of day it is and to lead them home. And they blew it and they're mad at all men. Feminists hate men. They're sexist. They hate men—that's their problem.[3]

— Jerry Falwell (1933–)

THE AWARD-WINNING HBO show *Sex and the City* chronicled the adventures of four women in their search for great sex and meaningful relationships. Carrie Bradshaw, the show's main character, attempted to capture in her columns the lives of those winning and losing in the game of love. Yet, in a very telling comment made during the series' nineteenth episode, Carrie confessed, "I write about sex, not love. What do I know about love?"

Carrie raised an interesting question. Are sex and love mutually exclusive? Can we experience great sex apart from the deep love developed through a familial relationship—a relationship based on mutual giving and vulnerability? Another of the show's characters, the uninhibited Samantha Jones, believed that we could. In fact, she questioned whether such familial relationships are even possible. During the fourteenth episode, she concluded, "Practically all the relationships I know are based on a foundation of lies and mutually accepted delusion."

Her words served as a stinging indictment of how she and many in the United States define relationships. It is sad that she did not see Christian-based relationships as offering much of an alternative. Could one of the foundational lies and mutually accepted delusions that Samantha alluded to have been how women have come to be perceived by our culture? And for those who are Christians, how has the biblical text contributed to that perception?

The way in which women have been perceived in Christendom has thwarted our ability to establish familial relationships that can lead to great sex. And although the ultimate goal of sexual ethics is not simply to have great sex, the creation of more intimate relationships that can lead to great sex is a highly desirable alternative to the consequences of oppressive relationships. But establishing familial relationships is hindered, in part, because of how women have been and continue to be perceived. Reading the scriptures through the lens of patriarchy has been used to justify advocating the male superiority as God ordained it. However, when we realize that these structures are a consequence of sin and not the order of things as ordained by God (as discussed in the Introduction), we can see that the ideal relationship is far from what historically has been perceived as God-sanctioned. Patriarchal structures prevent familial relationships—relationships based on mutual giving and vulnerability—from forming. Still, patriarchal tendencies are not solely limited to more conservative religious groups. Even within the more liberal mainstream society, women continue to be seen as less than men, especially when we consider that women are still not being paid the same as men for the same work performed at equal competency levels. For this reason, great, liberating sex can never take place until patriarchy in the relationship is dismantled and the full humanity of women is acknowledged in both the religious and the secular cultural spheres.

In this chapter, we turn our attention to the traditional role of women—specifically, how it is described within the biblical text and how that text has traditionally been interpreted. Although I recognize that most readers are already aware that patriarchy existed during biblical times and throughout the development of Christianity, I still think it is crucial to understand how the biblical text was and continues to be used to religiously justify the subordination of women. By reading the Bible with the eyes of those marginalized by the biblical text due to their gender, we can uncover how the overall structures during biblical times, as well as today, prevented women from realizing the full potential God created for them to live, even as they went about their lives maintaining a household, singing and laughing, falling in love, raising children, growing old, and dying in peace. By exploring how the Bible is read through the lens of patriarchy, we can begin to fully understand why Christian leaders are still determined to prevent women from fulfilling and performing certain roles in society.

In God's Image

If I were to ask readers to close their eyes and imagine what God looks like, most would picture a male body. Maybe the image that would come to mind is something similar to Michelangelo's renowned mural *The Creation of Adam* (1512) in the Sistine Chapel, in which God is illustrated as an old but well-built white man with a flowing white beard. Eurocentric art has taught, normalized, and legitimized a white male image of God. And it is this image of God that justifies patriarchy and influences a sexual ethics detrimental to women. No discussion concerning sexual ethics can take place until we first debunk God's purported male gender.

Most of us refer to God as a "He" without giving it a second thought because we construct "Him" in our minds as male. Yet the biblical text teaches us that when humans were created, they were formed in the very image of God. According to the first creation story found in Genesis 1:27: "God created *adam* in God's image, in God's image God created him, male and female God created them." Most Bibles read by Americans have translated the Hebrew word *adam* as "man." The verse is hence rendered: "God created man in God's image."

But is rendering *adam* as "man" the proper translation? In Hebrew, *adam* can be used to refer to a proper name, as in Adam, the husband of Eve. *Adam* can also be translated to refer to a male-gender individual, as opposed to the Hebrew word *issah* for "woman." And finally, *adam* can be used to refer to mankind, as in all of humanity. Now the text tells us that when God created *adam, adam* was created as male and female by God. So, if we translate *adam* to mean the person Adam, or render *adam* as "man" as opposed to a woman, does this mean that Adam the person or generic man was created with both male and female genitalia? Probably not. But what if we were to translate *adam* to mean humanity? Is humanity male and female? Yes, both males and females make up humanity. For this reason, when reading Genesis 1:27, "humanity" is a better translation for the word *adam.*

The fact remains, however, that for the vast majority of Judeo-Christian history, God has been thought of as a male, just as Michelangelo painted him on the ceiling of the Sistine Chapel. But what does it mean that we conceive of God as male, complete with a penis? If the functions of a penis are to urinate and to copulate, why would Yahweh need a penis? Or does the penis have a spiritual meaning? If men conceive of women as castrated by the Almighty Himself and as envious of what only God and men possess, then, the reasoning goes, should it not be natural for women to submit to men—who, unlike women, are created like God? In the nineteenth century, Sigmund Freud (1856–1939) came to the conclusion, from a purely secular standpoint, that women are envious of men's penises. If man, like God, has a penis, does it not stand to reason that all who have penises are closer to the perfect image of God? Following this line of thinking, the penis itself becomes a sacred object shared by God and males.

With this view in mind, it should not appear strange that in biblical times the great patriarchs of the faith, such as Abraham and Israel, placed great spiritual value on their penises by swearing oaths upon their genitals (Genesis 24:2–3; 47:29–31). More disturbing are biblical accounts concerning penises, such as the time God tried to kill Moses but was prevented by Zipporah, Moses' quick-thinking wife, who cut off the foreskin of her son's penis and rubbed it on Moses' penis, thus appeasing God (Exodus 4:24–26). Or King David's winning of his wife Michal through the gift of the foreskins of a hundred Philistine penises (2 Samuel 3:14).

What is important to note is that the sign of the covenant between God and man begins with the penis—specifically, cutting off its foreskin through the ritual of circumcision (Genesis 17:10–14). How then do women enter into a covenant with God if there is no penis to circumcise? It follows that to reserve that covenant for men only, the privilege of having a penis must therefore be protected at all costs from the threat of women. Hence the biblical enjoinment that if during a brawl, a woman "puts out her hand and lay hold of [a man's] genitals, then you shall cut off her hand and your eyes shall not pity her" (Deuteronomy 25:11–12).

It is true that the Bible refers to God as a "He," but God is also said to have eyes, ears, a strong arm, and so on. God is anthropomorphized and given human features so that humans' temporal minds can attempt to conceive of the eternal. The biblical text is not trying to tell us what color God's eyes are; rather, it is meant to convey the concept that God sees, so the act of seeing is understood by humans through the symbolical language of giving God eyes. The same concept is in play when the biblical text says God is a burning bush (Exodus 3:2) or a consuming fire (Hebrews 12:29). Does this mean God is combustive? No; the symbol of burning fire helps us to better comprehend that which is beyond comprehension. And when the Bible refers to God as a mother who would not forget the child from her womb suckling her breast (Is. 49:15) or as birthing Israel (Deuteronomy 32:18), this isn't intended to mean that God lactates and has a vagina; these too are symbols to aid our comprehension.

Contemporary scholars Paul Tillich (1886–1965) and Paul Ricoeur (1913–2005) were correct in asserting that one can only speak of or describe God through the use of symbols, connecting the meaning of one thing recognized by a given community that is comprehensible (such as *father*) with another thing that is beyond our ability to fully understand (that is, God).[4] As important as symbols are to help us better grasp the incomprehensible essence of the Divine, they are incapable of exhausting the reality of God. To take symbolic language literally (for example, God is exclusively male or female) leads to the absurd (for example, God has a penis or a vagina) and borders on idolatry (the creation of hierarchies in relationships according to who is closer to the Divine ideal). To speak of God as male, as fire, or as mother is to speak of God in symbols that, through analogies, convey limited knowledge for understanding what God is like.

The radical nature of the Hebrew God, as described in Genesis, is that unlike the gods of the surrounding Canaanite neighbors, Yahweh has no genitalia. The gods of the people surrounding the Hebrews were depicted in small statuettes about the size of a hand. If these gods were female they were manifested with large, pendulous breasts, broad hips, and prominently featured vaginas. The male god statuettes usually were depicted with large, protruding and erect penises. Even though this was the norm for fertility gods, the god of the Hebrews, who was also responsible for creating and sustaining all that has life, had neither breasts nor a penis. The revolutionary concept of the Hebrew god is that this God was neither male nor female and thus was male *and* female. In short, this God named Yahweh was beyond gender. For this reason it was considered blasphemy to make any graven image of the true God (Exodus 20:4), for such a God was beyond the imagination of finite minds.

To give God a penis is to subjugate women to all those who also have penises. As feminist theologian Mary Daly (1928–) wrote, "If God is male, then the male is God."[5] If men are gods, then women, because they lack a penis, fall short of divinity. Being less than men, women, as understood via the biblical text, were reduced to the status of property, incubators, the weaker sex, and the fallen Eve.

Women as Property

In the introduction we noted that God's perfect will for familial relationships was expressed in the verse "the man and woman were both naked, yet felt no shame" (Genesis 2:25). However, the introduction of sin into paradise led to the perversion of God's will for human relationships. Rather than man and woman finding their equality in the image of God, instead hierarchal structures were created. Patriarchy, being the first form of hierarchy, replaced the familial relationship originally established in the Garden. The consequence of the sin would be that the woman's desire would be for her husband, while he ruled over her (Genesis 3:16).

But, readers may ask, didn't God create a hierarchy in the Garden by making Eve subordinate to Adam? The biblical text does state that woman was created as Adam's helpmate (Genesis 2:18), leading Augustine (354–430 C.E.) to conclude that "Woman was merely man's helpmate, a function which pertains to her alone. She is not the image of God but as far as man is concerned, he is by himself the image of God."[6] The Hebrew word used for helpmate is *ezer,* from the root word meaning "support" or "help." It is the same word used throughout the scriptures when referring to God. "God of my fathers [who] was my *helper*" (Exodus 18:4). The Psalmist heralds God as being the "*helper* of the orphans*" (10:14) and assures the believer, "The Lord is with me, God is my *helper*" (118:7). In none of these cases, nor in any of the other places throughout the Bible in which God is referred to as our helpmate, does *ezer* imply subservience. We only assume the subordination or inferiority of the one called *ezer* when describing women. Maybe a better translation of *ezer* is the word *companion,* which connotes woman as a counterpart to man. Such a translation reinforces the hierarchy-free relationship originally created in Eden.

Nevertheless, the Fall was manifested by the transformation of woman's autonomy from a human being to personal chattel. Women became the property of men because they were perceived as naturally inferior, created by God either to be subordinate to men or as divine punishment for introducing sin into paradise—or both. Either way, as property, women became the extension of a man, and as such, any violation of a man's property became a direct violation of the man. This reasoning led to the female body—including the reproductive organs within her—becoming the property of the man who "rules over her." Her purpose for existence was reduced to the quenching of the lustful thirst possessed by man and to bear the man's future heirs.

Throughout the Hebrew text it is taken for granted that women are the possessions of men. (The biblical text also relegated children to a subordinate position under the patriarchal authority of the father. If they were to strike their parent (Exodus 21:15), curse them (Leviticus 20:9), or constantly rebel against their father's authority (Deuteronomy 21:18–21), they could be put to death.) The text does not seriously consider or concentrate upon women's status, but focuses on the fact that their identity is formed by their sexual relationship to the man: virgin daughter, betrothal bride, married woman, mother, barren wife, or widow. Woman's dignity and worth as one created in the image of God is subordinated to the needs and desires of men. As chattel, women are often equated with a house or livestock (Deuteronomy 20:5–7), as demonstrated in the last commandment, "Thou shalt not covet thy neighbor's house, wife, slave, ox, or donkey" (Exodus 20:17). Because women are excluded from being the subject of this command, the woman, like a house, slave, ox, or donkey, is reduced to an object, just another possession, another piece of property that belongs to the man and thus should not be coveted by another man.

The Hebrew Bible's attitude toward marriage mirrors what appears in the earlier Code of Hammurabi (eighteenth century B.C.E.), the legal codes of the Mesopotamian civilization that predated the Bible. Man, as the head of the family, had nearly unlimited rights and power over wives and children. Normatively, women were first under their father's authority, then with marriage they fell under the husband's rule. If a son were to outlive the father, he became the household head, with his mother falling under his authority. As property, a wife wasn't even considered part of the immediate family. For example, a priest was permitted to mourn the death of any member of his immediate family, except for his own wife or his married sister (Leviticus 21:1–4). Sexual activities such as prostitution, adultery, and incest were topics regulated under the category of property law. Participating in such acts concerned the trespass of another man's rights to his own property, not any violation of trust created within a mutually giving and vulnerable familial relationship. Intercourse with a woman who belonged to another man fell under thievery of the other man's rights to his woman's body and his right to legitimate offspring.

Although the unfaithful wife faced harsh punishment (death), the man reserved for himself the right to engage in intercourse with a multitude of women, even to the point of keeping, as possessions, as many as his means permitted. The great patriarchs of the faith, Abraham, Isaac, Jacob, and Judah, had multiple wives and concubines, and they delighted themselves with the occasional prostitute (Genesis 38:15). King Solomon alone was recorded to have had over seven hundred wives of royal birth and three hundred concubines (1 Kings 11:3). Even King David, a man after God's own heart, acquired a young virgin girl, the prettiest in all the land, to keep his bed warm during his declining years (1 Kings 1:1–3). The book of Leviticus, in giving instructions to men wishing to own a harem, provides only one prohibition, which is not to "own" sisters (Leviticus 18:18). The Hebrew Bible is clear that men could have multiple sex partners. Wives ensured legitimate heirs; all other sex partners existed for the pleasures of the flesh, or for creating political alliances. A woman, on the other hand, was limited to just one sex partner who ruled over her, unless she was a prostitute.

Adultery as a violation of trust within a loving relationship is a romantic modern concept that should not be read back into the biblical text. Patriarchy defined the commandment "Thou shalt not commit adultery" (Exodus 20:14) as an offense that can only be transgressed by women. The only time a man could be accused of adultery was if he trespassed on another man's "property," hence violating another man's rights (Leviticus 20:10). Ever wonder why the woman who was brought to Jesus, "caught in the very act of adultery" (John 8:3–11), was alone? After all, if she was caught in the *very act,* one would expect there to be another person in the room, right? But she and she alone was brought to Jesus because only she had sinned. Her sexual partner's marital status was irrelevant because patriarchy allowed him to engage in multiple sexual relationships. Consequently, no man needed to be brought to Jesus for punishment. But Jesus exposed the hypocrisy of patriarchy. When Jesus instructed those who were without this sin to throw the first stone, all the men walked away because they were no different from the one they accused.

If a man seduced (raped) a young virgin, he had but two choices: he either married her or paid her father a fixed sum. And even if the father refused to give his daughter in marriage, the seducer was still liable for paying the market value of her virginity. According to the biblical text, the true victim of the seduction was not the virgin girl, but her father. Her despoiling made her unsuitable for marriage, resulting in financial hardship for her father (her owner). The marrying off of one's daughters was in many cases an important political decision, made to create profitable alliances with other families. Virginity was such a profitable commodity that when an unmarried daughter was violated the father had to be compensated for damages (Exodus 22:15–16).

Because it was the father's responsibility to prove his daughter's virginity when she climbed into her new husband's bed (Deuteronomy 22:13–21), the daughter's virginity became the father's asset to be traded at a future date with another man. It goes without saying that no such requirement of sexual purity was expected of men. If shortly after the marriage the husband suspected his bride of being "used property," he reserved the right to annul the marriage—as Joseph planned to do with Mary, until in a dream he was supernaturally reassured by an angel and convinced to keep her (Matthew 1:19–24). It was crucial, then, to prove virginity, usually by the parents displaying the wedding night bedsheets with bloodstains caused by rupture of the female hymen during the initial intercourse (Deuteronomy 22:13–21). If there was no blood, a chicken was always kept handy in case its throat needed to be slit at the last moment to provide the precious proof.

As sexual property, women could be claimed as war booty (no modern pun intended). War turned women into spoils of war that, along with other valuable possessions, go to the victors. The common practice in war was for the "armies of Yahweh" to kill the men (Deuteronomy 20:10–18), disperse the spoils of war, and kidnap the virgin women to go into servitude or provide sexual pleasure. If a soldier was captivated by a captured woman, he was allowed to bring her into his home and make her his wife. A captured woman could be taken as a wife, as long as she was a virgin and from some distant land, so as not to snare her captor into a Canaanite cult (Deuteronomy 21:10–14). She was permitted a month to mourn her parents, but after the time of grief, the marriage was to be consummated. But with the passage of time, if her husband tired of her, he could allow her to leave. However, he could not sell her, for as the Bible states, "he had the use of her."

As property, any woman could be offered up as ransom to save the lives of men. During Abraham's visit to Egypt, he grew frightened of the Pharaoh on account of his wife Sarah's beauty. To save himself from being killed so that the Pharaoh could take over his "possession," he claimed that Sarah was his sister and offered her up in exchange for sheep, cattle, donkeys, slaves, and camels (Genesis 12:10–20). Now what do we usually call a man today who offers up a woman in exchange for monetary goods? This sexual transaction is repeated. Later on, Abraham did the same thing with Abimelech, king of Gerar (Genesis 20). His son Isaac followed in his father's footsteps by also offering Rebekah, his wife, to King Abimelech (Genesis 26:1–11).

Not only could women be offered up to save the lives of male family members, but they could also be sacrificed for the sake of male total strangers. A vivid example is illustrated in the story of Lot's daughters. One night, unknown visitors found a haven in Lot's home. When the presence of these foreign men became known throughout the city, the men of Sodom surrounded the house and demanded that the strangers be sent out so that they could be gang-raped. Lot approached the mob, hoping to protect the strangers taking refuge in his house. In appeasement, Lot offered the mob his two virgin daughters, encouraging them to "do to them as they see fit" (Genesis 19:7–8). In Lot's mind, his daughters were worth far less than the two strangers, only because the strangers were men.

A similar scenario is reported in the book of Judges 19–21. This time it was a Levite who found refuge, along with his concubine, in the home of an old man in the town of Gibeah. Again, as night fell, the men of the city surrounded the house and demanded that the Levite be sent out to be gang-raped. Like Lot, the old man went out to meet them, offering his virgin daughter and the Levite's concubine as ransom, insisting that the men of the town do with them whatever they saw fit. This time the townsmen took the concubine, raped her all night long, and left her for dead, lying at the door of the house where the Levite soundly slept.

The stories of Lot and the Levite priest illustrate that because women were property, they could be offered up for sexual abuse if this would save and secure the lives of men. And women, as property, could also be used to gain authority over a rival. The best way for a man to announce a public challenge to a political or social rival was by taking control of his possessions, specifically his women. This concept is demonstrated in 2 Samuel 15–16. In these passages, David's authority as king was challenged by his son Absalom. Absalom mounted a rebellion that forced David to leave Jerusalem. Upon entering the city, Absalom consolidated his power and authority. How? By pitching a tent on the palace's housetop, in the sight of all Israel, and then proceeding to rape all of his father's concubines. This was not a sexual act motivated by lust. Women, as sexual property, were the means by which Absalom could wrestle away authority from his father. Absalom was giving public notice that he had taken his father's place and was now in control of his father's possessions.

Women as Incubators

In patriarchy, one party must dominate (usually the male's role), while another must submit (usually women, children, and men conquered through war). A careful reading of the biblical text reveals that with few exceptions—namely, Deborah the Judge (Judges 4) and Queen Esther (Esther), each of whom maneuvered within the patriarchal structures to carve out for herself a space for leadership—women's identities were reduced to being extensions of their male counterparts, who were presented as the possessor of their female bodies. One of woman's main purposes for existing was to produce heirs, specifically male heirs—a theme often repeated throughout the biblical text. The barren matriarch Sarai offered her slave girl Hagar to Abram for rape so that he could have an heir (Genesis 16:2). Rachel, Jacob's wife, demanded of her husband, "Give me children, or I shall die!" (Genesis 30:1) as she competed with her sister Leah, also Jacob's wife, for his attention—an attention obtained through the birthing of men. Also, we cannot forget Hannah, the prophet Samuel's mother, who saw herself as worthless until God removed her barrenness (1 Samuel 1), or Michal, who was stricken with barrenness for speaking ill to her husband King David (2 Samuel 6:20–23). Even in the New Testament, Elizabeth, the mother of John the Baptist, rejoiced in her old age when she discovered that God had removed the reproach of her barrenness (Luke 1:24–25). For these women, barrenness was a humiliation.

Only through childbearing were women saved—a disturbing understanding of salvation, as reiterated by St. Paul: "It was not Adam who was led astray but the woman who was led astray and fell into sin. Nevertheless, she will be saved by childbearing" (1 Timothy 2:14–15). Is Paul—the promoter of salvation solely through grace, not works—actually implying that unlike men, women are saved through childbearing? No matter how we choose to interpret this scriptural passage to align it with our theological presuppositions, one thing is certain: salvation through childbearing is a concept rooted in patriarchy.

The early shapers of Christianity believed that the only purpose of a woman's existence was to procreate. In fact, Augustine went as far as to claim that it would have been better if God had placed another man in the Garden with Adam instead of a woman (the original Adam and Steve?), because another man would have made a more suitable companion. Because of the need for procreation, God instead created Eve.[7] Relying on Augustine's writings, the mediaeval scholar Thomas Aquinas (1225–1274) would conclude that insofar as Adam's purpose for existence was an end in and of itself, women's *raison d'être* was to procreate.[8] Probably no other Christian thinker better captured the concept of woman as human breeders than Martin Luther, whose advice for women was to "Bring that child forth, and do it with all your might! If you die in the process, so pass on over, good for you! For you actually die in a noble work and in obedience to God."[9] In other words, according to Luther, women, as human breeders, have an obligation to fulfill God's purpose for them, even if it costs them their lives.

But even though Christianity developed with the view that the sole purpose of women's existence—and of sexual intercourse—is procreation, the irony is that women were believed to contribute little to the reproductive process. Evidence for this view is most notable in the multiple genealogical lists found in the Bible, in which men beget men. Women were seen as passive objects that germinated the life source found only in the male semen. Until the advent of modern biology, Christian church leaders such as Thomas Aquinas, influenced by Aristotle (384–322 B.C.E.),[10] understood women as simply supplying the "formless matter of the body" required "in the begetting of men." It was the man who supplied the "formative power" of semen.[11]

If the only natural reason for participating in sex is procreation, then why have sex with a barren woman? Or, for that matter, have sex with a woman after menopause? With procreation as the sole purpose, to do so would be akin to sowing seeds in a desert. Likewise, sex with a menstruating woman is deemed an abomination because of her inability to conceive during this phase of her cycle (Leviticus 15:24). Such acts are said to be "unnatural" because they are contrary to what was understood to be the natural purpose of sex: conceiving heirs. Any sexual act that does not directly lead to human conception automatically is defined as "unnatural," be it oral sex, anal sex, homosexual sex, the use of condoms during sex, or sex for the pure sake of pleasure.

Women as the Weaker Sex

An underlying assumption found throughout most Christian literature is that men are physically and morally superior to women, who are the weaker sex (*sexus infirmitas*). According to 1 Peter, "husbands must treat their wives with consideration, bestowing honor on her as one who, though she may be the weaker vessel, is truly a co-heir to the grace of life" (3:7). Although equal in grace, still the purpose for the woman as the "weaker vessel" is to be ruled by the man. In his first letter to the Corinthians, Paul insisted that women must cover their heads because the woman is the "glory of man." Specifically, he wrote, "For man . . . is the image and glory of God. But the woman is the glory of man. For man did not come from woman, but woman from man. And man was not created for woman, but woman for man" (1 Corinthians 11:7–9). Augustine understood the order of creation in relationship to what he perceived to be a natural hierarchy. According to this understanding, because man came first, and woman came from man's side, he was created in the image of God while she was created in the image of man. God creates natural dualism: spirit-flesh, rational-emotional, subject-object, and male-female. Because man was closer to the spirit, he was a rational subject ordained to rule—and because woman was closer to the flesh, she was an emotional object ordained to *be* ruled. Thus, subjecting woman to man became the natural manifestation of subjecting passion to reason.

"But as the church is subject to Christ, so also are wives to be subject to their husbands in everything" (Ephesians 5:24). Just as the body had to submit to the spirit, which is superior, and the church had to submit to Christ, so too the wife had to submit to her husband. This logic concluded that prior to the Fall, man was superior to woman because he was closer to the image of God, whereas woman was inferior to man because she was created for and from man. For Augustine, patriarchy was not a consequence of sin, as we have argued, but rather God's will, which originated in the Garden. According to Augustine, "The Apostle has made known to us certain three unions, Christ and the Church, husband and wife, spirit and flesh. Of these the former consult for the good of the latter, the latter wait upon the former. All the things are good, when, in them, certain set over by way of pre-eminence, certain made subject in a becoming manner, observe the beauty of order."[12]

The prevailing wisdom within Christianity was, and for many conservatives continues to be, that conforming to the natural order of the universe is as beneficial for the beasts, wives, and children as it is for the man. John Chrysostom (347–407) could argue that patriarchy demonstrated God's loving-kindness, because it existed to protect women from themselves; because Eve sinned and led man astray, woman was now content and secure under the protection of man's authority. Chrysostom emphasized that women now *desired* to have their husbands ruling over them, for it was better to fall under a man's lordship than enjoy a freedom that would cast her into the abyss.[13]

Martin Luther continued this classical understanding of woman as the weaker sex. A wife, for him, was a "half-child" whose husband's responsibility was to care for her as though she was a child.[14] Luther traced women's inferiority to the creation story. He wrote, "Because Satan sees that Adam is more excellent, he does not dare assail him, for he fears that his attempt may turn out to be useless . . . Satan, therefore, directs his attack on Eve as the weaker part."[15] Woman's inferiority thus required man's governance for her own good.

The views of these Christian thinkers were formed through their reading of the biblical text in which the role of women, as being inferior to men, is normative. For example, although the church required that the first-born son (or male animal) be consecrated to the Lord, no such requirements existed for the first-born daughter (Deuteronomy 15:19–23). Woman's inferiority in religious matters allowed the man to whom she belonged (either her father or husband) to annul any pledge or vow she might have made to God (Numbers 30:3–15). Three times a year, God called all men to present themselves before God during the great national feasts. Women received no such calling (Exodus 23:14–19). They were frequently excluded from participating in temple rituals and festivals because they were deemed to be unclean due to their menstrual cycle (Leviticus 15:19). Likewise, they were forbidden to serve as priests, and priests could marry only virgins (Leviticus 21:1–9).

Women's supposed inferiority also prevented them from preaching to or teaching men, a practice still common among many churches today. The idea of women in positions of leadership was considered contrary to the laws of nature. John Calvin (1509–1564), in his commentary on First Timothy 2:12, stated: "Woman, by nature (that is, by the ordinary law of God) is formed to obey; for the government of women has always been regarded by all wise persons as a monstrous thing, and therefore, so to speak, it will be a mingling of heaven and earth, if women usurp the right to teach."

Still, in spite of women being perceived as the weaker sex, it was believed that they could still be used by God, but in a type of usage that only reaffirmed women's inferiority. If God used a woman as an instrument for God's revelation, she would be raised beyond both her human and female condition. She would demonstrate any authority not in her own right, but as one whom God uses in spite of her inferiority. In effect, she was no different from Balaam's ass, whom God used to speak a word of prophesy to the prophet (Numbers 22:26–30). God's use of a donkey to proclaim God's message did not make donkeys equal to man, and so it was with women, who, like jackasses, could speak for God but still remained unequal to men.

Women were considered the weaker sex, in part, because they were perceived to be the negation of men. Throughout the Hebrew Bible, the Law understood the legal concept of *person* to be male-centered; women (and children) were perceived to be incomplete males. Maleness was considered normative, the ideal. Anything that fell short of the norm fell short of God's ideal. Thomas Aquinas wrote that "woman is [a] defective and misbegotten" male—probably due to "some external influence, such as that of a south wind, which is moist."[16]

This ideology was manifested in how the physical differences between women and men were comprehended. Women's genitalia were viewed as the anatomical antithesis of men's. From as early as the second century until the eighteenth century, the woman's cervix and vagina were imagined as an inverted penis. Even the internal position of the ovaries was construed to be the counterbalance to the external location of the testicles. In this one-sex model, women had reached only a lower evolutionary stage of development; this categorized them as something less than fully human—a "defective and misbegotten" man. Their stunted and inverse "penis" only served to prove their deficiency as human, their lack of complete maleness.

Women as Fallen Eves

One of the major themes in Christian thought, still lingering to this day, is that women, represented by Eve, are the cause of sin and consequently the reason *man*kind was led astray from God's perfect will. According to this view, women's shapely curves are deemed to incite passion among holy men. They are the cause of man's disgrace and downfall. Because women lead men to lust, gender has to be regulated so as to restrain sex. Like their mother Eve, women are seen as the incarnation of temptation—specifically, sexual temptation. Tertullian (c. 160–220) proclaimed: "You [woman] are the one who opened the door to the devil . . . you are the one who persuaded [Adam] whom the devil was not strong enough to attack. All too easily you destroyed the image of God, man. Because of your desert, that is, death, even the Son of God had to die."[17]

Eve's action relegated all women to be subjugated to their men. St. Ambrose (339–97), the Bishop of Milan, voiced this conclusion: "[Adam] is found to be superior, whereas [Eve] . . . is found to be inferior. She was first to be deceived and was responsible for deceiving the man. The apostle Paul related that holy women have in olden times been subject to the stronger vessel and recommends them to obey their husbands as their masters. . . . The head of the woman is man, who, while he believed that he would have assistance of his wife, fell because of her."[18] Eve's culpability for humanity's Fall was echoed by Martin Luther, who noted that prior to woman, Adam ruled over all the creatures with everything being in good and proper order, governed in the best possible fashion. But along came Eve and became the source of all of Adam's trials and tribulations.[19]

Women were cast as the eternal temptress, responsible for arousing desire among holy men. Eve and all women who follow were the reason why men become sexually excited. Augustine maintains that a battle exists between the mind and aroused penises, which are caused by women.[20] According to the Bible, women tempted the angels themselves:

some time after the Fall, women sexually seduced angels with their long hair (Genesis 6:1–4; 1 Corinthians 11:10), disrupting the fixed natural order between celestial and mortal beings, resulting in offspring that were understood to be the source of malignant powers. Women, as the cause of human sin and cosmic evil, could not be trusted. Their lack of leadership and sexual seductiveness validated a subordination that cannot be surmounted. Maybe in some future heavenly abode women would become spiritually equal to men. But that was in the future. In the meantime, and in spite of their "shortcomings," women had to gracefully submit to men's authority. This was how God designed the male-female relationship. Or as John Calvin would explain, "The vulgar proverb, indeed, is that [the woman] is a necessary evil . . . given as a companion and an associate to man, to assist him to live well."[21]

Eve's association with the Fall made her the counterpoint to Mary, the mother of Jesus, who served as the medium by which the agent of the world's redemption entered history. Mary, as the eternal virgin, became the ideal model for Christian women to emulate. Women then were forced to choose between the mother and the temptress, between the virgin and the whore, and thus between the pivotal values of the ancient world: honor or shame.

In that world, a person's place in the ancient social order was marked by either acquiring honor or inducing shame. It was crucial for men to maintain or improve the honor of their family while simultaneously avoiding anything that might bring shame upon the family name. Generally speaking, honor was understood as male-centered, for through the man's participation in the public sphere, honor could be increased or decreased through his bold and aggressive actions when interacting with other men. Although honor was achieved in the public sphere, shame was created within the private sphere. Because of patriarchy, a woman who belonged to one man, yet was used by another, brought shame to the "owner" of her body. So to protect his honor, the man had to confine the woman to the household, where she could remain secure. Why? Because the locus of a man's honor was found in his words, whereas the locus of a woman's honor was found between her legs.

The residue of this ancient honor-shame value system can be seen throughout the development of Christianity. During the fifteenth and sixteenth centuries, merchants going away for business or crusaders off to liberate the Holy Land would protect the family's honor by fashioning a chastity belt for their wives. The belt was a metal contraption about the width of a hand, with a hole large enough to allow the wife to perform her necessary bodily functions, but small enough to prevent copulation. This chastity girdle fit over the wife's hips and contained a lock whose key the husband would take with him. He could leave with peace of mind that his sexual property was locked up and protected from trespassers (with the possible exception of the local locksmith). This drastic act was essential to ensure honor, because a woman who lost her "honor," in the words of Martin Luther, "is quite worthless."[22] Remaining tied to her domestic habitation forestalled shame. "As the snail carries its house with it," Luther informs us, "so the wife should stay at home and look after the affairs of the household, as one who has been deprived of the ability of administering those affairs that are outside and that concern the state."[23] Woman's redemption from Eve's influence, and from the shame she herself could bring upon the honor of her man's name, was to seek virtue, either through chastity (which becomes solely her responsibility) or by becoming a prolific mother. If she was a mother, her worth and respect increased proportionally to the number of males she birthed.

A Glimpse of Women Leaders

Women had two choices throughout Christian history: join a convent or get married. But whether a woman lived out her existence in a nunnery or in domesticity, she remained for the most part invisible within Christianity. True, women's voices can be found contributing to Christian thought; for example, Hildegard of Bingen (1098–1179), Julian of Norwich (1342–1416), and Teresa of Avila (1515–1582), to name but a few. But they are exceptions to the rule. And even when these voices rose above the male norm, they were still trapped in the social structures of male superiority. Women had to first reaffirm the weaker sex's position before being heard. Only then could they serve God by symbolically ceasing to be inferior women and instead becoming "men" capable of being used by God. For example, Julian of Norwich had to stress that in spite of the fact that she was a woman, God had still chosen her as a conduit for God's teachings. "But God forbid that you should say or take it so that I am a teacher, for I mean not so, nor I meant never so. For I am a woman, ignorant, feeble and frail. . . . But because I am a woman, should I therefore believe that I should not tell you of the goodness of God, since that I saw in that same time that it is his will that it should be known?"[24]

In effect, the church has insisted that women must first become "born-again" men if they are to have any hope of being servants of the Lord. The early church father Jerome (c. 345–420 C.E.) made this clear: "As long as woman is for birth and children, she is different from man as body is from soul. But when she wishes to serve Christ more than the world, then she will cease to be a woman and will be called man."[25]

Through faith, then, a woman could transcend her limitations of being trapped in a female body and aspire to be as useful and worthy as a man.

Ironically, Jesus didn't think being a woman was an obstacle to serving the Lord. Through deed, Jesus acted contrary to the normal expectations of his culture by conversing with women, either at the well (John 4:7) or in the process of carrying out his ministry (John 8:10). He included them as students (Luke 10:38–42) and as disciples (Luke 8:1–3).

According to Peter, one of the signs of the believing church was when "your sons *and daughters* prophesy" (Acts of the Apostles 2:17). This use of the word *prophesy* has little to do with predicting future events; to prophesy meant to proclaim God's words to God's people—what we today call preaching. The pouring out of God's Spirit is marked by both men and women preaching God's word, an action that in both past and present continues to be prohibited in many of our churches. Yet women throughout the New Testament occupied leadership positions in the church.

Some began churches, as in the case of Lydia of Philippi (Acts 16:11–12); others were teachers of men, as in the case of Priscilla, an instructor of Apollos of Alexandria (Acts 18:24–28); several were preachers, as in the case of the four daughters of Phillip (Acts 21:8–9); and various women were church elders, as in the case of the elected lady (2 John 1–5). They were among the first citywide evangelists (John 4:39) and the first to preach the Gospel of Christ's resurrection (Luke 24:9). Paul sends his greetings and encouragements to women who served as deacons, such as Phoebe (Romans 16:1); as apostles, such as Junia (Romans 16:7); and as pastors, such as Priscilla (along with her husband Aquila) in either Ephesus or Rome (Romans 16:3–5), Chloe in either Corinth or Ephesus (1 Corinthians 1:11), Nympha in Laodicea (Colossians 4:15), and Apphia (along with two others) in Colossae (Philemon 1–2). These women preceded those women who served as priest or bishops during the days of the early church or acted as patrons underwriting ministerial activities.

By the third and fourth century of the Christian church, the opponents of women clergy had succeeded in imposing the prevalent sexism of the secular culture on the church's structures, thus bringing to an end the mark of the pouring out of the Spirit, the preaching of their "sons and daughters."[26] Christ and the early church provided equality to women for church leadership, only to have, within a short time, the Gospel message distorted to justify women's subordination to men and their social structures. After the Roman Emperor Constantine's (c. 274–337) acceptance of Christianity as a state religion, there was a shift in worship practices from private house churches (the domain of women) to public basilicas (the domain of men). As the house church became public, new converts refused to accept women's leadership in public life. Theologians, like Augustine, began to proclaim women priests as a heresy.[27] By 352, during the Council of Laodicea, women were no longer allowed ordination, which suggests that before this time women were indeed ordained. Christianity created unjust practices—practices that prevent familial relationships (and in turn the great sex to which familial relationships can lead) from properly developing.

The Enduring Patriarchy

The brief historical overview of the role of women explored in this chapter reveals that women, since about the third century, have lacked—and in many cases still lack—the power to choose their role within the Christian church, whether it be creative, professional, or personal. Still, one can argue that the misogynistic views of women expressed by the giants of the Christian faith are ancient history, that Christianity today should not be judged by the sexism of former church scholars or by the societal norms of ancient times. But before we quickly dismiss how women used to be perceived by the church, we must recognize that much of what we define as our present Christian sexual morals continues to be based on and influenced by the historical understanding of woman as being the cause and contiguous perpetrator of sin. Today, with the strong cultural trend toward what is termed *political correctness,* the church has learned for the most part not to phrase male superiority in such misogynist fashion, yet the result remains the same—the understanding that women (specifically wives) should submit to men (husbands). Today, as in days of old, Ephesians 5:21–25 and Colossians 3:18–19 set up the marriage relationship in which husbands are commanded to love their wives but wives are commanded not to love, but to submit to their husbands. A few contemporary examples can illustrate this point.

James Dobson, popular psychologist turned political activist, wrote in his 1980 best-selling book *Straight Talk to Men and Their Wives:* "The primary responsibility for the provision of authority in the home has been assigned to men. . . . Whether women's activists like it or not, a Christian man is obligated to lead his family to the best of his ability . . . God apparently expects a *man* to be the ultimate decision maker in his family."[28] And although Dobson does make exceptions for women who might have to work outside the home for financial reasons, still, it is revealing that the section on women in his 1982 tome *Dr. Dobson Answers Your Questions* is titled "The Homemaker." A more recent and vivid example of the prevalent antiwoman Christian ideology presently being advocated can be found in the literature of Promise Keepers—a male Christian movement led by Bill McCartney, which serves as a backlash to the woman's equality movement. In *Seven Promises of a Promise Keeper* (1994), evangelist Tony Brown shares what men's response should be to their wives who want their husbands to be spiritually pure. The first thing, Brown says, "is sit down with your wife and say something like this: 'Honey, I've made a terrible mistake. I've given you my role. I gave up leading this family, and I forced you to take my place. Now I must reclaim that role.'" Brown is not telling men to *ask* that their role be returned; he is telling them to "take it back." He goes on to state, "I am convinced that the primary cause of this national crisis is the feminization of the American male."[29]

Women's submission to male leadership is also normalized by Tim and Beverly LaHaye, sex manual authors who wrote in 1978, "God designed man to be the aggressor, provider, and leader in his family. Somehow that is tied to his sex drive."[30] Ironically, Beverly LaHaye has spent most of her adult life working outside the home, going around the nation giving lectures as to why women should not work outside the home. This subordinate role of women within a marriage relationship was reinforced by the Southern Baptist Convention during their 2000 meeting, at which they inserted into the *Baptist Faith and Message* the following proclamation:

> A husband is to love his wife as Christ loved the Church. He has the God-given responsibility to provide for, to protect, and lead his family. A wife is to submit herself graciously to the servant leadership of her husband even as the church willingly submits to the headship of Christ. She, being in the image of God as is her husband and thus equal to him, has the God-given responsibility to respect her husband and to serve as his helper in managing the household and nurturing the next generation.[31]

In short, husbands are to love their wives and wives are to submit to their husbands, but this power relationship is defined as equality. Still, not all pronouncements that confuse the historical trend of subjecting women with the Christian message are locked in a semi-benign, quasi–political correctness of expressing equality while advocating submissiveness, as voiced by Dobson, Brown, the LaHayes, or the Southern Baptist convention. Take, for example, Pat Robertson's demonization of feminists. During his 1992 failed presidential run, he wrote a fundraising letter that stated: "The feminist agenda is not about equal rights for women. It is about a socialist, anti-family political movement that encourages women to leave their husbands, kill their children, practice witchcraft, destroy capitalism and become lesbians."[32] Pat Buchanan, another presidential candidate (in 1996 and 2000), wrote in his 1983 syndicated newspaper column, "Rail as they will about 'discrimination,' women are simply not endowed by nature with the same measures of single-minded ambition and the will to succeed in the fiercely competitive world of Western capitalism."[33] The Reverend Anthony Kennedy, vicar of the Church of England, while discussing female Anglican priests in 1994, wrote: "I would burn the bloody bitches . . . I can't see how a woman can represent Jesus, who was undoubtedly male, at the altar. I would shoot the bastards if I was allowed. For me, it's very simple. God made us male and female and as far as I'm concerned it's impossible for women to be priests."[34]

As these quotes demonstrate, most of our antiwoman views continue to be influenced by our lingering perception of women as property, walking incubators, or the cause of sin. Patriarchal rule, regardless of the benign spin proponents may attempt to give their views (for example, allowing that men and women are equal before God but given different gifts or roles), comes down to a fundamental premise: the inferiority of women. The Christian patriarchal ethics based on gender control presuppose unjust dominant-subordinate relational patterns that extend beyond women, as we shall explore in the next chapter.

Fostering Biblical Emancipation

Any serious discussion about fostering and maintaining a healthy sexual familial relationship cannot take place until we address sexism and patriarchy. The historical subjugation of women is among the primary reasons we encounter such difficulties in trying to have great sex. The patriarchy's dismissal of women as irrelevant to the creation of Christianity attempts to justify male claims of superiority and establishes a fear-based sexual ethical perspective. For sex to be great it must be free from unjust and abusive power relationships. This is not to infer that the only reason to eliminate patriarchy is so one can have great sex. Patriarchy should be eliminated because it is unjust and contrary to the basic gospel message of liberation for all who are created in the image of God.

When sex takes place in any hierarchical relationship in which women are subordinate to men, both parties are likely to be frustrated in their hopes for ultimate ecstasy. Sex may still be enjoyable, but to experience deep and profound pleasure is difficult, and some would say impossible. Why? Not because of the failure to employ bedroom maneuvers or maintain physical stamina, but rather because a familial relationship is absent. Great sex can happen only in an atmosphere that fosters mutual giving and vulnerability. It is mutual giving and vulnerability that creates intimacy, and without intimacy, sex cannot be great.

Patriarchy allows men the illusion that by possessing women as objects they somehow have possession and control over their own lives and existence. In reality, men as possessors of women also become subjugated to the very structures they create and establish for self-benefit. Why? Because those structures that privilege men with control also prevent them from fully experiencing the depths of intimacy, and that lack of intimacy prevents human fulfillment and closeness to God.

The greatest threat to mutual giving and vulnerability in relationships—and, by extension, to human and spiritual fulfillment—has historically been, and continues to be, the way in which women are perceived within patriarchy. Sex can never be liberated, or be liberating, as long as conditions in relationships prevent women from fully participating in the humanity created by God for them. As long as patriarchal structures define the personal and spiritual development of women, neither party in the relationship will be able to fully enjoy the passion possible through sex. This continues to be so even as well-meaning Christians often mention the need to return to a more literal interpretation of the scriptures. Unfortunately, most traditional readings of the biblical text, specifically on issues on sexuality, can prove to be quite unchristian, especially when the Bible is read through the eyes of patriarchy.

Again, Jesus' approach to women stands in marked contrast: it was quite antipatriarchal, if not downright liberative. In the Gospel of Luke appears a narrative that captures an exchange between Jesus and two sisters, Martha and Mary. According to the text: "In their travels it occurred that [Jesus] entered into a certain village. A certain woman by the name of Martha received him into her house. She had a sister named Mary who sat at the feet of Jesus to hear his words. But Martha was distracted with all the serving and said, 'Lord, do you not care that my sister left me alone to serve? Tell her then that she should help me.' Answering her Jesus said, 'Martha, Martha, you are anxious and troubled about many things when there is need of only one, and Mary chose the good part, which shall not be taken from her'" (10:38–42).

In this incident, Martha complains that she is overworked. Reading the usual English translations, we assume that she is overwhelmed with housework; however, the Greek word used in the text for serving is *diakonia,* a word usually translated as deacon. Hence, the work she is doing, and needs help in completing, is in relationship to her role as the deacon of this house church. Unfortunately, her duties and responsibilities as deacon deprive her of the opportunity to "sit at Jesus' feet," as her sister Mary did.

Mary, on this day, chose "to sit at Jesus' feet," rather than help Martha with her duties as the house-church deacon. To "sit at Jesus' feet" does not mean that there were no chairs available so she was forced to sit on the floor; to sit at someone's feet was, and still is, a euphemism for a teacher-student relationship. The student "sits at the feet" of the teacher, the rabbi. For example, we are told in Acts 22:3 that Paul sat "at the feet of Gamaliel"; that is, that Paul was a student of Gamaliel. During Jesus' time women were forbidden to touch the biblical text, let alone read or study it. Contrary to all social and religious regulations of the time, Luke is telling us that Mary was Jesus' student and disciple, just like the other twelve men sitting at his feet. In addition, both Martha and Mary are portrayed by John in his Gospel as well-known apostolic figures of the early church who were beloved by Christ (11:5). In the same way that Peter confesses the messiahship of Jesus (Matthew 16:15–19), so too does Martha as a spokesperson for the early church (John 11:27). And finally, through Mary's evangelism, many came to believe in Jesus (John 11:45).[35]

Jesus' commitment to debunking the patriarchy of his time can be seen in a retelling of the story through the eyes of marginalized women. In this retelling, the rabbi Jesus was received in the home of one of his apostles named Martha, who also served as founder and deacon of the house-church in Bethany in which she proclaimed God's word. On this day her sister Mary the evangelist sat at the feet of Jesus to study Torah. Martha asked the rabbi to have his student help with the duties required by the deacon, but the rabbi responded that studying Torah was just as important as serving.[36] Hence, the same biblical text that has historically been used to enforce the oppression of women instead, as we have carefully delineated, contains the very seeds of liberation by which patriarchy can be challenged.

2

LIBERATING THE BODY OF COLOR

The custom [of the Amerindians is] that the women do business and deal with trade and other public offices while the men remain at home and weave and embroider. They [the women] urinate standing while the men do so seated; and they have no reluctance to perform their natural deeds in public.[1]

—Juan Suárez de Peralta, a resident of Mexico in the late sixteenth century

Come on, sugar, I'm going to do you like a nigger, just like a nigger, come on, sugar, and love me just like you'd love a nigger.[2]

—The nocturnal comments of Jesse, the impotent white supremacy sheriff, to his white wife, in James Baldwin's *Going to Meet the Man*

I marry white culture, white beauty, white whiteness. When my [black] restless hands caress those white breasts, they grasp white civilization and dignity and make them mine.[3]

—Frantz Fanon (1925–1961)

DURING THE SUMMER OF 1994, the nation was captivated by what has been dubbed "the trial of the century." O. J. Simpson, "the Juice," was accused of murdering his wife Nicole Brown and her friend Ronald Goldman. O. J., probably the most successful running back in American football history, is black; his wife was white. Much can be written concerning Simpson's arrest and trial, but I wish to concentrate on just one aspect: the June 27, 1994, cover of *Time* magazine. For reasons still unclear, *Time* digitally altered the photo of Simpson to make him look darker. Why? They may have wanted to perpetuate the myth of the savage black man who endangers white women. Or more pragmatically, they probably thought that capitalizing on the myth would sell more magazines.

Responding to the mounting criticism of this alteration, James Gaines, as managing editor, wrote a response "to our readers" in the following week's edition. He acknowledged darkening Simpson so as to produce what is called a "photo-illustration." He blamed their poor judgment on having to make a snap decision during the wee hours of the morning (2 A.M.). He even admitted that tampering with the photo was, at best, "a risky practice." Still, as could be expected, he denied any "racial implication," while accusing the critics of being the real racists. "It is racist to say that black is more sinister, and some African Americans have taken that position," he argued. In other words, *Time* claimed that the real racists were the blacks, for complaining that O. J. was made blacker.[4] What the managing editor, like many white Americans today, failed to understand is that thousands of years of conditioning cannot be changed with a few decades of political correctness. The construction of race and its eroticization is so woven into white America's identity that it has become normalized in the way many whites have been taught by their culture to see bodies of color. To question this mind-set as racist only produces an incredulous response of innocence from those who have been socially taught to see the nonwhite as dangerous.

This is not the first time in U.S. history that a man of color has been characterized as being sexually dangerous to white civilization, specifically to white women. Probably one of the most blatant sexual demonizations of a black man occurred during George H. W. Bush's presidential campaign against the governor of Massachusetts, Michael Dukakis. In an infamous campaign ad, Dukakis was linked to a Massachusetts state prisoner, Willie Horton. Mr. Horton, a black man, raped a Maryland white woman while on a forty-eight-hour furlough. In a split television screen, Dukakis's face was placed next to Horton's, as if Horton was Dukakis' real running mate.

Some apologists might argue that the message was that Dukakis was soft on crime, and the criminal chosen just happened to be black, but such explanations are disingenuous. Tying the image of the black rapist with Dukakis was exactly the purpose of the campaign's designer. Lee Atwater, the mastermind behind the ad, issued a deathbed apology to Dukakis in the February 1993 issue of *Life* magazine. Fighting against an inoperable brain tumor, Atwater confessed that "in part because of our successful manipulation of [these] campaign themes, George Bush won handily. . . . In 1988, fighting Dukakis, I said that I 'would strip the bark off the little bastard' and 'make Willie Horton his running mate.'"[5] The message was clear: elect Dukakis and black men will be running loose to rape white women.

Such a message continues to be perpetrated today. In the closing days of the 2006 midterm election, the Republican Party replayed the "black men endangering white women" script. Harold E. Ford, Jr., the black Democratic candidate from Tennessee—who sought to be the first African American elected to the Senate from the South since the post–Civil War Reconstruction—has kept the Republican incumbent on the defensive in a race that was never expected to be competitive. With Ford and his opponent neck-and-neck in the polls, the Republican National Committee (RNC) financed a television spot of mock man-on-the street interviews, in which actors spoke sarcastically about Ford and his stands on some hot-button issues. Among the players was an attractive, white, bare-shouldered blond woman who says she met Ford at "the Playboy party." At the end of the ad, she looks directly into the camera, says breathily, "Harold! Call me," and winks. Even more incredible was the reaction of Ken Mehlman, chairman of the RNC, who insisted that he did not see a racial subtext to the advertisement.[6]

Making O. J. darker, disparaging a politician by associating him with black rapists, and portraying black politicians as wanting to have sex with white women are but three examples out of many that expose the intersection of sex and race in this country. No conversation about oppressive sexual structures can be complete without an exploration of how race is eroticized for the purpose of controlling bodies of color. This chapter will present a brief theoretical overview of the consequences of interlinking sexism, racism, ethnocentrism, and classism, illustrating how white heterosexual male privilege came to be structured within the Americas.

I Wanna Be a Macho Man

Sexism reflects just one aspect of what it means to be a "real man." It is therefore appropriate to expand our understanding of oppression to include all forms of prejudice imposed on those who fail to live up to the standards of being a white male with economic privilege. Male heterosexual superiority in the United States is as much about race and class as it is about gender. It would be naive to think that gender, race, and class structures of oppression exist as separate, isolated compartments. These normalized forms of oppression interact with, reinforce, and at times conflict with each other, yet their outcome is similar: to maintain white heterosexual male privilege (specifically within the United States, as well as many places throughout the world). All these forms of oppression are identical in their attempt to domesticate others; that is, to place the Other in a subordinate position. To fully understand how oppressive structures work, sexism, heterosexism, racism, ethnocentrism, and classism must be explored not as separate categories, but as a single unifying framework designed to privilege one group over all others. Because patriarchy has defined women as playing a lesser role than men, women—as we saw in the last chapter—have been viewed as being inferior to men. Likewise, because men of color—whether here in the United States or throughout the impoverished world—are seen as inferior to whites, Euro-Americans have been taught to project onto men of color passive characteristics so they could occupy the feminine space.

To be a man has historically implied a superior standard that carries Christian responsibilities. From those to whom much is given, much is expected. In the minds of those privileged with whiteness, a responsibility existed—what imperialists of old would call "the white man's burden"—to educate, protect, and Christianize nonwhites who, they believed, were unfortunate beings located at a lower evolutionary stage of development. This attitude continues today in the rhetoric of teaching "them" (for example, the Iraqis) democracy. The paternalism that men of empire showed toward their wives and children is extended to people of color, including men of color. These nonwhite men must be taught by those who are successful how to function in today's neoliberal world. Why? Because of the crass notion that history is forged by those with "brass balls." In the minds of those in power, women, nonwhites, and the poor fail to create or influence history because they lack the appropriate testicles. The potent symbolic power invested in the testicles both signals and veils white males' socioeconomic power.

To be called a self-made man, a man's man, or a real man is to recognize an ultimate achievement. Psychoanalyst Jacques Lacan (1901–1981) can help us understand this dynamic. To gaze into the mirror is to construct one's reflection through the negation of others. In other words "I am what I am not."[7] Using Lacan's mirror stage imagery, white males with economic privilege look into a mirror and recognize themselves as men through the distancing process of negative self-definition. The formation of their ego constructs an illusory self-representation based on the "lack of balls" projected upon those whom they consider and identify as inferior—be they women, the poor, or nonwhite males.

The resulting gaze of the white man with economic privilege inscribes effeminacy upon all those who "lack what it takes" to make history, provide for their family, or resist their subjugation to their domination. Women, the poor, and men of color become the nonmale. Constructing those oppressed as feminine has historically allowed white men to assert their privilege by constructing those whom they consider their inferiors as inhabitants of the castrated realm of the exotic and primitive.[8] The castrated male (read, racial and class Other) occupies a feminine space in which his body is symbolically sodomized as prelude to the sodomizing of his mind.

Seeing Dark Bodies

In the U.S. context, those men who are not man enough are those with nonwhite bodies, specifically blacks, Hispanics, Native Americans, and Asian-Americans. Even though they are emasculated for lacking "what it takes to be a man" they are still feared for having a penis. Because they possess a penis, they are still considered dangerous, for at any time they can threaten white civilization manifested as a white woman. Take the 2006 image used by the anti-immigrant organization Defend Colorado Now. "Wake up Colorado" appears above the image of a white woman in a stars-and-stripes Liberty costume reminiscent of a vintage illustration; she is leaning back in a chair, sleeping, vulnerable.[9] She is meant to represent the state itself. Below her are the words "Defend Colorado Now." To me, the image has an unconscious message for the viewer. Colorado, signified by a white woman, must be protected from the danger of Latinos crossing the border, for if she is not, her purity and innocence will surely be sullied.

Euro-Americans have historically been taught, through images in popular culture, that males of color are overly sexualized beings who invoke both fascination with and fear of their prowess. We've all heard about the exploits of hot-blooded "Latin lovers," or the locker-room remarks about the larger size of the black penis when compared to that of whites (although statistically speaking, all penises, regardless of color, are on average about the same length when flaccid: 4.8 inches). The stereotypical hot Latino Don Juan and the big-membered black signify the image of aggressiveness and carnality. The 1990 documentary *The Bronze Screen: One Hundred Years of the Latino Image in American Cinema* depicts how Latino actors like Ricardo Montalban were portrayed as the stereotypical Latin lover—an image heightened during the 1940s and 1950s as a result of America's "good neighbor" policies with Latin America. Sexual fear and awe of black men is evidenced by the popularity of modern plantation "bodice ripper" novels, and portrayed, to some degree, by the talented actor Paul Robeson in his various photographic poses and films like *The Emperor Jones*. Similarly the black, brown, red, and yellow female bodies are seen as sensual objects, available for consumption. The most recognized Asian example is the tragic Puccini opera *Madame Butterfly*, and the stereotypical image of Latinas as hip-swinging hussies was epitomized in the movie roles Carmen Miranda was forced to portray. Such media representations contribute to the cultural images of young white males hoping to learn the "art" of lovemaking from women of color, or nonwhite male bodies at the service of bored white females seeking to spice up their lives with an element of danger by going "slumming."

How did this understanding of dark bodies develop? People of color were historically perceived by white culture as wild creatures devoid of pure white blood; even those who lived in civilized societies were nevertheless seen as part savage. As whites projected their own forbidden desires onto darker bodies, they could engage in sex with these darker bodies, absolved of any culpability; those who were viewed as being evolutionarily closer to the heat of the jungle were held responsible for compromising the virtues of whites, through either their so-called seductive nature or their "black magic." To engage in sex with these nonwhite bodies gave whites an opportunity to lose themselves to primitive urges, heightening their momentary sexual experience while reinforcing these darker bodies' subjugation, as we will see throughout the remainder of this chapter.

Conquering the First Dark Women

The conquest of the woman of color by white males was more than a sexual conquest: it symbolized the conquest of land and the people who occupy that land. The travel diary of Columbus provides us with the first available account from the western hemisphere of the reduction of women of color to the status of objects to be conquered. On Thursday, October 11, 1492, he wrote:

> Immediately they saw naked people, and the admiral went ashore in the armed boat. . . . The admiral called two captains . . . and said they should bear witness and testimony how he, before them all, took possession of the island. . . . They [the land's inhabitants] all go naked

as their mothers bore them, and the women also . . . they were very well built, with very handsome bodies and very good faces.[10]

Columbus's first observation was not the lack of political organization of the island's inhabitants or the geographical placement of these islands in the world scheme. Rather, he eroticized the naked bodies of these inhabitants. In my reading of this entry, Columbus sees an open invitation to penetrate with the forward thrust of white civilization this new erotic continent, which awaited insemination with open arms and legs. These naked bodies and "empty" land merge the sexual and the economic preoccupations of the would-be conqueror.

How Columbus envisioned the world, as "a very round ball, and on one part of it is placed something like a woman's nipple,"[11] is very telling. The European conquest of the Americas began with the literal sexual conquest of the Native American woman—the land personified in a naked woman's body, specifically a naked indigenous woman's body. An incident involving Miguel de Cuneo, who participated in Columbus' second journey, illustrates this point. Cuneo attempted to seduce an indigenous woman given to him by Columbus (as though the woman as possession belonged to Columbus, who could dispose of his property in any way he saw fit). When she resisted Cuneo's advances, he whipped her and proceeded to rape her.[12]

Here we see the image of land and woman merge. Woman as land or land as woman was expected to wait to be vanquished, to be raped. Woman as land, specifically virgin land, awaited Columbus's seed of civilization. "Virgin land" was empty land: as the conquerors saw it, the indigenous population had not "used" the land; it was "untouched." Therefore, the Europeans could conclude that the natives had forfeited any aboriginal territorial claim and should acquiesce to being tamed by their conquerors.

Conquered Men as Emasculated

To justify the conquest of both the indigenous woman and the land upon which she lived, Native American men had to be gendered as effeminate, a process that occurred early in the conquest. By 1535 Gonzalo Fernández de Oviedo, chronicler of the colonization venture, referred to the Amerindians as sodomites, even though there is no hard evidence about attitudes toward homosexuality among the aborigines. Nevertheless, de Oviedo claims that for the Amerindian men, anal intercourse with members of both sexes was considered normal.[13]

By the eighteenth century, the supposed prevalence of homosexuality among the Amerindians was assumed. The Europeans saw the

Amerindian man as similar to other "primitives" of the world: that is, a homosexual and an onanist who also practiced cannibalism and bestiality. These sins against nature were seen as a threat to the institution of the patriarchal family and, by extension, to the very fabric of civilized society. The supposed effeminacy of the native people was further demonstrated by emphasizing their lack of body hair and pictorially displaying their supposedly small genitals. Simultaneously, the Amerindian woman was portrayed with excessively masculine features and exaggerated sexual traits,[14] justifying the need for manly Europeans to enter the land and restore a proper phallocentric social order under the guise of Christianity.

By constructing indigenous people—and, by extension, Third World people—as effeminate, the Europeans assigned to them what the Europeans believed was their natural function in life: service to the superior European white male. Colonization became a form of sexism, the domestication of the indigenous male. Juan Ginés de Sepúlveda (1494–1573), a Spanish philosopher and theologian who advocated that native people should be treated not as humans but as natural slaves, illustrated the masculine superiority of Europeans to Amerindians by saying that they relate "as women to men."[15]

By linking sodomy to cannibalism and bestiality, the Europeans believed their treatment of Amerindians was justified because they violated both divine rule and the natural order of both men and animals; thus the enslavement of the Amerindian was God's punishment for their sins and the crimes they committed against nature. Since civilization required tutelage, conversion of the American Indian became the justification for colonialism. Christian evangelism became a cover story for European power and privilege.

Owning Black Bodies

Eurocentric sexual norms that oppress people of color were not restricted to the Amerindians. The same framework that helps us understand the intersection of sexism and racism toward the Amerindians applies to African-Americans' experience. A famous illustration is the case of Thomas Jefferson and his slave Sally Hemings. Recent DNA testing confirms the longstanding rumors that Jefferson was the father of the children birthed by Hemings. Although attempts have been made to portray the Jefferson-Hemings relationship as consensual, Hemings' inability to withhold consent of her body, which was owned by Jefferson, makes him a rapist.

Under the social system that justified slavery, black women were considered the antithesis of the ideal genteel white woman, who advanced chastity and innocence. White women were symbols of purity and a product of a superior culture, whereas black women were seen as sexual animals to be trained and exploited. On the slave auction block, when the bidding slowed down black women were forced to disrobe to entice possible purchasers to pay a bit more for the nocturnal benefits of owning her body. Black female bodies existed for white male sexual exploitation; white female bodies had to be protected from the black male menace. (This does not discount the oppression of white female bodies—the physical abuse of female black bodies also served to warn white females of a fate that might also await them if they did not also passively submit to patriarchal rule.)

The taking of black female bodies by whites was not considered rape because African women, unlike their properly bred white counterparts, were considered to be closer to wildness, hence inherently licentious. As sexual savages they were construed as eager to be taken and ravished by any man, white or black. In the final analysis, they were held responsible for their own rape. In fact, the culture said black women really couldn't be raped because they were always the willing whore; it was the rapist who was the true victim for being seduced. As bell hooks reminds us, throughout the South, black slave girls soon after reaching puberty were property at the service of young Southern men needing sexual initiation.[16]

Such practices are not part of some distant past. This became obvious with the public revelation that segregationist leader and civil rights opponent Senator Strom Thurmond had fathered a child with his black maid during his youth. It was, and continues to be, a rite of passage for young white males of privilege to be sexually initiated by women of color, primarily black women. A recent revelation of this privilege can be witnessed in the March 2006 incident concerning Duke University's highly ranked and predominantly white lacrosse team (there is one black member). Several members of the team were accused of raping a black stripper. According to the twenty-seven-year-old alleged victim, she and another black woman were hired as exotic dancers to entertain a group of five men. However, when the women arrived at the house, they encountered more than forty men, all of them white, who proceeded to taunt them with racist epithets.[17] Although as of this writing the woman's accusation of rape has yet to be proven in a court of law, the point is that these white boys from families of power and privilege hired black women to sexually entertain them, continuing the tradition of assigning darker women's bodies the role of providing sexual gratification.

According to this view, the "taking" of black women (and by extension all women of color) could never be defined as rape because due to her seductive nature, she's always "asking for it." Rape could only occur when a white woman was involved. Slave masters were absolved of any blame for sexually "taking" their female through the passage of laws that defined all offspring of a black woman as inheritors of her slave status. As victims of her seduction, white men were not to be held responsible for siring offspring with their slave.

The Bible was masterfully used by those in power to justify the owning of black bodies. This was an easy feat; nowhere in either the Hebrew Bible or the New Testament is slavery categorically condemned. The supporters of slavery in the antebellum South were the ones who had the biblical chapters and verses to quote to justify their way of life. The abolitionists were hard pressed to find any biblical passage that outright condemned the institution of slavery. Even the rape of female slaves found biblical justification and was considered to be ordained by God. Specifically, Numbers 31:18 instructs conquerors as follows: "You shall keep alive all young females who have not had sex with a male for yourselves." This passage is part of Moses' instructions for treatment of the conquered people of Midian, who were now to be Israel's slaves.

No doubt, with the coming of the civil rights movement, most of these practices of reducing black female bodies to objects for white male consumption came to an end. Today, many Americans believe that the civil rights movement succeeded in eliminating most of our racist past; some now speak about living in a postracial world. But racism and ethnic discrimination persist. Political correctness may abound, but thousands of years of stereotypical attitudes and cultural lessons about bodies of color continue to influence how many whites view them. Consider, for example, the unresolved fate of Natalee Holloway. The blond, blue-eyed graduating honors student from Birmingham, Alabama, was on a senior trip with classmates on the mostly black Caribbean Island of Aruba when she disappeared in May 2005. Her disappearance became a major nationwide news obsession, as the media constantly kept us informed about any developments in this unfolding saga. Unfortunately, she has yet to be found. No one questions the tragedy for the young woman and her friends and family; still, far fewer Americans heard of Latoyia Figueroa, a brown woman who disappeared from the streets of Philadelphia around the same time. Both are young attractive women created in the image of God. Both have worth. Both deserve dignity. But based on the relentless media attention given to Holloway's disappearance, in comparison to the deafening media silence when blacks or Latinas disappear, one can only conclude that skin color determines who has greater worth and deserves more dignity in the eyes of the media. Does this mean the media is racist in its attitude toward black female bodies—the same attitudes that were prevalent in the pre–civil rights America? This is probably the wrong question to ask. What concerns us more here is how our views of darker bodies continue to be constructed after centuries of racist-based "legitimate" ways of understanding black female sexuality.

Blacks as Sexual Deviants

The African men who were shipped to the United States to serve as slaves were also defined as not being *real* men, like the Amerindian men before them. They could be strong as mules, but they were not considered to be men because they lacked the means of proving their manhood by providing for their family. Our nation's constitution relegated the black man to being just three-fifths of a white man.[18] Of course, we know that these men who labored to the point of death would have been capable of providing for their families had they not been slaves. Obviously, it was their white overlords who reaped the fruits of their labor. But, in a twisted form of logic, the overseer imposed a type of Christian work ethic that blamed the African and Amerindian man for not truly being men because of their impoverished condition. Paradoxically, while the African man was constructed as being less than a man, he was feared for the potential of asserting his lasciviousness, particularly with white women. Hence the stereotypical fear—a fear that still permeates white society—of blacks as rapists, even though most rapes that occur are intraracial, with the victim and perpetrator of the same race or ethnicity.

Labeling blacks (and by extension, all people of color) as morally deficient (considered to be evidenced by their so-called overly sexualized demeanor) only confirmed their preference for matters of the flesh over the rational. In the minds of white supremacists, all nonwhite bodies were, and still are, synonymous with unrestrained, primitive, hot sex. Because men of color are ruled by the flesh and not the mind, white control of their darker bodies is justified, to ensure, protect, and advance civilization. And how was this control maintained? Black men as sexual predators were controlled by lynching and castration. Black women as Jezebels simply got what they deserved and secretly wanted. These sexual acts of terror were justified as effective means of maintaining control over black bodies; blacks were seen as being ultimately responsible for the violence visited upon them.

Sex between a black man and a white woman was perceived as dangerous, if not deadly. The myth of the black man's excessively large penis (when compared to the white man's) and the white woman's small clitoris (when compared to the black woman's) meant the white woman had to be protected from being not just damaged, but permanently spoiled for white men's use.

On the other hand, the white society that depended on the slavery system constructed reasons to justify white men's having sex with their female slaves. According to a former slave from the Caribbean, "There was one type of sickness the whites picked up, a sickness of the veins and male organs. It could only be got rid of with black women; if the man who had it slept with a Negress he was cured immediately."[19]

These sentiments about blacks as wanton beings led twentieth-century philosopher Franz Fanon to sarcastically write, "As for the Negroes, they have tremendous sexual powers. What do you expect, with all the freedom they have in their jungles! They copulate at all times and in all places. They are really genital. They have so many children that they cannot even count them. *Be careful, or they will flood us with little mulattoes.* . . . One is no longer aware of the Negro but only of a penis; the Negro is eclipsed. He is turned into a penis. *He is a penis.* [italics mine]"[20] Fanon addresses the fears and forbidden desires that are at times projected onto African Americans, as well as other men of color—and the resulting fixation with the black penis that posed a threat to white civilization. The black penis had to be kept separate from power and privilege. This is why castration was viewed as an acceptable form of punishment for black men. At times, castration was part of the lynching ritual.

Finding Salvation with Hagar

Poor women, who are disproportionately of color, seldom have the luxury of controlling their own bodies. To feed their families and ensure their survival, some of these women find few options other than to use their bodies as commodities on the open market. Anyone who becomes vulnerable to sexual exploitation, whether consciously as a means for survival or against one's will, is a victim of injustice. There is no possibility of having great sex when vulnerability is demanded or forced from the other while the perpetrator guards his own vulnerability. Rape, incest, prostitution, and other forms of sexual misconduct are unjust not because they are sexual in nature, but because they take place in relationships that are not mutually giving, in which the vulnerability of one of the parties is abused. If pain, humiliation, and shame are forced on one who is powerless, then there is no familial relationship, whether the participants are married or not. The sex taking place in this nonfamilial relationship is unjust and thus immoral.

Take, for example, the relationship between the biblical patriarch Abraham and his wife's slave girl Hagar. All too often, when we read the story of Abraham and Sarah, the focus remains on the patriarch and matriarch of the faith. Unfortunately, the story of Sarah's African slave girl Hagar is either lost, forgotten, or silenced. But what would happen if we reread the story and made Hagar the center of the narrative? We might discover a message of hope, liberation, and salvation for poor bodies of color, specifically female bodies of color.

Unable to conceive, Sarah concluded that her barrenness was a curse from God. Taking matters into her own hands, she offered up her slave girl's body to Abraham, her husband. The Hebrew word used in Genesis 16 to describe Hagar is šiphâ, which means virgin. Hagar was a virgin who was forced to have sex with Abraham, by this time an old man. In other words, Hagar was raped by the patriarch of the faith—I say raped, because that is the term used when a woman is forced to have sex against her will. Hagar lost her personhood and instead became a womb to be used by Sarah—who owned Hagar's body—to accomplish Sarah's personal agenda. Hagar, who was an Egyptian, had no say as to who could enter her body. She, like so many of her African descendants, existed to serve the needs of those who owned her. For this reason, contemporary womanist theologian Delores Williams, in her book *Sisters in the Wilderness,* finds in the Genesis 16:1–16 and 21:9–21 account a rape narrative that resonates with the African American experience, specifically the experience of black women. As slaves, black women like Hagar were required to offer up their bodies at the whim of their owners. Not only were black female slaves required to satisfy their masters' desires, but they also had to face the humiliation and degradation of being "rented out" to other white men as concubines. Like her future descendants, Hagar was marginalized by gender, ethnicity, and class.

Yet Williams reminds us that Sarah's property, as a surrogate mother, experienced consciousness-raising. She became a model for all oppressed women, being the first woman in the Bible to seek her own liberation by fleeing Sarah's cruelty. Even though she was carrying Abraham's child, Hagar chose possible death in the desert, thus denying those who owned her any right to the fruits of her body. It was in the wilderness that God's presence was manifested, accompanying the outcast in the midst of her suffering. Surprisingly, the divine message instructed Hagar to return to Sarah and "suffer affliction under her hand." As disturbing as God's instructions were, returning led to her unborn son's physical survival. Born in the house of Abraham, her future son Ishmael also became an heir to the promise of God and, as such, an intruder to the covenant as understood by Jews and Christians.

At this point the unexpected occurred. Hagar, the lowly marginalized woman, gave God a name—a privilege extended to no other person throughout the scriptures. Only a superior, according to ancient custom, was able to name those who are lower in status. But here we have the first biblically recorded person to give God a name. Her actions became an overt strike against the predominant patriarchal structures of her time. And what name did this slave girl choose for God? *El Roi,* literally "the God who sees," a name that unites the divine with her human experience of suffering—for God sees the suffering of this marginalized woman.

The second time the Bible returns to Hagar, we find her again in the wilderness, not because she was fleeing, but because she was disposed of by those who owned her. Sarah eventually had her own son Isaac, but, fearing that her son's inheritance could be jeopardized by Abraham's first-born, Ishmael, Sarah orchestrated Hagar's exile. Again Hagar found herself in the desert facing death (a familiar scenario even today for domestic servants who, when they cease to be useful, are also discharged). Like poor women today, many of whom are of color, Hagar was robbed of subjectivity. Poor women today, like Hagar, exist as an economic commodity to be used to advance the privilege of those who have power over them. Homeless because of the unwillingness of the father of her child to shoulder his responsibility, she was abandoned. Alone in the desert, facing death, and questioning the promise God had previously uttered about the multitude of her descendants, she must have wondered about the blindness of this God whom she named *El Roi.* Yet this time God heard the cry of her son and rescued them.[21]

Hagar suffered from classism (as a slave), racism (as an Egyptian foreigner), and sexism (as a woman raped by Abraham). The biblical story of Hagar is a lens through which the Bible can be read. The story of the used and abused woman is a motif that resonates with many women of color. Even those who could be considered to be natural allies—women of the dominant culture, like Sarah—used Hagar's body to advance their own privilege. But the good news is that there is a God who is found in the wilderness, in the midst of the struggle of those on the margins of economic power and white privilege. Because God is found accompanying the disenfranchised, Hagar and her child Ishmael complicated the history of salvation by becoming part of God's promise to make a nation by using Abraham's seed.

3

THE BODY AND ITS PLEASURES

To indulge in intercourse without intending children is to outrage nature.[1]

—Clement of Alexandria

I must disfigure that face which contrary to God's commandment I have painted with rouge, white lead, and antimony. I must mortify that body which has been given up to many pleasures. I must make up for my long laughter by constant weeping. I must exchange my soft linen and costly silks for rough goat's hair. I who have pleased my husband and the world in the past, desire now to please Christ.[2]

—St. Paula (347–404)

CITING EMBARRASSMENT ON THE PART OF PARENTS to speak openly with their children about sexual issues, the Department of Health and Human Services in 2005 launched a website whose main purpose was to provide information on how to approach this delicate topic. Among the advice given was an emphasis on abstinence, a suspicion of contraceptives, and encouragement to obtain therapeutic guidance from professionals who share parents' values if their adolescent children experience "difficulties with gender identity or sexual orientation." As could be expected, several advocacy groups charged the government with using tax dollars to provide biased and inaccurate sexual advice to parents. Such organizations as the Sexuality Information and Education Council of the United States, the American Civil Liberties Union, Planned Parenthood, and the Human Rights Campaign charged that the Department's "misinformation" could end up causing severe damage to the health and well-being of adolescents.[3]

Regardless of the validity of the arguments used by such groups in their protest of the website, one truth is undeniable. The government's views on abstinence, contraceptives, and the "choice" to be gay as expressed on the website are rooted in a Christian—specifically, a conservative Christian—understanding of sexuality. The Department of Health and Human Services' attitudes toward sexuality, on which their advice and guidance are based, are but the latest manifestation of a historical Christian disdain for both sex and the body. Our modern-day aversion to, yet fascination with, the sexual can never be fully comprehended apart from this prominent Christian influence—a Christian influence that has reluctantly tolerated sex.

Sex as Sin

The Psalmist would sing "Behold, I was conceived in iniquity and in sin did my mother conceive me" (Psalms 51:5). Since the foundation of Christendom, believers in the Orthodox, Catholic, and Protestant traditions have offered these words up to God as part of their official prayers. Many have interpreted this scriptural passage to confirm that the sexual act responsible for conception is indeed a sin. Reciting this prayer affirms the supposed connection between sex and sin. But why would my very existence be understood as a product of the sin of sex engaged in by my married mother? Yet, rather than my existence being a product of love, this prayer supposedly emphasizes my unworthiness due to my mother's having had sex with my father. How did we as Christians arrive at such a conclusion?

Being in Body

The underlying assumption in Christianity that sex is "dirty" reflects a dichotomy that has existed in Christian thought for nearly two thousand years, between what was believed to be sacred (spirit) and what was defined as profane (the body). Most Christians have traditionally believed that the soul and the flesh are forced to struggle against each other for supremacy over the individual. Early Christian writers were strongly influenced by this antagonistic body/soul dualism, stressing the danger that new believers faced if they succumbed to the mortal body, as opposed to the immortal soul. That which is of the flesh was conceived as being corruptible, whereas only that which is of the spirit could expect to inherit the eternal. Or as St. Paul reminds us, ". . . flesh and blood is not able to inherit God's kingdom, nor does corruption inherit incorruption" (1 Corinthians 15:50). Though some will argue that the way in which Paul defined flesh and spirit does not necessarily support the argument in favor of the flesh-spirit divide, this divide still became a salient characteristic of Christianity.

It is not difficult for us to understand how Christians read their cultural context into Paul in determining why the corruptible flesh could not inherit the incorruptible spiritual world. After all, the body burps, emits foul odors, urinates, and defecates. With the passage of time the body begins to deteriorate, sagging and becoming wrinkled, and after death the body rots, decays, and decomposes, eventually becoming food for worms and maggots. The spirit, on the other hand, transcends the temporal effects of age and gravity. Although this flesh-spirit divide is foreign to the Hebrew Bible, it became a prominent feature of early Christianity through the influence of Neo-Platonic thought.

Stoic philosophy and its proclivity for devaluing the body also contributed to the Christian understanding of the body/spirit split. Their emphasis on obtaining inner peace through the human will's ability to control passions contributed to the overall pessimism regarding desire, specifically sexual desire. For the Stoics, marriage became the means by which self-control was practiced. The rational reason for engaging in sex became procreation. Although many modes of understanding gender and sexual reality developed during Christianity's early years, the body/soul cosmic split was among the most prevalent characteristics of that era. The early Christian scholar Tertullian expressed it succinctly: "Flesh is an earthly, spirit a heavenly, material."[4]

According to this way of thinking, the flesh, as inherently sinful, alienates believers from their bodies and, in turn, from their sexuality. Redemption came to be understood as a flight from the body—from the material toward the spiritual—an understanding that continues to influence the faith community today. For those seeking spiritual purification, hope for spiritual wholeness was and continues to be found in the process of freeing oneself from the sinful influences of one's body or by crucifying one's sinful flesh on Jesus' cross. Earthly pleasures are forsaken in remembrance of Christ's ultimate sacrifice—or, as St. Paul reminds us, "the one belonging to Christ crucified the flesh with its passions and lusts" (Galatians 5:24). Referring to a man engaged in sexual sin, Paul advised followers to "deliver such a one to Satan for destruction of the flesh so that the spirit may be saved in the day of Lord Jesus" (1 Corinthians 5:5). What develops from this body/soul dichotomy is a very antibody perspective, in which the body, in and of itself, is evil.

The early Christian faith, concerned with the believers' religious growth, sought spiritual development at the expense of the body, in which nothing good dwells. After all, Jesus recommended that we "cut off" those parts of the body that caused us to sin (Matthew 9:43–45). St. Paul illustrated this point when he wrote: "The fact is that I know that in me, that which is in my flesh, dwells nothing good, for while the desire to do good is present, in practice I cannot find the good. . . . What a wretched man I am! Who will deliver me from this body of death? . . . So then I with my mind truly serve God's law, and with the flesh the law of sin" (Romans 7:18, 24, 26). The danger the body poses for the believer is entangling the soul with the soiled flesh. For the true believer, no price is too great to pay to ensure the salvation of the soul. One of the leading early Christian thinkers, Origen (c. 184–254 C.E.), took Jesus' words in Matthew 19:12 literally and made himself a eunuch for the kingdom of God through castration.

God in the Flesh

Most Christians would be offended by the image of Jesus defecating or urinating. But if Jesus was indeed human, as we profess in our faith, then he had to have had such bodily functions. But as disturbing as it may be to some to imagine Jesus excreting bodily waste, many more people would find it blasphemous to imagine Jesus participating in any sexual act. Such anti-body views are then read into the life of Jesus, dehumanizing him through our pious sensibilities. But if we claim that Jesus was sinless (Hebrews 4:14–15), and connect this to the claim that Jesus did not engage in sex, we might falsely conclude that sex is sin, which is why Jesus abstained. One need only recall the controversy resulting from Martin Scorsese's 1988 film *The Last Temptation of Christ,* in which during a dream sequence Jesus envisions himself marrying Mary Magdalene. The concept of Jesus engaging in sex so enraged some arch-conservative Christians that they set fire to a Paris theater during a showing of the movie, resulting in the injury and death of moviegoers.[5] To the perpetrators, burning people alive was less repulsive than a movie dream sequence that explores Jesus' sexuality.

The idea of Jesus engaged in sex is highly sacrilegious because of how Christians have historically defined sex. The dualistic relationship created between the flesh and the spirit led to the development of practices that encouraged the denial of bodily pleasure in exchange for the pursuit of the spiritual. The danger of sex was that humans, specifically men, would lose themselves to the bondage of the flesh. Sexual pleasure had to be restricted by religious authorities to avoid what they ascertained to be detrimental to both the physical and spiritual welfare of the believer. The church perceived sex outside of what was constructed as an acceptable space, as something profane, wicked, evil, or sinful. Why? Because it celebrated and focused on the body, which, said the church, is dirty and temporal and thus distracted from the spiritual, which is eternal. Some early Christian sects (Gnostics, Marcionites, and other Syriac traditions) had such an aversion to the material world that they made salvation contingent on the renunciation of sex. This revulsion of the human body developed over the second century, influencing the evolution of Christendom.

Avoiding the Pleasures of the Flesh

From the middle of the third century through the start of the fourth, an ascetic movement developed, in part as a response to how the biblical text was interpreted, as in St. Paul's writings: "I chastise my body and subjugate it, lest when preaching to others I myself should be rejected" (1 Corinthians 9:27). In part, the ascetic movement was also the result of the Christianization of the Roman Empire (313) brought about by Constantine (274–337). Some Christians saw the faith becoming perverted with the trappings of the Empire's power and privilege. As a response, they fled to the desert to concentrate on achieving God's perfection in this life. They renounced wealth, property, power, privilege, comfort, family, and household responsibilities. And most of all, they renounced sex. Asceticism became the denial of bodily sexual pleasure and the repression of erotic desire, understood by the faithful to be a holy act of religious devotion required to enter God's service. Or as St. Anthony (c. 250–356) said, "the fibre of the soul is then sound when the pleasures of the body are diminished."[6]

Pain, suffering, deprivation, and self-mutilation were spiritualized, whereas love was desexualized so that desire for sex could be replaced with desire for God. Pleasure was found in self-denial so as to concentrate on things of the spirit rather than of the flesh. As a result, desire of sexual pleasure was demonized, an urge requiring suppression. Through pain, the opposite of sensual pleasure, the joy of salvation could be achieved. Suffering because of faith (as in the persecution of Christians) was replaced by suffering for faith (namely self-denial and self-repression). Pain and suffering no longer were derived from confronting injustices; rather, pain and suffering were romanticized for their own spiritual sake.

This understanding of violence in Christianity might help explain the popularity of Mel Gibson's 2004 film *The Passion of the Christ*. The audience witnessed Jesus, in all his humanity, being brutally tortured, ridiculed, and nailed to a cross, alone and abandoned—all the while being mocked by Satan. The gory scenes of torment being visited on Jesus throughout the film seem intended to support the doctrinal belief that suffering and death become salvific.

Forgetting that the cross is a symbol of evil allows for the easy romanticizing of those who suffer as some sort of hyper-Christians for the "cross" they are forced to bear. Such views tend to offer honor to the one suffering, encouraging a form of quietism in which suffering is stoically borne. What became the spiritual journey of the few early Christians seeking an ascetic life soon became the acceptable norm. Self-denial became an essential characteristic of Christian spiritual maturity. Salvation was marked by accepting, if not aggressively seeking, pain. No physical pain, no spiritual gain! Consequently, the painful act of self-flagellation (self-whipping) produced the necessary pain required before union with God could be obtained. This practice of self-flagellation originally grew out of the floggings administered as punishment to erring monks. Soon it was accepted as a religious expression that demonstrated the ascetic ideal—a practice approved and encouraged by the early Christian church. In 1349 Pope Clement VI prohibited the practice, but some Christians continued it, believing it brought them closer to God. Today groups like New Mexico's Hermanos Penitentes are believed to continue the practice in secret.

Although church leaders still recognized and respected the sex instinct as natural, they maintained (like the Stoics) that the sexual act should take place only for the purpose of procreation in marriage. Sex was a necessary evil—necessary as the means of preserving the species. For some early scholars, however, sex was to be avoided even by married couples. Anything but abstinence from sex would fall short of total emancipation from evil. Those who chose the ascetic life of abstention from all forms of sexual contact could gain the reward of living a more spiritual and pious life than those who married. Clement of Alexandria wrote, "If we are required to practice self-control—as we should—we ought to manifest it even more with our wives . . . sexual intercourse does no one any good, except that it harms the beloved. Intercourse performed licitly is an occasion of sin, unless done purely to beget children: A hired wife shall be accounted as a sow."[7] Tertullian went further, claiming that engaging in sex (even in marriage) and praying were incongruent. One could not engage in both sex and prayer, he insisted; one of the two had to be forsaken. Therefore, he stipulated, those who did marry because they were unable to control the passions of youth should in their later years strive to minimize intercourse with their spouse until they were able to renounce the activity.[8]

Augustine took this view even further. He saw no difference between what occurred in the marriage bed and sex between a man and a prostitute. Both were sinful; however, sex in marriage was permissible only for the purpose of reproduction.[9] The ideal marriage would become an asexual platonic relationship. When sex did occur for the sake of procreation, the man was to sow his seed into his wife—"the field of generation"—with the same dispassion exhibited by a farmer who sows his seed upon fertile earth—and women, like the earth, were to be subdued.

But Augustine saw pleasurable plowing as a problem. Any passion or lust demonstrated by the man while sowing his seed in the woman was due to the "horrible wickedness of the women who 'changed the natural use into that which is against nature.'"[10] If passion did arise during the sexual act for procreation, it was the woman, as seductive stimulus, who was responsible for inciting said lust. Or as Augustine put it, "Nothing so much casts down the mind of man from its citadel as do the caresses of women."[11] Nevertheless, in spite of the wickedness of women for inciting male passion, men were still required to love them. Augustine admonished men to love their wives as creatures redeemed by God, while simultaneously hating them for their corruptible flesh and the role their flesh played in conjugal relations. For Augustine, this love for one's wife was comparable to the love one must show to one's enemies.[12]

Marriage was ambiguously accepted only because of its ultimate purpose—procreation, even though the means of achieving this goal are considered to be a debauchery. But marriage, although necessary, had a spiritual cost. Jerome, a contemporary of Augustine, insisted that touching a woman, even one's wife, was something evil. To touch a woman excluded one from being able to commune with God. Consequently, the married man was unable to devote himself fully to God's will and purpose.[13] There was no middle ground for Jerome. As he advised, "either we pray always and are virgins, or we cease to pray that we may fulfill the claims of marriage."[14]

These views have persisted through the ages. Reiterating Augustine's assumptions on marital sex two centuries later, Pope Gregory the Great (540–604) would not condone marital sex for the sake of pure pleasure. Sex for any other reason except procreation was wrong, he wrote, because it reduced sex to a masturbatory act for the satisfaction of the male carnal nature. The purpose of wedlock was procreation; to abandon oneself to sexual pleasure exceeded the rights of marriage.[15] Even when engaging in sex for procreation, it was not free from sin because the pleasure associated with sex "tainted" the act.[16] Pope Gregory's view on sexual desire becomes clear when we see how he admired the way that St. Benedict (480–543), the founder and abbot of the monastery known as the Citadel of Campania, conquered his sexual desire through suffering. The pope recounts an episode of the saint's battle against the flesh:

> The moment [the Tempter] left, [St. Benedict] was seized with an unusually violent temptation. The evil spirit recalled to his mind a woman he had once seen, and before he realized it his emotions were carrying him away. Almost overcome in the struggle, he was on the point of abandoning the lonely wilderness, when suddenly with the help of God's grace he came to himself.
>
> He then noticed a thick patch of nettles and briers next to him. Throwing his garments aside he flung himself into the sharp thorns and stinging nettles. There he rolled and tossed until his whole body was in pain and covered with blood. Yet, once he had *conquered pleasure through suffering,* his torn and bleeding skin served to drain the poison of temptation from his body [author's emphasis]. Before long, the pain that was burning his whole body had put out the fires of evil in his heart. It was by exchanging these two fires that he gained the victory over sin. So complete was his triumph that from then on, as he later told his disciples, he never experienced another temptation of this kind.
>
> Soon after, many forsook the world to place themselves under his guidance, for now that he was free from these temptations he was ready to instruct others in the practice of virtue.[17]

Lest you think that by the twentieth century the Vatican had evolved a more liberated view of sex in marriage, consider Pope Paul VI, who in his 1968 letter, *Humanae Vitae,* still affirmed that the purpose of marriage was procreation, not fellowship—even though allowances were now made for nonprocreative marital intercourse. Only recently—with Pope Benedict XVI's first encyclical, *Deus Caritas Est (God Is Love),* released in 2006—has the church begun to concede that its view on sexuality has been somewhat "negative." He wrote, "Nowadays Christianity of the past is often criticized as having been opposed to the body; and it is quite true that tendencies of this sort have always existed."[18]

Continuing Influence of the Flesh

From our modern perspective, we can see that the extreme views on sex propounded by Augustine and his contemporaries were influenced by the societies in which they lived, as well as their personal life experiences. For example, we recognize now that Augustine's negative views on sexual pleasure even in "holy matrimony" were probably influenced by his illicit sexual experiences with the concubine with whom he had a child prior to his Christian conversion. In his writings, he reflects on this relationship as one based purely on the passions of sex, what he calls the "disease of the flesh," not love.[19] This apparent lack of love for his sexual partner clearly influenced his understanding of sex. When we study the life of Jerome today, it is clear that his views about the superiority of chastity over marriage were influenced by the promiscuous life he lived as a youth. He was obsessed with sex, and even when he attempted to escape the burden of the flesh by retiring to a monastic life, he was still haunted by memories of the female dancers he had witnessed in Rome.

Even though we can safely conclude that these great Christian scholars didn't derive their views of sexual morality solely from objective reflection on the biblical text, we must be careful not to dismiss the influence their writings still have over Christian concepts of sexuality and sexual mores in our society as a whole. True, when our modern, more progressive eyes read the words of these early Church fathers on sex in marriage, we quickly realize how outlandishly sexist and dated they are. Few today ever read these early writings, even though the concepts and world views expressed therein are woven into the very fabric of Christian thought. Yet although we may reject and laugh at the actual statements made by these early Christian thinkers, many Christians today are still uncomfortable with the link existing between the sacred and sensual. This apprehension is based on the foundational thoughts of Church writers such as these, even though the majority of the population may never have read their works, let alone know anything about them. Some of the very concepts Augustine developed in the early fifth century continue to define and influence how Christians (among both Catholics and Protestants) understand sex today.

For Augustine, sex was reduced to the genitals, something both uncontrollable and evil—a view that remains prevalent. The reason Adam covered his genitals with fig leaves, according to Augustine, was not modesty or shame; rather, because Adam's penis was erect and uncontrollably throbbing. Augustine succeeds in linking shame and sex to the Fall of humanity, which deserves God's punishment; he states that the erect penis signifies our will toward the flesh, over and against the spirit.[20] Augustine's argument that Adam's uncontrollably throbbing penis symbolized his rebellion against God redefined sex as the cause for expulsion from Paradise. And according to philosopher Michel Foucault, an erect penis "is the image of man revolted against God." Hence, the Christian problem with sex is desire itself.[21] Likewise, our throbbing penises or clitorises today, or our desire for them, continue to symbolize our choice of the things of this world rather than the Kingdom of Heaven.

Physical Union and Spiritual Rapture

For most of early Christian church history, sex was viewed as something requiring forgiveness, rather than something that can lead to spirituality. It is difficult to remember that there is another side to this coin, and that the antipleasure and anti-body strains, although powerful and influential, do not tell the whole story. Consider several biblical passages that seem to celebrate sexual pleasure: Proverbs 5:19 advises "Let [your wife] be the company you keep, hers the breasts that delight you every time, hers the love that ravishes you." Passages about Sarah the matriarch fondly recall her youth when her husband Abraham could sexually pleasure her (Genesis 18:12); the biblical text's last words about Moses, prior his death, inform the reader that in spite of his advanced years, his sexual vigor was not impaired (Deuteronomy 34:7). These passages illustrate the biblical witness to the importance of sexual pleasure. But sex is more than simply physical gratification. Sexual physical union, in a mystical way, reflects our spiritual union with God.

Singing the Song of Solomon

No other biblical book better exemplifies the celebration of sexual pleasure than the erotic poetry known as the Song of Songs. Contrary to the "pleasure as sin" mentality prevailing in the development of Christianity, the Song is unique because it vividly describes sexual yearning, refuting the prevalent fear of sexual desire. Here, sex is not reduced to the singular act of copulation, but encompasses the pleasure and passion that build toward a final release. How did such a lustful book ever make it into the Bible? After all, the book contains no mention of God, no guidance for ethical living, and no historical account concerning the Jewish people. What it does contain is an erotic description of female orgasm, wet dreams, allusions to oral sex, and the sexual frustration of not satisfying physical urges. Could its inclusion in the Word of God confirm that God's Word, contrary to Pope Gregory the Great or St. Benedict, avows sexual pleasure?

Since it became part of the Bible, early Hebrew scholars have read the Song of Songs as a love story, an allegory of Israel's love for God. Although all biblical writings were considered holy, the Song was considered among the earliest rabbinic texts to be the "Holy of Holies."[22]

Why would a biblical work celebrating desire and sexual intimacy be considered the "Holy of Holies"—the name for the special place in the ancient Temple where God's presence resided? According to the thirteenth century Torah commentator Rabbi Moshe ben Nahman, God is present among couples in the intimate moment of becoming one flesh. For example, the Sabbath God's holy day of rest was considered the ideal time for having sex, thus connecting a holy act with the holy day.[23] In effect, rabbinical commentators are insinuating that the bedchamber becomes the Holy of Holies. To express the concept of sexual intimacy as the Holy of Holies in a Christian understanding is to depict sex as holy communion.

Although not denying the postmodern possibility that a text can contain multiple meanings, it is important to stress from the outset that the Song of Songs is first and foremost a desire for and affirmation of sexual pleasure. The text never mentions procreation, and no attempt is made on the part of the biblical book to rein in, suppress, legislate, control, shame, or punish sexual expression. Quite the contrary. The text subverts the assumption that sex must occur only within marriage, as these two unmarried lovers (8:7b) play a coy cat-and-mouse game of searching for each other, describing their sexual arousal, lingering over past trysts, and anticipating the ultimate union. They burn for each other with a fire that comes from Yahweh, a fire that no flood can quench or drown (8:6–7). The text immediately starts with foreplay, demanding that the lover "kiss me with the kisses of your mouth," which taste "better than wine" (1:2). The sexual remembrances and desires of the lovers are celebrated throughout eight erotic chapters. As such, the book serves to counteract the anti-body aspects that developed in Christianity.

In her book *Exquisite Desire*, Carey Walsh illustrates the erotic and lustful sexual yearning laced throughout the Song of Songs by providing meaning to the ancient literary symbols used. For example, when the woman's breasts are described as "two fawns, twins of a gazelle" (4:5; 7:3), she explains that the ancient Hebrew mind would have instantly recognized what this description signified—that her breasts are "bouncy, dainty, and even in size (twins)." Elsewhere, her breasts are referred to as "clusters of vine" (7:8). Although today a locker-room description of women's breasts would more likely compare them to melons or grapefruits (depending on the size), to the ancient Hebrew mind, grapes were characterized as being hard, dark, smooth, ripe, and tart, probably signifying the oral pleasure of savoring, plucking, and nibbling upon the woman's hard, dark, smooth, ripe, and tart nipples.[24]

Fruits and their juices also become signifiers for body parts and the bodily fluids they distill. The constant enjoyment of "eating the choicest fruits" (4:16) becomes a double entendre for enjoying various sexual pleasures, specifically oral pleasures. The garden (of paradise?) that she opens for her beloved to enter is a euphemism for her vagina. Her garden (vagina) is locked up (4:12), but his "fountain" can make her garden fertile as streams of living water flow down (4:15). The beloved comes into the garden and eats and drinks from it (5:1); he comes down to her garden to enjoy it (6:2). In her garden are clusters of grapes (7:12), triangular in shape, surrounded by foliage, and gorged with juices.[25]

These lovers (who are not married, for her brothers wonder what to do with her on the day she becomes engaged [8:7]), are obviously intimately familiar with each others' bodies. "The curves of your thighs are like jewels, the work from the hands of an artisan. Your navel is like a round goblet that never lacks mixed wine. Your belly is like a heap of wheat, hedged all around with lilies" (7:2). He obviously has seen and enjoyed the woman's thighs, belly, and whatever the lilies represent! Likewise, she is familiar with his "belly [which is like] an ivory plate overlaid with sapphires" (5:14), no doubt a reference to his abdominal muscles, which are as precious as sapphires and carved as ivory. She craves the day when her beloved, like a bag of myrrh (a scent customarily used to enhance the lovemaking experience, per Esther 2:12 and Proverbs 7:16–18), lies on top of her, between her breasts (1:13). They have already been in the lovemaking "spoon" position, with his left hand under her head and his right hand embracing her (2:6; 8:3). They have fully drunk of each other's bodies to the point of recalling with fondness and desire the lasting pleasure of gazing upon the beloved.[26]

Such drinking is more than a simple metaphor. "I would make you drink the spiced wine from the juice of my pomegranates" (8:2). Remember, the seeds of a pomegranate that has been sliced in half can resemble a clitoris. If so, the pomegranate, red and hard, full of seeds, requires the dexterity of the tongue to retrieve its sweet and tart juice. Likewise, the woman's "juices" she so willingly wants to surrender can only be tasted through oral sex, leaving her with the expectancy of having her lover eat her "honeycomb with [her] honey" (5:1). These tasty treats of "honey and milk" can be found under the beloved's tongue (4:11). In an earlier passage the allusion to oral sex is more pronounced. "My beloved thrust his hand through the opening and I trembled to the core of my being for him. Then I rose to open myself to my beloved, my hands dripped with myrrh, pure myrrh off my fingers, on to the handle of the bolt" (5:4–5). In this passage, the hand of the beloved is found thrust into her "opening" causing her body to shudder in ecstasy. Opening herself to her beloved leads to fingers dripping with myrrh—the scent, as previously mentioned, employed for lovemaking. The same scent is found a few verses later on the lips of the beloved—"His lips are like lilies dropping flowering myrrh" (5:13), raising the question of how the wetness of the woman symbolized by myrrh is now dropping from the lips of her beloved. Later, in returning the favor, he is an apple tree and she gets to "taste his sweet fruit" (2:3).[27]

Subverting Patriarchy

But although she pines for her beloved to enter her garden, and opens it up for him to enjoy its ripened fruit, it remains "her" garden (8:12). His presence is by invitation only, thus subverting the prevalent patriarchal order evident throughout the rest of the biblical text. The Song of Songs not only celebrates sexual pleasure from a woman's perspective, but it achieves this pleasure because she maintains the autonomy of her garden. Reading the Song through a woman's eyes undermines an otherwise androcentric (male-centered) biblical text, overturning woman's supposedly subservient position in society. It is she—not her brothers, to whom she is required to submit—who determines who will romp through her garden. Because of her autonomy, she seeks her lover on her terms, cautious not to stir up or arouse love until it delights (2:7; 3:5; 8:4). Through mutual giving and vulnerability she gives herself permission to become intoxicated with the sweet wine of lovemaking. But at the end of the day, even though her beloved has tasted her choicest fruits and drunk in their juices, it still remains her garden—to be opened again for her beloved at a future time of her choosing.

The text reverses the normative patriarchal order of the day by making the woman's sexual desires and wants the center of the ethical discourse. In the Song of Songs, she is no longer an object, an extension of the male. Instead, she is her own subject who celebrates her sexuality without fear or shame. The woman of the Song seeks sexual intimacy with her beloved, quite apart from the patriarchal structures of her day. Besides desiring her lover's body, she also wants sex apart from a male dominant–female subordinate relationship. Love and sexual pleasure, for her, exist for their own sake! For this reason, the Song is more than simply an erotic psalm alluding to our love for God or Jesus. It is a protest song—protesting patriarchy.

The bold rebellion of taking control of her sexuality comes at a price. The city's watchmen, charged with maintaining the law and order of the patriarchal establishment (a law and order designed to justify and privilege male dominance), beat her (5:7). And although the Song does not end on this sad note to show the moral consequence of her actions, it does reveal the reality faced by women who chose to rebel against the law and order established to protect patriarchal privilege. Those women who attempted to determine their own destiny could expect a certain degree of hostility from the dominant male-centered culture.

Becoming One with Your Lover

Despite the societal consequences that befell the woman in the Song of Songs, the psalm teaches that both partners in a relationship have a right to become one through sexual pleasure, fulfillment, and satisfaction. What the lovers crave, what they ultimately desire, is to become one with each other. This process is possible when a familial relationship exists in a safe environment in which both lovers can be totally vulnerable, so that each can fully relinquish control over the partner and the self; in other words, they can lose themselves in each other. The possibility of intimacy among lovers can at times be forfeited due to a fear of it or, more specifically, a fear of not being in control and instead being taken advantage of. The pain of possible betrayal prevents some from becoming vulnerable and totally abandoning themselves to the other.

A 2005 study conducted by the University of Groningen at Copenhagen, Denmark, confirms this. The study showed that women genuinely achieve orgasm when the area of the brain involved in fear is deactivated. Brain scans taken of women being sexually stimulated by their partners showed that those achieving orgasm were able to do so only when fear (and high anxiety) was absent.[28] The study seems to indicate that only when vulnerability exists without fear and anxiety can great sex occur. Only then can climaxing be experienced as an ephemeral yet awe-inspiring burst of intense overwhelming pleasure, creating an ethereal state of being. When two lovers become one with each other, not only is pleasure heightened, but they create *shalom* for each other. The Hebrew concept of *shalom* is a complex word that denotes peace, solidarity, well-being, and wholeness. When *shalom* is connected to the Hebrew word *shlemut* (which connotes a concept of completeness), the highest level of peace is attainable. *Shalom* without *shlemut* can simply imply the absence of hostilities, but *shalom* with *shlemut* moves further, toward harmonious completeness. *Shalom* with *shlemut* can be achieved both in sexual union with one's beloved and in spiritual union with one's God. As sociologist Meredith McGuire reminds us, "important parallels exist between spiritual and sexual ecstasy."[29] Sex as a cause of *shalom* unites opposites. In the process of uniting opposites—spirit and flesh (matter), life and death, light and darkness, subject and object—wholeness, completeness, and solidarity can be achieved, as this rapture of sexual ecstasy dissolves the boundaries between the lovers. Entwined lovers' limbs make it difficult to ascertain where one person begins and the other ends. At the moment of orgasm, lovers' subjectivity dissolves as they lose themselves, each in the other. A transcendent altered state results. For lovers, this transcendent *shalom* with *shlemut* is achievable as they lose control of themselves in a safe environment of mutual giving and vulnerability and as they become one flesh.

Ultimately, becoming one is not limited to the lovers, for there is a divine nature in sexual intimacy. We can get to know God as well as we know our beloved. Jesus stated in his prayer to God, "That they [my disciples] all be one. As you Father are in me, and I am in you, may they also be one in us so the world can believe that you sent me" (John 17:21). As God the Father and Son are one in the Trinity (along with the Holy Spirit), so we too can become part of the Trinity, becoming one with God in similar fashion. The possibility of mystical union becomes possible through a Trinitarian awareness—that is, as three Gods in one is a mystery beyond reason, so too is the union of the human soul with God.

Becoming One with God

Saint Bernard of Clairvaux (c. 1090–1153), founder and leader of the monastery at Clairvaux that housed over seven hundred monks, delivered a series of eighty-six sermons on the Song of Songs from 1136 until the time of his death in 1153. He only got as far as chapter three, verse one. For seventeen years, Saint Bernard preached the erotic Song of Songs to celibate monks, many of whom had enjoyed worldly pleasures before renouncing them to join the order. Much time was spent on the allegorical kisses of Christ, seen as the union of two natures. Saint Bernard was not alone in his allegorical interpretation. As mentioned previously, early Hebrew scholars have read the Song of Songs as a symbolic representation of Israel's love for God, and later Christians interpreted the text to symbolize Christ's love for the church.

The casual reader of the biblical text will soon discover the recurring theme of God's (or Jesus') relationship to believers described as marriage, complete with sexual metaphors and the emotions sex produces—specifically tenderness, jealousy, and betrayal. The prophets of old would constantly describe God as the husband of Israel. "For your husband is your Maker and Yahweh of hosts is his name" (Isaiah 54:5). The prophet Ezekiel provides a more erotic example: "You developed and grew, reaching marriageable age. Your breasts are formed and your hair is grown, but you were naked and bare. I passed by you, gazed upon you, and behold, your time had come, the time for love. I spread my skirt over you and covered your nakedness. I swore to you and entered a covenant with you, declares the Lord Yahweh. You became mine" (16:7–8). In similar fashion, Jesus is portrayed as the bridegroom and the church as his bride (Matthew 9:15, 25:1–13). And remember, "to the bridegroom belongs the bride [the church]" (John 3:15).

But God's gentle wooing, offers of unconditional love, and the intimacy that comes with union, can quickly turn to violent jealousy. When God's people worshiped other gods, their unfaithfulness was likened to adultery. "As a woman betrays her lovers, so you, O House of Israel, have betrayed me" (Jeremiah 3:20). They were whores for rejecting God's love, deserving to be humiliated, crushed, and cast out, even to the point of being set up for gang rape (Ezekiel 23). In an allegorical tale, Jerusalem is described as Oholibah, whoring after Egypt even to the point of bestiality, becoming "infatuated by profligates big-membered as donkeys, ejaculating as violently as stallions" (Ezekiel 23:20). To symbolize God's marriage to a whore, he commands the prophet Hosea to do likewise. "Go and take for yourself a whore for a wife, and have children with a whore. For [Israel] has gone whoring away from Yahweh" (Hosea 1:2). So Hosea marries Gomer, paying fifteen silver shekels for her fidelity (Hosea 3:2).

Whether referring to God or Jesus, the paradigm used to describe experiencing the Divine is a personal relational model, specifically a marriage. But this is not some platonic asexual relationship. Contrary to the dualism of body and soul that was prevalent in the early development of Christianity, God is found in our sensuality. God is love, love understood as agape (unconditional) and eros (erotic), absent of any imposed human dichotomy. Divine-human relationships are biblically understood as being rooted in the ultimate intimacy between partners, with violation of fidelity described in sexual terms of unfaithfulness.

So if God can be found in our sensuality, where is God when a couple is engaging in sex? If it is true that God is present when two or more gather in God's name, and if it is true that God in Jesus lives in us, then is it also true that when a couple united in God have sex, God is also present? Is this an active presence? Does God's presence allow the couple to become cocreators with God? In the creation of one body? In the possible creation of new life? Such questions move us beyond reducing sex to a simple gift from God. Such questions ponder God's omnipresence (God is everywhere at all times) even at moments of extreme intimacy.

The concept of sex with God does not mean God is physical, for all Christian groups confirm and understand God as spirit. Rather, sexuality symbolizes ultimate communion. Sexuality becomes the means by which to understand the mystery of our oneness with God. If God's defining characteristic is love, then profound passionate love is the only foundation for any relationship between God and humans. Jesus answered the question "Which is the greatest commandment?" by stating: "You shall love Yahweh your God with all your heart, and with all your soul, and with all your mind" (Matthew 22:37). The love we are commanded to have for God imitates the love I hold for my beloved wife, because I love her with all my heart, all my soul, and all my mind. The spiritual rapture in which oneness with God is achieved, and the sexual union in which oneness with one's beloved is reached, produce similar effects. Sexual intercourse with my beloved becomes sacred because it is the ultimate celebration of love, and thus a precursor to the type of spiritual relationship and love celebration we can expect to have with our Lord! As great as sex is between humans, it is still but a pale reflection, a shadow, a poor substitute, compared with the ultimate intimate relationship we can expect to have with our God.

But how do mortals become one with God? In the same way we become one with the beloved—through mutual giving of each other in an atmosphere of total vulnerability. The Gospel of Mark expresses this paradox: "For whoever desires to save their soul shall lose it but whoever loses their soul for my sake and the gospel, this one shall be saved" (8:35). By losing control of one's life, a life in God is gained. But not only does the human become vulnerable, so too does the Divine. Vulnerable unto death! Life is achieved through self-negation, the giving up of control before a God also willing to become vulnerable and mutually give of Godself. The self and the Absolute find union in the self-negation of each.

The negation of the self means the emptying of one's appetites that hinder union with one's beloved, both the temporal lover and the eternal Beloved. Self-negation demands a death to self through a renunciation and rejection of possessions: the possession of power over the Other, the possession of "rights" over the Other, the possession of privilege before the Other. When the self dies in the Absolute (as expressed in Galatians 2:20: "With Christ I have been crucified, and I live, but no longer I, rather Christ in me"), the Absolute dies in the self. Union with God is the simultaneous self-negation of the Divine on the cross and the self-negation of the individual before that cross. At the foot of the cross, the dichotomy between sacred and secular ends as the Trinity makes room for humanity. Two spaces become one. The self becomes more than just "dust and ashes." The self, through its self-negation, becomes one with the Absolute.

For Juan de la Cruz (1542–1591), a Discalced Carmelite friar, becoming one with the Absolute is "the prayer of union," the indwelling of the Spirit of God in the soul. This *mystagogy* (the gradual initiation of the believer's soul into the mysteries of the indwelling Spirit by one's experience in this mysticism) is described metaphorically as a spiritual marriage between Christ and the soul, the soul possessing and being possessed by Christ. Juan de la Cruz wrote:

> The Bridegroom [Christ]: "Beneath the apple tree [the cross]: There I took you for my own, There I offered you my hand, And restored you, Where your mother was corrupted.". . .
>
> The Bride [soul]: "There he gave me his breast; There he taught me a sweet and living knowledge; And I gave myself to him, Keeping nothing back; There I promised to be his bride."[30]

Both Juan de la Cruz and Teresa de Ávila (1515–1582), a Carmelite nun, described the mystical union with God as a spiritual marriage in which the human soul's relationship with God is the mutual relationship existing in the Trinity between Father and Son. Not only does the soul get to know God, but through this relationship the soul gets to know itself. Love that leads to ultimate union creates the effect of a likeness between lover and object loved. For the soul to know anything, it must become like the object of its knowledge. De la Cruz wrote that this "union of likeness" of God and the human soul is what makes possible both self-revelation and a purely spiritual knowledge with God. God ceases to be an object and becomes instead another self spiritually present in the lover.[31] Mystical union with the Divine can best be understood as touches of "mutuality" in "accord with the intensity of the yearning and ardors of love."[32] This mutuality and equality existing between God and soul is expressed in love terms—love as eros in which God is "touched, felt, and tasted" and as such becomes the paradigm for relationships between earthly lovers.[33]

The biblical word used to refer to the union of God with the human soul is *yāda*, translated as "know," the same word used to describe sexual intimacy between a man and a woman, as in "Adam *knew* Eve his wife, and she conceived" (Genesis 4:1). Of the 949 times that *yāda* appears in the Hebrew Bible, 22 are direct references to sexual intercourse. This suggests *yāda* can be used as a double entendre. To "know" is to be vulnerable and exposed in more ways than one. Does the mutual self-negation of the Absolute and of the self imply such an intimate union? Yes, in a mystical or spiritual sense. Thus St. Paul, who can see but a "dim reflection in a mirror," would pine for the day when he would "know as fully as [he] is known" (1 Corinthians 13:12).

The writings of Teresa de Ávila reveal this type of intimate union, in which the soul becomes immersed in God, whose transcendence is understood as relational. For her, these mystical contemplations on being fully known by God lead to a burning desire for union manifested as ecstasy. Gianlorenzo Bernini's masterpiece, *The Esctasy of St. Theresa*, captures in marble the moment of Teresa's spiritual penetration, when the Divine and the human meet, embrace, and become one. The erotic sculpture, located at the Cornaro Chapel in Rome, reveals a swooning, toe-curled Teresa at the instant of rapture beneath the figure of an angel ready to impale her by thrusting his spear (a traditional phallic symbol) into her exposed breast. In her own words, she describes how she abandons herself to God with obvious sexual overtures:

> In [the angel's] hand I saw a great golden spear, and at the iron tip there appeared to be a point of fire. This he plunged into my heart several times so that it penetrated to my entrails. When he pulled it out, I felt he took them with it, and left me utterly consumed by the great love of God. The pain was so severe that it made me utter several moans. The sweetness caused by this intense pain is so extreme that one cannot possibly wish it to cease, nor is one's soul then content with anything but God. . . . So gentle is this wooing which takes place between God and the soul.[34]

Teresa encounters God, described in sexually symbolic language signifying a higher reality, one achieved through the vulnerable state of the self dying to itself. The use of sexually charged terms to describe her role as the "bride of Christ" obviously does not signify a physical encounter communicated to the intellect through corporeal senses, but a spiritual love that craves oneness in the same way passionate lovers do. Through self-negation, there is a mutual encounter based on a relationship between two subjects, as opposed to two objects. This act, which we call an encounter with the Divine, is the saving faith that mortal humans crave—a new life in God that transcends the physical and the grave. The core of union that occurs in the "center of the soul" becomes the *dolor sabroso* (the delicious pain) of Saint Teresa, the ecstasy of God's oneness with each individual soul.

But the "delightful union" of rapture vividly described by Teresa falls short of what she also calls the "true union," a union attained with a great deal of effort. Like any deep relationship between two lovers, it is a union of intimacy that takes place over time as two become one in more ways than the simply physical. For example, my wife and I have been one for so long that a simple glance, sigh, posture, or facial expression of one is fully understood by the other. No words are needed to convey what the other is thinking or feeling, such as how one partner begins a sentence and the other finishes it. Teresa described this true union with God in similar terms: "two persons of reasonable intelligence, who love each other dearly, seem able to understand each other without making any signs, merely by their looks." Similarly, God and the soul glance at each other "as these two lovers do: the Spouse in the Song [of Songs], I believe, says this to the Bride."[35]

Spiritual Ecstasy for the Everyday

The mystic union with God, like any healthy sexual relationship, moves from a delightful union, characterized as a short-lived passionate rapture occurring at the moment of climax, toward a true union of daily intimacy, characterized by the constant presence of the beloved. True union with God occurs in the everyday. Among many Hispanic theologians and believers, God, who takes on human flesh, still continues to enflesh Godself in the everyday lives and experiences of those who reside on the underside of society—those who live on the margins of power and privilege. An important element in ethical and theological reflection is what has come to be referred to as *lo cotidiano,* the Spanish word for "the everyday." The everyday experience of the world's oppressed people becomes the starting point in how God's presence is understood. The salvific experience of God—in the here and now, not just in some ethereal hereafter—is experienced by the marginalized in their daily struggle for dignity, justice, and civil rights. The spirituality of disenfranchised groups is contextual, making their everyday experiences the subject and source of religious thought.[36] Of course, God's presence cannot be limited to the trials and tribulations of those who suffer. Although it is true that God comforts those who mourn, God also dances with those who, in spite of hardship, rejoice! God is not present just in the struggle for life, but also in the passion for life's pleasure!

Like a beloved who shares in both the struggles and joys of life, God's presence testifies to God's love for us. The love God calls us to reciprocate becomes the standard by which all other human relationships are measured. This love becomes a moral imperative toward creating justice—the doing of love—toward our neighbors. This concept of connecting justice to love leads to the second part of "the greatest commandment": "You shall love your neighbor as yourself" (Matthew 22:39).

A SEXUAL ETHICS FOR
THE BODY

Nothing is so much to be shunned as sexual relations.[1]

—Augustine of Hippo

*The woman who is truly Spirit-filled will want to be totally
submissive to her husband. . . . This is a truly liberated
woman. Submission is God's design for women.*[2]

—Beverly LaHaye

AT THE CONSERVATIVE CHRISTIAN COLLEGE where I used to teach,
students often mentioned how much social and peer pressure there was
for them to marry on graduation. This mating ritual was affectionately
referred to by the student body as the "senior scramble" because many
partnering configurations were tried out in the hope of finding the perfect
eternal mate prior to receiving one's diploma. Because premarital sex is
considered a sin by many in the student body, some of these young adults
have redefined sex so that they can participate in it while maintaining
the position that they are not engaged in sexual activity. According to
several of my students (based on conversations and papers they wrote for
the class), explicit sexual acts such as oral sex, mutual masturbation, or
anal sex are not considered to be sex per se.

Research seems to confirm my students' experiences. According to
a seven-year study conducted by the National Longitudinal Study of

Adolescent Health, those who pledged to maintain their virginity until marriage were more likely to engage in other sexual acts, such as oral (six times more likely among both genders) and anal sex (four times more likely among males) than those who did not make such a pledge. Although they waited till marriage to engage in vaginal penetration with a penis, and got married sooner than those who did not pledge abstinence, they did not refrain from other sexual acts that included some form of penetration.[3] The definition of sex was reduced to mean only vaginal penetration by a penis. Hence, every form of sexual activity was acceptable and permissible as long as the woman could walk down the aisle on her wedding day with an intact hymen, taking great pride in maintaining her virginity until marriage. Such rationalization is not limited to adolescents and college students. We may recall that former president Bill Clinton used a similar definition of sex to rationalize his marital infidelity during the Monica Lewinsky scandal.

Unfortunately, the linguistic gymnastics performed by my former students so as to engage in a sexual union that they do not define as sex prevents spiritual rapture from truly occurring. Sex is transformed from a joyful physical and spiritual moment of ecstasy into a dirty, sinful act producing guilt, self-loathing, and regret. Not only are my students misunderstanding sexuality, but for the past two millennia so has the universal Christian church. The historical mores and traditions of Christians have been (for the most part) uncritically passed on from generation to generation. Many today continue to think that sex debases the soul. But sexuality is not some dark demonic force skulking in our innermost being that, unless restrained, dominated, or controlled, will lead us into a downward spiral of temptation, degradation, and spiritual ruin. As Christian ethicist James Nelson reminds us, "[Our] sexuality is a sign, a symbol, and a means of our call to communication and communion [with humans and the divine]. This is most apparent in regard to other human beings. . . . The mystery of our sexuality is the mystery of our need to reach out to embrace others both physically and spiritually."[4] To be human is to be sexual. Not that sexuality is the totality of the human experience, but it is surely a major aspect of what it means to be alive as humans. All who are or ever were human (including God in the flesh as Christ) have a need for right and just relationships with others. But the Christian view of sex as something sinful inevitably leads to unjust practices.

Sex is integral to power, and, as Michel Foucault reminds us, the locus of that power is the body. All cultures reflect, legitimize, naturalize, and reinforce their interests in part by how they define and construct sexual norms and values for the body. As we have seen in the first two chapters of this book, religion's proscriptions on sexual issues are a most effective form of social control, providing the means by which the dominant culture is maintained. Foucault asserts that "if repression has indeed been the fundamental link between power, knowledge, and sexuality since the classical age, it stands to reason that we will not be able to free ourselves from it except at a considerable loss: nothing less than a transgression of laws, a lifting of prohibitions, an irruption of speech, a reinstating of pleasure within reality, and a whole economy in the mechanisms of power will be required."[5]

Sex has been transformed into a tool to protect patriarchy. Sexual ethics was defined to perpetuate an unjust social order, mainly at the expense of women. Therefore, establishment of any justice-based social order will require a subversion of the normative sexual ethics of the dominant culture, which were and continue to be designed to privilege affluent males. To seek a liberationist sexual expression, sex must move beyond existing for the sole purpose of procreation or channeling lust.

Sex is a pleasurable experience, both physically and spiritually, designed to achieve wholeness and completeness—*shalom* with *shlemut*. Nevertheless, it cannot simply be reduced to a pleasure-seeking activity. And though both procreation and pleasure are, no doubt, part of the sexual experience, they are not its totality. For sex to be great, it must be justice-based—a justice consciously informed and developed from the perspective of those who are powerless, specifically those who suffer due to the existing patriarchal structures.

Correct Erotic Sex

Those who participate from a liberative-based ethical framework have given much attention to the theological concepts of *orthodoxy* (correct doctrine) and *orthopraxis* (correct action). In Eurocentric Christian theological thought, an emphasis on orthodoxy prevails. What is believed in one's heart and professed through one's mouth becomes crucial in defining what is and what is not Christian. One is saved through the doctrines one adheres to and not necessarily by what one does. As the apostle Paul reminds us, we are saved by grace, not by works, lest anyone should boast (Ephesians 2:9). But for historically marginalized Christian groups subsisting on the underside of the U.S. dominant culture (that is, Hispanics and African Americans), the emphasis is on orthopraxis—correct action. The actions one commits, specifically actions leading to a more just social order, are what define one's Christian commitment.

If Jesus is correct in stating that a tree is known by its fruits (Matthew 7:16), then emphasizing correct action neither limits nor dismisses grace, but instead concentrates on the "fruits" produced by the self-professing "tree." Praxis—that is, actions—become the outward expression of God's grace working in the new life of the believer. Theologies and ethical pronouncements are but human concepts developed by a people locked into and influenced by a specific social location determined by their place and time, attempting to perceive the ultimate reality of the Deity. History has shown us that at times, such theological and ethical pronouncements can be quite unchristian. One need only recall the Crusades or the Inquisition or simply review the first two chapters of this book to see that this is the case.

The quest for power over others dictates theological and ethical pronouncements concerning sex by relegating sexual acts to a binary system of what is permitted and what is forbidden. As such, sex is narrowly defined by what we do with our genitals. How we employ our genitals in one Christian culture or epoch may be defined as sinful, whereas a different Christian culture or era may deem it acceptable. Society is constantly changing, and sexual ethics must change to keep abreast. This does not mean that sexual ethics must change in order to "fit" the culture. The biblical principles of justice that call for attending to the needs of "the very least of these" (Matthew 25:31–46) must be reapplied by each succeeding generation to make sense in the evolving cultural ethos. If not, what the Bible has to say becomes irrelevant to the vast majority of Christians, as the credibility gap between the official church teaching on sexuality and the experience of most churchgoers continues to widen. Implementing biblical principles concerning sexual ethics does not mean developing new doctrines or ethical pronouncements. It requires developing more effective praxis, by debunking the stereotypes and biases of previous generations. Because any given group of Christians can be subject to oppressive social forces, Christianity is best determined by focusing more on the correct actions of the believer toward the disenfranchised and less on the official church's beliefs and doctrines.

In this book's reexamination of Christian sexuality, orthopraxis is a key concept. We can also use a more specific term that I have coined: *orthoeros*, meaning "correct erotic sex." All too often, when sexual ethics is discussed, religious leaders provide a list of "don'ts." In their attempt to construct a proper orthodoxy, a proper doctrine, they quickly move from saying sex is good (only in a heterosexual marriage) to developing a list of restrictions. But such lists, as developed over the past two millennia, have more often than not led to sexual repression and oppression. Sex as the epitome of sin fosters control through guilt, and labeling sexual desire as good but too powerful to contain means fear and coercion are used to ensure compliance with the sexual mores of the culture. History has shown that in the minds of past Christian leaders and believers, good Christians avoid sex, and if they engage in it they do so with as little pleasure as possible. So in the eyes of the Religious Right who presently are framing the Christian conversation on sexual morality, those who are openly gay, or engage in premarital sex, or are pregnant and unmarried, are blatantly flaunting their hedonism.

For more liberal-minded individuals (including some Christians), sex is reduced to a biological function, a private act between two consenting adults resulting from a dopamine-elevated state. Because of the liberal's presupposed dichotomy between the public and private spheres, sex clearly falls into the category of the private. For many liberal-minded individuals, sex becomes depoliticized—reduced to a personal choice that has no impact on the overall society. For others, sex is simply another bodily appetite, like eating or sleeping. It is simply what human mammals do, no more, no less. Therefore, as long as no one is being hurt by the sexual encounter, two or more consenting adults can participate in whatever sexual interaction they wish.

Neither the sexual legalism of conservatives nor the permissiveness of liberals provides a satisfactory basis for sexual ethics. Both sides of the spectrum overly emphasize the sexual acts, debating and seeking answers as to what is or is not sexually permitted. But if the message of the New Testament is the replacement of the Law with the new commandment of love—the substitution of works with faith—then orthoeros must concentrate on what it means to love my neighbor—more specifically, my sexually oppressed neighbor. The ethical act of unconditional love for the Other is what makes transformative relationships possible.

The main focus and concern of orthoeros is the sexual prejudices of those in power. Those whom society empowers usually impose restrictions on the powerless so as to enhance and secure their privileged spaces, as in the case of patriarchy. For this reason, it becomes crucial to construct a sexual ethics from the perspectives of the sexually marginalized—those subjected to sexual oppression. Those who are privileged by the present sexual patterns that cause oppression—specifically those who dominate their wives, partners, or supposed economic or racial "inferiors"—lack the moral authority to pass judgment on proper sexual relationships that may appear contrary to their so-called ethical vision. Under present normative sexual patterns lie the seeds for producing a justice-based sexual ethics, orthoeros, but only if we are willing to listen to the marginalized people's stories, learn from their experiences, resist the temptation to paternalistically fix the problem, and stand in solidarity with those abused by the present social structures—sharing in their pains and joys.

Our purpose here is not to limit what makes sex great but to enhance sexual pleasure and spiritual intimacy through the process of unmasking those oppressive structures put in place to control the "flesh" so that the "spirit" could flourish. In so doing we can make the words of the psalmist come true: "Steadfast love and faithfulness will embrace, justice and peace will kiss" (Psalms 85:10).

What Makes Sex Orthoeros?

To love and be loved is part of what defines our humanity. Correct erotic sex, orthoeros, occurs in a familial relationship of love and commitment, vigilant against any suffering of others due to that relationship. Orthoeros focus is on strengthening, securing, and supporting a mutually giving and vulnerable familial relationship. This familial relationship is not so much a set of rules as a way of being. The focus is not on the type of sex that occurs between individuals. How then is orthoeros established? For orthoeros to bloom, sex must be safe, consensual, faithful, mutually pleasing, and intimate.

Safe Sex: Taking Responsibility

For a relationship to be vulnerable, it must be safe—safe from harm, danger, and abuse. Irresponsible sex, as in the case of unprotected sex, can lead to sexually transmitted diseases and unwanted pregnancies. Such irresponsible sexual encounters can prove to be unhealthy, if not dangerous. Although these topics will be discussed in greater detail in Part Two of this book, for now it is important to note that the proper education in and use of contraceptives is a moral imperative. Safe sex calls for sexual responsibility, not prohibition or restriction.

The apostle Paul wrote, "Nothing to me is forbidden, but not all things do good. All things to me are lawful, but not all things build up. Let no one seek their own advantage, but each that of the other" (1 Corinthians 10:23–24). Sex is not forbidden, but not all sexual encounters are good or safe. No one should seek their own advantage through the use and abuse of others to simply gratify their sexual desires. Instead, each person should seek the sexual good of the Other. In this fashion, sex that brings no harm to self or others but also builds the other up, is safe.

For sex to be safe, it must move beyond the concept of conquest, beyond the "wham, bam, thank you ma'am" encounter. Sexual partners, specifically women, must be safe from the fear that after intimacy, in which both bodies and souls merge, she may feel as though she has been sexually used and emotionally abandoned. Likewise, vulnerability is threatened when, to counter the fear of abandonment, sex is used as a source of power to gain something, usually some form of privilege over and against the partner. And finally, safety also encompasses the absence of abuse and physical pain, which will be further explored in Chapter Eight.

Consensual Sex: Between Equal Partners

For sex to be mutually giving, we presuppose that both partners are mature and equal in power. By definition, this proscribes adults in full capacity of their faculties from engaging in sex with the mentally impaired, children, or subordinates at work. Even when mutual consent is given, an uneven relationship between the parties denies the existence of true consent. A mentally impaired person may agree to sex with a person having unimpaired mental capacities, not realizing all that is entailed in the encounter. A child may agree to have sex with an adult family member as a perverse understanding of love. A student or employee may agree to sex with their professor or employer in hopes of a better grade or job security, or simply out of attraction for the power the holder has over them.

No one should be coerced, tricked, pressured, forced, or threatened to engage in any sexual act that is contrary to their conscience or desire. In all these examples, because sex is not occurring in a mutually giving environment, it is unethical. Although these topics will be explored in greater detail in Chapter Eight, for now it is crucial to stress that for any sexual encounter to encompass mutual giving, both partners must agree on the roles they are about to undertake, even within a marriage. Consensual sex means the husband never forces himself or his will on his wife and overpowers her. To do so would be to forfeit the presence of God. For according to 1 Peter, "husbands must treat their wives with consideration, bestowing honor on her as one who, though she may be the weaker vessel, is truly a co-heir to the grace of life, least his prayers be hindered" (3:7). Setting aside the characterization of woman as a weaker vessel, the biblical principle here is that the man who fails to honor his wife will not have his prayers heard by God. His relationship to God is linked to how he treats his wife. I would add the same holds true for how she treats her husband.

Faithful Sex: Trusting in Vulnerability

Nowhere in the biblical text is monogamy established as the standard for all forms of Christian marriages, except as found in Titus 1:6, which requires Elders to be the husbands of one wife. Still, if our hope is for sex to be great, then both mutual giving and vulnerability must be present. Only then can the sexual relationship that is established be both nurturing and sustaining. Trust and safety from rejection or abandonment fosters the ability of both partners to feel vulnerable enough to mutually and fully give of each other, which in turn leads to a bonding that enhances the physical sexual experience. For this reason, any violation of this bond shatters fidelity.

If competition with a third party for the intimacy of one's partner defines the relationship, then the fear and the pain of broken trust and rejection prevent the establishment of an atmosphere of vulnerability. Instead of having trust—which allows a relationship in which partners feel it is safe to be vulnerable—envy, jealousy, mistrust, and competition can define the relationship, leading to feelings of rejection and anger. These feelings can prevent intimacy and bonding, and thus are not conducive to great sex. The partner who fears loss will, as a measure of self-defense, simply hold back. Multiple simultaneous sex partners can undermine a healthy vulnerability. Monogamous relationships create lifelong committed relationships in which sex affirms the ongoing union. The Book of Proverbs reminds men to "Rejoice with the wife of your youth, fair as a deer, graceful as a doe. Let her be the company you keep, hers the breasts that delight you every time, hers the love that ravishes you" (5:18–19).

Those who engage in any sexual relationship that is not familial (such as adultery) must remain cognizant of the future suffering it may cause for the betrayed partner and any children, and they must strive instead to ensure and preserve the fulfillment (physical and spiritual) of all who could be impacted by the sexual relationship. For joy, happiness, and ecstasy to occur, the rights and commitments of others beyond the two having sexual intercourse must be maintained.

Mutually Pleasing Sex: Giving and Receiving

To touch, to feel, to nibble, to fondle, to penetrate or be penetrated is more than simply sultry pleasure. It is trust—trust in a partner who will neither hurt you nor deny you pleasure. Improper sex occurs when conducted solely in search of self-serving pleasure, when love is absent from lovemaking. When the other is denied achieving the peak of sexual ecstasy, when the other is reduced to a commodity to be used and abused for self-gratification, or when the other, due to an uneven power relationship, is forced to participate in sexual acts against her or his will, then orthoeros is absent. Any sexual act, even within traditional marriage, can be abusive, oppressive, demeaning, or exploitive.

A love bathed in justice leads to great sex. For orthoeros to flourish, it cannot take place in an unjust and abusive relationship, whether personal or part of a larger social structure. Patriarchal sexual norms that assume a socially superior male-centered, pleasure-seeking aggressiveness, coupled with a socially inferior female passivity, undermines orthoeros because neither relationship is based on vulnerability or mutual giving.

Intimate Sex: Revealing the Inner Self

For some, having sex always with the same partner can become somewhat routine, predicable, if not repetitive. After the newness of physical passion starts to dwindle with the passage of time, we need not simply accept that sex goes from being red-hot to ho-hum. Great sex does not have to be perpetually linked to newer, younger, and hotter bodies, nor must the constant pursuit of new forms of pleasurable stimuli jade the enduring joy of sex. What makes sex great is not the act of obtaining physical gratification with and through another body, but the intimacy that comes with vulnerability. It is the intimacy created by two becoming one that enhances and heightens sexual pleasure, not the actual act of penetration. Through the process of revealing our inner self to our beloved, not only do we create intimacy, but we gain the power to heal our dysfunction by calming our deepest fears and satisfying our most intense yearnings. Even in the absence of penetration, whether due to illness, old age, or forced separation (such as war or imprisonment), sex can still remain great so long as it enhances intimacy.

Correct Erotic Sex as a Guide to Moral Living

Now that we know what constitutes orthoeros and therefore great lovemaking, the question remains, can this sexual ethic lead to proper justice-making? Can right relationships within the private sphere affect, influence, or impact relationships that occur in the public sphere? If private intimate relationships function in accordance with a hierarchical structure based on an active-passive oppressive model, we should not be surprised that this model is echoed in public relationships, in the marketplace, and in our government's domestic and foreign policies. Those policies mirror the patriarchal hierarchy existing in the household. First Peter clearly makes these connections. Believers are to be subject to the political structures of imperial Rome, even to the point of honoring the emperor (2:13–17), and they are to be subject to the economic structures imposed by their masters, even when masters are unfair (2:18–25). Similarly, women are to be subject to their "lords"—their husbands, even if their husbands are not believers (3:1–6). The same logic used to reinforce the obedience of women in the household is extended to the public sphere and the marketplace.

Injustice is the violation of vulnerability and the taking advantage of mutuality—in short, the abuse of power over another. The basis for most unjust social structures is the denial of bodily rights—denying the right to clothing, food, shelter, and health care for the body through economic oppression, or denying the right of the body to participate in the fruits of society because of its gender, skin coloration, or sexual orientation. Our society's obsession with the idealized white, heterosexual male body leads to injustices usually manifested in the form of classism, sexism, racism, and heterosexism. It is assumed that these idealized bodies are privileged to have power and control over poorer bodies, darker bodies, female bodies. This power and control, manifested as male-centered female-passive patriarchal sex, also legitimizes white male superiority while eroticizing domination. Pleasure is found in dominating—and for some, in a perverse way, in being dominated.

Christianity has been interpreted in such a way as to spiritually justify white heterosexual male supremacy both in the home and in the broader society. Failure to conform to patriarchal sex is understood to be a rejection of Christianity in general and "family values" in particular. Consequently, sexual justice cannot be understood apart from seeking class, gender, and racial justice. Orthoeros, by providing an ethical pattern for our most intimate human relationships, attempts to remedy these public injustices. Understanding that our body is the temple of the Holy Spirit (1 Corinthians 6:19), orthoeros holds that the body—that is, the flesh—is sacred because it is the receptacle of the image of God—the *imago Dei*. The body as flesh should not be considered a polluted and wicked vessel, as preached by early Christian leaders. In truth, as God's ultimate creation, the body is good—so good that God chose to enflesh Godself in the human body of a Jewish carpenter. Because God gives life to bodies by imprinting God's image on them, all life has worth and dignity. Sanctity of all life means the sanctity of all bodies containing life.

To seek justice deepens love for the other. Training one's heart to love others more deeply will positively impact one's love for one's beloved, and the ability to reach deeper levels of love can only enhance one's sexual encounters. Now if the major goal for justice-seeking is an equitable sharing of resources and power, then dismantling power structures designed to privilege one group at the expense of another becomes a major task for those seeking justice-based social order. If indeed such a social order exists in the bedchamber, then seeking justice "between the sheets" becomes an ethical issue. In this intimate space, power-sharing becomes the paragon for all other social relationships. This also means that there should be no difference between the patterns of intimacy in the private sphere and the overall socioeconomic structures existing in the public sphere. Pope Benedict XVI hinted at this in his 2006 encyclical *Deus Caritas Est*, in which he argues that a mature form of sex is unselfishly concerned with others, creating a type of love that leads to justice. He wrote, "Love looks to the eternal. Love is indeed 'ecstasy,' not in the sense of a moment of intoxication, but rather as a journey, an ongoing exodus out of the closed inward-looking self towards its liberation through self-giving, and thus towards authentic self-discovery and indeed the discovery of God."[6]

The Humanizing Power of Sex

What we do with our flesh in the privacy of our bedroom with our beloved is a virtue, because it is a means of learning how to selflessly love our beloved, the model for extending unselfish compassion for others. Sex humanizes its participants, providing a self-giving paragon by which to relate to others. Sexuality then ceases to be a private matter as it moves to the public sphere as a moral imperative. Even though sex may occur in private, it has social ramifications (as we will explore in greater detail in Part Two of this book). This means that, instead of being solely fixated on the genitals, sex provides the opportunity to move beyond the self toward the other. To desire sex is foremost a plea for communion, in which the psychological and physiological needs of lovers are met. Sexual fulfillment in a vulnerable and mutually giving relationship validates our humanity, because to be human is to be in relationship with our beloved, with our God, and with our neighbor. Although physical sex may be limited to the beloved, it gives us the opportunity to put the needs of that other first, which is the basis of Jesus' teachings, and also becomes the foundation for creating justice-based relationships.

Justice can be discovered in the quest for sexual passion. In turning from the domination-centered patriarchal sex hierarchy to search for a more egalitarian sexual relationship, we begin in the private sphere what needs to be manifested in the public. The one forced to be passive in a sexual relationship (in a heterosexual relationship, usually the woman) is reduced to a sexual object. She becomes a nonbeing, her personhood lost as she becomes simply an extension of her dominator. Before we can hope to make great sex achievable for all, we must first analyze the power structures that perpetuate the privilege of one group at the expense of the sexually marginalized. We must critically question the system of patriarchy, heterosexism, sexism, and their supporters. Yet when one voices the concern that the predominant sexual mores may foster oppressive social structures, one runs the risk of being labeled a libertine or a non-Christian by those who benefit most from reasserting their positions of power.

Let's be clear that seeking a sexual liberative ethic does not mean advocating a pseudo-religious permissiveness in which anything goes. To fully engage in a liberative sexual ethic is to fully rely on the power of God's grace while affirming *shalom* with *shlemut* for the self as well as for the beloved. From the get-go, a liberative sexual ethic dismisses any sexual relationship that prohibits *shalom* with *shlemut* from being established. Sexual abuse and exploitation are unequivocally defined as wrong and therefore evil. Liberation in and by Christ gives us the grace to explore how we can achieve *shalom* with *shlemut*. Will mistakes and errors occur in our quest for great sex? Of course, because we are humans. But if we recognize that failures and mistakes are themselves a powerful learning device that leads to personal growth, and if we understand grace as God's healing from wrong choices and painful experiences, then we can boldly move forward in our quest for great sex without fear of recrimination.

Nevertheless, fear of recrimination from sex runs rampant in many of our churches. For the Religious Right, a liberative approach to sexual ethics is considered antifamily. For them, regulating sexual activity is a crucial means by which cultural identity reinforces the prevailing social structures. According to Christian ethicist Marvin Ellison, "family values" has become the battle cry for reasserting "white, affluent, male hegemony as the necessary social mechanism for preserving both the family (read 'male-dominated, affluent families') and the capitalist social order."[7]

Reading the Bible for Correct Erotic Sex

It is undeniable that the Bible reflects the patriarchal norms of those who wrote it. This reality has led some to determine that the Bible cannot be relevant for those trying to construct any kind of sexual ethics for the modern world. But as tempting as this conclusion may be, it is erroneous. What we can learn from the Bible is that many parts of it can never be taken literally, especially if taking the text literally results in the oppression or death of others. Such literal readings only perpetuate its embedded injustices. Still, the biblical text can be a source of principles that call for a liberation from all forms of injustice, even those advocated by the biblical text. Within the text are the seeds to dismantle how the Bible has been used—and continues to be used—to reinforce the false consciousness of inferiority (specifically among women), which creates a barrier to enjoying great sex and true spiritual union.

The touchstone that all human relationships are to emulate and be evaluated against is the divine agape, as modeled by Christ. Jesus taught the importance of basing all relationships on this prescriptive form of love, which serves as a moral imperative. Obedience to the greatest commandment given by Christ—to love one another (John 13:34–35)—leads us to justice. Agape love can never be reduced to an emotional experience, although such feelings could and usually do become a symptom of the love praxis. Nor is it a paternalistic response to pity. Love is praxis—what one person does to, for, and with another. This is a love that binds the believer to the abundant life for and of the Other.

To love in this fashion is to question, analyze, challenge, and dismantle the social structures responsible for preventing people from reaching the fullest potential of the abundant life promised to them by Christ (John 10:10). For this reason, there is a connection between agape and justice based on an overall assumption of human worth and dignity. Surely to claim love for God while hating the Other reveals a clear lie, a falsehood. We cannot love God, whom we cannot see, while ignoring our sister or brother whom we *can* see (1 John 4:20). The gospel concept of agape love collapses the false dichotomy between faith (love the Lord your God) and ethics (love your neighbor as yourself). The love that liberates rests on acts of justice. Relationship with each other and with God becomes the source for moral guidance, capable of debunking the social structures erected and subsequently normalized by a culture operating through powerful dominance of the Other. Consequently, the basis for all ethical acts can be reduced to one verse, Galatians 5:14: "The whole Law is fulfilled in one word, Love your neighbor as yourself."

The Invention of Original Sin

Sin is what prevents us from loving our neighbor with the divine love of agape. But since early Christian history, sin has been associated with sex. Specifically, official church doctrine informs us that the original sin of humans, which is associated with sex, perverts all relationships with our God and with our neighbors. The tenet of original sin does not explicitly appear in the biblical text, although the account of the Fall (Genesis 3) provides tacit substance for speculation on the provenance of sin. It was the Babylonian Captivity (587–538 B.C.E.) that served as a catalyst for the inception of this doctrine. During this epoch, Hebrew thought was exposed to Persian ideology, specifically the prevalent dualism of good versus evil. The postexilic period saw the emergence of two theories concerning the fundamental origin of sin. Some linked this origin to an outside diabolic presence (that is, Satan) that forced its way into the human condition; others believed that sin was naturally inherent.

Although earlier theologians emphasized a solidarity with Adam, Augustine formulated a doctrine of *peccatum originale,* original sin, that graphically depicted humanity's complicity with Adam's rebellion by stating, "all sinned, when all were that one man [Adam]." Augustine grounded original sin in the act of copulation, probably due to his tormented thoughts over his own attitudes toward sex and exacerbated by his sexual urges, as revealed in his classic work *Confessions.* Elsewhere he argued that sexual shame was evident in all of society. Though original sin was a sin of the spirit, the bedlam Augustine himself had particularly experienced and also witnessed through his own unrestrained sexual desire led him to connect humans' original sin with sex.[8]

Sin, according to Augustine, was transmitted through the theory of "semenal propagation," which meant that in the father's semen was a generic spiritual substance *(foames peccatum)* that is transferred generationally. This helps to explain how a virgin birth was essential to ensure the birth of a sinless baby uncontaminated by the earthly father's sin-carrying semen. Every sexual act, even within a marriage, became the means by which original sin was transmitted, which meant that every sexual act was therefore sinful. His doctrine affirmed the ethos and practices of the early church, which was at the time renouncing sexuality for the ascetic celibate life. Clerics who chose and struggled with celibacy saw their sexual desires as undermining their quest for spiritual union with and full knowledge of God.

The problem with the doctrine of original sin as a stain on one's soul is that it ultimately roots all evil in Adam's original act of disobedience. In short, blaming the original sin of Adam (the Fall) for the sins of oppression prevalent in today's society is a questionable doctrine that obstructs ethical reflection. Doctrines are always being formed, reformed, and at times deformed. Most doctrines, either explicitly or implicitly, secure the power and privilege of those formulating the ethical pronouncements of the day. For example, "family values" is the present-day purity code used to condemn those whose sexual practices fall outside the Religious Right's moral vision. Today's cultural spiritual leaders are perpetuating their own doctrines that, in effect, turn the Christian church into a new form of prison.

The Church as Prison

For Christians, freedom from all sin, including original sin, is found in Christ. "If [Christ] sets you free, you are free indeed" (John 8:36). Although Christians may consider themselves to be "free," the reality for many, specifically women and gays, is that they are incarcerated in the church. The church, the local space in which liberation in Christ is found, has in many cases become an ornate prison. But not just any prison. Specifically, when it comes to sexuality, the church serves as a perfect paragon for a *panopticon*. The panopticon, as originated by the philosopher Jeremy Bentham (1748–1832) and later updated by the twentieth-century philosopher Michel Foucault, is a model prison designed to keep inmates under constant surveillance and scrutiny without their being aware of their observers.

The panopticon is designed in a circular pattern, with a guard tower in the center. The guard can easily gaze at the prisoners in their individual backlit cells. The prisoners, meanwhile, are unable to know when and if they are being watched by the guard, who remains unseen in the dark. Theoretically, constant surveillance coupled with the inability to know when they are being watched reduces the inmates' bad behavior, since they are always fearful of being caught. The gaze of the guard confers power on the observer while serving as a trap to those being observed, even when the surveillance is not constant. The mere possibility of being watched forces the object of the gaze to internalize the power relationship.

The prisoners who are being subjected to a field of visibility assume responsibility for policing themselves. The prisoner assumes the power relationship in which he or she plays the roles of both disciplinarian and disciplined, becoming the principal enforcer of his or her own subjugation. The guard could in fact be incompetent, a child, or even blind; it matters little. The prisoners, never knowing when or if they are being watched, will behave in accordance with the rules of the institution. In effect, the prisoners serve as their own guards.[9]

It is naive to view power as being centralized in the hands of the elite. Power is everywhere, forming and passing through a multitude of institutions. It is formed in relationships, which in turn sustain, advance, and maintain power. Power is most effective when it is exercised through a coercion that appears natural and neutral. Those who submit to societal norms and adopt the dominant culture's sexual (family?) values are rewarded with inclusion in the privileges the culture has to offer. But for those who challenge the prevailing sexual mores, punishment occurs in the form of marginalization and exclusion from power and privilege. The "punished" are labeled by those in power as sexual perverts or deviants because they refuse to conform to how society has constructed sexuality.[10] The panopticon, serving as a model for how oppressive power is sustained and maintained within the church, illustrates how women within the patriarchy can easily become its most vocal advocates.

The propaganda, political power, and coercive pressure exerted by the Religious Right is so seductive that many who are negatively affected by their pronouncements accept and perpetuate their ideology. For example, a woman can be recognized as a gifted CEO of a Fortune 500 company but in many conservative churches she is reduced to second-class status, prohibited from serving as a pastor, all the while being told that although males and females are equal they have different gifts and roles. But why is it that *her* gifts and roles are always passive in nature whereas *his* are active—privileged by leadership and power? She can sit on the bench of the U.S. Supreme Court, adjudicating the laws of the land, but she is prevented from standing behind the pulpit and pontificating on Leviticus. Well into the twenty-first century, the universal Christian church, rather than serving as the vanguard for the liberation found in Christ Jesus, usually finds itself still serving as the major legitimator of sexism (and heterosexism). Thus the Christian Church remains among the most discriminatory institutions in existence—perpetuating unjust social structures.

Excluding women (or anyone else, for that matter, due to their race, class, or sexual orientation) from leadership subconsciously contributes to imposed feelings of inferiority. Additionally, the imposition of a male definition on female bodies contributes to women's negative self-perception of their own bodies, all the while enhancing the male-centered view as normative. A false consciousness is established in which the excluded accept their inferior status as God-given in accordance with natural law. Learning to see their situation through the eyes of those privileged with power (in the case of women, men), some of those oppressed by the social structure become the most outspoken defenders, sustainers, and maintainers of the continuation of their own oppression within the church.

To insist that inequalities no longer persist within the church is delusional. No doubt some advances have been made with the times, but unfortunately such advances continue to be the exception to the norm. To establish orthoeros, the task is not to define the type of relationship (male-centered heterosexual marriage) in which sex can occur, but to establish biblically based principles of justice in all relationships, sexual and nonsexual, so as to dismantle the panopticon church.

Looking Forward

Throughout the first half of this book we have examined how Christianity has been misread to create, sustain, and enforce oppressive social structures. We have also examined that the way in which a liberative sexual ethic, grounded on the Good News of the biblical text that Jesus has come to give life and give it abundantly (John 10:10), can establish familial relationships that lead to great sex. But first, we must listen to the stories and voices of those most marginalized by the present sexual norms of the dominant male-centered culture.

In Part Two we will begin to explore how biblical principles that celebrate and call for great sex are applicable. Using the models for familial relationships provided in these past few chapters, we will proceed to issues dealing with same-sex relationships, celibacy, premarital sex, predatory sex, prostitution, pornography, masturbation, and marriage.

PART TWO

HAVING GREAT SEX

5

GREAT SEX IN MARRIAGE

Many men and women now in their sixties and seventies who have been disciples of Christ since childhood have preserved their [sexual] purity; and I am proud that I could point to such people in every nation.

—Justin the Martyr (c. 100–167)[1]

The church must help this society regain its sanity on the gift of children. Willful barrenness and chosen childlessness must be named as moral rebellion. To demand that marriage means sex—but not children—is to defraud the Creator of His joy and pleasure in seeing the saints raising His children. That is just the way it is.

—Al Mohler, president of Southern Baptist Seminary[2]

HILDALE, UTAH, IS PROBABLY one of the few locations in the United States in which the closest biblical text definition of the ideal marriage actually exists. Home to eight thousand members of the Fundamentalist Church of Jesus Christ of Latter Day Saints (an unaffiliated polygamous sect of the Mormon church), Hildale is the largest polygamous community in the United States. Carolyn Jessop, who escaped the Hildale community with her eight children, was one of the seven wives of a local motel owner. She was forced to marry this fifty-year-old man when she was only eighteen. Other women in the community have been as

89

young as nine when forced to marry. Ms. Jessop states, "Women in a polygamist culture are looked at as property, as a piece of meat. . . . We're not looked on as human beings with rights. The women are basically baby-producers. It's a difficult thing to break away from."[3]

The example of Hildale probably isn't what those clamoring for the establishment of marriage in line with a literal biblical interpretation have in mind. But as far as truly biblical marriages go, Hildale, Utah, can serve as a perfect blueprint.

What Is the Traditional Biblical Marriage?

Many today oppose same-sex marriages under the aegis of protecting the biblical definition of a traditional marriage. Yet traditional marriage as defined by Western culture does not have biblical roots and is incongruent with what is spelled out in the biblical text. In fact, it would be hard to find a modern-day Christian who would actually abide by a truly biblical marriage in practice, as the biblical understanding of marriage meant male ownership of women who existed for his sexual pleasure. On marriage, a woman's property and her body became the possessions of her new husband. As the head of the household, men (who usually married between the ages of eighteen and twenty-four) had nearly unlimited rights over wives and children. A woman became available for men's possession soon after she reached puberty; that is, when she became physically able to produce children. Most would agree that children, and the vast majority of teenagers, lack the maturity at this early stage of their lives to enter into a marriage as though they were adults. Yet the biblical model for sexual relationships includes adult males taking girls into their bedchambers, as did King David (1 Kings 1:1–3). If our society repudiates male adult-female child sexual encounters, then it must reject the Hebrew Bible's construct of marriage.

If a literal reading of the biblical text fails to provide a view of marriage acceptable to modern society, how then are we to use the Bible as foundational? This chapter will show that marriage as practiced in antiquity provides poor models for today's society. Jesus understood this and challenged the marriage arrangements of his time. This challenge is the basis for this chapter's description of what constitutes an orthoeros-based marriage. Here I will explore and define what is ethical in marriage and what can serve as prerequisites for great sex.

There are many ways in which the Bible cannot be a literal reference point or guidebook for modern-day marriages. Because the biblical understanding of the purpose for marriage was reproduction, marriage could be dissolved by the man if his wife failed to bear him heirs. In addition to reproduction, marriage within a patriarchal order also served political and economic means. Marriages during antiquity mainly focused on codifying economic responsibilities and obligations. Little attention was given to how the couple felt about each other. Wives were chosen from good families not only to secure the legitimacy of a man's children, but to strengthen political and economic alliances between families, clans, tribes, and kingdoms. To ensure that any offspring were the legitimate heirs, the woman was restricted to just one sex partner, her husband. If our society repudiates the concept that the purpose of marriage is for women to provide men with legitimate heirs, then it must reject the Hebrew Bible's construct of marriage.

Marriages were endogamous; that is, they occurred within the same extended family or clan, unlike the modern Western concept of exogamous marriage, in which unions occur between those from different groups. Men could have as many sexual partners as they could afford. Polygamy and concubinage were the norm and there is no explicit prohibition of these practices in the biblical text. Marriage was neither required in the biblical text nor universally accepted throughout Western Christendom as a prerequisite for sex. As discussed in Chapter One, a man during biblical times could engage in sex with whomever he chose: concubines, war booty, sexual slaves, and occasional prostitutes. If our society repudiates concepts like polygamy, concubinage, and sexual slavery, then it must reject the Hebrew Bible's construct of marriage.

Biblical marriage was considered valid only if the bride was a virgin. If she was not, then she was to be executed (Deuteronomy 22:13–21). Marriage could take place only if the spouses were believers (Ezra 9:12). And if the husband were to die before having children, then his brother was required to marry the widow. If he refused, he had to forfeit one of his sandals, be spit on by the widow, and change his name to "House of the Unshoed" (Deuteronomy 25:5–10). If our society repudiates concepts like the execution of nonvirgins, marriage only within the same faith tradition, and forcing brothers to sleep with their dead sibling's wife (and widows to sleep with their dead husband's brother), then it must reject the Hebrew Bible's construct of marriage.

Before marriage was elevated to a sacrament during the Council of Trent (1563), it was not regarded as sacred. The ideas that marriage had to be licensed by the state or sanctioned by the church are modern innovations to the biblical tradition. Before that time, even among Catholics, a simple proclamation of intent to marry, spoken anywhere, was sufficient for the couple to be considered husband and wife.[4] Marriage was mainly a civil arrangement, not officiated by clergy. The definition of marriage has always been evolving, from an understanding of marriage along the lines of property rights, to marriage as a means for procreation, to a family-dominated arrangement designed to protect wealth, to the more recent response to attraction, love, and mutual respect. Our modern definition of the traditional marriage based on love, trust, vulnerability, and commitment is neither traditional nor biblical. In fact, what we call the traditional marriage is quite a modern invention (dating from about the seventeenth century). Without hesitation we impose this modern concept of marriage on our culture, mistaking it for some historical or biblical norm.

Jesus Challenges the Ancient Marriage Traditions

The biblical view of the traditional marriage as portrayed in the Hebrew scriptures was challenged by Jesus. According to levirate tradition, as previously mentioned, if a married brother were to die, then it became the responsibility of the next brother to copulate with the widow for the purpose of siring a descendant (Deuteronomy 25:5–6). Any child born from such a union was considered to be the offspring of the deceased brother, not of the one who actually impregnated the widow—who, by the way, had no say in the matter. Now, during Jesus' time there existed a group known as the Sadducees who were associated with the priest, active in the Temple, and members of the Sanhedrin (the Jewish council of leaders). Although the biblical text lumps them with the Pharisees as opponents to Jesus' teachings, rabbinic literature has them opposing the Pharisees. Several Sadducees (who, ironically, rejected the concept of the resurrection of the dead) tried to stump Jesus through a clever question. They described a man who dies childless. His brother, in obedience to the Law, marries the widow, but he too dies childless. The same thing happens to the third and fourth and so on to the seventh brother. All marry the widow, and all die childless. Finally the widow herself dies. Now here's the question: On the day of resurrection, since she's been married to all seven brothers, to whom does she belong?

Jesus chides them by responding that in Heaven, men and women do not marry because they are like the angels (Matthew 22:23–30). Many have interpreted this passage to mean that there is no sex in Heaven—that men and women in their glorified resurrected bodies will be like angels—that is, asexual creatures. If Heaven is perfection, and if there is no sex in Heaven, then for those who want perfection the conclusion should be obvious: imitate the Heavenly model by minimizing, if not eliminating, sex on earth. However, there are some problems with such an interpretation. We know that according to Genesis (6:1–2), angels came to earth and had sex with women because they were attracted to the women's long hair (1 Corinthians 11:10). So angels are not asexual;

quite the contrary. Jewish tradition usually understood angels to be male,[5] with circumcised penises.[6] Nevertheless, today we assume the everlasting asexuality of humans in Heaven because we read our anti-body doctrines into the biblical text, thus obscuring Jesus' message.

If we were to reread the Sadducees' question, but this time replace one possession—woman—with another—donkey—we might better grasp the meaning of Jesus' response. A man owned a donkey. He died so his brother inherited the beast. When he died the third and then the fourth and so on to the seventh brother all inherited the donkey. All owned the jackass, and all died. Finally the donkey itself dies. Now here's the question: On the day of resurrection, since the donkey was owned by all seven brothers, to whom does it belong?

Jesus' response was not meant to imply that there is no sex in Heaven. He was specifically rebuking a patriarchal order that reduced women to possessions, no different from donkeys. Possessions, whether a donkey or a wife, are not "owned" in Heaven; they belong to no one. In Heaven, unlike on earth, they are not reduced to commodities belonging to the man and passed on to another on the owner's death. The traditional marriage of Jesus' time, based on male activity and female passivity, does not exist in Heaven because the wife ceases to be anyone's possession. She is her own person.

But why wait till Heaven? Shouldn't the Heavenly ideal be the model for relationships on earth, hence bringing to fulfillment the prayer "on earth as it is in Heaven"? Paul addresses this: "All baptized in Christ are clothed in Christ and there cannot be distinctions between Jew nor Greek (race), slave nor free (class), male nor female (gender), for all of you are one in Christ Jesus" (Galatians 3:28). The intent of the Christ event is for all—regardless of race, class, or gender—to share fellowship and community as equals because Jesus saves all of them equally. In Christ, the prevailing hierarchies undergirding power relationships are shattered. To maintain such a hierarchy, even under the guise of Christian discipline, is antithetical to the liberation proclaimed by the Galatians text, which finds no distinction between male and female in Christ.

Jesus' Message Is Lost

Women were to be equal to men, according to the gospel principles laid out by Christ. The writers of the New Testament were interested in issues dealing with justice and showed little, if any, interest in legislating personal piety. The issues that have become important to modern-day Christians (that is, sexual activity, drinking, swearing, and so on) were less important to Christ and his disciples than spreading the good word of God's love for all. The elevation of women as expressed by Paul (1 Corinthians 7:3–4) planted the seeds for the dismantling of patriarchy. Still, rather than take Jesus' teachings to their conclusion, the early church compromised between the ideal of Jesus' message and the reality of the times. The early church paradigm of equality (no male or female in Christ), as demonstrated in that first Christian community located in the Books of Acts (2:17), quickly reverted back to the patriarchal social structure that for the next two thousand years reinforced the subjugation of women in general and the wife in particular.

The domestic needs of men became the standard for formulating the ideal Christian feminine identity. Although the man is charged to love his wife as Christ loved the church, the wife is called to obey her husband, for he "is the head of his wife, as Christ is the head of the church. . . . as the church is subject to Christ, so too the wife to her husband in everything" (Ephesians 5:21–33). Marriage continued to be an arrangement in which the man found a person to satisfy his sexual desires, keep his household clean and orderly, and provide him with legitimate heirs. In domestic conflicts, his opinion always prevailed. As in biblical times, marriage was an institution intended to unite families for gain. Marriage was too important to leave to the whims of young adults. Families with sufficient economic clout arranged their children's marriages to ensure mutually beneficial economic and political arrangements. The primary goal was to forge a marriage that profited both sets of in-laws; if feelings of love happened to develop, so much the better.

During feudal times, marriage among the aristocracy was an arrangement designed to protect the lands and wealth of nobility. Because the poor lacked land and wealth, little attention was paid to the sacredness of common marriage among the serfs or to any claim they might have to sexual rights. Female serfs were always vulnerable to the feudal common practice known as *droit du seigneur* (master's right). The lords of the manor reserved for themselves the *jus primae noctis,* the right to deflower the bride of peasants residing on their lands. Economically marginalized women served as sexual objects to be used by young men of privilege for their sexual education. This practice survived in Christian America during the nineteenth century: as discussed in the second chapter, black female slaves were expected to satisfy their Christian masters' sexual desires. Because all blacks were seen as chattel, even if two slaves chose to unite before God in holy matrimony the civil and legal system refused to acknowledge any validity to the union.

As Eurocentric societies moved from feudalism toward capitalism, traditional marriage was again redefined. The woman's virginity prior to marriage and fidelity during marriage were important for the wealthy because this guaranteed that the man's earthly possessions would be inherited by a legitimate heir. Because the poor had no wealth requiring protection, there was no legal or civil need for an official marriage. In addition, the concept of the male as exclusive breadwinner was (and continues to be) unheard of among the poor. Although women of class were excluded from the workforce until about the mid-twentieth century, poor women and women of color were always expected to work, mostly in domestic roles, to help financially support the family. Even children, as recently as this past century, were also responsible for bringing home enough to eat. Women in poor families have always had to and still must work to earn money; the option of staying home to care for the house and children full-time is not feasible—it remains a class privilege disproportionately exercised by affluent whites. The nuclear family model of a full-time homemaker supporting a solitary male breadwinner didn't become the accepted norm in this country until the mid-twentieth century, thanks in large part to a growing middle class and the cultural reinforcement provided by the new entertainment medium of television. Americans were taught the ideal family hierarchy through shows like *Leave It to Beaver, Ozzie and Harriet,* and *Father Knows Best.*

After the Second World War, society underwent radical changes— changes whose roots stretch back to the start of the century with movements emphasizing "Negro" rights and women's suffrage. The demise of the Eurocentric colonial system globally with the rise of nationalistic movements in Third World nations, and domestically the rise of liberation movements (black, women's, gay) contributed to major transformations in the definition of a traditional family. In the twentieth century, increasingly marriage partners were chosen by those entering into the relationship, rather than their families. The fundamental reasons for marrying shifted from the political or economical to the emotional; specifically, marriage became an act of and commitment to love. Marriage evolved into a private and personal matter in which love and fidelity supposedly trumped political and economic concerns. Marriage became a romantic relationship that provided both partners with companionship and friendship designed to replace and surpass the natal family. What we today call "traditional marriage" is but the latest incarnation in an evolution that is still under way. Because for the most part our modern societies have determined that economic and political reasons to marry should no longer play a role in the establishment of a relationship, marriage has evolved into the development of a friendship on which love, fidelity, self-giving, and vulnerability can be built. For the rest of this chapter, we will examine the different elements and aspects of what constitutes an orthoeros marriage in light of biblical principles.

Seeking an Orthoeros Marriage

Sexual equality does not mean that the woman can now, like the man, have multiple sexual partners, but rather that the man, like the woman, finds fulfillment (and great sex) in fidelity. In the ancient biblical world (as well as both the Greek and Roman worlds), men were not expected to find full sexual satisfaction with just one person. It was acceptable for them to find sexual satisfaction through other outlets besides marriage. Marriage, as history has recorded, existed for the purpose of securing the legitimacy of the male offspring and stabilizing economic status. Hence the model for marriage as described in the biblical text falls short of today's ideal because it does not provide for the male's fidelity. Without fidelity, a justice-based relationship cannot take place. If indeed the body is the temple of the Holy Spirit (1 Corinthians 6:19), then the genitals must become the most sacred part of that temple—in effect the Holy of Holies to which all are denied entry except the one chosen.

But is monogamy natural? Among primates, humans are the only mammals that attempt monogamy. According to the government's most comprehensive survey conducted on the sexual practices of Americans, the National Center for Health Statistics found that over a twelve-month period, 18 percent of males between the ages of 15 and 44 had two or more female partners; 63 percent were monogamous (10 percent never engaged in sex and 6 percent hadn't had intercourse in the past year). Among women during the same time period and in the same age group, 14 percent had had more than one partner, and 68 percent were monogamous (8 percent never engaged in sex and 7 percent hadn't in the past year). Among those who are married, about 4.5 percent of all men and 3.8 percent of all women reported having more than one sexual partner in the past twelve months. It should be noted that a small portion of these percentages may not necessarily indicate infidelity; some of these marriages may have begun within the preceding twelve months; others may have been experiencing temporary separation.[7]

We humans may *say* we want monogamy, but our practice does not necessarily match our conviction. Still, questioning the naturalness of monogamy is probably the wrong approach. Instead, we should focus on the benefits, if any, of monogamy. Is it better for both the individual and society at large to advocate monogamy? A study conducted by The National Marriage Project revealed a strong case for monogamy. This nonpartisan, nonsectarian, interdisciplinary university-based initiative out of Rutgers conducted research and analysis on the state of marriage in America. The study showed that for men, more so than for women, marriage is a transformative event, changing men's behavior in particular ways. Married men end up leading healthier and more productive lives, working harder and doing better financially than unmarried men. Because of a stable routine, their job absenteeism, sick days, and quit rates are reduced, strengthening their workforce attachment. This is probably because these men are less likely to frequent bars, abuse alcohol, and engage in illegal drug use or other risky activities. Although it may appear acceptable for single men to be self-indulgent and carefree, such behavior is less acceptable for married men. The result of these trends is that married men earn 10 to 40 percent more than do single men with similar education and employment histories. They are more likely to spend time with relatives and become more involved in religious and community activities; hence they tend to be more responsible and involved fathers.

But are these married men happier? The survey found that the overwhelming majority (94 percent) claimed to be happier when married than when single. Seventy-three percent reported having a better sex life since getting married, and 68 percent said marriage has helped them become more financially stable. On this latter point it should be noted that on average, married couples create more economic assets than singles or cohabiting couples. Compared to those who were married, those who never married had 75 percent less wealth, and those who divorced and never remarried had 73 percent less.[8] The research seems to indicate that healthy marriages contribute to economic stability and personal fulfillment. Such an arrangement thus becomes one of the prerequisites for great sex.

The Consequences of Infidelity

If one of the characteristics of an orthoeros relationship is faithfulness, then the betrayal of fidelity jeopardizes the prospects for great sex. The biblical text has much to say about adultery. We begin our exploration by considering Mary, the mother of Jesus, who was suspected of being an adulteress. We are told by the biblical text that her betrothed, Joseph, was planning to informally divorce her for her unfaithfulness, but was stopped when he dreamt of an angel instructing him to marry the woman who was pregnant with a child that was not his (Matthew 1:18–25). Although believers in Jesus' messiahship usually accept the virgin birth as a tenet of faith, others who reject Jesus' claim do not necessarily subscribe to such a miracle. For some, Jesus was the bastard child of the Jew Mary and the Roman soldier Panthera. In fact, the title Jesus ben Panthera (Jesus son of Panthera) is not uncommon in the Talmud and other rabbinical writings. The third-century theologian Origen makes a reference to this accusation when he writes in defense of the virgin birth.[9]

Joseph's contemplation of ending his betrothal with Mary was not a result of broken trust. As already discussed, the modern definition of adultery (infidelity to one's marriage vows, regardless of gender) is quite different from the biblical understanding of the concept, which was understood as a property-related matter. Joseph considered ending his relationship with Mary because his rights to his property (her body) were trespassed. Women engaging in sex with anyone except their husbands were considered adulterers. A husband who suspected his wife of infidelity could, according to the Hebrew Bible, have her ingest a bitter elixir before the priest. If she survived unharmed, then she was faithful. But if her belly swelled and her thighs shriveled, then she was guilty of adultery (Numbers 5:11–31). It goes without saying that a man suspected of engaging in intercourse with a woman who was not his wife did not have to drink such a brew.

Although the Hebrew Bible defined adultery in such a way that it allowed men to have multiple sex partners, Jesus redefined adultery to assign men a share of the responsibility: "You have heard that it was said to the ancients, 'Do not commit adultery.'" But I tell you, that anyone looking at a woman with the intent of lusting after her has already committed adultery with her in his heart" (Matthew 5:27–28). Because Jesus specifically stated "anyone looking at a *woman* [with lust]," it must be assumed that his audience was composed only of men. We may wonder why he didn't address the possibility of women lusting after men. Was it because of the enduring sexist assumption that women lack sexual desire?

As I have noted, men could sexually amuse themselves with a multitude of sexual partners and never be guilty of adultery. But here, Jesus redefined adultery to include men. By making the woman the object of man's lust, Jesus expanded the definition of adultery to mean both literal and imagined intercourse with women other than the man's wife. Jesus redefined biblical marriage by characterizing it as an act of fidelity for both the woman *and the man*. Accordingly, any sexual act outside of the marriage by either partner nullifies the marriage by defiling it. Raising the bar on the definition of adultery to include husbands as well as wives, the writer of the book of Hebrews states, "Marriage is to be honored by all, and the bed is to be undefiled. Fornicators and adulterers will be judged by God" (13:4).

The Betrayal of Intimacy

If another characteristic for an orthoeros relationship is intimacy, then the danger of divorce and the rupture of the intimacy of oneness jeopardize the potential for great sex. When women were property, men could divorce them for "anything improper" (Deuteronomy 24:1). A man could discard his wife for whatever offense she might have committed that he perceived to be improper, even for something as trivial as disobeying a request. According to Ecclesiasticus (25:26), one of the Apocrypha books, "If [your wife] will not do as you tell her, separate yourself from her." And because women had no rights in and of themselves, they did not have the right to divorce their husbands.

When Jesus was asked how he understood the phrase "anything improper," he dismissed the question by redefining it. Referring to the creation story, Jesus annulled the right of husbands to divorce their wives because it contradicted God's initial intention of making two into "one flesh." Divorce was allowed by Moses because of the "hardheartedness" of men. But according to Jesus, "any man who divorces his wife. . . . and remarries, is guilty of adultery" (Matthew 19:9). As previously mentioned, the only way a man could be guilty of adultery at this time was to engage in intercourse with a married woman, another man's property. His marital status was irrelevant to the charge of adultery. But with Jesus' response, the man became the sexual property of his wife. If he were to divorce his wife and take on another woman, his first wife would maintain a sexual claim on him. Jesus' redefinition of divorce changed woman's identity as a disposable and divorceable piece of property. Patriarchy was challenged, as both spouses found equality as one flesh.

Probably one of the most important consequences of Jesus' pronouncement concerning divorce was the security it provided for women (mainly in theory; unfortunately, not in practice). Because women were dependent on men for economic survival, and because a divorce—both then and now—usually meant that the woman suffered more economically, women benefited from the indissolubility of marriage. True, this may not have ensured a happy or joyful marriage for the wife, but it did protect her from being thrown out of her home because of something her husband found improper about her. It is not surprising, then, that the early Christian church's main constituents were women, who through this teaching were given greater hope for a future of newfound security and protection.

Another consequence of Jesus' message was that it eventually brought an end to the practice of divorcing wives who proved to be barren. This greatly impacted the rich, who, wishing to secure their inheritance, could no longer insist that the fertile man could put away his sterile wife and take another to secure the eventual transfer of the family wealth. As the church developed along patriarchal lines, and the need to protect the riches of the wealthy became paramount, the granting of divorce (or putting away one's wife in a nunnery) for infidelity or impotence was reinstated in much of Western Christian society. England's Henry VIII provides a notorious example of divorce trumping biblical teachings. Protecting property rights and inheritances within marriage continues in modern days through the prenuptial agreement, whereby individuals wishing to protect their wealth agree that the personal property they bring into the marriage will not be jeopardized in the event of a divorce. Although such an agreement may make great business sense, I believe that to make provisions for a potential separation undermines a marriage that vows lifelong union. By making prior arrangements to safeguard wealth in the event of divorce, economics, rather than a familial relationship, is again made central to marriage.

With the Protestant Reformation, divorce was again redefined. Martin Luther allowed divorce for either the husband or the wife if their spouse was frigid or impotent. Luther writes: "[If a wife refuses to have sex] it is time for the husband to say, 'If you will not, another will; the maid will come if the wife will not.' Only first the husband should admonish and warn his wife two or three times, and let the situation be known to others so that her stubbornness becomes a matter of common knowledge and is rebuked before the congregation. If she still refuses, get rid of her; take an Esther and let Vashti go, as King Ahasuerus did."[10] Furthermore, Luther's high regard for marriage and disregard for sex outside of marriage led him to defend bigamy before God (but not before the secular authorities) as the better recourse to divorce or taking on a mistress.[11] Luther made this defense on behalf of a Protestant nobleman, Philip of Hesse, with the stipulation that the bigamy should be kept secret. It is important to note that Philip of Hesse was a valuable ally to Luther, responsible for forming a defense league of Protestant princes in the event the Catholic emperor tried to enforce his will on Germany. One wonders how much of Luther's pastoral advice was influenced by his own need for political protection.

Overall, divorce has historically been frowned on by the Christian church. So the question before us is whether modern-day Christians may divorce. St. Paul seemed to think they should be able to. In dealing with the question of divorce, Paul asserted that "God has called you to a life of peace" (1 Corinthians 7:15). Specifically, he stated that if a believer is married to an unbeliever who does not consent to the marriage, then the believer can separate and seek peace. But what if one spouse is abusive, physically or psychologically? And what if that spouse claims to be a fellow believer? Can they still separate? Absolutely. If a tree is known by its fruits, then the actions of the abusive spouse serve as a testament of unbelief. Although divorce continues to be a painful option, it may very well be the better of two evils. God has called the abused spouse to a life of peace.

Despite the fact that many Christians continue to see divorce as a spiritual failure, the U.S. divorce rate is presently twice what it was in 1960. Although it has been declining since hitting its highest point in the early 1980s, for the average couple marrying in 2005, the probability of divorce or separation during their lifetime remains close to 50 percent. The decline in divorce rates can be attributed to an increase in the age at which people first marry and their higher education levels, both of which probably contribute to more stable marriages. According to research, if one is well educated, earns a decent income, comes from a religious and intact family, and marries after the age of twenty-five without first having a baby, then chances of divorce are slim.[12]

Divorce is a painful experience that can have enduring consequences that impact one's ability to enjoy great sex. On a practical level, divorce (along with out-of-wedlock childbearing) is a major factor contributing to the increase in child poverty in the United States. According to one study, if the family structure had remained unchanged between 1960 and 1998, the black child poverty rate would have been 28.4 percent instead of the 45.6 percent that it was in 1998. Likewise, the white child poverty rate would have been 11.4 percent instead of 15.4 percent. According to one researcher, a single divorce costs the state and federal government about $30,000 due to higher usage of food stamps and public housing, as well as the costs associated with the increase in juvenile delinquencies and personal bankruptcies. In 2002, the nation's 10.4 million divorces carried an estimated taxpayer cost of $30 billion.[13]

In addition to the negative financial impact of divorce, it also negatively affects one's spiritual life. Divorce is considered to be spiritually painful because it tears apart the flesh that was made one in God. Still, there are circumstances in which divorce may be the best solution. As injurious as divorce can be to the soul and body, it can also at times be the means by which the soul and body can be saved. For example, the destruction of a human, created in the image of God, is a common sin inflicted through spouse abuse—physical, emotional, or psychological. At times the abused partner is left with choosing between staying in an abusive relationship or divorcing, neither one being ideal. But when divorce leads to saving or restoring a person's worth and dignity, then divorce may very well be the better option of the two.

Episcopal bishop John Shelby Spong suggests that churches should consider a liturgical service that marks the end of a marriage. Because divorce is a difficult and painful time for the couple involved, a service would bring together a caring congregation to love and support the couple separately through the anguish caused by their divorce. Additionally, it provides a spiritual opportunity to offer the pain up to God.[14] The issue of divorce for the Christian community should be less an attempt to control which couples can annul their marriage and when, and more about how it can minister to the pain experienced by divorcing couples.

The Right to Sexual Satisfaction

Sexual pleasure is God-given. This doesn't mean that sex should be our ultimate goal in life, or it becomes an idol. But this also means that sex isn't wrong. Sex is part of the human experience to be enjoyed, and that pleasure should not be limited to men. According to the Talmud, men are expected to meet and satisfy the sexual needs of their wives.[15] In the privacy of the bedchamber, couples can participate in whatever kind of sexually satisfying activity they choose. Their sexual activity, according to the Mishnah Torah, can be "natural or unnatural sex."[16] The right to achieve sexual satisfaction is confirmed in the New Testament. According to Paul (1 Corinthians 7:9), it is sufficient to justify entering into marriage. Even Martin Luther thought it was the "most disgraceful crime to produce semen and excite the woman, and [then] to frustrate her at that very moment [of climax by *coitus interruptus* (pulling out)]."[17]

Although some men may purposely choose not to sexually satisfy their partners, other are physically unable to do so due to premature ejaculation or erectile dysfunction. When men are unable to sexually perform for whatever reason, the cause is usually understood as biological. Men can turn to medicines such as Viagra, Cialis, Dapoxetine, or Levitra to correct their problem. But when it comes to women, the explanations and remedies given as to why they are unable to achieve sexual satisfaction are quite different. This is partially due to the lingering historical mindset that assumed women had no sexual desires. It wasn't until the 1920s that the woman's libido was "discovered" and emphasis was placed on her achieving sexual satisfaction. Secular sex manuals of that time placed the responsibility of sexually satisfying the woman on the male. Such manuals emphasized foreplay and clitoral stimulation, warning that leaving the wife sexually unsatisfied could lead to health problems for her. Women, it was said, had to learn how to have an orgasm because it did not come as naturally to them as it did to men.

It should therefore not be surprising that for women who today suffer from difficulty with sexual desire or response, the cause of the abnormality is usually understood to be psychologically based, rather than biologically, as with men. When Procter and Gamble tried to obtain

FDA approval in 2004 for Intrinsa, a testosterone patch for women designed to increase their sex drive, they were accused of creating a new syndrome for which they could market a profitable treatment. The results of a study presented at the 2004 annual meeting of the American Society for Reproductive Medicine showed that women with low sexual desire who used a testosterone patch had satisfying sex four times more often than they did before they got the patch. That study seems to confirm an earlier one conducted in 2002 published in the *New England Journal of Medicine*. Still, the FDA chose not to approve the patch in 2004, citing that not enough testing had taken place.[18]

An essential argument persists: emphasizing differences in sexual satisfaction based on gender. But mutual sexual pleasure is a healthy and liberating end unto itself, which can be enjoyed by both males and females. As such, couples should have full range to experiment and learn what brings them pleasure, as long as the familial relationship between them is not violated. For example, they should have the option of participating in oral or anal sex. Both are common enough in our culture, and the Bible does not implicitly prohibit them. According to a survey conducted by the U.S. Department of Health and Human Services, among adults ages twenty-five through forty-four, 90 percent of men and 88 percent of women have engaged in oral sex with an opposite-sex partner. In that same age group, 6.5 percent of men have had oral or anal sex with another man and 11 percent of women have had a sexual experience with another woman.[19]

Great sex is more than simply physical satisfaction, but seeking mutual pleasure remains an important characteristic of any healthy familial relationship. How each couple reaches sexual satisfaction remains their sole prerogative. As long as the characteristics of the orthoeros are not violated, then couples are free to define for themselves how they achieve sexual pleasure.

Choosing Children

In a 2005 column, Al Mohler, president of Southern Baptist Theological Seminary, wrote that couples who choose childlessness are guilty of "rebellion against parenthood [that] represents nothing less than an absolute revolt against God's design."[20] He bases his assertion on Psalm 127, which reads, "Children are a heritage of the Lord, the fruit of the womb a reward. As arrows in a soldier's hand, so are the sons of the young. Blessed is the man who has filled his quiver with them" (v. 3–5). Mohler advocates a "full-quiver" theology that disapproves of all forms of contraceptives. Only God, he argues, can decide when to open or close the womb; for mere mortals to practice birth control is akin to superceding the role of Divinity. If children equal blessings, then all that humans can do is have as many children possible so that a man's quiver can truly be full.

As disturbing as "full-quiver" theology may be, more distressing are Mohler's sociopolitical reasons for his stance. According to an interview he gave to *The Chicago Tribune,* Mohler explained that rather than being concerned with overpopulation, he was more troubled by underpopulation. Specifically he states, "We are barely replenishing ourselves. That is going to cause huge social problems in the future."[21] Now, as every grade school child knows, the world's population has been increasing with each year that goes by. According to the U.S. Census Bureau the world population, which was a little over six billion in 2000, is expected to be a little under seven billion by 2010, and will grow to over nine billion by 2050.[22] The U.S. population is also growing, from about 282,000,000 in 2000 to the 300,000,000 milestone reached in October 2006, with a projected 309,000,000 by 2010 and close to 420,000,000 by 2050.[23] If these scientifically projected increases are reliable, then we must ask, why is Mohler concerned about underpopulation? Underpopulation for whom? In other words, who are the "we" who are barely replenishing themselves?

The 2050 projections for U.S. population growth if present trends continue indicate that Euro-Americans will cease being the majority race in the U.S. The combined population growth of communities of color will make America a predominately nonwhite nation. Mohler answers my question as to who the "we" are in his August 15, 2005, blog: "[T]he tragic reality is that citizens of Europe and North America are now failing even to replace themselves in terms of children."[24] For Mohler and the Religious Right he represents, the call for "full-quiver" theology is white supremacy code-language advocating for the increase of white babies. Mohler's call is a race-based warning. It is a call for white fecundity, lest white America and Europe become overrun with "colored" children, which would only lead, per Mohler, to "huge social problems in the future."

Regardless of the racist overtones of Mohler's call for reproductive white sex, children, whatever their color or ethnicity, can indeed be a joyous product of sex. Still, when we engage in lovemaking, our conscious purpose is not necessarily to create a child; rather, we engage in sex for mutual pleasure—usually in the form of reaching orgasm—and intimate bonding. Yet although reproduction is not the sole reason nor the main purpose for engaging in sex, it is the original driving force that compels living things to have intercourse, and as such it does seem fitting that new life can be a product of two becoming one. Indeed, as a father of two children myself, I can unequivocally claim that my children are among the greatest blessings of my life. Like Al Mohler, who also has two children, my wife and I are not in "moral rebellion" against God because we have chosen to have no more.

Still, what about children being God's blessing? It is the height of biblical naiveté, as we have repeatedly seen, to impose modern concepts on ancient text. Children as blessings for their own sake are a relatively modern concept. Although the biblical text claims children are a blessing, this blessing was due to the economic value children had. Biblically speaking, children were an asset; like women, they were a man's property. If the union failed to produce children, a man had the right to put away his wife and choose another, in hopes that the new woman would produce offspring—preferably boys. In an agriculturally based society, the presence of children literally meant extra hands to work the field now and provide the parent with a form of economic security in the future. Children were needed to ensure financial support in old age, an ancient form of social security. The more children one had, the more financially secure one's farm became. But the size of families began to decline with the urbanization of society, along with advances in medicine contributing to longevity of life, population growth straining resources, and technology that reduced the number of people needed to work the soil. Still, in many societies throughout the world today where the social safety net has been dismantled (as in the case of China, India, and Russia) children remain a blessing because they serve as a hedge against the financial difficulties that may be expected in old age.

A disturbing story illustrating children's role as property appears in the book of Job, offending our present moral sensitivities, even though it made perfect moral sense during biblical times. We are told that all of Job's children, seven sons and three daughters, are killed by Satan on God's authority (1:2–9). This is but one of many calamities to befall Job, but no doubt among the most painful. By the end of the book, God restores all of Job's riches and properties, including, in a manner of speaking, his children. He actually fathers seven new sons and two new daughters, replacing those whom he lost earlier in the story (42:13–17). If children are seen as property, then the siring of new children to replace the old dead ones seems fair—kind of like the fourteen thousand sheep, six thousand camels, thousand oxen, and thousand she-donkeys that replaced Job's destroyed livestock. But if children are a product of love—a quite modern concept—then no number of additional children can ever assuage the grief or replace the sense of loss of the original ones.

Jesus changed the status of children by making them the ideal by which entrance into God's reign can occur (Matthew 18:3–4). Seeking the position of the least among us, the child became the means toward salvation. Children's identity ceased to be that of property; instead, they were a product of love. Jesus returned children (as well as women) to their status as human beings, instead of property in a patriarchal society.

Marriage to a Jealous God

One of the motifs found in the biblical text is marriage to God. In the Hebrew Bible, God is the husband of Israel, whereas in the New Testament, Jesus is the church's bridegroom. The prophet Isaiah proclaims that the Creator will now be the husband (Israel 54:5), who rejoices over his bride Israel as a husband rejoices over his virgin bride (Israel 62:2–5). Jesus would later refer to himself as the bridegroom at least seven times in the Gospels. The problem with this marriage imagery is how culture has historically defined marriage, specifically in a patriarchal structure. Because God—Jesus—is the husband, it's claimed by the patriarchal church that we, as the collective wife, must be servile and obedient, on earth as it is in Heaven. The wife, of a husband or of God, is commanded to submit and is expected to sacrifice her personhood for the one in authority. And if the bride proves to be unfaithful? Then she can be corrected through the use of savage violence. When Israel proves to be unfaithful to God, God strips her naked before her neighbors to be punished like any other woman who commits adultery. She is stoned and run through with the sword. Her house is set on fire while the full fury of a jealous God falls on her (Ezekiel 16:35–43).

When marriage is defined in this manner, it is a perversion that traps both the oppressed (wives) and the oppressors (husbands) in a social structure of domination, in which neither is free to engage in a familial relationship or in great sex. Both the wife and husband require liberation; that is, salvation from such a marriage arrangement, which manifests the essence of sin: oppression. This particular understanding of marriage with God is so perverse that it leads us further away from any type of intimacy with both God and our beloved.

In orthoeros, marriage is redefined to incorporate the qualities of a familial relationship. It is rooted in justice, and a new relationship is then possible with our beloved and with our God. This relationship becomes one in which a new level of vulnerability and mutuality creates the possibility of greater and more passionate intimacy. Moving away from patriarchy, this new marriage with our beloved is based on a relationship with God in which, as the prophet Hosea writes, "I [God] will betroth you to me forever. Yes, I will betroth you to me in integrity and in justice, in mercy and in compassion. I will even betroth you to me in faithfulness and you shall *know* Yahweh" (Hosea 2:19–20). Marriage ceases to be based on a dominate-subordinate relationship along the lines of a master-slave. Instead it becomes a deep friendship. Or as Jesus, the model for the perfect spouse, said, "No longer do I call you slaves, for the slave does not know what the master [husband] does. I will call you friends, because all that I have heard from my Father I have made known to you (John 15:15).

Only friends share equality, common respect, familiarity, and love. As the apostle Paul eloquently wrote, this is a love that is always patient and kind, never jealous, boastful, nor conceited. It is a love that is neither rude nor selfish, taking no offense nor becoming resentful. It is a love that does not rejoice in the other's failures, but rather delights in truth. Love is always ready to excuse, to trust, to hope, and to endure whatever comes (1 Corinthians 13:4–7). Only friends, be they our beloved or our God, can share the intimacy of this kind of love. Only friends can have great sex!

SEX AND THE SINGLE CHRISTIAN

But, wretched youth that I was—supremely wretched even in the very outset of my youth—I had entreated chastity from you [God] and had prayed, "Grant me chastity and continence, but not yet." For I was afraid lest you should hear me too soon, and too soon cure me of my disease of lust which I desired to have satisfied rather than extinguished.[1]

—Augustine

Onan must have been a malicious and incorrigible scoundrel. [Masturbation] is a most disgraceful sin. It is far more atrocious than incest and adultery. We call it unchastity, yes, a Sodomitic sin.[2]

—Martin Luther

IN THE LAST DAYS, when Jesus returns to establish his reign, one-hundred-and-forty-four-thousand people who are redeemed from the earth will stand before the Lamb of God, singing praises to the one who sits upon the throne. So the Book of Revelation tells us. What is the common characteristic held by these chosen people destined for the honor of standing in the presence of Jesus? According to the biblical text, "these are the ones who have not been defiled with women for they are virgins" (14:1–4). Regardless of the nagging technical questions this passage raises (whether this means that all one hundred and forty-four thousand people are male because they were not defiled by women, or that women who have not been defiled by women are also included), it is obvious that great importance is placed on the concept of virginity. When we also consider that one of the most important figures in Christendom (especially among Catholics and Eastern Orthodox) is the Virgin Mary—with the emphasis on *Virgin*—it is easy to conclude that the Christian interpretation of the biblical text is biased toward celibacy and, by extension, singleness.

Choosing Celibacy—Choosing Purity?

Contrary to popular belief, nowhere in Scripture is the concept of asceticism—the denial of sexual pleasure for the purpose of religious devotion—advocated as a lifelong practice for believers. Among biblical figures, with the exception of Jesus, the prophet Jeremiah is the only celibate mentioned. But this is mainly due to the impending doom (the Babylonian invasion) facing Jerusalem. Jeremiah's work of warning God's people prevented him from marrying and settling down. His singleness was a necessary choice so as to accomplish God's task; it was not a sign of ascetic devotion (Jeremiah 16:1–2). Even Jesus' singleness was neither a call to ascetic devotion nor a denigration of marriage, but rather a choice made so as to complete his earthly mission.

To the Hebrew mind-set, celibacy was unnatural. The Talmud states that anyone who is not married is deficient because they live for the self. In Judaism, embracing the other through marriage is an underlying component of being human.[3] If Aristotle is correct in labeling humans as "social animals," then our need to be connected, to be part of a social group, is probably best met through familial relationships.[4] In this case, the familial relationship need not necessarily be sexual. It can encompass the sexual intimacy of a couple, the deepness of a platonic friendship, or membership in a larger unit of a family. It does not take rocket science to figure out what the vast majority of scientific data indicates: that individuals who are in a loving relationship live happier, longer, healthier, and more fulfilled lives than those who are not.

Yet Christianity has made celibacy a more desirable state of being than marriage. This chapter will begin by exploring why. Although it is not the purpose of this chapter to discredit the choice of singleness, still, it will examine the consequences—at times negative—of forced celibacy. Furthermore, for those who willingly choose singleness as a way of life, this chapter will examine some of the struggles likely to be faced. The chapter concludes by attempting to apply an orthoeros stance to singleness, seeking the mean between the extremes of a culture obsessed with sex and the Christian component in that culture that advocates celibacy in singleness.

Discouraging Marriage, Encouraging Celibacy

The early Christian understanding of marriage was a major departure from Jewish thought. Although marriage was good, it was still considered secondary to a life of singleness and celibacy, for the celibate was considered holier and closer to God. Even Paul wrote, "The one given in marriage does well, but the one not given in marriage does better" (1 Corinthians 7:38). The ideal condition for the spiritual Christian came to be understood as permanent celibacy, for abstinence was an outward expression of an inward freedom from the corruptible flesh. Still, early Christianity attempted to broker a compromise between the ideal of living a celibate life and the reality of human sexual desire. Although the sex instinct was to be respected as being natural, men and women were not to abandon themselves to the "sinful flesh," for such abandonment harmed the spiritual and physical welfare of the believer. If celibacy was easily practiced, then the person should remain unmarried. If, however, abstinence was difficult, then marriage was a reluctant second choice.

Marriage therefore was recommended by Paul for those so over-wrought with sexual desires that they are incapable of submitting the flesh to the spirit by living a celibate life. "Concerning what you wrote, it is better for a man and a woman not to touch, but because of fornication, let each have his own wife and each her own husband" (1 Corinthians 7:1–2). Later in that same chapter, addressing widows and widowers, Paul discouraged remarriage. "But if they lack self-control, let them marry, for it is better to marry than to be inflamed" (v. 9). Based on these verses, asceticism was advocated and preferred by the church. But Paul's discouragement of marriage was probably due to his belief that Christ's return was imminent—he expected the second coming within his own lifetime (1 Corinthians 15:51–52; 1 Thessalonians 4:17). Why distract oneself with marriage and the worldly concerns a family generates when the end of the world was at hand (1 Corinthians 7:29–34)? To Paul, marriage was for those who are not "spiritual" enough to control their sexual appetites to spread the good news of Christ's impending return. Although to the first-century Christian mind-set celibacy made sense, this does not mean that marriage was forbidden or that celibacy was enforced. In his first letter to Timothy, Paul specifically railed against the satanic "lies told by hypocrites," who insisted that "marriage is forbidden" (4:1–3).

Still, the early church made it difficult to participate in a loving, celebrative intimate relationship within marriage. According to the commonly held belief, sex was a necessary evil of marriage; the more one abstained, the better it would be for the couple. Hence, the church warned against engaging in intercourse on Mondays (the day to remember the dead); on Thursdays (the day of Jesus' arrest); on Fridays (the day of Jesus' crucifixion); on Saturdays (the day to celebrate the Virgin Mary); and on the forty days before Christmas and Easter. In addition, sex was prohibited during a woman's pregnancy, plus the forty days after giving birth. In short, for over half of the year, Christians were to abstain from sex. And if a woman was pregnant, almost the entire year was off-limits.

Celibacy and the Clergy

Considering how much importance Christians have always placed on celibacy, it is not surprising that the Catholic Church mandates, to this day, celibacy among its clergy. What may be surprising to some is that this wasn't always the case. We know that the first "Pope" of Rome, Peter the disciple of Jesus Christ, was married, for one of Jesus' first miracles was the healing of Peter's mother-in-law (Matthew 8:14–15). We also suspect that Paul was either married or at one time married, mainly because most Pharisees strove to obey God's call to be "fruitful and multiply." Also, in his first letter to the Corinthians, Paul insisted on his right to enjoy food and drink, along with his right to take a Christian woman with him on his missionary trips, as have other apostles, including Peter (9:4–5). Who was this Christian woman he insisted could accompany him? His wife? Because marriage was the norm, it could be argued that unless otherwise stated, the normal marital status applies. In fact, for the first three hundred years of church history, the clerics of the faith were married. It wasn't until the Synod of Elvira (Spain), somewhere around the year 295 to 302, that celibacy was first legislated for churchmen, partly due to the negative views toward women detailed in the first chapter of this book. Canon 33 of the Synod of Elvira forbids bishops, presbyters, deacons, and others with a position in the ministry from engaging in sexual intercourse with their wives. If they disobeyed, they could be dismissed from their ecclesiastic duties.

Ironically, Paul mainly chose married men to be bishops, with only one limitation: that each have just one wife (Titus 1:5–6). He believed that abandoning sex altogether could lead to sexual immorality—in effect, giving Satan a foothold in exploiting men's weakness (1 Corinthians 7:5). But many took the church's views on celibacy seriously, threatening the family unit as those seeking "holiness" abandoned their families and joined monasteries (among them Augustine of Hippo, who abandoned his common-law wife of fifteen years). Even though celibacy was not legislated for clerics during the first three hundred years of Christian history, it was still expected for the higher grades of the clergy (for example, popes and bishops). Although priests could marry, it was seen as improper for them to do so after their ordination. This imposition of celibacy on the clergy was a struggle for the church hierarchy, as it was not universally accepted or practiced, although it remained the primary requirement for entrance into monastic communities. Only some six hundred years after the start of Christianity did the church start decreeing a celibate priesthood, leading to riots among the clergy.

It would be another six hundred years before the church officially imposed mandatory celibacy on the clergy with the 1139 Second Lateran Council, although Pope Leo IX (1048–1054) had ordered celibacy for the clergy some ninety years earlier. Married priests were threatened with excommunication, as were parishioners who took communion from such priests. In accordance with Pope Gregory VII's 1074 Council in Rome, wives of priests had their marriages annulled and their status reduced to that of whores and concubines, and their children became bastards. The fate that awaited these former wives (per the Synod of Melfi in 1089) and their children (per the Synod of Pavia in 1018) was to be sold into slavery. But it wasn't until the Council of Trent (1545–1563) that the church officially stated that celibacy and virginity were superior to marriage. Anyone who disagreed with this stance was declared anathema—that is, cursed by the ecclesiastic hierarchy of the church. As recently as 1954, in the encyclical *Sacra Virginitas*, Pope Pius XII reiterated the Council of Trent's conclusion that celibacy was superior to marriage.

Today, the mandate of celibacy for clergy is wreaking havoc on faith traditions like the Catholic Church. The celibacy vow has drastically reduced the number of priests who are able to carry out the functions of the church, such as consecrating communion. According to a Vatican working document, the ratio of priests to Catholics has gone from one for every 1,797 in 1978 to one for every 2,677 in 2003. In the United States the number is closer to one for every 4,723.[5] There is no indication that this trend will reverse any time soon. Unless changes take place in the Catholic Church, we can expect the clergy's numbers to keep dwindling.

Taking Refuge in Celibacy

For a small minority of the faithful, celibacy is a valid option. Additionally, choosing virginity and postponing sexual activity until one enters into a familial relationship may very well prove to be a wise choice for a multitude of reasons. It is unfortunate that our sexualized, media-saturated culture has made virginity and celibacy choices to be ridiculed. The 2005 motion picture *The 40-Year-Old Virgin*, starring Steve Carell, is a case in point. It stereotypes virgins as bumbling buffoons who are basically losers. Those who choose virginity or celibacy, especially for spiritual reasons, are derided and made to feel shame for their choice. If one of the characteristics of orthoeros is consensual sex, then the right to choose not to participate in sexual activities must be honored and respected. By the same token, celibacy should not be imposed on anyone.

The major problem with a church-imposed celibacy is that it contradicts the biblical text. Even though Paul advocated singleness over marriage, he insisted that celibacy was first and foremost a *charisma*—a gift. Thus it cannot be demanded of those who have not been given this particular gift. Besides, the gift of celibacy was given to certain individuals for the good of the entire faith community, not to indicate the moral superiority of some over others. But what if one's sexual drive were so strong that celibacy would be, to say the least, a challenge to maintain? Then the gift given to that individual was something else, something other than celibacy (1 Corinthians 12:4–30).

Still, in a patriarchal social structure, some women were able to find liberation in the bonds of celibacy. It was historically assumed that virginity saved women from the curse of Eve (Genesis 3:16)—specifically, male domination and the pain or possible death of childbirth. For centuries, women were under the authority of men: first their fathers, then their husbands. But nuns, although subject to the male hierarchy of the church, enjoyed a certain level of autonomy to pursue individual interests. Women could find liberation from sexual oppression in chastity. At the nunnery, young girls were encouraged to offer up their virginity as a sacrifice to Christ; in this way, as the brides of Christ, they could be saved from the sins of the world. Some went so far as to strap on a chastity belt and throw away the key.

This historical understanding of celibacy's benefits for women is taking on new meaning for both females and males of the modern world. Today, specifically among certain young Christians, celibacy is being seen as the Holy Grail, a requirement for membership in the new army of God. Virginity has become an organizational requisite for the defenders of God's ways during these "last days." These modern Christian virgins see themselves as the knights, warriors, and damsels of the coming kingdom of God. To engage in sex outside of marriage, according to Dr. James Kennedy of the influential Coral Ridge Ministries, is to participate in "an uprising against God." The popular evangelical conservative manual *Every Young Man's Battle* proclaims, "the world hasn't yet seen what

God can do with an army of young men free of sexual fevers. . . . you can remain pure so that you might qualify for such an army." This war imagery is continued by other authors, like John Eldredge in his bestseller *Wild at Heart*. On top of advocating abstinence until marriage, Eldredge claims that today's decadence is a direct result of men failing to assume the role to which God has called them. Women are frustrated by not being under the authority of men, he claims. What they want "is to be fought for" by men who are "hard-wired" for battle. These men must become modern-day warriors in the vein of *Braveheart* and *Gladiator* so they can whip their women back into their God-given assigned roles. To help these young warriors stay focused, organizations such as Abstinence Clearinghouse hold seminars and conferences called "abstinence teas" and "purity balls" (pun intended?). And what happens if one of these modern-day warriors of God falls by engaging in sex? They are always given the option of repenting, which will lead to their transformation as "born-again virgins."[6]

Obviously, some in our society hold extreme views on what it means to live the single life. There's a dichotomy between the drive for celibacy among born-again Christians and the sex-saturated mainstream culture that ridicules virginity. Both extremes are unhealthy for both the individual and the overall community. Orthoeros attempts to uncover the mean between these two extremes. But before exploring this mean, we will first examine the orthoeros stance on issues related to choosing a life of singleness.

Struggling with Singleness

It's not easy to choose singleness in a culture that glorifies sexuality. It takes concerted effort to reduce the constant bombardment of sexual images. Adding to the struggle of singleness is the paradoxical lack of proper information about sexuality. In our sex-obsessed culture, there's a lack of sex education to guide the individual and community in making proper moral and ethical decisions. How can an individual arrive at an orthoeros way of life when many in the Religious Right purposely prevent the free flow of information? How can we make Christian-based decision about contraceptives, masturbation, and dating in the absence of sex education?

Learning About Sex in a Sex-Saturated Culture

Influenced by the sexual ethics of the Religious Right, the U.S. government's sex education policy has aimed to reduce public school programs to an abstinence-only message. The Bush administration has backed this initiative with over $204 million in public funds.[7] Teaching sex education has been a hotly debated issue in the cultural wars of the past few decades. Since the start of both the new millennium and the George W. Bush presidency, the drive to make abstinence the only form of sex education in all public schools has seen its greatest gains. Wade Horn, an assistant secretary at the Department of Health and Human Services, insists that the best approach to sexual education is a clear and consistent message. According to him, to discuss birth control or provide access to contraception sends teenagers a contradictory message.[8] Sex education teachers are now more likely to focus on abstinence only rather than to deal with birth control methods. In 1988, one in fifty sex education teachers taught abstinence only. By 1999, the ratio was one in four.[9]

The abstinence-only strategy advocated by this particular administration is in reality a form of a virginity pledge that teaches adolescents to "just say no" to sex. A statement issued by the American Academy of Pediatrics agrees that abstaining from intercourse should be encouraged for adolescents, being the surest way to prevent sexually transmitted diseases (STD) and pregnancy as it focuses on delaying the initiation of adolescent sexual activity until adulthood.[10] This is a good and worthy goal. For most teenagers, their first sexual partner will probably not be their best choice. The younger the individual, the less mature they probably are about the impact of sex upon any relationship. The longer they wait to engage in sex, it is hoped, the more mature they'll be to deal with sex. Yet abstinence-only education has not led to more virgins, but rather to more abortions, teen pregnancies, and STDs.

According to the report on a 2002 survey conducted by the National Center for Health Statistics, among teenagers (fifteen to nineteen years of age), 46 percent of never-married girls and 46 percent of never-married boys had engaged in sexual intercourse, with 28 percent of females and 31 percent of males reporting sex with two or more partners.[11] A teenage female who is sexually active and refuses to use contraceptives has a 90 percent chance of becoming pregnant within a year's time.[12] According to another report, every year, about four million new sexually transmitted disease (STD) infections occur among U.S. teenagers. When compared to infection rates in other developed countries, U.S. gonorrhea and chlamydia figures are extremely high.[13]

Based on data from two large-scale government surveys, 75 percent of the decline in teen pregnancy was attributed to improved contraceptive use; the remaining 25 percent resulted from the increased practice of abstinence.[14] Although many teenagers are delaying vaginal intercourse until later years, other forms of sexual activity are still prevalent. The large percentage of adolescents participating in sex that excludes vaginal intercourse may be an attempt to prevent pregnancy, fulfill a virginity pledge, or both. Another study conducted by the National Center for Health Statistics found that among teenagers (fifteen to nineteen years of age) 55.2 percent of boys and 54.3 percent of girls had participated in oral sex. Additionally, 11.2 percent of boys and 10.9 percent of girls had engaged in anal sex. Among boys, 4.5 percent reported having oral or anal sex with a male; 10.4 percent of girls reported having had a sexual experience with a female.[15]

Unfortunately, a quarter of female teens and 18 percent of male teens used no form of contraception the first time they engaged in sexual intercourse. The 2002 study showed that those teenagers who used contraceptive methods were less likely to become pregnant or contract STDs, whereas those who did not use a contraceptive were more likely to become pregnant or contract an STD.[16] Another report found that, not surprisingly, nearly half (47 percent) of all unintended pregnancies in the United States in 1995 occurred among the 7 percent of women who did not use contraception.[17] But even when contraceptives are used, they are often misused. In a different study conducted at the University of Alabama, more than 40 percent of subjects reported an error in putting on a condom (not squeezing air out of the condom tip) and about a third reported misuse of the condom during intercourse (not holding the base of the condom during withdrawal).[18]

The consequences and costs of imposing the purity code of the Religious Right are staggering. Buying a $305 white gold "What Would Jesus Do?" purity ring (http://www.abstinence.net/store/00310.html), or $10 underwear decorated with stop signs (http://www.abstinence.net/store/00020.html), although cute, is simply not enough. Although the abstinence message may lead teenagers to delay vaginal intercourse to avoid pregnancy, it has not curbed oral or anal sex. And certain STDs—such as gonorrhea, chlamydia, chancroid, syphilis, and HIV—are still transmittable through oral and especially through anal sex. I believe that the lack of sex education contributes to the high STD incidence in the United States: one in five adults has an incurable sexually transmitted disease. The Centers for Disease Control and Prevention estimates that about nineteen million new cases of STDs occurred in the year 2004, with an estimated treatment cost of $19 billion.[19] About half of all STDs occurs among those in the fifteen-to-twenty-four age group.[20]

The abstinence-only campaign is not so much about promoting virginity until marriage as it is about blocking education about contraceptives. Adolescents who are already sexually active need appropriate education and counseling about how pregnancy and STDs can be prevented.

And although birth control is never 100 percent effective, it significantly reduces unwanted pregnancies, and certain types protect against STDs. Currently, no federal program exists that provides a comprehensive sexual education teaching both abstinence and contraception, even though providing such an education would accomplish the goals of both conservatives, who stress the importance of saving sex, and liberals, who stress the importance of safe sex. When we consider that U.S. teen birth rates are higher than in other comparable industrialized countries, partly due to their lack of information about contraception, it's apparent that comprehensive sex education is critical. Unfortunately, faith-based abstinence-only education generally does not provide information on contraceptive methods, except to discuss their failure rates.

Although a major focus in any sexual education program should be the mechanics of practicing safe sex, that education would be incomplete if it did not also incorporate the social and emotional components of intercourse. Specifically, education should also include discussions of dealing with peer pressure, avoiding being seduced to participate in acts one does not wish to engage in, and how to better understand sexual energy. Education should also encompass discussions about the state of mind for those entering into a sexual union: Does one partner see the act as an expression of love whereas the other sees it as recreational sex? What emotional consequences can arise from such mismatched expectations? Sexual educational programs should therefore cover the emotions associated with sexual activity—emotions like love, lust, fears (of rejection and abandonment), and fulfillment. Besides just teaching how to use a condom, sex education programs should also raise questions dealing with the familial relationship, like vulnerability and mutual giving. Such comprehensive information would provide students with the capacity to make better decisions for themselves.

Can Sex Be Safe?

Part of this abhorrence for contraception—even though condoms save lives—comes from our Christian history. Augustine insisted that for those who marry, procreation becomes a duty, an act of piety, and the primary purpose for entering into a marriage relationship.[21] He wondered if the sexual union between a husband and wife can even be called a marriage if they attempt to avoid having children.[22] He insists that a husband and wife who "procure drugs to cause sterility" are not truly husband and wife, but rather "merely use the good name of marriage to cover over their shamefulness."[23] Among many of today's churches (specifically conservative and moderate churches), sex outside of marriage continues to be considered a sin. STDs and pregnancy are seen as God's punishments for those who engage in sex outside of a heterosexual marriage, and contraceptives help the guilty to avoid these punishments; therefore, they should be denied that means of escape.

Such logic can prove deadly. For example, every year 3,700 women in the United States die from cervical cancer. The major cause (99.7 percent) of all cervical cancers is the human papillomavirus (HPV), the most prevalent sexually transmitted infection in the world, occurring at some point in up to 75 percent of sexually active women.[24] In the United States, half of all sexually active women between eighteen and twenty-two are infected. Although most cases do clear up, infections sometimes persist, causing cancer to develop decades later. Fortunately, researchers have developed a vaccine that has proven to be quite effective in clinical trials. GlaxoSmithKline announced in November 2004 that its Cervarix vaccine prevented 90 percent of new infections and 100 percent of persistent infections. Merck announced similar results in April 2005 and won FDA approval for its Gardasil vaccine in June 2006; as of this writing, Cervarix is not yet licensed. U.S. health officials hope to administer a vaccine to all girls when they reach the age of twelve. However, the Family Research Council, the political arm of James Dobson's Focus on the Family, vows to fight the vaccination of American girls. "Abstinence is the best way to prevent HPV," says Bridget Maher of the Family Research Council. "Giving the HPV vaccine to young women could be potentially harmful, because they may see it as a license to engage in premarital sex."[25] The message is clear: if you engage in sex, then you should be willing to live with its consequences—or as Maryland's teen pregnancy campaign slogan puts it, "You play, you pay."

Another reason for the hostility toward contraception is how it was understood theologically. Throughout history, church leaders equated (and many still equate) contraception with the murder of an unborn child. Semen was considered precious because it was believed to contain all the necessary elements needed to produce life. According to Aquinas, semen's purpose was to produce the next generation of humans. To ensure and secure the next generation, semen must not be improperly discharged. If sex's primary purpose was procreation, then any sexual act outside of heterosexual vaginal intercourse with some semen remaining in a fertile woman was an unnecessary waste of man's precious seed and thus a transgression against both God and the natural order—a "sin against nature."[26] Thus, not only were contraceptives off limits, but also masturbation, intercourse during a woman's menstruation, intercourse after menopause, and intercourse with a infertile woman.

Even when the Catholic Church accepted nonprocreative marital inter-course through Pope Paul VI's 1968 encyclical letter *Humanae Vitae,* it still maintained that the use of contraceptives was immoral (except for the rhythm method, per Pope Pius XI's encyclical letter *Casti Connubii*). Even the use of condoms as a way of preventing AIDS is frowned upon—proving once again that doctrinal adherence trumps lost lives.

The Private Sin

For many who are single, either by choice or by circumstance, mas-turbation provides a way of achieving sexual gratification and reducing sexual tension. According to the all-too-familiar joke, 90 percent of all individuals admit to having masturbated and the other 10 percent are lying. Most studies show that for the vast majority, masturbation starts around the age of ten and continues until death.[27] Despite the fact that almost every human being over that age has masturbated at some time, and even though there is no biblical justification for the prohibition of masturbation, it has long been considered a sin among Christians and still is, even today.

The original belief that led to this view was that the woman, as an incubator, only provided nourishment to the creation of life. The woman's womb was like a field waiting for the insemination of the male seed, which contained all the necessary substances required for human life. Within the male sperm existed the entire potential child. The womb, by contrast, was neutral, adding nothing to the child's genetic makeup. Therefore, to waste male sperm, as in the case of masturbation, was to literally destroy the potential for human life. For these same reasons contraceptive devices, by preventing pregnancy, waste the male seed, so by the same reasoning they are akin to murder. Religious leaders such as Martin Luther saw onanism as a sin more hideous than heterosexual rape, because at least rape was judged to be in accordance with nature, whereas masturbation was considered to be unnatural.[28]

Historically, medical authorities equated masturbation and sexual promiscuity with insanity. During the late fifteenth century, syphilis made its first appearance in Europe. Untreated, syphilis could lead to insanity. Early observation of this disease found a correlation between those who succumbed to the disease with those who were sexually active, specifically those who patronized brothels. The primitive medical establishment, unaware that syphilis was a sexually transmitted disease (a discovery that would not be made until the nineteenth century), concluded that those who engaged in excessive sexual activity, including masturbation, would become feeble-minded, if not insane.

During Victorian England, cages were constructed that fitted over the boy's genitals during sleeping hours to prevent masturbation. This cage was locked, and some were even spiked to prevent the boy from sexually stimulating himself. To "cure" those girls who wished to sexually stimulate themselves, a clitoridectomy (the partial or total removal of the external part of the clitoris) was an acceptable medical practice. Throughout the nineteenth and twentieth centuries, this medical procedure was accepted in English-speaking nations (until 1946 in the United States) as a means of stopping masturbation. The girl was "cured" because the procedure reduced the possibility of sexual arousal.[29] Although penis cages for boys are no longer used, the mutilation of women's genitalia continues to be practiced in a number of cultures. It is quite common in Indonesia and many countries of sub-Saharan Africa, east Africa, Egypt, Sudan, and the Arabian Peninsula. As of 2005, Amnesty International estimates that 135 million of the world's girls and women have undergone genital mutilation, and two million girls a year are at risk of this mutilation—approximately six thousand each day. The practice is so common that it has reemerged in Europe and the United States among immigrants.[30]

Another reason why masturbation was frowned on by the church was the belief that male sperm was a fluid that contained male energy, so that wasting this energy would also lead to feebleness. For this reason, an ascetic lifestyle, even within marriage, supposedly secured a long and healthy life. To constantly be losing one's seed was judged akin to Samson's getting a haircut, putting male strength and virility in jeopardy. Even today the common advice persists that boxers and other athletes should abstain from ejaculating, so as not to risk impairing their athletic performance in the boxing ring or on the field.

Early in the twentieth century the scientific community began to study and test the actual effects of masturbation. Even though masturbation has historically been thought to have negative physical and emotional consequences, the medical health community has found no negative correlation between masturbation and a person's physical or emotional health. In fact, recently researchers have suggested that men who regularly masturbate can reduce their risk of developing prostate cancer.[31] And there is no evidence of a cause and effect between masturbation and mental disturbance, with the possible exception of those who feel guilty because they believe masturbation to be a sin.

Despite these findings by the medical community, masturbation is still taboo among many modern-day Christians, leading many to struggle with a culturally imposed guilt. Some Christians who wish to refrain from masturbation will wear a masturband, a black plastic bracelet worn on the wrist. You continue to wear the band as long as you refrain from masturbating, but if you succumb, then you must remove the bracelet, making your hidden shame public. This prohibition is unnecessary when one considers that the Bible is silent on the topic of masturbation with the exception of a few verses. As detailed in Chapter Three, the Song of Songs (5:2–6) vividly describes a woman dreaming of her beloved "thrust[ing] his hand into the hole," only to awaken with her "fingers dripped with myrrh"—in other words, with her own wetness, the product of a wet dream.

The biblical story that has historically been used to condemn masturbation is the story of Onan, found in Genesis 38:1–11. According to the biblical text, Tamar married Judah's oldest son Er. However, Er offended God (his offense is unknown) and died as a result. Unfortunately he died childless. Following tradition, Onan, Er's brother, took Tamar to perform his duty of impregnating her so that a child could be born in his brother's name. But whenever Onan copulated with Tamar he would pull out before climaxing and thus spill his seed on the ground. God found this offensive, so he slew Onan. Christian commentators have historically understood Onan's sin to be masturbation, because he "spilled his seed on the ground"; *onanism,* a synonym for masturbation, is derived from his name. But Onan's sin was not masturbation. According to the text, he spilled his seed on the ground because he deliberately abdicated his duty of ensuring that his brother's name would continue. To be specific, his sin was avoiding his levirate obligation to his dead brother by performing *coitus interruptus.*

Many claim Jesus spoke indirectly about masturbation during the Sermon on the Mount: "You have heard that it was said to the ancients, 'Do not commit adultery.' But I say to you, that anyone looking at a woman to lust after her has already committed adultery with her in his heart" (Matthew 5:27–28). As discussed in the previous chapter, the emphasis of this passage may have more to do with debunking the predominant male view that adultery only applied to women, by suggesting that even gazing upon a women with intent was enough to make a man guilty. Still, because a certain degree of lusting is required to achieve climax during masturbation (especially for men), is Jesus stating that masturbation is akin to adultery? This question finds traction when we consider that in the verse that follows, Jesus stated that if our eye (by which we see the woman that we lust after) causes offense, it should be plucked out. Jesus then stated, "And if your right hand causes you to offend, cut it off and throw it away" (Matthew 5:30). Could this be a reference to masturbation, for what we do with our hand to complete the lust begun with the eye? Rabbinical literature seems to think so. According to the *Niddah* (a treatise found in rabbinical texts—the Mishnah, Tosefta, and both Talmuds—about the state of uncleanness), masturbation is referred to as "adultery by the hand"[32]—praiseworthy among women, but for men, the hand should be "cut off."[33] The physical purity code of the Hebrew Bible also labels those who experience wet dreams (whether or not they masturbate during their waking hours) as unclean and defiled, needing purification (Deuteronomy 23:11–12). Remember, according to the Jewish mind-set, unconsciously violating a purity law was not understood as a sin in the more modern Christian sense. It meant avoiding dirt—that is, avoiding becoming unclean—a concept that has shaped moral discourse. The individual experiencing a wet dream was not morally depraved, but dirtied by the body fluids.

We can conclude, however, that Jesus' focus during his Sermon on the Mount was not masturbation. He was replacing the traditional physical purity code with an insistence on maintaining a purity of the heart—a purity of intent. Paul wrote, "I know and am persuaded in the Lord Jesus that nothing is unclean by itself, except to the one who regards anything as unclean it is" (Romans 14:14). The issue of purity ceases to be about an actual sexual act (masturbation) and instead becomes about the intent of maintaining unjust sexual or social relationships (males, unlike women, engaging in adultery without penalty). If the act has the intent of continuing the objectification of the Other or of retarding a familial relationship, then for that person, that particular act (whether it be sexual or not) may be wrong. In Jesus' example he placed the emphasis on the intent of married men, who traditionally could never be guilty of adultery unless they had sex with another man's property. For such men, if even thinking of violating their familial relationship was enough to pronounce them guilty, how much more guilty would they be if they were to act on those thoughts?

Even without specific biblical censure to back them up, many claim that masturbation is detrimental because it is self-centered, due to its solitary nature and aim of self-pleasuring. This focus inward was believed to eventually cause separation between the individual and their beloved. But if we remember the church's antipleasure views as discussed in Chapter Three, it should not be surprising that it was prohibited, even though most people masturbate in this solitary way in their youth and still grow up to be involved in loving and healthy partnered relationships. Although a dimension of intimacy may be lacking in masturbation when compared to intercourse, masturbation can still create bonds between loving partners in many situations. Masturbation can enhance coupling, as in the case of injury, disability, or old age in which the use of one's sexual organs is difficult if not impossible. Masturbation can serve to bring people together emotionally, as in the case of couples separated due to travel, work, or war. Masturbating can help to heal grief, as in the case of widows and widowers. Mutual masturbation during foreplay, especially as a means of increasing the possibility of orgasm, brings lovers closer together, both physically and emotionally. Those who are not in a familial relationship may masturbate to relieve sexual energy along with the stress and tension it creates. Those who masturbate are often able to share with their partners suggestions on what leads them to an orgasm.

The biblical text is silent on the use of masturbation in situations like these. We don't have to be. Because of its potential of enhancing great sex, masturbation can play a role in the sexuality of Christians.

Hookups for the New Millennium

Andrea Lavinthal and Jessica Rozler recently published the best seller *The Hookup Handbook: A Single Girl's Guide to Living It Up*. They proclaim that dating is a thing of the past, something that "has gone the way of dinosaurs, eight-track players, and stirrup pants." In its place is the "hookup, the vague phrase used to describe what happens between two people who don't necessarily have any foreseeable future or even a hint of commitment." *The Hookup Handbook* attempts to "remove the emotional from the physical."[34] In a way, the book attempts to empower women by having them imitate men who see the gratification of their sexual urges, by whatever means necessary, as a birthright. But although having multiple sex partners might create the possibility of increasing sexual pleasure, it can never foster the intimacy of union—a fundamental ingredient to great sex. Throughout the book the authors suggest that the best way to remove the emotional (and, I might add, the spiritual) from the physical is through consuming large quantities of alcohol. But what Lavinthal and Rozler herald as the new way of creating relationships—sex without vulnerability and mutual giving—appears to have always been part of U.S. history. Hooking up is but the more modern reincarnation of the sixties' "free love," or the eighties' "recreational sex," or the more recent "friends with benefits." As the biblical text reminds us, "there is nothing new under the sun" (Ecclesiastes 1:9).

Hooking up—to use the present-day vernacular for sex without commitment to a familial relationship—is as old as sex itself. True, some eras and cultures were less open to the hookup than others. A polar opposite from our age of the hookup is England's Victorian society (which undoubtedly affected U.S. sexual attitudes), in which sex between married couples customarily occurred from once a month to once a year. According to Victorian mores, if a woman was to show any type of passion, then it was to be restricted to devotion to her children. Her value was in being a wife and mother. It was believed that a gentlewoman of class and refinement was incapable of enjoying sex. The apocryphal story has a Victorian mother advising her soon-to-be-married daughter that, when required to accommodate her husband's sexual needs, she should do as the mother had always done: "close my eyes and think of England." During the nineteenth century the Euro-American view of white women was transformed from the temptress of sexual sin to the seat of all virtue, purity, and innocence. For a white woman of the upper class to manifest sexual desires was a clear indication that she was both degraded and immoral. All references to legs were hidden because it was indecent to suggest that a woman had anything at all below the waist, hence an array of starched skirts, hoops, and bustles were worn that were impregnable by strong gusts of wind. During medical examinations women refused, out of modesty, to physically show or even verbally indicate the part of the body that ailed them. Even feminine hygiene was discouraged lest the washing of the genitals invoke lustful sensations that would lead to masturbation. The author bell hooks reminds us of the irony that although white women were being placed on a pedestal to be extolled for their virtues, the same time period saw the rise of sexual exploitation of black slave women and the formation of a massive underclass of poor white women forced into prostitution in Victorian England.[35]

Such attitudes about sex from the Victorian era, as well as the puritanical spirit of the early colonialists that shaped the U.S. sex codes, created a restricted sexual atmosphere throughout U.S. history against which the hookup and its precursors have rebelled. Political forces, through the power of the state, forged a moral code that perpetuated an antibody, antiwoman, antipleasure, and antijustice definition of sexuality.

Today's members of the Religious Right see themselves as the guardians of this tradition. A visit to the websites of some of these organizations (such as Focus on the Family) reveals their obsession with sex in the excessive numbers of links to articles dealing with this topic, particularly homosexuality. But there is more to Christianity than personal sexual piety, even though it appears we are left with only two extremes: the hookup, in which anything goes, and the Focus on the Family model, in which the Bible is reinterpreted to reinforce and maintain control over the culture through a puritanical patriarchal understanding of sex.

Seeking the Orthoeros Mean Between the Extremes

Marriage can never be reduced to simply the possession of a wedding certificate. It is meant to be the establishment of a familial relationship.

We all know of marriages that are marriages in name only because of how the partners treat each other. And when that relationship ends up in a divorce, it only confirms that a marriage was probably never truly established. Not all sex within marriage is moral, nor is all sex outside of marriage sinful. Two people who are both vulnerable and mutually giving to each other, but who engage in intercourse prior to a marriage ceremony, can be closer to the ideal of a familial relationship than two for whom intercourse occurs within a marriage not based on mutual giving and vulnerability. Marriage that lacks a familial relationship can be as immoral as marital rape.

It is interesting to note that the Hebrew Bible contains many sexual constraints, yet nowhere is premarital sex forbidden. Likewise, there is no explicit prohibition of sex prior to marriage in the New Testament. Indeed, there are a few examples in which premarital sex is accepted without a hint of moral outrage or indignation. In addition to the example of two unmarried lovers in the Song of Songs, as detailed in Chapter Three, the biblical text provides us with another example in Ruth. Ruth is a Moabite who marries Mahlon from the Jewish tribe of Judah. Her husband dies, and, rather than returning to her people, she accompanies her mother-in-law Naomi to Bethlehem, making Naomi's people her people and Naomi's God her God. These two women, one of whom was an illegal alien, living without a man in a patriarchal society, were marginalized and at the mercy of the generosity of others. Ruth was forced to pick the leftovers from Boaz's field after his laborers gleaned the harvest. Boaz eventually married Ruth, and she bore him a son who became King David's grandfather and a descendant of Jesus' lineage. But my point in retelling the story is how Ruth convinces Boaz to marry her. Remember, Ruth is a Moabite, and it was the Moabite women who once upon a time used their sexuality to lure Jewish men into worshiping false gods (Numbers 25:1–2).

In the third chapter of the book of Ruth, her mother-in-law Naomi grooms her and sends her to Boaz, who, after having his fill of food and drink, lies down in a heap of barley to sleep it off. While he sleeps, Ruth sneaks in and "uncovers his feet," lying down next to them. When Boaz awakens and asks who is in his bed, Ruth replies by saying, "I am Ruth, your handmaid. You shall spread your skirt over your handmaid for you are a redeemer." Boaz indeed redeems her by making her his wife, but not before spreading more than his "skirt" over her.

In the Hebrew vernacular of the time, *feet* was a euphemism for the male genitalia. The prophet Isaiah, describing how God will humble Assyria, states that the Lord will shave off the hair from his head and his "feet" (Isaiah 7:20). Isaiah is really referring to the pubic hair. Ruth initiated sex before she properly belonged to Boaz, hence his concern in verse 14 of that same chapter for protecting her honor by keeping secret the fact that she came to him on the threshing floor. Ruth's actions were acceptable among early rabbinical writers, some of whom permitted cohabitation without marriage under certain circumstances.[36]

The use of *feet* as a euphemism for *penis* raises an interesting interpretation of Jesus' encounter with a woman "who had a bad name in the town" (Luke 7:37). While he was dining at the home of a Pharisee, a woman who is described as a sinner waited at Jesus' feet, weeping. Her tears fell on his feet, which she then wiped away with her hair. Upon drying his feet, she covered them with kisses. She brought an expensive alabaster jar of ointment that she then opened so as to anoint his feet. The other guests were upset with this display, thinking to themselves, "How could Jesus be a prophet and let this woman with a bad reputation touch him?" (Luke 7:36–50). Why were they upset? Were they witnessing a sexual overture? Or are we making too much of the euphemism? As Freud might say, sometimes a foot is just a foot. Still, if there was sexual tension between this woman and Jesus, then Jesus transformed the event into something different, in the process enhancing the woman's dignity and worth by forgiving all of her sins.

Still, one cannot ignore the sexual references—viewed at the time as appropriate behavior—that appear in the non-canonical gospels. In the Gospel of Philip, Mary Magdalene and Jesus often kiss on the mouth, raising jealousy in the other disciples (55). The Gospel of Thomas has Salome commenting to Jesus that he has mounted her bed and eaten from her table (61). And fragments of the Gospel of Mary [Magdalene] have Peter saying to Mary that Jesus loved her more than any other woman, for he knew her well and loved her more than the apostles. Although these gnostic gospels were suppressed by the ecclesiastical authorities, and they are not considered by Christians to have any revelatory claims, they show that in early Christian history the sexual tension surrounding Jesus was not such a taboo subject as it is today.

How is sexual tension dealt with today? Young adults are told to wait until marriage to engage in sex. This might have been good advice in biblical times when girls were married off once they entered puberty. However, today's marriages are occurring much later in life. In 1960 the median age of first marriage's was twenty-three for males, twenty for females. By 2004, the median age had risen to twenty-seven for men—for those with a college education, it was one to two years older—and for women the median age had risen to twenty-five. The two reasons commonly cited by scholars for marriage occurring later are (1) longer years of education and (2) greater difficulties in gaining a secure foothold in employment. It appears that the prime time for men to seek their "soulmate" occurs at a later point in early adult life, usually between the ages of twenty-five and thirty.[37]

Is it then realistic to require individuals to wait until they are in their late twenties before engaging in sex? Whether we wish to proclaim it publicly or keep it closeted, the truth of the matter is that most Catholic, Orthodox, and Protestant followers today accept sex prior to a wedding ceremony as a proper response for a loving, faithful, committed, mature couple. Nationwide, marriage is ceding ground to unwed unions, as most people now live together before they marry for the first time. From 1960 to 2002, the number of unmarried couples living together increased by 1,100 percent. Over half of all new marriages are now preceded by the couple's living together, compared to virtually none just fifty years ago.[38] For the church leadership to only offer two choices, celibacy or marriage, shows how disconnected it is from the faith community sitting in the pews. If we insist that sex must wait until marriage, we reduce marriage to simply a license to have sex. Entering a marriage so as to engage in sex is unwise and by far the most inadequate reason to ever wed. Wrong reasons for marriage can lead to poor judgment in choosing partners. Such marriages, based more on lust than on love, can only contribute to establishing an unhealthy relationship that is supposed to last a lifetime. And when lust subsides, the absence of love prevents great sex from occurring.

Maybe we should be asking not whether we should engage in pre-marital sex, but rather whether we should engage in *prefamilial* sex. Before answering, we must remember that the discussion of premarital sex is not a defense of promiscuity. If a couple that has established a familial relationship engages in sex prior to marriage, shouldn't the church recognize and bless the existence of such a relationship? For intimacy to develop, vulnerability is required. Vulnerability does not happen overnight. Time is required to discover, explore, and trust each other. Great sex doesn't start in bed; it forms in the embedded memories shared by would-be lovers. Not just the positive memories, but the painful ones as well. Only after the intimacy that comes with time—enough to share and get to know as much of each other's totality as possible—can the intimacy of sex, the ultimate form of mutual giving, truly occur. For sex to be great, it must grow out of the bonds of a familial relationship. Only then does the pleasuring of each other increase with time, rather than decrease as the novelty wears off.

But don't studies show that cohabiting couples have a higher rate of divorce once they do marry—thus indicating that it is better to wait until a couple receives a marriage certificate before engaging in sex? Not necessarily. Although it is true that couples living together have higher rates of divorce once they marry, it is also true, according to more recent studies, that there is an exception to this rule: couples planning to be each other's spouses who have sex exclusively with each other.[39] That is, couples who have already established a familial relationship.

Hurrying into sex before establishing a familial relationship that is safe, consensual, loyal, mutually pleasing, and intimate runs the risk of having one's trust in the other abused. Sex without intimacy leads only to emptiness, disillusionment, shallowness, and pain. The process of becoming "one flesh" in a familial relationship creates bonds that are difficult and painful to sever, so it should be entered into with great care and caution. But the risk is worth it. Humanity's quest for intimacy is what makes sex great; anything else is but a cheap imitation. Only after a familial relationship is established and can be witnessed by all can the faith community, with integrity, speak on behalf of fellow believers in offering its blessing and providing its support to the relationship's success.

Let us not forget that it is the state, not the church, that determines what constitutes a legal marriage. If a right to marry does exist, it exists in civil society. Most Christians consider it a right to have a church ceremony. But in reality, marriage has always been a civil arrangement. Engaging in sex with a woman (even through force) was understood by ancient cultures to mean that the couple was engaged. Seducing a virgin into bed required the seducer to make her his wife (Exodus 22:16). This marriage, unlike others, could never be annulled, because he had forced her into sex (Deuteronomy 22:28–29). To recapitulate, among Catholics, marriage first was viewed as a sacrament in the twelfth century and incorporated into the church in the form of a compulsory ceremony during the Council of Trent in the mid-sixteenth century. Protestants like John Calvin, on the other hand, conceived of marriage as a holy ordinance.[40] At first the ceremony was the start of the marriage for the upper class, in which the bride's virginity was important not for religious reasons but as an expression of bourgeois class. Those from the working class continued to rely on consent as the means by which they established their common-law marriages. It was not until the mid-eighteenth century that the upper class began to force their marriage laws onto the lower classes as a political sign of respectability. Nevertheless, then as today, a marriage ceremony does not make engaging in sex moral or right; it is the proximity of a relationship to the familial ideal that makes it so. The fundamental question is, does the relationship produce love, trust, vulnerability, selflessness, and peace, or does it emanate possessiveness, self-gratification, fear, pain, and bitterness?

Even Luther supported the distinction between premarital familial sex and promiscuous fornication. He wrote, "[L]ying together in secret in anticipation of betrothal cannot be reckoned as whoredom, for it takes place in the name and with the intention of marriage, which spirit, intention, or name whoredom does not have. Therefore there is a great difference between whoredom and lying together in secret with the intention of betrothed marriage."[41]

If we can agree that the church's involvement in a wedding is to bless the union, then we must question whether the church has the right to delay offering its blessing until the union proves to be based on biblical principles of justice (not on the biblical description of marriage). Perhaps the church should be more discriminating as to which relationships should be blessed and which should not. Perhaps the church's blessing should be offered only after the union has been consummated—after the community of faith can bear witness to the type of relationship the two are forming. And if that relationship undermines justice, the church may reserve the right to withhold its blessing.

7

SAME-SEX
RELATIONSHIPS

---

*When lawlessness is abroad in the land, the same thing will
happen here that happened in Nazi Germany. Many of those
people [who were] involved [with] Adolph Hitler were
Satanists. Many of them were homosexuals. The two things
seem to go together.*[1]

—Pat Robertson

*The abortionists have got to bear some burden for [the
September 11 terrorist attacks] because God will not be
mocked. And when we destroy 40 million little innocent
babies, we make God mad. I really believe that the pagans,
and the abortionists, and the feminists, and the gays and the
lesbians who are actively trying to make that an alternative
lifestyle, the ACLU, People For the American Way, all of
them who have tried to secularize America. I point the finger
in their face and say "you helped this happen."*[2]

—Jerry Falwell

SPONGEBOB SQUAREPANTS, the silly frolicking sponge who openly holds
hands with a pink starfish named Patrick, was outed by Dr. James Dobson of Focus on the Family at a banquet held for members of Congress
during George W. Bush's second inaugural celebrations. It seems that the

absorbent yellow cartoon sponge had joined other supposedly questionable characters—such as Winnie the Pooh, Kermit the Frog, and Barney the Dinosaur—on a new video asking children to take a "tolerance pledge": a pledge to show dignity and respect for those who are different, whether it be different gender, race, ethnicity, faith, or, yes, sexual orientation.[3] Dobson's attack on a popular children's television character was reminiscent of a time when, a few years earlier, the Reverend Jerry Falwell led a crusade against the Teletubby named Tinky Winky, another popular children's television character. It appears that even though this particular Teletubby spoke with a boy's voice, he (she?) carried a purse and proudly displayed a triangle, the alleged symbol of homosexuality, on its head.[4]

Much can be revealed about a person in the sexual acts that person vehemently and loudly condemns—specifically the fear of gays, and more precisely the fear of possibly being perceived as gay. This was illustrated shortly after the March 1995 airing of *Jenny Jones,* a popular television talk show at the time. Scott Amedure revealed during the national broadcast his secret infatuation for coworker Jonathan Schmitz, who presumably was a heterosexual. Amedure was killed three days later by the object of his affection, Schmitz, who feared that everyone might now think he was gay.[5] This is just one example of pathological homophobia, but it mirrors the beliefs of many in our society, who think that avoiding the possibility of mistakenly being confused with someone who is gay requires the repression of all homosexuals.

The maintenance of a high-pitched religious fervor against homosexuals may intimidate some to simply stay in the closet while preventing others, who are struggling with their orientation, from admitting their true identity. Take, for example, Ted Haggard, the president of the National Association of Evangelicals (comprising sixty member denominations representing 45,000 churches across the United States); head pastor of the 14,000-member Colorado Springs mega-church, New Life; and confidant to President Bush. Rev. Haggard resigned in early November 2006 over allegations made by a former male prostitute that Haggard was a three-year client. Whenever any individual fails to deal with their sexuality in a healthy manner, it will manifest itself in destructive ways, not just for the individuals, but also the overall community. The humiliation Haggard faces is not limited to his person, but obviously extends to his family, his church community, and even to the spiritual ethos of the nation.

The Religious Right, of which Haggard is part-architect, has created a spiritual environment that is hostile to those who are homosexuals. A mere accusation is more than enough to destroy a reputation, family, and/or career. Whether Haggard is gay or not should be no one's concern except for his family or partner. It surely does not affect his ability to perform his job as a minister. Even James Dobson, responding to the sexual disclosures concerning Haggard, stated in a November 3, 2006, Focus on the Family news release that, "[Ted Haggard] has been used mightily to spread the Gospel of Jesus Christ in Colorado Springs and around the world." Haggard's sexual orientation, understood by the Religious Right as sin, did not impede God's ability to use him as an evangelist. Nevertheless, we live in a nation where being gay can become front page news. Why have we constructed a society so hostile to homosexuals that they must live a lie, even to the point of loathing their own identity? And if they are outed, why must they suffer similar trials and tribulations as Haggard, as if being gay, or accused of being gay, is some kind of moral travesty?

Again, Haggard's sexual orientation is not the issue. As this book goes to press, Haggard's saga continues to unfold. Regardless of how this story ends, Haggard, his family, and church community will never be the same. Ironically, the very hostile religious environment toward homosexuals that Haggard helped create and maintain appears to be turning on its own. Irrespective as to how one feels toward Ted Haggard, this is not a situation for rejoicing by those who oppose the Religious Right's particular views. Peoples' lives are being destroyed by an anti-gay social structure, regardless of who they are. Hopefully Haggard and company will learn the hard way what gays and lesbians face every single day of their lives.

The religious intolerance Haggard is experiencing derives from a line of thinking that insists homosexuals must be smoked out and persecuted, whether they are animated cartoon characters like SpongeBob SquarePants or, more seriously, are deemed a threat to our national security. After the first terrorist attack on the World Trade Center in 1993, our intelligence agency revealed an alarming shortage of Arabic-speaking translators. The mountains of data collected concerning possible terrorist attacks remain practically useless because of the backlog of critical information still untranslated. The backlog from 2004 alone encompassed 120,000 hours of potentially vital information concerning possible threats to our national security. Yet, since 1998, twenty Arabic-speaking government translators have been discharged from the military for being homosexual.[6] The United States had trained and skilled people who could do their job well and help save American lives, but because they are gay, this country has spurned their accomplishments and linguistic skills, despite their potential to prevent actions that could cost lives. Does sexual orientation really affect someone's ability to do their job well?

During the 2004 presidential election, same-sex marriage became a religious and moral issue that was successfully manipulated for electoral advantages, even though the issue of gay marriage did not originate from within the queer community but was a fear tactic developed by the Religious Right. More important than eleven states' subsequent passage of amendments banning gay marriages was the fact that people's fear of gay marriages was successfully used to generate support for the incumbent party in battleground states. The denial of gays' civil rights (here understood as the same rights presently extended to heterosexuals) has become a powerful political tool for the Religious Right.

When the American Association for Retired Persons (AARP) took a stance contrary to the president's Social Security plan, the conservative group USANext (whose CEO Charlie Jarvis formerly served as vice president of Dobson's Focus on the Family) set up a website showing two pictures. One, of an American soldier, was crossed out; the other, of two men kissing, carried a check mark. The caption read, "The real AARP agenda." The fact that the AARP never took a stance on same-sex marriage was irrelevant; $10 million was pledged by USANext to connect the AARP with same-sex marriage. This political ploy was well established during the 2004 presidential election, in which candidates deemed a threat by the Religious Right were portrayed as supporters of the so-call "gay agenda."

Even clerics who choose to minister to homosexuals as an expression of agape (unconditional love) are persecuted and silenced by more conservative religious hierarchy. In 1999, the Vatican officially ordered a priest and a nun from Maryland to end their national ministry to gay men and lesbians. According to the Congregation for the Doctrine of the Faith, the pair's ministry—which had been operational since the 1970s—had strayed from church teaching. Homosexual activity is immoral and evil, the Congregation said, and its participants suffer from an "intrinsic disorder."[7]

Overcoming Homophobia

But why is homosexually so condemned among conservative Christians? Throughout most of Christian history, as we have seen, the church insisted that one of the major purposes for engaging in sex was to procreate. If the purpose of sex is siring the next generation, then any sexual activity falling short of this goal was considered an abomination to God. Because sex solely between two men was considered an illegitimate waste of one's seed, it became labeled as deviant, as it deviates from the main purpose of sex. The coupling of two women were usually subject to less censure because, as described in earlier chapters, they were viewed as noncontributors in the creation of life, serving only as incubators. But overall, any same-sex relationship, like any other sexual act from which a pregnancy could not result, was *de facto* a sin. I would point out that the condemnation of homosexual sex provided some cover for the sexual peccadilloes of heterosexuals. The line of reasoning seemed to be that as long as heterosexuals do not engage in same-gender sex, they are not *really* morally depraved, regardless of how many promiscuous heterosexual relationships they might have engaged in.

In this chapter we will explore one of the most controversial topics in the Christian church, a topic that is at the root of several schisms within churches and denominations. It is not my intention to speak for the queer community. Instead, I approach this topic in an attempt to uncover how my heterosexual community causes marginalization and oppression. The chapter will first explore the common misconceptions about homosexuals, then review how the biblical text has been used to justify their marginalization, and follow up with a liberative reading of the Bible to establish an orthoeros approach to the topic.

Homosexual Myths

To maintain a societal norm of universal compulsory heterosexuality, myths about homosexuality must be fomented. For our purposes, we will explore just five of these myths. Probably the most popular is that homosexuality is a choice. If one's orientation is indeed a choice, then each of us must ask, "When did I choose my own orientation?" More than likely you would assert that we no more chose our orientation than we chose the natural color of our hair. But if we are to maintain the antihomosexual doctrine that same-sex activities are sinful, then we must also maintain that orientation is a choice, regardless of how much this may be refuted by scientific studies or our own experiences. If one indeed chooses to be homosexual, then one can choose to stop; in other words, one can be cured from gayness. At least this is what conservative Christians like Tim and Beverly LaHaye advocate. They write: "Can a male homosexual or a lesbian be cured? The answer to this question lies in an individual's being willing to accept Jesus Christ as personal Lord and Savior. If such a person is willing, a cure is possible, but so far there is little success in any other treatment."[8]

For many conservative Christians, there is no other allowable opinion than to say it's a choice, because if it is true that people are born gay, then it is God who made them gay. And what kind of sadistic God creates homosexuals so that God can justify the unleashing of God's wrath upon them? Here then is the crux of the problem. If all of God's creation is good, can God create an individual evil from birth, evil here understood as being gay? Homosexuality must remain a choice, because if God made one gay, then it is God who is to blame.

Regardless of what the Religious Right maintains, a portion of all humans are exclusively homosexual, and not by choice. This becomes obvious as we realize that homosexual identity is not limited to Western cultures. Almost every culture in the world has some form or manifestation of homosexual practices and behavior. Some even have reserved positions of honor, such as religious leadership, for gays. Even animals, as anyone who ever lived on a farm can attest, at times engage in same-sex acts and even form lifelong same-sex pair bonds. Throughout history, homosexuality has been celebrated, proscribed, tolerated, forbidden, and persecuted. With the fall of the Roman Empire, hostility toward homosexuality increased as the Church became more entrenched in the political sphere. By the sixteenth century, influenced by the Reformation, governments made sodomy a capital offense throughout all of Christendom. Considering the historical discrimination and violence homosexuals have faced, the stigma society places on them, and the many basic rights that are denied to them, why would anyone willingly choose to become homosexual?

In spite of historical and present-day persecutions, homosexuality has continued to exist. It is difficult to determine what percentage of the population is oriented toward the same sex, mainly because culturally imposed feelings of guilt, shame, and self-loathing influence how polls are answered. Nevertheless, in the U.S. government's most comprehensive survey conducted on American's sexual practices, the National Center for Health Statistics found that 90 percent of men in the eighteen-to-forty-four age range responded that they were heterosexual. About 2.3 percent of the men identified themselves as homosexual, 1.8 percent as bisexual, and 3.8 percent as "something else"; 1.8 percent did not answer the question. Among women in the same age range, 90 percent thought of themselves as heterosexual, 1.3 percent as homosexual, 2.8 percent as bisexual, and 3.8 percent as "something else"; 1.8 percent did not answer the question. Hence 4.1 percent of the population claims to be either homosexual or bisexual. Yet the same study showed that 6.5 percent of men admitted to having had oral or anal sex with another man and 11 percent of women had had a sexual experience with another woman.[9] There seems to be a disconnect between what people say they are and what they do. More are engaged in same-gender sexual acts than are willing to accept a nonheterosexual label. What is also interesting is that in other, earlier studies, the percentages identifying themselves as homosexuals do not appear to have increased over time, debunking another myth that as homosexuality becomes more acceptable within society, more would choose this lifestyle.

A second myth demanding attention is the reduction of the definition of homosexual identity to what is done with the genitals, and specifically which gender one prefers to have sex with. We distinguish between sexual orientation and the act of participating in sex with someone of the same gender. For those who do engage in same-gender sex, homosexuality is what one does sexually, not the totality of what one is. Like heterosexuals, homosexuals are complex beings whose total personality, feelings, thoughts, and actions are not governed by sexual orientation. They are parents and lovers, with children and siblings, working in blue- and white-collar jobs. They have always been in the military, in the clergy, and in high political office as presidents, prime ministers, and royalty. Therefore, any discussion of homosexuality must move beyond the genitals. Homosexuality is first and foremost an issue of identity, not sexual activity. We must keep our focus on orientation, gender roles, and gender identification.

A third myth is that homosexuality is either an illness, a mental disturbance, a sin, or an emotional disorder probably caused during childhood, and as such, can be cured or corrected. The Freudian-based explanation—that homosexuality is caused during the developmental stage of childhood by one's having a father who was either absent or hostile and an overbearing and overprotective mother—has been pretty soundly rejected by the psychological community. By 1973, the American Psychiatric Association had removed homosexuality from its list of pathological disturbances, followed in 1975 by the American Psychological Association's removal of homosexuality from its list of mental disorders. If indeed homosexuality is caused by the children's home environment, how then does one explain the homosexuality of John Schlafly (son of Eagle Forum founding president Phyllis Schlafly) or Mary Cheney (daughter of Vice President Dick Cheney)? Both were raised in ultraconservative households by at least one parent who has been at the forefront of denying gays and lesbians civil rights. Perhaps parenting skills (or a lack thereof) are not the cause of sexual orientation. It seems far more likely that sexual orientation is a natural predisposition, just as some people are naturally predisposed toward left-handedness.

The most recent studies, although not conclusive, seem to indicate biological factors cause *all* forms of sexual orientation. Orientation can be influenced by different levels of male and female hormones, structural differences of the brain, a hereditary phenomenon determined by chromosomes, or any combination thereof. Every major medical and psychological professional organization has concluded that orientation is predominantly determined by chemical, hormonal, and genetic conditions in the womb. No reputable medical or psychological professional organization makes the claim that homosexuality is a disease or a changeable pathology. But what exactly causes sexual orientation? We simply do not have, at this time, sufficient data to pinpoint the cause or causes of sexual orientation. But if indeed sexual orientation is the product of biological factors, then how children are raised does not determine their sexual orientation. The human condition of homosexuality, like heterosexuality and bisexuality, just is.

Any attempt, therefore, to "cure" homosexuality is as futile as trying to cure heterosexuality. There is no cure for one's orientation—only denial. Christian ministries, like Exodus International, that attempt to help homosexuals change their sexual orientation to heterosexuality are destined to fail. According to Exodus International's policy, "EXODUS upholds redemption for the homosexual person as the process whereby sin's power is broken, and the individual is freed to know and experience true identity as discovered in Christ and His Church. That process entails the freedom to grow into heterosexuality."[10] Although Exodus posts testimonies of successful conversions to heterosexuality, most of those ex-gay experiences fail to meet the test of time. Take, for example, the former chair of Exodus' board of directors, John Paulk, who also served as manager of Focus on the Family's homosexuality department, and who was recently discovered at a gay bar. Paulk's failure to be healed from his homosexuality, despite his public persona to the contrary, is more the norm than the exception.

Another organization, called Refuge, is geared toward teenagers. Refuge is a Love in Action ministry designed for young people ages thirteen through eighteen. This two-week boot camp (costing $2,000) attempts to cure teenagers of what they term are the "addictive behaviors" of pornography, drugs and alcohol, sexual promiscuity, and homosexuality through the use of therapeutic groups and individual counseling. Love in Action's executive director, John Smid, a self-proclaimed ex-gay who is also on the board of directors of Exodus, insists that the program's purpose is not to make homosexuals into heterosexuals, but to teach them how to live with and not act on their homosexuality.[11]

What organizations like Exodus and Refuge can accomplish is a repression of identity so one refrains from acting on one's homosexual tendencies. But there is no evidence that they have successfully changed the homosexual's orientation—that is, changed his or her attraction, longing, and fantasies for members of the same sex to the same feelings for members of the opposite sex. The real question to ask is whether

the experience of a homosexual who assimilates and conforms to heterosexual patterns should be normative for all homosexuals. Also, what
psychological damage is caused when people are forced to live contrary
to their identity—in essence, to live a lie?

Even if agreement is reached that homosexuality is an orientation one
is born with (usually, according to the Religious Right, akin to being born
with a disease or a disposition for gambling or alcoholism), the response
for treating this "condition" is either compulsory heterosexuality or
self-imposed celibacy. Compulsory heterosexuality violates the spirit of
Romans 1:26–27, which we will explore in greater detail in a later section.
Imposed celibacy, as we saw in Chapter Six, ignores Paul's assertion that
celibacy is a gift, a lifestyle few are called to follow, not something to be
forced on a third party.

A fourth myth about homosexuality attempts to limit any discussion
about sexual orientation to sexual organs. Depending on which sexual
organs you have, you are either male or female. But what happens
if the sexual organs you possess do not clearly indicate one gender?
Where do intersexual people fit in the current church debate over sexual
orientation? Intersexual individuals are born with a sexual anatomy that
does not neatly fit the accepted conventional ideas of male or female.
These are individuals who are born both male and female and neither
male nor female. For example, a person may be born with some cells
having the XX chromosomes (the biological definition of female) and
other cells with the XY chromosomes (the biological definition of male).
Others may be born with genitals that appear to be in between those of a
male and a female, with both a penis and a clitoris. Finally, the individual
can be born appearing as one gender on the outside but with the internal
anatomy of the opposite gender. How often does this occur? According
to medical research collected by the Intersex Society of North America,
medical centers call in specialists to determine sex differentiation for
children born noticeably atypical in terms of genitalia anywhere from
once in 1,500 to once in 2,000 births. Still more are born with subtler
forms of sex anatomy variations, some of which won't show up until
later in life.[12]

Sadly, as soon as intersexual children are born, many are rushed off for
"corrective surgery." A penis that is "too small" is removed to create a
girl, even though the penis would have functioned normally and in some
cases could even have attained the average size of penises upon reaching
puberty. What happens when this surgically created girl has sexual desires
for women when "she" reaches adulthood? Is he a lesbian? As can be
imagined, such procedures have caused intersexual adults great pain and
confusion, as they struggle with the stigma of being some sort of freak of

nature. Did God goof? Or is the Creator of all forms of life manifesting gender diversity—a diversity we refuse to accept because it does not fit neatly into our male-female, dominant-subordinate categories? Any attempt to create a biblical response concerning homosexuality must also consider intersexuality.

Surprisingly, the biblical text can provide intersexual individuals a model within the Divine nature. Central to Christian theological thought is the miracle story of Jesus being born of a Virgin (Luke 1:26–35). Not questioning the immaculate conception leads to some very interesting conclusions about Christ's gender identity. Biology teaches us that males have XY chromosomes and women have XX chromosomes. At conception, each parent contributes one of their chromosomes to the fetus. Women have only an X chromosome to contribute. If the man also contributes his X chromosome, then the fetus will develop into a girl because it has the combined XX chromosomes. If, however, he contributes his Y chromosome, then the fetus will develop into a boy because it has the XY chromosomes. Because there was no human male with an XY chromosome involved in Jesus' conception, he therefore had no Y chromosome.[13] This is further complicated when we consider that the Spirit who came over Mary has at times been theologically viewed as feminine. Both the Hebrew word (*ruah*) and the Greek word (*pneuma*) for Spirit are female gender. The literal acceptance of Jesus' virgin birth would conclude with his being not biologically a male, although he obviously was physically male. His circumcision attests to his having a penis. Was Jesus intersexual? When we further consider that Scripture and centuries of Christian theology reaffirmed that Jesus is the exact imprint of God's very being (Hebrews 1:3), we can begin to better appreciate Genesis 1:27, in which "God created humanity in God's image, in God's image God created him, male and female God created them." Both male and female and everything in between find their worth and dignity in the image of God fully revealed in the personhood of Jesus the Christ.

And finally, we must deal with the myth that homosexuality leads to pedophilia, literally the "love for boys." In this erotic-based relationship between adult men and adolescent boys, the boy as beloved takes a passive role and the adult is the active partner. As published on the website of the Family Research Council, the political arm of Dobson's Focus on the Family ministries, Robert Knight claims, "There is a strong undercurrent of pedophilia in the homosexual subculture. Homosexual activists want to promote the flaunting of traditional sexual prohibitions at the earliest possible age."[14] According to the Religious Right, pedophilia is not the only outrage that homosexuality leads to. According to the website of the American Family Association, chaired by Don Wildmon:

"Prominent homosexual leaders and publications have voiced support for pedophilia, incest, sadomasochism, and even bestiality."[15] In their minds, contrary to the empirical evidence available, to be gay means that one is more inclined to commit sexual crimes. But as we will see in the next chapter, pedophilia is a form of predatory sex and the abuse of power, not of homosexuality.

Complications with the Biblical Text

Most gays and lesbians are familiar with about seven biblical passages, which many conservatives use to either beat them into submission or condemn them for all eternity. Is it any wonder that some homosexuals reject the Bible and church (and, by extension, a faith) that is constantly hostile to their very existence? But the real tragedy is that the biblical verses hurled like missiles by these conservatives have been twisted to mean something far from the original intent of the biblical authors. The verses end up being interpreted according to the biases of a culture that fears and despises homosexuals.

Before examining these specific verses, it is important to first highlight several complications we find when an ancient text is literally applied to a modern society. The first complication is the fact that no specific word exists, either in Hebrew or Greek, that is equivalent to the English word *homosexual*, since both the word and the concept originated in the closing years of the nineteenth century. In fact, no biblical word exists whose meaning remotely defines the essence of how the contemporary word *homosexuality* is used today. Anal sex between men has historically been considered an aberration. It wasn't until the late nineteenth century that anal sex between men became the means of defining the total identity of a certain "species" of men. Nowhere in the biblical text is orientation mentioned. How then can the Bible condemn something it never mentions? Because both the Hebrew and Greek texts use euphemisms to describe same-sex acts, any interpretation of biblical passages alluding to homosexuality is fraught with difficulties. What the text does mention are cases of same-sex acts committed by heterosexuals, because in the minds of the biblical writers it was assumed everyone was heterosexual.

The Bible is silent concerning egalitarian same-sex eroticism. Still, there are a few instances in which the Bible refers directly to same-sex intercourse. When it does, the focus is on the sexual act as opposed to the person's identity or orientation. It is true that the Bible has taken a negative view of the sexual act usually connected with homosexuality. But it is also true, as we have seen throughout this book, that the Bible has been used to condemn all forms of nonreproductive sex as sin, including heterosexuality within marriage. The same logic used to debunk the biblical passages that supposedly condemn heterosexual sex is now needed to debunk the implicit and explicit biblical references made to homosexuality.

A second complication concerns the definition of homosexuality. Different modern cultures understand the word *homosexual* in different ways. According to the prevailing U.S. definition, two men engaged in a sexual act are considered gay. For many other cultures, only the one that places himself in the "position of a woman" is considered to be gay. As previously mentioned, sex with another man does not define homosexuality; only the one who is willingly penetrated is considered to be gay. The man who is in the dominant position during the sex act is able to retain, if not increase, his manliness because of the ability to penetrate. After all, penetration symbolizes superiority, because the one "on top" occupies that position both in the sex act and in societal power structures.

One simply needs to consider prison rape (a recent example that comes to mind is the atrocities committed by U.S. soldiers at the Abu Ghraib compound during the Iraqi war), which is clearly a brutal act of domination rather than mutual sexual attraction and love. Male-on-male rape is not about sex—it is about obtaining power through the demasculinization of the other, a violent act that humiliates and dominates the person forced into the passive position. T. J. Parsell said it well. In 1978, the lanky, pimple-faced teenager landed in adult prison for using a toy gun during a convenience-store robbery. While imprisoned, he was drugged and gang-raped. Recounting the event, he said, "What they took from me went beyond sex. They'd stolen my manhood, my identity and part of my soul."[16] Because the perpetrators of prison rape, whether they be fellow prisoners or military guards, are usually heterosexual, it would be more accurate to refer to what we call homosexual rape as same-gender heterosexual rape.

Third, most oppose homosexuality because of some gut-level disgust for the practice, or some deep-down fear that they themselves might possibly be gay. Few oppose homosexuality because some 7 verses out of 31,173 in the Bible says something somewhat negative about engaging in same-sex acts. I suspect that most first have a negative reaction—a reaction that the overall culture tells them is normal. Only then does the disgusted one reach for the biblical text to justify his or her feelings. But why is this normative reaction to homosexual relationships so hostile? I suspect it is because same-sex relationships challenge the gender-based hierarchical structures that have come to be legitimized in most heterosexual relationships. This is not to say that oppressive structures cannot exist in same-sex relationships; however, by their very composition, homosexual relationships can provide an alternative paradigm to the dominant-subordinate heterosexual relationship. The very existence of same-sex relationships can provide a corrective model for heterosexual relationships with a troubling dominant-subordinate imbalance, by providing a different paradigm that can refute the present prevalent patriarchal structures.

One final note: For many who disagree as to how a biblical text is interpreted on any number of issues, a compromise is usually proposed in which both parties simply agree to disagree. This strategy can usually be beneficial. However, when the interpretation fosters oppressive structures, then agreeing to disagree can never be an option. When the Bible's ancient words are used to support slavery, women' subjugation, and ethnic cleansing, then such interpretations must be condemned for Christ's sake. Interpretations that limit gay civil rights or advocate subjugation and oppression of homosexuals should also be challenged and condemned.

Biblical References to Homosexuality

Even those who apply a narrow-minded literalism to the Bible must admit that the scriptures fail to make a clear, decisive case against homosexual orientation. At best, the references to homosexuality are ambiguous, probably dealing with acts that are not what we today would consider to be same-sex relationships.

Implicit References

THE SIN OF SODOM (GENESIS 19:1–29 AND JUDGES 19:11–30). U.S. history has proven that most of its presidents, congressional leaders, and Supreme Court justices have been guilty of the sin of Sodom. Many of today's religious leaders, specifically most from the Religious Right, are also guilty of Sodom's sin. If truth be known, the author of this book is also guilty of the sin of Sodom. Even most of you who are reading this book are guilty of the sin of Sodom. This leads us to ask, what exactly is the sin of Sodom? According to the story, Lot, Abraham's nephew, received unknown visitors. On hearing of the strangers, the men of Sodom surrounded Lot's house and banged on the door, demanding, "Send them out to us that we may abuse and rape them!" If we believe most conservative preachers and biblical commentators, the sin of Sodom is homosexuality. Probably no other passage throughout all of scripture has been more consistently used as justification for condemning same-sex relationships.

However, biblical references to Sodom disprove such an assertion. Commenting on Sodom's sin, the prophet Ezekiel (16:49) wrote that Sodom's iniquity was the city residents' unwillingness, due to their pride and haughtiness, to share their abundance with those who were poor and marginalized. Amos (4:1, 11) prophesied the destruction of Israel for following Sodom's example of "oppressing the needy and crushing the poor." Likewise, referring to Israel as Sodom and Gomorrah, the prophet Isaiah stated: "Hear the word of Yahweh, O rulers of Sodom, listen to the law of our God, O people of Gomorrah! . . . Your palms are full of blood. Wash yourselves, purify yourselves, remove the evil of your doings before my eyes. Cease doing evil. Learn to do good. Seek justice, reprove the oppressor, be just to the orphan, contend for the widow (1:10–17)."

In all the passages throughout the biblical text in which Sodom's wickedness is mentioned, homosexuality is never listed as the cause for God's wrath. The crime of Sodom and Gomorrah, as elucidated by the scriptures themselves, is described as being a lack of justice done in the name of the "orphans and widows," the biblical euphemism for the disenfranchised. The noncanonical books that the Apocrypha comprises also attest that throughout early Judaism, Sodom's sin was regarded as demonstrating a lack of hospitality to strangers[17] and excessive pride.[18] Also, the early rabbinical writings that developed in the Talmud fail to make a connection between Sodom's sin and homosexuality.[19] Among the first to actually make such a direct connection between homosexuality and Sodom's sin were the Jewish philosopher Philo of Alexandria (c. 25 B.C.E. to 50 C.E.)[20] and Josephus (c. 37–100), who was commissioned by Roman authorities to write the history of the Jews.[21]

The sin of Sodom, as defined by the biblical text and the early rabbinical writings, does not refer to a loving relationship between two individuals of the same sex. Instead, it refers to the townsfolk's unwillingness to express hospitality to the visiting strangers. This could be why Jesus, when giving instructions to his disciples who were about to embark on a missionary journey, stated that those cities that refused them hospitality would face a worse fate than Sodom (Luke 10:1–12). The same xenophobia demonstrated by the Sodomites, who sought to physically rape the foreigners in their midst, is present today in the actions of those who economically rape the poor and the undocumented alien. Both in ancient Sodom and in the modern United States, the residents in power desire to subordinate the stranger, the undocumented, and the alien in their midst. Rather than using this passage to condemn homosexuality, today's preachers would be more biblically sound if they used Genesis 19 to show how First World nations economically treat the peoples of Third World nations, which is not so different from what the Sodomites hoped to do to the aliens in their own midst.

Even if some still insist that Sodom's sin was sexual in nature, the only argument that could feasibly be made is that same-gender gang rape perpetrated by heterosexual men is wrong—a position with which most liberals and conservatives, heterosexuals and homosexuals would find agreement. But even then, rape is not a sexual act, even though it is a violence involving sexual organs. Rape is foremost an act of domination in which pleasure is achieved through the humiliation and subjugation of the victim. The desire of mortal men to rape "heavenly messengers" was an attempt to subjugate the things of Heaven to the will of humans. It was an assault on God's authority! The sin of Sodom is not homosexuality, but unchecked heterosexuality in its attempt to dominate everything, even the things of God, with the male penis. Yet ironically, although Lot protects his guests from same-gender heterosexual gang rape, he shows no such qualms in offering up his two virgin daughters for gang rape, even though such an action would bring shame upon himself (Deuteronomy 22:20–21). In similar fashion, the attempted gang rape of the Levite in the Benjaminite town of Gibeah, found in the book of Judges, is not a desire for homosexual intimacy, but an attempt to demonstrate mastery over the foreigner by sexually subjugating him. In this case, when the Levite's concubine is offered, she is raped in his stead.

HAM'S GAZING (GENESIS 9:20–27). The story of Noah's flood begins with an account of sexual irregularities—the union of mortal women with heavenly beings (Genesis 6:1–4)—and ends with the sexual irregularity that takes place between Ham and Noah. According to the story, Noah invented wine. After drinking too much, he passed out naked in his tent. His son Ham "gazed" on his father's nakedness, and for this his posterity was cursed. Surely seeing your father naked should not cause divine retribution, or else most of us who ever saw our father without clothes (such as in the bathroom or changing clothes in a gym locker room) would be in trouble. To gaze on nakedness meant more than simply seeing. Gazing was a euphemism for desire. Ham did not just see his father with no clothes on, he sexually took advantage of him—a point reiterated in rabbinical writings.[22] Consequently Noah, on sobering up, exclaimed in horror for what Ham "has done to him."

Like the story of Sodom, this episode has nothing to do with an intimate homosexual relationship. It has to do with Ham asserting his power over his father by subjugating and humiliating him. It is interesting to note that among Ham's descendants are the Egyptians (who enslaved the Hebrews) and Canaanites (who stood in the Hebrews' way of possessing the promised land). Could it be that the writer of Genesis wanted to reveal that it was sinful and wicked for Ham (and through him, his descendants the Egyptians and Canaanites) to subjugate or humiliate the Hebrews? But if a sexual sin is to be found in this story, then it is incestuous rape. Again, conservatives and liberals, heterosexuals and homosexuals can agree that incestuous rape is wrong and sinful.

JESUS' COMMENTS (MATTHEW 19:12). At first glance it appears that Jesus says nothing concerning homosexuals. But on closer examination, what seems to be an implicit reference to gays appears in the Gospel of Matthew: Jesus' curious remark about eunuchs in response to a question about the advisability of disciples marrying. Eunuchs are castrated males. During Jesus' lifetime, singleness and celibacy were viewed with suspicion by Jews because such a lifestyle violated the divine call to be fruitful and multiply (Genesis 1:28). So when Jesus declared that (1) there are eunuchs and (2) they are made so for the sake of God's reign, he was no doubt referring to himself and those who would follow him as disciples. Not that Jesus castrated himself; rather, he had chosen a lifestyle of celibacy—metaphorically, as if castrated—for the sake of his mission.

What is interesting about Jesus' response is that he made two other references about eunuchs. He stated that there are eunuchs who are born eunuchs, and there are eunuchs who are made eunuchs. What was Jesus referring to? Due to castration, eunuchs were incapable of marriage. We know that some, like Nehemiah, were made eunuchs so as to serve as advisors to the king. Castration ensured that the ruler would not suffer shame due to his queen or a member of the king's harem having intercourse with the king's advisor. But what did Jesus mean by those who were born eunuchs from their mother's womb? How could a boy be castrated prior to birth?

Eunuchs, because they were unable to be fruitful and multiply, were considered sexual outcasts, unable to enter the assembly of Yahweh (Deuteronomy 23:1). In many cases, homosexuals are today's sexual outcasts, because they also face obstacles to entering or serving in God's house. We can see the reference to being born a eunuch as a reference to being born gay—probably one of the only biblical references to sexual orientation. The eunuchs of old are considered to be the predecessors of today's gays. Like those who choose celibacy for religious reasons, gay men are born with their genitals, but metaphorically castrated because they do not participate in so-called legitimate married life with a woman.

No doubt some would question this interpretation. Nevertheless, even if this interpretation is rejected, the good news is that the sexual outcasts, whether the eunuch of old or the homosexual of today, have a special place reserved for them in God's house. In Isaiah's messianic dream, the prophet proclaims: "Do not let the eunuch say, 'Behold, I am a dried up tree,' for thus says Yahweh to the eunuchs who keep my Sabbaths, and chooses things with which I am pleased, and take hold of my covenant. I will even give them in my house and in my walls a hand and a name better than sons and daughters, I will give them an everlasting name which shall not be cut off (56:3–5)" (I think the pun was intended).

Explicit References

Not only are there biblical Scriptures that implicitly deal with the issue of homosexuality, but there are also Scriptures that are more explicit. Historically, this handful of scriptures has been used as a proof-text by those attempting to prove homosexuality is an abomination. Consequently, any serious study of the biblical text requires a careful examination of these verses.

THE LAW (LEVITICUS 18:22 AND 20:13). The two passages in Leviticus dealing with homosexuality are part of what has come to be known as the Holiness Code (Leviticus 17–26). The meaning of the Hebrew word translated as *holiness* is better expressed by the English word *separate*. Thus, "I, Yahweh your God am separate (holy), therefore, you be separate (holy)" (Leviticus 19:2). Separate from what? From the Canaanites who previously occupied the land. The Holiness Code was the means by which proper rules of behavior were established to serve as the antithesis of the Canaanities' behavior. The Code concludes, "You shall not do the same deeds as were done in Egypt where you lived, nor must you do the same deeds as are done in Canaan where I am bringing you. You must not walk by their statutes. You must keep my judgments and walk by my statutes" (Leviticus 18:3–4). As a survival strategy for maintaining the ethnic identity and cultic purity of the Hebrews taking possession of a new land, the foreign customs and traditions of the surrounding "pagan" people had to be abandoned.

The penalty for violating Leviticus 18:22 and 20:13 (specifically the latter) was death. If these passages truly dealt with issues of homosexuality, then to take the Bible literally means that our response to homosexuals must not be to pray for them, to convert them, to cure them, or to deliver them from their sins. We are told to kill them. To take the Bible literally is to advocate the killing of all homosexuals. But not just homosexuals. A man who slept with another man's property had to be put to death for adultery along with the other man's wife (Deuteronomy 22:22). Brides who on their wedding night were discovered not to be virgins were to be stoned (Deuteronomy 22:13–21). (Of course, grooms who were not virgins had nothing to fear.) Because some groups throughout history have taken the Bible literally, the perpetrators of these sexual "sins" have indeed met such fates.

Homosexuals have historically been burned at the stake, stoned, imprisoned, and hospitalized. Even today, gays face violence through gay-bashing—treatment ranging from harassment to beating and even death. One would hope that most Christians today would cringe at advocating the killing of homosexuals. But unless we advocate the murder of all homosexuals, we are not taking the Bible literally. This again raises the issue of biblical interpretation. Could these passages of the Holiness Code calling for the death of men having sex with men be ignored, just as we ignore earlier passages of the Code that impose the death penalty on disrespectful teenagers (Leviticus 20:9), adulterers (Leviticus 20:10), and blasphemers (Leviticus 24:15)?

A more profound question to ask is, "What are these passages really discussing?" Because the word *homosexual* does not exist in the biblical Hebrew language, the direct translation for *miskebe' issah,* as used in Leviticus 18:22 and 20:13, is "not to lie with a man as with a woman." To do so is a *to'ebah,* an abomination. *To'ebah* (and the synonym *shiqquts*) translated as *abomination* is neither a moral nor an ethical term, but a technical cultic term denoting something ritually unclean due to a crossing of boundaries. Other abominations include the improper use of incense (Numbers 16:40); offering a blemished animal as sacrifice (Deuteronomy 17:1); eating unclean animals such as shellfish (Leviticus 11:10), dead carcasses (Leviticus 11:11), and any part of the pig or other animals with cloven hoofs (Deuteronomy 14:4–8); remarrying a former spouse (Deuteronomy 24:4); and having sex with a woman during the seven days following the start of her menstrual period (Leviticus 20:18–24; Ezekiel 18:6). On this last point it is interesting to note that although Christian conservatives like Tim and Beverly LaHaye condemn the "abomination" of homosexuality, they are comfortable with the "abomination" of sexual intercourse during the wife's menstruation.[23]

Why is it ritually unclean to "lie with a man like with a woman"? The answer can be found in the prior verse, specifically Leviticus 18:21, which prohibits the offering of children as sacrifices. By linking these two verses, is the condemnation of a man lying with a man an abomination because it refers to the "sacred sex" acts that occurred in pagan cults? Same-gender sex was widely practiced in the ancient world, with a special class of prostitutes serving these needs in many religious establishments, such as the temple prostitutes who resided in the brothel of Ishtar's Temple in Babylon. Lying with a sacred male prostitute (referred to in the Bible as qadesh) was considered an abomination because it followed the ritual practices of the pagans, specifically the Canaanites. The Israelites were warned not to allow their sons to become sacred prostitutes, nor to bring their "dog wages" into the Temple of Yahweh (Deuteronomy 23:19). Israel was to avoid the ritualized sex that was part of the Canaanites' religious experience, formerly adopted in Hebraic worship (1 Kings 14:24; 15:12; 22:47) and not fully eradicated until King Josiah's reign (2 Kings 23:7). Therefore, homosexual orientation is not an abomination. However, homosexual acts based on a power relationship that degrades and humiliates one party forced against their will into a passive position is indeed an abomination—a stand that can be taken by most conservatives and liberals, heterosexuals and homosexuals.

Before focusing on the New Testament, I should note that no prohibition is made throughout the Hebrew Bible concerning lesbianism—what the Hebrews called *mesolelot,* literally "women who rub." The absence of penile penetration in a lesbian relationship was construed as an absence of sexual intercourse. Besides, women were perceived as already being passive, and they had no honor to lose by being placed in a passive role by another woman. If we choose to be literal, a biblical argument could then be made for same-sex female relationships. In fact, several rabbinical writings mention that although a priest was forbidden from marrying a harlot, he was still allowed to marry a woman who was sexually active with another woman.[24]

REMAINING FAITHFUL TO ONE'S NATURE (ROMANS 1:26–27). This particular verse is embedded in a larger section specifically dealing with idolatry, the exchange of "the glory of the immortal God for worthless imitations" (Romans 1:23). Paul rails against the unnatural worship of created things that are found in nature (like birds, animals, and reptiles) in favor of what should be the natural worship of God as evidenced throughout nature. Paul is speaking not about homosexual orientation, but about exchanging what is natural for the unnatural. Unfortunately, reading the text with a heterosexual bias presumes that the term "unnatural" must be a reference to some sort of homosexual activity—for acts that are considered not normal and unnatural in heterosexual sexual activity are therefore abnormal and unnatural, deviant and filthy sexual acts.

In his reference to sexuality, Paul is speaking about heterosexual men who have forsaken "natural intercourse" to be "consumed with passion for each other." Basically, his theme is that it is wrong to change one's nature. Today we can say that it is wrong to change one's orientation. Heterosexual men should not exchange their nature for homosexual practices, as was common among heterosexual slaves and prostitutes who were forced into homosexual activities. Paul is criticizing the fact that heterosexuals were forced to engage in homosexual activities against their will. Likewise, if we are to remain faithful to this principle, homosexuals should not exchange their nature (orientation) for heterosexual practices. Each group should remain faithful to its own orientation.

Also in this biblical passage is a reference to women "turning from natural intercourse to unnatural practices." This is the only place throughout the entire Bible in which lesbianism is mentioned. Or is it? We shouldn't assume that "unnatural practices" here refers to women engaging in same-gender sex. Again, that would betray our heterosexual bias. In keeping with the case that Paul is making against exchanging what is natural for what is unnatural, "unnatural practices" could be a reference to women acting contrary to the patriarchal norms of the time—perhaps a crossing of the boundaries that circumscribe proper household roles, based on the requirement of women's passivity.

PAUL'S COMMENTS (1 CORINTHIANS 6:9 AND 1 TIMOTHY 1:10). Paul's writings must be read from a Greco-Roman social context, because he wrote his epistles both to and from within these cultures. It would be an error to read Paul's references to same-gendered sex using a twenty-first-century understanding of homoerotic relationships, rather than the existing cultural ethos of his own time. To the ancient Greeks (specifically Plato and Aristotle), the ideal form of love, the deepest form of friendship, could occur only between men, for only then, they believed, would reason and passion be joined together. The highest level of love could not occur between a man and woman, basically because of her passive role, which undermined any rationally based equality. Certainly a man could enjoy physical pleasure with his wife; this was necessary to ensure procreation. But only with another man could he achieve deep companionship through the highest and purest form of spiritual love.

Throughout ancient Greek culture, pederasty was both accepted and extensively practiced as a type of male initiation rite. Great military leaders such as Alexander the Great encouraged homoerotic relationships in their military forces. Because lovers were willing to die for each other, military troops were organized by pederastic relationships in which the adults taught the youth valor, bravery, and manliness. (So much for the "don't ask, don't tell" policy of our modern military!) Greek same-gendered relationships were the product not of homosexuality but of, as Martti Nissinen calls it, an "institutionalized bisexual role behavior . . . [which] assumed that everyone was able to love both genders."[25]

Greek homoerotic customs influenced Roman culture, with the possible difference that although Greek same-sex relationships were generally among those in the aristocratic class (and thus between social equals), Roman same-sex relationships usually occurred between a master and his slave. In addition, male homosexual prostitution was both legal and commonly available. It wasn't until 342 C.E. that gay marriage was outlawed, but the law was routinely ignored, with few penalties imposed on the offenders. Until then, gay unions were such a part of Roman culture that even the military genius Julius Caesar was involved in a relationship with King Nicomedes of Bithynia, earning Caesar the pejorative title "Queen of Bithynia"—not because he was engaged in a same-sex relationship, but because he took the passive role in the relationship, the role of slaves and prostitutes. Passivity meant, and still means, social subjugation. By Caesar's taking on the female role and becoming the object of someone else's sexual desires, his dignity was brought into question.

It is to this Greco-Roman world that Paul writes his letters to the Gentiles. The Greek word appearing in these passages that is usually translated as *homosexual* is *arsenokoites* (the 1 Corinthians passage also includes the Greek word *malakos*). The translation of these words as *homosexual*—a term that did not exist until the late nineteenth century—has led many to the conclusion that gays will never inherit the kingdom of God and that they are destined for everlasting damnation. Such reasoning led some—like Reverend Fred Phelps, a Baptist preacher in Topeka, Kansas—to protest the memorial service of Matthew Shepard, who was brutally murdered for being gay in the small Wyoming town of Laramie. Fellow church members waved antigay signs that read: "No Fags in Heaven," "God Hates Fags," "Matt in Hell," and "No Tears for Queers."[26] The reverend's church, Westboro Baptist Church, developed a website, the "Perpetual Gospel Memorial to Matthew Shepard." The site displays a photo of Shepard literally "burning in hell" with a link that permits site visitors to hear Matt's tortured screams from the depths of the inferno.[27] Interpreting *arsenokoites* and *malakos* as used in these passages to mean homosexuals, Reverend Phelps concludes that gays and their supporters deserve such violence. "Not only is homosexuality a sin, but anyone who supports fags is just as guilty as they are. You are both worthy of death."[28] According to statistical data compiled by the FBI, of the 9,035 hate-crime offenses reported in 2004, 15.7 percent (or 1,418) were crimes committed due to the victim's sexual orientation.[29] That's almost four hate crimes a day aimed at homosexuals, thanks to the biblical justification offered by individuals like Reverend Phelps. He and his church have even protested funeral services across the nation for fallen soldiers of the Iraqi War. Phelps defends his actions, contending that the death of American soldiers in Iraq is God's punishment of this country for harboring gays.[30]

But *arsenokoites* and *malakos* do not refer to what we today understand to be an intimate homosexual relationship. *Malakos* literally mean "soft," a term that refers to "effeminate boys" when used in other ancient literature. This could also be a reference to a pederasty relationship in which the male who is penetrated is taking the "soft" or passive position of a woman. *Arsenokoites* is harder to translate because the term appears to have been coined by Paul; it doesn't appear in other ancient literatures, nor is it used much by subsequent authors. *Arsenokoites* seems to denote the passive role taken by male prostitutes. When we consider that Strabo, a Greek historian, geographer, and philosopher who was a contemporary of the emperor Augustus, writes that there were over a thousand prostitutes (male and female) working in Corinth out of the Temple of Aphrodite,[31] and that male prostitution was extensively practiced in Greece, we can reasonably conclude that the 1 Corinthians and 1 Timothy passages refer to these male prostitutes—particularly the 1 Corinthians passage. It seems that these passages condemn pedophilia and male prostitution—a condemnation that most conservatives and liberals, heterosexuals and homosexuals would share today.

SLEEPING WITH THE ANGELS (2 PETER 2:4–8 AND JUDE 6–7). God's punishment of Sodom and Gomorrah for their "shameless ways" and "unnatural fornication" is mentioned in both of these passages. If these verses are read with the presupposition that the sin of these ancient cities was intimate same-sex relationships, then the logical conclusion is that the passages condemn homosexuality, with warnings of divine punishment. But a closer examination reveals that the authors of these biblical books were not referring to our modern understanding of homosexual orientation. The 2 Peter passage begins with a reference to sinning angels, and in the Jude passage the subjects are angels who traded "supreme authority" for "spiritual chains." These two biblical passages refer to the Genesis 6:1–4 account of angels having sex with mortal women and, in doing so, disrupting the natural order separating humans from the divine. The "shameless ways" and "unnatural fornication" in the passages in 2 Peter and Jude are sexual intercourse between celestial and mortal beings. Why then mention Sodom and Gomorrah? Because the men of Sodom attempted to gang-rape Lot's guests, who were angels. The townsfolk's unnatural lust for angels is being condemned, not homosexuality. And again, both conservatives and liberals, heterosexuals and homosexuals can agree that sex with angels is probably not a good idea.

Cruising Through the Bible

Author and pastor Timothy Koch provides a methodological approach
to Scripture that he terms "cruising." Cruising is how some homosexuals publicly find and connect with each other in a culture hostile
to their existence. For Koch, cruising through Scripture helps him
discover individual characters who are friendly to his gay male identity, others that are hostile, most who are apathetic, and as he says,
"a few really hot numbers." His cruising is not an attempt to vali-
date his existence, explain away Scripture, or attempt to force homosexual interpretations onto multiple texts. Instead, he is reading the
Bible with a queer eye, looking for signals to pick up that would res-
onate with his orientation.[32] Using this methodology, we can explore
three such stories.

David and Jonathan

> The soul of Jonathan's was knitted with the soul of David, for
> Jonathan loved him more than his own soul. . . . Jonathan and David
> made a covenant, because he loved him more than his own soul. . . .
> Saul spoke to his son Jonathan and all his servants to have David
> killed. But Saul's son Jonathan exceedingly delighted himself in David.
> So Jonathan told David, "My father Saul is seeking to kill you so
> please be watchful, especially this morning. Stay in some secret place
> and hide. . . . Saul's anger glowed against Jonathan. And he said to
> him, "You son of a rebellious perversion. Don't I know that you
> have chosen the son of Jesse to your shame, and to the shame of
> the nakedness of your mother? As long as the son of Jesse lives on
> this earth, you shall not be established, you or your kingdom.". . .
> Then Jonathan rose from the table in the heat of anger . . . he grieved
> for David and how his father had shamed him. . . . In the morning
> Jonathan went out [to where David was hiding]. . . . And there they
> kissed each other, and they wept with each other with David weeping
> more. And then they left [for the last time, swearing to be faithful
> to the covenant they made. Some time later, when David learned of
> Jonathan's death in battle, he laments:] "I am distressed over you
> my brother Jonathan, you were very dear to me, your love more
> wonderful than the love for a woman." [1 Samuel 18:1, 3; 19:1–2,
> 30–31, 34–35, 40–42; 2 Samuel 1:26].

If we were unaware that this is a biblical tale, we might well suspect it
of being a gay love story. But knowing it's in the Bible will likely change

the meaning for most readers. We must question whether we can read the scriptures for what they literally say, without our biases and homophobia imposing certain meanings on the text. I'm not saying that David and Jonathan were bisexual (they each had wives), nor am I saying that they weren't. I'm simply pointing out that these passages raise questions about their relationship.

Prior to this story of the parting between Jonathan and David, we are told that David was a very handsome man with beautiful eyes (1 Samuel 16:12). Interestingly, we are told earlier that Saul, Jonathan father, was also very handsome, the most handsome man throughout all the land of Israel (1 Samuel 9:1–2). We are first introduced to both Saul and David with a description of their stunning good looks. These two beauties developed a relationship with each other. David became Saul's armor-bearer, who would entertain Saul with his music-making; in return, Saul grew to love David (1 Samuel 16:21). We know that in several ancient cultures, such as Greece, a pederastic relationship between the adult warrior and his beautiful younger war companion was common. Perhaps similar relationships existed among the Israelites. Saul's anger toward his son Jonathan could have been partly fueled by jealousy now that David was loved by a younger man. Was Saul upset that his own son supplanted his relationship with David?

In a matter-of-fact way, the biblical writer informs us that David and Jonathan wept and kissed during their final farewell, an outpouring of love not witnessed when David departs from his wife. There is a reference to their entering a covenant (marriage?) of love, one that is greater than that of a woman's love. And then there's Saul strange comment to Jonathan of choosing David to his shame and then referencing his mother's nakedness. Such a negative sexual reference, at least in Saul's mind, indicates his suspicion that something sexually "indecent" was taking place between his son and David.

Ehud and Eglon

The Moab king Eglon ruled over Israel. But God raised the left-handed Ehud to deliver the people. After the Israelites presented their tributes to their foreign ruler, Ehud whispered to the king that he had a secret to share. The king immediately cleared the room to be alone with Ehud. Then Ehud reached under his garment to take something out, using his left hand (the hand used in ancient culture to deal with private body parts and their functions). What was King Eglon expecting—or hoping—that Ehud might pull out from under his garment? Was Ehud pretending to be gay so as to kill the foreign despot, or was his reputation already known by Eglon, as indicated by the king's lack of fear in securing a private chamber for them?

To the king's surprise, Ehud pulled out a very long knife and stabbed the king in a place where the "fat" (cheeks?) closed over the blade. We can only wonder exactly where on his person the king was stabbed (Judges 3:22). Again, without much fanfare, the biblical text simply describes a relationship that makes more sense in the context of the participants' willingness to engage in a homosexual activity.

The First Christian Church

One of the first challenges faced by the early church was whether to include non-Jews. Should Gentiles be required to convert to Judaism and *then* become Christians? More specifically, should they first be required to be circumcised? Acts 15 records the controversy that took place at Antioch. "Unless you are circumcised in the tradition of Moses, you cannot be saved," exclaimed those who came from Judea to disrupt Paul's mission. Even the most faithful to God can expose the prejudices lurking in their hearts—as demonstrated by Peter, who refused to eat with the Gentiles. Interestingly, this is the same Peter who faced criticism for visiting the home of the Gentile Cornelius, a Roman centurion (Acts 10–11). Still, while Peter was in Antioch, when men of Jerusalem arrived to insist that Gentiles must first be circumcised before being saved, he avoided eating with the uncircumcised (Galatians 2:11–14).

The controversy was eventually settled in favor of the Gentiles. They could become Christians without first having to become Jews. Today, a similar controversy exists. This debate centers not on whether men must cut off their foreskin to become Christians, but whether the queer community must cut off their identity, their orientation, before they can become Christians. In many cases, the Church requires that they first become heterosexuals before becoming Christians, adopting a heterosexual lifestyle contrary to their being. When gays state that they can be both gay and Christian (like the uncircumcised Gentile Christians of old), their critics—specifically in the Religious Right—argue that they cannot be true believers. For if they were, they would have been cured of their gay identity or, at the very least, have repented of what they are. Yet homosexuals insist on perceiving the Divine through their own gay eyes. To do otherwise seems blasphemous to them.

How might gays respond to those people who pressure them to assimilate into the heterosexual culture? Paul's rather earthy rebuttal is worth noting. He told those Gentiles, "I wish that the ones causing you to doubt would castrate themselves" (Galatians 5:12).

Homophobia as a Paradigm for Oppression

Up to this point, this chapter has examined heterosexism as one aspect of oppression. But to truly examine the interconnectedness of heterosexism with other models of oppression (classism, racism, and sexism), it behooves us to expand our present concept of homophobia (the fear of gays or of being gay) into one that encompasses all forms of oppression imposed on those who fail to live up to the standards defined by the dominant culture. For purposes of discussing oppression, homophobia presents a useful paradigm: it is obviously the oppressor's (that is, homophobic heterosexuals') construction, designed to help members of that group (particularly males) understand how they link being a "real" man with the subordination of all whom they see as nonmales.

Traditionally, gender has been defined as a set of innate social traits that are essentially linked to a biological sex. Males are expected to behave aggressively; women are to behave submissively. These traits have been almost universally accepted as the norm. But in reality, such sets of behavior, deeply rooted in the political and religious heritage of a people, are socially constructed by a given society, imposed to legitimize the power of one group over another. Those who are perceived as aggressive seize the opportunity to lead, and those who are perceived as weak end up as followers. The logic goes that to be a woman means to be passive during the sexual act; by extension, her role during sex illustrates her passivity in society. But such passivity, as we have seen in this chapter, is not limited to women. Ascribing a male-female binary structure to all of society blurs the biological distinctions between males and females, as gender-appropriate roles cease to be limited to a person's particular biological sex.

The reasoning continues: only those who penetrate are males, even if they are biologically women (as in the backhanded male compliment "she got balls"). All others are females (even if they are biologically male). Penetration thereby comes to symbolizes manliness. To accuse a man of being penetrated is to question his manhood. To be placed in the position of a woman, that is, a passive role, invites shame at the expense of honor. Those dominated by another man's penis, whether literally through intercourse or figuratively through the symbolic penetration of being socially dominated, cannot assume the active male role of leadership. They are unfit for any power-based status, because taking the passive position indicates the loss and surrender of power. But for the one penetrating (regardless of biological gender), the ability to place the male other in the position of a woman indicates superiority and domination. He (usually a "he") can subdue both women and men. Sexual aggression is a means by which power can be exercised over the other. The ultimate conclusion is that only those with penises (real or symbolic) are aggressive enough to forge a society. Homosexuals and women, as well as nonwhite males and the poor (both of which are feminized by their low status and lack of power) usually fail to influence society because they are perceived as lacking that power of penetration.

Thus the man's penetrating penis provides the personal capacity to dominate others, especially his adversaries. The resulting gaze of the dominant culture's male assigns effeminacy to others who do not have a penetrating penis by which to "make" history, or "provide" for their family, or "resist" their subjugation. Women, nonwhites, and the poor usually end up becoming the "not male." But those who are deemed to be "real men" cannot rest easy in their position. They fear that their masculinity—which is defined by the power they exert—would be forfeited if any suggestion or allegation of passivity or vulnerability was successfully made. This is borne out in the accounts offered by many of those who bash or murder gay men. They justify their action by stating that the victim "made a pass at them." What did the gay victim see in the eventual attacker that would lead the victim to suspect that he too might be gay? In the mind of the homophobic, killing the homosexual becomes a necessary process by which manhood can be aggressively reclaimed—and thus prove that one is surely not passive. In a similar fashion, homosexuality is to be feared because it subverts patriarchal social patterns in which men are to be "on top"—never penetrated.

Those who refuse to prove their manhood are relegated to the feminine sphere. Constructing the oppressed as feminine has allowed men of the dominant culture to assert their privilege by viewing those they oppress as inhabitants of the castrated realm of the exotic and primitive. Like benevolent fathers, they then have the duty and responsibility of all those with penetrating penises to care for, provide for, and protect those underneath. Those on top dominate, control, lead, and protect. Those on the bottom follow and obey. This is the prescribed natural order, as manifested both in the bedroom and throughout a culture's social structure. In the minds of the males of the dominant culture, it is bad enough to be forced into a passive position. It is worse to "choose" to be passive. They became enslaved by the inferiority engraved on their flesh by the dominant culture's ethos.

Societal structures of oppression (racism, classism, and sexism) cannot be fully dismantled while homosexual civil rights continue to be denied. As long as these oppressive social structures continue to exist, many will be denied the great sex that is their birthright.

This discussion raises a number of fundamental questions. How then can homosexuals freely develop the familial relationships that lead to great sex? What are the sexual moral responsibilities of gays and lesbians? What must homosexuals do to live in accordance with biblical principles? And there is one answer to all three questions: exactly what is expected of heterosexuals. You are to love the Lord your God with all your heart, with all your soul, and with all your mind, and to love your neighbor as yourself. What is expected from homosexuals in their relationship to God and to their fellow humans is no different from what is expected from heterosexuals. No more and no less. Having multiple sex partners violates orthoeros among homosexuals as well as heterosexuals—not because sex is wrong or evil, but because having multiple partners prevents the possibility of having great sex within a familial model. Just like heterosexuals seeking familial sexual relationships, homosexuals are also called to become vulnerable and to enter into a mutually giving relationship with their beloved.

And what should be expected from the church of Christian believers? To openly support their commitment to all familial sexual relationships.

PREDATORY SEX

---

*Rid society of prostitutes and licentiousness will run riot
throughout. Prostitutes in a city are like a sewer in a palace.
If you get rid of the sewer, the whole place becomes filthy
and foul.*

—St. Thomas Aquinas[1]

*Just when . . . a man needed a bit of peace and privacy in
his own home, who should start spouting texts and
interpreting God's word in his own home, women. . . . It was
well known that with a woman, a dog and a walnut tree, the
more you beat 'em the better they be. Equally "natural" was
the duplicity of women. According to proverbial wisdom
they were saints in the church, angels in the streets, devils in
the kitchen and apes in bed.*

—Sheila Rowbotham, commenting on the prevalent attitudes
of colonial Massachusetts[2]

THE STORY OF SUSANNA does not appear in the Hebrew Bible, but it
can be found in the Septuagint, the first Greek translation of the Hebrew
Bible. Protestant Bibles do not carry the story, but it does appear in the
Apocrypha, a set of books that are not awarded the same revelatory
authority as the biblical canon. Catholics include the story in their Bibles,
appearing as chapter 13 of the book of Daniel.

The story revolves around the beautiful Susanna. She is falsely accused of adultery by two respected elders. These men brought false testimony against Susanna because she spurned their sexual advances, choosing death before dishonor. A trial was held, and she was convicted. But God heard Susanna's pleas for succor. The Spirit descended on a young Daniel, who, through clever questioning of the two elders, revealed their falsehood. Susanna was saved, and the would-be seducers were condemned to death.

Susanna's plight is the same predicament faced by many women today. Either they must give in to the sexual advances of men who have power over them, or they confront dire consequences. And although death may not necessarily be the norm, loss of employment, loss of reputation, and loss of self-respect are. We see Susanna's story privately and publicly repeated in the highest pinnacles of power as well as in the lowest stratum of society.

Uncovering Sexual Abuses

If our goal continues to be the pursuit of great sex, then the abuses visited on others in order to achieve self-gratification undermine any hope of achieving our goal. No doubt, few would openly make a case in favor of sexual abuses like rape or violence toward women and children. So why discuss them here? Because the way in which the biblical text has historically been interpreted in Christianity through the years has contributed to the creation and propagation of abuses that remain not so well hidden in many churches. Did your pastor preach a sermon about domestic violence this year? Or some time during the past five years? Has your pastor ever preached such a sermon? If your church is like most, then you know that the answer is disappointing. It is bad enough when churches turn a blind eye to sexual abuse, and it is worse when churches simply dismiss sexual abuse. Take the example of Dr. Robert Gray, the former pastor of Trinity Baptist Church in Jacksonville, Florida. In May 2006, he was arrested and charged with two counts of capital sexual battery after two of his alleged female victims reported he abused them when they were six years old. Since his arrest, twenty-two other people, including one man, have come forward accusing Gray of sexual abuses. Unfortunately, because these abuses involved children older than twelve, Gray cannot be prosecuted on these cases due to the statute of limitations. These abuses are inexcusable, and to trivialize them reduces the magnitude of the situation. During a three-day conference of the Southwide Baptist Fellowship in October 2006, which was scheduled to meet at Trinity Baptist Church prior to Dr. Gray's sexual abuses coming to light, Jerry Falwell, the keynote speaker, said: "When you hit a bump in the road"—Falwell then mentioned the six months of challenges the church has been facing—"forget the bump in the road. That's all it is. You've got to move on."[3] It is disturbing that for some, a loving relationship between two individuals of the same sex is an abomination before the Lord, while the rape of children by a prominent pastor is simply "a bump in the road." With all the talk about when not to have sex and who not to have it with, churches have done a poor job in engaging their congregations to deal with sexual practices that bring harm, if not death, to the most vulnerable members of society: women and children.

As we examine these abuses in this chapter, we will implement an orthoeros approach to discover ethical responses to sexual sins. Finally, the chapter and this book will end with a liberative reading of the Bible to explore ways in which both victim and abuser can find redemption and healing in Jesus and his message of radical love and liberation.

The Abuse of Sexual Power

Whenever sexual favors are demanded to ensure professional or economic gain, or when refusing to provide sexual favors might threaten one's professional or economic security, sexual harassment has occurred. The Bible provides examples of men in authority who misused their power for sexual gains. One familiar story is that of King David, who from the roof of his palace gazed at a neighbor bathing. David, probably the original Peeping Tom, orders the object of his desire, Bathsheba, to his chambers, where they engage in intercourse (2 Samuel 11:1–5). In most sermons I have heard on this passage, Bathsheba is portrayed as one of the "bad girls" of the Bible. Most of these preachers—male preachers, that is—speak of her seductive powers; specifically, how she led astray a man after God's own heart. But we must ask, who had power in this relationship? It was David, as king, who held the power of life and death over people like Bathsheba. When the king sent his messengers to fetch Bathsheba, did she really have the option of turning down the most powerful man in the land? The only response she could offer would be something like "Yes sire, I am but your humble maidservant, let your will be done." Unfortunately, this is not the only biblical record of a sexual predator. A woman forced to sleep with a man of power for the sake of her survival is nothing new, and the Bible is filled with these stories.

Even our own national leaders are part of the problem. Former president Clinton abused his power to force his will on a young woman. Even if Monica Lewinsky made the first sexual advancement to confirm consent, she is still the victim of sexual harassment, just like Susanna. Why? Because of the power dynamics that were present. Using one's power to obtain sex, whether one be the president of the United States or the king of Israel, is immoral. Not because of the sex itself (setting aside the issue of marital infidelity), but because power (which has been deemed sexy by society) was inappropriately used at the expense of violating vulnerability and mutuality. No matter who commits the crime, sexual harassment has one common denominator: empowerment of one party, usually a man, at the expense of the disempowerment of another, usually a woman. Sexual harassment is one of the means of maintaining social control over women.

Sexual abuse, of course, encompasses more than harassment carried out by economically powerful men against women in their employ. Sexual abuse is committed against wives and young children, against prostitutes and prison inmates, against college students, the elderly, and young teenagers. It crosses all economic, gender, orientation, and racial lines.

Victims of rape have been attacked by an abuser (whether stranger or family) who is usually motivated by strong negative emotions like hate, anger, or revenge—*not* by sexual arousal. The assailant has a desire to demonstrate power over the Other, a power achieved through the Other's humiliation and subjugation. Sexual abuse is not limited to physical violence, however; it also encompasses verbal intimidation, intentional degradation, public humiliation, spiritual manipulation, and economic deprivation. Not only does the physical and psychological damage caused by sexual abuse affect the one sexually victimized, but its influences are also visited on the next generations; as the biblical text reminds us, "visiting the iniquity of fathers upon their children, and on their children's children, to the third and to the fourth generations" (Exodus 34:7). Sexual abuse in one generation has a way of manifesting itself in future generations. A perverse understanding of sexuality develops, which is then taught to the next generation, thus preventing descendants of sexual victims from fully enjoying sex, partly due to a learned unhealthy understanding of sex.

Obviously all men are not sexual predators, but unfortunately almost all women have been sexually harassed at least once. It is important to acknowledge that men too can be victims of predatory sex and sexual abuse, in both heterosexual and homosexual partnerships. But for this chapter's purposes, we will focus on the majority of victims—women and children—whose abuse has been more systemic and institutionalized throughout history. We must remember that violence toward women—whether it be physical, sexual, or psychological, whether committed by a family member, acquaintance, or stranger—is first and foremost about power, specifically property and political power. Violence—even rape—has little to do with sex, even though sex becomes the means by which power is demonstrated. Nor is violence a result of the perpetrator's "losing control" in a relationship. Violence is a means of maintaining control over the conduct, thoughts, beliefs, and actions of the Other.

All in the Family

Of all the women that are murdered each year in the United States, one third are killed by their husband or boyfriend.[4] Another 1.5 million women are assaulted each year by an intimate sexual partner, and another million are stalked by someone they know.[5] According to a national survey, 34 percent of women had been sexually coerced by their husband or their intimate partner during their lifetime.[6] Of those who reported sexual violence, 64 percent of women and 16 percent of men claimed abuse at the hands of a current or former spouse, cohabitating partner, boyfriend or girlfriend, or a date.[7] Eight out of every ten rape cases involved a perpetrator known by the victim.[8] And as shocking as these statistics may be, they fall short of accurately illustrating the violence women face at the hands of their significant others. Why? Because the majority of all forms of sexual assaults are not reported to the authorities, hence the data collected greatly understates the true magnitude of the problem.

Violence in a relationship is not limited to the physical. It also includes

- Psychological violence, by creating an environment that leads the abused partner to feel depression, anxiety, suicidal, and low self-esteem
- Social violence, by restricting access to services and other relationships
- Health-based violence, manifested by engaging in high-risk sexual behavior (unprotected sex, promiscuity, or trading sex for necessities)
- Economic violence, by controlling the finances so as to maintain the partner in economic deprivation
- Public violence, through a deliberate pattern of public humiliation

These forms of violence in a relationship—and physical violence in particular—are a manifestation of power that can be used to teach the recipient of the abuse to conform and obey. With time, the actual violence ceases to be necessary. The mere threat of its use is sufficient for the one abused to docilely obey. Power is internalized as victims learn to police themselves. As a form of survival, of self-preservation and protection, the victim (more often than not a woman) learns to behave in the appropriate manner—a manner that reinforces her status of imposed inferiority. Such self-disciplining can only lead to the undermining of one's self-worth and dignity.

Marital rape, or any other manifestation of sexual violence, is a distinctly painful violation for the woman who has placed her trust in a man—a trust whereby she willingly has given him her body in the past, a trust that may even have produced children. Yet seldom is this form of abuse reported, usually due to a desire to protect the abuser. Other reasons for keeping silent include deep feelings of love for the children, desire to protect children (if any) from finding out, commitment to or obligation for the family, and strong religious beliefs that demand submission from the wife.

Religious Support for Domestic Violence

Not surprisingly, both the biblical text and institutionalized Christianity have been complicit in creating and supporting this sexual violence against women. The concept of women as property led early Christian fathers like St. Augustine to the belief that beating one's wife was a God-given right and obligation, an appropriate way for men to maintain male authority. By canon law, husbands were entitled to beat their wives. Consequently, this legal precedent has influenced a Western jurisprudence that has a long tradition of turning a blind eye to cases of domestic violence and absolving husbands from the charge of raping their wives. As recently as 1976, marital rape was legal in all fifty U.S. states.

The assumption that a woman's body is the personal possession of her spouse is the ever-present consequence of a Christianity defined so as to reduce women to creatures subordinate to male authority, and a secular media that objectifies women to sell products. Men are taught by their culture and their faith that they have full access to their wives' bodies—wives who are commanded by God *Him*self to submit. Yet the ultimate violation of vulnerability in any marriage is the taking of a spouse's body against her will.

But women are not the only ones victimized by this abusive relationship. Men too are trapped by these social structures. One of the participants of the Presbyterian Special Committee on Human Sexuality (1988–91) made a profound observation. He wrote, "I can only conclude that battering—at least in part—is a substitute for tears. As little boys, men are taught that 'big boys don't cry,' and that when threatened or hurt, they should learn to 'stand up and fight like a man.' Being deprived of human tears, they, in turn, victimize women as a means to live out the impossible cultural assignment to control the feminine within themselves."[9]

Linking Class to Sexual Abuse

All of us, regardless of gender, age, race, class, or ethnicity, are possible targets for sexual abuse. There are, however, several vulnerability factors that increase the risk of victimization. They include gender (78 percent are women[10]), age (for 54 percent of women raped and 75 percent of men raped, the rape occurred before their eighteenth birthday[11]), and high-risk behavior (substance abuse[12]). One factor not usually considered is class.

Among poor women of the world, sexual abuse is a greater threat. Poverty is more than simply a state of economic being. In many cases, it represents the loss of innocence for girls. As Marcella Althaus-Reid reminds us, the poor girls and young women of the world are easy targets for sexual exploitation. Forced to live in crowded slums in which violence and promiscuity thrive, "girls get raped before puberty or married as adolescents as part of the few available economic transactions offered, except for several forms of prostitution and sexual bondage."[13]

Among the poor, women are more affected by their economic status. Economic deprivation forces women to depend on men for mere survival. As such, they lose control of their own sexuality, at times forced to exchange sex for food—food not just for themselves but, in most cases, for their children. But of course poverty is not limited to the extreme conditions found in undeveloped countries. Even in wealthier industrialized nations, economics that privilege an elite group create sexual danger for those who live on the underside of that wealth. Poverty and limited education possibilities influence high-risk decisions about sexuality, decisions that place women in more vulnerable situations.

No matter whether she is rich or poor, however, the female victim of rape must face the attitudes of people who feel she bears at least some responsibility for the attack. When reading a newspaper report of a rape, the first questions that come to mind may well be, What was she wearing? Was she drinking? What was she doing in his room late at night? Why was she walking down that deserted street alone? A Christian history that has continuously viewed women as the cause for inciting male sexual passion has taught us that men are not expected to control their sexual urges; it is the woman who is responsible. It doesn't help women to be told that their proper response to the threat of rape, as expressed by early

Christian thinkers, is to commit suicide rather than allow the rape. In ancient cultures, as well as in some cultures today, a violated women is expected to restore honor to her family name by killing herself. The fact that she is still alive after being raped proves she did not try hard enough in resisting the attack. Death before dishonor is part of our collective consciousness. Hence, all victims of rape are held somewhat culpable.

Rejecting the Biblical Justification for Sexual Violence

Unfortunately, the biblical text does not lay out a clear moral mandate against rape that can be used by contemporary Christians. As we've already pointed out, in the Bible, rape is a crime against property, an assault against the woman's husband or father as property owner. This is a crime punishable by death. If the woman fails to cry out for help, then she too must be put to death, unless the attack occurs in the countryside far from earshot. If the victim is a virgin, then the rapist reserves the right to pay her father three times the original marriage price in order to marry her (Deuteronomy 22:23–29). The biblical text even provides examples in which mass rape is called for. The most notable example is found in the book of Judges 19–21, in which Israel went to war against the tribe of Benjamin.

After winning the battle, the Israelites swore never to give their daughters to the Benjamites as wives. But with time they came to regret their oath, for they realized that its implementation could mean the loss of one of the twelve tribes. To remedy the situation, the other tribes of Israel, after great bloodshed, captured four hundred virgins from Jabesh-Gilead, giving these possessions as wives to the six hundred surviving Benjamites. Still, this was not enough. More virgins were needed to meet the needs of the Benjamites. So Israel advised the Benjamites to lie in wait in the vineyards of the town of Shiloh; when their young maidens came to dance during the Lord's feast, they could capture wives for themselves and take them back to their land. Hence the kidnapping and subsequent rape of these young maidens finally resolved the dilemma caused by men of honor who swore not to give their possessions (daughters) in marriage to the Benjamites.

The most disturbing aspect of the narrative is the silence of God. Nowhere does the text provide comfort to the abused women or to the reader of the story. Nowhere are we informed of how God viewed these atrocities. No reassuring words demonstrate God's contempt for such actions.

So, what do we do with such stories as we search for a biblically based orthoeros moral code? We can read disturbing passages like these through the gospel mission of Jesus Christ as elucidated in John 10:10: "I came that they may have life, and have it abundantly." Because the Christian faith is rooted in Christ's purpose—to provide life abundantly, both temporal and eternal—any biblical text or interpretation of that text that prevents life from being lived abundantly is anti-Gospel and thus needs to be rejected. Here we follow the lead of Jesus, who taught us to reject biblical passages such as "an eye for an eye and a tooth for a tooth" in favor of the love commandment that undergirds all doctrines and ethics (Matthew 5:38–42).

Sexual Abuse of Children

Any casual reading of the biblical text reveals several incidents of incest—that is, sex among close family members. In fact, if we begin with the assumption that there were only two individuals created by God—Adam and Eve—and that all of humanity today is directly descended from these two humans, then obviously brothers and sisters born to this first couple had to intermarry to start the growth of the population. A literal reading of the creation story means that we are all descendants of incestuous relationships.

Even so, more explicit biblical depictions of incest can be found in the story of Noah, who was sexually taken advantage of by his son Ham (Genesis 9:20–24); Lot, who was made drunk by his two daughters so that they could seduce and become impregnated by him (Genesis 19:30–38); Nabor, Abraham's brother, who married his niece (Genesis 11:29); and Jacob, who married two sisters (Genesis 29:21–30; Leviticus 18:18). We also see that Abraham married his sister (Genesis 20:12), and Amram, Moses' father, married Moses' aunt (Genesis 6:20), in direct violation of the biblical prohibition of marriage between near–blood relatives, as in the case of brothers and sisters (Leviticus 18:6–18). Additionally, Reuben, Israel's oldest son, had intercourse with his father's concubine, his brother's mother (Genesis 35:22), and Absalom, King David's son, also had sex with his father's concubines (2 Samuel 16:21). It should be noted that women as the possession of men became an extension of men; hence to engage in sexual intercourse with your father's possession—as in the case of Reuben and Absalom—is considered an incestuous assault on the father (Leviticus 18:8), usually with the aim of dominating the father through the conquest of his property. Hence this form of incest was the most grievous because it challenged patriarchy. Then there is that incestuous verse in the Song of Songs in which the protagonist of the poem wishes that her beloved was her brother, also nursed on the breasts of her mother, so that when they meet in the streets, they could kiss without fear of impropriety (8:1). Finally, there is the disturbing story of Amnon, King David's son, who rapes his sister Tamar (2 Samuel 13:1–22). What makes this story even more troubling is how Tamar's sexual violation is handled by the men in her life. A conspiracy of silence develops in which Tamar's pain becomes immaterial to how the story unfolds. The tragic story ends with King David weeping—not for Tamar the victim, but for the loss of his sons Amnon (the rapist) and Absalom (who rebelled against his father's authority on the pretense of defending Tamar's honor).

In contrast to these disturbing biblical passages, Jesus pays special attention to protecting children from abuse. According to the Gospel of Mark, Jesus took a child, set him in front of the crowd, and stated that it would be better for anyone who proves to be an obstacle to this child's development to be thrown into the sea with a great millstone around his or her neck (9:37, 42). Although most have interpreted this passage to refer to children (of all ages) within the faith (that is, baby Christians), it is important to note that Jesus couches his comments in a section dealing with sexual immorality—cutting off one's sinful hand or foot and plucking out one's sinful eyes (9:43–48). As pedophilia was an acceptable sexual custom of the Greco-Roman world, children, specifically boys approaching puberty, were highly vulnerable. It would have been in character for Jesus to pay close attention to the smallest and most vulnerable among the crowd, the children.

From 2001 to 2003 in the United States, the following sexual offenses toward children (eighteen years old and younger) were reported to the authorities: 125 cases of forcible fondling (85 of which were on infants less than a year old), 18 cases of sexual assault with an object (13 of which were infants), 34 cases of forcible sodomy (of which 25 were infants), and 61 cases of forcible rape (of which 39 were infants).[14] The problem is more common than what these FBI statistics indicate, usually because such abuses are seldom reported to protect the predatory family member. According to the Children's Bureau of the U.S. Department of Health and Human Services, it is estimated that 90,600 children were sexually abused in the United States in 2003 alone. That comes to about one out of every five hundred children.[15] Let's consider just one of them.

When Justin Berry, a thirteen-year-old, hooked a web camera to his computer, hoping to meet other teenagers online, he instead received instant messages from adult men, all wanting to chat and be his friend. At first they were very complimentary, nonthreatening, and ready to provide Justin with gifts. One "friend" taught Justin how to set up a PayPal account; another showed him how to develop a wish list on sites like amazon.com. Before long, Justin was receiving all sorts of gifts, including sophisticated computer hardware to transmit images that were not so grainy. One day someone offered Justin $50 to sit bare-chested in front of his webcam for three minutes. What the heck, thought Justin, I sit by the pool with my shirt off for nothing. What began as a simple request to remove his shirt progressed to removing his pants, then his undershorts. Soon he was videoing himself showering, masturbating, or having sex with prostitutes. Some of his online friends suggested meeting, which led to sexual molestation. His online "friends" numbered more than 1,500 individuals who paid him hundreds of thousands of dollars. Among these friends were teachers, lawyers, doctors, and businessmen.

Justin is not alone. Most pornographic sites contain photos of naked teenagers. One website in particular claims to feature 140,000 images of "adolescents in cute panties exposing themselves on their teen webcams." One online portal that markets for-pay webcam sites lists about 585 teenager-created sites.[16] According to interviews with a nationally representative sample of 1,501 youths ages ten to seventeen in 1999, approximately one in five children with Internet access was sexually solicited on-line, while one in thirty-three received an aggressive sexual solicitation (that is, the solicitor asked to meet the child, call by phone, or send regular mail, money, or a gift).[17] Some, behind their bedroom's closed doors, only a few feet away from Mom and Dad, become online porn stars with the help of online adult "friends."

Because children and most teenagers lack the maturity to enter into a familial relationship of mutual giving and vulnerability, sex with children is always abusive. Hence, any sexual contact with a minor—regardless of consent or invitation—constitutes abuse. Abuse is not limited to the physical. It can also entail forcing children to watch pornography; taking pictures of children either nude or with sexually explicit overtones; exposing oneself to children; treating the child as an adult in conversations about sex (if mainly to derive pleasure, as opposed to providing education); administering unnecessary enemas or other toilet practices; and frequent "accidental" opening of the bathroom or bedroom door while the child is undressed. The consequence of abusive experiences, whether physical or psychological, is that children may develop into sexually dysfunctional adults, robbed of the chance to have consensual great sex as adults.

There is a common myth that homosexual men are more likely to sexually abuse children than are heterosexual men, a myth that has been proven false.[18] In fact, the typical pedophile is a heterosexual. They are usually not strangers, but relatives or close family friends of the child.[19] It would be a grave error to assume that men who have sex with boys are homosexuals, a mistake presently being made by the

Catholic hierarchy. During 2002, revelations of priests engaging in sex with children—going back several decades in some cases—came to light. More horrifying than the sexual abuse of children was the disclosure that bishops and their dioceses had covered up the abuses to avoid a scandal. Pedophilic priests had been moved from one parish to another, providing them with new opportunities for abusing more children. Similarly, as of the writing of this chapter, we are witnessing the unfolding drama occurring within government, specifically the allegations that for years the Republican leadership for the House of Representatives did nothing while Congressman Mark Foley of Florida sent sexually explicit text messages to underage pages. In both government and the church, public relations had trumped the protection of the little ones.

As part of its response, the Catholic Church and the Religious Right, aligned with the Republican Party, decided to scapegoat gays, even though in the case of pedophilic priests, the church vigorously denies this tactic. Still, in November 2005 the Vatican released a document that will exclude most gay men from the priesthood. Candidates for the priesthood must have overcome homosexual tendencies at least three years prior to ordination as a deacon, making it almost impossible for any man with a basic gay orientation, even though he is celibate, from ever becoming a priest. The only way a gay celibate man can ever be ordained is if he remains closeted.[20]

Seeking Violence to Achieve Spiritual and Sexual Gratification

Reading the ascetic life of saints raises the questions about a possible relationship between seeking God and sadomasochism. Does the quest for physical pain itself become a form of sexual pleasure? The concept of sadomasochism, a composite of both sadism and masochism that developed several centuries after the ascetic life of saints, might help us better understand the ambivalent relationship between agonizing sexual pleasure and agonizing physical pain. Sadism, named after the Marquis de Sade (1740–1814), is the practice of inflicting violence on the other person to stimulate one's own sexual pleasure. Masochism, named after Leopold von Sacher-Masoch (1836–95), is the practice of deriving sexual satisfaction and pleasure from receiving pain and being violently dominated. The underlying assumption of sadomasochism is that constant exposure to pain will eventually become pleasurable. The cultivation of this new stimuli will slowly replace the ability to become sexually aroused by any other means, such as genital stimulation. The infliction or receiving of painful stimulus becomes necessary to experience intense and extreme sexual arousal. Are the extreme cases of self-denial and self-mutilation practiced by the early Christian ascetics in their desire to pursue heavenly pleasure a sanctified form of sadomasochism? If so, we have developed a faith in which the ultimate desire to please God is satisfied through the prolongation of pain.

The Christianity that developed found pleasure in the state of being dominated by God. The pleasure received from sadomasochism is not so much the pain received or inflicted, but rather the knowledge of control over another. In the early Christian ascetics' renunciation of sexual pleasure, did they turn God into a dominatrix? If so, this creates an image of a God who erotically desire humans to self-inflict pain, as though God would take pleasure from humans' repression of pleasure. The idea of God as dominatrix would then seem to justify the repression of those who fall short of the ascetic ideal. Furthermore, because of the intertwining of religion and politics, the sexual repression that developed in Christianity also became manifested in the political arena, as the state became more and more intermingled with the Church. Political repression that brought pain to commoners in this world was offset with the promise of heavenly bliss in the next.

As explored in the third chapter of this book, there was a certain sadomasochism in the religious antipleasure views of the early Christian believers, who linked pain—specifically, the self-deprivation of sexual pleasure—with salvation. Self-denial of the flesh's desires was deemed essential for achieving an elevated spiritual plateau. Even the theology of atonement, developed by Anselm of Canterbury (1033–1109), has a sadomasochistic aspect. According to this theology, God's honor was offended by the sins of humans (specifically original sin), so he had to respond: either by punishing humans (because God is all holy) or by demanding a substitute—a sacrifice to take the place of the offending humans (because God, after all, is merciful). Hence the need for Jesus to die on the cross, shedding his blood to compensate for the iniquity of humans. In other words, God, to satisfy God's vanity, must humiliate, torture, and brutally kill God's child Jesus, rather than the true object of God's wrath, so that God can be placated. The problem with Anselm's theory is that it casts God as the ultimate child abuser who is satisfied by the domination, humiliation, and pain of God's child.

So what about sadomasochism (S&M) in human relationships, in which bondage, humiliation, and physical pain serve as the ultimate aphrodisiac and arousal comes from an overt dominant-subordinate power relationship? Because of the abuse many women face in relationships marked by domestic violence, there is much concern about whether S&M should be considered an acceptable sexual practice. If we insist that the concept of orthoeros offers guidelines rather than rigid rules, then we cannot rule out S&M. If consenting adults in a familial relationship in the privacy of their bedchamber mutually choose to engage in S&M, then, like any other sexual activity, it should occur only in the context of orthoeros code: that is, in a context in which unconditional love is linked to a justice-based relationship. Such sexual acts can only be entered into with an uncoerced agreement to remain safe, sane, and consensual. If S&M becomes a form of role-playing, then clear signals and open communication are required to delineate the boundaries between, on the one hand, play and pleasure, and on the other, violation and pain. Fantasy role-playing can only be acceptable if both parties remain in full and complete control of what is occurring. There's a fine line between mock sexual games and the terrifying feeling of having no control over what is happening to you. When either party loses this type of control, their vulnerability and trust are betrayed.

Sex for Sale

When I was studying and teaching at Temple University, I had a regular commute through the streets of Philadelphia to reach the campus. I still remember how, at Lehigh Avenue and Broad Street, I would always see the same two or three women standing on the corner, waving at passing cars. They did not look like Vivian Ward, the fictitious streetwalker played by Julia Roberts in the movie *Pretty Woman*. Nor did they appear joyful about the work they were doing, as professed by Xaviera Hollander in her memoir *The Happy Hooker: My Story*, later made into a film staring Lynn Redgrave in the title role. The women I observed each day were neither pretty nor happy. They were broken women, empty-eyed, in search of their next meal ticket. It did not take a sharp eye to see they were unkempt and unwashed, showing outward signs of substance and physical abuse. Now I'm not implying that the women at Lehigh and Broad are representative of all prostitutes; still, they do demonstrate the cost to a woman's humanity when she is reduced to a commodity for sale, an item that depreciates with the passage of time and constant use.

Hollywood producers—most of whom are men—would like to perpetuate the fantasy of happy, pretty women who willingly enter the "profession" of prostitution, in part to ease the conscience of the men who pay for their sexual services. But this so-called "victimless crime" is an illusion, shattered by the testimonies of the many women who are forced to sell their bodies to feed themselves and, in many cases, their families.

By Men, For Men

Prostitution can never lead to great sex because it lacks a familial relationship. Prostitution is immoral not because it involves sex, but because it relies on exploiting the vulnerability of women or men who exchange their worth and dignity for a few dollars. Regardless of some who attempt to portray prostitutes as fully liberated women in control of their sexuality, the truth remains that it is a system predominantly run by men to service men and profit men. Prostitutes are treated like objects, created and condemned by the same male-centered society that benefits from their existence. Without a doubt, prostitution is among the most male-dominated and sexually abusive social structures in existence.

Yet the woman who is forced into prostitution for economic reasons is defined and scorned by her sexual activity. She becomes a "whore." But what do we call a Solomon who had seven hundred wives of royal birth and three hundred mistresses (or concubines)? Men who visit "whores" are usually known by more complimentary terms: *player, playboy,* or the neutral *john.* Men are not negatively defined by their sexual activity, and they are seldom held liable for procuring the sexual services of women.

Regardless of society's bias against prostitutes, in Jesus' eyes, they would enter Heaven before the religious leaders of his day who observed God's commands and dictates (Matthew 21:31). Perhaps Jesus understood that these women were the oppressed victims of a so-called victimless crime. This "profession" hardens the prostitute's life, aging her before her time and placing her in dangerous situations in which bodily harm and even death are constant possibilities. Still, these prostitutes provide the solution for the dilemma faced by men wishing to engage in sex without the complication of a relationship with a wife (or mistress). Even regular visits create no legal obligations. Intercourse is reduced to a commercial transaction. The man gets what he wants—sexual climax. And the woman gets what she needs—money to survive.

The Bible distinguishes between secular prostitution and prostitution connected with a religious cult. The biblical text appears to treat secular prostitution as natural and necessary. Among the sexual laws appearing in the Hebrew Bible, none forbid a man from visiting a secular prostitute. For example, when Judah goes to a prostitute (Genesis 38:15–16) or when the Israeli spies do likewise in Jericho (Joshua 2:1) or when Samson spends the night with a prostitute (Judges 16:1–3), these women are not stigmatized. None of the secular prostitutes who serviced these holy men of God are condemned; rather, most of them are portrayed as heroines, with two of them finding a favorable spot in Jesus' genealogy (Matthew 1:3, 5). Yet if a man married and discovered on his wedding night that his bride was not a virgin, then he had the right to have her stoned for having "played the harlot in her father's house" (Deuteronomy 22:21). What made prostitution wrong in the Hebrew Bible was not the exchange of money for the chance to copulate, but rather the removal of intercourse from the social system that reduced women to property in a hierarchical male-centered power structure.[21]

A Detestable Thing

It seems that the only biblical text condemning prostitution appears where the practice is linked to temple worship. Remember, Yahweh's principal nemeses were the male fertility god Baal and the female god Asherah. Priests of these fertility gods practiced what is called an imitative or homeopathic magic.[22] The rituals practiced by these priests, consecrated to fertility gods, were based on the law of similarity, which maintained that like produces like. Because they thought that an effect resembled its cause, these priests believed that they could produce any desired effect merely by imitating it. The ritual, intended to create fecundity for crops and livestock, consisted of sexual acts by and with temple prostitutes in the sanctuary in imitation of what they hoped to accomplish in the fields. Both male and female served as temple prostitutes. Despite their important role in ensuring a good harvest, the temple prostitutes were banned from God's people as a "detestable thing," occupying the lowest level of social status (Deuteronomy 23:19).

None of Yahweh's priests could marry a prostitute (Leviticus 21:7), and if one of the priest's daughters were to become a prostitute, her father was obligated to burn her alive (Leviticus 21:9). Yet Jesus' dealings with prostitutes seem to have been influenced by the book of Proverbs. Although the proverbs look down on the prostitutes as the antithesis of wisdom (Proverbs 7), the condemnation is mainly reserved for the man that hires her services. It is he who is the fool, frittering away his wealth (Proverbs 29:3). Consequently, Jesus was not afraid to associate with women with bad reputations (Luke 7:36–50) and to use prostitutes as positive examples for religious leaders to emulate (Matthew 21:31). It seems Jesus recognized that in a patriarchal social order in which a woman's primary means of survival is to surrender to the authority of a father, husband, or son, the woman without a man has little choice but to earn her meals by selling her body. It is not the woman who is to blame, but the men who designed the social structures that prevent her from surviving apart from a man. They create the circumstances that force women to turn to prostitution, then take advantage of her situation by using her services.

The New Testament advises us to "flee from harlotry" (1 Corinthians 6:18). When the council of apostles in Jerusalem decided on the required obligations for converting Gentiles, they called on them to abstain from anything polluted by idols, from *porneia,* from the meat of strangled animals, and from blood (Acts 15:20). *Porneia* is a Greek term that originally meant consorting with prostitutes. Could its proximity to "anything polluted to idols" be an overall prohibition of participating in foreign cults that involved temple prostitution? One is left wondering if the translation of this term throughout the New Testament as "sexual immorality" or "fornication" should be replaced by a more accurate translation: as a prohibition of participating in cultic worship involving temple prostitutes rather than secular prostitution. Regardless, most biblical translators and commentators have come to accept the term as a reference to sexual immorality in general.

When Paul gets around to specifically condemning prostitution, he does so by equating it to adultery (1 Corinthians 6:9). The author of Hebrews (13:4) does likewise. In an interesting twist, Paul appeals to reason by claiming that a Christian who becomes one with a prostitute makes Jesus one with a prostitute (1 Corinthians 6:15–17). After all, if we are one with Christ and become one with a prostitute, doesn't that makes Christ one with the prostitute? Unfortunately, his point has been interpreted to underscore the unworthiness of prostitutes and the horror of their uniting with Christ. Yet such an interpretation contradicts Jesus' positive references to and encounters with prostitutes. Perhaps it is not the prostitute who causes the defilement but the Christian male who unites with her. This male Christian becomes defiled for objectifying the woman, using her as a commodity. It is not the prostitute who is unworthy to be connected with Christ, but the Christian male who secures her services who is unworthy. If indeed Christ *is* "the least of these," then Christ is the prostitute—the used, and abused woman of today's society. Because the prostitute is among today's crucified people—that is, her life, dreams, hopes, worth, and dignity are crucified so that men can be saved through the breaking of her body—she is Christ in the here and now. Christ is found not in the perpetrator, but rather in the perpetrator's victims.

A Crucial Social Function

Prostitution was tolerated as a lawful immorality throughout most of Christian history because it was seen as protecting virtuous Christian wives from the lustful demands of their husbands and maintaining harmony in the political sphere. Its absence, it was believed, would disrupt society, casting it into a debauched chaos. Early Roman moralists, such as Cato the Censor, Cicero, and Seneca, regarded prostitution as necessary because it prevented men from breaking up the marriages of others. During the Crusades, prostitution increased. Pious warriors for the Lord were not expected to abstain from intercourse just because they were away from their wives. According to calculations kept by the Templars (the Order responsible for keeping records of the Crusades), thirteen thousand prostitutes were needed in one year alone just to satisfy the desires of these saintly warriors.[23] St. Thomas Aquinas—relying on the writings of Augustine, who urged husbands to go to prostitutes rather than commit adultery (with another man's woman)[24]—believed that prostitution, like a sewer, served a crucial social function. Besides relieving the wife from her husband's sexual advances, it was believed to be a safety valve to reduce sodomy, adultery, rape, incest, and domestic violence.[25] In Aquinas's mind it was better to exchange money for sex than to relieve sexual "lust" within a marriage.

The Curia—an ensemble of ministries responsible for assisting the Pope in governing the Catholic Church—partially financed the building of St. Peter's Cathedral in the Vatican through a tax on prostitution. The sum collected was four times more than what Pope Leo X expected to collect from the sale of indulgences in Germany. Yet it is the sale of indulgences that is most remembered as the main means for the construction of St. Peter.[26] History seems to have forgotten that the cathedral was partially built on the backs of women—or more accurately stated, women on their backs. With the coming of the Protestant Reformation, church authorities began to focus on prostitution as an aspect of adultery. Martin Luther used harsh comments when referring to both adulterers and prostitutes. He attempted to eradicate prostitution, but eventually left the brothels alone, concerned that their closure might create social unrest.

Sex Slavery in the Twenty-First Century

In October 2000, a businessman from California's Silicon Valley was charged in a scheme to bring a thirteen-year-old Vietnamese girl to the United States to be his sex slave. Although Michael Rostoker, president and chief executive of a San Jose electronics firm, pled not guilty, he was convicted in 2003 for agreeing to pay the girl's family $150,000. His punishment: fifteen months in a federal prison. In a culture in which women continue to be commodified, the idea of purchasing a woman, for a few hours or for a lifetime, should not appear too strange to us.[27]

When we think of sexual slavery, we usually imagine it to be a horrible practice of the distant past, abolished in the nineteenth century along with all other forms of slavery. We might even be reminded of the patriarch of our faith, Abraham, who had sex with his wife's slave girl Hagar (Genesis 16:3). However, sexual slavery is not so rare in our modern times. Sexual slavery is a form of forced prostitution; in the United States and other industrialized nations it victimizes immigrants, often those from Asian countries. Of the 600,000 to 800,000 humans entrapped into sexual slavery worldwide, 80 percent are female and up to 50 percent are children. It is estimated that 14,500 to 17,500 foreign nationals are trafficked to the United States each year. According to the FBI, traffickers in human flesh pocket $9 to $10 billion in annual profits.[28] Women from impoverished nations are either kidnapped or promised jobs in First World nations, only to be forced into prostitution once they arrive. Others participate in "legal" mail-order bride schemes, lured and enticed by the glittering promise of First World nations. Those who are promised jobs usually sign a contract for work in their country of origin, thus enabling the traffickers to clear them through customs without question. But once they arrive, the "owners" of these women and children usually confiscate their passports, airline tickets, and meager financial resources, making the slave completely reliant on the owner. The same holds true for mail-order brides, who are ripe for abuse due to the barriers they face: limited financial resources, enforced isolation, elimination of access to social agencies, ignorance of their legal and immigration rights, and an overall imbalanced relationship in which the bride's immigration status is dependent on her husband.

But sexual slavery is not limited to immigrants; many are enslaved in their own countries. According to a University of Pennsylvania study, hundreds of thousands of U.S. citizens run a high risk of being trafficked in the United States, three hundred thousand of them as child prostitutes. Other organizations have estimated this number to be as high as eight hundred thousand. Of the 1.6 million children who run away from home each year, approximately 40,000 of them will have some type of involvement in or brush with sexual trafficking. The typical age range of the children first used in prostitution is eleven to fourteen, and some are as young as nine.[29]

Another form of sexual slavery is tied to the sex tourism that draws men and women from industrialized nations to developing countries. And sex slavery flourishes in places where the U.S. army is stationed. Take the example of South Korea, where hundreds of trafficked women, mostly from former Soviet bloc countries and the Philippines, are forced to work as prostitutes in bars patronized by American servicemen.[30] Sex slavery flourishes because of market demand—mainly male sex buyers creating a profitable incentive for traffickers to meet that demand. Yet the women and children ensnared in this lucrative "business" cry out to be rescued. According to field research done in nine countries, 89 percent of those forced into prostitution want to escape.[31]

Sexual Images for Sale

A hypersexualized media and a violent porn industry serve as backdrop for any discourse on sexual abuses and crimes. Still, many would defend the graphic display of sexual images, including violent sexual images, as an expression of free speech or creative art. But is there a line between art and pornography? Or is any nakedness immoral, requiring covering up? Michelangelo labored seven years over his masterpiece *The Last Judgment,* situated behind the altar of the Sistine Chapel. On its unveiling, a collective gasp was heard throughout the audience, for all the figures, including Jesus and his virgin mother, were naked. Quickly, a concerted campaign sprang up to remove the offensive artwork, led by Pietro Aretino. He even tried blackmailing the sixty-plus-year-old Michaelangelo about his amorous relationship with the handsome young Tommaso di Cavalieri. When Cardinal Carafa ascended to the papacy as Paul IV in 1555, he ordered the fresco's removal. But this would have required destroying it, and the protest from the many artists of the Renaissance forced him to reconsider. He finally decided to hire one of Michelangelo's students, Daniele de Volterra, to paint clothes on the offending figures. He became known as *Il Braghettone,* the Breeches-Maker.

Breeches-makers have existed throughout history. One of the most recent breeches-makers is former U.S. Attorney General John Ashcroft. Among his first official acts on being appointed was to hang blue drapes in front of a bare-bosomed Art Deco statue of Justice in the Justice Department's lobby.

But why would the image of the nude body be considered evil, dirty, or sinful? Is pornography's aim to excite and titillate wrong? After all, the biblical text is silent about the morality of erotic literature—a possible indication of its permissibility. In fact, the Song of Songs serves as an example of erotic literature found in the biblical text. The issue to consider is not whether viewing pictures of naked people is moral; rather, the real question revolves around the objectification of the human body—more often than not, the female body. In light of Jesus' switch from a purity code based on the physical to a code based on intent, it is important to explore the intent of art containing nude bodies and the consequences of that art.

We begin by realizing that there is not one form of pornography. Pornography is a multifarious phenomenon of which certain elements are incongruent with the hope and goal of achieving great sex. As is true for the actual act of intercourse, pornography that focuses on sexual self-gratification as its final goal (as opposed to a familial experience), especially at the expense, abuse, or degradation of another (usually women and children) is unjust. Erotic literature or art that celebrates the joy of orthoerotic sex is not immoral; what proves problematic is the emphasis on the erotic divorced from the love-based familial.

Pornography can be understood as any verbal or pictorial medium that portrays a sexually explicit subordination. This subordination occurs when a subject is dehumanized as an object, thing, or commodity; when the subject is portrayed as enjoying pain or humiliation or being raped; when the subject is depicted mutilated, bruised, in pain, hurt, or in bondage, or in a position of submission or servility; when body parts are displayed so as to represent the person as only those parts, void of personhood and subjectivity; when subjects are displayed being penetrated by objects or animals; when sex is juxtaposed with scenes of subjects in filth, or being injured and tortured. Though the vast majority of subjects are women, there is also pornography that depicts children, men, and transsexuals.[32]

Pornography is a multibillion-dollar industry. The shame felt by the previous generation of being seen going into an adult theater has been eliminated, thanks to videotapes and DVDs, cable, and the Internet. We now have access to pornographic material from the privacy of our homes. Even cell phones, with their advances in technology to deliver full-motion video, are seen as a lucrative new means of pornographic distribution. Just as ring tones can now be purchased and downloaded (a $453 million business in 2005), so too can pornographic images. Xobile, which started in April 2005, charges 44 cents to watch a two-minute video clip. The company is growing at a rate of six thousand new customers a month.[33]

Sex sells. It sells by exploiting the most powerful sexual organ in the human body—the brain, which is capable of conjuring up a sexual fantasy world. It sells by exploiting those who become addicted to pornographic material, probably fueled by centuries of religious training that portrayed sex as something dirty, evil, and wicked. Everything from clothes to deodorant, from cars to pasta, taps into this sexual fantasy world, promising that their product will get you more sex. But sex is not only used to sell products. Sex is profitable in and of itself. In 2004, Americans spent somewhere around $10 billion on adult entertainment, more than was spent on Hollywood's box-office receipts of almost $9 billion in 2005. Over the last generation, pornography—once a business operated out of seedy storefronts and adult theaters—has gained mainstream acceptance, thanks in part to leading porn divas like Jenna Jameson. Consumer demand is so strong that it has seduced some of America's biggest brand names, which are now making millions selling erotica to America. In 2002, Comcast, the nation's largest cable company, reported $50 million from adult programming. Big hotel companies like Hilton, Marriott, Sheraton, Hyatt, and Holiday Inn report that 70 percent of their in-room profits are derived through their in-room pay-per-view television systems, a service used by over 50 percent of their guests.[34]

What then are the consequences of pornography? Although social science lacks sufficiently sophisticated techniques and tools to definitively prove what damage, if any, can be caused by pornography, concerns about the effects of pornography persist. A recent survey concerning the sexual health of the family concluded that "a pornographic media culture may contribute to unrealistic expectations of what [men's] future soul mate should look like. Influenced by the sexy images of young women on MTV, the Internet, and the runway in televised Victoria's Secret specials, men may be putting off marriage to their current girlfriend in the hopes that they will eventually find a combination 'soul mate/babe.'"[35] Additionally, pornographic material sends the message, especially to youth, that "everyone except you is doing it," which is in direct conflict with the official societal stance, "just say no." Another concern is the increase of plastic surgery on private parts. Comparing oneself to the images on the screen has led some men to surgically lengthen their penises. Women have also gone under the knife for procedures to nip the inner labia, plump the outer labia, or simply tighten the vagina. Some have gone so far as restoring the hymen, all in the hope of increasing her partner's sexual pleasure.

Probably the major concern about pornography is the objectification of women and men (and in many cases children). The object of the one gazing is portrayed as being devoid of all characteristics that define their personhood. The women (usually it's women) on the pornographic screen have no dreams or aspirations, no wants or desires, except one: to bring pleasure to a man. They are simply reduced to a collection of digitally enhanced body parts. They are no more than a pair of long legs, empty eyes, a tight rear end, and large breasts that never sag. One set of body parts is no more important than another set, assuming of course that these parts are equally young, tan, and trim. These cyber-women do not exist in the real world. They are simply masturbatory objects. These women are presented as easily aroused and eager for sex with anyone who happens to be at hand. One is left wondering how these images created about promiscuous women, mainly by men, affect the society's perception of and attitude toward women. Flesh-and-blood women who do not measure up to the air-brushed beauties laid out in the Victoria's Secret catalogue, or whose body proportions fall short of the Barbie-doll ideal, are deemed undesirable.

A fantasy world is created in which accidental meetings turn into sexual encounters, in which sexual conquest is enjoyed by the prey as much as by the hunter. In which "no" really means try harder and you'll get what you want. In which sexually transmitted diseases or the possibility of pregnancy do not exist. This fantasy world stresses power over another rather than sharing power with an intimate.

The issue here is not whether pornography should be censored, but whether the current discussion about the public manifestation of erotica should continue to be controlled by and for men for the sole end of profit. Only when those who seek great sex have joined the discussion can we hope to address all aspects of the issue.

Pornographic Violence

One of America's most popular television series, *CSI*, began its January 2005 episode with the severed head of a woman tucked into a newspaper sales box. As the show progressed, her decapitation was shown to an estimated twenty-eight million viewers through the cinematic device known as the flashback. Although brutal depictions of male victims also exist, women are usually the victims of the more graphic forms of violence. It appears that violence against women has become a popular plot for family entertainment. Although some of us still may be disturbed that the severing of a woman's head is common fare for the general primetime viewing audience, we may not be aware that the darker corners of the World Wide Web are filled with images of forced rape, gruesome female torture and mutilation, and the sexual humiliation of women.

It is one thing to gaze at pictures of naked bodies; it is quite another when explicit sex is paired with explicit violence. The use of violence in pornographic literature in the form of "bondage" and "discipline" conveys the false message that for sex to be good, it must contain an element of pain. The same woman who fights off her sexual attacker in one scene is in the next enjoying the afterglow of sexual ecstasy. A "victim" enjoying her assault contributes to the mythology that (1) women secretly enjoy being forcibly taken against their will, and (2) women are really asking for it. It would be simplistic to propose a direct cause and effect between consuming pornographic violence and committing acts of sexual violence; human nature is far too complex for such reductionist explanations. Yet it would be naive to assume that such connections do not exist. The false reality created in the small screen does influence viewers' perceptions and world views. Studies seem to indicate that exposure to sexual violence contributes to the acceptance of both the "rape myth" (that women secretly want to be physically taken and ravished), and violence in relationships.

Could it be that pornographic violence reinforces and socializes patterns of domination? Several studies conducted by the American Psychological Association, the American Psychiatric Association, and the National Institutes of Mental Health agree that viewing violence desensitizes people to cruelty, alters perceptions of reality, and increases aggressive behavior. Further studies indicate that when men view scenes of violence that are linked to sex, their perception of sexual reality is distorted, their attraction for comparatively less exciting partners is decreased, they are primed to perceive women in sexual terms, they perceive sexual aggression as appearing less serious, and they are more prone to the possibility of inflicting sexual violence.[36]

One disturbing pattern in the Hebrew Bible has unfortunately continued in some form to the present day. In biblical times, it was common practice for one faction to kill the men of the other faction, steal their possessions, and take their women for sexual amusement, exportation, and servitude. This linking of the violence of war with sexual violence against women has found a new expression in our modern world, specifically in the U.S. war in Iraq.

Consider Chris Wilson, a twenty-seven-year-old entrepreneur who runs an amateur porn site. He created the site in 2004 by asking men to post naked photos of their wives or girlfriends. Videos can also be posted showing them engaging in different lascivious acts. U.S. soldiers serving overseas became major clients of the site. Wilson offered these soldiers free membership in his site in exchange for pictures depicting daily life in Iraq or Afghanistan.

It's true that the vast majority of these pictures and videos are from the battlefield. They include photos of a captured Saddam Hussein, videos of Iraqi soldiers being trained, one U.S. soldier showing off a bullet wound to his shoulder, companies of male and female soldiers coping with military routines, and various candid shots of everyday street life. Some of the photos are of naked female soldiers stationed in Iraq posed with machine guns or grenades. It was these photos of naked female soldiers that led the Pentagon to investigate the site in October 2004. They then attempted to block their personnel's access to the site.[37]

Also among the photos are gruesome pictures of the mutilated victims of war, many of whom were blown apart or burned, in direct violation of the First Protocol of the Geneva Convention. One photo shows a dead Iraqi with his intestines hanging from open wounds. Another is of a man sitting in a car with his head blown off. Several of the grisly photos are of severed body parts: a foot, an arm, a head. Still another shows a man's head with his brains seeping out of a head wound. In some of the photos and videos, American soldiers in uniform are laughing and joking next to the corpse. These pictures are violent, gory, brutal, and disturbing, and often accompanied by flippant and crude comments made by those who posted them. Most comments joyfully justify the horrific image. One photo of charred remains appears under the headline "Cooked Iraqi"; one of the postings is simply the words "Burn baby, burn!" Juxtaposed under these pictures are links to videos showing women engaged in explicit sex.

On September 27, 2005, the army began a preliminary inquiry to investigate the gruesome photos and the gore-for-porn arrangement between U.S. soldiers and Wilson's site. Within twenty-four hours the inquiry concluded that no felony had occurred. They claimed a failure to find evidence proving that the graphic photos of dead Iraqis were taken by American military personnel.[38] It would appear that disciplinary action is more likely to be taken when naked pictures of female soldiers are posted on the web than when the photos are of gory, disfigured corpses of Iraqis.

Whether on the battlefield or in the movie house, violence is condoned, but sex must be covered up. A feature film that violently degrades women can receive a PG or PG-13 rating as long as it does not show frontal nudity. But if nudity is shown, it is rated R: Restricted, for the young who must be protected from such images. The societal message is clear: a naked woman being slashed to death by a knife is fine for the youth to watch as long as no breasts are shown. But if breasts do make it onto the screen, then the scene must be restricted for mature audiences. Just compare the uproar that followed Janet Jackson's breast-baring stunt during the 2004 Super Bowl half-time show with the deafening silence in response to the portrayal of violence against women depicted in most television dramas. Frankly, I would rather have my children see breasts naturally presented than see a knife slashing through covered-up breasts.

And therein lies the problem with the debate on pornography. For the Religious Right, pornography is wrong because it is sexual. But if sex is great and ordained by God, how then can it be wrong? It is not the naked body revealed that is obscene, but rather the dehumanization of that body. Pornography is wrong because of its ever-increasing connection to violence and its degradation and objectification of women and children.

Christianity has failed to provide an alternative to pornographic violence, due mainly to its own complicity. Christianity can be accused of incorporating the basic theoretical patterns of violence. A spirituality of domination, in which the faithful find joy and fulfillment in submission, is the norm advocated. I wonder how our sexuality would be manifested if we were to instead celebrate relationships based on a spirituality of mutuality, cooperation, and companionship, rather than on patriarchy.

Hope for Redemption?

Can there still be hope after the familial relationship is brutally betrayed, after vulnerability is shattered, after the trust implicit in mutual giving is taken advantage of? The very message of Jesus, the message of the Gospel, is one of liberation—a liberation that at times is procured through subversion. This subversive reading of the scriptures can provide a means by which to overcome the sexual abusive structures in which individuals find themselves.

A glance at Jesus' genealogy reveals an interesting set of ancestors: women, some of whom were illegal aliens. What's so extraordinary about including these women in Jesus' genealogy? Their inclusion runs contrary to the patriarchal assumption that only men can beget men.

Among the women featured is the Canaanite Tamar, who had to trick her father-in-law Judah so that he could meet his obligation of caring for her. She played the prostitute and had intercourse with her father-in-law to obtain the levirate right of siring a child in the name of her dead husband (Genesis 38). Next, there is Rahab, the Canaanite prostitute of Jericho, who used her trade as cover to hide the Israeli spies. In so doing, she made a preferential option for the Israelites and stood against her own people, causing their death and destruction (Joshua 2). Another of Jesus' ancestors is the Moab Ruth, who violated modern Christian sensitivities and engaged in premarital sex with Boaz to ensure her financial future (Ruth 3). She is followed by Bathsheba, who was raped by King David. To make matters worse, her husband was murdered by the king to cover up his sexual misconduct (2 Samuel:11). And finally there is Mary, the mother of Jesus, whose unusual matter of becoming impregnated raised an enduring suspicion of adultery.

All these women share a common bond: they survive acts or reputations of sexual immorality, which for at least two—Tamar and Bathsheba—come at the hands of sexual predators. But before rejoicing at how the liberating message of Christ can bring redemption to those under the suspicion of sexual misconduct, we are forced to deal with those passages in which no sign of redemption seems to be present. In *Texts of Terror,* Phyllis Trible reexamines four women's narratives in which redemption does not appear. We are presented with women like Hagar, the Egyptian slave girl who was exploited by her master Sarah and forced to have sex with Abraham. She was finally cast away, left to die in the desert. Her salvation came not because she found favor in God's eyes but on account of her son Ishmael (Genesis 16:1–16; 21:9–21). Then there is Tamar, the daughter of King David, who was violently raped by her brother (2 Samuel 13:1–22). We are also presented with an unnamed concubine who was gang-raped all night only to be slaughtered by her owner the next morning and dismembered into twelve pieces (Judges 19:1–30). And finally, we are presented with Jephthah's daughter, who was sacrificed by her father as an offering based on a foolish vow he had made. We cannot help but wonder why God provided a ram to take Isaac's place when he was about to be sacrificed (Genesis 22:11–14), but no ram was offered for Jephthah's daughter (Judges 11:29–40).

What is most troubling about these biblical narratives is God's silence. Nowhere in the text do we find confirmation that God is angered, upset, concerned, or incensed about the violence these women faced. Nowhere does God shed a tear over their fate. Their inclusion in the biblical narrative raises disturbing questions about God. Or are the authors of these texts so steeped in patriarchy that their misogynistic views are simply projected onto the deity? Because men don't care about the condition women find themselves in, then God also doesn't care. To find redemption, one is forced to read into the Bible one's own theology of hope and liberation. Aware that the text itself is silent concerning the outrage of the sexual violence faced by these biblical women (and, by extension, millions of women today who also face sexual violence), we are forced to reread the text with an eye toward solidarity. Even though these biblical victims of sexual violence preceded the Christ event, and even though the promise of some future Messiah thousands of years away would have provided little comfort to these women in the midst of their abuse, still the message of the Gospel is that all the victims of sexual predators—present and future—are Christ crucified. Christ crucifixion is not an act of substitution for our sins, as posited by Anselm of Canterbury; rather, it is an act of solidarity in our unjust suffering.

The victims of sexual abuse are among today's crucified people. They can find solidarity in a Christ who was also abused, beaten, broken, tortured, and humiliated. And God was silent during Christ's abuse, leading him to cry out, asking why God had abandoned him (Matthew 15:34)—just as God was silent during the sexual abuse of these five biblical women, and as God appears to be silent during the abuse of so many today.

The responsibility we are given, as daunting as it may appear, is to dismantle the patriarchal structures that foster sexual abuse. The hope we are given, as fleeting as it may appear, is that there is a resurrection after crucifixion. Is this glimmer of hope enough? Only time, love, liberation, and redemption will tell.

NOTES

Preface

1. Peter Kiefer, "Berlusconi Chastity Countdown," *New York Times,* January 31, 2006.
2. Michel Foucault, *The History of Sexuality,* Vol. 1, trans. by Robert Hurley (New York: Vintage Books, 1978), 156.

Introduction

1. Luis G. Pedraja, "Trinity," in *Handbook of U.S. Theologies of Liberation,* ed. by Miguel A. De La Torre (St. Louis: Chalice Press, 2004), 53.

Chapter 1, Liberating the Female Body

1. Becky S. Drury and Frances B. O'Connor, *The Female Face in Patriarchy: Oppression as Culture* (East Lansing: Michigan State University Press, 1999), 61.
2. "Table Talk," *Weimarer Ausgabe,* II:1975.
3. www.mediamatters.org.
4. See Paul Ricoeur, *Interpretation Theory: Discourse and the Surplus of Meaning* (Fort Worth: Texas Christian University Press, 1976), and Paul Tillich, *Theology of Culture* (Oxford: Oxford University Press, 1959).
5. Mary Daly, *Beyond God the Father: Toward a Philosophy of Women's Liberation* (Boston: Beacon, 1973), 19.
6. Augustine *On the Trinity* XII:7:10.
7. Augustine *The Literal Meaning of Genesis* IX:5:9.
8. Thomas Aquinas *Summa Theologica* I:92:1.
9. Martin Luther, "On Married Life," *Weimarer Ausgabe* X:2
10. Aristotle *On the Generation of Animals* I:21.
11. Aquinas *Summa Theologiae* II:2:26.

12. Augustine *On Continence* I:23.

13. Chrysostom, Homily 17, *Homilies on Genesis* 36.

14. Luther, Sermon on the Second Sunday after Epiphany, *Weimarer Ausgabe*.

15. Luther, "Lectures on Genesis," *Luther's Work* I.

16. Aquinas *Summa Theologica* 1:92:1.

17. Tertullian *The Apparel of Women* I:1:2.

18. St. Ambrose *Paradise* 4:24.

19. Luther, "Table Talk," *Weimarer Ausgabe* I:1046.

20. Augustine *On the Grace of Christ and Original Sin* 2:41.

21. John Calvin *Commentaries on the First Book of Moses Called Genesis* 1.2.18.

22. Luther, On Marriage Matters, *Luther's Work* XLVI.

23. Luther, Lectures on Genesis, *Luther's Work* I.

24. Julian of Norwich *Revelations of Divine Love: The Shorter Version* VI.

25. Jerome *Commentary on Ephesians* V, 3:5.

26. Karen Jo Torjessen, *When Women Were Priests: Women's Leadership in the Early Church and the Scandal of Their Subordination in the Rise of Christianity* (New York: Harper San Francisco, 1995), 2, 6–7, 11, 33.

27. Augustine *About Heresies* 1:17.

28. James C. Dobson, *Straight Talk to Men and Their Wives* (Waco, TX: Proven Word, 1980), 64.

29. Tony Brown, quoted in John Swomley, "Promises We Don't Want Kept," *The Humanist*, Vol. 56, No. 1 (January–February 1996): 35.

30. Tim and Beverly LaHaye, *The Act of Marriage: The Beauty of Sexual Love* (Grand Rapids: Zondervan, 1978), 34.

31. "The Family," *Baptist Faith and Message*, XVIII.

32. Maralee Schwartz and Kenneth J. Cooper, "Equal Rights Initiative in Iowa Attacked," *Washington Post*, August 23, 1992.

33. Mimi Hall, "Pat Buchanan's Strong Words Get Second Look," *USA Today*, February 22, 1996.

34. Vivek Chaudhary, "Vicar Opposing Women Priests says 'Burn Bitches,'" *Guardian* (London), March 9, 1994.

35. Elisabeth Schüssler Fiorenza, *But She Said: Feminist Practices of Biblical Interpretation* (Boston: Beacon Press, 1992), 64–65.

36. De La Torre, *Reading the Bible from the Margins,* 125–27.

Chapter 2, Liberating the Body of Color

1. Anthony Pagden, *The Fall of Natural Man: The American Indian and the Origins of Comparative Ethnology* (Cambridge: Cambridge University Press, 1982), 174–75.

2. James Baldwin, "Going to Meet the Man," *Going to Meet the Man* (New York: Dell, 1965), 210.

3. Frantz Fanon, *Black Skin, White Masks* (New York: Grove Press, 1967), 63.

4. James R. Gaines, "To Our Readers," *Time,* Vol. 143, No. 27 (July 4, 1994): 4.

5. "Atwater Apologizes for '88 Remark about Dukakis: Bush Campaign Chief Linked Convicted Murderer Willie Horton, Democratic Candidate," *Washington Post,* January 13, 1991.

6. Robin Toner, "In Tight Senate Race, Attack Ad on Black Candidate Stirs Furor," *New York Times*, October 26, 2006.

7. Jacques Lacan, *Écrits: A Selection,* trans. by Alan Sheridan (New York: Norton, 1977), 1–7.

8. Elizabeth Grosz, *Jacques Lacan: A Feminist Interpretation* (London: Routledge, 1990), 115–45.

9. http://www.defendcoloradonow.org/images/wakeup_colorado.jpg.

10. *The Journal of Christopher Columbus,* trans. by Cecil Jane (New York: Potter, 1960), 22–24.

11. Ibid., 16.

12. Tzvetan Todorov, *The Conquest of America: The Question of the Other,* trans. by Richard Howard (New York: Harper & Row, 1984), 48–49.

13. Peter Mason, *Deconstructing America: Representations of the Others* (New York: Routledge, 1990), 56–57.

14. Mason, 67, 173.

15. Luis N. Rivera Pagán, *A Violent Evangelism: The Political and Religious Conquest of the Americas* (Louisville: Westminster/John Knox Press, 1992), 135.

16. bell hooks, *Ain't I a Woman: Black Women and Feminism* (Boston: South End Press, 1981), 28–29.

17. Joe Holley and Christian Swezey, "Rape Accusation Against Lacrosse Players Roils Duke," *Washington Post,* March 30, 2006.

18. U.S. Constitution, 1:2.

19. Esteban Montejo, *The Autobiography of a Runaway Slave,* ed. by Miguel Barnet, trans. by Jocasta Innes (New York: Pantheon Books, 1968), 42.

20. Frantz Fanon, *Black Skin, White Masks,* trans. by Charles Lam Markmann (New York: Grove Press, 1967), 157–59, 170.

21. Delores S. Williams, *Sisters in the Wilderness: The Challenge of Womanist God-Talk* (Maryknoll, NY: Orbis Books, 1993), 1–33.

Chapter 3, The Body and Its Pleasures

1. Clement of Alexandria *Christ the Educator* II:10:95.

2. St. Jerome, Letter CCIII to Eustochium, 15:1.

3. "Groups Object to Government Web Site about Sex Issues," *New York Times,* April 3, 2005.

4. Tertullian *To His Wife* I:4.

5. Steven Greenhouse, "Police Suspect Arson in fire at Paris Theater," *New York Times,* October 25, 1988.

6. Athanasius *The Life of Anthony* 7:2.

7. Clement *Christ the Educator* II:10:97–98.

8. Tertullian *On Monogamy* I:3.

9. Augustine *The Literal Meaning of Genesis* IX:7:12.

10. Augustine *The City of God* 14:23–24.

11. Augustine *Soliloquies* I:10:17.

12. Augustine *Our Lord's Sermon on the Mount* I:15:41.

13. Jerome Epistle XLVIII to Pammachius 14.

14. Jerome Epistle XXII to Eustochium 22:7.

15. Pope Gregory *Pastoral Care* III:27:28.

16. Pope Gregory Epistle XI to Brunichild, Queen of the Franks.

17. Pope Gregory *Dialogues* 2:2.

18. Pope Benedict XVI *Deus Caritas Est* (*God Is Love*) I:5.

19. Augustine *Confessions* VI:12:21.

20. Augustine *The City of God* XIV:19, 21.

21. Michel Foucault, *Religion and Culture: Michel Foucault,* ed. by Jeremy R. Carrette (New York: Routledge, 1999), 186.

22. Mishnah "Tractate Yadayim" 3:5.

23. Ramban, Iggeret HaKodesh, 2.

24. Carey Ellen Walsh, *Exquisite Desire: Religion, the Erotic, and the Song of Songs* (Minneapolis: Fortress Press, 2000), 65, 88.

25. Ibid., 124–25, 130.

26. Ibid., 66, 101.

27. Ibid., 86, 106–09, 125, 128.

28. Michael Le Page, "Orgasms: a Real 'Turn-off' for Women," *New Scientist* No. 2505 (June 25, 2005): 14.

29. Meredith McGuire, *Religion: The Social Context* (Belmont, CA: Wadsworth Publishing Company, 1997), 66.

30. Juan de la Cruz *The Spiritual Canticle* 23, 27.

31. De la Cruz *Ascent of Mount Carmel* 1:4:3–4.

32. *The Spiritual Canticle* 13:2.

33. *Ascent of Mount Carmel* 2:32:2.

34. Teresa de Ávila, *Life of St. Teresa,* trans by J. M. Cohen (Harmondsworth, UK: Penguin, 1957), 210.

35. *Life of St. Teresa,* 27.

36. Miguel A. De La Torre, *Doing Christian Ethics from the Margins* (Maryknoll, NY: Orbis Books, 2004), 36–37.

Chapter 4, A Sexual Ethics for the Body

1. Augustine *Soliloquies* I:10:17.

2. Beverly LaHaye, *The Spirit-Controlled Woman* (Irvine, CA: Harvest House, 1976), 71.

3. Hannah Brueckner and Peter S. Bearman, "After the Promise: The STD Consequences of Adolescent Virginity Pledges," *Journal of Adolescent Health,* Vol. 36 (April 2005): 271–78.

4. James B. Nelson, *Embodiment: An Approach to Sexuality and Christian Theology* (Minneapolis: Augsburg, 1978), 17.

5. Foucault, *The History of Sexuality* (1978), 5.

6. Pope Benedict XVI *God Is Love* I:6.

7. Marvin M. Ellison, *Erotic Justice: A Liberating Ethics of Sexuality* (Louisville: Westminster John Knox Press, 1996), 12.

8. Augustine *City of God* XIV:18.

9. Michel Foucault, *Discipline and Punish: The Birth of the Prison,* trans. by Alan Sheridan (New York: Vintage Books, 1995), 202–03.

10. Foucault, *The Foucault Reader,* 60–61; Foucault, *History of Sexuality,* 93–101.

Chapter 5, Great Sex in Marriage

1. Justin the Martyr *The First Apology* 15.

2. "First-person: Deliberate Childlessness & Moral Rebellion," *Baptist Press News,* July 27, 2005.

3. Nick Madigan, "After Fleeing Polygamist Community, an Opportunity for Influence," *New York Times,* June 29, 2005.

4. Stephanie Coontz, "The New Fragility of Marriage, for Better or for Worse," *Chronicle of Higher Education,* May 6, 2005.

5. 1 Enoch 15:7; 2 Enoch 30:11.

6. Jubilees 15:25–27.

7. William D. Mosher, Anjani Chandra, and Jo Jones, of the U.S. Department of Health and Human Services' National Center for Health Statistics, "Sexual Behavior and Selected Health Measure: Men and Women 15–44 Years of Age," *Advance Data from Vital and Health Statistics,* No. 362 (September 15, 2005): 1–3, 10.

8. Barbara Dafoe Whitehead and David Popenoe, *The State of Our Unions: The Social Health of Marriage in America* (Piscataway, NJ: The National Marriage Project conducted by Rutgers, 2004), 5–6, 13.

9. Origen *Contra Celsum* I:32.

10. Luther, The Estate of Marriage, *Luther's Work* XLV.

11. Luther, letter to the Hessian Chancellor Johan Feige, July 1540, *Briefwechsel* IX.

12. Whitehead and Popenoe, 21–22.

13. Ibid., 13, 21.

14. John Shelby Spong, *Living in Sin? A Bishop Rethinks Human Sexuality* (San Francisco: HarperSanFrancisco, 1988), 188–89.

15. Nedarim, 15b.

16. Mishnah Torah, Issurei Biah, 21:9.

17. Luther, Lectures on Genesis, *Luther's Work* VII.

18. Lynn Crawford Cook, "Meeting Women's Desire for Desire," *Washington Post,* September 20, 2005.

19. Mosher, Chandra, and Jones, of the National Center for Health Statistics, "Sexual Behavior and Selected Health Measure," *Advance Data,* No. 362 (September 15, 2005): 1.

20. Albert Mohler, "First-person: Deliberate Childlessness & Moral Rebellion," *Baptist Press News,* July 27, 2005.

21. Vincent J. Schodolski, "Pitter-patter of Little Feet Isn't for Them," *Chicago Tribune,* November 27, 2005.

22. U.S. Census Bureau, Population Division, International Programs Center, http://www.census.gov/ipc/www/world.html.

23. U.S. Census Bureau, Population Division and Housing and Household Economic Statistics Division, http://www.census.gov/population/www/pop-profile/natproj.html.

24. http://www.albertmohler.com/commentary_read.php?cdate=2005-08-15.

Chapter 6, Sex and the Single Christian

1. Augustine *Confession* VIII:7:17.

2. Luther, Lectures on Genesis, *Luther's Work* VII.

3. Yevamot, 63a.

4. Aristotle *The Theory of the Household* I:2:9–10.

5. Ian Fisher, "Uninvited Guest Turns Up at Catholic Synod: Issue of Married Priests," *New York Times*, October 7, 2005.

6. Jeff Sharlet, "The Young and the Sexless," *Rolling Stone*, Issue 977/978 (June 30–July 14, 2005).

7. Russell Shorto, "Contra-Contraception," *New York Times Magazine,* May 7, 2006.

8. Associated Press, "Doctors Denounce Abstinence-only Education," MSNBC, July 5, 2005.

9. Jacqueline E. Darroch et al., "Changing Emphases in Sexual Education in U.S. Public Secondary Schools, 1988–1999," *Family Planning Perspectives,* Vol. 32, No. 5 (2000): 204–11, 265.

10. American Academy of Pediatrics, "Statement by the American Academy of Pediatrics for the Hearing by the House Subcommittee on Health House Energy and Commerce Committee," *Welfare*

Reform: A Review of Abstinence Education and Transitional Medical Assistance, April 23, 2002.

11. Joyce C. Abma, Gladys M. Martinez, et al. of the U.S. Department of Health and Human Services' National Center for Health Statistics, "Teenagers in the United States: Sexual Activity, Contraceptive Use, and Childbearing, 2002," *Advance Data from Vital and Health Statistics* 24 (December 2004): 1.

12. The Alan Guttmacher Institute, *Sex and American Teenagers* (New York: AGI, 1994).

13. Jacqueline E. Darroch et al., *Teenage Sexual and Reproductive Behavior in Developed Countries: Can More Progress Be Made?* (New York: AGI, 2001), 29–30.

14. Heather Boonstra, "Teen Pregnancy: Trends and Lessons Learned," *Guttmacher Report,* Vol. 5, No. 1 (February 2002).

15. Mosher, Chandra, and Jones, of the National Center for Health Statistics, "Sexual Behavior and Selected Health Measures," *Advance Data* 362 (September 15, 2005): 21–22.

16. Abma, Martinez, et al., "Teenagers in the United States," *Advance Data* 24 (December 2004): 1.

17. Robert Hatcher, *Contraceptive Technology,* 17th ed. (New York: Ardent Media, 1998), 216; and Haishan Fu et al., "Contraceptive Failure Rates: New Estimates from the 1995 National Survey of Family Growth," *Family Planning Perspectives,* Vol. 31, No. 2 (March/April 1999): 56–63.

18. Reuters, "Study Finds High Rate of Errors in Condom Usage," MSNBC, August 16, 2005.

19. Lawrence K. Altman, "Officials Report Mixed Picture on STD Rates," *New York Times,* November 9, 2005.

20. Hillard Weinstock, Stuart Berman, and Willard Cates, Jr., "Sexually Transmitted Diseases Among American Youth: Incidence and Prevalence Estimates, 2000," *Perspectives on Sexual and Reproductive Health,* Vol. 36, No. 1 (January/February 2004): 11–19.

21. Augustine *The Excellence of Marriage* XIII:15; XVI:18; XVII:19.

22. Ibid. V:5.

23. Augustine *Marriage and Desire* I:15:17.

24. J. Groopman, "Contagion," *New Yorker,* September 13, 1999, 44–49; F. N. Judson, "Interactions Between Human Papillomavirus and Human Immunodeficiency Virus Infections," *Scientific*

Publications, Vol. 119 (1992): 199–207; and J. M. Walboomers et al., "Human Papillomavirus Is a Necessary Cause of Invasive Cervical Cancer Worldwide" *Journal of Pathology,* Vol. 189, No. 1 (1999): 12–19.

25. Debora MacKenzie, "Will Cancer Vaccine Get to All Women?" *New Scientist,* Vol. 2495 (April 18, 2005): 8.

26. Of God and His Creatures, III:123.

27. Brian Alexander, "Unleashing Your Wild Side," MSNBC, May 31, 2005.

28. Luther, Lectures on Genesis, *Luther's Work* VII.

29. For a complete review of clitoridectomy procedures in English-speaking Western nations, see Mary Daly, *Gyn/Ecology: The Metaethics of Radical Feminism* (Boston: Beacon Press, 1978), 240–45.

30. http://www.amnestyusa.org/women/violence/female_genital_mutil-ation.html.

31. "Masturbation Cuts Cancer Risk," BBC, July 16, 2003.

32. Babylonian Talmud Niddah, 13 a–b.

33. Mishnah Niddah, 2.1.

34. Andrea Lavinthal and Jessica Rozler, *The Hookup Handbook: A Single Girl's Guide to Living It Up* (New York: Simon Spotlight Entertainment, 2005), 1–3, 9.

35. bell hooks, *Ain't I a Woman: Black Women and Feminism* (Boston: South End Press, 1981), 32.

36. Ramban *Responsa* 2.

37. Whitehead and Popenoe, *The State of Our Unions* (Piscataway, NJ: The National Marriage Project, 2004), 7–9, 11.

38. Ibid., 25.

39. David Myers and Letha Dawson Scanzoni, *What God Has Joined Together: A Christian Case for Marriage* (New York: HarperSanFrancisco, 2005), 29.

40. Calvin *Institutes* IV:19:34.

41. Luther, On Marriage Matters, *Luther's Work* XLVI.

Chapter 7, Same-Sex Relationships

1. *700 Club,* January 21, 1993.

2. *700 Club,* September 13, 2001.

3. Inside Track, "Group Puts Squeeze on SpongeBob as Gay Icon," *Boston Herald,* January 21, 2005.

4. "Gay Tinky Winky Bad for Children," BBC News, February, 15, 1999.

5. David W. Dunlap, "Shameless Homophobia and the 'Jenny Jones' Murder," *New York Times,* March 19, 1995.

6. "The Price of Homophobia," *New York Times,* January 20, 2005.

7. Gustav Niebuhr, "Vatican Tells Priest and Nun to End Their Gay Ministry," *New York Times,* July 14, 1999.

8. LaHaye and LaHaye, *The Act of Marriage,* 275–76.

9. William D. Mosher, Anjani Chandra, and Jo Jones, of the U.S. Department of Health and Human Services' National Center for Health Statistics, "Sexual Behavior and Selected Health Measures: Men and Women 15–44 Years of Age," *Advance Data from Vital and Health Statistics,* No. 362 (September 15, 2005): 2–3.

10. http://www.exodus-international.org/about_exodus_policy.shtml.

11. Alex Williams, "Gay Teenager Stirs a Storm," *New York Times,* July 17, 2005.

12. http://www.isna.org.

13. Edward L. Kessel, "A Proposed Biological Interpretation of the Virgin Birth," *Journal of the American Scientific Affiliation* (September 1983): 129–36.

14. www.frc.org/insight/is93f1hs.html.

15. www.afa.net/homosexual_agenda/homosexuality.pdf.

16. Carolyn Marshall, "Panel on Prison Rape Hears Victims' Chilling Accounts," *New York Times,* August 20, 2005.

17. *Book of Wisdom* 19:13–17.

18. Ecclesiasticus 16:8.

19. Sanhedrin 109a; Baba Batra 59a; and Erubim 49a.

20. Philo of Alexandria *On Abraham* XXVII:137–141.

21. Josephus *Antiquities of the Jews* XI:3.

22. Sanhedrin 70a.

23. LaHaye and LaHaye, *The Act of Marriage,* 286–87.

24. Yebamoth 76a.

25. Martti Nissinen, *Homoeroticism in the Biblical World: A Historical Perspective,* trans. by Kirsi Stjerna (Minneapolis: Fortress Press, 1998), 60.

26. Tom Kenworthy, "Anti-Gay Forces Incite Shouting Match at Wyoming Funeral," *Washington Post*, October 17, 1998.

27. http://www.godhatesfags.com/memorial.html.

28. Arizona State University, March 11, 1998.

29. Federal Bureau of Investigation, *Crime in the United States 2004: Uniform Crime Report* (Washington, DC: U.S. Government Printing Office, 2005), 67.

30. "Anti-gay Church Protests at Soldier's Funeral," *Associated Press*, August 28, 2005.

31. Strabo *Geography VIII* 6, 20.

32. Timothy R. Koch, *Cruising as Methodology: Homoeroticism and the Scriptures, Queer Commentary and the Hebrew Bible*, ed. by Ken Stone (Cleveland: Pilgrim Press, 2001), 169–80.

Chapter 8, Predatory Sex

1. Aquinas *Summa Theologica* II:2.

2. Sheila Rowbotham, *Women, Resistance and Revolution* (New York: Random House, 1972), 17–18.

3. Bob Allen, "Falwell Terms Clergy Sex-Abuse Case 'Bump in the Road,'" Ethics Daily, October 31, 2006: http://www.ethicsdaily.com/article_detail.cfm?AID=8088

4. Federal Bureau of Investigation, *Crime in the United States 2004: Uniform Crime Report* (Washington, DC: U.S. Government Printing Office, 2005), 23.

5. www.cdc.gov/ncipc/factsheets/ipvfacts.htm.

6. Kathleen Basile, "Prevalence of Wife Rape and Other Intimate Partner Coercion in a Nationally Representative Sample of Women," *Violence and Victims*, Vol. 17, No. 5 (2002), 511–24.

7. Patricia Tjaden and Nancy Thoennes, *Full Report of the Prevalence, Incidence, and Consequences of Violence Against Women Survey* (Washington, DC: U.S. Department of Justice, 2000), 1–2.

8. Ibid.

9. *Presbyterians and Human Sexuality 1991* (Louisville: Presbyterian Church U.S.A., 1991), 40, as quoted in Daniel C. Maguire, "Men, Male Myths, and Metanoia," *Body and Soul: Rethinking Sexuality as Justice-Love*, ed. by Marvin Ellison and Sylvia Thorson-Smith (Cleveland: The Pilgrim Press, 2003), 178.

10. Tjaden and Thoennes, *Full Report of the Prevalence, Incidence, and Consequences of Violence Against Women Survey* (2000), 1–2.

11. Ibid.

12. H. Champion et al., "Adolescent Sexual Victimization, Use of Alcohol and Other Substances, and Other Health Risk Behaviors," *Journal of Adolescent Health,* Vol. 35, No. 4 (2004), 321–8.

13. Marcella Althaus-Reid, *Indecent Theology: Theological Perversions in Sex, Gender, and Politics* (London: Routledge, 2000), 49.

14. Federal Bureau of Investigation, *Crime in the United States 2004: Uniform Crime Report* (Washington, DC: U.S. Government Printing Office, 2005), 359.

15. National Clearinghouse on Child Abuse and Neglect Information, *Child Maltreatment 2003: Summary of Key Findings* (Washington, DC: Administration for Children and Families, U.S. Department of Health and Human Services, 2005).

16. Kurt Eichenwald, "Through His Webcam, a Boy Joins a Sordid Online World," *New York Times,* December 19, 2005.

17. David Finkelhor, Kimberly J. Mitchell, and Janis Wolak, *Online Victimization: A Report on the Nation's Youth* (Alexandria, VA: National Center for Missing & Exploited Children, 2000), ix.

18. American Psychological Association. *Understanding Child Sexual Abuse: Education, Prevention, and Recovery* (Washington, DC: American Psychological Association, 1999).

19. Office of the Assistant Secretary for Planning and Evaluation, *Male Perpetrators of Child Maltreatment: Findings from NCANDS* (Washington, DC: U.S. Department of Health and Human Services, 2005), 12–15.

20. Congregazione per l'Educazione Cattolica, *Circa I Criteri di Discernimento Vocazionale Riguardo alle Persone Con Tendenze Omosessuali in Vista Della Loro Ammissione al Seminario e agli Ordini Sacri* (Rome: The Vatican, 2005).

21. L. William Countryman, *Dirt, Greed, & Sex: Sexual Ethics in the New Testament and Their Implications for Today* (Philadelphia: Fortress Press, 1988), 164.

22. Sir James George Frazer, *The Golden Bough: A Study in Magic and Religion* (New York: Macmillan, 1951), 12.

23. Richard Lewinsohn, *A History of Sexual Customs,* trans. by Alexander Mayce (New York: Fawcett Premier Books, 1958), 69, 135.

24. Augustine *On the Good of Marriage* 8, 12.

25. Aquinas *Summa Theologica* II:2.

26. Lewinsohn, *A History of Sexual Customs,* 157.

27. U.S. Attorney Northern District of California, press release, November 18, 2003, http://www.usdoj.gov/usao/can/press/html/ 2003_11_18_awards.html.

28. U.S. State Department, *Trafficking in Persons Report* (Washington, DC: U.S. Department of State Publications, 2005), 13–14, 19; and U.S. State Department, *U.S. Cooperates with Europe to Combat Sex Trafficking* (Washington, DC: U.S. Department of State International Information Programs).

29. Chris Swecker, Assistant Director, Criminal Investigative Division Federal Bureau of Investigation, statement before the Commission on Security and Cooperation in Europe, United States Helsinki Commission, June 7, 2005.

30. William H. McMichael, "DoD Team to Investigate Sex-slave Charges in S. Korea," *Army Times,* December 9, 2002.

31. U.S. State Department, *Trafficking in Persons Report* (Washington, DC: U.S. Department of State Publications, 2005), 8.

32. Catherine A. MacKinnon, "Not a Moral Issue," *Feminism and Pornography,* ed. by Drucilla Cornell (New York: Oxford University Press, 2000), 185–86.

33. Matt Richtel and Michel Marriott, "Ring Tones, Cameras, Now This," *New York Times,* September 17, 2005.

34. *60 Minutes,* "Porn in the U.S.A.," CBS News, September 5, 2004; Matt Richtel, "A Night to See the Stars Actually Wearing Clothes," *New York Times,* January 10, 2006.

35. Whitehead and Popenoe, *The State of Our Unions: The Social Health of Marriage in America* (Piscataway, NJ: The National Marriage Project conducted by Rutgers, 2004), 9.

36. Myers and Scanzoni, *What God Has Joined Together,* 43–45.

37. Chris Thompson, "War Pornography," *East Bay Express,* September 23, 2005.

38. Thom Shanker, "Army Investigates Photos of Iraqi War Dead on the Internet," *New York Times,* September 28, 2005; Shanker, "Army Inquiry Finds No Evidence G.I.'s Gave War Photo to Web," *New York Times,* September 29, 2005.

THE AUTHOR

BORN IN CUBA months before the Castro revolution, Miguel A. De La Torre and his family came to the United States as refugees when he was six months old. At the age of nineteen, he began a real estate company in Miami, Florida, and became active in local politics as a candidate for the Florida House of Representatives. The company was a financial success. Convicted by the biblical passage concerning the "Rich Young Ruler" (Luke 18), De La Torre dissolved his thirteen-year-old firm and attended Southern Baptist Theological Seminary to obtain a Master's in Divinity. During his seminary training he served as pastor to a rural congregation. Lacking opportunities within the church structure due to ethnic discrimination, De La Torre continued his theological training and obtained a doctorate degree. The focus of his academic pursuit was social ethics within contemporary U.S. thought, specifically how religion affects race, class, and gender oppression. He specialized in applying a social scientific approach to Latino/a religiosity within this country, Liberation theologies in the Caribbean and Latin America, and postmodern/postcolonial social theory.

Since obtaining his doctorate in 1999, De La Torre has authored numerous articles and more than ten books, including the award-winning *Reading the Bible from the Margins* (Orbis, 2002); *Santería: The Beliefs and Rituals of a Growing Religion in America* (Eerdmans, 2004); and *Doing Christian Ethics from the Margins* (Orbis, 2004). He presently serves as associate professor for social ethics and director of the Peace and Justice Institute at Iliff School of Theology in Denver. Within the academy he is a director to the Society of Christian Ethics and the co-chair of the Ethics Section at the American Academy of Religion. A scholar-activist, Dr. De La Torre has written numerous articles in popular media and has served in several civic organizations.

INDEX

A

Abortions, 115, 118, 130

Abraham, 16, 20–21, 23, 47–49, 59, 142, 166, 176, 183

Absalom (son of David), 22, 166–167

Abstinence, sexual, ix–x, 50–51, 55, 71, 83, 86, 109–118, 120, 127, 138, 145, 169–170; better than marriage, 58, 109–113

Abuse, sexual. *See* Predatory sex

Adam and Eve, 5, 8, 15, 18, 23, 25, 27, 58, 67, 83, 113, 166

Adultery, 19–20, 65, 77, 97–99, 106, 108, 121–122, 146–147, 159, 161, 174–175, 183

AIDS. *See* STD

Althaus-Reid, M., 164

Ambrose, St., 27

Amedure, S., 131

American Academy of Pediatrics, 115

American Association for Retired Persons, 133

American Family Association, 139

American Psychiatric Association, 136, 181

American Psychological Association, 136, 181

American Society for Reproductive Medicine, 103

Amerindians, 36, 41–43, 46

Amnesty International, 120

Amnon (son of David), 167, 184

Amos (prophet), 143

Anal sex, 24, 42–43, 70–71, 103, 116, 135, 140, 167, 175

Angel, 21, 68, 92–93, 97, 158; tempted by women, 27–28, 92, 144, 151

Anselm of Canterbury, 170, 184

Antony, St., 54

Apphia the pastor, 30

Aquinas, T., 23–24, 26, 118, 158, 175

Aristotle, 24, 109, 149

Asceticism, 54–55, 83, 109–110, 120, 169–170

Ashcroft, J., 177

Augustine of Hippo, 18, 23–25, 27, 31, 56–58, 70, 83, 108, 112, 117, 163, 175

B

Balaam, 26

Baldwin, J., 36

Barrenness, 19, 23–24, 48, 89, 99, 118

Bathsheba, 160, 183

Benedict, St., 57, 59

Benedict XVI, 57, 80

Benjamin (tribe of), 165

Bentham, J., 84

Bernard of Clairvaux, St., 64

Bernini, G., 68

Bestiality, 43, 65, 140, 178

Bible, x–xiii, 4, 6, 10, 17–21, 24, 26–27, 52, 59, 67, 73, 86, 89–92, 98, 103, 105–106, 108, 113, 121–125, 129, 157–158, 160–161, 172–174, 181; emancipating, 33–35, 47–49, 81–82, 134, 139, 152–154, 166, 184; and homosexuality, 134, 139–154; to justify oppression, 1–4, 14–15,

Walking in
Daniel's
Shoes

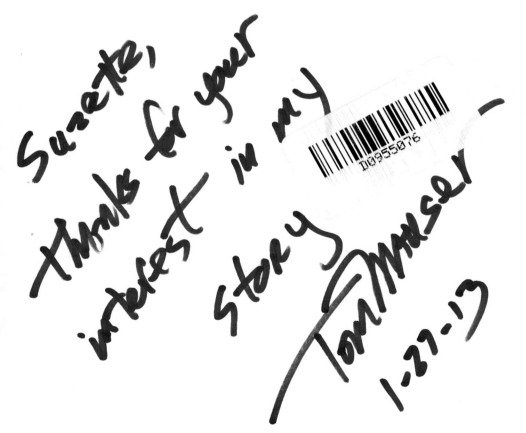

Sweeta,
Thanks for your
interest in my
story
Tom Mauser
1-27-13

Walking in Daniel's Shoes

A father's journey through grief, controversy, activism, and healing following his son's death at Columbine

TOM MAUSER

Walking in Daniel's Shoes

A father's journey through grief, controversy, activism, and healing following his son's death at Columbine

First printing 2012

ISBN 978-0-9853021-1-5
LCCN: 2012907669

ATTENTION CORPORATIONS, UNIVERSITIES, COLLEGES, AND PROFESSIONAL ORGANIZATIONS: Quantity discounts are available on bulk purchases of this book for educational and gift purposes, or as premiums for increasing magazine subscriptions or renewals. Special books or book excerpts can also be created to fit specific needs. For information, please contact Tom Mauser at safemauser@yahoo.com

Table of Contents

PREFACE

Imagine sending your child off to Columbine High School on April 20, 1999—and he didn't return. I've heard many parents say they couldn't imagine what it would be like to go through such an experience. I can imagine it, for I lived it. My son Daniel was murdered that day at Columbine.

I will share my journey, writing about "that day" and the days, weeks and years thereafter, here in the epicenter of this earthquake called Columbine. This is *my* story. My wife and daughter experienced this tragedy along with me, so I will describe our family's experiences, but I cannot tell my wife's or daughter's stories. Those are their stories, not mine.

This is a father's story, an account of shock, pain, grief, advocacy, joy, struggle, healing, triumph, questioning, honoring and renewal—and of trying to find meaning in it all. This is a story about a father's love for his son. It is a story of one victim of gun violence in a nation infested with an epidemic of gun violence.

I felt driven to tell Daniel's story so he would not be forgotten, so the world could learn more about one of the victims and not only about the killers. So why, you might ask, did it take thirteen years to write this book? For one thing, it wasn't clear to me when my story of Columbine ended—it's something I've been living ever since April 20, 1999. More important, for years I satisfied my desire to tell Daniel's story through the memorial Web site I established to honor him, and where I described Daniel and the things being done in his name.

But not all could be told on Daniel's site. Some stories were too long or didn't seem right for that format. And there were stories that were still too painful to write about and share at the time. Enough time has now passed. I'm ready to share the rest of my story.

Something else that drove me to write this book are the many letters and emails from people from all over the world. Some are from a new generation of curious young people who have an interest in Columbine, saying they were not old enough to understand what really happened at Columbine at the time, or that their parents shielded them from the tragic story. Some are adults who say they didn't follow the Columbine story closely when it happened but want to learn more about it now, especially about the victims and how their families are doing. I want to satisfy their thirst for more information and understanding, providing a parent's perspective.

I have also been driven by the fact that school violence, bullying and gun violence still persist in America. Some people hoped Columbine would bring the nation to its senses and bring about an end to school violence—but that hasn't happened. We need to talk about why that's so.

Some people insist Columbine is 'old news' that has lost its relevance and that we need to "move on." Perhaps many people have done so. But I continue to hear from people who still remember where they were and what they were doing when they heard the news about Columbine, just as my generation remembers the assassination of President Kennedy and as the Great Generation remembers the attack on Pearl Harbor.

Many people still wonder how such a horrific thing could happen. It bewilders them because the Columbine killers were intelligent and came from ordinary, well-to-do families, not from broken, poor or single-parent households. So why did it happen? We'll never know for sure, but I'll share some of my thoughts.

I will not give in to the temptation to sensationalize this story or make it overly morbid in order to sell more books. I am writing this book on my terms. I will not provide all the gory and investigative minutiae of the tragedy at Columbine nor describe all of the many controversies that surrounded it. One can read other books for that. I will present some of the details, though, insofar as some are needed to provide a framework and others were meaningful parts of my experience of Columbine.

I hope this book will provide a new perspective. I hope it provides an understanding of what it's like to be in the middle of such a high-profile tragedy. I hope it convinces more people to become active in changing our gun laws and our social attitudes toward guns. I hope it provides a helpful glimpse of my experience to others who are dealing with grief. Finally, I hope this book succeeds in demonstrating how a father's love for his son can drive him to demand change in the world around him.

Tom Mauser

BEFORE READING...

I would like to share with readers a few observations about some of the language and references offered herein.

Columbine has become such a part of my life that it has become part of my vocabulary, as it has for America's. "Columbine" has become a single word descriptor, a euphemism for a school shooting or a school massacre, so that's how I will use it. A news story mentioning that students were "planning a Columbine" is understood by most people. People know you're not referring to the state flower of Colorado. So, in this book I refer to something as happening "after Columbine," not as "after the shooting massacre at Columbine High School in Littleton, Colorado."

When I speak of the "Columbine families" I am speaking about the parents of the twelve students murdered at Columbine and the spouse of the teacher murdered at Columbine, as well as their immediate families. I am not referring to the families of those injured at Columbine or of all families within the larger Columbine community.

I understand that in following this tragedy one cannot help but examine the killers. But in doing so, undeserved attention would be given to them. Too much attention has already been showered upon them. Therefore, I will often refer to the killers in the Columbine massacre as just that—the Columbine killers, or as H&K. I will not print their names frequently herein and give them the attention they sought through bloodshed. But neither will I irrationally avoid mentioning their names. I will use them sparingly.

I struggled with how to refer to those whom I opposed in the course of my gun control advocacy. My opponents were nothing if not varied. Some were friendly NRA members or gun owners who disagreed with me but acknowledged my point of view and treated me with respect. Others were quite the opposite—gun extremists who showed only contempt for my point of view and were lacking in a basic level of civility.

Those with whom I most often sparred were gun rights activists who were zealous and uncompromising in their beliefs about gun laws and the role of guns in our society. In this book I generally refer to them as "gun activists" to distinguish them from those who are merely gun enthusiasts or pro gun in their outlook. As a group, gun activists include many people who are NRA members—but certainly not *all* NRA members. I would, however, put most members of the more fanatical and fervent gun groups, such as Gun Owners of America, in the gun activists category.

This book is not arranged in chronological order of my experiences. It is chronological in general but is primarily arranged by topic area. For that reason, to avoid any confusion, I have provided a chronology of major events in the appendix.

There are a number of stories that do not appear in this book. When I began writing this book in 2009, I did not have a goal in terms of how many words or pages. I simply wrote away. When I was finished writing, in the latter half of 2011, I had written over 175,000 words. This was far too much for a standard-sized book, and yet my story was not one that could be told in two books. So, I reduced it. I will eventually place these other stories and viewpoints on Daniel's Web site or in a blog.

A unique aspect of books today is the opportunity to share one's story in multiple formats. That is, I can provide links to photos, videos and documents that help expand on my experience. Even if you purchased an electronic version of this book you can view the photos in the book. At the back of the book are multiple links to, for example, a YouTube video showing Daniel at different ages. There are also links to documents referenced in the book as well as photos.

Chapter 1

That Horrific Day

Tuesday, April 20, 1999, started out no differently than any other day. I jumped out of bed. Shaved. Took a shower. Meditated. Ate breakfast. Headed off to work. Put my nose to the grindstone. I don't remember what time I woke up or what I ate or whether I saw my kids before I left for the office. All of that has been overshadowed by other memories of the day.

Late that morning I was supposed to head off to the southern Colorado city of Pueblo to attend a public transit conference. Along with fellow employees, I planned to leave the office at about noon. I was frantically cramming to get as much work done as possible before leaving the office.

Sometime around noon a coworker came into my office, wearing a concerned look on her face. I was running late and hoped her interruption was a brief one.

"You live in south Jefferson County, don't you?" she asked.

"Yes," I replied, wondering how her inquiry could possibly be more important than my trip. I was always energized by these transit conferences, and I didn't want to leave late and miss part of it.

She went on, seemingly knowing the answer to the previous question. "And you have teenaged kids?" She received the response she was expecting. "And do they go to Columbine High School?"

I was growing more impatient, fearing this conversation would prevent me from scarfing down my lunch before leaving. "Yes," I told her, "my son Daniel goes there."

She urged me to come to the Mt. Evans conference room, saying that something was happening at Columbine High School. I reluctantly agreed to join her. In the room, the television was on and ten or twenty people were gathered watching news coverage. Having employees watching news coverage on the television was unheard of in our offices. It was fairly hushed, and all eyes were focused intently on the TV screen. On the news, helicopters were buzzing around. Police had surrounded the school. It was reported that shots had been fired. *Shots* were fired? How could *that* be?

Then came images of students fleeing the school grounds, and parents hugging terrified teenagers. Word must have gotten around that I had a child at Columbine. I sensed some people looking at me with concern.

Shots were fired?

ONE IN TWO THOUSAND

I must admit I wasn't overly concerned as I first watched. This was Columbine High School, after all. And even if there was a shooting, Daniel would not be involved. He was a good kid. He wouldn't be the target of violence, and he certainly wasn't foolish enough to get in harm's way if there was trouble. Other kids might be at risk, but not Daniel. Besides, there were two thousand students at Columbine. He was just one of two thousand students. Only one of two thousand.

As we watched, the situation at the school seemed to worsen. Police were hunkered down behind SWAT vehicles. Fellow employees began showing more concern toward me. My staff encouraged me to go home, but I saw no reason to do so. We watched in horror as a boy's limp body dropped from a second-floor window to the roof of a SWAT vehicle and waiting police officers.

I tried to call home, but the line was continuously busy. When I finally got through, there was no answer. A little while later I got a call from my wife, Linda. She sounded concerned. Certainly more so than I. She was fearful because she had not received a call from Daniel. That was no surprise, I thought to myself, given he didn't have a cell phone, given how busy Denver's phone lines had suddenly become with this developing crisis, and given how hard it would be for Daniel to find a phone to use.

Linda had just come from the county's Columbine Public Library. The library and Leawood Elementary School, each within a half-mile of Columbine High School, were serving as destination points for students who had escaped the developing crisis. Linda said there were sign-up boards at both the library and Leawood. Officials were asking the students to sign it so their parents would know they were safe. She hadn't noticed Daniel's name on the board at the library, but she said in the mess of writing it was hard to read names.

She had left the library out of frustration and suggested that I leave work and go to Leawood School and look at the board there. She was going to stay home to await a call from Daniel. I agreed, finally giving up any thought of going to the conference that afternoon. I asked my staff to leave without me. After Daniel got home, I could go to Pueblo and the conference. People would understand why I was late.

My staff asked if I had a cell phone so I could stay in touch with Linda, since it was a thirty-minute drive to my home. I did not; I was a holdout, feeling I had no need for a mobile phone. Our office had a spare, however, so I checked it out for the day.

I hated the thought of using that phone—mostly because I had no idea how to use it. It was an old, boxy phone from ages past, nearly the size of a large shoe box with its charger. It was a clunker that made strange noises. But it was my only option for reaching Linda—and good news.

One of my employees, Steve Ellis, offered to drive me home. *Why would I need a ride?* I thought to myself. It seemed ridiculous to leave my car at the office, 15 miles from home. But Steve implored me to accept, saying it was better that I not drive at a nerve-wracking time like this. He emphasized that I could use the mobile phone while he was driving. That made sense, so I accepted his offer.

As we drove, I repeatedly tried calling home but couldn't get through. The entire phone network was jammed. You'd have thought that the Denver Broncos had just won the Super Bowl and a tornado had touched down and Madonna was making a guest appearance at Southwest Plaza Mall.

A FRANTIC SEARCH

Steve dropped me off at home. When I walked into our house, Linda was wearing a deeply concerned look on her face. Questions started frantically flying between us. *Where was Daniel? Why hadn't he called? In what room would he have been in when the crisis started? With the phone lines so busy, would he even be able to call? And if he escaped, how would he be able to get home, since he didn't drive yet? Might he have gotten a ride with a friend?*

Leawood Elementary was just a couple of miles away from our home, north up Pierce Street and east a few blocks. But I couldn't travel that way, Linda told me. Pierce Street and others around Columbine High School had been closed off. I had to make a circuitous detour a few miles to the east on Coal Mine Road, north on Platte Canyon Road, then west on Bowles Avenue.

I listened to radio news coverage as I drove. I heard a reporter describe the arrival at a hospital of a fifteen-year-old-boy who had been shot and injured. Daniel was fifteen. My heart suddenly sank. For the first time I seriously worried about him. *What if the boy at the hospital was Daniel? Why hadn't we heard from him? What the hell was going on at that high school? Shots were fired? Gunshots? This cannot be happening! This cannot be real!*

The parking lot at Leawood School was full, and nearby street parking was taken. I had to park blocks away. Police cars and media trucks were everywhere. As I approached the school, I saw something that simultaneously brought me a rush of joy as well as apprehension. There, walking toward me was Jeremy Baker, Daniel's best friend, along with his father. *Thank God Jeremy was safe,* I thought. *Then Daniel must be safe.*

But there was a voice in back of my mind asking why these two good buddies weren't together. I asked Jeremy if he had seen Daniel.

"No," Jeremy answered, with a concerned look. He said he thought Daniel might have been in the cafeteria or library at the time the shooting started.

I moved into the school. Walking toward me were teary-eyed parents and their kids, heading for safety and freedom. I wanted *desperately* to be one of them, to find Daniel and just go home. I wanted a happy ending like theirs. I wanted this nightmare to be over. *Where the hell was Daniel?*

Things were rather hectic there. I looked around but there was no sign of Daniel in the gymnasium or any hallway. The gymnasium was serving as a kind of command post for school officials and the police, as well as for students who had escaped Columbine and were waiting for their parents to retrieve them—though there weren't many remaining. It didn't seem like anyone there could help me. The police just asked me to be patient without sharing anything about what was going on at the school. Nothing seemed to be happening. People were must milling round, with blank or anxious looks on their faces.

Some people were there to help out. My next door neighbor, Pete DeFillipis, was one of them. He's an ex-fireman, so it's in his blood. His son had escaped the school unharmed, yet Pete stayed for hours.

The crowd there ebbed and flowed, he told me. He further explained that kids who escaped Columbine would be brought to Leawood, usually in school buses. But no school buses arrived while I was there.

When students were taken inside from the buses they were asked to place their name on one of the sign-in boards. I checked them but didn't see Daniel's name on any list. The listings were a mess. Some of the writing was impossible to read. That was not surprising. How could you expect kids to write legibly after they'd just escaped from what must have seemed like hell?

There was nowhere else to look. I waited for about a frustrating hour or so, with little to do but react any time a door opened to the outside or a policeman walked in the room. There was no television on, and no announcements were made about what was going on. I wondered why they weren't doing something more to get our kids so we could all go home.

At one point I noticed that Colorado Governor Bill Owens was standing in the front of the gym. He was a pro-gun Republican, and at

that time the state legislature was engaged in the passage of three controversial pro-gun bills, including one that would have made it much easier
to obtain concealed weapons permits. It was unlike me to be so daring,
but I approached the governor and told him I was desperately looking
for my son. I scolded him: "Maybe if you and the legislators weren't trying to make concealed weapons easier to get, we wouldn't be having this
problem! Look what's happening here at Columbine with guns!"

The governor mildly chastised me, saying it was not the time or place
to be talking about such things, that we needed to concentrate on helping these kids, not talking about guns.

He was right; it was not the appropriate time for such an inquiry,
but I felt I had to voice my concern about our gun-crazed culture and
laws. Who would have imagined that this liberal Democrat would soon
be working with the governor—a conservative Republican governor—to
promote gun-control measures?

I kept trying to reach Linda with that dreadful mobile phone, but
I couldn't get through. I searched out uncrowded spots in a hallway to
make my calls because I was so embarrassed by the loud, strange sounds
coming from that monstrosity. In other circumstances my silly struggle
with it could have come from the script of a TV sitcom. But this was
certainly no comedy.

WAITING AND WAITING FOR A BUS

The crowd in the school began to dwindle. At one point officials announced they had set up a special room for parents whose children were
not yet accounted for. That seemed like a good idea to me. I wanted to
get away from that gymnasium where I had to endure the joyous reunions
and whispered speculations about what was happening at Columbine.

I went to this "waiting room," where there were perhaps fifteen to
twenty-five people. I do not know who was in there with me, or which of
the other victims' parents were there. I didn't speak to anyone there; I was
in another world. As we waited along with crisis counselors the school
district had provided, we were told that one more bus with kids who had
escaped was on its way to Leawood. That was the first bit of good news
I had heard.

One of the counselors spoke to me, but I have no recollection of our conversation. I was distracted. I was in distress. Fifteen minutes passed. We waited. Thirty minutes. Why the hell was it taking so long?!?

I still had little idea what was happening at Columbine. Nobody was giving us information. At one point, a teenager came into the room, and I overheard him tell someone, "They're saying there could be twenty-five students killed."

Twenty-five kids killed? *Killed?* My God! Why were they keeping us in the dark? How could someone kill twenty-five teenagers in our high school? And what the hell was I doing, sitting helplessly in a room with a bunch of counselors? This wasn't helping me find Daniel.

After about forty-five minutes in that room, I realized a bus was probably not coming. Even if the police were interviewing the students on the buses, it shouldn't take this long for a bus to get there. Later I discovered that someone had made a terrible mistake. There was no final school bus. We were all sitting there in hopeless anticipation for a bus that was not coming.

A FUTILE RETURN TO HOME

I left the "waiting room" and stopped to talk with my neighbor, Pete. I told him I couldn't stay any longer, that I needed to be home with Linda. He promised to keep me informed of any news.

As I walked down the sidewalk toward my car, my pace suddenly picked up, until I started running at top speed, and I began crying in a panicked whimper. I quickly got in my car and sped away. I wasn't about to return home taking the long detour I took to get there. But I was unsure of how to get out of this neighborhood and wondered if I could reach Pierce Street without running into a police barricade. As I drove, I sped up and began driving wildly. I was desperate to get home. This car was a prison that kept me from a reunion with Daniel.

I hit a speed bump on Weaver Avenue so hard it threw the car into the air. I was crying out loud, wanting to find Daniel, wanting the comfort of home. I had little idea what I was doing. I wasn't at Leawood being counseled, and I wasn't at home to greet Daniel. I was in purgatory.

As I approached Weaver Avenue's intersection with South Pierce Street, my way home, a policeman manning a blockade witnessed my reckless driving. He stepped partly into the street and signaled for me to stop. "Why are you driving so recklessly?" he asked sternly.

"I can't find my son! My son! I've got to get home to my family! Where is my son?"

The policeman admonished me. "Sir, the way you're driving you might not make it home alive to see him. Or you could harm someone else. You've got to get a hold of yourself!" I assured him I would calm down and begged him to let me get home to my family. He didn't detain me or issue a ticket. I calmed down a bit and drove less erratically, but I was still whimpering and my heart was pounding in my chest.

When I arrived home, I didn't find the comfort my heart sought. Linda had a somber look. There was no news. Daniel hadn't called. The police hadn't called. *Where was Daniel? Might he be wisely hiding in a safe place in the school? Was he in the library at Columbine? Or the cafeteria? Which was the safer place to be? Or could he have been shot?*

We were helpless. Waiting. Worrying. Wondering.

In the early evening, some neighbors came by to see if Daniel made it out okay. Friends were calling to ask the same. We could say nothing other than, "No, he's not home yet. We haven't heard from him. We're hoping he's okay."

A FUTILE RETURN TO LEAWOOD

Out of options and full of questions, I decided to go back to Leawood Elementary to see if there were any updates. Two neighbors, Greg Lobser and Val Meyer, offered to drive me there. There were far fewer people and less activity at Leawood. The mood was solemn. Did these people know something I didn't know? I went back to that awful "waiting room," but after getting virtually no new information, I told my neighbors I didn't want to stay there. It was just too damned depressing. I didn't want to be talked to by a counselor.

Pete was still there. Officials wanted to make sure they could stay in touch with me, especially given how tied up the phone lines were. Pete had a cell phone, so he agreed to be a point of contact for us with the police.

I hadn't eaten since breakfast, so we stopped at the quickest and most convenient spot: the McDonald's on Coal Mine Avenue. It was a place I rarely ever set foot in. But I had eaten no lunch. I could tell the place was on edge. The girl who waited on me must have sensed something was wrong. She handed me my order and said, "There won't be any charge."

BACK AT HOME AGAIN

The concerned calls from family and friends continued. Our daughter, Christie, was a thirteen-year-old middle school student whose school was put in a lockdown that day. After school Christie went two doors away to the home of her friend LizAnne Brovsky. The Brovskys offered to have Christie stay at their house for the night. What a blessing that was, being able to remove Christie from the frightful environment at our house.

Pete called. He later told me it was an unbelievably difficult call to make. Police needed a description of what Daniel was wearing. *How the hell would I know? And why are they asking this?* I had to ask Linda for that information. She remembered exactly.

Pete called again. This time Linda answered the phone. Police needed Daniel's dental records. *Dental records? How were we expected to hold out a sliver of hope after being asked for dental records?* We wondered in anguish. *All we did was send our son to school that morning, and here we were, facing the prospect of having to identify his body. How could this be happening to us? Why couldn't Daniel just show up and put an end to this horrific nightmare?*

About ten neighbors and friends were solemnly gathered together in our family room, watching the news and waiting, making small talk, trying to be positive. There was endless speculation about whether Daniel might have been in the library or cafeteria. Our next door neighbor, Monica Lobser, described it as "the longest night."

At about 11:00 p.m., the doorbell rang. It was a sheriff's deputy. He said there was still no definitive news; they didn't have any further information. He said there might still be students in the school, but authorities would not enter much of the building because of the potential for more bombs. They were going through the school inch by inch, looking for unexploded bombs and students, he told us. They hoped they'd be able to get more information and call us in the morning. *Not until the morning?*

We told friends and neighbors who were with us to head home. What we all needed was a good night's sleep. Everyone was stunned by what was unfolding. They shared hugs, said good night, and went home with hearts heavy with sadness, emptiness, confusion, and frustration.

It had already seemed like a day in hell, and now there would be a long, seemingly endless night before we could find out more news. We were exhausted and emotionally spent. Daniel could be in that school, bleeding to death, and police weren't moving to get to him. My hope was that he was hiding in a closet or a classroom, smartly waiting things out. But, good Lord, it already had been almost twelve hours since the shooting started. Why wouldn't he have come out of hiding? Why weren't the police looking for him more aggressively?

Eventually, Linda and I went to bed, but I knew I wouldn't sleep, not knowing whether my son was alive or dead. How could I sleep when my son could have been calling out helplessly for help, or bleeding to death?

I decided to go downstairs so I didn't toss and turn and wake up Linda. In the basement, I turned on the television to watch what had happened at Columbine that day. I began wailing and crying, and talking to myself in whimpers—or perhaps I was calling out to God. "Where is Daniel? Where is Daniel? What if Daniel is dead? Lord, I don't want to lose my son!"

Linda was two levels above me in the house but apparently heard me anyway. She couldn't sleep either. She came down and put her arms around me, and we cried together. We both had already reached the conclusion that Daniel might no longer be with us on this earth.

APRIL 21

We managed to get a little sleep that night, but we were up early to make sure we didn't miss the call from the sheriff's office. I'm an optimist by nature, so I still held on to the faint hope that somehow Daniel was alive. Perhaps holed up in a room somewhere, injured but alive. But with each passing, painful minute, my optimism couldn't sustain me. The hope that came with a new day quickly faded. I had a terrible feeling in my gut. Things were too quiet.

When the authorities finally called at about 8:00 a.m., it was only to tell us that they still couldn't give us a report, saying they were carefully going through the school and would call us as soon as they could report something definitive. *Almost a whole day later and they couldn't tell us about our son? What were they doing over there?*

Margi Ness, a work colleague and friend of ours, had been scheduled to arrive at the Pueblo conference the previous evening. But after learning that Daniel had not come home, she chose to come to our house instead that Wednesday morning. She arrived at about 9:00 a.m. We later learned that she feared she would see hordes of TV cameras and police blocking the street, but there was nothing. At first she felt relief, but then she wondered if it were too quiet.

She said that ringing our doorbell felt ominous. Both Linda and I invited her in, then we stood in a circle in the hallway, hugging and crying. "We don't think he made it. We think he's dead," Linda said, shaking.

The waiting continued. We were joined by more friends and neighbors as the morning went on, including Ron Claussen, who was a friend and deacon at our church. We all sat together helplessly in the family room.

GONE

It wasn't until late morning that a sheriff's deputy and two victims' advocates came to the front door and asked to speak to Linda and me. We all stepped into the living room. They didn't beat around the bush. They gave us the news we so dreaded: Daniel was dead.

My son was dead. How the hell could he be dead? I just saw him the day before. All we did was send him to school. He was not a troublemaker or a drug user or a gang member. He was becoming so ready for the world, and I was so unready to deal with this.

Linda and I didn't break down in tears or become hysterical. The news was anticlimactic, and we were in shock. The officers went into the family room and spoke with the others who were there with us, then left.

The victims' advocates stayed and spent time counseling us. One of them was too overbearing and Linda found her to difficult to deal with. Margi asked the advocate to leave the house.

We entered a parent's ultimate nightmare, from which there was no escape. It became painfully obvious that our lives were about to change in a dramatic way.

Chapter 2

Daniel Conner Mauser

He was our first born, arriving at 8:46 a.m. on Saturday, June 25, 1983. He measured in at 7 pounds and 14 ounces, and 19.5 inches long.

I remember the night well. We had practiced for the birth. Arriving at the hospital in plenty of time on late Friday evening, I was supposed to "assist" Linda through her labor, being a Lamaze "coach" during the pushing stage. I tried, but wasn't very helpful. I'm one of those wimps who doesn't like to be in a hospital and is queasy at the sight of blood. The waiting and the pushing went on well through the night. I was woozy but I was there when our son finally arrived the next morning—and I didn't pass out! It was an amazing experience. I had my camera to record some of it. Linda could have done without the camera, but I persisted.

We named our son Daniel Conner Mauser. Daniel was chosen for its connection to the Biblical character Daniel as well as Linda's fondness for Elton John's song of the same name. Conner was Linda's maiden name. She was an only child, so it was our way of carrying on her family's name.

Daniel was a wonderful blessing. He was a smiling and entertaining baby and toddler. Linda quit her job to be with him. He seldom had health or behavioral problems. I had a demanding job as director of a small, private nonprofit agency on the other side of the city, but I tried not to let it consume too much of my time. I loved being a father to this baby boy.

A GREAT KID

Like his parents, Daniel was fairly shy. He was talkative and playful with his family and close friends, but not as much with those with whom he was not familiar. He was an easy-to-please, easygoing kid who wasn't prone to complaining or whining.

Daniel was always well-mannered, respectful, and obedient, never getting into serious trouble. He was inquisitive and an avid reader who earned good grades in elementary school. I take little credit for that; Linda was the one who challenged our kids and kept them on track in school.

In sixth grade, he struggled somewhat with depression. Linda was concerned enough to send him to a therapist. Apparently he was feeling stress after he'd had a bout with pneumonia and had missed a lot of school. He felt his teacher was pressuring him too much to catch up. He coughed excessively after several weeks, although the doctor had given his okay for a return to school. Fortunately he recovered and seemed to snap out the depression after a few months.

Daniel was a Cub Scout and Boy Scout for a few years. I was the one who usually took him to the Scout meetings, though it was Linda who provided much of the help with his projects.

Daniel and I especially enjoyed going to Boy Scout camps together. The most notable was a weekend winter camp in the mountains in the middle of January. When we arrived at camp, where it was below zero, we discovered that Daniel had somehow forgotten to bring his winter coat. I was irate, but fortunately one of the Scout leaders had an extra coat. The first morning the boys laughed about how well they slept as opposed to their dads, who were crammed together with them into tents but unable to sleep because of the fathers' snoring.

Once school projects intensified early in middle school, and as he became more engaged in piano lessons, Daniel dropped out of the Scouts. He had progressed and earned the basic badges, but he wasn't overly

enthusiastic about staying with scouting long-term. Since I was never a Scout myself, I wasn't terribly helpful in encouraging him. But we did both enjoy the time he was a member.

In middle school Daniel was selected to be in the gifted and talented program. He played chess and won second place in a Denver metro tournament as a member of the school's chess club team. He won two National Science Olympiad awards, presented to the top ten scorers in general science knowledge.

Although bright, in middle school he struggled for a while. It wasn't that Daniel was becoming a typical rebellious middle schooler; he just seemed disorganized and undisciplined at times. Linda worked with him, and it began to make a difference.

By his sophomore year at Columbine High School, Daniel was hitting his stride. He was doing well in classes, particularly in the sciences. Students said Daniel was quiet in class, but he also was a "go-to guy" if they were uncertain of an answer. He was always willing to help others out.

Daniel was an occasional babysitter who played with and took an interest in the children for whom he cared. He was a Junior Volunteer at Swedish Hospital for two summers, helping in the pharmacy. Perhaps it was because of that hospital experience, along with his excellent grades in math and science, that he expressed some interest in working in the medical or medical research field. He loved computer and Nintendo games. We played the Super Mario Brothers game together, and he quickly

advanced through the game's skill levels. It didn't take long for him to be so good that I'd have to wait far too long for him to finish playing through his round. I was no match for him, so we stopped playing it together.

I bought a stand-up foosball table, thinking that maybe I'd have more of a chance of competing at something other than a video game. Wrong! It didn't take long for his skills to better mine. I learned to accept that he was going to beat me most of the time, so I merely tried to reduce his margin of victory when we played. It was usually me asking him to play. At one point I could tell he became bored playing with me, but most of the time he agreed to play. He did it for me. That's the kind of kid he was.

He loved the challenge of playing board and party games. When Linda and I played charades or trivia and knowledge games with other adults, Daniel would insist on playing with us rather than hanging out with his sister or other kids. If he wasn't quite competitive enough for a particular game, he would volunteer to read the questions or participate in some other way.

Like his dad, Daniel had a keen interest in current events and social issues, becoming a regular reader of *Time* magazine and a frequent viewer of "60 Minutes."

His English teacher wrote that she always appreciated his wit, and apparently his French teacher adored him. Daniel traveled to France with fellow Columbine students in spring 1999. We're glad he was able to take that special trip before his death. The last photo we have of him is with his fellow students on that trip.

Like me and my mother, he sometimes worried too much about little things. For instance, he often warned me if the gas tank in the car was getting low. If the warning light came on, he became very vocal, insisting that we stop to fill the tank immediately.

TACKLING WEAKNESSES

Linda worked with Daniel and Christie on their schoolwork and in developing a vision for what they wanted to achieve. I was more the playful and wild-and-crazy parent who teased and entertained his kids.

Linda asked Daniel what activities he wanted to take on at Columbine but without pushing him in any particular direction. To our surprise, he made two amazing choices. Daniel was certainly not someone you'd expect to ever voluntarily speak in front of a group of people other than his closest friends. Yet he shocked us by saying he wanted to join the debate team at Columbine. He excelled there and was awarded several excellent and superior ratings.

He participated in a variety of debate formats—cross-examination, Congress, and Lincoln-Douglas—and earned membership in the National Forensic League. Topics he debated included alternative energy sources, genetic engineering, and the rights of journalists to conceal sources.

Slender and tall, Daniel was not very athletic. He played soccer for a couple of years when he was young, but he didn't have much killer instinct to kick the ball into the net, and he was too shy to be a great team player. We introduced him to skiing, though he was never great at it. In his early teens Daniel played baseball on a YMCA team, in a league far less intense than the Little League. He enjoyed it, and I know he appreciated that I was there for most of his games.

Despite his lack of athleticism, he wanted to play a sport at Columbine, so he joined the cross country team—again, with no pushing from us. As a freshman, he ran with the squad but never made the team. But he stuck with it, running in practices and cheering on his teammates at the meets.

It was an important lesson I think he taught the world: Take on your weaknesses! He sought to overcome his own limitations. He didn't take the easy way out, by doing only those things with which he was comfortable. He challenged himself.

HIGH ACHIEVER

Daniel did well in his freshman year at Columbine High School, but he excelled in his sophomore year, becoming a straight-A student. A couple of weeks before he died, Daniel's biology teacher told Linda that Daniel would be receiving an award for the outstanding sophomore biology student. It was supposed to be a secret. Daniel never found out.

Weeks before the Columbine massacre, Daniel applied for membership in the National Honor Society, whose competitive membership is based on academic achievement, service to the community and teacher recommendations. In September 1999, Daniel was accepted into the society. That same month we attended a ceremony to accept Daniel's membership. We were so proud of his accomplishment yet so saddened he was not there to accept the award or to demonstrate to the world the talents he had to share.

A DINNER TABLE FAMILY

To know Daniel you need to know his family. We were a close family that found time to do things together. We almost always ate dinner together. There was no sneaking off to watch the TV or play on the computer. We ate together, talked together, and exchanged stories and ribbed each other.

Daniel's mother, my wife, is extremely loving. Linda was born in 1951 in Illinois and adopted by Joe and Virginia Conner of Colorado. She grew up on a farm outside Longmont, north of Denver. She was the only child of a ranching father and elementary school teacher mother (both now deceased).

Linda is a graduate of Longmont High and the University of Colorado–Denver, where she earned her bachelor's in English. She has worked as a legal secretary and paralegal. She's an avid reader, and has been a member of various book clubs and Bible study groups. She is a master of board games, especially ones requiring knowledge of vocabulary, like Scrabble and Bananagrams.

She could be counted on to volunteer at our kids' schools. She's been a downhill and cross-country skier, tennis player, hiker, poker player, and swimmer. She considers herself a feminist, yet chose not to work outside of the home for most of the years when Daniel and Christie were growing up. It was a choice and financial sacrifice we made to allow for more nurturing of our children. It turned out to be an ominously fortuitous choice that allowed us to spend more precious time with Daniel.

I was born in 1952 and raised in Finleyville, a small town south of Pittsburgh. I'm the youngest of four children of a coal miner, Edward Mauser, and his homemaker wife Helen (both now deceased). Neither was well educated, having only reached the seventh grade. I was proud of the fact my dad took on the task of building the house in which I was raised. He did much of the work himself over four years, with some help from friends and a few contractors.

My father died of cancer when he was fifty-four and I was just ten. Life was tough, with my mom collecting Social Security survivor benefits. She supported us by cleaning homes and offices. It wasn't easy, since she had never learned to drive, relying on the bus system, my siblings and me, friends, and employers to get around.

I'm a graduate of Monongahela (now Ringgold) High and the University of Pittsburgh, where I earned a bachelor's in political science and urban studies in 1974 and a master's in public administration in 1976. Shortly after graduating, I visited Colorado on vacation and moved to Denver that fall to get a new start on life, in a state with a better job market. I met Linda at a New Year's party in 1979, and we married in May 1981.

Like Linda, I enjoy downhill skiing, tennis, poker, board games and hiking. I like bicycling, climbing the easier 14,000-foot mountain peaks, and exploring the mountains and their old ghost towns. I'm a good photographer but my biggest passion is music.

I have an active sense of humor. I am witty, a practical joker, and a good joke teller, especially if the joke involves relaying it in a foreign accent or certain character type, given my ability to speak with a number of foreign accents.

Eighteen months after Daniel's birth, his sister Christine Leigh arrived in October 1985. They were a great pair, and Daniel was a terrific big brother, watching over Christie. They played with kids in the neighborhood, yet spent lots of time entertaining each other.

Christie and Daniel were close, though their personalities were somewhat different. In most respects, Daniel was much more like Linda—shy, introspective, intelligent, and calm. Christie was like me—a bit more outgoing, not quite as disciplined, and a bit wild and crazy. Daniel would roll his eyes at his sister, a budding thespian, and in an exasperated tone exclaim, "Theater people! Oh, my God!" Linda thinks he prided himself on being a rational sort of fellow, not given to drama of any sort.

Christie is slender, with blue eyes, a light complexion, and long, silky blonde hair. She learned Tae Kwon Do, liked art, writing, cats, and bike riding. She did well in school, and enjoyed drama and acting. She followed in Daniel's footsteps, volunteering at Swedish Hospital.

LASTING IMAGES

We exposed our children to the world, taking regular visits to the zoo, the children's museum, IMAX nature movies, and the natural history museum. We believed in showing our kids the world around them. Among the places Daniel and Christie visited: Washington, D.C.; Los Angeles; San Diego; Pittsburgh; Orlando; Sarasota (where Daniel was stung by a sting ray in the shallow water of the ocean); Yellowstone; Niagara Falls; Mt. Rushmore; Las Vegas; Grand Canyon; Zion, Bryce Canyon and Arches National Parks in Utah; the coast of Maine; Boston; and New York City. And we visited nearly all the favorite scenic spots here in Colorado. Daniel loved telling stories to others about the misfortunes from our trips.

We seldom used a camera at home in my childhood, perhaps because we were poor, so there are few pictures of me as a child, other than formal school portraits and a few photos I was given by other people.

I was not about to let that happen to my kids. I was often playfully ridiculed about being a pest with a camera as Daniel and Christie grew up, especially by Daniel, who didn't like having his picture taken when he was a teen. The family tired of my, "Wait! Don't move! That's a great shot! Oh, maybe not. Wait, I want to take an 'insurance' shot in case that didn't work out. Come on, Daniel, smile. No, not a fake one, a natural one!"

By taking tons of shots I ended up with some terrific photos of my kids. I preferred taking photos of them in everyday settings, being themselves, and snapping the photo at any moment rather than after a staged "Cheese!" I also rented a video camera for nearly every one of the kids' birthday parties.

The ridicule I faced for taking so many photos, and all the money I spent on photos and video equipment, was certainly worth it. I'm so happy I made a pest of myself. I relish those photos and videos. They're irreplaceable.

DRIVING DAD CRAZY

Daniel reached a milestone late in 1998, when at the age of fifteen and a half, he qualified to get his driver's permit. One evening I asked him to go to the grocery store with me. It was a ruse. Instead I drove to the parking lot of our church, pulled in and signaled for Daniel to get behind the wheel.

"What are you doing, Dad? I'm not ready for that. I'm waiting, so don't push it."

I was shocked and disappointed. I assumed he would jump at the chance to drive a car for the first time, but he wasn't ready. With a school trip to France coming up, as well as other school projects, Daniel had made an agreement with Linda that he would hold off on taking driver training classes until summer vacation. I was hoping I could get him to drive anyway. But he seemed in no rush to learn. He was determined to honor his agreement, so we just drove back home. He never did get behind the wheel of a car.

CLASSMATES

Daniel achieved many things. But high-profile popularity was not one of them. He was too shy. Yet to many fellow students he will be remembered for his helpfulness, his smile, and his gentle personality.

We received numerous letters and Web site messages from Daniel's classmates after the massacre. If there was anything that could bring me to tears, it was these messages. I rarely went to school events, and knowing Daniel was so shy, I worried about how he got along with other students. When I received these touching, personal messages, I was greatly relieved and moved.

Renalda of Denver didn't attend Columbine but wrote: "I had the opportunity to meet Daniel once at a debate meet I was not even going to attend, but was dragged to by some friends. Daniel and I conversed shortly, and it was clear that his intelligence was bright and strong. He taught me a few things in the short time we talked. I will always remember your son. The impact he had on me in such a short time was great."

Natasha from the town of Parker says she only met Daniel a few times at cross country meets, "but I remember how genuine and sincere he was. He just stuck out in my mind the first time I met him. I didn't know him, yet he simply said, 'Great race!' one day, and I was like, wow, he honestly made my day by congratulating me before my coaches even did."

Devon Adams reminded us that "Moose" was Daniel's nickname in debate class. "So appropriate—it's a large, amusing but quick and fierce-when-it-needs-to-be animal."

Peter simply told us: "Dan was my friend. That's the most wonderful thing that I can say. In its simplicity it is what I will cherish."

Angie wrote: "I knew who Dan was, I was lucky enough to have 5th hour with him in American Literature class. He always had something to add to our class conversations and when no other student had anything to say or knew anything to say, Dan would always speak up. He was a very smart kid. I never got to know him, but I looked through the Web site and learned a lot about who he was and I only wish that everybody could have gotten to know that side of Dan, including me. I know he was shy because although he was involved in the classroom discussions, he never really talked otherwise."

One girl, Leann, wrote as if she were writing to a still-present Daniel. "I remember debate class and the quiet boy, who I was sure was about to make the best argument. I remember how you used to get excited when Sergio or someone else from class would get involved in a heated debate. I just wanted to write and say that I haven't forgotten you and I never will."

Video of Daniel on YouTube (see link in Appendix).

Chapter 3

Reality Sets In

The pain of losing Daniel would not go away. Every new task, every new duty brought waves of pain: calling family members to inform them of the tragic news, fielding calls from friends and coworkers asking whether Daniel "was safe." I was unprepared for this anguish. But then, how does one prepare for the death of one's child? Nobody close to me had been through it. Lord, how were we going to handle this? How was Christie going to handle this?

How do you grieve when you're also having to deal with excruciatingly painful tasks like funeral and burial arrangements? I didn't want to have to think about choosing a casket and cemetery for Daniel or what music and readings I wanted for his funeral. Just a few days before that I was talking with Daniel about his debate class, I was playing a game of foosball with him. How could it be I was suddenly having to deal with burying his body? How was it he could be a murder victim?

How was I going to get through this?

FAMILY COMFORT

Early on I was warned by a victims advocate that it was possible Linda and I would grieve in different ways, and it could put a serious strain on our marriage. An old high school friend who was a doctor called to express condolences and during our conversation cautioned me that the death of a child can put a very heavy burden on couples. Their early guidance was extremely helpful advice because Linda and I did indeed discover that we grieved in different ways.

My immediate family flew out to be with us. My brother and sister from Pittsburgh, and my brother from Houston, flew out as soon as they could, along with members of their families. Others came from all over the country to comfort us, including an elderly man who was a next door neighbor from my childhood, an old college roommate living in California, and a cousin from Pennsylvania.

Missing was my mother. If ever there was a blessing in the curse of Alzheimer's disease, this was one. My mother, who had just turned ninety-one, was in a nursing home and was a fair way along in her struggle with the disease. She was not tuned in to what was going on around her, so had no idea what happened to her grandson.

My mother adored Daniel. She loved to rock him in her arms and take him for long walks. If she had been alert and aware of what had happened to her precious grandson, she might have had a heart attack, despite having a strong heart that eventually kept her alive until she was ninety-nine. But if not struck by a heart attack, she certainly would have suffered from tremendous heartache. She was a nervous and emotional person; she would not have known how to deal with the shock of losing her precious grandson. She probably couldn't have withstood the flight out to Denver. And I can't even imagine her being able to endure his funeral. It was best she was oblivious.

Being surrounded by family helped me greatly. Linda, conversely, had no immediate family members. She is an only child, and within the previous decade her parents had passed away, as had her Denver aunts and uncles, none of whom had any children. On one hand, she at least had the experience of grieving their deaths, but on the other hand they were all elderly, which was hardly comparable to the loss of her son. Without her own family members to lean on, she relied on my family and her good friends, particularly her best friend Marlene.

I don't recall a lot of what was happening those first few days, just bits and pieces. I can't imagine how we survived. How did we manage to sleep at night—or did we? Did we remember to feed our pets? How did the laundry get done? We were numb, shell-shocked. I think we were operating on automatic pilot, just carrying out some normal routines as we normally did but hardly aware we were doing so. Other tasks were carried out by our friends and family members, who bought groceries and ran errands we needed, like taking our dog to a kennel because the commotion was just too much for him. Linda and I rarely ventured outside our house unless we had to attend to a duty related to the upcoming funeral.

I recall the great conflict I felt on a couple of occasions when I came across people at our home who were engaged in a slightly upbeat conversation that included a funny story or laughter. For a moment I found myself livid with them, wondering how they could be so insensitive at such a tragic time. At the next moment I debated whether I should perhaps be grateful to them, for intuitively I realized they were also numbed by this loss but probably recognized the need to reflect positively on Daniel's life and to avoid being somber all the time.

I recall a disappointing visit from our parish priest, who brought with him Denver's Catholic archbishop, Charles Chaput. We were honored that Denver's top Catholic official would come to our home to offer his condolences, but the visit was awkwardly formal and they seemed so stiff that it didn't bring much comfort to us. They didn't stay long, not even sitting down with us, saying they had others to visit.

THE MEDIA ONSLAUGHT

A victim's advocate provided me with a flyer—"Your Rights with the Press"—outlining how to deal with the media. Its subtitle was "You have the right at all times to be treated with dignity and respect by the media." The paper included tips such as:

You have the right to say "no" to an interview even if you have granted previous interviews.

You have the right to select the spokesperson or advocate of your choice.

You have the right to select the time and location of an interview.

Intuitively I knew most of the tips and had had a little exposure to the media, but it still helped to read them, for I certainly wasn't prepared for the onslaught that was about to come.

The media circus came quickly. Once the names of the victims were released, we started receiving calls. My neighbors were concerned about the disruption that might be caused by the media and curious onlookers. A day or two after the massacre, they asked police if they could block off our cul-de-sac to keep the media and others at bay but were told they could not do so. Some did the next best thing—they parked their cars on the street to fill up the available curbside parking. That way any reporters had to park elsewhere and walk to our house and be seen by others, rather than easily clog our street and quickly approach our house.

At first I simply told those in the house with us to get rid of any reporters that called or came to the door. A day or two after the massacre, I was told a reporter was speaking to neighbors to get information about Daniel. That evening a call came from a reporter at one of Denver's daily newspapers seeking information to write a story summarizing Daniel's life. I refused to take the call, being in no mood to deal with the media.

I reconsidered, though, once I realized I was being given an opportunity. My neighbors perhaps could tell a heartwarming story about Daniel, but I was the one who knew all about my son's life. The world needed to know about him. I didn't want an empty or incomplete story next to Daniel's photo in the newspaper. The world needed to hear about Daniel Conner Mauser.

I excused myself and broke away from the crowd. I went to the basement, where in about thirty minutes, after conferring with Linda, I quickly wrote a short summary of Daniel's life. I made a cold call to the switchboard of the newspaper and told them who I was and that I wanted to fax them a story about my son. Now the world would hear about Daniel from his proud parents.

DEALING WITH THE ONSLAUGHT

We were receiving dozens of phone calls every day. We didn't have caller ID, so we couldn't screen calls. Friends and relatives were calling, so we couldn't ignore them. There were so many calls that we asked the people helping us to filter them. News agencies from all over the world wanted to talk with us but very few succeeded.

I was fortunate to work with someone with expertise in dealing with the media. Our state agency's public information manager, Dan Hopkins, offered his help and that of his staff to deal with the crush of media attention.

I felt guilty accepting Dan's help. He had plenty to do already, and this was a personal issue, not part of his job duties. But, as he pointed out, since it quickly became known that I was a CDOT employee, he was getting lots of media calls from reporters angling for information from him, so he was getting calls anyway.

I accepted his offer. Within an hour or two Dan and one of his staff members came to my house, downloaded pictures of Daniel, as well as my summary of Daniel's life, and made it available to the media. We agreed to funnel all media calls to Dan's office. I told Dan I was willing to talk to the media about Daniel. He thought it would become too overwhelming; I was still in a fog and not watching a lot of television coverage, so I wasn't fully aware of the widespread and worldwide coverage of this tragedy. I wasn't thinking about how some of the questions would be difficult, how reporters would drill me with questions about the killers and the causes of the massacre, and how much time it would take to deal with the media.

It quickly became evident the media requests were too numerous. I backed off my offer to respond to most media requests, and limited the interviews to just a few major national and local news outlets. In the first ten days I spoke to just a few reporters, and only by phone; I didn't provide live, or radio or television interviews.

Most of the media representatives who called our home were kind and understanding, according to those who answered our home phone. But it was different for Dan, probably because calls were referred to him and he was serving as the "traffic cop" for access to me. He said some in the national media were rude and aggressive, requesting attention as if it were his obligation to provide information to them. This was especially true of national talk radio programs and a few magazines.

There were some horror stories. Allegedly a *People* magazine reporter had the nerve to show up on the doorstep of one of the Columbine parents at 9:00 p.m. in the evening, asking for an interview. Other reporters were seen by our neighbors surreptitiously lurking around our cul-de-sac, perhaps looking for an unusual story or waiting to pounce on us if we left the house.

The local media usually were more respectful and recognized that we deserved our privacy. But there were a few exceptions. For instance, a Boulder newspaper reporter came to our front door without announcement within the first couple of days. I naïvely assumed that reporters would not be so rude as to intrude on a family at such a tragic time.

A few days after the tragedy, a local television station managed to get through to me on the phone and offered to provide video footage of Daniel's upcoming funeral, more or less in exchange for an interview. I believed it was an inappropriate offer, a deceitful attempt to gain access to me. "Pool" coverage of the funeral had been arranged, meaning only a few journalists and one television crew would be there, and they would share their video feed with all media outlets. I called the station and spoke to the news director, whom I told in no uncertain terms how disgusted I was with their offer and how I would never speak to them again if they tried such a maneuver.

ACTS OF KINDNESS

There were many acts of kindness that took some of the burden away from what was happening. All Columbine victims' family members and out-of-town guests were offered free airline tickets to Denver from United Airlines and free rooms at local Marriott hotels. We were offered free funeral arrangements and a free cemetery plot, though these costs were later covered by a victim's assistance fund.

A steady stream of friends and neighbors brought food and flowers and offered condolences. About a half-dozen people at any one time helped manage all the chaos in our home. (God bless them all!) One of the duties involved calling our friends and relatives to break the horrible news.

We were overflowing with food trays sent by friends and neighbors—more than we could handle. Food was everywhere. We had to ask neighbors to refrigerate some of it for us, or even simply take it and eat it themselves. The food trays came in handy, for in those first few days I don't think we ate any sit-down meals; we grabbed something, threw it in the microwave, scarfed it down, and went on to the next painful task or conversation.

The house overflowed with flowers, many from complete strangers. I appreciated the thoughts they represented, but there were simply too many flowers, and they had a negative side. The arrangements, some of them huge, took up too much space in a house already overflowing with well-wishers and food. Worse, for me, however, was the smell and sight of them: I felt as if our house was a funeral home. I hated to discard them, but I asked our visitors to take some of them home with them.

One particular act of kindness occurred within the first couple of days. Chuck Blaskovich, a neighbor on our cul-de-sac, came to our house and asked for a photo of Daniel. He returned within a day with twenty or so large buttons bearing one of my favorite photos of Daniel. We distributed them to family members and others who wore them to the funeral and other events over the next few days. I continued wearing the treasured buttons at numerous public events for years thereafter. I still have one of the buttons left. The pin is badly bent and barely functions, but it is still precious to me.

LASHING OUT

By the end of that first tragic week, I began thinking of the role that easy access to guns seemed to play in the massacre at Columbine. I thought of how a number of pro-gun bills were breezing through toward passage in the Colorado legislature in February. I was concerned enough back then that I wrote a letter about the bills to my state representative. I was so upset with the tone of some pro-gun letters to the editor in the *Denver Post* that I cut them out and saved them, determined to respond with my own letter to the editor. I never got around to it.

On the Saturday following the massacre, I separated from others in the house in the morning and went to the basement to use the phone. I looked up the names of two or three of the men who wrote those pro-gun letters to the editor and made cold calls to them. This was not like me. I was not someone who found it easy to confront others, particularly in this way, and I was someone who did not easily get so upset. It was as if it were another person who was doing this, another person who was seemingly blaming these innocent people for gun violence.

I recall little about the calls I made that morning, except that I chided them, asking if they had any idea what it was like to have a child murdered with a gun. For some time I didn't think about the calls until I learned later about two of the men I called. I was told that one of my calls, ironically, was made to the brother of Anthony Fabian, who years later turned out to be an adversary of mine when he became president of the Colorado State Shooting Association, the National Rifle Association chapter in the state.

I also discovered I made a call to a Michael Lantz from the Denver suburb of Lakewood. In July 2000, Lantz wrote to my state representative, Don Lee, because he read about an ongoing disagreement about gun control between me and Lee. Lantz apparently wanted to complain about me to Lee; I was made aware of the letter a year later when Lee tried to use the letter to discredit my lobbying work. In the letter, Lantz reported to Lee that he received an unwelcome phone call from me just after Columbine. Lantz claimed that I began speaking immediately after he answered the phone, telling him "to give up (his) worship of guns" and demanding that he promise to do so. He said I would not allow him to answer.

Lantz wrote that when he was able to respond, he insisted he did not worship guns and he believed everyone had a right to own or not own a gun. When I again told him to give up his worship of guns, he said he hung up on me. In the letter, Lantz wrote that I called again less than a minute later and again questioned his support of guns, then hung up. Lantz wrote that he told his wife he felt threatened by my call and thought about reporting it to the police, but didn't, though he wished he had reported my "threat."

I'm sure my call to Lantz was disturbing and unwelcome, but it was hard for me to think of my call as a "threat." Why would he think that a man whose son was just murdered might threaten a stranger who had done him no harm? Perhaps Lantz had never experienced such tremendous grief and could not imagine how a grieving father might lash out at those who seemingly support lax gun laws that could lead to teens gaining easy access to weapons.

I wish I had never made those phone calls. Although I'm ashamed of what I did, I can also forgive myself because I recognize my state of mind at the time. I was distraught and angry about weak laws that made it so easy for the wrong people, like teenagers, to gain access to guns. I lashed out at these two men because it was convenient to direct that anger at them at that moment.

ACTS OF PAIN

I dreaded the duties associated with laying Daniel to rest, particularly going to the morgue to identify his body. I had seen that scene play out on television shows, but that was hardly preparation; I was not ready to live through it myself. How the hell could I possibly keep my composure through such a painful ordeal? Fortunately, though, we were informed that authorities had dental records and a good enough description of Daniel and his clothes to identify him definitively, without the need for us to go to the morgue.

But we could not escape other dreadful responsibilities. The trips to the funeral home and cemetery were very long, quiet ones. The funeral home was only a few miles away, but the cemetery was in Golden, more than 20 miles from home. I still recall the route I took to get there and the mellow Nicholas Gunn music I played during the trip to try to soothe our nerves.

We had to pick out a casket for Daniel. I didn't want to deal with it. I didn't care much about which casket to choose and didn't see the need to deliberate about the cemetery plot. I just wanted to get it over with. I would have been willing to just hand over the responsibility to someone else if I could have.

We had to arrange for a headstone and a cemetery plot location. As we spoke to the cemetery representative, we suddenly came to the realization that Daniel was going to be buried there alone forever if we didn't do something to change that. We couldn't let him be there alone, so we decided to purchase two plots for ourselves next to Daniel, which added to the painful paperwork.

Because of Daniel's interest in debate, he wanted Linda to buy him a nice suit, which she did shortly before he died. He wore it only once—at Easter. Linda decided it was appropriate to have him buried in it, along with photos of his favorite cat and first pet, Alfred, and *Star Wars* videos.

We had to select a day and time for his burial, and arrange for a funeral Mass, along with the songs and readings for the service. Because our church parish was also home to other Columbine victims, our priest suggested a joint wake Friday night for Daniel, Kelly Fleming, and Matt Kechter. He also suggested a joint funeral Mass on Sunday evening, though it would only be for Daniel and Kelly, since Matt's funeral Mass was planned for a different day.

I was not thrilled about having joint services, but I also understood the burden placed on our church by the massacre: three of the slain students and one of the seriously wounded were parish members, and the church also had to deal with numerous teens in shock and a crush of media.

MORE ANGUISHING NEWS

I was upset that we were having trouble getting information about the funeral arrangements. The funeral home informed us they wanted to schedule the funeral and burial yet didn't know when the authorities would give them Daniel's remains. They had to proceed, scheduling a Sunday funeral Mass and a Monday burial. Yet by Thursday they said they still didn't have Daniel's body and were unsure when the viewing could be. We were appalled that we had to wait so long for our son's body to be released, especially in a case where it was known who committed the crime and how Daniel was killed. It was distressing to think his body had to wait so long before being embalmed.

I was distressed when I realized there wasn't going to be much time for the viewing at the funeral home. Where I grew up, burials were not quick. Viewings were usually open casket, they lasted at least a couple of days, and it was an important family gathering.

Late Thursday evening, after most of our friends had gone, the mortician called to say he finally had been given Daniel's body. He suggested having the viewing starting at noon on Saturday and going through Sunday afternoon. That wasn't much time, but he told me there was little they could do. He indicated they would be rushing just to have his body ready for the viewing time on Saturday, since he had been shot in the face and extra cosmetic work was needed to prepare him.

My body froze in shock. *Shot in the face?* It was the first time I had been told that disturbing news. Shot in the *face?* How the hell could someone shoot my son in the face? What kind of person could look at another human being and shoot him in the face? They were questions that rushed through my distressed mind during a painful pause that seemed to last forever. I composed myself as best I could, then timidly asked whether it was going to be okay to continue with the planned open casket for the viewing.

Margi witnessed me on the phone during this conversation. I may not have spoken anything in response at first, but apparently I was far from silent. She said she will never forget the sound that came out of my mouth with the news from the mortician about Daniel being shot in the face: "It was a sort of scream accompanied by a low, guttural noise—total and complete anguish. It was horrible."

I wanted to see Daniel beforehand to decide whether an open casket would be appropriate, but the mortician said it wasn't that simple. There wouldn't be enough time before the viewing, because they had to plan for one or the other. He tried to assure me they would be able to present Daniel well, yet I couldn't help but think how I didn't want people to remember him as disfigured.

Linda told me not to worry, but I ignored her advice. I was distraught. The funeral home consented to let us see Daniel just before the viewing began. There would be little time to change our minds; we were told to plan for an open casket.

At the funeral home, I was relieved when I saw Daniel's face. He was not disfigured; in fact it was difficult to see his injury. Still, it was difficult to look at him. For me it was not the case that Daniel "looked good." He looked okay considering how much time elapsed before the mortician was given his body. But to me the body looked little like Daniel. The last time I saw him he was teeming with life, not unanimated, motionless and pale. This was a young man so full of life just a few days ago. I wanted that Daniel back.

Daniel at Glenwood Hot Springs Pool

Chapter 4

From Dust to Dust

April 1999 was the second wettest April recorded in Denver history, with 5.86 inches of rainfall, some of it in the form of miserable, slushy snow. That rainfall was about a third of what semiarid Denver normally gets in an entire year. It also was the seventh coldest April, with an average temperature of 42.6 degrees Fahrenheit. That was especially true for the days following April 20, as the weather mirrored the gloom that surrounded our household and the community.

There were so many dark, wet, cold days that even now I get an awful, depressing, sinking feeling when the weather is damp, chilly, and rainy in the days following each Columbine anniversary.

THE WAKE

On Friday night, April 23, the wake was held for Daniel, Kelly, and Matt. Most of the twelve hundred seats at St. Frances Cabrini Church were taken.

Not only had Linda picked the scripture reading for the wake, she wanted to read it. She had been an excellent "proclaimer" at our church, reading Bible verses during Mass, but I worried about whether she would be up to the task on this night. She was a strong woman, but this was such an extraordinarily grueling situation. I was concerned that she might break down. I could certainly understand if she did, but I wondered why she wanted to put herself through that. I went to the altar to stand with her and support her as she read. But it was me that looked and acted upset and stressed out, not Linda.

It was unbelievable how strong and brave she was that night. She spoke calmly and gracefully. She didn't drop her head or become tearful. In a great dedication to Daniel's spirit, she even looked up at the audience frequently as she read from Romans verses 8:31–39.

These are verses that ask, "If God is for us, who can be against us? Who will separate us from the love of Christ? Will trouble, or distress, or persecution, or famine, or nakedness or danger, or sword?...neither death, nor life, nor angels, nor heavenly rulers, nor things that are present, nor things to come, nor powers nor height, nor depth, nor anything else in creation will be able to separate us from the love of God in Christ Jesus our Lord." It was an amazingly fitting and positive reading she selected for that occasion.

When the priest gave people the opportunity to say something about any of the teens, Linda was the second person that made her way to the microphone. I had no idea she was going to do so. I had assumed it would be others who spoke at these events, not family members. I could not believe her strength to once again face the crowd.

"I just want to say how pure Daniel was in his heart," she began. She related to the crowd how Daniel reacted while reading J. D. Salinger's *Catcher in the Rye*. The book is a rite of passage story about the book's main character, Holden Caulfield. Linda told how Daniel had remarked, "I don't think there are that many phony people out there. I think Holden was way too cynical." It was a sign of the positive (maybe even a little naïve) view of the world that Daniel held.

Daniel had taken a class trip to France just a few weeks before the massacre. Linda fondly remembered Daniel asking what she would like him to bring back for her. She wanted some good chocolate. But to her surprise, he returned home with a gold cross necklace that he bought at the majestic Mont Saint-Michel church and monastery on the French coast. She showed the crowd the necklace. "I just really can't believe what it meant to me. I really think it was a sign to me. I really do believe that."

The next person to approach the altar was Christie. Again, I felt disbelief. I had no idea Christie would also be speaking and was so proud of her for having the strength.

"I have a lot of great memories about my brother. But my favorite is the last time I talked to him, which was on Tuesday morning [April 20]. He was just leaving out the door and he said, 'I love you,' and I said, 'I love you, too.' I was really shocked. I knew he always loved me, but he didn't say it that often. I felt pretty special about it at school that day because usually he only said 'I love you' on holidays or Christmas."

The crowd chuckled at her observation, making for a needed tension reliever. I chuckled for a moment also, but then I sobbed, for it was such an amazing story, such an amazing sign of comfort to us. It was the first I heard her relate that story. Perhaps Christie had tried to tell me about it but I had been too distracted.

More people went to the altar and spoke of the three slain students. But not me. I just sat there. Where were the words? It's not often that I'm a man of no words, but that night I had no voice. I could say I wasn't prepared to speak, or that I thought the speaking was just for other than family members, or that Linda and Christie had already spoken. That's what I told myself as I sat there, but those were just excuses.

I just sat there. I could have overcome those excuses for not speaking. But I didn't. I never went to the altar to speak. It's not that everything had already been said. I could have talked about how playful Daniel was, how he loved to help others, how he tried to overcome his shortcomings by taking them on directly. But I just sat there. I'm still ashamed of myself for not speaking. I don't know why I failed to speak up, but I think it was something that motivated me later to do other things to honor Daniel in such a public and vocal way—to make up for my failure to speak up to honor Daniel that night.

THE BOWLES CROSSING MEMORIAL

Sunday, April 25, was yet another dismal and dreary day with scattered showers. We once again endured the painful task of greeting people at the funeral home, but not for very long. We decided to attend a community memorial service being held for all the Columbine victims. It seemed appropriate to attend the service, given that it was a gift from the community and since Vice President Al Gore, General Colin Powell, and Governor Bill Owens were among the dignitaries who would speak. I felt very conflicted by our decision. On one hand, I felt I had an obligation to be at the funeral home to greet and thank those who came to pay their respects. At the same time, though, it was agonizing to be there. My family assured me it was okay to attend the memorial service and that visitors would understand.

The memorial event was held in the Bowles Crossing shopping center. A makeshift stage was positioned at the top of the steps of a theater complex. The standing-room-only crowd packed into the theater parking lot.

Before the event began the Columbine families had a private audience inside the theater with the dignitaries. We met them as we walked through a reception line. It was humbling to be in the presence of the Vice President of the United States and a hero like Colin Powell, knowing they had come here to comfort us. But at the same time I couldn't ignore the realization that we were all there only because my child and others had been murdered. I was grateful for their presence, but they couldn't undo what had happened.

After the reception, we were all led to a special seating area in the front of the crowd. There was no announcement of our arrival, but some in the front of the crowd must have figured out who we were as we marched out, for we noticed the sad, reverent looks on their faces as we proceeded to our seats.

I'll never forget how Bruce Beck, stepfather of victim Lauren Townsend, acknowledged the crowd with the sign language signal for "I love you"—a raised thumb, index finger and pinky finger. I had to ask Linda what the sign meant. It became something I often flashed to crowds when I spoke, and ever since that day it's been something my family flashes at home with each other to show our love for each other.

More than seventy thousand people were packed into the parking lot and beyond. Survivors of the massacre, brothers Jonathan and Stephen Cohen, sang their song, "Columbine, Friend of Mine," which had become an instant favorite in the Denver community. The speakers offered comforting and inspiring words, but I heard only some of what they said, for I was mostly thinking of Daniel and the difficulty of the coming days.

THE FUNERAL MASS

We left the memorial service before the crowd proceeded to nearby Clement Park for another ceremony because we needed to prepare ourselves for Daniel's 5:15 funeral Mass. It was a joint service for both Daniel and Kelly Fleming. As we arrived by funeral limousine at the church, special measures were taken to whisk us into the church to avoid the media, the curious, and people who wanted to talk personally to us before the Mass.

The church was teeming with people. A closed circuit television was set up in the gymnasium to accommodate an overflowing crowd. I was humbled as I occasionally glanced up to see various friends, coworkers, and people I hadn't seen in years there to pay their respects to Daniel.

Linda and I were asked if we would be willing to close Daniel's casket at the beginning of the service. I volunteered to do so, probably because I wanted to make up for not speaking at Friday night's wake, and because I remembered my mother sobbing and leaning over to kiss my father just before he was laid to rest when I was a child. It was a painful yet rewarding and symbolic act, as I leaned over and kissed Daniel on the forehead, and gently said goodbye.

It was a beautiful service, presided over by Archbishop Chaput. There was no need to worry about speaking in front of the crowd, no need to worry about whether he was in a better place. We took solace in the beautiful music and the comforting words offered to us.

DANIEL'S BURIAL

Daniel was buried the next day, six days after the massacre. It was a small but moving ceremony at Mt. Olivet Cemetery, open only to family and close friends. Afterward, my family members and others who had come to Denver to be with us ate lunch together at a restaurant near the cemetery. Then everyone said goodbye as they headed off to their destinations.

It was wonderful to have these family members and friends with us. But when they all left at once after lunch we suddenly felt terribly alone. We had each other, and we knew intuitively that our friends and even strangers would be there to comfort us in the coming weeks and months. Still, at *that* moment, as our friends and family departed, we felt dreadfully alone. I will never forget the absolutely empty, dark, frightful feeling as Linda, Christie, and I left the parking lot alone and drove home in painful silence.

As much as the chores and ceremonies of the last few days were difficult and painful, they at least kept us focused, and perhaps a bit distracted from the hollowness of life without Daniel. While our departing friends and family were returning to some degree of normalcy in their lives, we were returning to a different home. We were returning to an empty home—a home without Daniel—and to a home and life with seemingly nothing good to look forward to.

Chapter 5

The Massacre at Columbine

The massacre at Columbine, there are still people who are unclear about what happened there. Some people continue to repeat misinformation about it. Some people have told me they simply didn't want to hear the horrific details, didn't care about it, or were young and shielded from the news by their parents.

Much has already been written and documented in great detail about what happened on that dark day. I won't provide all the gruesome details and minutia in this book, but I will cover the basics. This information is primarily culled from law enforcement reports and reliable news reports.

MASS MURDER ON THE MENU

At 11:14 a.m. on the morning of April 20, 1999, Eric David Harris, eighteen, and Dylan Bennet Klebold, seventeen, walked into the cafeteria at Columbine with murder on their minds. They carried two large duffle bags, each loaded with a 20-pound propane tank bomb, and placed them on the floor next to some tables and walked away, assuming they and the two bags would be unnoticed in a sea of students and backpacks.

They set a timer to detonate the propane bombs. The time was carefully selected by Harris, based on his prior observations of the cafeteria, so he could kill the maximum number of students. He determined that 11:17 was the time they could kill hundreds of students.

Harris and Klebold proceeded to their cars in the parking lot outside the cafeteria. Their plan was to wait for the explosion and then shoot survivors as they fled the building. The killers waited with two shotguns, a TEC 9 handgun, a Hi Point 9mm carbine rifle, and 76 homemade explosives.

The two propane bombs did not detonate, as the killers had planned. Many people can be thankful for that. But having failed to wreak death and havoc, they decided to use the guns and other explosives to kill their classmates. They scrambled to the top of a small hill on the west side of the school, where they had a view and clear shots of the outside exit from the cafeteria and well-traveled sidewalks.

AN END OF INNOCENCE

The Columbine killers stood on high ground in their infamous trench coats, worn so they could hide their long guns, along with backpacks and duffle bags, where they stashed their sawed-off shotguns, ammunition, and bombs. They began firing upon students at about 11:21. First they shot two students who were sitting on the grass eating lunch. Then they shot three students exiting the cafeteria. Then more students were shot. The killers were also lighting and tossing explosives.

The Jefferson County Sheriff's community resource officer for the school, Neil Gardner, was eating lunch a short distance away from the school when the shooting began. After being alerted of trouble by a school custodian at 11:22, he arrived on the scene in his car at 11:24, with lights flashing and siren blaring. The killers realized their shooting spree would not go unchallenged, as they and Gardner exchanged gunfire. None of the three was hit.

Meanwhile, in the cafeteria, teacher Dave Sanders and two custodians recognized the danger and told students to get under the tables. As the students became more aware of the danger around them, a number of them rushed out of the cafeteria and proceeded up the stairs to the second floor of the west wing.

Teacher Patty Nielsen, looking out the west entrance doors on the second floor to see what was happening, was hit with glass as the doors were shattered by a bullet. She retreated into the nearby library, which was located above the embattled cafeteria. She ducked behind the main counter and called 911, while also yelling at the fifty-four students in the library to take cover under the tables. If any of them had run to the outside hallway, there is a good chance they would have run into the killers.

Facing fire from Gardner, the killers took cover in the school using the west entrance door, where Patty Nielsen had been injured moments before. They fired shots at fleeing students in the hallways. Hero Dave Sanders, who had directed students to safety, was shot and crawled into a science classroom with the aid of teacher Richard Long.

At 11:27 the killers were in the hallway outside the library, firing their weapons and setting off bombs for three minutes, but not hitting any students. Teacher Patty Nielsen, still in the library with students, continued talking with a 911 operator. She told the operator she heard bombs and gunfire in the hallway just outside the library. The operator told her help was on the way.

NO LONGER A REFUGE

At 11:29 the killers entered the library. Exact times of events are known because of the recording of Nielsen's 911 call. The killers shouted at the students to "Get up!" None of the 54 students rose. They fired one shot into the room as they entered, injuring one student. Then they shot and killed a student as they walked toward the west windows of the library. They shot out the windows as they took aim at the police and fleeing students. The police returned fire. It was like a war zone.

Then the library became an execution chamber, as the killers walked around taunting students, then shooting them. Some were shot and some were spared. Some who were shot were known to the killers. One spared student was in one of Harris's classes but not a friend. Harris told him, "We're killing people!" then asked him to leave. He did.

At one point Harris moved a gun too close to his face as he fired. The recoil smashed the gun into his face, resulting in a bloody, injured nose. He was likely in pain, for eyewitnesses reported he was suddenly much more agitated.

HORRIFIC, LIFE-CHANGING SOUNDS

Near the end of the shooting spree in the library, Eric Harris approached Daniel, who, like the others, was hunkered down under a table. According to various reports from witnesses, Harris taunted Daniel by calling him a geek, and reportedly referred to him as "four eyes" because he wore glasses.

At 11:34:55 Eric Harris fired a bullet from the Hi Point Carbine. It pierced Daniel's hand but probably was not life-threatening. Daniel pushed a chair at Harris. Daniel paid for that act of defiance and self-defense, as Harris called out, "Get up!" and at 11:34:57 fired another bullet, this time into Daniel's face. The bullet entered near his nose and traveled into his brain, likely killing him quickly. God rest his soul.

The public has heard the beginning portion of the 911 tape, as the killers entered the library. The public has not heard the tape thereafter, as the Columbine killers went on their shooting spree in the library. And it never should. It is a disturbing recording of the sound of hell on earth, of hatred, of horror, of death.

The families of the victims were given the opportunity to listen to the recording. Linda had no interest in listening. It was a year or more before I chose to do so. I just wasn't ready for it before then. I knew it would be agonizing to hear it, but for some unknown reason I felt compelled to listen so that I could hear the distress, hear the sounds Daniel heard in his last moments of life. (I listened a second time to the tape as I was writing this book.)

It was one of the most disturbing experiences of my lifetime, listening as two monsters terrorized a group of innocent students and took sinister delight in killing them. When I listened to the tape, I did not cry. The experience was beyond such emotions. I simply sat in utter disbelief and shock.

I could not hear much of what was being said by the killers and their victims, unless they were especially loud. Much of what was reported came from eyewitness accounts or from police use of special methods for detecting sounds on the tape. Listening on a small cassette tape player didn't reveal those fine details, but I wasn't about to complain. I was hearing more than I could handle as it was. I could hear students crying out in shock, screaming "Oh my God!" and I could hear the killers calling out "Woo!" and "Yahoo!" as they shot classmates. I could hear each of the many shots fired. I sat in disbelief as I listened to the momentary, horrific sounds that marked the end of ten human lives.

I also heard the shots fired at 11:34:55 and 11:34:57. I sat there thinking of how that second shot ended the life of my son. Could there possibly be a more horrific, solitary sound that a parent could hear?

SEVEN MINUTES OF DESTRUCTION

In seven minutes, Eric Harris and Dylan Klebold killed ten students and wounded twelve others in the library. The other students in the library were not singled out for execution. We will never know why. My belief is the killers showed their power over others by demonstrating how they had the ability to choose between life and death. They relished it. But also, when they saw the faces of kids they knew and were suddenly faced with the reality of shooting them, perhaps the killers saw themselves for the cowards they were and had some second thoughts.

At 11:36, the killers left the library and walked through the science area. They apparently made eye contact with some students in the rooms, but did not attempt to break into those rooms. But they were not done. They threw some pipe bombs into the cafeteria from the hallway above.

At about 11:44, the killers entered the cafeteria. One of them fired several bullets at one of the propane bombs that had failed to detonate at 11:17. He was likely trying for the destructive explosion they had been hoping for earlier. And they were probably hoping to end their lives at the same time. But they failed once again.

At noon they left the cafeteria and returned to the library. By then most of the surviving students had departed. One of the killers fired a gun at the police from the library window. At around 12:06 p.m., the killers committed suicide in the library by shooting themselves in the head.

When the rampage was over, Cassie Bernall, Steven Curnow, Corey DePooter, Kelly Fleming, John Tomlin, Matt Ketchter, Dan Rohrbaugh, teacher/hero Dave Sanders, Rachel Scott, Isaiah Shoels, Lauren Townsend, Kyle Velasquez, and Daniel were dead. God rest their souls.

Injuries ranged from slight bullet grazes to paralyzing injuries. The injured were Brian Anderson, Richard Castaldo, Jennifer Doyle, Austin Eubanks, Nicholas Foss, Sean Graves, Makai Hall, Anne Marie Hochhalter, Patrick Ireland, Michael Johnson, Joyce Jankowski, Mark Kintgen, Lance Kirklin, Lisa Kreutz, Adam Kyler, Stephanie Munson, teacher Patti Nielson, Nicole Nowlen, Jenna Park, Kacey Ruegsegger, Valeen Schnurr, Charlie Simmons, Daniel Steepleton, Mark Taylor, and Evan Todd.

The aftermath on the west side of Columbine High School, where you can see plywood covering the shattered windows of the cafeteria and library.

IN THE LINE OF DUTY?

At no point during what I described above did law enforcement enter the school and engage the killers. They were outside the entire time. There were law enforcement officers from the Jefferson County Sheriff's Office, which had jurisdiction, and from the Denver Police Department, Arapahoe County Sheriff's Office, and other agencies.

Many people were upset that law enforcement officers didn't enter the building and seek out the shooters. They claimed that Patty Nielsen was lied to when she was told help was on the way. They insisted the police should have stormed the library once they were aware of the carnage taking place there, based on the 911 call. They claimed that the killers could have been stopped. They asked why law enforcement didn't act quickly and questioned why they would even bother responding to the scene if they weren't going to seek out the killers and do something to protect the students inside the school.

Law enforcement responded that the shooting in the library happened too quickly for the officers on the scene to evaluate the situation and stop the massacre in time.

The larger criticism was that officers took too long to enter the school, regardless of whether they could have made it into the library in time to save lives. Law enforcement responded that they were following what was standard operating procedure (SOP) at that time for such situations. SOP called for law enforcement to create a perimeter so the perpetrators could not escape, and to develop a plan for negotiating with the perpetrators. Unfortunately, this procedure does not account for situations where the perpetrators are simply seeking to mow people down and are suicidal, with no intent to negotiate.

With not much to do other than create a perimeter and exchange some gunfire with the killers, there was little the police could do to stop the killers as they went on a shooting spree. I don't blame the police on the front lines for that. I know there were many officers who were frustrated their orders were not to enter the school. Those orders came from Jefferson County Sheriff John Stone and his top commanders. They were responsible.

Stone's office was aware of what was happening in the library. There was some confusion as to how many shooters were in the school and who they were, but there should have been no doubt about the destruction going on inside the school, based on teacher Patty Nielsen's 911 call from the library.

People must judge for themselves whether the sheriff made a reasonable response under the circumstances. But the verdict is in on the SOP used at Columbine, as is clearly evidenced by the fact that it is *no longer* the SOP. Instead, police follow an "active shooter" SOP, which calls for more direct engagement with a shooter in such situations.

Although one can dispute the circumstances and danger that surrounded the police during the first thirty minutes of the massacre, I believe there is simply no excuse for what happened to teacher/hero Dave Sanders.

Sanders was the teacher who stayed in the school during the massacre to help students. After being shot, he found refuge in a science classroom. He was bleeding badly. Students posted a sign in the window of the classroom, in plain sight of police officers: "One bleeding to death." Those students watched in horror as Dave Sanders slowly died. More than two hours after the last shots were fired by the killers, two hours after they had committed suicide, Sanders drew his last breath.

What's especially troublesome is that it's also possible that some of the students who died in the library might have been alive during this time the sheriff refused to enter the school and their lives might have been saved if quicker action was taken.

Sheriff Stone said he could not put his officers into danger, given that the killers also had bombs that might have been set to detonate. It's true that was a possibility. But there are many situations where officers' lives are at risk. We should always be careful not to needlessly send them into harm's way, but in a case where there has not been gunfire for two hours and a human being is known to be bleeding to death, many found the sheriff's caution inexcusable.

That caution spilled over into the next day. Daniel's death was not confirmed by the sheriff's office until noon of the next day. We were told investigators were moving slowly and deliberately into the school and securing it cautiously. We were never told whether Daniel was even in the library, let alone whether he was shot, yet they would have known from interviewing survivors from the library that Daniel was there and was shot.

Some said we should be thankful that Columbine changed the way police respond to these shooting situations. Perhaps, but I don't believe Columbine was the first situation calling for an active shooter reaction. To me the SOP should have been questioned long before April 20, 1999. But, more important, it should have been questioned on April 20, 1999. On the battlefield, there are SOPs, but officers have the ability to *adjust* to the situation at hand. So, too, it should have been at Columbine. Sheriff Stone and his commanders were given the ability to reason. It's a rotten shame they chose not to use it that day.

Chapter 6

Prelude to a Massacre

The tragedy that took place here happened in an ordinary school in an ordinary American suburb. It did not occur in a violent or troubled school or one infested with gang activity. It did not happen in a transient, dysfunctional community down on its luck. That's what was so frightening to many Americans—that Columbine was just too much like their own school and community.

The massacre was not the result of a "random" act of violence. It was not the result of someone "losing it." It was not the result of students shooting indiscriminately into a crowd in a fit of rage. It was much more sinister than that, and its seeds were sown over a period of time. The Columbine killers' journals, investigators' interviews of friends and classmates, as well as investigative news reports, provide some insight into their behavior and motivations—insight that could also indicate how this tragedy could have been prevented if someone had been aware enough to put together all the pieces.

NO, NOT LITTLETON

To many, Columbine High School seemed like the last place something like this would happen. Sure, it was a school with bullying, cliques, and favoritism toward athletes—but is that so unusual in America?

I received emails from a few people who claimed there was something seriously wrong in the Littleton community itself—dark secrets that somehow led to this tragedy. Nonsense. That's just a way for them to deny that it could ever happen in their own community. This community is no different than thousands of other sprawling suburbs in America.

Where did it happen? It's important to note that while most news reports described Columbine High School as being in Littleton, and while some people who live in the Columbine area often say they reside in Littleton, neither is true.

Littleton is a suburban city of over 50,000 people that lies a few miles east of Columbine High School, in neighboring Arapahoe County. The school and the community surrounding it lie in southern Jefferson County. Much of the area was first developed in the 1970s and 1980s when it was mostly farm land and open fields. The area chose not to become an incorporated municipality or to be annexed into another city. The Columbine area happens to have a Littleton *mailing* address, getting it from the nearby Littleton post office, so some people refer to the area as Littleton, while others refer to it as Columbine or simply as south Jeffco.

The Columbine community, lying at the base of the foothills of the Rocky Mountains, has over a hundred thousand residents. The area is marked by small hills, shaped by creeks streaming down from the foothills. It's a mostly white, middle-class area dominated by single-family homes, situated over a dozen miles southwest of downtown Denver.

What happened here in Columbine could happen anywhere. There were no dark secrets. The only thing that was different was that the Columbine community was home to Eric Harris and Dylan Klebold.

LEADING TO THAT DAY

We often hear that school shooters are antisocial loners and outcasts. The Columbine killers were outcasts, but they were not so isolated that they didn't have any other friends. Unfortunately, none of those other friendships was strong enough to break the fatal bond between the two killers, who fed off each other's rage and dysfunction.

Dylan Klebold was born and reared in the Denver area, and seemed to have a relatively normal childhood. Eric Harris moved to Denver when he was in middle school, after his father retired from the military and settled back in his home state. Harris may have been hampered by being a "military brat," a child forced to move from school to school as his father changed military assignments, thus making it hard for him to develop strong friendships. In fact, in his journal, Harris made reference to the difficulty of moving around.

Middle school is the place where the Columbine killers met each other and began their friendship. In their first year at Columbine High School, they appeared to fit in. But things changed in their sophomore year. Like many high school students, they hated school and their classmates, but it seems their hatred ran much deeper than that of most others.

The killers were teens who spent lots of time playing violent computer games. They hung out with kids who were different, kids who wore dark clothes and combat boots. A few of their friends were part of a loosely allied group that was referred to as the Trench Coat Mafia. This group saw jocks, overtly religious Christians, and others as exclusive cliques and as their rivals, if not enemies. The two were seen by others as loners and outcasts who had difficulty fitting in with the mainstream. Harris and Klebold dressed like members of the Trench Coat Mafia and were friends of some of its members, but they were largely on the fringe of the group, not bona fide members.

The two worked together at a local pizza joint. There their playfulness took a more dangerous turn that was a precursor to future behavior, setting off firecrackers and small explosives outside the restaurant. Once Klebold crossed the line when he brought a pipe bomb to work and was disciplined by his supervisor.

Klebold was shy and awkward, but he wasn't taunted as much as Harris, probably because he was well over six feet tall and his presence was a bit intimidating. Harris endured more bullying. He was smaller and more outspoken in a way that turned other people off. He also had a chest deformity known as a "hollow chest," which caused him to be slightly hunched forward. As a teen he underwent surgery for the deformity, but apparently it did little to help. There were reports he was sensitive about it making him look "different" and weaker in physical strength.

BECOMING CRIMINALS

The killers were bored and angry teenagers. At first their rebellion involved firecrackers and pranks. Then it turned to careless, foolish theft. In January 1998 they sat in a parking lot near Chatfield Reservoir and spoke disparagingly about someone who had left electronic equipment and other possessions inside a van parked there.

Harris and Klebold broke into the vehicle and took the electronic equipment and a briefcase, saying it was the owner's fault for being so careless. But they weren't very good thieves; they were caught shortly after the crime by a sheriff's deputy who came upon the scene and could tell something was wrong based on the behavior of the two teens. They were charged with theft, criminal mischief, and criminal trespassing. For a while they were punished by their parents by not being allowed to hang out with each other, but eventually they got back together.

They were sentenced to a juvenile diversion program administered by the district attorney's office. They performed some community service and received counseling. It seemed like a reasonable sentence for two kids who did pretty well in school and hadn't been in trouble before. But the judge was not told by police authorities about other possible criminal activities by the killers, including setting off pipe bombs.

Klebold and Harris made fools of the diversion program. They were released early in 1999 with complimentary remarks from an official of the program, who wrote, "Eric is a bright young man who is likely to succeed in life." It's amazing how Harris managed to be released from the program without at least a warning to his parents. He provided answers on a program questionnaire that were either revealing or indicative of a smart-ass. On the questionnaire, Harris checked that he had difficulties with depression, anxiety, anger, homicidal thoughts, loneliness, mood swings, obsessive thoughts, and temper. There's no evidence that program officials acted on his ominous responses.

WEB-FILLED HATE

Brooks Brown was a sometime-friend of the killers. Things changed when Harris blamed Brown for vandalizing a neighbor's home. When

Brown's mother claimed it was Harris who committed the crime, the vandalized homeowner called police and implicated Harris. He became enraged.

By early 1998 Klebold and Harris had their own Web site where they wrote of their contempt for many around them, including Brooks Brown. Brooks's parents met with the sheriff's office and informed them of a threat made against their son on the site. The Browns gave the police twelve pages of Harris's violent writings, including statements such as:

> *"You all better hide in your (expletive) houses because I'm coming for EVERYONE soon, and I will be armed to the (expletive) teeth and I WILL shoot to kill and I WILL (expletive) KILL EVERYTHING."*
>
> *"I am the law, if you don't like it, you die. If I don't like you or I don't like what you want me to do, you die. God I can't wait until I kill you people."*

The Web site also indicated that the pair had been making and detonating pipe bombs. Apparently this didn't mean a lot to the Jefferson County Sheriff's Office detective who met with the Browns, for he never returned the Browns' phone calls after that visit.

NO QUESTIONS ASKED

In December 1998, the killers went shopping for guns. They took Klebold's friend, Robyn Anderson, to the Tanner Gun Show. The show is a regular fixture in Denver, conducted a few weekends every year. Firearms are sold by both licensed dealers and private (unlicensed) sellers. The would-be killers examined guns and asked Anderson to buy three guns they spotted. Two were shotguns, and one was a shorter gun, a Hi Point 9 mm Carbine. The killers assumed they needed Anderson to purchase the guns for them because she was eighteen and they were both seventeen at the time.

According to Anderson, the gun sellers should have known it was a "straw purchase"— a purchase by one person on behalf of another person who is prohibited from making the purchase. She claimed it should have been clear because the killers were the ones who asked the questions and checked out the weapons.

Anderson purchased the firearms from a private seller, not from a licensed dealer. She testified before a legislative panel that as she and the two boys walked around the gun show, Harris and Klebold "kept asking sellers if they were private or licensed. They wanted to buy their guns from someone who was private and not licensed because there would be no paperwork or background check…I was not asked any questions at all. There was no background check…I would not have bought a gun for Eric and Dylan if I had had to give any personal information or submit any kind of check at all." If she had purchased from a licensed dealer, she would have had to fill out paperwork and pass a background check.

Early in 1999 Klebold and Harris returned to the Tanner Gun Show. They met with Philip Duran, a man they knew from the pizza restaurant, and his friend Mark Manes. They found out Manes was a gun aficionado and had a collection. At the gun show they apparently decided there was another type of weapon they wanted to add to their arsenal. Not long after going to the gun show, Duran became the middle man in a deal to purchase an Intratek TEC DC-9 semi-automatic handgun from Manes. Because it was a handgun, rather than a long gun or rifle, it was illegal for Manes to sell it to minors, and illegal for Duran to act as middleman in arranging the sale. They would later be convicted and sent to jail for those crimes.

SIGNS, SIGNS, EVERYWHERE SIGNS

The Columbine killers showed signs of disaffection and violence, even in class projects. They made a video entitled, *Hitmen for Hire*. In the video, much of which was filmed inside Columbine High School, Harris and Klebold played the part of hit men dressed in black trench coats and sunglasses. Outcasts, nerds, and other picked-on kids could turn to these assassins in order to take care of bullies who were harassing them. They used crude gun replicas, not real ones. The video was not completely dark in its mood, nor was it played all for laughs. The pair was angry when the teacher would not show the video to others.

In a creative writing class he took with Klebold, Harris wrote a gruesome story based on Doom, the video game he loved to play. Doom was a popular first-person shooter game which featured Satanic imagery and a space marine that killed the undead and demons. Harris also wrote an essay from the point of view of a bullet being fired from a gun. In psychology class, when given the opportunity to submit dreams for analysis, Harris shared with his classmates that he dreamed about shooting people.

Klebold turned in a story in creative writing class about a man coming into a town and using guns, knives, and bombs to kill popular kids who mocked him. The teacher found it disturbing and inappropriate. Klebold dismissed the concern, saying, "It's just a story." When the teacher spoke to his parents, they did not seem worried, allegedly making a comment about "trying to understand kids today." With the Klebolds' consent, the teacher turned the writing assignment over to a guidance counselor. Apparently there was no follow up.

Rumors and stories about the behavior of the Columbine killers filtered through the high school. Some students heard about Harris and Klebold's love of bombs. Some teachers complained about the two, and some knew they were depressed and angry. Still, little happened to the would-be killers, except that Klebold was caught and punished for cracking into the school computer system to gain access to locker combinations so he could plant harassing notes. The two continued to plod along with their plan for destruction.

In March 1999, the killers and some friends went to an isolated, forested area known as Rampart Range to fire their weapons. The foothills area south of Denver was known for such gun forays. Phil Duran and Mark Manes, the two men who had arranged the sale of the TEC 9, were with Klebold and Harris. Video of this event was shot and later was released to the public. It shows them firing sawed-off shotguns and the TEC 9 handgun, laughing and making ominous remarks about the damage their guns could do.

NOWHERE MEN

These two teens were about to leave high school. Their miserable high school experience was about to end. Why were they not willing to just leave it behind them? New lives could start for them—or at least for Klebold. The day before the Columbine massacre, Klebold's father sent an initial payment for a college dorm room to the University of Arizona.

Harris, on the other hand, had made no such plans. He was pushed by his parents to register for classes and get a summer job. Harris contacted a U.S. Marine recruiter. The recruiter came to their home five days before the massacre, but he learned that Eric was taking the drug Luvox, an antidepressant, which disqualified him. Some people speculated that Harris's rage was driven by being turned down for the Marines; others saw the plan to join the Marines as a diversionary ruse.

And how did the killers spend their last weekend on Earth? Klebold was at a place surrounded by some of the people he hated so much, an event that stood for the mainstream school that he detested—the Columbine prom. Klebold's date was Robyn Anderson, the teen who had bought three guns for the killers. Harris did not go to the prom, but did have a date for part of the night, then went to the after-prom party at the high school alone and met up with Klebold and other friends, all of whom could have easily become victims of the cafeteria bombing they planned.

ARMED AND DANGEROUS

The killers needed plenty of ammunition for their firearms. Harris ordered gun magazines (also known as ammunition clips) from a gun shop. In his journal he mentions that a clerk from Green Mountain Guns called his home. His father, who owned guns, answered the phone. When the clerk told the elder Harris, "Your clips are in," he simply told the clerk he hadn't ordered any clips. Eric wrote in his journal that his father never asked whether the caller had the right phone number, and acknowledged that if either the clerk or his father had just asked another question or two, his plans might have been ruined. But they weren't.

On the day before the massacre, Harris rounded out their ammunition supply, picking up 100 rounds that Mark Manes had bought for him at a Kmart store for 25 dollars—a purchase that would become the subject of a significant scene in Michael Moore's documentary, *Bowling for Columbine*.

Chapter 7

The Earthquake
Called Columbine

The massacre at Columbine wasn't a singular event impacting a single group of people or a single community. It was like an earthquake, with concentric circles moving out countless miles from the devastated core, the impact lessening as the distance grew. It was like an earthquake, with a calming after the disaster, followed by recognition of the devastation and aftershocks that rattled nerves even more.

MOVING OUT FROM THE EPICENTER

I certainly was aware my family and I were not alone at the epicenter. I saw the devastation around me. Obviously there were the fourteen other families who tragically lost loved ones, along with their extended families, friends, neighbors, classmates, coworkers, church congregations, and others at the innermost circle of destruction.

Also at the core were the injured students and their families. Some of the students had multiple gunshot wounds; some had to undergo years of rehabilitation; and two were paralyzed and unable to walk. While some of the injuries were less physically damaging, they were no less emotionally taxing. The burden on these students was tremendous. Some continued to recall the horror of coming face-to-face with the flash of a firearm aimed directly at them or the explosion of a homemade bomb callously tossed their way. Others likely felt "survivor's guilt," wondering why they were spared while others lost their lives.

It was difficult for some of the injured to recover. One turned to drugs. One dropped out of high school. One's father left home, apparently in part because he couldn't deal with his son's injuries. One injured girl said she couldn't go into a library anymore. Another always looked for exits before going into a public place.

A LOSS OF YOUTHFUL INNOCENCE

Many of the survivors of the library executions no doubt wondered why they were spared. But just as tragic, they had witnessed something horrific—the deliberate murder of ten students over a ten-minute period as they hunkered helplessly under tables while listening to the taunting of two murderers, fearing they were the next to be shot.

Within a year or two of the tragedy, one student who was in the library indicated a willingness to speak to me about her experience there, making the offer through the school. I declined the invitation; I wasn't ready to hear it.

Other students who suffered after the tragedy were those who were in the science classroom along with teacher Dave Sanders. They were there for hours, watching Sanders bleed to death, wondering what was happening around them that prevented the police from saving the life of this hero.

And there was the devastation experienced by the other students and teachers at Columbine High School. Many of them had a friend or student who was killed or injured. Most found themselves fleeing the school, wondering if they, too, were about to be shot. Some experienced the shock of hearing gunshots or of seeing a classmate lying injured on the ground. Some likely experienced survivor's guilt.

One student was so frightened she had to sleep with her parents for a time after the massacre. Some of the kids were afraid of the sound of television news helicopters, fire alarms or sirens; in fact, parents were notified in advance if Columbine High School planned to test its fire alarms because of students who couldn't deal with the noise. Some students were frightened when they saw a group of students running down a hallway because they were afraid something terrible had happened and that kids were running for their lives.

After the massacre, Columbine students were moved to Chatfield High School for the remainder of the 1999 school year. Balloons were put up as part a welcoming gesture, but had to be taken down because it was too frightening to some students when the balloons accidentally popped. The school changed the sound of the fire alarms so students wouldn't hear the same haunting noise they heard on April 20. Chinese food was the entrée served in the cafeteria that awful day, so for about a year it was eliminated from the menu. The school was much more sensitive about the movies and videos shown, as even World War II movies with guns being fired frightened some students.

A CITY, A STATE, A NATION, A WORLD REACT

It was amazing how America and the rest of the world reacted to the tragedy at Columbine. I was unaware of some of it because I was preoccupied with my own pain and tasks those first few weeks. I became more aware of the massacre's reach as we were flooded with sympathy cards and letters of support from around the world.

In the midst of so much pain, the world sent us an outpouring of love. In Denver, many things came to a respectful, shocked stop. Denver's baseball team, the Colorado Rockies, had some players whose children attended Columbine-area schools. Out of respect for the victims' families and the community, the Rockies postponed two games and wore Columbine High School patches on the right arms of their uniforms for the remainder of the season. Denver's hockey team, the Colorado Avalanche, postponed their opening two NHL playoff games.

We received hundreds and hundreds of expressions of sympathy in the mail, along with many Teddy bears, angels, crucifixes, and other objects of affection. Some mail was simply sent to us in care of the school itself. The school was closed off for months, so we drove to other locations every week or so to pick up another box of letters and donated items.

Some letters arrived at our home with an incomplete address, such as "Daniel Mauser's Family, Littleton, Colorado" or "Mausers, Columbine High School, Colorado." The post office knew who we were and made the effort to get them to us.

Many messages came from perfect strangers. Some came from people who said they had a special connection to Columbine. We received an email from a father in Illinois in June 1999, who wrote: "We recently moved to Illinois from Littleton, and I'll never forget the look on my 16-year-old stepdaughter's face when I told her of the terrible events at Columbine that day. She only said to me, very quietly, 'David, please find a list.' I think she knew what I'd find. I printed off the names and held my breath as I sat down with her and the list. She was silent and ashen. I asked if she knew any of the victims, but I already knew the answer from the look on her face. She pointed to Daniel's name and that of Lauren Townsend. She had known Daniel from 6th grade and Lauren from summer volleyball. She is still having some difficulty processing this loss."

A MAKESHIFT MEMORIAL

Directly next to Columbine High School is a large, multi-purpose park known as Clement Park. It quickly became an impromptu memorial where people could express their feelings and pay their respects.

A red Acura Legend and a brown Chevy pickup became an early magnet for people coming to the park. They were vehicles driven to the parking lot the morning of April 20, but not driven home that day. The vehicles of victims Rachel Scott and John Tomlin became instant shrines, overflowing with memorial items—flowers, Teddy bears, hearts, crosses and other religious items, handwritten notes and posters, candles, poems, and countless other objects.

A burgeoning number of people came to the park. At first memorial items were placed around trees and other objects. Then the commemoration became more organized, with people bringing in display tents, most with tables placed inside, where items could be stacked and protected from the elements.

Walking around the park, you couldn't help but smell the sweet aroma of the hundreds of floral arrangements. You could learn about the victims from the crosses in the ground, where people had strung newspaper clippings and personal stories. On the fences surrounding the park's tennis courts were strung bed sheets and huge poster paper displays with words of condolence from schools and organizations all over the nation.

A week or so after the massacre, I watched the late evening news alone, drinking wine to try to relax before bedtime. Linda had already gone to bed. I watched a news story about a group of people in an open tent in Clement Park, gathered around a group of candles, despite the darkness and the cool, damp weather. I was so moved I promptly drove to the park. There I came across a group of mostly young people from a church in the nearby suburb of Englewood. They were praying for the victims. I told them who I was and that I was grateful for what they were doing. They gathered around me and prayed for Daniel and my family, an experience that brought tears to our eyes.

I returned to the makeshift memorials in Clement Park on a number of occasions—usually by myself, because Linda found it too sad to visit. It was heartening to see thousands of people paying their respects to the victims, knowing that many of them did not know the victims personally. I was overwhelmed by the amount of reverence shown by the crowd. There was no laughing, no trivial chitchat, no loud talking. Mostly I heard whispered conversations, crying and sobbing, or somber silence.

It was an unbelievably moving experience to overhear students talking about the victims and watch them cry for the victims. Daniel was shy and not a popular student, so hearing someone say something about him moved me to tears. I don't think anybody recognized me as the father of one of the victims, as I hadn't yet made any media appearances. I wanted to thank anyone who mentioned him, but I was too overwhelmed with grief. I imagined that Daniel's spirit was there in the crowd with me, taking it all in, so I convinced myself I didn't need to thank them.

Once I brought my own item to the park. I wanted to make Daniel more real than was possible with the black and white newspaper photos being displayed. I made copies of a number of photos of Daniel and pasted them onto a small poster board and wrote on it, "May the lives lost here not be lost in vain. Daniel Mauser's dad."

I put it in a visible place outside rather than in a tent, but with so many items arriving each day and with the wet weather, it became a bit beaten up and lost amid the massive collection of memorial items.

Nonetheless, during a local newscast the photos were included in a news story about Columbine, and I was amazed to talk to strangers months after the tragedy who told me, "Oh, yes, I remember seeing your photos in the park."

THE CROSSES

One of the more popular sites people visited in Clement Park was Rebel Hill, the small knoll that overlooks Columbine High to the northwest. It was 30 or so feet high, likely built from soil left over from construction of the school. Fifteen crosses, each eight feet high, were placed on the crest of the hill to represent each of the victims. There were some smaller sets of crosses throughout the makeshift memorial grounds, and they were more accessible, but these particular crosses drew far more attention. Thousands of people flocked to the hill as if on a pilgrimage.

Linda and I decided to visit the celebrated crosses. May 2 was a cool, damp Sunday, as were so many of the days after the massacre. As we entered the park, we found ourselves near the base of Rebel Hill, close to the front of the line rather than the end of it. We saw hundreds of people snaking their way through the park in a line so long we couldn't see the end.

We thought of leaving rather than enduring a long, painful wait. But we asked ourselves whether we as parents of a victim should have to endure such a wait. We spoke to an elderly pair of women who were in line near the base of the hill, explaining who we were and asking if we could join them. They graciously agreed to let us "jump line" and comforted us. We all trudged slowly along up the steep, muddy hill. It certainly wasn't an easy trek under those conditions, especially for the women, one of whom was eighty-one years old. Neither of them knew any of the victims but had driven from miles away to pay their respects.

The top of the hill was a solemn and emotional place. The two crosses placed there for the Columbine killers had become controversial and were removed a few days before we arrived. We read what was posted and draped on each cross, but it was difficult for us to pause for long at Daniel's cross. It was still unreal for us. Even though we had already been grieving, when we looked at his cross it felt as if we had just discovered that Daniel was dead.

AFTERSHOCKS HIT THE COMMUNITY

Just as communities devastated by an earthquake must often endure fear and damage from aftershocks, so too did the community of Columbine experience unexpected, devastating aftershocks in the weeks and months following the massacre. Columbine was a community on edge.

In August 1999, three swastikas were found etched on the inside and outside of the school. One small marking was scratched into a brick wall and two were found inside a girls' bathroom. In September, security was tightened in Jefferson County schools after five high schools received a series of anonymous threatening letters.

On October 19, on the eve of the six-month anniversary of the massacre, a student threatened to "finish the job" started by the Columbine killers. On the next day, about a quarter of the students stayed away from school, and another quarter went home early. The student making the threat pleaded guilty and was ordered to perform community service.

On October 22, tragedy struck the Columbine inner circle. The mother of one seriously injured girl went into a nearby pawn shop, asked to see a gun, pulled a bullet from her pocket and loaded it into the gun while the clerk looked away, then fatally shot herself. The girl's mother was diagnosed with depression even before the massacre, and the stress of seeing the suffering of her paralyzed daughter was too much for her to endure.

That month the CBS Evening News aired a portion of the surveillance videotape from inside the Columbine High cafeteria. The tape came from an emergency preparedness video created by a local fire department group and shown to a gathering of school administrators at New Mexico Tech and videotaped by an Albuquerque TV news reporter. The video quickly went viral. It was yet another piece of Columbine evidence not shared with the Columbine parents by the sheriff's office in advance.

In December news broke of the disturbing "basement tapes." These were videotapes recorded by the Columbine killers in the weeks and days before the massacre and discovered in the Harris home. On them, the killers ranted about their hatred for fellow students and for humanity in general.

The tapes themselves were only half the painful story. Columbine parents also were extremely upset about the timing of the release of the tapes, coming right before Christmas, as well as the way they were re-leased—to Time magazine. There was no warning given to Columbine parents, which broke commitments from the sheriff. Many of us were livid and called for the resignation of Sheriff Stone.

In early December 1999, just as the community was hoping to gain from the warmth and hopefulness of the Christmas holiday season, a Columbine student received a threat in a chat room from someone who warned her not to go to school Thursday, December 16. The threat read: "I need to finish what begun and if you do I don't want your blood on my hands."' The threat, which was later tracked to a young man in Florida, forced the cancellation of classes December 16 and 17, delaying final exams.

On the day the threatening email was received, Columbine parents were treated to dinner by a group called Holiday Express, a band from New Jersey that performed during the Christmas season at places that have been struck by hard luck or tragedy. They came to Littleton to pro-vide some much needed holiday cheer.

The next evening they performed a rousing holiday concert for the Columbine community on a cold evening in the parking lot of the high school. Both evenings were a fun and wonderful treat, but they were somewhat overshadowed by the email threat, cancellation of classes, and all the controversy and anger surrounding the basement tapes. It was tough enough to deal with the first Christmas without our child, let alone those other hurtful distractions.

SHOCKWAVES EXTEND INTO 2000

Other events continued to test the nerves of the community. In January 2000, our low-crime suburb was shocked by the news that the body of eleven-year-old Antonio Davalos was found stuffed in a trash bin within a mile of Columbine High School. A twenty-eight-year-old man, once a friend of the boy's family, was arrested for his murder.

A month later, two Columbine High School sweethearts were shot to death in a Subway sandwich shop just a half mile from the school. The bodies of Nicholas Kunselman, fifteen, and Stephanie Hart, sixteen, were discovered inside a Subway shop where Kunselman worked. Police didn't believe robbery was involved in the crime. The case has never been solved.

Another person was found dead from a gunshot in the parking lot of a local Burger King, just a half-mile from Columbine High School and near the Subway shop. The death was determined to be a suicide, but nonetheless the community was uneasy with the news of yet another shooting death.

A year after the massacre, the community learned a high school basketball player at Columbine, who lived just a few blocks from us, committed suicide in his home. He was a star player and had so much promise. He had witnessed teacher Dave Sanders's death in the science classroom and had also been a friend of Matt Kechter, one of the students killed at Columbine.

The Columbine community tried hard to rally and prove its strength, using a "Columbine Pride" campaign, complete with "We Are Columbine" signs and bumper stickers. I preferred the stickers that read, "We Are All Columbine," for it more accurately reflected how America should view this and other tragedies. After all, if there were problems in our community, they were no different than the epidemic of thoughtless gun violence infecting the entire nation.

MINISTER CAUGHT IN THE MIDDLE

The turmoil even reached a church deep in the heart of Columbine. Reverend Don Marxhausen was senior pastor at St. Philip Lutheran Church, a nine-hundred-member congregation in the community. The Klebolds had briefly tried out his church about five years before the massacre. Tom Klebold was a Protestant and his wife Sue was Jewish. Their tryout at the church didn't last long. After the massacre, remembering their tryout at the church, and probably recognizing the dilemma the Klebold family was facing in terms of funeral arrangements, Marxhausen sent word through the grapevine that he would help the Klebold family if asked.

The Klebolds responded to the minister's overture. Marxhausen officiated at a small, private memorial service for Dylan Klebold a few days after the massacre. About a dozen people attended the service at a mortuary about 20 miles away.

Some people condemned Marxhausen for conducting the service. Long-term members of St. Philip left the church ostensibly because of the Klebold memorial service. I was disappointed by that reaction but certainly not surprised. Despite what Klebold did, I believe he was entitled to a memorial service, for we are all children of God. If he was somehow not entitled, that was God's judgment, not ours.

Some in the congregation were unhappy because Marxhausen officiated at the Klebold funeral or because he expressed understanding toward the Klebolds. Others contended that Marxhausen's trouble was related to the fact he spent so much time on the Columbine issue and counseling students. Others contended it was because he was outspoken.

Others countered that the parish council and congregation were supportive of the memorial service, but said they were disappointed in Marxhausen's programs. Some were angered because he took a sabbatical while the congregation conducted a 1.7–million-dollar expansion campaign a few months after the massacre.

Tension was so high a mediator was brought in, but when the mediator was unable to resolve the issues, Marxhausen resigned. He said at the time he did so "to avoid a bloodbath." There was nothing terribly wrong with the minister or his congregation: Mass murders and the emotions surrounding them have a way of stirring up raw emotions and creating turmoil.

AFTERSHOCKS AT HOME

Aftershocks hit our home through our daughter Christine. Some of her friends and classmates in seventh grade were understanding and supportive, but others were not. Some said insensitive things to her and accused her of "getting too much attention."

We thought of pulling her out of school but didn't. The school allowed her to skip classes to attend counseling sessions along with the siblings of three other Columbine victims. The ensuing bond was helpful, since most other students had no idea what these children were dealing with as a result of the massacre.

In eighth grade, the situation with classmates got worse. She again faced accusations of getting too much "attention" and not "getting over 'it.'" In particular, a few students called attention to the fact one girl's disabled brother had died, leading to statements that "She got over it. Why can't Christie?"

Life at school became hellish for Christie. She says some teachers were good to her, some were not. She felt one teacher in particular, rather than give her too much attention, seemed to go out of her way to ignore her and treat her poorly. Christie made some new friends but even a few of them turned on her. She admits she sometimes asked to leave class to see a counselor just as a means of getting out of class, out of schoolwork, and away from the hassles she was facing. At times she "just wanted to be left alone, because nobody seems to understand what I'm going through."

One student stole Christie's journal and began to tell other students lies about what was in the journal, claiming, for example, that Christie was suicidal. Christie felt the girl was doing it not necessarily to hurt her but as a means of getting attention for herself. The mother of the girl who stole the journal reported to the school that Christie might be suicidal. Christie was not suicidal, but she certainly was upset that someone stole her journal and was spreading rumors.

Christie told school officials she felt she was being harassed by the girl who stole the journal, but the school seemed more concerned with the rumor she was suicidal. The school seemed unwilling to address the harassment, and eventually suggested that perhaps it was better for her to finish the school year away from the school, studying from a tutor. Linda and I thought they were dodging Christie's problems, but we decided to accept their offer to provide the tutor, figuring the school wasn't going to be any more responsive to Christie's problems.

The following school year, Christie was supposed to start her freshman year at Columbine High School. We just couldn't send her there, but not because we thought it wasn't safe. It was largely because we couldn't expect her to walk through those hallways, and frankly, because Linda and I weren't about to enter the school and pretend everything was okay.

We were also reluctant to send Christie to either of the two other nearby Jefferson County high schools, given our lingering anger at the school district over several issues and their unwillingness to share any information they had about the behavior of Harris and Klebold.

We took a chance and enrolled her in Mullen High School, a nearby Catholic school. Tuition was expensive and the transition was difficult for Christie because she did not know anyone there, had no background in Catholic elementary schools, and was not interested in the sports programs that were revered there. She finished the year but was clearly not comfortable there.

For her sophomore year, we enrolled Christie at Arapahoe High School. It was ten miles away, in a neighboring school district. Our neighbor, Monica Lobser, was a teacher there, so we felt comfortable that she would help introduce Christie to the school and provide a useful support system for her. Christie fit in much better there and didn't seem to face as much attention as "that sister of a Columbine victim." She graduated from the school in 2004.

MORE PAIN ON WEST DAVID AVENUE

Less than two years after Columbine, another earthquake struck our cul-de-sac.

Christie was like a big sister to Ali Meyer, a girl a couple of years younger who lived across the street. On Saturday night, February 10, 2001, Christie and Ali took a short walk to a nearby convenience store. As they were crossing the intersection of the wide, four-lane South Pierce Street, the light changed, so they scurried to get to the other side. Christie ran a few steps ahead of Ali. Suddenly Christie heard the horrible sound of Ali being struck by a passing vehicle in the last lane they crossed. The vehicle sped away.

Christie screamed as she looked back to see Ali, who had been hurled down the street by the impact. Her body was lying motionless by the side of the road 93 feet away from where she had been hit. Passers-by stopped to help, and soon the police showed up. I received a frantic call from a crying and distraught Christie. I immediately ran to the scene. There I found the police taking measurements and putting up crime scene tape. The ambulance had already left. The police interviewed Christie as we sat in a police cruiser.

What made the accident more tragic was the fact that Ali's parents were nearby when it happened. They were returning home at the time, driving north on Pierce Street, when they saw that a small crowd had gathered around someone lying by the side of the road. They called 911, then went to help, only to discover their daughter was the victim.

Ali was rushed to Swedish Hospital for treatment then later transferred to Children's Hospital, where she remained in the intensive care unit for five weeks, unconscious and in critical condition, with multiple fractures and internal injuries. She was moved to the rehabilitation unit, where she officially came out of a coma, though she was barely conscious.

The driver who struck Ali was pursued by a witness who said the driver eluded him by turning off the SUV's headlights and pulling down a side street. But the elusive driver did not escape detection. The impact of the vehicle hitting Ali was so strong it knocked the front license plate off the driver's Ford Explorer.

The driver, Dennis McNamara, must have realized he would be caught, given the pursuit, the car damage and the missing license plate. He called the police to turn himself in before they arrived at his house. He was taken into custody and later given a blood alcohol test, which showed he had been drinking.

McNamara lived less than a mile from us, in the same subdivision. His two children attended the same school as Ali. He pleaded guilty to leaving the scene of an accident and driving while impaired. He was sentenced to two years of work release, in which he was allowed to work his daytime job and spend the rest of his time in jail.

McNamara was required to perform community service and was placed on probation for ten years. It was a lenient sentence, largely because the compassionate Meyers family didn't want to see McNamara's children suffer. The sentence was also light considering that McNamara had a drinking-and-driving conviction ten years before and given that Ali's condition later took a tragic turn.

Eventually Ali returned home from the hospital to be in familiar surroundings. She began recovering from the physical injuries she sustained, but still had many hurdles to overcome, including brain damage. She had little control of her body, had to be fed through a tube, and spent her time in a wheelchair. She couldn't talk; she occasionally communicated by moving her head and blinking responses when asked questions. The Meyers built a large addition on their house with a special bedroom and bathroom for her.

On the morning of November 22, 2002, Ali unexpectedly passed away. (God rest her soul.) It was a shock to everyone, since she was slowly showing signs of improvement.

Ali's struggle put a terrible burden on Christie. She had lost her brother and now a good friend, but I credit Christie with dealing with it well. She visited Ali, followed her progress, and was hopeful about her prospects. In most respects she handled it better than I. Dealing with Ali's recovery and eventual death was difficult for me. Despite my own experience of tragedy, I was not as supportive of the Meyers as I should have been. I found it difficult to visit Ali, and I did not comfort the Meyers as much as someone in my situation should have done.

I had complained about how some parents didn't seem to understand how to deal with grieving parents like Linda and me during our time of grief. Yet when I was put in the same situation, I likewise froze and became unsure of how to deal with my grieving neighbors. It was a hard lesson. I found myself becoming more forgiving of those about whom I had complained.

Go to: www.danielmauser.com/spontaneous.html to view photographs from the spontaneous memorial in Clement Park.

Chapter 8

Swirling Controversies, Twirling Lives

I s it possible in this country to live through human tragedies without the stain and strain of controversy? Can we allow people to grieve without having their actions and motives questioned? Can people stop telling victims how they should grieve? Can we question how murderers are to be memorialized or characterized? Can victims call for investigations and the release of information without being called vindictive or disrespectful of law enforcement? Can they seek to turn tragedy into positive change without being labeled as publicity hungry or money-grubbers?

APPARENTLY NOT.

That's the sad reality in America. In many cases of school shootings and similar tragedies, controversy often befalls the victims and the community. There are disagreements over who was to blame for the crime or whether more could have been done to prevent it, disputes over how to treat the perpetrators, arguments over lawsuits, and battles over whether to release certain crime information. Columbine was no exception. Given its multiple victims, a questionable law enforcement response, lawsuits, a public school, gunfire, and teenaged mass murderers, the Columbine massacre was not going to be without disagreement and controversy.

Perhaps the storm was inevitable, but that didn't make it any easier to accept. The constant din of controversy, both real and perceived, exacerbated the pain felt by the Columbine families. Some of the controversy was related to beliefs and actions of the Columbine families, but some was outside of our control or did not directly involve us, and yet at times it seemed we were held responsible. These controversies made our healing more difficult and were an undeserved burden on those of us at the epicenter of the tragedy.

HERE, THERE, AND EVERYWHERE

Everyone seemed to be weighing in about some aspect of the Columbine tragedy—the media, public officials, writers of letters to the editor, and the public in general. It's hard to avoid controversy when the media is so closely covering an event. Often they were thoughtful when covering the many touching human interest stories surrounding Columbine, but other times they looked for tantalizing news that kept the public immersed in the Columbine story. They were more than happy to interview someone with a grudge or an accusation, regardless of their standing or integrity. After all, controversy and conflict *sell*.

Newspaper columnists and radio talk-show hosts were paid to keep the public fired up over Columbine issues. Little seemed off limits. For example, some weighed in about whether autopsies of all the victims should be made public. Was there really anything of consequence in those autopsies that would shed new light on the massacre? It seemed their motive was simply an overactive sense of morbid curiosity.

There were plenty of cynical, media-crazed people in the public taking it all in. The tone of some letters to the editor and comments on talk radio was simply without compassion or understanding. They denounced the police, school district, teachers, and even the Columbine parents, often without foundation.

RELIGIOUS DISPUTES

Controversy engulfed the Columbine tragedy even before our children were laid to rest. The public memorial service conducted April 25 at the Bowles Crossing shopping center was a solemn event, but even it stirred a commotion.

An ecumenical group of religious leaders spoke at the event, including the Denver Catholic Archbishop, a rabbi, and two Protestant ministers, but some of what was said was far from ecumenical. One of the ministers was Franklin Graham, son of evangelist Billy Graham. He asked the crowd, "Do you believe in the Lord Jesus Christ? Have you trusted him as your savior? Jesus said, 'I am the way, the truth, and the light. No man comes to the Father but by me....' It is time for this nation to recognize that when we empty the public schools of the moral teachings and the standards of a holy God, they are indeed very dangerous places."

Jerry Nelson, pastor of Southern Gables Evangelical Free Church in Littleton, also spoke. He related a story of two dying women in a Nazi concentration camp. When a Jewish woman expressed despair about how the other's God could have allowed this tragedy, the other woman said, "I only wish you knew my Jesus." The pastor then explained to the crowd, "What she was saying is this: There is only one rational way to live without despair in a world of such pain, and that way is to know the son of God, Jesus Christ."

A few religious leaders, particularly rabbis, black ministers, and liberal Protestants, were upset. They all complained about how the event had been turned into an evangelical church service intended to exclude those who were not "born again" Christians. Some people complained that Graham used his speech for political purposes—to advocate for school prayer. Others claimed the speeches were evidence there were "Christian cliques" at Columbine High that added to the factionalism among students.

Writers of letters to the editor took sides. Judy Wallace of Englewood wrote in the *Denver Post*: "If I had been the parent of a child who died at Columbine and he/she didn't fit into the 'born again Christian' category, I would have been extremely hurt by the insensitivity of the service."

Others criticized those who complained about the preachers. Martha Lucas of Denver wrote in the *Post*: "If liberal Christians find Franklin

Graham's message about accepting Jesus offensive, they don't have to listen to him… For the reverends and rabbis to insist on intolerance in a setting like this is inappropriate." Still others said an event including public officials should not have had religious speakers.

I did not speak out about the controversy back then; I was stunned and angry at what I heard but I was too preoccupied to react. But I will now. Although I'm a Christian who believes—like many of our Founding Fathers—that government should not promote a religious belief, I did not feel the memorial service should have been secular. I welcomed the presence of religious leaders to give us comfort. But I also expected it to be an event that brought people together to mourn our children's deaths and to provide hope to the community.

The two preachers told the crowd the only hope was through one religious belief. Telling a crowd that was likely of varied religious beliefs that one particular faith was the only "rational" way to avoid despair was hardly a way to bring people together. It was intended to make people feel separate, providing comfort only to those of that particular faith.

Religious differences are a sign of how we as people are unique and different. As long as we have such divisive proclamations in a service intended for mourning, then we're only going to continue to have unhealthy religious conflict rather than tolerant religious differences. It's too bad that Graham and Nelson didn't take the time to think of whether their words were welcoming or hurtful, or think of how they would have felt if they had a different religious belief and sat in the audience and listened to those exclusive messages.

Controversy arose involving which victims were asked "Do you believe in God" by the killers and who did or didn't say "yes" in response. During the massacre in the library, it was reported by one student that Cassie Bernall was asked moments before she was fatally shot if she believed in God and that she had answered "yes." Following Cassie's death, her mother wrote a book, *She Said Yes: The Unlikely Martyrdom of Cassie Bernall,* about her daughter's turbulent teenage life, spiritual conversion, and martyrdom. Some Christians alleged that the Columbine killers hated and mocked religious students and targeted them.

This account of Cassie saying "yes" was later challenged by another student in the library who claimed the exchange took place between

Dylan Klebold and Valeen Schnurr, a student who was seriously injured, and that it was Schnurr who had said "yes." It became generally accepted that the exchange was mistakenly attributed to Bernall. Some people were critical of the publishing of the book and for the martyrdom attributed to Bernall, but her parents were simply reacting to the reports they were originally given and sharing her heartrending story with the world, as we were all want to do.

It didn't matter who said "yes." What matters is that the Columbine killers hated many people and were finding any number of excuses for murder. What matters is that there may have been other students that day who were devoted Christians who would have answered "yes," but that there also may have been kids who would not have responded at all, or would have responded "no" yet could have been just as devoted in their love for God. The test of one's devotion is found in how one lives one's life, not in how one responds under duress to two disturbed murderers pointing a gun at you.

Separation of church and state became a contentious issue after the school district invited victims' parents and other community members to paint ceramic tiles that would be placed in Columbine's hallways—a project that was planned before the massacre. Tempers flared when the district determined some of the tiles needed to be pulled off because they didn't meet the district's criteria. Tiles could not include references to the massacre, names or initials of the students, Columbine ribbons, religious imagery, personal messages, references to the shootings, or anything obscene or offensive.

There were some Columbine parents who included their child's name, words about their child, crosses, and religious phrases on their tiles. They were upset their tiles were removed. Some sued the school district, saying they were being denied their First Amendment rights. The case made it all the way to the U. S. Supreme Court, which ruled in favor of the school district's right to restrict content.

Linda and I did not participate in the tile project. We could understand why the school district wanted to prohibit religious imagery in its school, given the desire of some Christians in this nation to theocratize our schools and government. We could understand why the school would not want an overabundance of massacre-related tiles on its wall. But we also felt the district handled the tile project and its response poorly, and that its list of prohibited items was so long as to make the project sanitized into meaninglessness, especially for the Columbine parents. There seemed to be little reason to invite the parents' participation under such guidelines.

CROSSED OVER CROSSES

Even crosses were enmeshed in heated disputes. A carpenter from Illinois placed fifteen crosses at the top of Rebel Hill in Clement Park—thirteen for the slain and two, written in a different script, for the killers.

Reactions to the two crosses for the killers were mixed and emotional but mostly negative. Some said their inclusion represented a Christian act of forgiveness and an attempt to begin the healing process. Others were outraged, feeling their inclusion inappropriately equated the killers' deaths with the victims and seemed to inappropriately offer a blessing of sorts.

The father of one of the victims removed and destroyed the two crosses for the killers on April 30, about two days after they were erected. A similar controversy brewed many weeks later when a local church planted fifteen trees on its grounds as a memorial. Some of the Columbine parents dug out the two trees commemorating the killers. We were not among the parents who removed the crosses or trees, but we nonetheless received a few nasty letters from people that were upset and seemed to hold all the Columbine families responsible.

I understood how it would seem to some that the placement of fifteen crosses could be seen as healing and an acknowledgement that the killers also tragically lost their lives. It is not my belief as a Christian that the killers are automatically destined for hell or not deserving of a cross. I believe God makes that judgment, not us.

After a young man in Erfurt, Germany, killed sixteen students then himself, people reacted with sadness and anger but not bitterness. During a solemn memorial event, sixteen candles for the victims were lit, along with a seventeenth, which was set apart from the others. The killer was included, but separated.

At the Rebel Hill memorial, the carpenter who placed the crosses did not ask for the opinion of those most affected by the tragedy. It was insensitive to include the crosses for Klebold and Harris right with those of the other victims. Someone felt the time was right to begin the process of healing and forgiving, but what made them think the families of the victims were ready?

It would have been more appropriate to set the crosses for the killers apart from the others. The killers lost their lives, too, and they had grieving parents and friends, but they died after brutally ending the lives of our loved ones. The way the killers died was different, the way they were mourned was different, so likewise their crosses should have been handled differently. Different lettering was not enough.

Ideally it would have been best to ask all the parents how they felt about the crosses. But that would have been almost impossible to do at the time. We were in grief, not in the mood to be surveyed. I think the best to do then would have been not to challenge those hearts that were so damaged, to not include crosses for the killers or to have the crosses in a separate and removed location.

LAWSUITS AND INVESTIGATIONS

Lawsuits were filed after other school shootings, including those at Jonesboro, Arkansas; Springfield, Oregon; and West Padukah, Kentucky. Columbine was no different. The lawsuits filed in the wake of Columbine produced a variety of reactions from the public—mostly negative.

Some people seemed to believe lawsuits represented outrageous or greedy behavior, overlooking the fact that not all suits are monetary. Many suits filed in the aftermath of tragedies like this are aimed at forcing the release of information from parties associated with the crime— law enforcement, people associated with the killers, or others. It's an unfortunate fact that some attorneys of those parties recommend against full disclosure, except for that which might exonerate their client, for they fear that disclosure might expose something harmful to their client and lead to a lawsuit. That often is counter to the interests of the families of murder victims, who want to learn all they can about the crime. Such was the case with Columbine. We had no assurance we were getting all the information. We often felt we were stonewalled. Lawsuits were a way of breaking down those walls.

The public and media sounded off about whether the killers' writings, videotapes, and other materials should be released to the public. It was a no-win subject for Columbine parents to weigh in on: If you spoke out saying these materials should not be released to the public, you were criticized for selectively and hypocritically opposing full disclosure and for not allowing the release of materials that might help experts better determine the state of mind of the killers. If you spoke out in favor of full disclosure of these materials, you were criticized for helping to encourage copycat attacks.

The Columbine families often found themselves being asked to weigh in on what seemed to be an endless lineup of investigations and study groups formed in the wake of the massacre. The following are among the most visible:

- The Governor's Columbine Review Commission, a group charged with conducting a review of the massacre and how it was handled. Particularly notable in its proceedings was the fact it was snubbed by Sheriff John Stone and Undersheriff John Dunaway, who refused to testify, saying they couldn't do so because they were conducting their own investigation.
- The Columbine Task Force, a community group assembled by Columbine's Republican state representative, Don Lee, to look into the general causes of the massacre. Predictably, it stayed away from the issue of how easy access to guns played a role.
- The primary crime investigation, conducted by the Jefferson County Sheriff's Office, which dragged on for a long time.
- The volatile investigation that looked into the allegation that one student was killed by friendly fire from a Denver police officer— an untrue allegation that led to the resignation of a sheriff's officer whose lies fueled the allegation.
- The Columbine Records Task Force, that sought to facilitate the full public disclosure of the remaining, undisclosed Columbine investigative records.

DISPUTED LICENSE PLATES

Even a simple effort to make a commemorative state license plate to honor Columbine and collect funds for the victims was dragged into a heated debate. It happened because the divisive issue of abortion was injected into the Columbine fray.

A bill was introduced in the state legislature to create a special license plate to honor the victims of Columbine. The bill proposed that the commemorative license plate feature a rendering of the columbine, the state flower, along with the words, "Respect Life." Some legislators, pro-choice advocates and others, objected to the use of the "Respect Life" phrase because of its common use as the tag line by those opposed to abortion rights. These opponents claimed some people would purchase the plate not out of respect for Columbine, but in order to make a political point, tying the Columbine murders to the need to stop abortion.

I didn't support the "Respect Life" phrase and instead would have preferred "Never Forgotten" or "We Are All Columbine" on the plates. I believe we all need to "respect life," but I objected to one interest group needlessly hijacking the Columbine tragedy and tying it to their opinion regarding abortion. It bothered me that many pro-life advocates also support the death penalty and are often NRA supporters. It disappointed me that some pro-choice advocates might choose not to purchase the Columbine license plate simply because of the "Respect Life" moniker.

Linda agreed that the choice of "Respect Life" was politically motivated, but she did not feel the victims of Columbine were being slighted by most who chose the plate. I eventually came to accept the plate despite my reservations, feeling that if pro-life advocates obtained the Columbine plate primarily to make a political statement rather than to honor the Columbine victims, it was unfortunate but beyond my control. Both of our cars now display the Columbine/Respect Life license plate.

Chapter 9

Daniel's Shoes

aniel had his own room, on the opposite end of the hallway from ours, on the second floor. After he died I avoided his room as much as possible. There was no good reason to go in there anymore. Daniel was no longer there.

Within a few weeks of the massacre, Linda and I talked about the fact that we had to deal with Daniel's belongings. Disposing of one's deceased child's belongings is something no parent should ever encounter. It was a task we put off, but we knew we couldn't put it off forever. Finally, at one point it seemed it would be easier to deal with than putting it off and having to clear out his belongings from a stuffy, dank room that had become even more lifeless and depressing. We concluded we wouldn't be purging Daniel or erasing his memory, we would simply remove things that would not be needed any longer. We would keep some objects to remember him by, but toss others away.

THE DIFFICULT PURGE BEGINS

Daniel's clothes were a reminder of him but most were not a reminder of specific events, so it was a bit easier to dispose of them. There was satisfaction in knowing they would be used by someone else when we donated them to a charity.

It was not a total purge. Daniel had grown to the point where he was slightly taller than I, and it was naturally the source of lots of ribbing: "Hey, Tom, it looks like Daniel is taller than you now! Is that true?" In a good-natured way, I always insisted it wasn't true.

Daniel was thinner than his aging and slightly expanding Baby Boomer dad, so I could not fit into his pants. But since we were both a men's size medium, I kept a few of his nicer polo shirts that didn't scream out "I'm in high school!" I have worn them proudly ever since. Nobody else knew they were Daniel's. I still have and wear two of them. I wear them sparingly, though, for I want them to last a long time.

The toughest things to dispose of, and one of the last I gave away, were Daniel's foosball game and other sports items. There was no reason to keep them, especially since he and I were the only ones who played with them. The foosball game took up space in the basement, and I had to pass by it painfully every day on my way to the computer room, so it had to go. But deciding to whom to give the game and sports items became a major task.

I decided it might seem too morbid to ask one of his friends. Maybe they'd be honored to have them, but if they weren't comfortable they might be reluctant to tell me so. I decided it was not enough to just have these items donated by means of a curbside charity pickup. I wouldn't know where they'd end up. These were Daniel's things; they could not be given up that easily or anonymously. I had to see them get into someone's hands. I had to see them go to someone less fortunate, in Daniel's memory.

I called a Boy's Club and asked if they accepted such items. They indicated they would accept them and would either use them or send them home with one of the boys. I stuffed the foosball table, Daniel's baseball glove, a football, and a few games into the back of my Subaru Outback and drove to a Boy's Club in a poor southwest Denver neighborhood. I did so later in the evening, close to closing time, so there wouldn't be many boys there. I carried the items into the club. An employee asked if I wanted help carrying the rest of the items in. I didn't; it meant a lot for me to carry them in and complete the task myself.

It was especially difficult to carry the foosball table inside, so it went last. It wasn't that I didn't want to give it up. It was that I wanted to let someone know how important that game was to me and to know it belonged to a very special teen. But I knew I couldn't do that; they couldn't tell boys these were items from a boy who had died, for that might seem too depressing or morose. Instead, I set the table down next to the other items and tried to keep my composure as I told the employee who I was and that I'd appreciate them finding a home for my son's things. I wasn't quite able to finish. I started to sob. The employee began to thank me and talk to me, but I had to excuse myself and leave before I completely lost it. I did lose it, but fortunately it was not until I reached the car.

Most of Daniel's belongings were gone, but the task of purging was not without a thoughtless omission: We failed to consult with Christie. Years later she finally spoke up and indicated she wished we hadn't moved so fast in purging his room, as she felt there might have been some memorable belongings that she would liked to have kept.

THE RIGHT SIZE

I never took Daniel shopping for clothes or shoes, since that was Linda's domain, so I had no idea what size shoes he wore. As we cleared out Daniel's closet, I came upon a pair of tennis shoes. Reeboks. White with a slight bit of black trim. Linda said she thought they were size ten and a half. I was amazed; that was my size, too. I tried them on, and they fit perfectly. How appropriate.

There was something special about those shoes, but it wasn't until many months later that their symbolic meaning fully struck me. Early in 2000, a national organization, the Silent March, announced plans to bring one of its events to Denver. The Silent March calls attention to gun violence by collecting and displaying pairs of shoes to represent the people who have died in shootings, thus reminding the public in a powerful way about those who are no longer with us.

In advance of Colorado's event, a number of organizations collected footwear. The goal was to collect 4,223 pairs of shoes to represent American children and youth killed with guns in a single year. The Silent March event was held April 11, nine days before the first anniversary of Columbine. I spoke at the event, on the west steps of the State Capitol in Denver, and I wore Daniel's Reeboks. When I finished speaking, I took off the shoes and had the honor of placing them among all the hundreds of shoes on display on the steps.

Tom speaks at Silent March event, April 11, 2000.

Many in the crowd were brought to tears. There were others like me who brought the shoes of a loved one who had perished. After the event, the shoes were donated to charity, but I retrieved Daniel's Reeboks. I decided they would serve as an ongoing reminder to others of the pain of losing one's child to gun violence.

From time to time over the next few years, I wore those shoes to a number of events, including some described in this book, and spoke. I also wore them around the house and yard casually—yet not so often that they became excessively worn. Now I don't wear them at all; I'm just saving them.

NEW SHOES, DEEPER MEANING

The Reeboks became less symbolic and special in 2004. Five years after the massacre—I don't recall that the length of time was ever explained—the Jefferson County Sheriff's Office called the Columbine families and informed us they were prepared to turn over the possessions of our loved ones that had been cataloged as evidence. We had long ago been given Daniel's backpack and books from the library and his locker, but nothing else. The remaining belongings they had were the clothes he was wearing that day. I didn't want his clothes; I did not even want to see them. I assumed they might be bloodied. I knew they would be too painful to keep. There was no good to be found in keeping them.

I asked the police if they had his shoes. My heart jumped with joy when they told me they did. Could these also be size ten and a half? Would they be free of blood stains? I took time off from work and drove to the sheriff's office as soon as I could to pick them up.

I identified myself when I arrived. After a short wait that seemed like forever, an employee descended stairs from the second floor, holding a clear plastic evidence bag. I thanked her and rushed into the lobby of the building, sat down and examined my prized possession. There they were—a dark pair of Vans tennis shoes. They had no visible blood stains and they looked like they might be my size. With a tremendous sense of anticipation, I took off my shoes and tried on Daniel's. My heart soared; they fit perfectly!

I couldn't wait to try them out. But I was not about to be as casual about wearing them as I was with the Reeboks. Since these were the shoes he was wearing when he died, they were hallowed to me. Perhaps some people might find that notion strange or even dreadful, but to me, the shoes were energizing, enabling, and inspiring.

I have proudly told people I was walking in Daniel's shoes, to honor him, by doing what I think he would have wanted me to do. My use of the shoes was meant to symbolize that I would try to prevent future Columbines and future gun violence so that other parents would never have to walk in the shoes of their murdered child.

I treasure the guest book entry submitted through Daniel's Web site by Michael Williams from New York: "I was touched by how your son moved you with one thought that was so important to him. In our lives we hope that our children will follow in our footsteps, but you actually walked in HIS. What a wonderful opportunity for you. I'm sure he looks down on you every day and tells everybody 'That's my Dad.'"

Yes, I'm the dad walking in his son's footsteps and wearing his shoes. My public speaking and activism were less frequent by 2004, but anytime I spoke to an audience about Daniel or gun control, or when I protested against the NRA, or when I attended a Columbine memorial event, or when I visited elected officials in the halls of Congress, I have worn those Vans shoes. I only wear them on these special occasions. I intend to keep them in good shape for the rest of my life, for someday they'll be passed on to my children and grandchildren.

Chapter 10

Taking That First Step

It was a simple question asked innocently at the dinner table. Initially it was brushed aside, but later it launched a push for change. That one question led me to become consumed by an issue and propelled me into the spotlight, making me a target of praise, controversy, anger, and derision.

THE QUESTION

My family was preparing to eat dinner one evening about two or three weeks before the Columbine massacre. Daniel often shared the excitement of classroom discussions at the dinner table. On this evening, he posed a question to me as we waited for Linda and Christie to join us at the table. He brought up a subject area we had never discussed before. It wasn't something that was a topic in his debate class, but rather a subject that came up in a conversation with debate classmates.

"Dad, did you know there were loopholes in the Brady Bill?"

I knew the Brady Bill was a law passed by Congress sometime in the 1990s, under the leadership of James Brady, President Ronald Reagan's press secretary who was seriously injured in the assassination attempt on Reagan. Despite incurring a serious injury that kept him in pain, in a wheelchair, and with impaired speech and movement, Jim and his wife Sarah Brady fought bravely for more than a decade for a law requiring anyone purchasing a gun to first pass a criminal background check. In 1993 the Bradys' efforts resulted in passage of a law that prevented criminals and mentally deranged people, like the one who shot Brady and Reagan, from purchasing a gun at a gun shop.

No, I didn't know about loopholes in the bill, I told Daniel. I must not have shown much interest, because our conversation was a short one.

Guns were never something that were a part of my life, nor were they alien or frightening to me. There were many hunters where I grew up, including neighbors, relatives, and my oldest brother. I grew up with respect for hunters. My father didn't hunt, none of my close friends hunted, and there was never a gun in our home, so I never hunted or had the opportunity to handle or fire a gun in my youth. Daniel, on the other hand, had once fired a rifle while at Boy Scout camp.

When I was in college in the early 1970s, I took a beginning level debate class. We spent the entire semester debating just one issue: gun control. Students were required to alternate between the pro and con position. On one hand, gun violence wasn't something that had directly impacted my life. When I grew up we didn't hear of school shootings, we rarely had people "going postal," and we didn't have "wing nuts" amassing arsenals of military-grade weapons or blowing up federal buildings.

On the other hand, I recall how gun violence became a concern to my family following the shootings of John and Bobby Kennedy and Martin Luther King, Jr. I recall the shock of watching television coverage of a 1966 shooting rampage in Austin, where a sniper killed 14 people and wounded 32 others from a 28th floor observation deck of a college building.

After arguing both sides of the issue in class, I concluded that I favored gun control. But it was nothing I could really wrap my arms around, as there was much less talk of gun control at that time, so I was drawn to other social issues.

Daniel's inquisitiveness was making him consider his views on gun control, yet I did nothing to advance the conversation. I didn't even tell him about my college debate class. How ironic it is to look back and see the connection between Daniel and me both being drawn to the gun-control issue based on our debate classes, and how unfortunate that I didn't engage him in conversation about it.

Two weeks later, Daniel was shot—with a gun purchased through one of those gaping loopholes in the Brady Bill. What are the chances of such a thing happening? This was no mere coincidence. I wasn't someone who believed that people were given life-changing "signs," yet suddenly I believed I had clearly been provided with one.

PROTESTING THE NRA'S INCURSION

A week or so after the Columbine massacre, our friend Margi Ness asked if I were going to the protest against the NRA's national convention. I hadn't been following the news closely, so I didn't know about the protest. I was astounded with the irony of the NRA holding its national convention in, of all places, Denver—just ten days after the Columbine massacre.

A group of people were going to protest the NRA's presence, Margi said. A crowd would hear speakers on the west steps of the State Capitol, then march around the hotel where the NRA was meeting. She asked if I wanted to go. I was reluctant at first. My life was still a mess at that time. I had so much on my mind, so much pain to deal with. But as I thought about it, I decided I had to go. I couldn't ignore Daniel's dinner table question.

Margi offered to give me a ride to the protest. I accepted her offer, since I knew it might be difficult to drive after what might be an emotionally difficult experience. And I didn't want to go the protest alone among so many strangers.

A day before the protest I took one of my favorite photos of Daniel—one showing the sweetness and innocence of a twelve-year-old—to a FastSigns shop. I asked to have a large sign made. On one side of the sign I wanted the words, "My son Daniel died at Columbine. He'd expect me to be here today," and on the other side, "My son died at Columbine. Don't let his death be in vain." And on both sides, I wanted Daniel's photo. And I needed it done in one day. The manager looked at me with sad eyes and promised it would be done, at no charge.

The protest was sponsored by the Colorado Coalition Against Gun Violence. I called its executive director, Ted Pascoe, and told him who I was and that I would like to attend the protest with a sign honoring my son. He asked if I would like to speak. I told him I would bring a written statement to distribute but that I just wasn't sure if I would be in the mood to speak. I left him dangling.

I wrote an essay expressing my thoughts on the Columbine shootings, gun control, and the NRA. I remembered the local Kinko's store had made an offer to the Columbine families to provide free photocopies, so I printed 450 double-sided copies for the crowd.

When I awoke that Saturday morning, May 1, 1999, I still didn't know if I wanted to—or could—speak from the podium. I wanted to see how I felt and how many people were there. There would likely be others there to express their thoughts, so at first I told myself I would be satisfied being near the podium, letting my sign do the talking.

When Margi and I arrived at the capitol, there were far more people than I expected to see. Just a month before, CCAGV drew about 400 people to a rally in protest of pro-gun bills streaming their way through the state legislature. But on this day, the grassy area on the west side of the state capitol was packed and overflowing. The crowd was estimated at 12,000.

Margi and I made our way through the crowd, toward the capitol steps, where I sought out rally organizers. As we walked through the crowd towards the podium, I could tell a hush fell over those around me as they read my sign.

When I reached Ted, he again asked if I wanted to speak. I told him I still wasn't sure, showing him the meager 450 copies of the statement I brought. I asked him if any other Columbine parents were there and planned to speak. I had met some of them in the past few days, but had no idea how they felt about the NRA or whether they knew about this event. Ted told me no other Columbine parents were speaking.

Damn, I thought to myself, *the crowd should hear a victim's perspective, so it's going to have to be mine.* A sign and an essay weren't enough. I knew that my speaking could have a tremendous impact, so I decided I had to do it.

SPEAKING MY PEACE, DANIEL'S PEACE

After a number of other speakers got the crowd fired up with some fairly harsh statements denouncing the NRA, it was my turn. I handed my sign to someone near the podium as I stepped to the microphone after being introduced.

It became very quiet. I was a bit nervous, looking out at the hushed sea of faces. I occasionally spoke publicly at work, where I was comfortable doing so, or when I entertained a small crowd with one of my humorous slide shows. But never had I spoken to a crowd of this size, and certainly never under such emotionally difficult circumstances.

I don't recall much of what I said, except for what was recorded and played by the media. I had no prepared speech; I ad-libbed, randomly echoing some of the thoughts from my written essay.

"I am here today because my son Daniel would expect me to be here today. If my son Daniel had not been one of the victims, he would be with me here today.

"Something is wrong in this country, when a child can grab a gun so easily, and shoot a bullet …." I couldn't control my emotions and became speechless. I couldn't get out the words. My head dropped; I bit my lip and closed my eyes as I tried to compose myself. How could I say those painful words? The pause seemed like a long time, but was actually only a second or two. "…and shoot a bullet into the middle of a child's face," I continued, as I pointed to the picture of Daniel on my sign, "as my son experienced. Something is wrong."

I did not condemn the NRA and gun owners, but instead drew a contrast between hunting animals and people. "There are good hunters—many," I began. "But the time has come to understand that a TEC 9, semi-automatic, 30-bullet weapon like that used to kill my son, is not used to kill deer. It has no useful purpose." (Months afterward I received mean-spirited emails from gun activists saying my son was not shot with the killers' TEC 9. That was true, but I did not know that at the time of my speech.)

Other speakers were strident in their attacks on the NRA for not canceling the convention. But I did not criticize them for meeting in Denver ten days after the gun violence at Columbine. I had worked in the private nonprofit world, and it made sense that the NRA might have bylaws requiring it to go on with an annual membership meeting.

I heard that the NRA convention normally consisted of a huge trade show and other events, but that it had been stripped to just the annual membership meeting. Thousand of NRA members cancelled their travel plans, hundreds of vendors lost out and hotels lost visitors. In my speech I questioned why the NRA felt the need to cancel its convention. If they felt absolutely no responsibility for the Columbine tragedy or America's gun violence, I asked the crowd, why not go ahead with the full convention?

It was reported that most convention activities were called off because of sensitivity to the tragedy at Columbine, but I believed the NRA abandoned them because it didn't want the world to look at its trade show. The NRA might normally welcome the media to its conventions as a public relations opportunity to recruit members and portray itself as a mainstream organization. But in this case the NRA could not take the chance the media would cover the trade show floor with its shocking and upsetting display of firepower, particularly displays of assault weapons and high capacity magazines that skirted the assault weapons ban in effect at that time. Those weapons would have upset many mainstream Americans. Yet if the NRA strictly prohibited news cameras from the trade show floor, the media and public would have been critical of the NRA for being so secretive, questioning what they were hiding.

I think the NRA also cancelled the convention because of the risk some of their more vocal members would speak to the media and make insensitive statements about gun control and Columbine that would be embarrassing to the organization.

After the speeches were finished, the crowd marched a few blocks to the Adams Mark Hotel, where the NRA meeting was being held. Initially there was some concern about being able to fulfill the plan to encircle the one-square-block hotel. But given the size of the crowd that day, there was no problem—we surrounded the hotel with people to spare!

I walked with my sign, along with a bevy of volunteers shielding me from the media and from potential trouble from NRA supporters. There was mostly silence and respectful behavior from our marchers, our soldiers of peace. A few pro-gun people were there, but aside from a few verbal barbs, there were no conflicts.

HESTON'S RANTING

As we marched outside, NRA President Charlton Heston was inside, giving NRA members a speech that questioned how anyone could possibly be mad at the NRA and insisted that its members simply loved their freedoms.

The NRA members booed loudly as Heston told them Denver's Mayor Wellington Webb had asked the group not to come to Denver. Heston told the crowd, "This is our country. As Americans we're free to travel wherever we want in our broad land.... Don't come here? That's offensive. It's also absurd because we live here." Rather than address what some people thought was insensitive behavior for proceeding with its meeting, or even mentioning that they could not legally cancel the meeting, Heston chose instead to speak about the group's *right* to be there. But the community wasn't questioning its *right* to be there, it was questioning its sensitivity to the situation.

Heston tried to portray the NRA as a poor, misunderstood victim, while at the same time demonizing the NRA's critics. "Still they say don't come here. I guess what saddens me the most is how that suggests complicity. It implies that you and I and 80 million honest gun owners are somehow to blame, that we don't care." Heston was appealing to all gun owners, not just NRA members, trying to draw them in to his attack on the NRA's critics.

Heston couldn't fathom what might upset the community about the NRA meeting in Denver after the Columbine massacre. "They say we'll create a media distraction, but we were preceded here by hundreds of intrusive news crews. They say we'll create political distraction, but it's not been the NRA pressing for political advantage, calling press conferences to propose vast packages of new legislation."

Rather than address why there might be sensitivity surrounding the NRA meeting, Heston attacked the widespread news coverage of Columbine. Yes, the news coverage of Columbine was intrusive, as well as intensely overwhelming. Much of that was because America was in shock and wanted to know more. It wanted to know more so it could better understand how to prevent future tragedies.

Would Heston have preferred that we provide less coverage and know less? Was he like gun activists who think there will be fewer shootings if we just had less news coverage of shootings? That was not going to happen.

Rather than address why there might be sensitivity surrounding the NRA meeting, he attacked gun control advocates for "pressing for political advantage" by calling for new legislation in the wake of the Columbine massacre. Yes, they were calling for legislation, but they were simply responding to what many Americans were calling for. Likewise, Heston was responding politically to his members who insisted that "we don't need any more gun laws."

The rally was the event that launched me into my role as an outspoken advocate for gun control. My speech and the march outside the hotel kindled my personal advocacy, but I was especially stirred into action by hearing the news coverage of what was said inside the hotel by Heston and other NRA speakers. Their statements helped solidify my commitment to my role as a gun control advocate.

Chapter 11

Well- Yet Ill-Prepared

Almost overnight I thrust myself into the spotlight and became a new voice for those seeking reasonable gun laws. I had stepped up onto a soapbox, but was I ready to be in the spotlight?

Daniel's words to me about loopholes in the Brady Bill two weeks before Columbine were the reason I was willing to step up that day on the west steps of the state capitol. But it was adrenalin and my dedication to Daniel that got me through that speech, and I benefitted from speaking to a receptive and sympathetic audience.

It all sank in that evening as I watched television coverage of my speech and read about it on the front page of Denver newspapers the next morning. I knew I had made an impact. I knew people would be expecting to hear more from me. I assumed my phone would soon be ringing with media requests. But I wondered whether I was up to it.

In the twenty-four hours after my speech, and even after I started receiving additional media exposure, I went through a lot of self-reflection and serious questioning. I struggled with the pros and cons of getting more deeply involved with the gun-control cause, questioning whether I was ready to take up this mantle.

WHY THE GRIEVING ONES?

As I pondered whether I was prepared to fully dive into gun-control advocacy, I was comforted with the realization I would not be walking alone. Although at first I felt very alone standing in front of that crowd at the capitol, I knew there were many people who went before me and many people from whom I could learn, such as Jim and Sarah Brady.

Other parents had become advocates for change after the loss of a child, such as the many moms who spearheaded Mothers Against Drunk Driving (MADD). I thought of Marc Klaas, whose twelve-year-old daughter Polly was kidnapped at knife point from her mother's California home during a 1993 slumber party and later strangled. I admired Marc for becoming an outspoken advocate for child safety, giving up a lucrative business to pursue an aggressive agenda that included tougher sentencing for violent predators.

It was comforting to know others had succeeded in becoming advocates for change in honor of their child. But that did not mean I was adequately suited to handle the emotional burden. That did not mean I was willing to make the kind of personal sacrifice made by those like Marc Klaas. That did not mean I had what it took to be successful.

It bothered me that many in our society so often looked to those who suffered a great loss to step in and rally others for change, whether the issue was drunk driving, drug abuse, or weak gun laws. Victims' families are emotionally drained and devastated, so why look to them to point out the obvious need for change?

BUMPER STICKER ACTIVIST

Philosophically, I had no problem taking on the gun-control issue. I had been supportive of gun control ever since I examined both sides of the issue in college, though I hadn't acted on it in any significant way and knew few details about the issue.

At one point in the 1980s, as the recipient of mailings from various organizations supporting a variety of social causes, I received a mailing from an organization promoting gun control. My interest in gun control was sparked by an increasing level of gun violence and by the heroic efforts of Jim and Sarah Brady to change gun laws. I sent a donation to the organization and in return received a packet that included a bumper sticker. With two young children at home, that's about all I was willing to do: write a check and throw a bumper sticker on the car.

I mentioned this cause to a friend, and he commented about seeing the organization's "no handguns" logo—a handgun within a square and a line through it. "You're not going to put that sticker on your car, are you?" he asked.

I was perplexed by his question, until he elaborated. "Do you realize what could happen? Do you want some gun nut to get mad at you and 'key' your car or pop a bullet into it? What if Daniel and Christie are in the car? Those gun nuts are nasty."

That possibility seemed rather farfetched to me, but I took his advice. I didn't put the sticker on my car, and for years my interest in the issue waned. I never again made a contribution to a gun-control organization—until 1999.

Ironically, my interest in the gun-control issue abruptly surfaced early in 1999, prior to the massacre. There was newspaper coverage of a bill in the Colorado legislature that would have made it easier for individuals to obtain permits to carry concealed guns. It was something that didn't make sense to me, not because I thought people shouldn't be allowed to defend themselves, but because it seemed unwise to put many more guns in our midst and in the hands of untrained people. Colorado law already allowed the police to issue concealed weapons permits to those in need, at their discretion, but this bill forced the police to issue the permits to virtually anyone. I wrote a letter to the editor about the issue and also to my new state representative, Don Lee.

PREPARED FOR REALITY

I recognized that the danger of becoming a grieving advocate was that one could develop unrealistic expectations about how much change could really be accomplished. One's failure to bring about change could lead to a lot of frustration and anger at a time when one is emotionally vulnerable and sensitive. On the other hand, it occurred to me that my career helped prepare me for this advocacy. I had already learned first-hand that it was difficult to change laws and attitudes overnight.

For more than thirteen years I had worked for the Colorado Department of Transportation. The primary focus of CDOT was the building and maintaining of highways, but my years there had been spent as a manager of a small program that provided federal transit grants to local bus programs.

In the transportation field there was an ongoing debate between highway and transit advocates. Highway advocates argued that most transportation resources should be invested in our highway system. Their more extreme advocates accused public transit advocates of trying to destroy the highway system by siphoning off funding for transit systems and trying to force people to use transit. They insisted Americans cherished the "freedom" they felt when using their automobile.

Transit advocates like myself responded that buses also needed highways, and that most transit users also owned cars, so it would be foolish for us to advocate for destroying the highway system. We argued that society could not build its way out of traffic congestion or rely solely on one mode of transportation. We insisted it was unrealistic to think a workforce going to work at about the same time could expect its highway system to have enough lanes to handle all those cars without significant delays.

Transit advocates pointed to America's foolish transportation choices, such as buying SUVs despite the fact they were gas hogs that drove up demand for gasoline, and inevitably, its price. We acknowledged that Americans cherished the "freedom" they thought their automobile provided, but argued that at the same time they were strangled by its troublesome consequences: traffic congestion, energy-wasting suburban sprawl, poor air quality, and billions of dollars spent on highway lanes and so-called "free parking."

Highway supporters rarely offered realistic solutions to congestion, dependence on foreign oil, or poor air quality. They simply promoted more highways lanes as the only answer, even though that solution was not at all sustainable or healthy. As quick as they got the lanes they demanded, those lanes would fill to capacity, leading their advocates to call for even more.

America's mindset about cars had been in place for years, so many of us in the transit field knew it could not be changed overnight, even in the face of overwhelming evidence that dependence on single occupancy vehicles was unsustainable.

It struck me that the gun debate was amazingly similar. Gun activists defended the status quo—weak gun laws and easy access to guns—even though the country had already been going in that direction for years and gun violence was worsening. They said the solution to gun violence was to have more guns, yet more guns only led to more gun violence. They spoke of freedom but refused to address the many consequences of that freedom, such as guns easily getting into the wrong hands, and offered no realistic solutions.

My career prepared me for a cause whose beliefs were not easily or quickly accepted by the public. It prepared me for a struggle where opponents would stubbornly advocate for the impossible: freedom without consequences.

DOUBTS

There were other reasons I was a good candidate to become absorbed in a social cause: I had always taken a deep interest in public policy matters. I was a "child of the sixties," someone who believed in the need for personal activism as a means of improving society. I was a political science and urban affairs major in college and looked forward to a career in public service. One of my great thrills in college was twice driving to Washington, D.C., and standing in line in the middle of the night to get a spectator seat at the Senate Judiciary Committee's Watergate hearings.

I was a concerned citizen who read the newspaper thoroughly and never failed to vote in a congressional election. I wrote letters to the editor concerning current events, letters to my elected officials, and letters to businesses when dissatisfied with service or dismayed with corporate policy. I was active in my church and had served on the board of my condominium association.

But with those plusses also came doubts. Although I was involved in those activities, I was rarely "on the front lines." I was a sideliner. I was against the war in Vietnam and attended a few small anti-war rallies, but I did little more than that. I was never active in party politics, other than carrying a few campaign leaflets. I never got deeply involved in any causes and never took a leadership role in them.

I was a high-energy multi-tasker, but I questioned whether I would have the stamina to sustain that level of energy while I was grieving and under emotional duress.

SPEAKING OUT?

Even if I didn't serve as a leader, I had the potential for being an effective speaker. Unlike many people, I was not uncomfortable with public speaking. I spoke in front of peers at work and occasionally entertained large audiences with my humorous slide shows. My voice projected well, I enunciated my words effectively, I made effective eye contact with my audiences as I spoke, and I was good at summarizing my speaking points.

On the other hand, most of any of my public speaking presentations were to captive, friendly, and receptive audiences. Those public speaking experiences were hardly relevant to what I would face as a gun-control advocate. How would I function when I was speaking about an issue for which I didn't have years of experience? How would I feel about speaking under duress or somberly as a grieving father, after being so well known for upbeat presentations and for making people smile and laugh? And how would I cope when faced with people who were hostile toward my gun-control message?

I was competent at public speaking, but it didn't come naturally to me nor was it because I was an extrovert. I was shy around strangers and lacking in self-confidence. One person who inspired me was late night comedian Johnny Carson, who apparently was somewhat introverted and uncomfortable with public speaking but relaxed "in his element" as a comedian in the environment he controlled. Likewise, I was able to place myself into another world when I spoke. I could usually present comedy material without laughing or even cracking a smile, and I wouldn't notice if someone nodded off when I spoke.

But I was only comfortable so long as I was somewhat in control, "stayed on message" and was at ease with my audience. These audiences associated with the gun issue would mostly be strangers and my issue was a contentious one. I was not effective at thinking on my feet or responding to tough or unexpected questions. I was poor at responding to unexpected interruptions and was even bothered if I faced a friendly heckler at a slide show. These weaknesses made me doubtful about how I would hold up if I became emotional or if I faced tough questions from reporters or debate opponents, or if I faced belligerent pro-gun hecklers.

TIME FOR A DECISION

Was my family ready for me to commit to this cause? Weren't they the most important consideration? Would they be supportive? Didn't Christie need my time and attention? Would this emotionally draining advocacy work threaten my ability to support my family emotionally during a difficult time and add to the burden I would have trying to cope at work? Unfortunately, I stubbornly ignored those troubling questions when I thought about becoming an advocate.

I wasn't very sincere in seeking Linda's support. I knew she largely agreed with me philosophically about the need for gun control, but I also assumed she would be concerned about me diving into the gun-control issue. She knew how I could be hard on myself, how impatient I could be, and how I sometimes put too much energy into projects and exhausted myself. I knew she would be concerned about how a mild-mannered person like me would deal with this chaotic and highly charged issue, and whether I could handle the stress.

I largely avoided any discussion with Linda on whether it was wise to dive into it. Once I told her wanted to get involved in gun-control advocacy, I figured she'd assume I would likely do it regardless of whether she objected, because she knew how stubborn I was and how strongly I felt about Daniel's words to me about the gun law loopholes. She told me she would support my work but that she would not join me in it, as she didn't want that kind of public exposure and pressure when she was grieving.

Perhaps one of the greatest drawbacks I faced in weighing whether to move forward was my own personality. I was not a person known for being impulsive or for taking big risks. I usually thought things through before diving into something new and different. I tended to avoid controversy and was not very assertive. When I spoke at the NRA protest I threw aside my usual caution. I was working on gut emotions and adrenaline—anger at the NRA and love for Daniel. I simply wasn't thinking of the consequences or about what it might lead to in the future. But could that feeling be sustained?

On the day after the NRA protest, as I expected, the media came calling. I received a call from an NBC *The Today Show* producer asking if I would be willing to appear on the show on Tuesday, May 4, from Littleton. That forced me to decide whether I was "in."

For once I allowed emotion to trump my reliance on logic and reason. It all came down to the feeling I needed to respond to Daniel's words. Daniel was not there to debate the issue, so I would be there for him. I needed to be the new member of the debate team. I was in.

ONTO THE NATIONAL STAGE

I agreed to appear on *The Today Show* but then one of the disadvantages of such an appearance occurred to me—the time difference. A 7:00 a.m. appearance on the Today show means 5:00 a.m. in the Mountain Time Zone. I was thrilled with the prospect of being on near the beginning of the show, but it would be difficult to get up that early. I hadn't returned to work yet and I wasn't sleeping well, so I was sleeping in late many days to make up for it.

The show's producer wanted me on the set well before 5:00. She asked if I wanted a car to pick me up for a ride to the interview, which was being held in one of the numerous media tents still stationed in Clement Park. It seemed ridiculous to get a ride to go just two miles, but I decided to accept her offer in order to reduce the stress on me and to ensure I made it to the right tent. Unfortunately, that meant leaving home much earlier than if I was driving there myself.

I arrived well before 5:00 a.m. and only then learned I was not appearing until sometime after 5:30, not in the first half hour of the show. At about 5:15 or so, there was a crisis. My crisis. I discovered I had forgotten to bring my button with Daniel's photo on it. It was that 3-inch wide button that was given to me by my neighbor Chuck and was something I wore nearly everywhere I went. I certainly wasn't about to appear on national TV without it. I told one of producers I needed a ride back home to get the button.

The producer was not enthralled with the idea. He was concerned I would miss the interview, so he insisted I stay, despite my insistence I knew how long it would take to go home and return. I sternly informed him I would not proceed with the interview without Daniel's button. He reluctantly capitulated, and the driver and I made it home and back again in time.

I was interviewed by Matt Lauer from the show's studio in New York. It was my first experience of having to respond to questions being fed to me through a tiny earpiece carrying a tinny voice. I found it difficult to concentrate on questions put to me by a faint voice of someone I could not see.

I stumbled over a few of my words at first but then settled in. He asked why it was so important for me to be outside the NRA convention (because Daniel would have wanted me there and because of Daniel's words to me about the Brady Bill loopholes). He asked if I had been a gun-control advocate before Columbine (only slightly, and not actively).

He asked whether I held the NRA responsible for Columbine. Perhaps gun activists assumed I would respond with a resounding, "Yes!" But I did not. "I don't think they have a direct responsibility. Certainly not. But I think it is an indirect responsibility because they have promoted the proliferation of guns in this country."

Lauer also asked how I felt about the parents of the killers. I thought back to that flyer given to me by a victims assistant that said I didn't have to answer a media question if I chose not to. It was too early for me to start condemning the parents, I thought, since a lot of information about the massacre still was not known. "It's hard for me to say at this point, Matt. I think we have to let time dictate that, and I really don't want to get into that right now."

Relief came when he asked me to describe Daniel. That's really why I was there, to tell Daniel's story. I was tired of all the attention being given to the Columbine killers. I was thrilled to be given the opportunity to describe Daniel and tell the world the story of how Daniel overcame his weaknesses. While I spoke, many of the photos of Daniel I had sent to the show were displayed. I was a proud father, delighted beyond belief that America would now know more about him.

ON TO THE WHITE HOUSE

At the beginning of that same week my friend Margi informed me that First Lady Hillary Clinton was conducting an event at the White House that Saturday, on the eve of Mother's Day, to address children's lives lost to gun violence. Margi had a friend who knew someone that worked on the White House staff. Margi mentioned to her friend that she knew the parents of one of the Columbine victims.

After being told of the first lady's event, Margi inquired whether I might be considered to participate in the event. She was told that since so few days had passed since the Columbine tragedy, the White House staff was reluctant to approach me about appearing at the event, but that they wouldn't rule out having me if I requested to attend.

I wanted to attend. If they were going to reflect on gun violence and its terrible toll on parents, I wanted to be there to talk about this most recent example of gun violence. Contacting the White House through the person Margi mentioned, I asked if I could attend and speak. The official agreed, saying I'd have ten minutes to speak.

The White House official asked me to provide a copy of my speech in advance for review. I went through multiple drafts. I didn't finish it until the day before the event, on Friday, my flight day. I faxed it to the White House with little time to spare. I worried officials would want to change or significantly shorten my speech, but they didn't ask me to change a word.

I wasn't sure of what to expect at the event. After arriving at the White House on Saturday morning, I, along with the other speakers, attended a private reception with the first lady. What an exciting place to find myself! I got to meet America's first lady as well as some inspiring women who, like me, had experienced the loss of loved ones to gun violence.

After the reception we were escorted into the East Room, which was filled with well over a hundred people. Six people were scheduled to speak. I was the only male speaker and next to last to present, right before the first lady. I was greatly honored to be asked to introduce the first lady when I was finished speaking.

SPEAKING FROM THE HEART

I listened as the other speakers told their stories of gun-related tragedy. Children shot. Lives turned upside down. Lives needlessly wasted. I felt so much pain listening to them, yet I also felt a kinship with them.

At first I was nervous about speaking. This was an audience of strangers. The women who spoke before me were all eloquent, so I felt pressure to likewise do well. But most nerve wracking was just the fact that, after all, I was speaking at the White House in front of a national audience.

When I speak to audiences, I normally follow a general written outline, or preferably, I ad lib, as I did at the NRA protest. I don't like to read a speech verbatim, because I usually don't like other speakers who do so. I like to look at my audience, though in doing so I get flustered trying to find my place in my outline.

Because I had to present the White House staff with my speech, I felt I couldn't afford to ad lib. I needed to find a happy medium, by reading it so many times that I could remember it well, not lose my place but also looking up to make eye contact. I worried about getting too choked up, and it was made worse by the fact the speakers before didn't "lose it."

To calm down I reminded myself their losses weren't as recent and that the pressure I was facing was nothing compared with what I had just been through. Besides, many of those in the room were people who had lost loved ones to gun violence or worked in the field of grief counseling or law enforcement, so I was speaking to a sympathetic audience who would not care if I stumbled or if I cried or if I lost my place.

When it was my turn to speak, I started by giving thanks for "all the cards, prayers, and condolences we've received" from all over the nation. "My son Daniel died that day along with..." Then I spoke the names of all the victims, slowly, looking right at the audience, for I knew that would be more dramatic and meaningful than reading the names. I had memorized the names alphabetically, and refused to look down at my script as I recited their names. I thought it was a poignant moment, but then I forgot two of the names momentarily and stumbled slightly as I added them on at the end. That temporary omission of their names bothered me immensely, particularly because they were the two students who were minorities.

I told the audience how I had waited in painful anticipation for word about Daniel's whereabouts, and of how I and other parents whose children weren't accounted for had been asked to wait in a separate room and told there was one more bus with students yet to arrive. I told the audience that I felt many American parents were likewise in a waiting room of sorts every day, waiting for that school bus to arrive, hoping their children are safe from violence, yet worrying that something tragic could happen.

I risked political incorrectness by mentioning religion, linking the solution to gun violence to core Christian beliefs. Just three weeks before Columbine, I told the audience, Christians celebrated Easter and reflected on how Jesus Christ sacrificed His life on our behalf. I emphasized that the message in Christian teachings is that we all must sacrifice for the love of each other. From that I concluded that to deal with gun violence would require sacrifices by parents, by the entertainment industry, and by those who promote gun shows, manufacture guns, and advocate unlimited access to guns.

Finally, I spoke about how I admired Daniel for his drive to address his weaknesses and urged America to "likewise address its weaknesses, including its culture of violence."

When I reached the end I felt I had done a good job that would make Daniel proud. There was much to be pleased about. In about twelve minutes I was able to express my thanks, reflect on Daniel, relate my experiences of that horrific day, and offer a general solution. I managed to stick closely to my written speech while also looking frequently at the audience, and I didn't lose it emotionally. It was something I think Daniel could be proud of.

Most of the speech can be found on YouTube (see link in Appendix).

Chapter 12

Becoming a Full-Time Advocate

Almost overnight, I became a leading voice for those seeking reasonable gun laws. Because of Daniel's words to me I was willing to take up the mantle, but the lessons I was learning and the people I encountered over the next few months firmed up my willingness to play a larger role in pushing for stronger gun laws. In the months following the massacre I was stirred into a deeper activism as I learned more about the gun issue, as I met others who had suffered losses due to gun violence, and as I heard of other shocking stories of gun violence.

ENCOURAGEMENT

In the months following Columbine I met a number of people who became gun-control advocates as a result of losing loved ones. During one trip to Washington, D.C. to participate in a press conference promoting a gun-control bill, I attended a reception where I met people like Steve Young of Skokie, Illinois, who lost his son to gun violence and became a gun-control advocate. From him and others I learned what it was like to both grieve and be an advocate for change.

I was exposed to a greeting I would hear again over the years: "Welcome to the club. Sorry to have you as a member." It was a "club" to which nobody would want to belong—one consisting of parents who lost children to gun violence. Many in the "club" offered me advice on how to deal with grief and described how the pain decreased over time but never went away. They all seemed strong and determined to fight for change and not accept what had happened to them.

Like so many others in this tragic situation, they were determined not to see others experience the same pain. Bonds were formed quickly with these new heroes of mine, and I have crossed paths with a number of them over the years. Along with Daniel, they became an inspiration to me.

JESSICA'S TRAGEDY

Early in the summer of 1999 my resolve to do something about gun laws was strengthened by the tragic story of Jessica Gonzales of Castle Rock, a suburb of Denver. It was a story that demonstrated what happens when government doesn't take gun laws seriously enough.

Early in the 1999 legislative session, before the Columbine massacre, the legislature passed a bill that changed the way Colorado conducted background checks for firearms purchases. States had the choice of initiating background checks themselves and accessing both federal and state databases of criminal records, or just checking federal databases by letting the checks be conducted directly by federal officials. Our legislators were told the biggest problem with having the checks conducted by federal officials was that they were not set up to catch restraining orders or records of seriously mentally ill persons, because those records were usually filed at the state level and were usually not available to federal officials. Colorado had been conducting checks with state employees, but legislators and Governor Bill Owens opted instead to save money by having the checks conducted by federal officials.

Not long after their decision on June 4, 1999, Jessica Gonzales obtained a domestic restraining order against her husband Simon requiring him to remain at least 100 yards from her and their three daughters except during specified visitation time. On June 22 her husband took his three girls to an amusement park, but he didn't return at the promised time.

Simon Gonzales went to a gun shop and bought a gun while his daughters innocently waited in his truck. Shortly thereafter he fatally shot seven-year-old Leslie, eight-year-old Katheryn, and ten-year-old Rebecca. Next he drove to a police station where he opened fire and died in a shootout with police, most likely an intentional case of "death by police."

Simon Gonzales was prohibited from purchasing that gun because a restraining order had been issued against him. But that restraining order did not show up in the database used by federal officials conducting the background check, so he was easily able to purchase a gun. It was a prime example of why we have to take our gun laws seriously and do all we can to keep guns out of the wrong hands, and be willing to pay to do it. Not long after this tragedy, Governor Owens temporarily reversed the legislative action administratively and found a way to pay for initiating background checks at the state level.

A SAFE BIRTH

In May 1999 I made a call to Ted Pascoe of the Colorado Coalition to Prevent Gun Violence, the group that organized the May protest against the NRA Convention. I asked about a bill that was just voted on in Congress.

During our conversation he informed me two political activists were holding a news conference the next day to announce the formation of an organization that would lobby for gun-control laws: SAFE Colorado. SAFE, which stood for Sane Alternatives to the Firearms Epidemic, was created by Arnie Grossman, a writer and Democratic Party political strategist, and John Head, an attorney and Republican Party activist. Following the Columbine massacre these partisan opponents became convinced that bipartisan action was needed to enact stronger gun laws.

I was excited about it and wanted to be there for the historic first press conference, so I decided to invite myself. I called John Head and asked if I could join them. He asked me to speak. I gladly welcomed the opportunity.

During the press conference, John and Arnie announced SAFE Colorado would be lobbying the Colorado legislature, pushing for stronger gun laws. They developed an effective model for bipartisan action. Along with John and Arnie, the organization's board of directors also consisted of two Democrats and two Republicans, all prominent figures in the community: a former Colorado attorney general, a former Colorado secretary of state, a rabbi and an attorney. Two former Colorado governors—Republican John Love and Democrat Dick Lamm — served as honorary chairmen.

Before leaving the press conference, I informed the media I would be doing some lobbying of my own. I told them I was going to protest at the Denver offices of U.S. Senators Ben Nighthorse Campbell and Wayne Allard, who had just voted for an NRA–backed bill that supposedly addressed the loophole in the Brady Law that allowed criminals to purchase guns at a gun show without a background check but which was largely a sham because it made the background check voluntary not mandatory.

Some of the media followed me to Campbell's office. I carried the same sign I carried at the NRA protest a month earlier, but modified to say "Shame on Senators Campbell and Allard." Before marching I entered the offices of the senators and told the staff I was disappointed with their votes and that I would be marching outside to register my displeasure.

Campbell's staff became alarmed when the media showed up in his office and began filming me. They quickly invited me into an office to talk in private about his vote. I thought their concern was not genuine, that they only wanted to keep me away from the news crews. When they were done talking with me I protested outside the office. The media did not follow me to Allard's office, so his staff ignored my protest completely.

A COURAGEOUS, BIPARTISAN MOVE FOR CHANGE

During summer 1999, political pressure increased for changes in gun laws. The Colorado Coalition Against Gun Violence, others and I urged Governor Owens to convene a special session of the legislature to act on gun-control legislation. The governor rejected the calls, saying it was premature to do so and that it was unclear what bills would be reasonable.

That summer, Owens and democratic Attorney General Ken Salazar (who later became U.S. Senator and Secretary of the Interior) jointly conducted a youth violence summit. Numerous experts participated in the summit, which had a big public turnout, myself included. Despite the unwieldiness of the proceedings, the summit did manage to produce some reasonable recommendations.

Five of its recommendations were related to gun laws. In a refreshing show of bipartisanship and common sense, the governor and attorney general announced they would support those five changes in gun laws and would send them to the legislature for consideration. The bills would ensure the following:

- Require that juvenile crime records be included when gun purchase background checks are conducted.
- Outlaw, at the state level, third-party purchases of weapons for people who cannot legally buy them for themselves—otherwise known as "straw purchases."
- Raise the age for purchasing a handgun in a private sale from eighteen to twenty-one.
- Require adults to safely store firearms so they're not accessible to minors.
- Close the so-called "gun-show loophole" by requiring background checks on all purchases at gun shows.

The first two proposed bills were considered somewhat neutral by gun activists, but they insisted the remaining three were unacceptable gun-control measures. It was a shock to the gun activists that Governor Owens would support such measures, since he was a solid supporter of the NRA. But it wasn't as big a surprise to me. I saw him at Leawood Elementary School the day of the massacre; I think that day's tragic events had an impact on him. Even he could see the time had come for change and we couldn't simply say that all gun restrictions were off limits.

Governor Owens paid a price for supporting these measures, as more extreme members of the gun rights movement openly criticized him, labeling him "Governor Gun Control" and picketing him at some Republican events. Even his Republican friends in the legislature were cool toward the proposals. When Owens gave his opening speech at a joint session of the 2000 legislature, his fellow Republicans applauded his major remarks but most snubbed him by not applauding his remarks about the five gun measures.

A JOB OFFER

The governor and attorney general's agenda was a great boost to those of us who wanted to see changes in Colorado's gun laws. It gave me hope, but it also brought apprehension. It was becoming increasingly difficult for me to work and carry out my advocacy. As a public employee, I had to be especially careful not to conduct gun-control activities on the job, yet it was easy for the media to track me down at work. Since I didn't have a cell phone, they naturally tried to reach me at work, then were frustrated when I offered to return their calls in the evening from home yet told them I didn't want them calling me directly at home and disturbing my family.

Throughout that summer, I received numerous requests to speak at events and to the media, but only sometimes did I agree. Every time I spoke at an event that took place during regular work hours, I had to request time off. It was too difficult for me to try to make up the work at other times because my evening and weekend hours were already occupied with other family and Columbine-related activities. I had little choice but to use up vacation time. It was becoming obvious this newfound advocacy was not going to be sustainable for the intense, four-month upcoming legislative session.

Late in 1999, SAFE Colorado asked me to become a paid lobbyist in 2000, pushing for passage of bills in the upcoming state legislative session. It didn't take a lot of thought on my part; it seemed to be the place for me to channel my energy. But two conditions had to be met before I would agree to serve: first, I needed to be granted an unpaid leave of absence from my job so I could return once the lobbying work was done; second, SAFE Colorado had to provide me with the same salary and benefits I received as a state employee so my family wouldn't have to sacrifice because of my change in employment.

My request for a leave of absence for up to one year was approved by my department's executive director. SAFE Colorado agreed to pay my regular salary, though it couldn't duplicate all my current benefits. I was willing to accept that, knowing it would be difficult enough for a new nonprofit agency to raise funds to pay my salary. SAFE made the commitment to raise the money, and I took the gamble that they'd be able to deliver.

In January 2000 I began work as the director of government affairs, unaware of just where this journey would take me.

Daniel with horse he rode on a trail in the mountains near Fairplay, Colorado, 1998

Christie and Daniel with their cocker spaniel, Marcus

Chapter 13

Derailed

I was not a stranger to state government and the legislature. I was a middle manager in a state agency, a political science major in college, and an avid follower of current events. But a lobbyist I was not. I did not personally know any legislators, though I knew of many by name and reputation. I knew no lobbyists or exactly what they did. I was familiar with the legislative process in general but certainly not in detail. I was shy around strangers, people in authority, and those with a high degree of self-confidence. I was a fish out of water and not well prepared to serve as a lobbyist.

SAFE Colorado did not have a professional lobbyist, so I was somewhat on my own. On the other hand, SAFE's board was made up of people with political experience. Also, my arrival and my name were well publicized, so it seemed that might open some doors.

John Head, SAFE's co-president, provided me with space in his law office. For the first few days I sat in my office, helplessly wondering what the hell I was supposed to be doing. I knew I should have been purposefully wandering the halls of the State Capitol, but I dreaded talking to legislators at that early point. A salesman I was not—it just wasn't normal for me to make cold calls on strangers trying to convince them to support something I knew many of them had little interest in supporting.

Within the first week or so of the legislative session, gun bills were being introduced right and left. Some were pro gun, including the three that had been tabled the year before "out of respect" for Columbine. I guess the "respect" had expired. Some were gun-control measures and some were unquestionably pro gun. Others were neither pro nor con but gun related. Some were "competing" bills, covering the same issue, just mixing and matching certain components.

When the dust settled, a total of 23 gun-related bills had been introduced! Most seasoned lobbyists don't take on that many bills, so how would I, a novice lobbyist, handle the workload? With so many gun bills up for consideration, I would have to pick my battles, focusing on those with the most impact, primarily the five being supported by the governor and attorney general. Some of the gun-control bills had little chance of passage since they were sponsored by Democrats in the Republican–controlled House and Senate.

Even those bills with the support of the Republican governor and Democratic attorney general were not shoe-ins. There were a few Democrats who leaned strongly to the pro-gun side. The Republicans held a comfortable margin as the majority party, and most were conservatives and devout supporters of the NRA, but there were at least a few moderates we thought we might win over on a few issues. The NRA was also reminding legislators of its presence, spreading $25,000 in campaign contributions among some legislators just before the session began in January.

THE FIX

The gun lobby already knew it had to deal with the specter of Columbine, but now it had to deal with a new element: the father of a Columbine victim. My presence, though, probably didn't change their game plan much. If concern over Columbine led to any gun-control bill winning wide support, the gun lobby likely planned to resort to its usual arsenal of tools: push to amend the bill in a way that weakened it, add loopholes that would make the bill hard to enforce, or attach a "poison pill" amendment that made the bill unacceptable even to those otherwise supporting the bill.

Slowly I came out of my shell and approached a few Republican legislators, but quickly I became discouraged as I heard a similar refrain from many of them, almost as if it had been rehearsed. They included variations of the same theme: "I'm very sorry for your loss. I cannot imagine the pain you've endured. It's terrible what those two evil boys did at Columbine. We have all been so profoundly affected. I'm sure there will be things we can agree upon, but we see things a bit differently on the need for more gun laws. None of them would have changed what happened. After all, those boys broke over 20 laws..." To me it seemed the fix was in.

To make matters worse, I was not terribly effective as a lobbyist. I was better at speaking to the media and testifying on bills before legislative committees than I was at being a strategic lobbyist. I was overwhelmed trying to follow so many bills. It was hard to determine how to divide my time. Much of my day was spent talking with other lobbyists who were working for clients sympathetic to my cause, such as the police chiefs. They gave me tips on the legislative process and informed me of key contact people for certain bills. They were helpful but it was no substitute for my talking one-on-one with legislators.

I was not assertive enough in trying to make a pitch to legislators if I thought they might not support my bill. I was even reluctant at times to approach the moderate Republicans and Democrats we needed, convinced some were unwilling to appear at all conciliatory because of fear that word of their openness might be discovered by the NRA. On some occasions when I spoke to legislators I could tell they looked around to see who saw us talking, perhaps fearful the NRA would find out they were conversing with the enemy. I also felt uncomfortably unwelcome after hearing that my presence in the capitol made a few legislators "uneasy" because they felt it was inappropriate for me to be there as a full-time "grieving parent" lobbyist rather than a professional lobbyist.

I was not adept at identifying and corralling possible "swing votes"— those legislators not necessarily committed strongly to either side of an issue and potentially willing to swing your way on a vote. I was also ineffective at "counting votes," that is, knowing how many legislators are likely to vote for or against a bill so you know whether you are ready for a vote or should wait until more support is gained. I was too green, an outsider, too introverted, and not politically skilled enough to be effective at counting votes.

TWO BILLS ON TARGET

There were two important gun bills before the legislature that were not among the five originally presented on the governor and attorney general's list. One was sponsored by my state representative, Don Lee. I was greatly disappointed in Lee, for despite being Columbine's representative he clearly was in the pocket of the NRA. But I will at least credit him for sponsoring House Bill 1243, which required parental consent for the transfer of a firearm to a juvenile. This bill was a response to the fact Robyn Anderson was not charged with a crime for transferring the three guns she had bought in a straw purchase for the Columbine killers.

Many people, including me, were upset that what Anderson did wasn't considered an illegal straw purchase because the guns were purchased from a private seller and not a licensed dealer. Many were surprised to hear it was legal to purchase certain firearms for a minor so long as the purchase was a "private" one, and legal for someone to transfer a long gun to a minor. Perhaps it was a naïve belief that only family members would ever purchase a gun for a minor. House Bill 1243 closed that loophole, requiring parental approval for transfer of a gun to a minor. The bill was passed and signed into law by the governor.

The other important gun measure, Senate Bill 125, was a response to the tragedy that befell Jessica Gonzales, the mother whose daughters were shot by her estranged husband, who was able to purchase a handgun despite being prohibited by a restraining order. The bill made permanent the governor's administrative action to reinstate the state taking the lead role in conducting background checks.

Despite the lessons learned from the Gonzales case, some gun activists opposed the bill, painting it as intrusive gun control. The bill benefitted from being sponsored by a Republican and by the fact SAFE

Colorado was not overtly pushing it, thus sparing it from being labeled as a measure supported by gun-control activists. We left much of the lobbying to the governor. The bill passed and was considered a major victory for Governor Owens, though he again faced ridicule from some gun activists.

DEATH SENTENCE

Two of the five gun bills promoted by the governor and attorney general—both opposed by the gun lobby—failed miserably early in the session. One would have raised the age for purchasing a handgun in a private sale from 18 to 21 and the other would have required adults to safely store firearms so they were not available to children. The two bills not opposed by the gun lobby were passed. One required that juvenile records be included when gun purchase background checks are conducted, and the other made straw gun purchases a state crime and not just a federal crime.

A number of pro-gun bills were approved and signed into law. One particularly insidious bill prevented civil lawsuits against the gun industry by local governments. Some American cities had been filing suits against the gun industry based on allegations it wasn't doing enough to keep guns out of the hands of criminals. The gun lobby considered these lawsuits harassment and frivolous, and convinced legislators to deny local governments the right to sue.

One by one, gun-control bills were defeated by the NRA–friendly legislature. Clearly the gun lobby was still well in charge at the capitol one year after Columbine. But there was still one remaining gun-control bill supported by the governor and attorney general that hung in the balance—one that had a strong connection to Columbine. And to Daniel.

THE GAPING LOOPHOLE

The remaining bill, the most hotly debated one, would have closed the so-called gun show loophole.

People who deal in, manufacture, or import firearms are required to obtain a Federal Firearms License (FFL). A dealer is defined as any person who is "engaged in the business of selling firearms at wholesale or retail."

The term "engaged in the business" refers to those who devote time to dealing in firearms as their livelihood through "the repetitive purchase and resale of firearms." Generally speaking, anyone who maintains a retail location to sell guns is considered "engaged in the business" and as such must obtain a FFL and comply with certain regulations.

A person who makes only "occasional" gun sales or sells from his or her personal collection or for a hobby is not considered "engaged in the business" and is not required to obtain an FFL. Sellers not required to obtain FFLs are generally referred to as private sellers or gun collectors.

The Brady Law of 1996 set forth a new requirement for all FFLs: every person who attempts to purchase a gun must pass a criminal background check to make a gun purchase. An FFL is required to contact a law enforcement agency, which then reviews government records to ensure that the purchaser is not a prohibited buyer. Prohibited buyers include people convicted of felony crimes (serious crimes, as opposed to misdemeanors), people against whom there is a restraining order, chronic drug or alcohol abusers, fugitives from justice, and people who have been legally adjudicated as mentally disturbed (not merely someone with a mental illness).

These background checks have prevented hundreds of thousands of firearms sales to prohibited purchasers. But as written, the Brady Law has a fundamental weakness, thanks to a gaping loophole promoted by gun lobbyists: it only applies to sales through FFLs. If you're a prohibited purchaser, you are still able to buy a gun from a private seller. It's illegal to do so, and it's illegal for anyone to knowingly sell a firearm to a prohibited purchaser, but because these private sales are conducted without a background check, a private seller normally has no way of knowing whether the buyer is a prohibited purchaser.

Nowhere is this loophole more prevalent than at a gun show, where hundreds of firearms are sold under one roof by many sellers. Both FFL gun dealers and private sellers do business at gun shows. The gun lobby would have you believe most private sellers are ordinary citizens selling a few guns from their "personal collections." Some are, but many are large gun merchants with hundreds of firearms for sale, and many sell at multiple gun shows. These gun sales may not be their only source of income, but it's more of a business than a mere hobby, as in the case of Oklahoma City bomber Timothy McVeigh, who for a while seemed to support himself buying and selling guns at gun shows as a private seller.

Federal gun regulators don't have the resources to investigate whether these big-time sellers are "engaged in the business." Besides, if they became aggressive in their investigation of these private sellers, they would be condemned by the gun lobby.

A REMEDY TO THE LOOPHOLE

House Bill 1242, sponsored by Democratic Representative Ken Gordon of Denver, would have closed the loophole. The bill was simple. It required all purchasers at a gun show to undergo a background check. Since private sellers at gun shows aren't authorized to obtain background checks of their customers through law enforcement's system, the bill required private sellers to conduct the background check through an FFL at the gun show. To ensure there was such an FFL available to conduct background checks, the bill required the operator of a gun show to arrange for at least one FFL to conduct background checks for private sellers.

In late January 2000 the bill was sent to the House Judiciary Committee for its first test. It got off to a dramatic start when Representative Gordon arranged to have Robyn Anderson testify before the committee. I understood why her testimony might be helpful for the bill, but I wasn't looking forward to being at the committee meeting to hear her. I had never faced her, and I didn't want to be in the same room with her. It was stressful enough attending court proceedings in 1999 for the two young men who illegally transferred the TEC DC-9 to the killers, but this was worse, because the gun used to kill Daniel was purchased by Anderson, and she was not arrested for what she did. I knew it would be emotionally draining to listen to her and then face a barrage of questions from the media.

INTERRUPTED BY AN HONOR

In the end, I was not there for Anderson's testimony. A few days before the hearing, I received an unexpected call from the White House asking if I would appear in the House of Representatives gallery during

President Clinton's State of the Union address to Congress. What an honor, but what a dilemma! How could I turn down such a request? But I wasn't sure I should go, since House Bill 1242 was scheduled for committee testimony on that same day. I desperately wanted to testify in support of the bill, as this was the only remaining gun-control bill with any chance of passage.

I presented my concerns to SAFE Colorado's board of directors. They encouraged me to go to Washington, saying that being at the capitol would honor Daniel and possibly provide a spotlight on our work. Furthermore, the committee hearing would probably be just one of a few such hearings, while there was just one State of the Union speech. Secretly, of course, I was relieved because it spared me from facing Anderson.

I called the White House and confirmed my attendance. They asked me to keep quiet about my appearance until just before the event. That was fine with me. I didn't want to distract attention from media coverage of HB 1242 just as we were building momentum.

I left for Washington on the evening of January 26, the day before the address. The next evening I was given a ride to the U.S. Capitol and led to my assigned seat in the House gallery. I had no idea what to expect, although White House staff had mentioned I would be sitting near the first lady. I knew that some guests were specifically recognized by the president during the State of the Union address, but I didn't know if they all were, and the staff didn't mention anything to me about being singled out.

I was surprised to see I was seated only two rows from the railing of the balcony and midway down the right side. I assumed the first lady sat front and center in the balcony, which was some distance away, so I was confused. As I introduced myself to others around me, I discovered I was sitting right behind Henry Aaron! Yes, Hammerin' Hank, baseball's all-time leader in home runs at the time, right there in front of me!

A while later an entourage entered and sat near us. It included First Lady Hillary Clinton and daughter, Chelsea. They didn't sit in the center of the balcony after all; they sat on the right side, not far from me, so we greeted each other.

A short while later, President Clinton arrived amidst the usual fan-fare. I gazed down on the floor of the House, seeing many political leaders I was familiar with from watching the news. What a treat for a political science major! Here I was in the midst of this great (though often boring and theatrical) American annual tradition. I listened as the president spoke about welfare reform, education, and other national priorities.

He continued: "Again, I ask you to pass a real patients' bill of rights. I ask you to pass common-sense gun safety legislation. I ask you to pass campaign finance reform. I ask you to vote up or down on judicial nominations..."

I wondered whether that was all he was going to say about gun safety legislation. (He dared not call it *gun-control* legislation.) He then spoke at length about health care but not about the patients' bill of rights he brought up earlier. I feared the same would happen to his call to pass common-sense gun safety legislation, that his one brief mention of gun safety legislation would be the end of it. After all, the Republicans controlled Congress and they were in the pocket of the NRA, so perhaps Clinton decided not to expend political capital on a hopeless cause.

HONOR FOR DANIEL

When the president was about halfway through his address, he surprised me by returning to the gun-control issue by speaking of Columbine. "Soon after the Columbine tragedy, Congress considered common-sense gun safety legislation to require Brady background checks at gun shows, child safety locks for all new handguns, and a ban on the importation of large-capacity ammunition clips." My heart jumped as he talked about gun laws, but also sank as I thought, *Oh, God, here we go again with talk about Columbine. I don't want to have to hear about Columbine and keep my composure. What next? Will the cameras pan up to show the grieving Columbine father sitting there as soon as the word Columbine is spoken?*

Clinton went on: "With courage, and a tie-breaking vote by the vice president, the Senate faced down the gun lobby, stood up for the American people, and passed this legislation. But the House failed to follow suit.

"We've all seen what happens when guns fall into the wrong hands. Daniel Mauser was only fifteen years old when he was gunned down at Columbine. He was an amazing kid, a straight-A student, a good skier."

My heart raced. Daniel was being honored by the President of the United States to a national audience! I was a mess of emotions. I had a huge lump in my throat. I was about to cry but knew I couldn't possibly do that. I needed to be strong. What if a camera was on me? I was sure a camera would be on me, as these events were so closely choreographed.

"Like all parents who lose their children, his father, Tom, has borne unimaginable grief," Clinton continued. "Somehow Tom has found the strength to honor his son by transforming his grief into action. Earlier this month, he took a leave of absence from his job to fight for tougher gun safety laws. I pray that his courage and wisdom will move this Congress to make common-sense gun safety legislation the very next order of business."

Clinton wanted to recognize me in the gallery, so he called me out. "Tom, thank you for being here tonight. Tom Mauser, please stand up."

I already was standing up, as was everyone around me. We had all stood up and applauded after Clinton called on the lawmakers to make gun safety legislation the next order of business. Even though we were all standing, I was probably easy for the audience and cameras to spot. I was the one wearing a button with the photo of a teenage boy. I was the one who had stopped applauding, his hands clasped in front of him, with a look that said, "What the heck is happening here? I'm embarrassed and humbled."

For about 20 seconds the TV cameras were on me as I received a standing ovation from everyone present. It was a greatly humbling experience. Unsure of what to do, I simply bowed my head in recognition and mouthed the words, "Thank you, Mr. President."

I was awed by the recognition, given that I hadn't yet accomplished anything in terms of changing laws. The bar had certainly been set high for me.

After the address, I was escorted out by a White House staff member. While making our way through the capitol lobby and a flurry of activity, I was asked if I would speak on camera with NBC's Tim Russert. After meeting Hammerin' Hank Aaron, I could speak with the biggest home-run hitter in TV political coverage? You bet I was willing!

As I waited for Russert to finish other interviews, the White House staffer was perhaps a bit surprised as I unexpectedly encountered House Speaker Dennis Hastert and majority leader Dick Armey, who was an unabashed gun activist. Like me, the two were waiting to be interviewed. I surprised myself by strolling up to them, introducing myself, and asking, "Would you please close the gun show loophole? It's really ridiculous to allow this loophole, don't you think?"

Hastert and Armey were caught off guard and unsure what to say, perhaps wondering if any reporters were within earshot. My heart was pounding as it hit me that I had really stepped outside of my comfort zone. I don't recall exactly what they said, but it was a typical political response that avoided my question. I wasn't satisfied with their reply, but I didn't expect to be. It was a short encounter, but what counted was that they had been challenged by a plea from the heart of a victim of gun violence.

BACK TO WORK

The next day I returned to reality in Colorado. The gun show loophole bill was still in play, so the Washington experience quickly became history. I received a few media inquiries about being honored by the president, but I didn't focus on pushing that story, for the emphasis was on HB 1242.

I learned that Robyn Anderson testified before the committee, telling the committee how she made the purchase at the Tanner Gun Show and insisting she would not have bought guns from a licensed dealer because she would have had to fill out paperwork associated with a background check. Some legislators and pundits condemned her testimony, insisting that because of her reprehensible behavior she could not be believed. They also asserted Anderson was trying to save her own skin by making it look as if the problem was the loophole in the Brady Bill, not her own actions. However, she had already been cleared of any charges, so there wasn't much she had to gain by testifying.

I was pleased to hear that HB 1242 passed out of the House Judiciary Committee on a 7–6 vote. But because there was a small "fiscal impact"—a cost to the state if the bill were implemented—it had to be approved by the House Appropriations Committee before reaching a vote in the full House.

There was more high drama in the Appropriations Committee. Representative Gordon shocked the hearing room as he pulled out and held in the air a .22-caliber Ruger pistol he had recently bought from a private seller at a gun show without undergoing a background check. There were gasps and statements of outrage from Republican legislators. I was also shocked initially, but I also understood the point he was trying to demonstrate. Gordon assured committee members the gun was not loaded and that he had cleared his actions with the House speaker and capitol police.

What bothered me during the Appropriations Committee hearing was that much of the testimony was not about fiscal impact, it was about the bill itself. It angered me to think the bill was not being debated based on whether the small cost to the state was worth it in terms of the lives that could be saved.

Having failed to kill the bill in the Judiciary Committee, the gun lobby worked hard to win votes on the Appropriations Committee. So did our side. The bill was getting a lot of media coverage, so the pressure on committee members was tremendous.

The Republicans held a majority on the committee, so it was expected that a great deal of pressure was put on them by the party and the NRA to defeat the bill, for we were confident we had all the Democrats on our side. We focused on three Republican members: a moderate, Steve Tool, and two suburban Denver women, Debbie Allen and Nancy Spence, who were conservative but not aligned with the far right.

We worked hard to win Tool's vote, so we just needed one of the female legislators' votes. Allen was considered the most likely swing vote because she was running for a Senate seat that fall. We felt that opposing this popular bill would be detrimental to her election chances in that district. The governor's chief lobbyist said he had talked to Debbie Allen five times in an effort to persuade her to vote for the measure. SAFE Colorado put tremendous pressure on her, too, delivering flyers door-to-door in her district.

Although the focus was on Allen, I was still hopeful we could win over Spence, because she was a strong supporter of bills related to kids and education.

An amendment was offered, with SAFE Colorado's knowledge, in response to concerns voiced by gun activists that gun buyers' names not be kept in any federal databases. But even that was not enough to placate the gun lobby. In the end, when the vote was taken, we got the votes of all the Democrats and of Tool, but we lost all the other Republicans. We lost by a vote of 6–5. To this day I have not forgiven the Republicans for caving in to the gun lobby, especially Debbie Allen and Nancy Spence, for I don't think they were following the will of their constituents nor were they voting based on the fiscal impact. The vote was a political hatchet job, doing the will of the gun lobby. I had the pleasure of delivering campaign fliers door-to-door for Allen's opponent and of seeing her lose the Senate race that fall.

I was shocked and devastated by the vote on HB 1242. My mind told me there was a good chance we would lose the vote, but my heart so much wanted my mind to be wrong. I wanted a victory for common sense, a victory for Daniel. I felt that passage of this bill would be enough of a victory that I could end my lobbying in a few more weeks. I wanted to return to my normal job and my normal life, but that was not to be.

I tried instead to look forward. It was time for Plan B.

Daniel and his Grandma Mauser

Chapter 14

Taking It to the Streets

By late February 2000, less than two months into the legislative session, I was discouraged and disgusted. The legislature failed to close the gun show loophole, even though polls indicated more than 80 percent of Coloradans supported doing so. The session lasted until early May, but the Republican majority had decided to take up most of the gun-related bills in the first few weeks of the session, likely so they could quickly pass their pro-gun bills, dismiss the gun-control measures, and move on to other business before the public expressed disgust with what they had done in the aftermath of Columbine.

My lobbying work was mostly done and I was burned out, given my ineffectiveness, the NRA's influence, and the intransigence of most Republicans. I felt I had largely failed. I wanted to be back at my regular job and out of the pressure cooker by the end of the legislative session in early May, with at least some success in strengthening the state's gun laws. But it didn't look like that was going to happen. The gun-control bills were mostly dead in the water. Only a couple of moderate gun-related bills were passed and signed. Meanwhile, the pro-gun bills had much better luck. It seemed unreal that one year following the Columbine massacre Colorado's legislature was passing pro-gun bills and rejecting common-sense gun legislation. What good could now come of my efforts?

A NEEDED BOOST

SAFE Colorado's board believed strongly that closing the gun show loophole was critical. Since the bill that would have done so had failed in the legislature, SAFE decided the time had come to shift gears. I continued to lobby for and against the few gun-related bills that remained, but SAFE Colorado and I began to devote most of our time and effort to closing the gun show loophole by attempting to put the issue to a vote of the people of Colorado.

We received an early boost to our efforts from President Clinton, who was interested in helping us promote the campaign. The White House called and informed us that Clinton's schedule would allow him to stop in Denver on April 12 to promote our efforts to close the loophole. SAFE's leadership asked me how I felt about having such an event eight days before the first anniversary of the massacre.

I was a bit concerned with the timing and the fact I assumed my family and I would be under a lot of stress as we approached the anniversary. In addition, I imagined some people in the community would be critical of what they'd say was a political event so close to the anniversary. However, I told SAFE I was agreeable with going ahead with that date because there would be no date that would satisfy some critics and no date on which I could escape the reminders of Columbine.

As expected, when news of President Clinton's planned visit became public, some in the community voiced objections, saying he was politicizing the gun issue at a time too close to the anniversary, when emotions were high. Some insisted Clinton was coming for a partisan event at taxpayer expense. Governor Owens, despite fully supporting our efforts to close the gun show loophole, announced his refusal to meet with Clinton during his visit, saying he shouldn't be coming to the state for the purpose of pressuring Congress to pass federal gun laws. I was disappointed with Owens's position. After all, there was no specific legislation in Congress at the time to close the gun show loophole. However, I knew Owens probably didn't want his support for closing the gun show loophole to be associated with a Democratic president when he was taking a lot of heat for the gun-control measures he was supporting. His objections were a way of appeasing his pro-gun critics.

Our rally was held at the Colorado Convention Center, where the president and the leaders of SAFE Colorado were on a stage in front of a few thousand cheering people. The rally was not a partisan event—there were both Republicans and Democrats attending and speaking at the rally.

Tickets were given away for the event in advance. As a means of not making it too easy for troublemakers to get tickets and "crash" the event, we required most people to phone in for tickets and pick them up at an office and show identification. Fortunately, there was only one bit of trouble inside the rally, and it was from a screaming man with a sign who was upset about a foreign-relations issue, not about gun control. He was removed from the crowd.

Outside it was a different story. I, along with a few others, arrived early for the event to meet with the president, so I didn't have to wait in line outside as most others did. Because of security screening, it was taking a long time for ticket holders to enter the convention center to attend the rally. They were forced to walk through a gauntlet of gun extremists waiting outside for them, both before and after the rally. Fortunately, police kept the extremists behind waist-high barricades in a large area near the convention center, but the event attendees couldn't help but hear and see their message.

Some of the pro-gun demonstrators wore camouflage, some came dressed in Revolutionary War garb and some wore t-shirts with the name of a new gun extremist organization, the Tyranny Response Team. They carried signs condemning gun control and equating it to Nazism. Many who attended the SAFE Colorado rally, including high school students, received their first exposure to the rudeness of gun extremists. The extremists chanted and used bullhorns to harass the rally attendees, shouting insults and profanity, condemning them for taking away the protesters' "God given rights" and taunting them for attending the event.

Some claimed that gun-control measures, such as criminal background checks for gun purchasers, made it harder for women to quickly obtain guns for self-protection. Some ridiculed women for supporting gun control and refusing to carry a gun as a means of preventing rape.

Although the scene was unpleasant outside, the event inside was a great success. It was much like a pep rally. Clinton and I both spoke to the crowd, expressing disappointment with the legislature's failure to close the gun show loophole and explaining why it was important. Clinton urged the crowd to take action in Colorado and wished us well in our efforts. The lively and supportive crowd lifted my spirits immensely, helping me overcome my disappointment in my lobbying. The event energized me and gave me hope.

THE PEOPLE GET TO DECIDE

The gun lobby had its way with the legislature, but the time had come to let the people decide by putting the issue to a vote on a statewide ballot. To do so in Colorado, promoters of a citizens' initiative needed to develop language following certain legal guidelines. The language then had to be approved by a special legislative committee. Once approved, that language would be placed on petitions, which had to be signed by a certain percentage of eligible voters in order for the measure to be placed on the ballot.

SAFE Colorado was well prepared to conduct a campaign. Its board of directors included some seasoned politicians who knew the political system and understood public policy. The board hired a team of experts to run the campaign. Wally Stealey, a seasoned political expert, was hired as campaign manager. An exceptional legal firm well-versed in ballot initiatives, led by attorney Mark Grueskin, was hired based on its outstanding ballot initiative expertise. Stan McKee, Cynthia Stone, Elaine Calzolari, and John O'Donnell were hired to run SAFE's campaign office, serving as office manager, communications director, special events coordinator, and fundraiser, respectively. Office volunteers such as Patricia Gilman and Karen Mather worked tirelessly on the campaign, as did many others.

The SAFE Colorado board and the legal team developed an excellent strategy. The ballot initiative they drafted was similar to the gun show loophole bill that failed in the Colorado House but was slightly stronger. The NRA and Republicans had a chance to pass a moderate version of the bill, but since they obstinately refused to do so, they would now face an amendment that didn't make some of the concessions that were offered during the legislative session within House Bill 1242.

SAFE made another important strategic decision. In Colorado a citizen initiative can be presented to the voters on the ballot either as an amendment to the state constitution or as a statutory amendment. A constitutional amendment is directly written into the state's constitution and therefore is not open to revision except by another vote of the people. As such, the gun lobby could not easily change the law, but it also meant the new law couldn't readily be revised if a minor problem was discovered. It was this latter aspect, and the reluctance of many of us to overburden our state constitution with numerous amendments, that concerned the SAFE board.

A statutory amendment is more flexible. In essence, it is a legislative bill passed by the people. As such, it can easily be changed or overturned by the legislature in a future legislative session like any other bill. Despite that risk, the SAFE board decided to present the bill as a statutory amendment. They felt we could work hard to pass the bill by a wide margin, with a mandate so strong the legislature wouldn't dare try to gut or overturn it.

SIGN IN, PLEASE

The initiative language was sent to a legislative committee for review to ensure it met legal (not political) requirements. As expected, the gun lobby challenged our language for Amendment 22, saying it wasn't clear enough, but the committee ruled in our favor and accepted our language.

SAFE Colorado moved ahead, shifting into petition gear. We needed to get 62,500 valid petition signatures to get the amendment on the ballot. Given that some signatures would be ruled invalid (because, for instance, the petition signer's signature or printed name didn't exactly match what was in official voting records), we set a goal of getting at least 100,000 signatures.

Some organizations pay people to collect petition signatures. By paying signature collectors, organizations may be recruiting people who only do it for the money. Such petition collectors may go overboard to get signatures because they are paid per signature collected, which can lead to sloppiness and signatures that are later found to be invalid.

SAFE's board wisely decided it would use only volunteers. They felt that with the great groundswell of support for closing the gun show loophole, it would be possible to recruit lots of volunteer petition carriers. Use of volunteers would also demonstrate the groundswell of support for Amendment 22. We successfully recruited a large cadre of volunteers and staff who knew how to properly carry out the petition process.

We had an exceptional public relations and media campaign, led by Cynthia Stone, SAFE's director of communications. She arranged to have the first petition signatures collected at a rally on the west steps of the state capitol on May 3, 2000. The event was staged at the same place where the protest against the NRA convention had been held in 1999.

The first signature collected at the rally was that of Republican Governor Owens. The second was that of Democratic Secretary of State Ken Salazar The third signature came from Denver Mayor Wellington Webb. My signature followed, as did those of other dignitaries, including some state legislators. How symbolic it was to sign the petitions in front of the building where the NRA managed to convince legislators to thwart the will of Coloradans by refusing to close the gun show loophole.

Governor Owens summed up the effort well, telling the crowd that "nobody should be concerned about a background check other than the criminals and kids who won't get weapons" with this amendment in place.

The petitions then went out to those in the crowd. In another symbolic move, as the rally ended, many volunteers fanned out and walked down Denver's nearby pedestrian mecca, the Sixteenth Street Mall, and collected hundreds more signatures.

Over the next few weeks, petition carriers went to supermarket parking lots, art festivals, Colorado Rockies baseball games, and to their neighbors' homes, and returned with a flood of signatures. Volunteers reported a few cases of opponents being rude, but mostly the process went smoothly.

While the signature collection process proceeded, four gun-owner groups, with some help from the NRA, tried to stop our initiative in various courts. In Colorado, a ballot initiative is limited to only one subject and its sponsor must estimate the cost of the initiative to taxpayers. Our opponents argued in lower courts that our initiative was misleading, that it covered more than one subject and that we failed to adequately measure its cost. When they didn't get a favorable ruling in lower courts, they took it to the State Supreme Court. On July 3, 2000, the Supreme Court ruled against the arguments of the gun groups, giving us the green light to move ahead.

We had a deadline to meet in order to turn the petitions over to the secretary of state's office, but we finished with lots of time to spare. When we tallied the petitions we found we had gathered *110,000* signatures, more than enough to overcome gun lobby challenges.

SPELLING IT OUT

A creative ceremony was arranged to have petition gatherers join SAFE members who would deliver the petitions. It attracted a lot of media coverage and an enthusiastic crowd. On August 2, 2000, we gathered once again on the west steps of the capitol. In front of the podium, we laid out the thousands of bundled petitions. Police were nearby in case someone tried to disrupt the event or damage the petitions. Twenty-three people standing behind the podium held up signs, each containing a single letter, which collectively spelled out "close the gun show loophole."

After I and a few others spoke to the gathered crowd, I led a long, single-file procession to the secretary of state's office, carrying the bundles of petitions and the signs spelling out our message. I was wearing Daniel's shoes. Cameras rolled as we walked the three blocks to the elections office. It was an incredibly symbolic statement about the power of ordinary people petitioning their government for change.

I announced our arrival at the office and dropped off the first bundle of petitions, all to the clicking and whirring of news cameras. Then came dozens of petition carriers, one-by-one, dropping off their bundles. It was a joyous and triumphant moment, and a fitting tribute to Daniel. Within a week or two the secretary of state certified that we had an adequate number of valid petition signatures to place the amendment on the ballot that fall. This was our biggest victory up to that point. We couldn't let it be our last. But the gun lobby still had plans to rain on our parade.

Tom speaking at a rally on the west steps of the state capitol before delivering 110,000 petition signatures, August 2, 2000.

Chapter 15

Coloradans Get to Decide

We were on the ballot! Now it was time to convince the people of Colorado once and for all that Amendment 22 was reasonable and needed. Early polling showed that more than 75 percent of Coloradans supported closing the gun show loophole. We assumed our opponents would do anything to chip away at those numbers by creating doubt, discrediting SAFE Colorado, arguing it was an affront to gun owners, spreading fear, and raising more legal challenges. We were right.

USING THE COURTS

Pro-gun groups had already gone to court in the spring to stop our effort. Despite being ruled against by the State Supreme Court, gun activists continued to mount legal challenges against us. In September they went to lower courts, arguing that when their earlier legal challenges were filed, SAFE Colorado should have stopped its petition-collecting process until a final ruling was issued.

Our legal team argued it would have been unreasonable for SAFE Colorado to stop its petition drive every time a legal challenge was filed.

They insisted that the Supreme Court had already ruled that there was no set starting time to gather signatures as long as petitioners were willing to take the risk that the wording on the ballot could be changed by the courts and the signatures collected up to that time thrown out. SAFE Colorado had undertaken the risk that it would have to begin its petition drive all over again if it lost a court ruling.

If gun activists had won their case, they estimated about 90,000 of SAFE's 110,000 petition signatures would have been invalidated, because they were collected before the July 3 State Supreme Court ruling. But those ninety thousand personal declarations were not invalidated. We didn't have to start over because lower courts ruled against this legal challenge of gun activists. So the activists again took their case to the State Supreme Court, and on October 10 the Court ruled against them once again!

In all, six legal challenges were filed against Amendment 22, and every one lost. It was a hassle that cost us money, and it was a slight distraction from our campaign, but overall the gun activists' efforts backfired because it helped keep Amendment 22 in the news, providing us free publicity and an opportunity to condemn their actions.

Every time a court ruling came down, SAFE's communications director was ready with a press release and I made myself available to the media. Because the issue was related to Columbine, and because it was summer—a slower news time—the media were more than willing to offer me a chance to speak. I usually told reporters I wondered why my opponents didn't want the citizens of Colorado to get a chance to vote on Amendment 22. "What are they afraid of?" I usually asked. "Why are they relying on the courts rather than the voters?"

FULL STEAM AHEAD

Our campaign went ahead despite the legal challenges. I spent some of my time doing something that wasn't natural for me: making fundraising calls, visiting personally with potential donors, and attending fundraising events where I spoke. I'm not a very good salesman, but the fundraising work was a necessity.

I spent much of my time speaking to the media and to the public. Sometimes organizations called us asking for a speaker on Amendment 22 and sometimes it was me calling to offer myself as a speaker. I spoke at Rotary Club meetings, churches, colleges, television and radio stations, political party gatherings (I even spoke at a couple of local Republican Party gatherings!), and at numerous other settings. When I was the only speaker, I didn't exploit my exclusive access to my audience. I made a point to present the arguments of my opponents and my responses to them.

On some occasions I debated someone opposed to Amendment 22. I preferred that format because it was symbolic of my walking in Daniel's shoes, doing something he loved— debating. Plus I feared that when I spoke alone some people might be reluctant to ask tough questions of the father of a Columbine victim. Some might be polite in person but not supportive of Amendment 22 in the voting booth. In the debate format the audience heard both sides of the issue.

RESPONDING TO THE ABSURD

I became familiar with all the arguments of my opponents and loved the challenge of responding to them. "Amendment 22 is an attack on private gun sales!" many argued. But the fact was that Amendment 22 simply made private gun sellers play by the same rules as licensed dealers. Why should private sellers be allowed to let a gun slip so easily into the hands of a criminal just because they are a private seller? It was illegal for private sellers to knowingly sell guns to a prohibited purchaser, so why not provide them the means to conduct a background check?

Opponents argued it was possible to get a gun without a background check through a private sale arranged between two individuals or through a classified ad. They argued that private sales at gun shows should not be treated differently from those other private sales.

I countered that gun shows were events open to the public where there were usually hundreds of guns from which to select. It didn't make sense to operate under two standards at a gun show, requiring a background check at one table but not at another. I insisted that my opponents actually were making an excellent argument for conducting background checks on *all* private sales, not just at gun shows, and that it would be an effective step in keeping guns out of the wrong hands. I told audiences that SAFE Colorado wasn't proposing such a far-reaching step at that time but thanked gun activists for making such a strong case for universal background checks covering all gun sales.

Another common assertion of our opponents was that criminals didn't go to gun shows. "Why would they go to a gun show when they can buy them on the street?" they asked.

I responded that the reason was simple. Criminals would go to gun shows for the same reason any other person would go—the wide selection of firearms under one roof. In Colorado, thousands of prohibited purchasers attempted to buy firearms from a gun shop but were denied. There was absolutely no reason to believe they likewise wouldn't try to make a purchase at a gun show, especially if they discovered they could purchase from a private seller without a background check to stop them. Furthermore, some prohibited purchasers, such as those who had a restraining order against them, might not even be aware they were prohibited buyers.

Opponents were adamant that honorable private sellers would never allow a criminal to make a purchase. My response: "How do you know someone is not a felon or a wife beater or a chronic alcoholic? Can you tell from their looks? No, you have to conduct a background check, which is what Amendment 22 is designed to do."

Some of the arguments against Amendment 22 were based on its specific provisions. For example, opponents criticized the broad reach of the amendment, including the requirement that a background check be conducted for sales on the entire grounds of the gun show, including the parking lot, as well as transactions that were started at the show but completed later. Our reasoning was simple: We didn't want a private seller skirting the law by telling a potential buyer, "Psst! We can skip the paperwork. Just meet me outside."

Amendment 22 allowed licensed gun dealers to charge up to a $10 fee for conducting a background check. Gun activists claimed $10 was unreasonable and would wipe out private sellers. I responded that it wasn't reasonable to expect licensed dealers to conduct background checks for their competitors for free, since they had to take time to call in to the Colorado Bureau of Investigation to check criminal records, just like they did for their own sales. The amendment leveled the playing field at gun shows, since the loophole gave an unfair and dangerous competitive edge to private sellers. Many private sellers exploited that edge, posting signs that read "no background check required," "no waiting here," or "no paperwork." Such signs were an invitation to prohibited purchasers.

Some gun dealers supported Amendment 22 because they didn't think it was fair that some gun buyers could bypass paperwork associated with background checks by going to a private seller, but no individual gun dealer spoke publicly in favor of the amendment, likely because they knew they would face the wrath of gun activists and possibly become the target of a boycott.

MISUSING THE SECOND

Naturally, some opposed Amendment 22 as a violation of their Second Amendment rights. I enjoyed responding to that argument. I would simply ask my opponent: "How in the heck does this infringe on your Second Amendment rights? If you're a law abiding citizen, and you pass the background check, you're able to purchase a firearm. How is that an infringement? How is that any different from the background checks now being conducted by FFLs at gun shops?"

I stressed that the Second Amendment conveys the right to bear arms but does not allow one to escape the responsibility of ensuring that a felon or other prohibited purchaser doesn't gain access to firearms. Our nation doesn't allow prospective teachers to bypass background checks, nor does it allow people to bypass the security check at an airport, so why should we let people bypass a background check for gun purchases?

Opponents argued that private sellers should be excused from administering background checks because they were private transactions and therefore exempt from any government oversight. I countered that there was nothing sacred about a private sale or seller. If you sell your car to another person, as a private individual, you still have an obligation to transfer and notarize the public title documents just as you would if you were going through a car dealer. Public documentation protects us all.

Furthermore, the gun sold by a private seller is just as deadly as a gun from a licensed dealer.

In desperation, some opponents resorted to the "fatalism" argument: if prohibited purchasers were turned away at a gun show, they would get a gun somewhere else, such as the black market or a newspaper ad. In other words, we can't stop all sales of guns to prohibited buyers, so why try?

I told my audiences we had to remain positive about what could be done to prevent guns from getting into the wrong hands, and that closing the loophole was one of them. I insisted we couldn't afford to give up doing background checks just because we knew some people would try to get around them.

If felons, drug abusers, and wife beaters decided they had to go elsewhere to make their purchase, fine! Making them go elsewhere could lead to their being caught, reported, or otherwise getting into trouble. We shouldn't make it easy for them to purchase a firearm, and particularly not right under our noses in a public place like a gun show.

SLIPPERY SLOPPINESS

One of the most common assertions of gun activists was that Amendment 22 was a first step by gun-control advocates to pass more and more laws. This, they claimed, would eventually lead to the elimination of all gun rights, denying the right of self-protection, and banning and confiscating of all firearms—the proverbial "slippery slope" argument.

It was typical of gun activists to portray gun-control proposals in this way and argue that something more sinister was being planned. They tried to create fear among gun owners while avoiding the question of whether a particular gun-control proposal might actually help keep firearms from criminals, kids, and the mentally deranged.

I reminded audiences that the Amendment 22 vote was not about confiscating or banning guns. The initiative language was short and simple, and there for them to read. Only one proposal was being brought before the voters: to close the gun show loophole. Period. Any other proposed laws would have to be put to the voters or legislators to consider, and they would be decided on their merits and within the Constitution.

Amendment 22 needed to be considered based on what it was, not on the speculative fear that it might somehow "lead to something else." Still, the most devoted gun activists adamantly clung to the slippery slope argument because most of their other arguments were not clicking with most voters.

BECOMING THE ISSUE

When opponents couldn't get traction with voters they occasionally tried to sidetrack the debate by making *me* the issue, focusing on my motivations or my state of mind. They often maintained that my advocacy represented merely an emotional "feel-good" or knee-jerk reaction to Columbine. The massacre certainly was the impetus for Amendment 22, but the easy availability of firearms at gun shows was a wake-up call for many Coloradans, not just for me. Amendment 22 was responding to a real need to close a gaping loophole, just as the Jessica Gonzales case called for closure of another loophole. Wanting to prevent future tragedies was not an "emotional, knee-jerk reaction," I told my audiences. Instead, it was my opponents who were reacting without reason by making outrageous claims about Amendment 22.

It was not uncommon for opponents to try to win points with an audience by first expressing sympathy for me, often to the point of being overly patronizing, then following that with "but we cannot allow our sympathy for Columbine to guide our public policy. We feel for these victims. We understand Mr. Mauser's pain. But no law will bring back Mr. Mauser's son, and no law would have changed what happened that terrible day at Columbine."

I responded that I was not engaged in this debate to bring Daniel back. It was too late to undo Columbine. I simply wanted to prevent another tragic shooting by ensuring guns were not easily available to a child or a criminal.

Some gun rights advocates tried to make an issue of the fact I was being paid for lobbying and at an annual salary ($72,000) they considered too high. Apparently they thought I should volunteer my time in order to be legitimate or rightfully devoted. I responded that that my family could not be expected to have me work for nothing.

In October 2000 an hour-long, weekly public affairs program on a Denver public television station was devoted to Amendment 22. Two women spoke in opposition to Amendment 22 and two in support of it. I was not there to speak for Amendment 22, as I was overseas at the time.

Near the end of the program, the host, moderate radio talk show host Peter Boyles, gave each side of the debate a chance for a closing statement. Linda Gorman, a researcher for the Independence Institute, a conservative/libertarian think tank, summarized for the opponents. She chose to take a cheap shot, bringing up something that had not been discussed during the debate.

"I'm glad that the legislature protected me from the gun-control lobby, which is paying Tom Mauser seventy grand a year to go around arguing for gun control—"

Boyles interrupted her, interjecting sarcastically, "Oh yeah, Tom Mauser had his kid killed at Columbine, to hell with him...."

Gorman continued. "No, no, but that does not mean that you guys can take away my right to self defense, or that you can waste resources promoting laws that simply draw money out of legitimate crime enforcement into things like background checks, which simply let criminals get guns whenever they want and keep law-abiding citizens from defending themselves."

Boyles allowed Gorman to finish, then added a final comment. "Tom Mauser left his job, the money he got to support his family. He quit after his son was killed at Columbine. He's not getting a paycheck from his company. He's getting a check from this organization (SAFE Colorado) to do this. Now, these people, the NRA and others, hire people every G.D. day. They get paid all the time to do these things, and here's Tom Mauser, whose son is brutally murdered. You know, we could have ended this show without your doing that on Tom Mauser!" Gorman said nothing.

Boyles emphatically instructs his guests to stay in their seats until well after the credits rolled at the end of the show. But he was so disgusted with Gorman's attack that he shook his head and walked off the set before the credits finished scrolling.

HELP FROM OTHERS

Well over $2,000,000 was spent on the Amendment 22 campaign. SAFE Colorado raised far more money and from many more sources than its opponents. That was no surprise, given that we had so much more support from the people of Colorado. Nearly all the opposition dollars came from the NRA.

The opposition ironically painted themselves as the underdogs, which, of course, is so seldom the case in legislative battles. They tried to make an issue of the fact that some of SAFE's money came from well-heeled Colorado liberals. It did, but it's likewise true that most of the Republicans supported by the NRA were getting campaign contributions from well-heeled conservatives.

They also made an issue of contributions from the Brady Campaign in Washington, D.C., as well as some from other "out-of-state interests." I simply responded that nearly all our opponents' money came from the NRA's national headquarters, which was located in Virginia.

They had few individual donors, while we had hundreds and hundreds. The NRA easily could have outspent us, but I think they were smart enough to know it was a losing cause. They likely made a contribution because they were expected by some of their members to put up a fight, regardless of the merits of Amendment 22.

A HERO WEIGHS IN

Most major newspapers in the state endorsed Amendment 22. So did all four living former Colorado governors: Democrats Dick Lamm and Roy Romer, and Republicans John Love and John Vanderhoof.

But one of our biggest boosts came from Senator John McCain, who agreed to tape two television commercials in support of Amendment 22. Americans for Gun Safety, a moderate gun-control organization, arranged and paid for the commercials.

McCain's commercials put opponents in a corner. "I'm John McCain with some straight talk…I believe law-abiding citizens have the right to own guns. But with rights come responsibilities."

Our opponents were being marginalized by support from Republicans like McCain. It was not easy for them to attack the motives of an

American hero, but the more extreme gun activists did so anyway. "The only people that respect him (McCain) are the press," Dudley Brown, executive director of Rocky Mountain Gun Owners (RMGO), told the *Denver Post*. "What's one more liberal Republican on their train?"

VICTORY!

We were confident of victory as election day neared, yet we remained cautious. We kept working hard to ensure a wide margin of victory to better protect against future legislative attacks on the bill.

On election night, we held a party in a small art museum and awaited the election results. I was elated when, early in the evening, all Denver television stations declared Amendment 22 a winner, with a 70 percent "yes" vote!

Our celebration was boosted even more with word of a similar victory against the gun lobby that night. A similar citizens' initiative to close the gun show loophole was passed by the voters in Oregon by a margin of 60 percent to 40 percent. That was reassuring, indicating that if there had been a "Columbine factor" impacting Colorado's vote, it was only a slight one. Voters had overwhelmingly supported closing the gun show loophole in two western states.

After word of the passage of Amendment 22, SAFE Colorado's leaders spoke, then introduced me. I gave one of my better speeches that night, perhaps for no other reason than it allowed me to be more upbeat. I was able to offer my reflections on gun control, honor Daniel, and size up our opponents, all in a more relaxed manner flavored with some humor.

After being introduced, I fumbled around with some papers and pretended to look confounded, telling the audience I had misplaced my speech. Then I pulled out a piece of paper with numerous holes poked in it. "Oh, these are the arguments of the NRA for opposing Amendment 22!" I dismissively tossed the paper to the floor.

Then I pulled out a business card, claiming it was that of Dudley Brown, the leader of RMGO. "What's this? Oh, a business card for Dudley Weapon!" I dismissively flipped it onto the floor.

Next I pulled out a legal-sized piece of paper. "Oh, look, another petition! Stan, are we still taking petitions?"

Perhaps it's not as funny on paper, but my delivery was comical and the crowd loved it. Those who had only ever witnessed my serious advocacy side were perhaps surprised to see this other side of me.

I paused briefly, then smiled broadly with a jubilant look. "What a sweet night! And what a sweet victory. And what a sweet journey this has been for me," I told supporters, pausing briefly as I bent over and reached to the ground before standing erect once again, holding a pair of Reebok sneakers, and continuing, "in Daniel's shoes!

"We're here because the legislature failed to do its job. We're here because our leaders failed to lead. We're here because the NRA and the gun lobby badgered, bought, and bullied the legislature to ensure the gun show loophole wasn't closed. So we decided to let the people of Colorado do the leading. And you know what? What it really came down to? The NRA just simply couldn't badger, buy, or bully the people of Colorado!"

I went on to speculate that the NRA lost so badly "because people just got sick and tired of the same old rhetoric and old clichés," along with their constant excuses for gun violence and the absence of reasonable laws. "But, most of all, voters were fed up with the negative, hopeless message of the NRA and the gun lobby that says, 'Well, criminals are gonna get guns anyway.' What happened in Colorado was that people turned to the positive message that we offered—that they *could* do something positive to keep guns out of the hands of kids and criminals."

I expressed my hopes for the future, calling for "our voices to be heard in the halls of Congress, so that all Americans see the closing of the gun show loophole. Let our voices mark the dawn of a new day, when we take a serious look at our gun laws, a day when the NRA is treated for what it really is—a tiny special interest group that has wielded power disproportionate to the size of its membership."

I summed up my role in passing Amendment 22, telling the crowd that some mistakenly thought I was founder or the brains behind SAFE Colorado. "No, really what I have done is provide a face for this movement, the face of a victim of gun violence. I've provided a soft, reasonable voice that matches and complements this common-sense amendment. And I provided a story—it's Daniel's story, a story that makes people realize that we are all victims of gun violence. And we are all capable of doing something about it. And we did so, tonight. It's the work that you all did that made it happen. It is your victory, along with Daniel's. You should all be so proud of what you have done here tonight. Thank you and God bless you all."

Video available on YouTube (see link in Appendix).

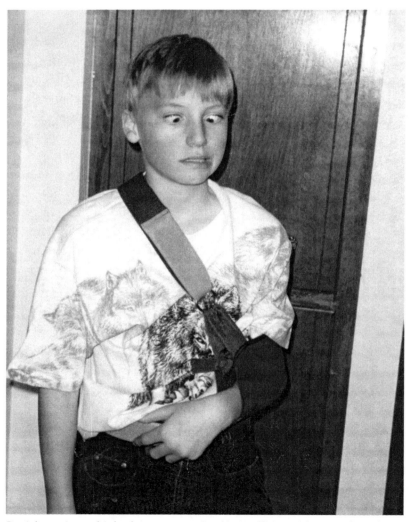

Daniel reacting to his broken arm, sustained in a collision with a snowboarder while skiing

Chapter 16

How Does One Deal With Such Grief?

There was satisfaction in lobbying to change gun laws. I felt a great sense of accomplishment after helping to close the gun show loophole in Daniel's name.

My advocacy was often referred to as "turning grief into action." But I'm not so sure I agree with that term, for it implies I somehow converted my grief into something else. I managed to put aside some of my grief while I was an activist, but it was temporary. It would be wrong to think I eliminated or conquered my grief. Far from it.

I constantly dealt with grieving Daniel's death. I didn't somehow "overcome" my grief in those early years. The best I could do was put it aside for periods of time. But I returned to it every time I was asked about Daniel by a reporter during an interview, every time I mentioned Daniel when giving a speech, every time I opened my wallet and saw Daniel's photograph, every time I walked by his room or saw his photo on the wall.

It was satisfying and heartening to hear people compliment me on the things I was doing in Daniel's name. But frankly the messages from other people that most resonated with me were those that so accurately reminded me of what I was dealing with every day, such as:

- "There is no greater loss for a parent than losing one's child."
- "No parents should ever outlive their child. No parents should ever have to bury their child. It's simply not the natural order of things."
- "I can't imagine what I would do if I were to lose one of my children."
- "You're having to bear an unimaginable pain."

These messages might seem overly somber, but they effectively served as a realistic reminder and acknowledgment of my pain, and assurance it was okay to be in such anguish.

POORLY PREPARED

I was a poor candidate for dealing effectively with deep grief. Prior to April 20 I had lived a good life and had never faced terrible adversity. I had not endured major health, financial, or job crises. I lost virtually no one close to me to a tragic death, so I had rarely experienced deep grief.

Those who know of my earlier years might question that observation. After all, my father died when I was only ten years old and he was only fifty-four. That would seem to be a pretty traumatic experience for a child, but the fact is my father's death was not a great loss to me at the time.

My father was not close to his four offspring. We rarely went on vacations or outings together. We rarely even went out together for dinner, and I have no memories of him playing a game with me or running with me in the yard.

His selfish weekday routine was nearly always the same: he expected dinner on the table shortly after he arrived home from his job at the coal mine, read the newspaper, then went to drink and socialize at the local Moose Lodge. Little of his time was spent with his kids.

My brother Jim, seven years my senior, was a good Little League baseball player, but my dad rarely watched him play games. When I reached Little League age, my dad was asked to take me to a tryout and signup session. After the session, at home, he made it clear he wasn't about to drive me regularly to baseball games if I signed up. Perhaps it cut in to his precious time at the Moose Lodge. I was devastated. I never joined the Little League. It was hard to forgive him for that.

To this day, I have only two positive recollections of my father. The first was an annual ritual in which he took me to the Moose Lodge on a Saturday afternoon to visit Santa Claus. The second was another particular instance in which he took me with him to the Moose Lodge. I was about seven or eight years old. Perhaps he had to babysit me that evening and had no choice in the matter, because I don't recall him ever doing this on any other evenings. I remember being thrilled, for he introduced me to his drinking buddies, showered some attention on me, and let me play the coin-vended bowling machine. It's sad that these two seemingly insignificant events made such an impression on me.

I feared my father. He had a fist fight with my oldest brother. He drank a lot and was not what I'd call a "happy drunk." My father and mother quarreled frequently, and it frightened me. The arguing often began in the kitchen, where they would slam the door behind them so I couldn't see. But they could not hide the shouting and the pushing and banging of furniture I heard. I don't recall ever seeing my mother with any bruises or injuries, but it was still a traumatic experience to hear their clashes.

In his later years my father suffered from cancer and black lung disease. I assume they may have increased his feelings of anger and misery, but it was still no excuse for his abuse or for making our home a miserable and fearful place to live.

I don't remember feeling sorrow when he died. For me it was just an event, a time I saw my mother in grief, a time I was impressed by how many people showed up at his funeral. Whatever grief I felt was not about losing this man but about not having a father like other kids did, and in seeing my mother left alone to struggle financially.

BETTER PREPARED

After having so little experience with losing loved ones, I was ill prepared for deep grief. In some respects Linda might have been better prepared. She had lost both her parents and some aunts and uncles within the previous few years. More important, she sought help in dealing with her grief after Columbine. An avid reader, she quickly picked up a number of books about the grieving process. But not me. I'm a slow and easily distracted reader, so I rarely read books. Consequently, I went lacking for advice on how to handle my grief, except for what Linda shared with me when I was willing to listen.

We agreed on the need to seek a grief counselor. The first one we saw wasn't a good fit. We didn't like his style or his reaction to us. We selected another counselor and visited her regularly for a year or two, and she helped us. Friends, clergy, and people who've lost loved ones can be of help with grief, but for us they were more useful in terms of providing general comfort. It was difficult to share some of our deepest pain with those closest to us without causing concern, so a counselor was especially helpful because she could be more objective and honest.

As a nurturing mother who gave up a career to spend more time with her children, Daniel's death was especially hard on Linda. After years of nurturing Daniel and having such a profound impact on shaping him, it was catastrophic to have him suddenly taken away in such a senseless way. In little ways I was able to release some of my grief through my activism, but Linda didn't have such an outlet, as she was a more private person. To make matters worse, between my job and activism I was often not at home to provide support in some of her difficult times. She had to do much of her grieving alone. Furthermore, I think Daniel's death was tougher on Linda because Daniel's persona was much more like hers than mine.

HURTFUL REMINDERS

During the first few years after the massacre there were things that caused me great pain rather unexpectedly. For example, I would often become sad simply thinking of places that I associated with Daniel. Prior to Columbine I attended national conferences and often would stay an extra day or two to visit city landmarks, national parks, or other popular spots. Having been an urban studies student, I loved visiting other cities and studying their architecture, history, and transportation systems. Daniel was developing an appreciation for some of the same things.

A few times the family flew out to join me at the end of a conference, but usually I was alone. Often I would tell my family I planned to take them to particular places I visited. Even now, when I think of some of those places, like Glacier National Park, it saddens me because I am reminded that I got to visit them but Daniel did not—and never will.

Sometimes I've been asked if I am sad going to places I often went with Daniel, such as his elementary school or favorite restaurants. I know some parents move away to escape those painful reminders. Actually, I managed to adapt to going to such places, perhaps because I saw them so often I grew accustomed to them. Instead, the sites that I found painful to visit were ones we only visited once or a few times but which for some reason I associated with him, such as a baseball field where I took him for a few YMCA baseball games and the playground at Observatory Park, a place I took him occasionally as a means of trying out different playground sets. I simply don't let myself go near those places.

PAIN IN CHURCH

Church should be a place where we find solace, but for me there was a recurring painful experience at a church event that's supposed to be a blessed and joyous one. Immediately after a child is baptized at Columbine United Church, the place where we worshiped after leaving the Catholic Church in 2002, the congregation is asked to turn to the back panel of the hymnal and sing "I Was There to Hear Your Borning Cry." The lyrics are positive and uplifting, but for a while I could only see them in a negative light.

I tried to be a good congregant and sing along during the joyous ceremony, but for a few years I could not sing the opening lyrics:

I was there to hear your borning cry,
I'll be there when you are old.
I rejoiced the day you were baptized,
To see your life unfold.

I could usually get out the first line, but when it was time for the second, I became mute. A huge lump would form in my throat and I would move my lips slightly in a faint attempt to mouth the words along with the congregation, but all the while I was holding back tears and feeling immense agony.

For me the lyrics were a painful reminder that Daniel's life would not play out, and I would not be there to see him grow old. I obviously knew these baptisms were for others' children, but I could not help but reflect on Daniel's baptism and his shortened life, and the fact these children being baptized most likely would live into adulthood, while I would not see Daniel's life fully unfold.

While not as choked up as I was with those opening verses, I also found myself struggling with some of the next verses.

> *In a blaze of light you wandered off*
> *to find where demons dwell*

These haunting lyrics reminded me of the blaze of gunfire that took Daniel off to heaven and of the demonic actions of the teens who killed him.

> *You were raised to praise the living Lord,*
> *to whom you now belong.*

These lyrics innocently referred to the young child being baptized belonging to God, but for me they were another stark and sullen reminder of Daniel being with God and not me. Intuitively I knew I was twisting these lyrics and making them a reminder of death, an incomplete life, a sudden and tragic event, and a child in heaven—but I found it hard to follow intuition and common sense.

The hymn ends with the repeating of the first verse. By that point I was usually able to compose myself. The baptized child was being walked down the aisle and presented to the congregation on my side of the church, so I was usually able to accept the fact it was a joyous occasion for the family of the baptized child, and not only a terrible reminder of the loss of Daniel.

This hymn lasted only a few minutes only every few weeks, yet it made a painful impression on me. It's only been in the past three or so years that I've been able to sing all the lyrics and come to grips with and sing the hymn.

ENCOUNTERING DANIEL?

For the first year or so after Columbine it was sometimes difficult for me to encounter a teenage boy that looked a little like Daniel. I could easily become sad even seeing a teenage boy riding his bike with his dad or viewing a magazine photo of a teenaged boy having fun with his father.

The most painful experience took place in the parking lot of a nearby King Soopers supermarket. As I walked from my car toward the store, I noticed a young man, probably about fifteen or sixteen years of age, walking ahead of me. I couldn't see his face, but he was fairly tall, thin, and blonde, and had a bouncing walk eerily similar to Daniel's.

I slowed down. I was walking behind Daniel, I thought to myself. What a cruel trick, to have a teenager so similar to Daniel, just out of reach. I lost the teen once he walked into the large store. I rushed to get what I needed and rushed back out. I was reluctant to encounter the boy. I don't know why. Maybe I was afraid his face might look like Daniel's, or maybe I was afraid I would be disappointed that he did *not* look like Daniel. The experience haunted me, but after that one painful experience those awful look-alike sightings ended.

DREAMING OF DANIEL

I'm someone who often has vivid recollections of dreams. Linda can confirm how bizarre some of my dreams are, because I often tell her about them. My dreams have a wide variety of strange subjects and characters, and rarely seem to return to the same theme.

Within the first few years of the massacre, though, I experienced a disproportionate number of dreams about Daniel that were somewhat consistent in their circumstances and detail. In the dreams Daniel would suddenly reappear in my life, and he was usually about seven or eight years old. At one point in the dreams I'd realize he should not be with me and alive. In the dream I realize I have been specially blessed to have him back with me.

I would find myself overjoyed to have Daniel there but was very protective of our "secret." Throughout the dream, I would wonder how I could keep this secret from the world, whom I could tell, and how I could keep him in hiding yet still able to attend school and be part of the world. For a while I'd be ecstatic being with Daniel, but nearly always Daniel simply disappeared from the dream and I forlornly told myself that he wasn't supposed to be with me anyway. It was always a bit tougher to get out of bed in the mornings after those dreams, for I had a terrible feeling of loss and of having been tormented with his brief presence.

PAIN FOR JEREMY

For a number of years after the massacre, during the Christmas holiday Daniel's best friend Jeremy would visit us. It was thoughtful of him to think of us during the holidays. Unfortunately, I couldn't stand it when he visited.

It's not that I was somehow angry that Jeremy survived. It was hard on me because he was such a graphic reminder of Daniel. I'd say to myself, "Here's Jeremy, but where's Daniel?" At times they were inseparable. I watched Jeremy grow each year and couldn't help but wonder what Daniel would look like and what he'd be doing with his life. It was also difficult to see him because I felt grief for Jeremy, who had lost his best friend.

I acknowledged those things to myself, yet I still couldn't stand to see him and couldn't get beyond thinking that Jeremy was such a painful and vivid reminder of Daniel's absence.

Whenever Jeremy visited, Linda was always a gracious host, engaging him in conversation and asking about his life. She was stronger and better able to deal with having Jeremy there. I usually sat there and said only what I needed to in order to be polite. All the while, I had a huge lump in my throat and fought back tears. I couldn't wait until he left.

I've shared these feelings with Jeremy. I've told him there was nothing wrong with him visiting us and he was thoughtful to do so. I told him I was grateful that he came to visit us but that at the time it was just too upsetting to see him and not Daniel.

I also told Jeremy that with the passage of time I learned to deal with his visits. They evolved into something that actually relieved me, for I had worried about how Jeremy was doing after losing his best friend. Seeing that he was growing up, dealing with this tragedy, and making something of himself made me feel better.

GO DIRECTLY TO GRIEVING, DO NOT PASS GO

I experienced some triumphs in my advocacy and found healing in a number of wonderful interventions, and I was able at times to find a way to channel some of my grief. But there also was agony. I was on a sickening rollercoaster ride. It wasn't uncommon to take two encouraging steps forward and then one giant step backward.

My journey through grief was filled with tears, anger, despair, marital conflict, and apathy. They were all part of my experience. I strived for peace of mind and the satisfaction of doing something positive in Daniel's name, but I never let myself think my struggle would be without a lot of setbacks. It was not.

Columbine victim John Tomlin's truck turned into a shrine in the Clement Park parking lot

Chapter 17

Signs Pointing to Healing

When disaster strikes, most people at some point want to pull themselves together and try to find a degree of normalcy—even though they know nothing may be "normal" any longer. They search for healing wherever they can, whether in their homes, in their workplaces, in their hearts. I was no exception. I wanted to laugh and play again; I wanted my life to be something like it was before.

It wasn't going to be easy. I realized I had to work at it and look for healing wherever possible.

NORMALCY AT THE OFFICE

One place I needed to find some normalcy was my place of work, where I spent so much of my life. I thought it might be helpful to return to a familiar setting where I could occupy myself with something that could take my mind off the stress of grief. But that wouldn't be easy; I was completely absent from the office for three weeks after the massacre, so I was unsure how it would feel upon my return.

There were about ninety people in the division where I worked. I was concerned about facing a parade of people coming to my cubicle to express their condolences and asking how I was doing, how I was coping. Fielding one or two questions was manageable, but I feared facing a multitude of inquiries. At the same time I was also fearful that I might find myself feeling very alone if people avoided me because they were unsure of what to say.

Consequently, I took a proactive approach. I decided to carefully plan my return to work, announcing May 12 as the date of my return in an email to all employees and inviting them to a "welcome back" of sorts. I wrote to my coworkers that I preferred to come back and speak to them as a group rather than individually, so I could satisfy their curiosity but avoid the painful telling of Daniel's story multiple times.

I wrote an outline for my presentation, as well as a brief handout for those who didn't make it to the meeting, summarizing the primary messages I wanted to share with them. The outline and handout attempted to answer the questions I assumed people were wondering about: How were my family and I doing? What had the past three weeks been like? Did I welcome their questions?

Ironically, the gathering was held in the Mt. Evans Room, the same conference room where I watched the tragedy of Columbine unfold on April 20. I began the event by thanking everyone for all their cards, calls, visits, and memorial gifts. I emphasized that nobody should worry about whether or not they should have visited, or offered help, or called or sent a card earlier; I assured them there was no book on exactly how to react to such a tragedy.

I briefly described what happened on April 20, starting there at work and leading up to finding out Daniel had been killed. It was painful to tell it, but I knew I had to do so to satisfy their curiosity and avoid having to repeat the story later. I teared up as I spoke about the days following the massacre and about the wonderful signs of comfort we experienced that helped get us through it all.

I told them how I was coping with my tragic loss. How we read every letter we received. How it helped to talk with others who lost a child. How our faith played an important role. I shared with them how Linda and

Christie were doing, that Christie had returned to school and that it might be a tough road for Linda being home alone. I told them that Linda and I were seeing a grief counselor.

Naturally I talked about Daniel. It wasn't as difficult to do as I had feared, for I was so proud to tell the story of his life. Perhaps it was harder for them to hear it told.

I made some guesses about what life at work might be like for me and how they might approach me. I first admitted that I couldn't be sure how I'd adjust, but that I expected to experience both healing and grief. I told them I assumed I was well enough to work productively but that a profound feeling of deep sadness could simply come over me at any time because the loss of one's child is not something a parent can ever completely get over.

I speculated that some of them might not know what to say to me but that it was understandable. I countered that it might likewise be difficult for me to know what to say to them or to know whether it was "appropriate" to laugh along with them or to join in a conversation if I was feeling sad. I suggested that they not question whether it was okay to have an upbeat conversation with me for fear that I might be feeling miserable. I told them that by and large they should just go on as normal but not expect me to always be fully engaged. I told them I thought work was a place I might find some normalcy but that I might not be highly motivated and might at times have trouble concentrating.

I told them I preferred not to encounter people asking me with a concerned look and an exaggerated voice, "So how are you *doing* today?" I told them I expected it would be a long and difficult road back for me and that constantly being asked that question was not helpful. I suggested that if someone really needed to know my mood at a given time or how I was progressing that they might consider asking my staff or someone else close to me.

I insisted that I didn't want to be treated differently, that if they needed to challenge me about a work issue or about something I had done they should not avoid doing so just because I had lost my son.

I told them I had developed very strong gun-control beliefs. I assured them I respected their beliefs if they felt otherwise but that it was probably best for them not to challenge me about my beliefs for the foreseeable future. I acknowledged that people had a wide range of beliefs regarding gun control and insisted I didn't want people to verbally support my beliefs just to please me.

I asked what their experiences of Columbine were, but few spoke up; I suppose it was just too difficult for them to talk about. Finally, I responded to questions they had of me.

It was an emotional event, with many tearful faces in the room, yet I think that "putting it all out there" was helpful. It seemed my efforts paid off. My colleagues largely followed my wishes. I didn't face repeated questions about the events at Columbine and I wasn't constantly questioned about how I was feeling on any particular day.

HEALING THROUGH LAUGHTER

One small way I tried for a return to more normalcy was through something in which I had a talent—making people laugh. But I wondered when it was even permissible to laugh, and especially to make other people laugh, after you've lost a child. Who expects a grieving parent to make a practice of making others laugh?

For a number of years I had presented humorous slide shows to entertain people. I have a collection of hundreds of zany slides—from funny road signs to crazy office situations to silly animal poses, taken mostly from humor magazines. Each show I assemble is unique, weaving slides into a certain theme, whether for a transportation meeting or a retirement party or a roast. I give each show a unique ethnic slant and story line, using my uncanny ability to impersonate various ethnic accents. Among my "characters" are a cranky Russian, a stuffy British man, "Father Guido Sarducci" from Saturday Night Live, and an east Indian.

After my slide shows had become a regular fixture at Colorado transit conferences and lost some of their novelty, I reached out to new audiences by offering my services to other state transit conferences. It was a way to be creative, make a few bucks, and visit other states, sometimes with my family.

Early in 1999, I agreed to perform at an October statewide transit conference in Traverse City, Michigan. After the massacre, the conference sponsors told me they would understand if I canceled the appearance. But I insisted on keeping my commitment. I felt no pressure or obligation to do so. I believe I was driven to proceed because I was looking to do something fun and positive again—making people laugh. Perhaps subliminally it was a way of telling people I was doing better, though I guess I didn't quite feel comfortable doing so at home, fearing people closer to home might think it strange or inappropriate for me to give one of my zany slide shows within a few months of the death of my son. In Michigan I would be presenting mostly to strangers who didn't know my sad story.

I went to Traverse City and gave an amusing presentation at a luncheon, posing as a Russian transportation official making fun of America's transportation system. The crowd was told after my slide show only that I was the transit manager from the Colorado Department of Transportation. I was pleased with the laughter and the resounding applause, but I could not let it end like that. I could not simply pretend to be some zany guy who merely came to entertain them.

I thanked the crowd and told them it meant a lot to me to be able to present to them. I told them it meant so much because in April my son had been killed in the Columbine massacre and that I wanted so much to see a return to fun things in my life, like doing slide shows again. A hush suddenly fell over the room. I saw a number of shocked and tearful faces in the crowd.

Before I walked off the stage I told the crowd there was one thing they could do in appreciation of my performance and in honor of Daniel: visit his Web site. As I began to pass out the business card with the Web address, the audience broke into applause again. It was a reassuring moment for me. In the following weeks I received a number of wonderful email messages from people who were in the audience, making it an even more worthwhile trip.

SPIRITUAL HEALING

It takes a lot of help to deal with immense grief and loss, and certainly my faith in God and my long-held spiritual beliefs about death helped me tremendously. I had often contemplated the unfairness of life, how so many good people died too young, how utterly tragic it was that children died, and how so many catastrophic events of nature claimed so many innocent lives. Seldom did I ever question how it was that "God could let these things happen." But would I feel the same way after my son was murdered?

When Daniel died, I didn't find myself "mad at God" the way some people are when tragedy strikes. I realized that it was not God that pulled the trigger that day.

It has always been my rather simple view of life that God never intended to give us a perfect world. If we were given a world without pain, what appreciation would there be for joy? If we were given a world where there were never any tragic losses of loved ones, would there be as much appreciation for them? If we were assured of living without pain, would we really value life as much—or would we even come to expect such a privileged existence from God?

I strongly disagreed with those people who wrote me saying, "God has called Daniel home to be with Him as an angel ...." I recognize it is a sentiment based on some people's religious beliefs, but I don't agree with that thinking. I respect and appreciate their intent to express words of comfort, but I don't believe that a loving God would take a child to "be with Him in heaven" because "He needed another angel." That's nonsense. I believe He is willing to wait and already has enough angels. He doesn't need to recruit more and deny children their time on earth with us, nor would a loving God want to.

To me this "angel" talk is just a way of trying to erase pain by elevating our loved ones to sainthood and making an excuse for why they couldn't remain here on Earth. It seems such talk is aimed at making one feel guilty for not being willing to "sacrifice" their child. I believe in people sacrificing for each other, but not in offering up a child's life to a God in search of angels. I do not find it sinful to defiantly tell God you'd rather not give up your child and that it was better for Him to just wait.

When a child is murdered, the cause is found here on earth, and the blame rests here on earth. Let's not somehow attribute it to a God looking for angels. Some deaths are simply unpreventable, and we are usually the ones responsible for the deaths that are preventable, not God.

God gave us both sorrow and joy, happiness and sadness, wealth and poverty, life and death. The challenge remains for us to develop an understanding and appreciation for all of them, and to not begrudge God because we think we did not receive our fair share of the better gifts from life.

After all, are we not taught as Christians that God has something wonderful in store for us after our lives on this earth? So why do so many Christians go to extraordinary medical lengths to extend their lives by just a few days and live so much in fear of death? I'm not suggesting we shouldn't value our lives and our time here, or that we should want to die, but we need to have a more realistic view of death and the afterlife that's consistent with Christ's teachings. I'm still grieving Daniel's loss and furious about it. But I have accepted it.

WHAT DANIEL WANTS

Many people have spoken about Daniel being "in better hands" in heaven and looking down on us and smiling. I don't know anything about what heaven is like, but I do believe he somehow is looking down. It is helpful to imagine what he is saying and thinking as he looks down.

I certainly can't imagine Daniel saying, "Mom and Dad, I hope you're both miserable and inconsolable down there. I'm in a better place, but I hope your pain is deep and that you're miserable for the rest of your lives without me. I hope you're never able to smile or have a fun day. Please cry over me every night and never get over my death. Never forgive those who killed me. Allow my death to haunt you, and while you're at it, make sure Christie is also miserable."

No child would think or say such a thing—and certainly not Daniel. But if we're ever too burdened with deep grief over the loss of a child, aren't we ignoring the wishes of that child in heaven? If we truly believe in a glorious life after this one, would we want to live it there wishing grief on our loved ones? Of course not! And neither do our children. So if our children don't want us to be burdened with agonizing grief, then why should we let ourselves be miserable, heartbroken and burdened with agonizing grief?

I refuse to think Daniel wants me to remain inconsolable and despondent. I want him to feel relieved. I'm not going to feel guilty about being able to smile and laugh and live a full life. We can't let misery and constant grief upend our lives. We cannot let ourselves feel guilty for outliving our children or for returning to something close to a happy, normal life. That's no way to honor and remember our children.

That is not to say my life has returned to "normal." It hasn't. That is not to say I haven't cried for Daniel many times. I have. I love him and miss him and selfishly wish he were still with us, not God. But I cannot let grief overtake me, and I'm sure that's the way Daniel wants it.

OBSESSING ON SIGNS

I have always been perplexed by my fellow Christians who give so much attention to "miracles" and "signs." I'm referring in particular to those who obsess on things like the Shroud of Turin or a random earthly object that somehow resembles the Virgin Mary.

My bewilderment is based on my perception that these people have the need to prove to others (or is it to themselves?) that God is still present in this world. It makes me wonder if their search for miracles is cloaking some degree of doubt. Why obsess about witnessing such miracles and mystical signs? If one truly believes in God, why repeatedly insist on such miraculous signs as confirmation of His presence?

My belief is that the signs of God's existence, presence, and wonderment are all around us if we are open to them. Why obsess about these reminders of God's existence and demand more proof? God's presence is in the beauty of a forest, the cry of a newborn, the fluttering wings of a butterfly, the gleam in the eye of a child. We've got the evidence of His everyday presence, so why have this fixation on finding signs from God? Instead, what we need are more signs of our humanity toward one another as signs of God's presence.

Having said all that, I must confess I have witnessed what I consider signs of comfort from God. Perhaps some would even call them miracles. I didn't look for them. They were presented to me. I wasn't exactly prepared for them, but there they were. I was amazed when they occurred, and perhaps only accepted them as signs of God's presence once I noticed a few of them and could no longer deny them or pretend they were mere coincidences.

The first sign is one I related earlier when I described how Christie told the story at Daniel's wake of how he surprisingly told her on the morning of April 20, 1999, that he loved her—something "he usually only said on holidays." One can't but wonder what prompted those words on that day. Could that have been a mere coincidence?

The events on April 25, the day of Daniel's funeral Mass, also could not have been mere coincidences. It was a cloudy, unsettled day, with spells of rain. The rain cleared for most of the community memorial service that afternoon. When we entered the church for the Mass at about 5:00 p.m., it was cool and overcast, but not raining, as if we were being welcomed in peace. Just as the Mass began, the rain started again. You could hear it outside during the silent moments of the service.

Near the end of the Mass, the caskets of Kelly Fleming and Daniel were moved from one side of the altar area to the other for the final prayers. Suddenly the rain stopped again and bright sunlight shone through one of the small windows on the west side of the sanctuary. The healing light bathed the two caskets in their new location. It was unbelievably touching to see the change in weather and the brilliantly illuminated caskets. Mere coincidence?

MORE SIGNS

We buried Daniel the next morning. It was another day of unsettled weather, like most of the days following the massacre. A small group of family and friends went to the grave site. The funeral procession traveled 20 miles to Mt. Olivet Cemetery. Linda, Christie, and I sat quietly in the spacious funeral limo as we made the long and painful trek.

As we drove north along C-470, a four-lane freeway on Denver's western edge, Linda and I both noticed a small herd of deer peering at us from a field on a small rise a short distance away, near the Morrison exit.

This highway, skirting the edge of the foothills of the Rocky Mountains, was known for occasional deer crossings. But the area where we saw the deer was open, not wooded, and was on the city side of the highway, not the foothills side. To have a herd of deer in such a place at that time of day seemed unusual. They just stood there, looking toward the highway, as if paying their respects. To us they represented Daniel's gentleness and were a sign of God's comfort, telling us not to worry, that Daniel was in a better place.

As we continued the drive, the sky was overcast. But as the burial ceremony started at Mt. Olivet, the sun suddenly broke through a circle that opened in the clouds above us and shone brightly on the burial ceremony. The sun was so intense that, as someone with significantly thinning hair, I was concerned I'd get a sunburned scalp.

One gets a good view of much of the city from Mt. Olivet, so I could tell the sun was not shining on most of Denver. It was shining down on Daniel. It was a sign that we should not be in so much pain, that Daniel was safe.

AND THEN AGAIN

For months after Daniel's burial, whenever I drove along C-470 I'd look along the highway for deer. Perhaps I was a doubting Thomas, questioning whether our sighting of deer on the day of Daniel's burial was actually a common occurrence. Instead, I never saw a herd of deer like I did that one day—until two years later.

On April 20, 2001, the second anniversary of Columbine, Linda and I drove to Daniel's grave. I remarked that I had forgotten to look along the highway for deer. But Linda told me *she* had been watching. She, too, had been in search of that same sign from God but had not seen any deer.

We already were near the end of C-470, where it merges with I-70, about two miles north of the Morrison exit. There was just one small area of open space before the land became filled with housing subdivisions and businesses. And yet it was in that spot, at the north base of Green Mountain, that we suddenly saw a large herd of deer just yards from the highway.

Once again it was not the time or place you'd expect to see them gathered. They weren't facing the highway in seeming reverence the way they were a year before, but it was still amazing. Once again we felt moved by what we thought was another clear sign of comfort from God.

When we arrived at the cemetery, the weather was dark and unsettled. After we arrived at Daniel's grave, though, the clouds broke for a while and gave us wonderful sunshine, just as had happened the day we buried Daniel.

I was humbled and awed by these events, though I'm reluctant to call them "miracles." I'm sure other grieving parents have had similar experiences. I believe that God does reach out to us, whether it is in profound or subtle ways. But we have to be open to them and accept them.

We cannot expect to be continually comforted or reassured. Every year we go the cemetery on the anniversary of Columbine, and every year I look for the deer. I've never seen them again along the highway, but not finding them isn't a disappointment. I can't expect God to continue with these outward signs when He has already done so and has given me so many other blessings.

Chapter 18

Healing in Many Places

Icouldn't expect to continue finding these special spiritual signs of comfort as I did following Daniel's death. I would need to find healing in my everyday life. At first that was difficult. I hoped I would find some peace in my daily ritual of practicing Transcendental Meditation, a technique where one sits solemnly in a quiet place for about twenty minutes, with eyes closed and silently reciting a meaningless sound. I had been practicing TM for at least twenty years and it normally relaxed me, but for weeks after the massacre I was unable to meditate. I was too upset, and too often I found myself unavoidably picturing Daniel hunkering under that table in the Columbine library, wondering how he felt. I had to stop practicing TM for a while, for it was not healthy.

I discovered some healing in the simplest of things. Like music. And in the most unlikely of places. Like Guatemala.

MUSICAL HEALING

Although I can't sing well, play a musical instrument, or even identify notes on a musical scale, I am a music junkie. I'm always surrounding myself with music. The CD player in the car is nearly always on, blaring if I'm traveling alone. The MP3 player is on when I'm walking to and from my bus and light rail rides.

I have spent a small fortune on hundreds and hundreds of CDs. I'm addicted. I like a wide variety of types of music—oldies from the late fifties through the eighties, rock, jazz fusion, New Wave, New Age, Cajun, Celtic, and folk. Often my mood determines what type of music will be played at any given time.

But what kind of music was appropriate after losing Daniel? Most of my collection was inappropriate for soothing me. The Beatles and the Beach Boys could normally be counted on to lift my spirits, but not now. I couldn't pretend that things were fine by just rocking down the highway blasting the Doobie Brothers or John Hiatt.

Just as upbeat music was not appropriate, I also found it too painful to listen to certain soft music. A friend sent us a CD on which he compiled some of his favorite classical music tunes. He pointed out that one, Samuel Barber's *Adagio for Strings*, was used for noted funeral processions. I easily could tell; it was unbelievably sad.

I was a mess if I listened to *Adagio*. I usually got a huge lump in my throat and was frozen with grief. Despite that, I have to admit I purposefully listened to it on a number of occasions. I have only played it when I've already been in a particularly sad mood. I suppose I felt the need now and then to return to that sad state I experienced in 1999.

I would allow myself to slip into melancholy, playing Adagio or certain mellow New Age songs, but there is another type of music that was and still is impossible for me to deal with. It is classical or any other form of music featuring multilayered, high female voices singing in what I call "angelic voices." I'm guessing this music is just too painful because it reminds me that Daniel is surrounded by angels in heaven. While intuitively I'm happy Daniel is in heaven, that's not where I want him to be. I can't stand the sadness that goes with that painful and haunting reminder.

INSPIRED BY CINDY

We received dozens of music tapes and CDs following Columbine, mostly from strangers. Most were spiritual and religious in nature. While

I appreciate the donors' generosity and intentions, I found most of them useless. I'm just not touched by so-called Christian inspirational music that's filled with general words about healing and faith in God.

Instead, I found myself listening to certain New Age music that was mellow yet uplifting, by artists such as David Arkenstone, Nicholas Gunn, Peter Kater, Deuter, George Winston, and David Lanz. I found comfort and relaxation in their music, perhaps because they were instrumentals without the distraction of lyrics.

A number of months after the massacre I received a letter from a woman named Cindy Bullens, a noted songwriter, soloist, background singer, and guitarist since the 1970s. It included her autobiographical album, "Somewhere Between Heaven and Earth." Cindy's letter expressed her condolences and told us the CD had been written in honor of her precious daughter, Jessie, who died of cancer in 1995 at the age of eleven. Cindy wrote and performed the album.

I quickly discovered the album was an inspirational, joyous, and sorrowful masterpiece. It meant much to us because it was written and performed by someone who also tragically lost a child. It wasn't "religious" music, but it sure was spiritual.

The lyrics are a celebration of the life of her daughter, of her slow and painful slip into death, and the aftermath for Cindy. But it's not simply a somber album. It presents the wide range of emotions one feels at the time, from despair, to hopefulness, to anger, to disbelief, to acceptance, to misery, to triumph. It's not just helpful for people experiencing such a loss; others willing to experience these emotional feelings can appreciate it too.

The beat ranges from gentle acoustic to upbeat rock, reflecting the range of emotions here. The lyrics are awesome and so is the music. The fitting opening song, "In Better Hands," contain lyrics that especially touched me.

You know I wish I could be grateful
Instead of full of fear
The kind of love that you gave me
I can't replace with tears.

And though I'll never feel that love again
Never again
Well, I can take some kind of comfort in
Knowing you're
In better hands, in better hands

The title track, "Somewhere Between Heaven and Earth," contains an eloquent message:

But there's no rhythm in the rain
There's no magic in the moon
There's no power in this pain
Till somewhere between heaven and earth
I can find you again.

If I could one more time
Feel your hand in mine
Hear your voice call my name
And whisper sweet good night.

Then there'd be rhythm in the rain
There'd be magic in the moon
No such thing as love in vain.

After a number of Columbine families played the CD they had received from Cindy and had made contact with her, she offered to perform for us in person. We gladly accepted. She flew to Denver and performed for us in the sanctuary of Columbine United Church. Many of the Columbine parents attended, with no media or outsiders invited. Cindy seemed touched and honored to be with us, and we felt the same way. It was an amazing evening full of tears, hugs, joy, and understanding.

HEALING IN GUATEMALA

For years we had been donors to an organization called the Christian Foundation for Children and Aging. CFCA assists children and elders in poor nations throughout the world. We made a monthly donation to the program, helping Evi, a disabled girl in Guatemala. We chose her in part because she was just a day older than our daughter Christie.

We designated CFCA as a charity for memorial gifts after Daniel was killed. Because the organization received many donations mentioning Daniel, CFCA asked us if we would be willing to let them conduct a special fund drive in Daniel's name. They said the greatest need in Evi's community, San Ixtan, was a new school, so they proposed to raise money to build one.

I was concerned because I did not have the time to devote to raising funds. But CFCA insisted they didn't want our time, except to help write the text of the appeal that would be mailed. I was willing to help but wondered how they could possibly raise enough money to build a *school.* And what if they came up far short? CFCA assured me I needn't worry, that it would cost only about $31,000 to build the school. It would be a simple cinderblock building. But still—only $31,000?

After we agreed to help and provided some text, CFCA mailed a special appeal to its regular donors, telling Daniel's story and asking for contributions. CFCA raised more than $78,000! We were astounded and humbled by the success.

CFCA's president, Bob Hentzen, who resides in Guatemala, asked us to travel there to see the results of the fundraising. Linda, Christie, and I did so in March 2000. I took a break from my SAFE Colorado lobbying job to spend an eye-opening week in this impoverished nation.

Mr. Hentzen took us to San Ixtan, located in the southern portion of the country, near its border with Honduras, where we were shown the recently completed school building. It was a six-room elementary school. Although rudimentary by American standards, it was certainly functional. To the left of the building, only a short distance away, was another structure that was about half completed. I asked Mr. Hentzen what it was. "Oh, that's the fourteen-room middle school," he told me very matter-of-factly. The money CFCA raised was also helping to pay for that structure! Workers couldn't complete it in time for our visit, but there it was, a framed-in structure standing as another wonderful memorial to Daniel's memory. We were astonished they were able to do so much with so little money.

They held a reception for us, including an outdoor Mass said in Daniel's memory in a courtyard between the elementary and middle school. The Mass served as a dedication ceremony for the school. Most in attendance were students. Evi was there, along with her aunt. Evi's mother could not be there because she was working in the fields, picking coffee beans. She couldn't afford to take a day off from her job.

The school girls wore sparkling white blouses and plaid skirts, as in many traditional Catholic schools in America. The boys wore bright white shirts and dark pants. All wore dazzlingly shined black shoes. Streamers lined the walls. A student choir sang beautiful hymns throughout the service. A colorful bouquet of flowers adorned the front of the makeshift altar. On the altar stood a large, framed photo of Daniel.

Mass conducted in San Ixtan, Guatemala, as part of the dedication of the school built with funds raised in Daniel's name.

I was an "A" student in Spanish many years ago, but I had done little to keep my knowledge current. Nonetheless, during the Mass I could understand much of what Hentzen told the crowd in Spanish about Daniel and of how we came to be there that day. It was heartening to have this group of strangers learning about Daniel, yet also strangely sad to hear the story of his death in a foreign tongue.

It was a moving ceremony that brought tears to our eyes, because we were reminded of Daniel's death and could imagine Daniel's innocence when he was the age of these children. But they were also tears of joy, for it was humbling to know that Daniel's death had motivated people in America to help these children have a better place to learn.

LA BIBLIOTECA BENDITA

The Mass was an incredibly emotional event, but we were not yet prepared for what was coming next. We knew that more money was raised than what was needed to build the school, but we were unclear about how the remaining funds were being used, other than our general impression that it was being used for some kind of school building.

Following the Mass, we accompanied Mr. Hentzen to another community, San Lucas Toliman, 80 miles to the northwest, where they were using the remainder of the donated money.

We were amazed at what we saw in this city of about 20,000 people, built on the shores of Lake Atitlan. Despite its size, the city lacked much of the basic infrastructure —public facilities, restaurants, businesses— that one would expect to see in an American city of that size.

We were greeted by Father Greg, a priest from Minnesota who had faithfully served in this country for more than thirty years. We attended Mass in his historic church, which was built in 1572.

After Mass we were presented with gifts, including an attractive embroidered shirt, a lovely embroidered blanket, and a wonderful wood carving sculpted by a villager depicting "Daniel in the lion's den." The carving was particularly special to us and is still prominently displayed in our home.

We were then taken to the Catholic school on the church campus, where we visited a room that served as the only library for this large community. The room, which also functioned as a meeting and all-purpose room, contained a large table, a few book shelves, and some books. That day, students from the University of Illinois who were volunteering their time during spring break ate lunch there.

Hentzen informed us they were constructing a new library with the additional funds raised in Daniel's name. What a fitting tribute, given that Daniel had died in the library at Columbine! We were moved to tears.

Hentzen said the San Lucas community had included a library on its "want list," and it was being built out of necessity, not because of the Columbine connection. It was yet another sign that a powerful force was somehow at work in this tragedy. To this day I still get emotional when telling the story of the blessed library in Guatemala.

While visiting the school, we were taken to every one of the classrooms. In each room, smiling, wide-eyed, excited students gave us handwritten notes, thanking us for the library and expressing condolences. It was an amazing, heartwarming welcome I will never forget.

A nun stands at the entrance to the library in San Lucas Toliman, Guatemala, built with funds raised in Daniel's memory.

Next they took us to the library site, adjacent to the school and church. Only the cinderblock walls were up. We were again surprised to discover how much could be built with so little money. It was a two-story building, constructed with special sealants to prevent mold growth in this humid climate. Amazingly, the money also would purchase books, computers, a television, and a VCR.

In the years following our trip, I received emails and letters from a number of Americans who have traveled to San Lucas Toliman to visit or volunteer. They have sent us pictures of the completed library. Above the doorway at the entrance are the words "*Bienvenidos a la biblioteca, en memoria* a Daniel Mauser." Welcome to the library, in memory of Daniel Mauser. On a book case is a large, framed photo of Daniel.

These travelers have shared heartwarming stories from the library, including how many of these poor children spend hours there reading and working on computers, and how at an annual city parade, a group of students representing the library carries a parade banner with Daniel's name and photo. Visitors who were our friends or members of our church, or simply Denver residents who knew of Daniel's story, told us how they were warmly welcomed by the church staff.

How touching it is to hear that these children learn in a library built with money raised in Daniel's name. How could one not feel healing from that?

OVERWHELMING EMPATHY

Each experience on that trip was enormously heartrending. This Third World country is impoverished. Banks and other businesses are patrolled actively by guards with automatic weapons at the ready. Nicer homes are protected with walls and barbed-wire fences. This is a nation that had been torn apart by 36 years of civil war.

Despite that devastating backdrop, we observed a people full of optimism, appreciation, and friendliness, and in the schoolchildren we saw hope, energy, and enthusiasm. We developed an appreciation for how much we have in America—and for how much we take for granted. The strength of these people inspired us and their suffering provided us with a context for our own suffering. I actually felt guilty as an American, knowing we have so many material possessions yet are so unappreciative, knowing we can be such whiners about the possessions we *don't* have, and knowing that despite all our resources we are unable to deal with so many chronic problems—crime, drug and alcohol abuse, broken families. And gun violence.

When we visited each of the classrooms at the school, the schoolmasters presented our story as if we were an inspiration for the children to model. On the contrary, their pain and suffering, coupled with their optimism and friendliness, was healing inspiration for us.

Chapter 19

Ocean Star

Within just two or three weeks of the tragedy, Linda brought up a subject that surprised, touched, and astounded me. She asked me how I would feel about adopting a child, and in particular, a girl from China. It was something we had never talked about before. *My God*, I thought to myself, *we just lost our son; why are we talking about adoption? How in the hell could I think about having a new child in our home?* I thought that maybe she was just dreaming, trying to fantasize something positive to get her mind off this nightmare we were living. She was not.

AN UNEASY DECISION

Linda was serious. Adoption became a hot topic full of spirited discussions, largely because of my reluctance to take it seriously. In the weeks after the massacre, we made a habit of taking walks around Johnson Lake in Clement Park as a means of relaxing, getting some much needed exercise, and getting away from it all. It was there that Linda kept bringing up the subject, much to my frustration.

It seemed too soon after Daniel's death, and I was concerned adoption could be a way of dodging or hiding our grief. I was concerned about the expense, too; we certainly hadn't planned on adopting, so I fretted about spending thousands of dollars on something that seemed so uncertain and risky. I worried about whether the Chinese children might have health issues that would burden our lives. And there were my selfish concerns about the time I wanted to dedicate to the gun-control cause and about how raising a young child would greatly delay my eventual retirement.

One of my biggest objections was that I felt we were too old to take this on. Linda and I were both forty-seven years old at the time. My father was just fifty-four when he died, so I was worried about my longevity. Linda was adopted, so we had no idea of her birth parents' health history or longevity.

I had memories of being in elementary school and high school with no father to encourage me, no father to play with, no father to teach me how to drive. I didn't want that to happen to my child if I died young. And I worried that adopting a child at this age meant we would be well into our sixties by the time the adopted child entered high school.

Linda and I went through some of those issues ourselves. My parents were forty-four when I was born. Linda's parents were forty-two when she was adopted at birth. Linda and I had both felt somewhat awkward when we were in high school and our parents were in their far-from-hip sixties during the hip sixties. It's not that we weren't loved, but we had trouble relating to parents who were so much older than our friends' parents (by *our* standards) and seemed so much more old-fashioned.

And there was the critical issue of considering Christie's needs. Might this adoption draw much needed attention away from her? How would she deal with us devoting so much attention to a toddler when she was in great need of our time and affection?

FINDING ACCEPTANCE

Over a period of a few weeks and at least a dozen discussions, some of my concerns subsided as I thought more about them. Even though my dad died so young, my mom was then ninety-one, so the longevity question was somewhat neutralized. Furthermore, I spoke with an extended family member about her willingness to adopt our child in the event anything happened to us before Christie was an adult, and she was willing to do so.

As for our being old when the child would be in high school—so what? We thought we were probably more hip than our parents, relatively speaking, and having Christie around would aid that a bit. It was something we could work on.

Linda and I were in good health, so it didn't seem like we were taking a big risk. Knowing we'd need to keep up with a child would likely prompt us to stay in better shape. Linda knew of a few people who adopted Chinese girls, including a teacher at Daniel's elementary school, and their children were healthy. Best of all, Christie loved the idea of having a younger sister. She and Linda thought it would be a great healing experience for all three of us.

To pay for the adoption, we could use the money we were given by the community through the United Way's Healing Fund. What better way could there be to "give back" to everyone while also using it for our own healing?

We also felt a child would give us hope in the midst of despair, and that it would be a tribute to Daniel, not a cloaking of pain. Our adoption would be part of our remembrance of Daniel. We felt he would be proud of our decision. We often spoke of how the time we would have spent with Daniel as he went through high school and college could instead be spent helping a child in need. It was a done deal—I was "in."

WHY CHINESE?

We moved on to the details. We agreed on a Chinese adoption for a number of reasons. One was practical: at our age, it would be difficult if not impossible to adopt domestically, unless we chose an older child. Chinese adoptions were much more forgiving about the age of the adoptive parents. Linda had her heart set on an infant or toddler because she wanted to make more of an impact on the child over a period of time, and she feared taking on an older and perhaps troubled child who might have emotional issues at a time we were so emotionally fragile ourselves.

There was another issue as well. Most Chinese adoptees are girls, and choosing a female would avoid any possibility of a boy somehow being "compared" to Daniel, consciously or not.

When Chinese girls are abandoned it's usually because of social and economic factors, particularly China's one-child policy. Because of the country's population explosion and crowding, the government imposed a limit of one child on most citizens, particularly in cities. There were enormous penalties for violation of the law.

Boys are usually preferred in their traditional society, because boys carry on the family name and especially because they are the ones expected to take care of their parents as they age. Wives are expected to follow suit—caring for her husband's parents, not their own. If you are only allowed to have one child, and you want that one child to care for you in your old age and you want a child to carry on your family name, it's not hard to understand why girls might be at risk in China. As a result of this gender bias, girls are occasionally abandoned. Normally they are left in public places where they will be found.

One of the positive characteristics of China is its emphasis on family. Their nation is more family-centered than America. But being so family-oriented can have drawbacks. If you are someone *without* a family, like these abandoned girls, you will have a more difficult life. You will always have a difficult time answering questions about your parentage, and some people may look down on you for not having a known family lineage.

Domestic adoptions weren't encouraged by the Chinese government nor were they socially acceptable in China at the time. As a result, there weren't many options for getting these girls out of orphanages beyond foreign adoptions, and only a small percentage of these children were adopted. More recently, though, attitudes and policies in China have changed. The government has placed many more restrictions on foreign adoptions, has loosened its one-child limitations, and has been more accepting of domestic adoptions.

SIGN HERE...AND HERE...

We dove into the adoption process, beginning with the paperwork in July 1999. There were dozens of documents to complete and procedural steps to go through, such as visits by a social worker. But after all we had been through in our lives, those inconveniences seemed like nothing. We submitted our final documentation in December 1999. We knew there was then a bit of a wait ahead for us, but that was acceptable, given our need to journey farther along in our grieving process.

We used an outstanding adoption agency based in the Denver area. Chinese Children Adoption International (CCAI) is a nonprofit agency headed by a Chinese couple, Joshua and Lily Zhong, who handle Chinese adoptions with a passionate devotion and a dedicated paid and volunteer staff.

Late in summer 2000 we experienced the sheer joy of "match day," the day CCAI gave us pictures of the girl we would be adopting, along with a few items of vital information, such as height and weight. We were told her given name was Liu Hai Xing ("lee-yu high sheeng"). Liu was a reference to the city she was from—Liuzhou, an industrial city in southeastern China, close to Vietnam. Hai Xing translated to "ocean star."

Liu Hai Xing was given the birthdate of November 22—someone's estimate of the date, given that she was abandoned. That date was of special importance to me as a Baby Boomer as it was the tragic day President John Kennedy was assassinated, a day so vivid I can still remember where I was when I heard the news.

Liu Hai Xing was abandoned in a phone booth near a police station when she was about two weeks old. She spent less than a month at an orphanage. Although many abandoned children spent long periods of time in orphanages, if not their entire childhood, a trend was developing at that time toward placing some in foster homes. Children in orphanages were well cared for, but they didn't get the same personal attention and nurturing as found in foster homes. Liu Hai Xing was placed with a foster mother, a woman who had become an empty-nester after her son went off to college.

We were given the opportunity to request another child after being given the pictures and vital information. Adopting parents were given only one such opportunity to reject a match. But on what basis would we *reject* this match? We were not selecting jewelry! In the three photos they sent us Liu Hai Xing wasn't smiling nor was she particularly animated, but hers was a lovable face and one to which we were drawn. How could we say no?

TRIP OF A LIFETIME

The next exciting piece of news we were awaiting was our travel date. In September we were informed by CCAI that we were scheduled to leave for China on October 12 and would be gone for two weeks. We immediately made travel plans. Christie would miss two weeks of school and have lots of makeup work if she went with us, but there was no hesitation about her going with us. It would be a terrific learning and emotional experience for her.

At the time I was working on the campaign to gain voter approval of Amendment 22. I'd be gone for two of the final three weeks leading up to the election, which are usually a critical time in a campaign. The SAFE Colorado board was supportive of my adoption and granted me time off. Fortunately the polling numbers were good, so I could afford to be away.

When adopting through CCAI, adoptive parents take the trip with a travel group, usually consisting of up to ten sets of parents. In our case, two travel groups went together, so there were twenty sets of parents. They came from all over the country. Most were married couples, but some were single women. Some were empty-nesters with biological children, some were going for a second Chinese child, and some were becoming parents for the first time. Some brought along friends, grandparents, or their other children.

We first flew to Hong Kong, where we were able to spend a day sightseeing and adjusting to jet lag. Next we flew to Nanning, a city of four million that serves as the capital of Guangxi province, where Liuzhou was located. Adoptive parents were required to process the adoption in the provincial capital of the child they're adopting. In Nanning, as in every city we visited, CCAI had staff on site to help us, lead us, and translate. It was a smooth and professional process with hardly a hitch. We stayed at a top-notch hotel in the middle of the city, and one that was apparently accustomed to entertaining Western guests, given its restaurant menu and numerous items written in English.

ANTICIPATION

On the evening of our second day in Nanning, the children were scheduled to be delivered to us, one by one, in our hotel rooms between 7 and 9. At about 6:30 I was alone and hanging out in an art shop in the lobby of the hotel, too antsy to simply sit in our room waiting. Suddenly I heard a large, noisy group of adults and looked at them walking through the lobby. They stood out because they were wearing more traditional Chinese clothing than others in the hotel. But what really made them stand out was the fact they were carrying many wrapped-up toddlers. There was an air of excitement surrounding their entry, so I stepped out of the shop to watch their parade.

These were probably our babies! And one of them no doubt was our Liu Hai Xing. Suddenly I realized I was like the groom just before a wedding trying to sneak a peek at his bride. *That's forbidden*, I told myself. *I can't be looking at them. I can't spoil the moment, seeing Liu Hai Xing before Linda and Christie. I've got to wait. That moment is reserved for our hotel rooms.* So back into the art shop I went, feeling a bit guilty.

I peeked out the door of the shop until I noticed that the parade of babies had proceeded up the elevators. I immediately went up to my room and shared the good news with Linda and Christie. "They're here, they're coming!" I told them with excitement in my voice, as if I thought it wasn't going to happen as planned. But when? How much longer would we have to wait?

It seemed like an endless wait. Sometime after 8 there was a knock at the door. We welcomed a group of about four men and women into the room. One was holding Liu Hai Xing. We didn't know if they were representatives of the government or from an orphanage. It didn't matter. We only cared about getting our new child.

All these months of waiting came down to this one moment. We were excited but tried to be calm. It was an awkward feeling, wanting to politely listen to the information they had to share with us, but also wanting to just snatch our toddler from their arms and say, "Hey, we've raised two kids before; we can handle it from here. Thank you. Bye."

Just as we had been told in advance about Chinese tradition, Liu Hai Xing was dressed in many layers of clothing, despite the warm weather.

We wondered how any child could stand such heat. I wanted to unwrap her right then and there.

The adults explained a few things to us. They were a bit difficult to understand, but we probably were too distracted by the excitement to listen to them anyway. Part of what they talked about involved the differences among rice formulas. Beyond that, perhaps they were describing her health history, or detailing the terms of the limited liability warranty...we didn't care! We just wanted them to hand over our little girl!

The whole time Liu Hai Xing was screaming and crying. After about ten minutes the adults left her with us. She continued to scream and cry. And scream and cry. We weren't first-time parents; we'd had lots of experience with crying babies, yet it still was a bit bothersome. I couldn't help but be stricken by fear: *What if she doesn't bond with us?*

Who could blame this toddler for her incessant crying? She was in a strange place with these strange, light-haired, light-skinned people with oddly shaped eyes! Probably the only words she heard from us that were remotely familiar were our rudimentary attempt at "*Wo i nee,*" Chinese for "I love you." But that was hardly enough to soothe her. No amount of holding or clowning around could calm her down. She continued to scream and cry for at least an hour. Eventually she cried herself to sleep.

ACCEPTANCE

After an hour or so our little girl woke up. Within a few moments she opened up to us, examining us as we were likewise doing to her. She was especially mesmerized by Christie's long, blond hair. Within a short while she gave us her first smile. It seemed we were forever bonded from that moment.

We immediately fell in love with this cute, charming, well-behaved toddler. We were hungry for discovering more about her—what she ate, how she played, what she liked to do, what amused her. We were grateful there was plenty of time to do so.

All the parents and their newly adopted girls were given time together. We made a few trips around the city in two large tourist buses, undergoing a brief medical exam at a clinic, shopping at a baby goods store and a large grocery store, and visiting a large cultural museum that offered many exhibits with English translations and exhibits that featured the area's history and architecture. One evening an impromptu birthday party was arranged by the parents in the large lobby of one of the upper floors of the hotel, using bed sheets strewn on the tile floor.

We took Liu Hai Xing on a number of walks around the area, to parks and shopping areas. At first we wondered how the natives here would feel about us walking around with a Chinese baby. We feared Nanning might not be quite as accustomed to Western visitors as cities like Shanghai. We were told the Chinese government didn't go out of its way to publicize these adoptions of Chinese girls by foreigners. Before our trip one adoptive couple told me they were stopped by an elderly woman on the street who abruptly pulled out the front of their Chinese toddler's diaper—to see if it was a boy they were "taking!"

Our concerns quickly melted away. We were amazed at the reception we received from the people we encountered. One might think such an overcrowded nation would be impersonal and cold, especially toward strangers walking these Chinese babies through the streets, but nearly everyone we came across seemed welcoming. Unlike America, where one is accustomed to people masking their reactions to strangers, it was not uncommon for people to smile broadly at us, and some would even point at Liu Hai Xing and openly make comments to each other. Some even looked back at us as we passed, sometimes pointing and giggling, still buzzing about what they had seen. We didn't get a single disapproving look.

I'll never forget the experience of walking through a shopping mall and having a grandmotherly woman stop us, smile, and signal that she'd like to hold our baby. Well, perhaps it wasn't a signal—she practically took her from the stroller before we could protest! I felt insecure, worrying if she would check to see if this was a boy we were "taking." Or what if this woman would win over our daughter, given her friendly and more familiar Chinese appearance and ability to speak to her in a familiar sounding language? After all, we were still strange intruders who had cared for Liu Hai Xing for only a day or two at that point.

But, lo and behold, not long after the woman took the child from the stroller, Liu Hai Xing started crying. The elderly woman was fit to be tied. She reluctantly handed our bundle of joy to Linda and the crying stopped. She was comforted in her mama's arms. What a delightful and reassuring moment. Nice try, grandma, but this child was right at home in the arms of her new "may may" (mother).

WINDING DOWN

All the parents went on a fantastic side trip to the tourist city of Guilin, where we took a boat cruise on the majestic Li River. The area is known for its spectacular, rounded limestone karsts that look like either a spire or half an egg sticking out of the ground—thousands of outcroppings hundreds of feet high, creating a picturesque landscape. We were told the Chinese prefer to visit these odd mountains in months when there was a misty rain and light fog that created a mystifying atmosphere. October was not supposed to be one of those months, but it was for us. There was a light mist and clouds scattered throughout the river valley, creating a beautiful, mystical scene without drenching us or hiding the karsts.

All that was officially left to do was take our children to the polluted city of Guangzhou (formerly known as Canton), where we would process the adoption at the American consulate. Most CCAI adoptive parents experience the pleasure of staying at the famous White Swan Hotel, which is near the American consulate. Unfortunately, because of a large conference, we couldn't stay there. Instead, we spent two nights at a four-star business hotel. It was amusing at times, watching the reactions in the hotel restaurant, given the contrast between the serious businessmen in suits and a laid-back group of American parents with their loud and playful Chinese toddlers.

We then flew back home, through Hong Kong and San Francisco. A couple of Denver television stations had offered to meet us at the airport to record our arrival. It would have made for a nice Columbine healing story, but I knew we would be arriving late at night and would be exhausted and wanting our privacy, so I refused their offers and kept our arrival time a secret. In fact, we didn't have anyone greet us there. We arrived in Denver safe and sound, feeling triumphant but exhausted.

A BLESSED NAME

We gave our daughter the name Madeline HaiXing. For her middle name, we simply combined Hai Xing into one word for simplicity, but making the "X" upper case to distinguish the two separate words—though we assume it will rarely be spelled that way. Hopefully Madeline won't curse at us as she grows older for giving her that middle name, given how people will no doubt struggle with its spelling and pronunciation.

The derivation of Madeline's first name is a special story and one that brings a lump to my throat and tears to my eyes when I tell people about it, even to this day. The choice of the name Madeline came from Christie. She suggested it after Linda gave her the opportunity to select it, with just a suggestion that perhaps the name start with the letter "m" to go with our last name. Christie later said she's not sure why she picked the name, speculating she might have been influenced by the French children's book series of that name, though adding it certainly was not a favorite of hers. Oddly enough, Linda and I simply accepted her choice with virtually no discussion or debate.

A number of months after we brought Madeline home, someone asked Linda: "Did you choose the name Madeline because of the letters?" Linda didn't understand what she meant, so the woman elaborated: "Well, did you pick the name because when the letters are scrambled it spells Daniel M?"

It was one of those remarkable revelations that stops you in your tracks. We did not know about the letters when the name was chosen. Even though there's an extra "e" in Madeline when the letters are scrambled, it was nonetheless another amazing, special blessing in our healing process—a blessing named Madeline, a blessing growing from Daniel M.

A BLESSING

There were no regrets about the adoption. Madeline was a happy, healthy, inquisitive, sociable, intelligent child. There were no bonding problems. Her positive attitude and upbeat personality were a great blessing to us at a time we really needed them.

I get a bit perturbed when people remark that our daughter is lucky to have been adopted by an American couple. It bothers me that what some people apparently mean to say is that our daughter is lucky to be out of communist China and lucky to be with us here in America.

Madeline might be better off in terms of the cultural difficulty of being an orphan in family-centric China. I don't agree, though, with the simplistic, xenophobic argument that she's better off in America because of our wealth and political system. We are a great nation, but that does not mean we should believe that every child is somehow better off under our wings.

We are the lucky ones, for having been blessed by *her* presence in *our* lives. What we have given Madeline is a healthy family environment, but she has given us much more in return. She has filled a hole in our hearts.

Christie and Madeline and their rat terrier, Diego, December 2011

Chapter 20

New Family Bonds

O ne of the unexpected and inexplicable consequences of the massacre was the disappointing desertion or drifting apart of some
friends. Some friends didn't know how to handle our tragedy, or
didn't know what to say to us, or perhaps felt uncomfortable around us.

I wondered why my old graduate school roommate never contacted me following Columbine or even in the thirteen years since then to
express condolences. I wondered why we received condolences from so
few of the members of the two "small church community" groups we
belonged to at one point; these groups brought people together in each
others' homes to share their faith in Christ in intimate settings, yet it
seemed there was little closeness with many of these people.

Linda wondered why a certain friend just seemed unable to engage in
any discussion of the grief she was going through, seemingly preferring to
talk about anything *but* Linda's pain.

We were left to wonder why some people became estranged. Had
we failed to acknowledge their expressions of sympathy? Was it my gun-
control advocacy? Or was it just too challenging for them to deal with us
in our situation? I'm guessing it was mostly the latter.

NO ONE KNOWS

It was disappointing that we lost a few friends, but we more than made up for it with new ones. I made new friends in the gun-control movement, including others who had lost loved ones to gun violence. Thanks to our adoption of Madeline, we became close friends with a special group of parents from the Denver area who went to China with us in 2000. We still gather together with them for birthdays, Chinese New Year, picnics, vacations in the mountains, and for our girls' "Gotcha Day"—the anniversary of the day our girls were handed over to us in China.

But of all the new relationships we developed, none was as important at the time as the one that developed among the families of the Columbine victims.

Prior to the massacre we knew none of the families of the victims nor did we know any of the students killed or injured at Columbine or even their names. It was a large school, and the victims were from different graduating classes. I assume Daniel knew some of them, but because he was shy and had a small circle of friends, none was likely close friends of his.

The first time we came across some of the Columbine families was at the funeral home, where three of our children were laid out. My extended family members reached out and met some of the other Columbine family members there and conversed with them, but I was far too upset to talk to anyone outside my own circle. A few days later we encountered most of the victims' family members at the community memorial service, but there weren't many opportunities to speak with them at length.

One month after the massacre we gathered together at a church to be consoled by President Bill Clinton and the first lady. The Clintons graciously met and conversed with each family individually, so there was quite a long wait for them to make it to each family's table. During that time many of the families eventually strolled around and connected with each other. A month or so later one of the Columbine families extended an invitation to gather and socialize at their church in an informal setting. But it was the next gathering, for a picnic a few weeks later in Littleton's Ketring Park, where a new bond was formed among the Columbine families.

It started out as a picnic on a lazy summer afternoon but talk quickly turned to the murder scene. Some of the parents were angry that the Jefferson County school district was going to use the library at Columbine High School after the school reopened in the fall. The district planned to remove the bloodied books and carpets and cover up the bullet holes in the room where ten of our children were murdered.

We were in disbelief. How could they expect us to ever set foot in that school? How could they possibly expect students to step into that library again, given what happened there? We heard of one girl who was so shaken by what happened that she couldn't set foot in *any* library, let alone *that* library! Did school officials really think it was just a matter of cosmetics, that they could merely cover over the marks of a massacre?

We would not allow the library to reopen as if nothing had happened there. We were committed to having the library torn out and replaced. It became a cause that brought us together. A number of us showed up at subsequent school board meetings to advance our request. The board listened to us but showed little willingness to change course.

As someone who worked in the public sector and followed public policy, I understood the school district could not easily justify the destruction of a structurally sound facility and the spending of considerable taxpayer dollars to build a new library when it had more pressing facility needs. But school administrators should have offered alternatives. Worse yet, they did not initiate any meetings with us to ask us how we felt about their plans. After all, most of our children had died in that room and it likely would be viewed as a horrific death chamber for a long time to come.

When it seemed the school board was not receptive to our request to close and replace the library, it became clear we would have to turn to the community. The families began to meet regularly to develop strategies for pressuring the school district to replace the library, to recruit others to help us, and to raise funds to replace the library quickly in order to minimize disruption to the students of Columbine during construction.

We received lots of help from others in our quest, in particular from community members who were shaken by what happened at Columbine. Rita Kahn, a community activist and fundraiser extraordinaire, became our major advisor. She was joined by Lynne Bruning, a community development specialist at the University of Colorado Center for Community Development, who served as our meeting facilitator and organizer. There were others who assisted, too numerous to name here.

MOVED BY HOPE

The Columbine families created a private nonprofit organization to lead the effort and to solicit and distribute the proceeds of our fundraising efforts. We named it Healing Of People Everywhere—HOPE. The Denver Foundation agreed to collect and disburse the proceeds on our behalf, since we didn't yet have tax exempt status or the capacity to handle large amounts of money.

We developed a plan of action. Rather than replace the library with another one in the same location, we proposed to build an extension of the school to the west and place the new library there. The existing library was above the cafeteria. We proposed to remove it, including its floor, creating an atrium. This raised ceiling in the cafeteria would have inspiring artwork that would gently commemorate the victims.

It was not an easy sell. A few people in the community spoke out against the plan in the media, saying it was a waste of resources to build a new library when it was not needed and when there were far greater school needs.

At first the school district was reluctant to accept our proposal, concerned about how long it would take to raise the amount of money needed, the need for a temporary library, the short time in the summer available to build the atrium, and the potential for disruption of classes in the fall if work was not completed. For a while they insisted that we have most of the needed funds raised before starting any work. We felt that was an unreasonable requirement. We worked tirelessly to convince the district to let work begin that upcoming summer, even though we were far from raising all the needed funding.

We pleaded with the community to support us—and they did! In January 2000 the school board agreed to the construction of the atrium that summer. In doing so it was taking a leap of faith, for there was a risk that we'd come up short in our fundraising and construction would be halted. By that point we had raised barely enough money for the library removal and atrium construction, and not the larger amount needed for the new library construction, which was intended to start in 2001.

We set a clear goal of raising the amount needed for the entire project —$3.1 million. At first money began pouring in, but then the pace slowed, as we were in the midst of a mild recession. Construction and supply firms, particularly with the leadership and generosity of Jeff Mack of Turner Construction, began to offer building materials and labor at reduced or no cost.

School groups and others throughout the nation raised funds through bake sales, car washes, garage sales, and other special events. The heartfelt stories of people's efforts were overwhelming, such as the dollar bill sent in by a female jail inmate and elementary school students collecting thousands of coins in donation jars. We received contributions from more than 4,600 individuals and organizations.

When the contributions slowed, we sought more local and national publicity. Columbine parents Dawn Anna and Ann Kechter were valuable spokeswomen, appearing on *The Today Show* and other venues to make a plea to the nation. When we came up short of money at a critical time, local community philanthropists stepped up with healthy donations that put us over the top.

In the end, we exceeded our fundraising goal in cash, volunteer hours, and donated services and materials. It was a hard-fought group effort, though something for which I take little credit. Some of the parents participated in numerous fundraising events, but my only contribution was time at HOPE meetings. I did not play a leadership role, and because I was so preoccupied with my gun-control efforts, I was not fully engaged in the effort. Furthermore, I didn't make myself visible in the fundraising effort because I realized I could be a lightning rod due to my gun-control activism. I didn't want to give those who were opposed to gun control a reason not to contribute to HOPE.

The atrium was completed in August 2000, in time for the new school year. The ceiling was adorned with a beautiful mural of a Colorado forest canopy of aspens and evergreens. The mural–actually twenty different paintings–consists of four large central canvasses and sixteen other paintings that float on "cloud" figures suspended from the ceiling. At the atrium's opening ceremony, Dawn Anna aptly described the special meaning and purpose of the ceiling artwork: "We wanted heads to be lifted, not hung, wondering 'where did that child die?' When you walk into the atrium, you have to walk with your head held up. The entire room lifts your spirits."

In 2000 and into 2001 we watched as the new library was built. Our dream became a reality on June 9, 2001, when a larger and more technologically advanced library was dedicated. It was a heartfelt triumph for the families of the Columbine victims who worked so hard at a difficult time in their lives, and for the community that gave so generously.

TRIUMPHANT, BUT

The HOPE work was satisfying, but it was not without its pain. During much of our effort, in 2000, I was working full-time as a gun control lobbyist, going right from an emotionally charged job to the emotionally charged HOPE meetings. Right from the frying pan to the fire. The HOPE project was rewarding, but the meetings were not always a positive experience, given our frustration in working with the school district, the maddening stories being swapped about the latest controversy in the Columbine investigation, and all the raw emotions associated with Columbine.

Linda usually didn't go the meetings because we didn't want to leave Christie alone at home too often. In reality Linda didn't want to be at the meetings anyway. For her they were just too painful a reminder of Columbine, with all the conversations about the crime scene and the latest controversies. She had little interest in the issues related to construction and fundraising. She probably would have preferred that I not even go to the meetings, given that she saw how I often came home exhausted, glum, or angry.

FAMILIES OF THE INJURED

At times I've been asked whether the families of the slain and injured connected with each other well. It wasn't often we had an opportunity to gather together. There was an instance in 2000 when all the victims' families were given complimentary tickets to a Bruce Springsteen concert in Denver, complete with a catered reception with Bruce and his band prior to the concert. Many families of both the murdered and injured attended, and some good connections were made there, but it was the exception.

There wasn't anything deliberate about the lack of connections, nor was there any kind of discord. It's just that our experiences and healing were different. The loss of our loved ones strengthened the connections among the families of the slain. Perhaps it seemed more challenging for some of the injured and their families to deal with us, since our experience was so different. Perhaps some of the injured felt "survivor's guilt."

The Columbine families deliberately invited the families of the injured to join in the HOPE effort. Not a lot did, but a few were regular participants and others helped out at times. The HOPE project managed to provide a strong bridge between the families of the slain and the families of the injured.

There didn't seem to be as strong a connection among the families of the injured. I'm not aware of them ever getting together as a group. That's no surprise, given that there were significant differences in the level of care having to be provided by those families. The injuries ranged from severely crippling to minor—though I hesitate to call them minor injuries, given the trauma of having been in the middle of a massacre.

LIKE FAMILY

The Columbine families became like a new family to us. We didn't have a lot in common with many of them—we came from different faith backgrounds and had differing views on some of the causes of the Columbine massacre. But what we had in common—devotion to our murdered loved ones—was all that mattered.

In those first few years, we didn't gather just for HOPE meetings. We also got together for picnics, Christmas gatherings and other events, including a wedding and a graduation.

The annual Never Forgotten dinner, conducted two weeks or so after each Columbine anniversary, usually brought together nearly all of the

Columbine family members. It was an event sponsored by the local Clear Channel radio station chain, along with other co-sponsors. They set up a trust fund that annually provides thirteen $5,000 scholarships in the names of each of our loved ones.

The winners of the scholarships were graduating high school students from the Denver area who were exemplary in their community activities and focused on helping others. At each dinner we sat at tables with the student winning the scholarship in our child's name, along with their family members, the teacher who nominated them, and a member of the media that introduced the student at the award ceremony.

It was usually a bittersweet event for Linda and me. On one hand, we got to visit the Columbine families and show them how Madeline and Christie were growing up. There was a hopeful side, as an exceptional student learned about our child and often spoke their praises when they accepted their scholarship in front of the assembled crowd. In later years the selections of scholarship winners were especially gratifying to our family, as they were somehow related to Daniel's legacy. For example, one winner raised money for the poor in Guatemala, another was Chinese, and another was a blind teen who ran on his school's cross country squad.

On the other hand, the announcement of each scholarship included a short bio of the victim. It was heartening to hear Daniel's story told, but it was yet another reminder of the heartbreaking reason we were there in the first place.

After the eleventh year, interest in the event among the Columbine families waned. While the scholarship continued, the dinner event was discontinued.

There were also many negative events that brought us together. There were the hearings aimed at trying to force the release of evidence, the court hearings for the two young men who supplied the handgun to the Columbine killers, and the hearings for a bill that would have created a formal legislative investigation of Columbine. These events were necessary evils, but I should have followed Linda's lead and avoided more of them. I hated to be there, for they were such stark reminders of the pain we were dealing with, yet I also felt I could not simply leave all the dirty work to the other families.

Occasionally Linda has lunch with a couple of the other Columbine moms, and some other friendships have developed among the Columbine families. But in recent years, the Columbine families have seldom gathered together, nor do we see them unless we run across them by accident. Perhaps we don't gather because we don't need each other's support as much as we did in the past.

But we will never forget how we all helped each other get through this pain and tragedy. We usually felt so comfortable being with each other. We could talk about how we were feeling without wondering whether we were boring the other person or making them feel uncomfortable. People often tell us they "have no idea what you're going through." They're right. They don't. But these twelve other families knew what we were going through. They knew what it was like to be experiencing immense grief. They knew what it was like to be at the epicenter of this earthquake.

The new HOPE library at Columbine High School

Chapter 21

www.Healing

Those who lose a child to tragedy in this Internet era have a far-reaching source of healing unavailable to previous generations. Parents can now memorialize their child in a direct, heretofore unimaginable and public way. They can ensure their child will not be lost in obscurity. They can tell the story of their child, provide vivid photographs, create a guest book for visitors, and correspond with them.

People all over the world can Google the name of a victim or the location of a shooting tragedy and follow links to learn about the victims. No longer do people have to dig up old magazines or microfiche files at the library to learn about the victims of a shooting.

Sadly, many people will focus only on the names and stories of the killers. But that can change somewhat if we make information about victims readily available for those who care enough to seek out their names.

GROWING FROM A SEED

Four days after Daniel's death, a stranger from our area spoke briefly with me at the funeral home and planted a seed. Drew Kerin was a Republican activist who served as a legislative aide to our state senator.

During a short conversation he suggested I set up a Web site to honor Daniel so the world would not be fixated on the killers but instead on the stories of the victims. I was in no shape to act on it immediately, but the idea stuck with me.

At the time, I used the Internet for email, but I wasn't an active visitor of Web sites, particularly personal or memorial ones. Nonetheless, the thought of telling the story of Daniel's life took root within me in the weeks following the funeral, and I quickly went into action.

If ever there were an angel on earth for Daniel, it was Erik Koskinen. He was a coworker in the information technology office of my division. I asked him for advice on how I could find someone to help me set up a Web site, since I was clueless about how to proceed.

Erik insisted on doing it himself. I didn't know him all that well because I didn't work directly with him, but he was someone who was deeply moved by what happened at Columbine. In fact, he was there at the state capitol on the day of the NRA protest and offered me moral support.

He asked me for pictures and text, and took care of the rest. He created a great template. Over the coming weeks I'd bring new materials to work, and he'd take them home and within a day or two they were up on the Web site he created.

I don't know how Linda and I found the time or energy, but we were teeming with new material for the site. It was love for Daniel gushing out, as we told the story of his life and related what we were doing to honor him.

Next I printed business cards promoting the Web site. The card was headed, "Celebrating His Life." On the card was the message, "Since his life was taken at Columbine High School on April 20, 1999, we have been dedicated to keeping Daniel's memory alive. We created a Web site to focus on his wonderful life rather than his tragic death.... Please visit www.DanielMauser.com."

I handed out the card any chance I got. I popped them into envelopes when paying bills. When I spoke to reporters, I handed them the card and asked them to get more information at the site so I wouldn't have to field so many painful questions about Daniel. When I spoke to groups, I handed the cards to the audience and told them they could thank me for my presentation by visiting Daniel's Web site. I've distributed thousands of these cards over the years.

VISITORS TO THIS NEW HOME

The company that hosts the website offers a helpful tracking system that provides all kinds of statistics about activity on the site. For example, the Web site attracted an average of more than 7,000 hits per month in the first year, dropping to about 6,600 by 2003, but then growing to more than 9,500 in 2005 and 13,000 in 2008. That's not a lot of hits by most business standards, but to me it was amazing when I thought of it as 250 people a day learning about my son. It struck me that probably only a few hundred people on this earth knew who Daniel was when he was with us, yet now tens of thousands of people were getting to know him!

It has also been astonishing to see where the visitors come from. Many foreign visitors can be identified by country of origin, as many of them have ISP extensions such as ".al" (Albania) or ".bz" (Brazil). I can track how many visitors come from various countries. How could a parent not be moved by seeing that people from faraway places like Belgium, Malaysia, and Kenya were learning about their child?

AN ONSLAUGHT OF LOVING MESSAGES

The guest page was a place where people could leave us messages. We've received thousands of personal notes. We have read every one of them, and in fact still have printouts of many of them. At first there were too many to respond to, but as time went on we were able to reply to most of them.

Dr. Kathleen Johnson of Atlanta, a total stranger, was the first to make an entry in the guest book. It was a fitting first message, for its themes and sentiments would be repeated by so many other writers over the ensuing years:

> *"I think of Daniel every day. I think of you, his family, every day. I will always remember all of you. I could tell from Daniel's picture that he was exactly as you portrayed him...a gentle spirit.*

Somehow, even though I did not know Daniel, I experience his loss. My prayers and thoughts are with you. Thank you for this Web site. May God hold you close and ever so connected with the gentle soul that was given to you as your son."

Many messages started with similar lead-ins, including "You don't know me, but...." Or "I still remember where I was and what I was doing when I heard the terrible news...."

Writers tried their best to lessen our grief. "I wish there were something I could say or do to ease your pain ..." was a common message. Many offered words of encouragement: "Remember that they took a life, not a spirit!" "The shortest candle shines the brightest." "Daniel will live on in all of our hearts."

A DIFFERENT MEANING TO PRAYER

I have never been a very prayerful person in the traditional sense. Even though I was raised as a Catholic, I was rarely one to recite prayers at length, and never one to pray a rosary. I would memorize the prayers in the Catholic liturgy that were recited during the Mass and could remember them well, but seldom did I think deeply about what they truly meant.

I thought of myself as a more practical, logical Christian, reflecting on the life of Jesus and about how we should lead lives modeling His. I seldom offered intercessory prayers for others. I saw little purpose in praying for others, believing that, instead, I should do something more directly, like giving my time or money, not "merely" praying.

If someone lost a loved one, I rarely would say a prayer for them. I felt that God was going to determine the fate of the deceased person not my prayer. God wasn't going to count up the prayers offered for different people and determine their fate in heaven or hell based on a count of prayers. There was nothing fair in that. It seemed more practical to talk to and comfort the person who suffered a loss, though, truth be told, I often failed to do even that. I was lousy at offering condolences, let alone prayers.

My experience with Columbine and with Daniel's Web site has turned my view of intercessory prayer upside down. I still don't believe

God counts up prayers, but I have come to better understand that prayers aren't so much something directed at God, but rather, at each other. Sure, we can ask God to intervene, but then we'd just be on the sidelines waiting for God to act. We were not put on this earth for the purpose of being observers on the sidelines. We cannot expect all good to flow from God. We have to be participants and interveners.

Our prayers and reaching out can help to heal, not necessarily because they result in God taking action, but because they result in *our* taking action. Our prayers, particularly those shared with those who've lost a loved one, help to surround and comfort them. That's what so many people did for us. The Web site gave them the opportunity to do so. And I felt the power of their efforts.

Dawn Swann from Quakertown, Pennsylvania, summed it up well: "It must be amazing to receive an entire country's prayers...." Yes, it was amazing. I cannot begin to tell you how comforting the messages were. Christians are taught we are all provided with God's spirit. So when you hear from so many people offering prayers, you're getting a good serving of that spirit. I cannot realistically say to God that I feel terribly lost and alone in this grief, for He would say to me, "Have you not heard those I have sent to you? Have they not told you they were praying for you? Did they not take the time to show you they cared for you? Have they not comforted you?"

Yes, they have. It's been part of my healing.

The love was mutual. Even when my eyes glazed over some of the repetitious themes in the messages, I nonetheless looked at the name of the person who wrote it and in my own way said a prayer—by simply reading the name, speaking to God, and saying how happy I was to hear from that person, confirming that they were a special person to reach out to us.

NAVIGATING TO DANIEL

It was interesting to see how people discovered Daniel's Web site. Many visited the site after reading about Daniel in a newspaper or magazine article. Some were led to the Web site after reading *She Said Yes*, the book about Columbine victim Cassie Bernall. Many, like Nicole Hayek of Rochester, Minnesota, visited "after I went to a program tonight by

Darrell Scott and was deeply moved." Darrell, the father of Columbine victim Rachel Scott, travels all over the country speaking to schools and community groups about the need for kindness and compassion, and the dangers of bullying.

One mother brought a tear to my eye when she wrote, "I ran across your site by searching for 'words of comfort' on the computer. I lost my only child, David, at age 16 last September. He was walking on the sidewalk when he was hit by a hit-and-run driver."

There were other ways people connected with Daniel's site. Some writers had the same last name, wondering whether they might be related to us. A few, like Dan from Mobile, Alabama, made another ironic correlation, based on our last name. He wrote, "I came across your Web page searching for information on an old 7mm Mauser that was taken in on loan by the pawn shop where I work part time." From another writer, "I was searching for information on Mauser rifles but was delighted to find Daniel's site." (Mauser is a German arms manufacturer, maker of a famous line of bolt-action rifles and pistols from the 1870s and still made today.)

TEEN WRITING

It was always pleasing to get messages from teenagers, because they represent hope for future generations and are often more insightful and honest in their writing. Many said Daniel reminded them of themselves or of a particular friend, and many indicated they would love to have known him.

Kevin McC. from California demonstrated impressive compassion for a fourteen-year-old boy when he wrote, "I never knew Daniel, nor anyone else at Columbine. But I would like to know what I can do to pay my respects, and find out more about the lives of these wonderful spirits." I was touched by such a message from a teen boy living far away, so I wrote back, telling him he had *already* paid his respects in countless ways, and that he could do more by Googling the names of other victims to learn about them.

Another touching story came from a teen in St. Albans Bay, Vermont, who wrote how he read about Daniel in an article in Rosie O'Donnell's magazine: "It made me, a 15 year old male, cry…Oh, my God. Anyways, I was reading the magazine in my dentist's office, the nurse came for me. I waited till I was done reading the article before going in. I had to explain to the dentist why my eyes were so red."

ENCOURAGEMENT AND REFLECTION

I was pleased when I received words of encouragement for my gun-control efforts, since I was sensitive to the fact some people might think it inappropriate to include my gun-control beliefs on the site. It was heartening to hear from people like Michele K. from Omaha, who offered up: "More of us are on your side than the other, even if we don't always express it." From another writer: "You made so much more of an impression than Charlton Heston, who burbled about the land of the free and the home of the brave. The brave don't shelter behind guns. They come out and they make themselves vulnerable, as you have. God bless you."

A teacher in Littleton reflected on how we raise our children. "We need to revisit the way we raise males in America. We teach them to hide their feelings. Eventually they are unable to recognize their feelings. Some of the greatest men have been gentle men. We ask girls, 'How do you feel?' We ask boys, 'What do you think?' There's something wrong with that."

Helen Smith from New York reflected on her reactions to Columbine, Daniel's Web site, and lessons for her teenaged daughter. "Although I saw the news about Columbine, at the time I was going through a stressful time in my life and chose to turn the TV off. I recall saying things like, 'The news can really run a topic into the ground' and 'enough already.'

"Looking back now I realize that is what so many of us do, we tune out the world so that we don't have to deal with reality. After reading the 'Rosie' article about Daniel, I found myself crying. The picture of you holding up your son's sneakers hit home. Your son was a real person. He put on his sneakers each day just like my kids do and he went out and enjoyed life like all kids should. I would like to apologize to you for turning off the TV. Daniel was a person who died needlessly and will not be the last until we all leave the TV on and get angry enough to choose to take action from what we are seeing."

COMFORT ON DIFFICULT DAYS

Daniel's Web site provided many comforting messages, but some were especially moving. They were messages that reassured us of the positive side of humanity, messages that brought us hope, or inspired us, or brought tears to our eyes or raised our spirits high.

I especially appreciated words of comfort and encouragement on those days that were so difficult: the Columbine anniversaries, Daniel's birthday, Father's Day, and Christmas. I knew that many people wouldn't remember Daniel's birthday, or were too busy on holidays to write, so I was especially thrilled to get messages on those days.

Shannon B. from Littleton wrote on one of the Columbine anniversaries, saying that Daniel reminded her of her 11-year-old son, Scott, who is "sensitive, loving and is interested in computers and science, too. Scott's birthday is, sadly, April 20th. He cried last spring on his birthday, and told me he hated having his birthday on the same day as Hitler's birthday and the Columbine tragedy."

David P. of Lafayette, Indiana, offered a beautiful Christmas message: "I thought about how peculiar a holiday like Christmas is, because it's a holiday that invokes polar opposite feelings for people." Some enjoy it, he said, while others dread its sorrow and pain. "I did some searching on Columbine and their families and I found this site. I've learned about the life of one of those lost, someone not so different from this 29-year old in some ways. The black and white newspaper photos are two-dimensional in many ways. This site has added three dimensions and color to that photo; I have been given an idea of the person Daniel was and always will be. After spending the past half hour here, I can tell you that it feels like the Mauser family has given 'me' a Christmas gift."

COMFORTING CONFIRMATION

It was reassuring to hear positive feedback about the Web site itself. I love to play devil's advocate with others (and myself) and can be sensitive about what others think of me, so I was apprehensive about creating a memorial Web site, concerned that some might view it as too somber or morbid, or that it was too focused on "victory" and not enough on the sadness that goes with the loss of a child. Might it seem like the product of a parent gratuitously boasting about his child, given that only two of the other Columbine parents had established a site like this, and neither was lengthy? Thankfully I received few criticisms of the site itself—except, as expected, from gun activists.

I was surprised to hear so many people *thank* us for putting up the Web site and for sharing Daniel's life with them. Very common were the words of Kathleen P. of Boston: "My children are all safely tucked into their beds tonight and I thank God for that, but thank you for putting your pain out there for people like me who take day-to-day things for granted."

From S. Smith of Dunnellon, Florida: "You have created something here that brought tears to my eyes and joy to my heart. Your affirmation of life, your love of hope and your desire to live beyond the terror of Columbine truly inspire…. Thank you for making your son real to me, and thank you for taking the time to make him real to the world."

"What a beautiful remembrance for your son Daniel," a woman wrote. "I could feel all the love you have for Daniel as well as the sorrow of losing him in such a terrible, senseless way. I saw no hatred expressed for the two gunmen. That must be the reason that so much love was for Daniel. There was no time for hateful feelings or a place for hate in this lovely remembrance of him."

Renee, a woman from Tennessee who lost her brother Michael in a tragic accident, described our Web site in a way I had not thought of before: "I applaud you for being able to celebrate your Daniel's life as I have celebrated my brother's life. I remember being told that I could use my brother's death to make myself *better* or I could use the experience to become *bitter*…I chose to strive for *better* as I would not want my brother's death to create something so negative…you reminded me of that today when I visited Daniel's Web site and looked at the precious pictures."

Laura, a woman from Jonesboro, Arkansas, scene of an earlier tragic school shooting, wrote, "I know your son IS proud of you. I believe much of his strength and character came from you, just as now your strength is coming from him."

HELPING OTHERS

Some of the most moving messages we received were from people who said they were somehow helped by the events at Columbine or by reading Daniel's Web site. Chris W. of Sparta, Wisconsin, warmed our hearts when he wrote, "I have had some problems at school and I have changed a lot because of this Web site, it really changed me. I have talked to my dad about the problems and I've been getting help."

"Punk Girl" told us in late 1999 that "It just might make you feel better to know something. I have had a very big problem with anger. Not near as bad as Eric and Dylan, but I bet their problem wasn't too bad a long time ago, either. I don't want to end up like they did, hurting innocent people. So I have gone to get some help for my anger and have been doing really well for a while now. I will keep getting help for my anger. Thanks for your Web site."

KN of Waco, Texas, who wrote to us in 2002, said he was thirteen years old and hinted at his personal problems: "It took me a while, but I finally realized that what I was doing was wrong. I was very fascinated with the tragedy, but for all the wrong reasons. I was basically obsessed with Eric and Dylan.... People treat me the same way that people treated them, like I am nothing, just a menace to society. I understood where Harris and Klebold were coming from.

"But now, as I look at your Web site, this is the only Web site that has touched me enough to realize the error of my ways. Eric and Dylan weren't harmless boys who got made fun of, as I used to think, but two monsters. Horrible, hideous creatures that felt no remorse for anyone or anything.... If any of this makes sense to you, I'm thankful, because it took a lot of courage to write this to you. Today was a day that opened my eyes for the first time in my short life."

A WORLD CRYING

I knew the pain from the Columbine tragedy was overwhelming in my community, but I was amazed at how the nation reacted. Jessica C. from Ocean City, New Jersey, confessed, "I don't think I've ever cried and mourned over people I didn't know before, however these shootings will be engraved on my heart for life."

Jennie A. from Austin, Texas, wrote, "I am at work, people keep asking me if I'm ok, they walk in and see tears in my eyes. I have shared your story with a few of my coworkers and they leave my office with tears in their eyes also."

Nothing struck me as emotionally, though, as stories of men crying, because it reminded me of my own crying and because "men aren't supposed to cry," and even when they do, they usually don't admit it. Yet some did.

William of Houston shared his deep feelings, saying, "I am a grown man of 39 years and I found myself in uncontrollable tears as I tried to view your site." The words of a junior high teacher brought a lump to my throat as I read of his experience. "I have been looking over your Web site today while my students are testing. Luckily they have not been paying much attention, as I have been crying a bit."

One anonymous man, after viewing Daniel on a YouTube video, wrote, "It's been nine years already and I'm not an emotional guy. I don't even think I have cried in two years. But this made me feel so bad. It made me feel guilty for not appreciating life enough. It's sad that Daniel didn't get the chance to make something of himself. Somehow I feel like he deserved it more than I do. It makes me feel like I owe him something."

REFLECTIONS ON DANIEL

The purpose of the Web site was clearly stated: to celebrate Daniel's life. As a father, I found it fulfilling to be able to tell Daniel's story, and doubly fulfilling to have people reflect on their impressions of him. After all, isn't that what we want from parenting? To pour our love and caring into our children, then see it result in a child so full of love and promise that it impacts others and leads them to compliment your child?

Colorado's Lori Ann observed, "Your son seemed to be such a gentle person and you really can see the light of God behind his beautiful eyes." Similarly, Kerry K. from California wrote, "He had the face of an angel, innocence and kindness radiated from his picture."

From Mike, a junior high geography teacher in Oklahoma: "I have known some students with similar qualities as Daniel and I can tell that he was the type of young man that every parent would dream of having as a son, that every teacher would dream of having as a student, and that I am sure every child would love to have as a parent… I can feel his spirit and yours inside me, and I am going to think of your family every day, as I try to teach and coach with the love this world so desperately needs and my students deserve, and I dedicate what I do to Daniel. I am going to let him be my example."

Scott in Tennessee referred to Daniel as "an ordinary kid who became a hero just for being who he was." And from Dan in New York: "These emails from strangers are, I'm sure, of little solace to you, but remember that there are thousands upon thousands of people who have learned about Daniel and have great admiration for who he was, and who are trying to be better people because of this massacre. That is a legacy that few of us will ever attain."

MESSAGES THAT ESPECIALLY TOUCHED OUR HEARTS

Linda and I were rather shocked at the email we received from Valerie in North Carolina: "I'm 52, am raising a six year old that I have raised since he was two. He was neglected and emaciated…I was going to adopt him but I have health problems. Forgive me if I appear selfish in this request, but you seem so loving. Would you please consider this child for adoption? We would be forever grateful." We were humbled by her request but unable to help her.

Bryan Devine, an elementary school teacher in Cincinnati, shared Daniel's Web site with his class and led a discussion of it. The students then sent us a scrapbook they filled with Daniel's pictures and their own personal messages to us.

"By looking at the pictures and reading about Daniel and his life, my kids felt a personal connection to him," Devine wrote to us. "It was interesting to see that most of them spent their time looking at the pictures of him when he was about their age. We discussed how important it is to discuss feelings and not let things build up inside you. One boy raised his hand and discussed his sister's death that had occurred four years earlier. I knew of this but he had never discussed it openly. I was so proud that he was comfortable enough to do this. Many other students chimed in and it was one of those days as a teacher that I just sat back and let the class discuss issues that are usually very difficult to open up about. I really feel Daniel's site helped to make this possible and our class community grew tighter because of it."

I give my heartfelt thanks to all who wrote. God will not forget your kindness.

Daniel as a toddler

Chapter 22

How Could They Be Admired?

I knew they were out there; I had heard of their Web sites. I never visited any of them, as I had better things to do than read the thoughtless and sick ranting of Harris and Klebold sympathizers and admirers. Fortunately, I never encountered these H&K admirers or their writings in the first few years after Columbine.

I didn't go looking for them, but within a few years, they came looking for me. I started getting messages from them through Daniel's Web site.

IMPOSSIBLE TO IGNORE

What can you say to teenagers who admire murderers or say your child deserved to die? I couldn't believe these teens learned nothing from Columbine and somehow justified violence as the killers' only way out of their misery. Was there nobody out there throwing a life preserver to these misguided admirers, these lost souls? For me it was one of the bigger heartaches growing out of Columbine—that there were teens who admired the Columbine killers, and that some saw nothing wrong with taunting the parents of one of its victims.

A few of them would say they were sorry for what happened to Daniel, that it never should have happened. Nonetheless, they still expressed understanding for how Harris and Klebold could have become so desperate, usually indicating they had been bullied themselves.

Most expressed not a word of sympathy or understanding. From "vampyr" in Scotland came, "Daniel and all the other victims deserved to die. Eric and Dylan should be worshipped like the gods that they are. I mite just shoot my whole school too, cuz i know what its like to be put thru the every day hell that Eric and Dylan were, and they made the right decision to kill everyone that they did."

From Brian in Louisiana came: "Get over it. He [Daniel] wasn't as innocent as you sometimes think. He helped to torment those 'outcasts' as did all of the Columbine students. I can't say I feel sympathy for him, because I don't. How can I feel sympathy for a type of person so like those I have suffered through with their abuse for so long?"

VIDEO MISSIVES

Early in 2008, I added a new way of sharing Daniel with the world, posting videos on YouTube, one a tribute showing him at different times of his life. While I received many positive responses to the videos, they exposed me to a new, younger audience and resulted in my receiving even more disturbing postings from H&K (Harris and Klebold) admirers.

From someone identifying him- or herself as "Storm the School" came the message: "I could be an asshole and an idiot like most of these REB and VoDKa fans, but I won't. All of the people who lost their lives deserved it. Eric and Dylan deemed them unfit and executed them. No human should survive the nuclear holocaust that will soon come if humans don't smarten up. School shootings are the next best thing, so hail Reb hail Vodka." (Note: Reb and VoDKa were Harris and Klebold's nicknames for each other.)

From both "KriegUndFausTrecht" and "hardkoregamer999" came the same message: "Eric and Dylan sure owned them all."

I was deeply troubled by these messages. Obviously, if two Columbine students were capable of wreaking havoc and mass murder, there was a chance there were others who were capable of the same. Was I hearing from potential copycats?

What especially troubled me was determining *how* to respond. At first I did what I thought was most appropriate. I ignored them. As one young man wrote after reading one of the repulsive messages on the YouTube comment board, "I think [he] is just some emo kid from the suburbs who hates his parents and is trying to be 'Internet Tough.' Anyone can write anything on the computer."

Christie added to that observation, speculating that most of these nasty emailers are what's referred to as Internet "trolls," people who send inflammatory or provocative messages with the primary intent of evoking an emotional response. They're especially known for posting hurtful messages on memorial Web sites in order to cause grief to families. They're people who may want to feel power over someone unknown to them by trying to see whether they can elicit a reaction of outrage, anger, or fear. They likely do so because they may have little power or authority in their own lives. They're easily able to do so using an impersonal means like the Internet. I was angry at them and could not believe people could be so cruel to a grieving father, yet it was easier to hope these were thoughtless, conscienceless trolls than it was to imagine they were raging teens who actually admired H&K and had the potential to become violent.

But isn't that what we *all* hope? Don't we all want to believe that these are just blustering teens who couldn't possibly be dangerous? Isn't that the kind of denial that too often leads us to ignore warning signs?

How do I know I'm not getting a message from a disturbed student who is about to go on a shooting spree? What if I am one of those people to whom they are sending a message to signal their intent? What if they view my not responding to them as a sign that maybe their violence doesn't matter or that I don't care?

It was difficult to determine the state of mind of these emailers. Were they teetering on the edge of rage, or were they just acting out their anger? I wanted to neither condemn nor condone them, for fear of sending the wrong message. Despite reading their despicable words, I felt that if I simply cursed at them, it might add to their anger and confusion, yet I also certainly couldn't disregard or condone their threatening language.

I decided not to take that chance. If I were playing into the prank of an Internet "troll," so be it. I felt I could not sit there and read this trash and not respond. After all, that's how we so often get into trouble—by ignoring troubled kids. I decided to engage them, even though I recognized I was no substitute for a psychologist or counselor.

I decided I'd respond to the H&K admirers when it seemed appropriate. My responses would focus on the reminder that school shootings were real and final, not something theoretical or a fantasy within a video game. I knew I had to proceed cautiously. I had to avoid the temptation to give my gut reaction to their messages, yet also could not soft-pedal my approach.

TRYING TO REASON WITH KM

One of the early H&K admirers with whom I engaged in email conversations, whom I'll refer to as "KM," started off callously. He repeatedly referenced *Natural Born Killers*, a gruesome movie about killing sprees that was a favorite of H&K's.

Referring to Daniel, he wrote, "Another unfortunate casualty of NBK (Natural Born Killers). Simply collateral damage, though. I must say, if you're really Daniel Mauser's father, you have become quite a zealot. Blindly fighting against firearms because your little boy took a round to the face. Emotion has indeed blinded you. Long live Reb and VoDKas' message."

I wrote back, confirming that I was Daniel Mauser's father and questioning why he was an admirer of two murderers who couldn't deal with their problems. In reply, he questioned why I chose to protest against firearms instead of bullying.

I acknowledged that bullying was a factor at Columbine but that "the punishment for bullying is NOT death. There has always been bullying and always will be." I told him what a great kid Daniel was, as were the other victims. I told him he spoke of my son "taking a bullet to the face" flippantly as if it were some sort of game.

KM fired back, calling me "ignorant" and condemning me for ignoring what he saw as the real problem: bullying. "I'm not sure if you lack the courage to stand up to the real problem, or if you're just blind, but either way you're not doing anything to stop school shootings."

I sternly responded that Daniel was nerdy and the likely victim of bullying, too. "But he didn't freakin' shoot somebody for it. Bullying

WAS a big factor at Columbine, but again, since when is it normal to kill someone because they bullied you? Besides, H&K didn't even kill those who bullied them. They killed just about ANYone." I explained why I focused on gun control and asked whether he had ever experienced the death of a loved one.

"IF you wanna communicate by means of childish, demeaning insults, I don't have the time or patience; go waste your time elsewhere," I told KM. "Those who resort to anger and insult are usually hiding frustration and a lack of content. You seem to care about this issue, so surely you can do better."

KM did "do better," writing back without the glibness or condemnation of earlier messages. "All right, now I have an understanding of why you have chosen to rally against the firearms industry. But why not rally to have harsher punishments implemented on bullying?" I felt like we had at least made a connection and our discussion was more civil. I concluded he was someone who was bullied himself, or at least knew of someone who was bullied, and that he might not be a candidate to harm others.

LOSING McD

One young man in his late teens, whom I'll refer to as "McD," wrote that "[The killers] owned your son, lol," along with some vile taunts. I wrote back, telling McD that "they 'owned' no one. They were losers with no control of their own lives. This is no laughing matter. My son was shot in the face and died. Have u ever dealt with the murder of someone u knew?"

"No, I have never dealt with a murder of someone I knew, but I wouldn't care. When my dad died I shrugged it off." I was pleased I had elicited a response, but I was a bit shocked to read his claim that his father died and to see his callous reaction to it. I couldn't help but wonder if his defiance were related to having lost his father.

I knew the feeling of having lost a father at a young age. "I'm sorry to hear you lost your father," I wrote, and told him my father died when I was ten and that he was abusive and a heavy drinker, yet someone who down deep inside probably cared for me. I then challenged him, asking, "is your hard-assed, alienated, cavalier attitude really just masking some feelings about losing your dad?"

He didn't respond to that question, but he did at least momentarily show a bit of humanity, saying, "I'm sorry about your losses as well, especially when Daniel isn't going to be home for Christmas this year." But then he switched to condemning my gun control efforts.

My response back was sarcastic, and in hindsight I wish I had just left it alone. "Gee, after about six messages you finally say a word of sympathy. Took you long enough, didn't it? Some human being you are, not unlike the 100s of gun nuts who've written me insulting and even hateful mail…"

He replied, "I don't give sympathy easily, its not because I am a jerk, it's because I do not believe in it. Weakness is something Eric hated. Natural Selection. Oh, and there were 15 people shot in the massacre—don't forget the real victims, Eric and Dylan. No one ever helped them."

McD continued ranting against gun control, but for me his statements sympathizing with the killers were just too much to handle, especially when he wrote,

How can you deny that he was owned? Eric KOd your son.

Eric Harris – 1

Daniel Mauser – 0

Eric Harris WINS!

I stopped corresponding with him. I felt I had at least forced him to understand the pain of a grieving father, the reality of gun violence, and how his admiration of the Columbine killers was so harmful. I can only hope McD's dark views of life did not manifest themselves in a harmful way.

A NEW WAVE

Starting late in 2011 I received an onslaught of postings from a new set of H&K admirers. With dozens of messages arriving within a three-month period, I assumed the writers were connected in some manner. Virtually none of them expressed a word of sympathy. Many taunted me with simple messages like "Eric & Dylan were martyrs!" and "E&D were the true victims." The primary message of most was that the students shot at Columbine were intentionally shot because they were bullies, as evidenced by the fact that victims in the library were singled out, while others were spared—allegedly because they were not bullies. Despite the inherent frustration in dealing with these admirers, I responded to most of their postings, challenging their reasoning.

But there was no reasoning with these devotees. When I insisted that Daniel was a gentle, nerdy, shy kid and not a bully, they replied that even nerds can be bullies and that I was obviously biased and blind to my son's bullying. I conceded that it was possible Daniel might have been indifferent to H&K or looked the other way if he saw them being bullied. But, I told them, that could have been true of many kids. I asked them whether that was something for which one deserved to be shot? Most didn't answer that question, but some insisted it was deserved.

Virtually none of the admirers responded when I asked how it could be that H&K selected their victims yet, in the case of the bomb, attempted to kill everyone in the cafeteria, not selected bullies. None responded to my insistence that H&K were simply murderers.

After three months of these messages and their recurring themes and taunts, I tired of responding. It was difficult saying all I wanted to say in 480 keyboard characters, so in February 2012 I posted a new video on YouTube in which I responded to the admirers of H&K. I indicated I thought many of them were simply trolls and told them they ought to "get a life" and that when they grew up—if they ever grew up—they'd look back and realize how repulsively they behaved. For those who wrote because they were bullied, I asked why they felt the need to harass me, since I was not the source of their problem. I asked them if their behavior, which amounted to Internet bullying, made them any better people than the bullies they condemned. I added that I thought it was ludicrous to treat H&K like heroes, because they did little to stop bullying. I reminded them that their heroes were the many people before them who had been bullied and survived it. I told them the ultimate revenge against their tormentors was to make something of themselves rather than be only bitter and defeated.

THEY'RE OUT THERE

I will always second-guess how I responded to these troubled admirers. Should I have contacted law enforcement? Should I have been easier (or harder) on them? But the point is not how I handled them, but that we must all learn to deal with these troubled people.

After all, they're kids in your community. Maybe they're kids in your school or your child's school. It doesn't matter that they may not be your neighbor. It doesn't matter whether they are a product of a broken home or that you can blame all their dysfunction on their parents. What matters is that they are out there. In the end, they're your kids. They're our kids. If we fail to do something about these troubled, bullied, disaffected kids, we're going to continue to suffer tragedy. If not when they're in high school, then when they're in their twenties…or thirties…or….

Chapter 23

The Absence of Civility

There's an ugly side to being a gun-control advocate. My colleagues in the movement can confirm it with their own stories of the rudeness and hostility they have encountered. Many elected officials could also tell you about the rudeness they face dealing with gun activists, but most would be too afraid to be publicly critical of these bullies they encounter for fear of repercussions.

When you join the gun-control movement in a high-profile way, you quickly discover the stunning lack of civility exhibited by many of your opponents. It's common to be confronted with insults, taunting, biting sarcasm, intimidation, belligerence, and even seething hatred. Gun activists often refer to themselves as law-abiding gun owners. Most are, but many routinely violate the laws of common decency. You needn't be an advocate to experience it. Just look at the blogs of gun activists or newspaper Web site responses to letters to the editor that promote gun control.

Intuitively I knew there were cruel and detestable people in this world, but it was so much more vivid and intimidating when I was the direct target of their nastiness.

PRANKS, INSULTS, CONFRONTATIONS, AND WORSE

Some of the opposition directed at me by gun activists was mild. For example, I received mailed invitations to join the NRA and at least five times pranksters signed me up for subscriptions to gun-related magazines like *Guns and Ammo*. When I received the subscription invoices, I returned them with a note explaining that I did not want to subscribe and the reason why my name had been subscribed.

Even years after Columbine, I was needled. A few months after the tenth anniversary, I received a manila envelope with Colorado state Senator Greg Brophy's name on it. In it was a form letter, signed by Brophy, inviting people to join Rocky Mountain Gun Owners, the gun extremist organization that claims the NRA is "too soft" on gun issues. I mailed the entire package to Brophy's home address along with a letter that asked him to remove my name from the mailing list and questioned whether the mailing was an in-your-face move or someone's idea of a practical joke. I also informed him of the taunting I had received in the past from RMGO members.

A few weeks letter, I received another letter with Brophy's return address, but in a different type of envelope, so I assumed he was responding to me. Instead, it was another copy of the membership invitation letter. I wrote to Brophy again, then emailed him. I also spoke briefly to a member of his staff, but Brophy never responded to me.

Those were mild examples of taunting compared with the mean-spirited messages that began to arrive not long after I became a gun-control advocate. Our phone number was listed, and I was the only Tom Mauser in the Denver directory, so it wasn't hard for gun activists to find me.

A few weeks after the massacre, Christie, who was thirteen at the time, answered the phone and was greeted with the ranting of a gun activist who didn't even bother to ask for me. He delivered a vulgar tirade against gun control. Linda also took a few nasty calls. Soon after, we requested an unlisted number.

Not long after the massacre I received two handwritten cards postmarked in Des Moines, Iowa, signed "Richard W. Pope." Among other things, he called me a "weak, pitiful man who is trading on the dead body of your son to get your name in the paper."

A similar letter, dated May 14, 1999, came shortly after my appearance at the protest against the NRA convention. It was signed by Terry Chelius, who operated the Chief's Rest Ranch and Hunting Lodge in Whitewater, a remote town in western Colorado. He wrote, "Get a life, Tom, don't use this deal for your own agenda. I realize that you have probably never had anyone listen to you before and this is a great vehicle to get your 15 minutes of fame, but try to get on with your life. Put your ball cap on straight, get a job and buy a good gun."

I responded with my own letter, telling him he had a lot of nerve sending such an unwelcome letter to me, adding that he had no idea what it was like going through what I had gone through.

Chelius, a Vietnam veteran and former Colorado State Trooper, defiantly responded that September. "Please, find a job, with all the spare time you have it would seem you could combine your obviously questionable IQ with your other vague attributes and make minimum wage somewhere sweeping out a gun store… As an adult I would expect more from a grieving father than to try for his 15 minutes of fame through the tragic death of his offspring …" I never wrote back. (Note: In 2008, Mr. Chelius pleaded guilty to charges of welfare fraud.)

Once I set up Daniel's Web site, email from gun activists arrived through the guest book page almost immediately. Not all were mean-spirited messages. Some were respectful and offered words of sympathy. Robert Boyce of Bucksport, Maine, wrote to me in 2000, "I would just like to say God bless and keep you in his tender loving care. I am a gun owner and a member of the NRA. I don't believe guns kill people but rather the people that abuse them. May God bless." It was one of the more respectful ones written by someone identifying themselves as an NRA member. Still, I wonder why he couldn't just have written without the clichéd "guns don't kill people" comment. Would he have chosen to write without that comment?

Most emails were less than congenial. I could usually tell the direction emails would take by the opening statements. Many gun activists who wrote didn't express a simple salutation like "Hello" or "Mr. Mauser," let alone express a single word of sympathy for my loss of Daniel. They launched right into attack mode. Other writers, such as Aaron from British Columbia, Canada, would express some sympathy, then shift to assailing my advocacy: "I am truly sorry about your son, to lose someone you care about is not a treat, I know, but the way you're whoring his death like this doesn't exactly make you out as the grieving father."

UNSAFE AT SAFE

Once I began working as a lobbyist for SAFE Colorado in 2000, the nastiness accelerated and intensified. When we were fully engaged in our Amendment 22 campaign, we received dozens of pieces of vicious mail. Much of it was directed at our co-presidents, some was directed at all of us, and some was directed at me.

Staff members did not show me most of the nasty mail. They felt I was dealing with enough pain. But one message was so hostile it could not be ignored. The unsigned letter, postmarked in Denver, was from a man claiming to be a Vietnam combat veteran. After condemning our efforts to close the gun show loophole and insisting he would ignore any gun-control laws, he berated me. "Whatever happened to the concept of 'grieving in private?' Stop trying to assuage your guilt feelings by taking away my rights…. If you ultimately succeed in your goals, I suggest that you may want to start carrying a handgun yourself, Tom Mauser, because I may decide to kill YOU."

That was enough of a threat that I presented it to the police. There was little they could do, though, since it included no name or return address.

Another letter, postmarked Grand Junction, Colorado, was not quite as direct in its threat, but just as malicious: "God damn you must be a proud son of a bitch with all the publicity…. You should have gone to work instead of beating the drum over your dead son's grave for more gun laws…if that poor kid [Daniel] could see what a fuck-up his old man turned into, he'd shit his pants. I'm [sic] are not wishing you any bad luck but I'd watch my back from now on if I was in your shoes." It was signed "Art Jenson, Grand Junction," but the phone book had no such person listed. I suspect it was someone too cowardly to use his real name.

E-NASTINESS GOES ON

After Amendment 22 was passed I was in the public eye far less often but rude messages continued. Reverend William A. Sladek, a minister from eastern Colorado, sent an email a month after the 2001 terrorist attacks, writing, "In light of September 11th, I'm surprised you didn't disappear into the cave you crawled out of.... You're an enemy of freedom and the people of this great nation if you think your agenda supercedes [sic] the state of war this nation now faces.... Get a life, you pathetic idiot."

Janice Peterson sent an email to state Representative Ray Rose, a legislator who twice sponsored a bill that would have weakened Amendment 22. She copied me on the email, which congratulated Rose for "standing up to" me. About me, she wrote, "I can't think of too many people in this state who are more despicable, more selfish and more unjustly given attention than this disreputable person...I think four years is more than enough time for him to have pushed his donkey cart around in an effort to justify his existence."

Kimmy Estrada, like a number of other critics, accused me of thinking my loss was somehow more significant than others'. "You aren't the only one who has lost someone...yours doesn't trump anyone else's loss. You need to deal with it, privately." She became a repeat emailer, often taunting me when, for example, there was a court ruling in favor of gun rights.

Among the most common themes were that I was demeaning, disgracing, and diminishing Daniel's memory, that I was trying to avenge his death, that I was "profiting" from my advocacy, and that I was intent on pushing for the confiscation of all guns.

Mean spirited messages didn't come only from "rogue" members of gun rights organizations. I also received one from someone in a leadership position. Ray Hickman, who was serving as the Northern Coordinator of Rocky Mountain Gun Owners, wrote a letter to me in June 2000 and was not shy about assailing me: "Every case of anti gun activism following a tragedy such as Columbine has been by Liberal socialist pukes who hate the Bill of Rights.... Get on with your life and stop being the PAID whore of the Bell Campaign and SAFE Colorado."

I assumed opponents living nearby in my neighborhood would be less callous in their attacks. Not so. In 2004 I distributed campaign flyers in my immediate neighborhood. When I rang doorbells I gave my name and told the resident who I was campaigning for. One elderly man living a few blocks away recognized my name. Despite his seeing that I had five-year-old Madeline with me, he launched into a loud and acerbic attack on my gun-control advocacy, saying he was a war veteran and didn't appreciate fighting for rights only to have them taken away by me. Madeline was frightened by his conduct.

In 2006 I went door-to-door in support of a candidate and handed out my personal endorsement statement. Al Arrowood was upset that my statement was critical of Mike Kopp, a pro gun Republican candidate for state Senate who wrote in his campaign material, "I support no gun control, period." Arrowood wrote to me, "You lost any sympathy from me about your son when, while in DC on business during the events of Columbine, I heard your anti-gun advertisements. You wasted no time in politicizing your son's death. As a father and a grandfather, I find that morally reprehensible. Your son needed a better father. I feel great loss for your son, but you have no credibility with me when you callously use his death to politicize, and you're still using his death to politicize. Have you no decency?"

RESPONDING BACK

I replied to many of the pro-gun writers, even though I knew I wasn't going to change their minds any more than they were going to change mine. I did so because it enabled me to relieve my feelings of anger and was good practice for challenging their arguments, given that many were presenting the same arguments that Americans were hearing or reading in everyday life. It took time to respond to them, but so many themes were constantly repeated I was able to simply cut and paste responses I stored in a catch-all document.

I challenged them, often responding, "Why did you bother to write me? Do you not think I get lots of rude and nasty emails from gun activists who attack me? Did you really think your mean-spirited email would change my opinion, or did you just think you'd feel self-satisfied telling a father whose son was murdered just how wrong he was about gun control?" Rarely did they respond back.

I found it rather ironic that some of the writers spoke about their religious faith or about the need for more religious teaching of our youth as a means of reducing gun violence. I wondered how they reconciled their religious beliefs with the rather rude and uncaring messages they sent me. I wrote back to many of them suggesting, "Since you speak of your Christian faith, I'd like to ask you if you think your email to me was written in the spirit of Christ. Would you please share with me the name of your minister/priest? I'll write and ask if *they* think your letter was written in the spirit of Christ." It was no surprise that most either didn't respond, or said they weren't practicing church-goers, or told me it was "none of my damned business."

So how should I view these mean-spirited messages and their authors? How should I react? Chris S. from Albany, New York, summed it up well when he wrote, "Just know that there are so many more of us whose hearts go out to you and your family than there are of uncaring idiots. Ignorance rears its ugly head in so many hateful ways. I can't help but feel sorry for these people because they have no compassion. They must be living pretty miserable and unhappy lives. I just hope that none of them gets to you. You will always have your beautiful boy in your life. No one can take that away from you. He'll always be with you and keep you strong. Just remember that there are so many of us who care about you and our love and support are so much stronger than anything negative you might hear from ignorant people."

MISPLACED BLAME?

I've heard gun activists claim the incivility and animosity directed toward me is harmless and a *natural* reaction from people who are concerned their Second Amendment rights will be stolen from them. Some claim my complaints about mean-spiritedness is a distraction from the issue at hand (Second Amendment rights) and is an unfair attack on average, law-abiding, patriotic, gun activists who should not be blamed for the rude behavior of a few "bad apples."

I'm not convinced we're talking about just a few bad apples. I've received hundreds of mean-spirited messages, and I've read many menacing pro-gun postings on Web sites, so I can't help but conclude they constitute just the tip of the proverbial iceberg.

There are tens of millions of gun owners in America. I'm not criticizing them as a group. The great majority of them are not members of the NRA or any other gun-rights organization. Most are responsible gun owners, and they weren't usually the ones sending me the mean-spirited messages—it was the gun activists. When my opponents accuse me of attacking all responsible gun owners or all NRA members, it's because that's a quick and easy way of demonizing me and making me the issue rather than addressing the real issues surrounding gun violence and weak gun laws.

I do not denounce or blame all NRA members for the rude behavior of some gun activists. I recognize that many do not tolerate this misbehavior. Yet at the same time, it disappoints me that rarely have I heard responsible NRA members and gun activists publicly condemn this incivility and insist on a courteous dialogue. They usually remain quiet. Why? Either they don't care, or more likely, they too are intimidated by these gun activist bullies. Just as there are police officers who feel pressured to honor the "blue code" and not turn in dishonest cops, there likewise could be responsible NRA members and gun activists pressured not to criticize their rude comrades-in-arms.

As a whole, these gun activists are the most belligerent, mean-spirited group of people I have ever encountered in my lifetime. I believe many have become so myopic and obsessed with their gun advocacy that they can't deal with gun control in a civilized manner. They can't stand victims speaking out like I do because it makes the problem real to people. So they resort to intimidation and bad behavior.

As long as there are NRA leaders and right-wing Republican politicians who use hostile rhetoric against those who support gun control, there will continue to be mean-spirited missives and a lack of civility. Their rhetoric is endemic of a movement that has crossed the line and is just not willing to have a civil discourse on the gun-violence issue in America. If responsible gun-rights supporters don't want to be tainted by this viciousness by others in their midst, then they damn well ought to at least publicly rebuke those who use this rhetoric and these intimidating tactics. After all, silence is complicity.

LOSING AN ADVOCATE

What is most bothersome is that the voices of incivility can successfully intimidate those who might otherwise join the fight for stronger gun laws. A prime example of this occurred less than a year after Columbine.

It began with a tragic shooting in Wakefield, Massachusetts, on the day after Christmas in 1999. Michael McDermott walked into the Internet consulting company where he worked and opened fire with an AK-47 semiautomatic rifle with a 60-round, large capacity feeding device and a 12-gauge pump-action shotgun. When he was done, he had fired 49 bullets and unloaded six shotgun shells. Thirty bullets hit their target, killing seven of his coworkers.

A week or two after that massacre, I received a call from a woman who was a relative of one of the victims. She told me the victim's family was considering issuing a statement advocating restrictions on assault weapons such as that used by the killer. She had visited Daniel's Web site and was impressed by my gun-control advocacy. She wanted to know what it was like for me to be grieving my loss and also supporting gun control.

But the woman's major question to me was one I didn't want to hear. "Do you get harassed by gun activists?" The woman said one of the victim's family members lived in the South and was concerned about what might happen if he advocated gun control. My heart sank as I wondered, "Why must I be the one to throw cold water on her interest?"

I could not lie to her. After eight months of being an advocate, I told her, I had received some nasty phone calls and letters. But, I told her, trying to put it in the best light, the troublemakers were small in number and there was great satisfaction in seeking change in the name of my son. I told her we needed to do what we could so that others didn't face gun violence like our loved ones had.

She thanked me, but I never heard from her again. That family apparently never made a statement about gun control. It was a heartbreaking disappointment, but I had to accept that some people were suffering enough and didn't wish to bring more pain on themselves and their families. This failure to recruit the woman also made me far more determined to continue and strengthen my gun-control efforts because I knew there were other victims who could not or would not speak up. It helped me realize that not only was I speaking up for Daniel, I was speaking up for other victims.

We cannot allow people to intimidate those among us who wish to speak up for common sense gun laws. We cannot expect extreme gun activists to voluntarily tone down their harsh rhetoric, change their radical beliefs or end their incivility, so we must instead grow our numbers in the gun-control movement, speak with a louder voice, strengthen our resolve. and win people over—using civility.

Chapter 24

Facing the Opposition

The calls and letters I received from some gun activists were often unpleasant, but at least they were at a distance. My face-to-face encounters with gun activists were often more unnerving and threatening. Most of the encounters involved gun activists who weren't interested in courteous debates and formality. Many didn't feel bound by the normal protocol of respectful human interaction. These activists were like some talk show enthusiasts—more interested in irately expressing their anger and their distaste for anyone who disagreed with them than in engaging in civil discourse. They liked to carry signs, shout pronouncements through bullhorns, and taunt their opponents. Etiquette and restraint were words not normally found in their playbook.

FACE TO FACE

One of my first encounters was in March 2000. Gun-control hero Jim Brady was in Denver for a SAFE Colorado fundraising event at the Grand Hyatt Hotel. When I arrived alone that evening, there were a few dozen gun activists lining the sidewalk outside the hotel, carrying signs and bullhorns, with a few participants dressed in Revolutionary War garb. Many were members of the Rocky Mountain Gun Owners or a new group of gun extremists calling themselves the Tyranny Response Team.

They chanted slogans about not surrendering their guns and protecting the Second Amendment. I had to "run the gantlet" down the sidewalk through their ranks. It was a bit unnerving, since they recognized me. Some called out to me. I stopped and spoke to a couple of the protesters who seemed to be leaders of the group, along with others who joined them, for I was not about to let them intimidate me.

Some complained about my taking away their rights and knowing nothing about guns. Some chastised me for not being willing to debate them on gun issues. I pointed out that I recently participated in a debate about gun issues at a local college and that some gun activists were present. That was not good enough for them. They insisted that I debate them on "their territory." What that really meant was they wanted me to appear in a setting where they were the primary audience, where they could badger me without having to follow the usual rules of decorum.

After a short while I excused myself and went inside to the event, where there was a buzz among the attendees about the extremists outside and the comments and behavior they observed as they entered the hotel. When I left the event, I was concerned the protesters might still be there and that I might be targeted for harassment, so I requested and received an escort from a security guard to my car a couple of blocks away.

My experience that night was only the beginning. There were more events that year at which the TRT, RMGO, and other pro-gun groups showed up to protest. On Mother's Day 2000, dozens of rallies were held in cities across the country under the banner of the Million Mom March, an organization that was formed in response to Columbine to call for stronger gun laws. I spoke at the rally in Denver, which was held in Civic Center Park. Linda went with me. As expected, the TRT was there with its legions to protest our event. I hoped that since this was a large park with numerous entry points we would be able to enter without being noticed.

We were not so lucky. A couple of TRT members spotted me entering the park and approached us. They taunted me for "trying to take away their God-given gun rights" and for not debating them. Linda had already heard me describe my experiences with them, but this was the first time she encountered it personally. She was shocked at their brazenness. I felt awful that she had to endure it, but there was little I could do. She accepted the challenge, agreeing we could not cower to them. But unlike the encounter I had at the Grand Hyatt Hotel, I didn't bother engaging them in conversation.

One thing that struck me that day and at subsequent events was the fact the local media didn't seem to report the foul-mouthed language and bad behavior of these extremists. I speculated the media didn't want to report such unpleasantness on the air and didn't want to stir up these activists and face possible retribution.

INTIMIDATION

Another incident took place in summer 2000 after a debate on Amendment 22 with Bob Glass, the outspoken leader of the Tyranny Response Team and owner of a gun shop.

After the event, I left Denver's public access TV station with Cynthia Stone, SAFE Colorado's director of communications. After we separated and walked to our own vehicles, I noticed that Glass was not far behind us. As I began to pull out of the parking lot, I saw he was the passenger in a pickup truck. The truck stopped shortly after it had pulled out of its parking space, blocking the lane of traffic. Glass got out and walked toward the front of Cynthia's car. He started to argue with Cynthia as she approached her car. At one point, after Cynthia entered her car, Glass leaned onto the hood of her car and started yelling at her and slapping his hands on the hood. Cynthia was stuck there, since a car was parked behind her and the pickup truck was in front of her. A short while later Glass got into the truck and left.

All this time I was frozen in place, sitting in my car wondering what the hell was going on and what I should do. I told myself to get out to defend Cynthia and confront Glass, yet I feared I was being set up for a fight, which was something typical of TRT tactics. I also told myself that perhaps the situation wasn't that serious, that Glass was joking around, yet I knew better. I just wasn't sure what the hell to do.

I felt some comfort when I noticed Fred Holden, a conservative activist, walk into the parking lot as this was going on. He had been in the studio with us. I thought his presence might defuse the situation. Glass surely wouldn't do anything foolish in front of Fred. Holden stopped short of the confrontation and got into his car, but he couldn't get out of the parking lot because the pickup was blocking him. He yelled at the pickup driver to move. At about that time, Glass returned to the truck and left the scene.

A few days later I contacted Holden and asked what he witnessed in the parking lot. He recalled being blocked, but said he did not see Glass harassing anyone. Without Holden's corroboration, it wasn't worth trying to have Glass charged with harassment. Besides, we wanted to keep our "eyes on the prize"—passing Amendment 22—and not let ourselves be distracted by a side show.

A CHURCHLY CONFLICT

One particularly unnerving confrontation occurred in August 2000 as we were campaigning for Amendment 22. Cynthia Stone and I traveled north to Fort Collins to speak at a meeting of the local Million Mom March. The meeting was held at the Plymouth Congregational Church. I was asked to speak to group members after they finished their business meeting.

When we arrived, we saw a contingent of about twenty or so Tyranny Response Team members. As usual, they were carrying signs; some were dressed in Revolutionary War garb and others were wearing black TRT t-shirts. It seemed unusual because they were there on the church grounds, which was private property, not out on the public sidewalk. As on other occasions, we were taunted as we walked past them into the church hall.

We went to a small room in the church to prepare our materials, waiting until the Moms finished their business meeting. As we walked down a hallway toward the meeting room to join the Moms, we saw the church minister speaking with a police officer and some TRT members. I wondered what that was all about and why the TRT members were inside the church building. Why would the minister allow these troublemakers in?

Why would the police let them in? After all, this was the Million Moms meeting, not a city council meeting.

As I began my presentation, about fifteen TRT members filed into the room. I was shocked by their entry but was not about to stop speaking and give them any attention. Most of them stood in the back of the room, often speaking to each other and glaring at the seated crowd. If the police hadn't been there, it probably would have been worse.

As I spoke, they mumbled and made gestures, acting like a gathering of junior high students. When it came time to take questions from the audience, they raised their hands. I decided I wouldn't ignore them; they'd probably become even more rowdy if I did. I wasn't going to be intimidated by them, so I looked right at them as I fielded their loaded questions. "Why are you trying to take away my God-given rights?" "Why won't you let me protect myself?"

Near the end of my presentation some TRT members began getting more rowdy and restless. One TRT member was snapping photos. Another was videotaping the meeting and the crowd. At one point one of the women told the man standing immediately behind her with the video camera to stop taping. She put her clipboard in front of the camera. The man holding the video camera, George Keifer, claimed the 5-foot 1-inch, 105-pound woman pushed the clipboard into his camera, knocking it into his eye and "causing a minor facial injury." Keifer cried out, claiming he had been assaulted, insisting he would press charges and that "the Moms" were lying when they claimed to be peace loving.

A similar incident occurred a number of weeks prior to that in Boulder, where a gun-control advocate pushed back hard against a TRT member who was blasting his bullhorn into the man's face. In that case, the TRT pressed charges and again claimed their opponents were the aggressors. It was all just part of the TRT's theatrics and intimidation.

At the end of the Moms meeting, one of the TRT members sarcastically told me, "Mr. Mauser, I appreciate your getting $72,000 a year on the corpse of your son." Rather than taking his bait by getting angry, I instead turned to a local newspaper reporter who was standing there and told him that the protesters' presence and behavior only served to make me more passionate about my cause.

After the event we were informed that because the Moms had announced the meeting in the newspaper, the police were pressed by the TRT to rule it was a "public event" and that the TRT could enter the meeting. A policeman apparently told the TRT members he preferred that they leave, but they chose to do otherwise. A day or two later, though, the police reversed their ruling, acknowledging that the TRT could have been asked to leave that night. But by then it was too late to undo what happened.

UNWANTED!

TRT members apparently never got over the passage of Amendment 22 in 2000. In fall 2001, they decided to take it out on me. Their Web site included a notice with a photo of me in the center, similar to an FBI "wanted" poster seeking the capture of criminals and placed in post offices. The poster announced that I was "Wanted for: Crimes against civil liberties." It announced "secondary charges" for "conspiring with fanatical Nazi style groups" and "for fraudulent profiting from the death of his son."

The poster went on to describe me as someone who gets "violently angry," is "anti-American," and "has made thousands of dollars off of memorial scams." It advised people that "any help in this matter is strictly confidential" and that if I were seen, "contact local officials or contact us online at www.trtnational.com."

In early October, just after I spoke at a gun-control workshop, some letter-sized copies of the TRT "wanted" posters were placed on telephone poles in my immediate neighborhood. I didn't take them down. They were just trash; trash like that speaks for itself and could only hurt their cause in the eyes of reasonable people.

MARCHING TO MY HOME

The "wanted" poster incident prompted me to check the TRT Web site occasionally. There I noticed an announcement that the TRT was coming to my house on the evening of Friday, December 14, 2001, which was the eve of Bill of Rights Day. The TRT was going to demonstrate against what they considered was my attack on the Constitution.

I wasn't sure what to expect, but nothing surprised me when it came to these extremists. I felt I had an obligation to contact the police to let them know what was happening. I didn't want problems for my neighbors and I didn't want to call the police at the last moment if there were a problem. I told the police I wasn't going to incite a confrontation and had no intention of engaging these screwballs, but that I thought the police should have a heads-up in case there might be crowd control or traffic problems. The sheriff's office—the same one I had come at odds with over Columbine issues—said they would assign someone to keep an eye on things. That was about the extent of our conversation.

I didn't want the protest to be a surprise to my neighbors, so I delivered a flyer to everyone on my cul-de-sac informing them of the planned protest. "I'm sorry this is happening," I wrote, "especially at this time of year. But there is nothing I can do. There is nothing specific that led to this. Ostensibly the protest is connected with Bill of Rights Day, but I think they just want to intimidate me." I informed them I would not engage or confront the TRT, that I had asked my gun-control allies to stay away, and that I had not contacted the media about the event. These are things the TRT would have hoped for as a means of creating a circus atmosphere and shining attention on themselves. I was not about to hand them that attention.

I asked my neighbors not to confront the TRT protesters. My neighbors obliged, but with one clever twist. One neighbor came up with the brilliant idea of placing their trash cans on the sidewalk that evening so the TRT members would have to walk around them onto the street as they marched. The next day wasn't trash day—they simply saw a suitable way to convey a message to the protesters what they thought of them!

When Friday night came, I took my family out for dinner and a movie. I wasn't enthused about the appearance of "running" from the TRT and letting myself seemingly be intimidated, but on the other hand, if the TRT protesters were going to make a lot of noise, it wouldn't be much fun to be at home anyway. Besides, not being there would likely defuse the situation and frustrate them.

Before leaving home I decided to leave a little message for the TRT. I took a large, framed photo of Daniel and set it on the front lawn. I placed a desk lamp next to the photo, and shone the light on the photo of Daniel so they would be reminded of why I do what I do.

Not long after the scheduled starting time, about eight people showed up for the protest. For much of the time they apparently just stood in front of our house, holding candles. The weather was mild for December, so a few teenaged boys from the cul-de-sac hung around the driveway across the street shooting basketball. They were both curious and concerned about what might happen that evening after visiting the TRT Web site. But they felt safer after noticing a few marked police cars driving up and down the cul-de-sac prior to the protest. They were intrigued when they noticed a couple of strange and unfamiliar cars with tinted windows parked on the street, assuming them to belong to undercover cops.

When the teens went to a house to the east of us and stood outside, they were somewhat unnerved when a TRT member started taking pictures of them. This was one of TRT's ways of trying to intimidate people—by taking photos and placing the least complimentary ones on their Web site along with various rants or insults aimed at that person. Fortunately there was no contact or conflict between the teens and protesters.

The event was a flop. It was short and got virtually no attention. Perhaps the turnout was poor because some TRT members realized there was no evidence there would be a confrontation or counter-demonstration. They got no response from me nor were they getting calls from the media. They later claimed it wasn't a protest march but merely a "candlelight vigil" in front of my house to grieve "the death of the Bill of Rights at the hands of Tom Mauser." Yeah, whatever.

DEPRIVED OF RIGHT TO HARASS

More dramatic than what happened at my house was what happened before the protest. The police had observed the TRT as they gathered at a nearby strip mall before marching to my house. One of the TRT leaders, Duncan Philp, decided to drive to my street to make sure nobody had gone directly to my house rather than to the strip mall gathering point.

As he left the strip mall parking area, he was stopped by a sheriff's deputy and ticketed for minor traffic violations, including making an improper left turn, driving without a seatbelt, and driving without a valid license. (Philp had a New Mexico license and a Colorado post office box, yet claimed he lived in Wyoming.)

Philp later challenged the traffic charges in court, claiming they were invalid because his violation was on private property (the strip mall), meaning he could not be stopped by police. Prosecutors eventually dropped the charges.

Philp then sued the two Jefferson County deputy sheriffs who ticketed him, claiming he was being harassed by police simply for exercising his First Amendment rights to free speech and assembly—that is, protesting at my home. Jefferson County offered to settle with Philp rather than have the case drag on. Philp accepted their offer of $20,000.

Philp wasted no time in gloating about his victory, sending me an email the day after the settlement, on October 10, 2002, writing "... thanks for the twenty thousand Tommie, I will use it to by a brand new Barret .50 cal. See ya at the next rally Tommie. I win you lose." The Barret .50 cal is a powerful, long, large-caliber sniper rifle that uses large cartridges and was designed for the battlefield to puncture armor and destroy targets from long range. Something told me I had not heard the last of Duncan Philp.

Chapter 25

Go Directly to Jail

One threat against me went too far. On December 2, 2006, I received an email with the subject line, "Watch your ass."

I will be protesting your house real soon. I will disrupt your life and I will be armed.

Your Friend
Duncan Philp

PS. I now run the TRT and I have a militia at my disposal. So you better be afraid be very very afraid.

I hadn't received an email from gun extremist Philp for at least a year or more, and my gun-control activities weren't in the news at that time, so I wondered what suddenly motivated him to write. I was concerned because the message arrived a few days before Bill of Rights Day, the same day Philp and the TRT held their "vigil" at my house four years earlier. The TRT seemed to be inactive for some time, but with Philp saying he was now leading it, I worried he might try to do something over the top in order to get some publicity. I didn't savor the thought of another protest at my home, but I wasn't about to cower at his threat by responding immediately or by going to the police, as I assumed he wanted me to do. I waited a day or two, then sent an email response:

"I guess I'll just expect the same group of five or six people. Whatever. Congratulations on your promotion. Merry Christmas."

I hoped my dismissal of his threat and my unwillingness to take the bait would lead to indifference on his part. But I was wrong. A response came immediately.

Tommy boy

You better watch out you better not cry because the TRT is coming for you. Maybe not your house maybe your office maybe a smear campaign. You are a fucking loser and your son was a gay homo that got shot by some other gay homos in a lovers spat.

Duncan Philp

His response angered me to no end. He seriously crossed the line of civility, making a contemptible attack on Daniel and threatening to come to my workplace. Since they failed to arouse a response at my home in 2002, I was concerned the TRT might try to cause a commotion at my office. I had no choice but to tell my supervisors as well as building security officials about the possibility. I told them about the protest at my house and the taunting. I dreaded the embarrassment and distraction that could be caused by these unpredictable and misbehaving gun zealots. We agreed, though, not to inform employees about the threat.

I did tell Linda about the threat. She became concerned for my safety and for the disruption that might befall our family. When Bill of Rights Day came, we went out for the evening, just in case protesters came to the house again. This time I didn't inform my neighbors of the possibility of another protest on the block, especially since I saw nothing about a protest on the TRT Web site. Fortunately, Bill of Rights Day came and went without a protest. I was relieved and hopeful that Philp's threat had subsided.

Two weeks before Christmas, I took a day off work to do some Christmas shopping. One of my employees called my cell to alert me about a warning that had been issued at work. An email was sent by management to all headquarters employees, informing us that a Denver police officer would be posted in the main building the next two weeks as a result of a threat received in the front office.

Given the timing I naturally assumed that the warning was related to the email threat directed at me and that the TRT was following through with its emailed threat. I was livid about the impact this was having on my coworkers and worried that my activism had become a liability. But when I returned to work the next day, I spoke to our security manager and discovered he thought the threatening email was just a "general threat" against the agency by a disgruntled person, not a specific threat and probably not related to me. I was relieved, but still concerned about the strange coincidence of its timing.

I hadn't bothered responding to the second email. I saw no point in giving this cretin the pleasure of knowing I might be fearful or impacted by these e-mails. But perhaps my lack of reaction is what led to a third message, which took a decidedly more threatening turn.

I have a laser site on my 50 cal as well as a home made silencer. I have spotted planes flying into DIA [Denver International Airport]. I could easily shoot one down so do not take any trips for a while. I am not saying I would do some thing but you never know you fucking NAZI pig. You want to take away my right to own a gun because your loser son got shot. Fuck you you god damn bastard. Duncan Philp

This email went too far over the line to ignore. After all, a .50 caliber rifle is said to be capable of shooting down some airplanes. I called the Jefferson County Sheriff's Office and told them about the emails I had received. I was reluctant about doing so, for I feared Philp was purposely trying to draw them into this dispute, given his successful lawsuit against the sheriff's office after the protest at my home. On the other hand, I also feared that Philp, who seemed to be an antisocial recluse, might be "losing it." What if he really did want to cause trouble or harm? I didn't want something awful to happen to me, my family, or my coworkers, and then have it discovered after the fact that I didn't report the email threats to law enforcement.

I gave background information to sheriff's officers, including the 2002 home protest and past emails I had received from Philp. I assumed there was little they could do. I didn't go the media with the story for I worried Philp would welcome media coverage.

SURPRISE ARREST

Shortly before Christmas the sheriff's office informed me they had made an arrest. They said the case was more serious than I likely had thought, primarily because of the veiled threat to shoot down an airplane. In a post-September 11 world, such threats are taken more seriously.

Six law enforcement officers, including an agent from the FBI, approached Duncan Philp in a Wyoming parking lot—with guns drawn—and took him in for questioning.

Philp told the police another pro-gun activist, Darren Morrison, who had a long-running dispute with Philp, had been trying to discredit him in a number of ways, including bogus emails. Philp insisted that Morrison was probably the one writing to me, in order to get Philp in trouble.

In a quick and shocking turn of events, the police tracked Morrison down and interrogated him. Morrison, a 45-year-old father from Fort Collins, confessed to the crime. In January 2007 he was charged with harassment, and he quit his ten-year job as a janitor for Colorado State University.

I was in disbelief that Philp was not the culprit and regretted that I had implicated him. I reviewed my old emails and noticed the email address used by Morrison was slightly different from the one used by Philp. But given the emails' blunt and taunting language, I had little reason to question whether it was Philp that was writing.

ATTEMPTED APOLOGY

Late in January 2007 I received an e-mail apology from Darren Morrison. It began, "I am very sorry for the emails I send to you … It was very wrong and very distasteful what I had done. I did not intend to hurt you, only Duncan [Philp] but in my anger I did not think my actions through."

The long, rambling email related at length how, even though he was a fellow gun-rights activist, he had come into conflict with Duncan Philp. He claimed that Philp had been harassing him and his family for years. He maintained it started when he was asked by the TRT to bring his children to a protest of a gun-control gathering "because the TRT wanted to look like they were family friendly." Morrison complained when Philp screamed obscenities at the rally, and claimed Philp defied his complaint by pointing his bullhorn directly at Morrison's young son, allegedly causing an earache and ringing ears for a week.

Morrison admitted that after that incident he visited a TRT Internet forum and complained about Philp. Morrison claimed the dispute escalated, with Philp posting nasty messages posing as Morrison. Morrison asserted he also got crosswise with Philp because he objected to the TRT's plan to protest in front of my home, and that Philp harassed him with Internet postings when Morrison ran for a seat in the state legislature.

Wait a minute! Was he serious? Darren Morrison ran for public office? This man, who thought nothing of sending vile e-mail to a man whose son was murdered, who boasted he could shoot down an airplane, had run for a seat in the Colorado House of Representatives? A quick check on the Internet confirmed that he indeed had run for a seat on the American Constitution Party ticket, but lost.

"I know the years of abuse by Duncan do not any way excuse me for what I have done. I thought also that what I sent you would strength you cause [sic]. I am really sorry about what I have done. It make [sic] me sick to my stomach thinking about how I hurt and maybe scared you. I will have to go to court this spring and I will owe up to it and pay whatever fine and do what ever community service. I am going to cash in my retirement saving to pay the fine and then move out of the state far away from Duncan. Duncan shot his own dog for barking and waking him up so I should not have ever messed with him."

RESPONDING TO THE MENACE

I wrote back to Morrison a few weeks later. My email began, "Thanks for writing to explain yourself …. I'm not quite sure, to tell you the truth, what to make of your e-mail to me. On one hand, I am an overly trusting person, so I'd like to believe you are being truthful and remorseful. Yet…I can't help but wonder if your email was something suggested by someone (like your attorney) as a means of trying to get me not to go to the media or not to ask for a stronger penalty."

I relayed to him in painful detail a description of the many impacts that his "despicable act" had on me and my family. I mentioned, for example, that "it was a bit disturbing to have the police advising (me that I) ought to be more cautious in moving around out in the public." I told him I wondered what I had done to deserve needing to put on more outside lighting and being more watchful at nighttime.

I asked Morrison, "Why did you think this would not affect me, since even you acknowledge what a gun nut and threat Philp is? It was ridiculous if you thought there were no risks to you in doing what you did. For the life of me, I can't imagine how you thought this would come down on Philp after you and he had already had conflicts. Did you think he'd simply be arrested? What outcome did you expect?"

But after condemning his actions at length, I closed with, "Having said all that, and getting it off my chest, let me say I appreciate your statement of remorse…I appreciate that you've acknowledged the terrible and stupid mistakes you made. It is indeed something that hopefully has taught you a lesson. Like me, you and your family must move on from and return hopefully to some degree of normalcy. May you find peace."

HIS DAY IN COURT

On Friday, June 1, 2007, I was present in Jefferson County Court for Darren Morrison's hearing. A small crowd assembled outside the courtroom prior to the hearing. There in the hallway I recognized Morrison from a newspaper photo. I was sure he also recognized me, and it appeared he was thinking of approaching me.

I was conflicted. At first I was tempted to talk to him, just to see in person what he was like as a human being. I wondered what his demeanor would be as he faced the consequences of his actions. But I avoided any eye contact, deciding I simply wanted to see justice done and did not wish to encounter him before the hearing.

I'm glad I avoided him. Before the hearing began, I was approached by law enforcement officers and asked to step into a meeting room to speak with the county prosecutor, two sheriff's officers, and an FBI agent. They shared with me the disturbing news that although Morrison may have expressed remorse to me, he was posting nasty email messages to other gun activists even after he was charged in January. They also said Morrison's airplane threat was more serious than I thought. For a short while Denver International Airport was "on alert" and notification of Morrison's threat was sent to the director of the FBI. With that news, I lost any inclination to show a degree of mercy toward this misguided man.

I proceeded to the courtroom, where I waited as some other cases were dealt with. I sat alone, wondering who the others in the audience were, whether they were there for Morrison's hearing or for another. On the other side of the courtroom I spotted Duncan Philp. I was glad he was nowhere near me.

Judge Judy Archuleta announced it was time for Morrison's case. The prosecutor laid out the details of the charges against Morrison, telling the judge about the impact of the airport threat and insisting that "his actions display a lack of concern and disrespect for authority and unwillingness to control his behavior." He referred to the "childish behavior" of Morrison's disagreement with Philp and asserted he "is abusing his privilege to use the Internet" and "thinks his rights to express himself freely allow him to do whatever he wants."

I testified against Morrison, telling the judge about the impacts of Morrison's actions on me and my family, just as I had reported them to Morrison, saying he was playing with people's lives. I resisted the temptation to personally attack him and call for a maximum sentence. My words spoke for themselves, leaving Morrison's fate in the hands of the judge.

Duncan Philp asked for an opportunity to address the court, and the judge reluctantly allowed him to make a statement about the impact of Morrison's actions on him. Philp insisted he was the real victim in this case. He was bitter about his arrest and also used his time to lambaste Morrison's other attempts to defame him and to cite other inconsequential political and philosophical battles he had with Morrison.

Morrison, who was not represented by an attorney, was given an opportunity to speak to the court. He apologized to me and to his family: "What I did is inexcusable." He asked to be spared jail time, saying he already was unemployed and it would have a devastating impact on his family. For a moment I pitied this poor, pathetic man. For all his email bravado, he shrunk down to size in the courtroom.

Morrison's decision not to hire an attorney was a mistake, for I'm sure an attorney would have advised him either not to testify or to greatly limit his remarks. After apologizing, Morrison began firing comments at Philp. It was a long-winded and feeble attempt to make excuses for his despicable actions. Just as Philp had done, he described in ridiculous detail the philosophical disagreements between him and Philp, as if any of us in the courtroom cared. It was "theater of the absurd," as I told one reporter, with two grown men spatting like spoiled little children.

Judge Archuleta then pronounced sentencing for Darren Morrison, ordering Morrison immediately to jail for five days and putting him on a year's probation. He was also ordered to perform 60 hours of community service and to stay away from guns, the Internet, and my family for one year. He was handcuffed on the spot and led off to jail, looking very shocked.

I was glad to see that justice had been done. I have never heard another word from him or the TRT since that day. I can't quite say the same for Duncan Philp, who recently posted a message on my Facebook page attacking the "violence" of "gun grabbers."

Chapter 26

Daniel vs. Goliath

I was more than willing to take on any cause in honor of Daniel. I was willing to walk anywhere in his shoes, but in so doing on the gun issue I was treading into dangerous territory. The NRA was arguably the most powerful lobby in the nation. Some would even say it was a march into futility, a walk into a battle with a powerful Goliath.

MISGUIDED

Many gun activists insisted I despised guns and gun owners; therefore, I hated the NRA because it represented them. Nonsense. It's true that I have little but scorn for the NRA organization, but it's wrong to think that's because it defends guns and is made up of gun owners. It's wrong to think that I oppose everything the NRA does and stands for. And it's certainly wrong to think that I have scorn for everyone who's a member of the NRA.

I received hundreds of letters and emails telling me, in some critical or sarcastic fashion, that I was badly misguided for "blaming the NRA for what happened at Columbine" or for "blaming the NRA for the death" of

Daniel. Why must gun activists take the mere criticism of the NRA and twist it into an unwarranted allegation that I hold it directly responsible for the massacre at Columbine? Why? Because it's easier to demonize me and exaggerate my position than it is to discuss the reality of gun policy and gun violence in America.

What I have blamed the NRA for is the irresponsible promotion of weak gun laws that make it far too easy for the wrong people to get guns, the promotion of an anything-goes gun culture, the encouragement of the unlimited proliferation of all types of dangerous weapons, and for vehemently opposing gun laws that would help keep guns out of the wrong hands. If not the NRA, who *would* you hold responsible for these things?

My scorn for the NRA is not misplaced. My scorn is not based on irrational fears. It is based on my observations and experiences.

THREE EASY STEPS

The NRA is no doubt a powerful communicator. In the field of political opinion, it has largely won the coveted battle of getting one's message out. The problem is that much of the message it conveys is often exaggerated and bears little resemblance to the truth.

The NRA's tactics are simple. First, when proposals are brought forth to change or add gun laws, it inevitably tells its membership that the proposed gun law is an infringement of an individual's Second Amendment right to bear arms; they do so regardless of what the proposed law really does, regardless of whether that law might reduce gun violence, and regardless of the fact that no right in the Constitution is absolute. Second, it gets members angrier and more engaged by telling them their gun rights are about to be stolen away by gun-grabbing gun-control advocates whose ultimate goal is to confiscate their guns and deny them the right to defend themselves. Third, it repeats steps 1 and 2 over and over and over.

The NRA is one of the most powerful lobbies in America, if not the most powerful. There are a number of other organizations at the national and state level that promote gun rights, such as the Gun Owners of America, but none has anything approaching the clout of the NRA. Many of these other organizations are more extreme in their defense of the Second

Amendment, so they have a tougher time gaining as much support from Congress and the public.

The NRA benefits from appearing to be less extreme than other pro-gun groups and from having a larger membership base. But that does not mean the NRA is moderate or that it can speak for mainstream America or that it does not take extreme stands.

A CLOSER LOOK

The stated goals of the NRA are to protect the Second Amendment of the Bill of Rights, to promote firearm ownership rights, marksmanship and firearm safety, and to protect the right to hunt and to use guns for self-defense. It has played a key role in promoting competitive firearm sports. In its safety and shooting sports roles it has done a commendable job. There is a need for such an organization, and it is appropriate that hunters, sportsmen, and gun owners have a voice for their interests.

I believe, however, that the NRA has overreached its purpose and has disproportionately shifted its efforts to its political and lobbying objectives, morphing into a hard-edged, aggressive, right-wing political organization that has moved farther from mainstream America and has alienated some of its base membership.

The NRA says it has four million members, including hunters, sportsmen, target shooters, antique gun collectors, policemen, and others. But many did not join the NRA with the intent of supporting its political agenda. Some joined when they registered for a training class or because membership was necessary for participating in a competitive shooting sport. Many are not fanatical gun activists or the type of people who have written mean-spirited letters to me. In fact, some have written to me indicating they are ashamed of the actions of the NRA.

This is "not your father's NRA," to put a twist on a phrase popularized in advertising. A description I heard a number of years ago sums it up well: The NRA has developed a *Field and Stream* membership but a *Soldier of Fortune* leadership. For those unfamiliar with these two references, *Field and Stream* is a respected, mainstream hunting and fishing magazine. *Soldier of Fortune* is a right-wing, testosterone-laden magazine for those who like to read about mercenaries, weaponry and conflicts around the globe.

How did the NRA become such a powerhouse? I think much of its success resulted from its aggressive response to the declining number of hunters in America. This decline was not based on some sinister conspiracy by liberals or animal-rights activists or people who hate hunting. It was mostly tied to the increasing (and I would argue unfortunate) urbanization of our nation. That urbanization resulted in less land being available for hunting and shooting ranges, longer treks to reach hunting grounds, and decreasing interest in traditional pursuits on the part of young people, who became more interested in sedentary distractions like video games. Consequently, the gun industry needed to find new customers for its wares, and the NRA was poised to help the industry find them.

Our ever-increasing urbanization also led to increasing tension among urban dwellers, which in turn led to an increase in crime. As people became more fearful of that crime, they felt the need to arm themselves. Unable to sell as many hunting firearms, the gun industry responded to an increased demand by producing smaller and cheaper handguns, as well as military-type assault weapons seen in the media, to attract a wider customer base.

At the same time, given America's weak gun laws, cheap handguns easily got into the hands of thugs and gang members, making it easier for them to tool themselves as criminals. Firearms also easily got into the hands of people who weren't necessarily the criminal element, but who quickly found themselves leaning that way with the newfound power inherent in firearms. That led to a greater increase in crime, which in turn led to an escalating increase in firearm purchases by a fearful public—the proverbial vicious circle.

As shootings became more commonplace, particularly in some high-profile cases, lawmakers at the national, state, and local levels naturally called for stronger gun-control laws. Those calls for restrictions were not good for a gun industry that was losing its hunting rifle sales yet seeing increased sales of cheap handguns and high-powered military style firearms. That created a terrific opportunity for the NRA to come to the rescue.

The NRA riled up its membership base with its talk of gun rights and confiscation. It recruited new members, particularly people who felt compelled to buy a gun for protection but who were told their right to protect themselves was being taken away, and people from the right wing who vehemently opposed any limitation on rights and liberties. The NRA has been successful in boosting its membership every time major gun-control proposals have been introduced, including the ones following the Columbine massacre, fueled by its alarmism and name-calling. These tactics helped build a huge campaign war chest and power.

A NO NONSENSE LOBBY

The NRA became effective at rallying its membership, calling upon them to put pressure on their elected representatives to oppose any and all gun-control measures. The NRA used direct mail and email, its state chapters, and "phone trees" to bombard elected officials with calls and letters. It urged its members to vote only for candidates who received a high grade on the NRA's voting scorecard.

"What's wrong with that?" some have asked me. "Isn't that the American way? Aren't they just using the American system to protect their interests and promote their beliefs?" If it's carried out in a truthful and courteous way, it would be. But what makes the NRA stand out is the way it goes about doing its work—by stirring up fear, demonizing its opponents, and relentlessly badgering elected representatives.

The NRA relies on macho, military-style discipline and peer pressure, calling on its members to toe the line and not compromise. It appoints hard-edged members to its board of directors, such as controversial rocker Ted Nugent. Some of its most active and vocal members are more prone to expressing their distaste for gun control in strong and belligerent language—not unlike many angry, conservative talk radio listeners. The NRA usually sends in well-paid, polished lobbyists to rub elbows with legislators, but it relies upon its members' no-nonsense, in-your-face behavior, which is not bound by the normal diplomacy found in legislative environments, to get its way.

RENEGADE INDUSTRIES

The NRA is in some respects similar to the tobacco lobby of years ago, before it eventually imploded with the truth about tobacco's health impact. It was tough for the tobacco lobby to win over the general public by proclaiming the virtuousness of tobacco and tobacco farming subsidies, so the tobacco lobby instead "played hard ball" with members of Congress, making hefty campaign contributions, urging smokers to demand their right to smoke wherever they pleased, and lying about the health effects of smoking.

Similarly, the NRA can find it hard to win the sympathy of many Americans when there are so many stories of deadly shootings in the United States and questions about its unwillingness to compromise on gun issues. The NRA can't rely much on public relations efforts, finding it harder to count on outdated and senseless clichés to win support from an increasingly educated population outside its base. Instead it relies on firing up its membership, legislative badgering, and hefty campaign contributions to get its message across. The NRA fights any suggestion that gun violence is a societal healthcare issue, instead insisting that gun violence results from the poor personal decisions of individuals. Its emphasis is on rights, not on lost lives.

The NRA's strategy has served it well, although its influence and image are slipping, especially among younger people, women, and professionals.

The NRA is a very unforgiving lobby. It's not enough for elected officials to vote with the NRA *some* of the time. The NRA expects them to toe the line *all* the time. Both political parties fear the NRA because of its strong-armed tactics. Few dare to upset the godfather of all lobbying groups—unless they're in a very secure seat at election time.

This lobbying giant has become a Republican political action committee. Because the unimpeded exercise of liberties is the mantra of conservative Republicans, who dominate their party these days, it's a natural marriage. There are also Democratic politicians who are supportive of the NRA, but often it's a matter of survival. In the South, in parts of the country where there are lots of hunters, and in "swing" districts where politicians are sensitive to power lobbying, these Democrats don't want to have the NRA attacking them, so they find it far easier to give in. Unfortunately, gun-control advocates haven't garnered enough strength to fight back.

There's another overlooked factor behind why so many Democrats fear the NRA. The Democratic Party has traditionally been the favored party of union members and blue-collar workers. Gun policy became a cross-cutting issue. Although many blue-collar workers oppose the pro-business, pro-wealth, anti-union stance of Republicans, some are sportsmen and tend to be pro gun, especially if someone riles them up with macho talk attacking "gun grabbin' liberals." If the NRA is able to convince just a few of them that Democrats were trying to take away their gun rights and their guns, it could help sway the election of a Republican in a district with a close party registration split.

THE NRA BLACKLIST

Evidence of how desperate the NRA is to maintain its stronghold on elected officials and how determined it is to punish those who dare oppose them was evident in a discovery a few years ago that the NRA published a long list of people and organizations it believed were "anti-gun." It was essentially their "blacklist."

Their list was representative of the arrogance, isolation and unforgiving nature of the NRA. Organizations on the blacklist read like a who's who of mainstream America: they included the National Association for the Advancement of Colored People, YWCA, National Education Association, AARP, American Medical Association, League of Women Voters, and the St. Louis Cardinals.

The list of "anti-gun" religious groups was certainly ecumenical, ranging from the U.S. Catholic Conference to B'nai B'rith to the United Methodist Church. Also on the list were newspapers and magazines, as well as personalities such as Oprah Winfrey, Bruce Springsteen, Matt Damon, Walter Cronkite, Shania Twain, Britney Spears, Sean Connery, and Julia Roberts—to name just a few.

They all made the mistake of doing something that upset the NRA— such as supporting a gun-control campaign or speaking out for gun-control laws. The NRA is not one to forgive. They'd rather retaliate. The NRA's top executive, Wayne LaPierre, tried to justify the NRA's attack on those on its "anti-gun" list on NBC's The Today Show, saying, "Our members don't want to buy their songs, don't want to go to their movies, and don't want to support their careers. They cherish the Second Amendment that much." Perhaps they do, but I believe that gun-control activists and mainstream Americans cherish their loved ones far more than the NRA's members cherish the Second Amendment. The organizations on the NRA's list are simply concerned about America's epidemic of gun violence.

THE NRA'S SPY

An even more outrageous example of the gall and paranoia of the NRA was revealed in a *Mother Jones* magazine expose in 2008. Their story revealed that a woman known by many as Mary McFate, who worked within the gun-control movement, was actually a paid spy working for the NRA.

For more than ten years, McFate worked for a variety of state and national gun-control groups. She volunteered her time to serve on boards and coordinate activities. All the while, though, Mother Jones alleged McFate was paid to snoop for the NRA by a Maryland security firm, just as she had done a few years earlier by infiltrating an animal-rights group.

Mary was living two lives. She used her maiden name in her spying work, but she lived a separate life in Sarasota, Florida, as a patriotic member of the Daughters of the American Revolution under her married name, Mary Lou Sapone. She didn't just spy, she befriended many leaders in the gun-control movement. Many of those leaders are people like me who have lost loved ones to gun violence. She betrayed our trust. All this despicable woman cared about was getting information on the gun-control movement's activities that would benefit the NRA.

I recall meeting Mary on a few occasions, although I didn't get involved in any projects or lengthy conversations with her. But Ted Pascoe, who coordinated the protest against the NRA convention ten days after Columbine, remembers Mary. Just a few days after the tragedy at Columbine, McFate showed up at Ted's office and volunteered to help with the protest. She was in Ted's one-room office every day for the week prior to the protest and was privy to all the planning discussions. She could afford to fly to Denver, of course, if she was being bankrolled by the NRA.

There are spies in the corporate world, but this is not the corporate world. This is the nonprofit world, the world of helping, the world of competing ideas. It should not be a world of cutthroat tactics and devious behavior. It should not be a world where one betrays people in grief.

The problem is that we in the gun-control movement are trusting people. We're not devious or paranoid. We're in the movement because we want to save lives, to make our nation safer for our kids and our families and our neighbors. When someone shows up and says they feel our pain and want to help us, we take them at their word. We don't expect that they are contemptible liars paid to spy on us. But that's exactly what Mary was.

Mary's spying was revealed during depositions given during an unrelated 2003 lawsuit by members of the security firm with which she was associated. After the Mother Jones story broke, Mary McFate suddenly dropped out of all her gun-control activities and slithered back to her home in Florida. Mary and the NRA could have simply denied the allegations but instead have refused to comment.

FROM HIS COLD, DEAD HANDS

There was no more visible advocate for the NRA than actor Charlton Heston, who served as the NRA's president for six years. For many NRA members, and many in the public, he will be forever remembered for one particular image.

It was an image of Charlton Heston, at various NRA meetings, holding up an antique 1874 rifle, boldly declaring, in a deep, angry voice, "From my cold, dead hands!" He didn't need to complete the statement; his supporters could easily fill in the rest. Heston was essentially saying, "To take this gun and my Second Amendment rights away from me, you'd have to kill me and pry the gun from my hands."

To me this act represented a pathetic and ironic statement about the gun rights movement. In reality, Heston could have kept his antique rifle because America didn't have any desire to take it from him. The gun he used to make his audacious display was a gun that at least provided a fighting chance to one's opponent or potential victim. It could not be concealed in one's waistband. It didn't house a magazine holding thirty bullets. It couldn't be fired semi-automatically. It couldn't reliably hit targets long distances away. It couldn't easily pierce metal. It didn't fire bullets specially designed to do maximum harm upon entering human flesh.

What Heston didn't seem to understand was that what brought so much pain to so many Americans was not that antique rifle he so proudly displayed to his legions. He could have kept that rifle until the day he died in 2008, and he could have taken it to his grave with him. We couldn't have cared less about it.

America's problem is not Heston's antique gun; it's the cheap handgun, the assault weapon, the exceptionally lethal bullets and the weak gun laws. They're the things the NRA has come to be known for defending without hesitation.

Heston should have shown his defiance more honestly and realistically. He should have stood there with an AK-47 assault rifle in his hand, equipped with a flash suppressor, pistol grip and a thirty-bullet magazine. Completing the picture would be Wayne LaPierre, NRA's executive vice president, standing next to him with a cheap handgun tucked away in his pants, holding a copy of the Brady Law in one hand and a lighter in the other. Heston would call out, "From my cold, dead hands," while LaPierre would flick the lighter and set fire to the copy of the Brady Law, calling out defiantly, "And here's what America can do with its background checks and other gun laws!"

Now *that* would have more accurately reflected the NRA's beliefs than the ridiculous theatrical use of the benign, antique rifle. It was no accident that Heston held up an old relic. There was a reason why Heston did not hold up a cheap handgun or assault weapon: it would have marginalized him and shown the real NRA to America. It would have turned more Americans away from the NRA.

Chapter 27

In the Belly of the Beast

Protesting the NRA convention in Denver was not enough. For me, dialogue must accompany protest. I wanted dialogue with those who supported easy access to guns, because I had many questions for them. I knew my questions were on the minds of many Americans. And who better to ask than Charlton Heston, the NRA president? After all, he had such a righteous image, having portrayed Moses in Hollywood's *The Ten Commandments*. Surely this admired man would be willing to answer the questions of an innocent victim of gun violence.

A LETTER UNANSWERED

And so it was that on May 11, 1999, less than a month after Columbine, I wrote a letter to Heston (the letter can be found at www.danielmauser.com/HestonLetter.html). In it I asked what practical purpose there was to assault weapons like the TEC DC 9 handgun used at Columbine and questioned him as to why the NRA opposes attempts to outlaw this and other similar types of assault weapons. Given Heston's Biblical roles, I asked if he believed that if Jesus were on earth physically that He would care at all about the "right" to own a gun.

I genuinely thought I would get a response from the NRA on behalf of Heston. I assumed the reply would say little of substance and would ignore my probing questions, but I thought, perhaps naively, officials would at least respond to offer condolences and to deflect the bad publicity directed their way as a result of Columbine. I was wrong.

Late that summer and into fall 1999 I made three calls to NRA headquarters, indicated who I was, and asked whether I would be receiving a response to my letter. Twice I spoke with a man who identified himself as Jim Keplinger. All three times I was told Heston was busy but that I would get a response. I received nothing.

In March 2000 I had the peculiar opportunity to meet the NRA's chief executive on common ground. Jim Brady, Wayne LaPierre—the NRA's executive vice president—and I attended an event in Denver in which we voiced mutual support for a program that targets criminals possessing guns. LaPierre looked uncomfortable as we stood together after we were introduced backstage, and he said little. I casually handed him an envelope that contained my letter to Heston and a personal note to LaPierre that politely requested a response to my original letter. He put it in the pocket of his suit jacket. He never responded to the request.

In fall 2000 I called NRA headquarters and again complained about getting no response to my letter. A few weeks later I got a call from a woman named Suzie, who said she had been asked to provide me a response. She asked me to fax her a copy of my original letter to Heston. I did so, optimistically thinking I finally was going to hear from them. But again, no response.

The NRA did not even send a simple note acknowledging receipt of my letter. It was as if I didn't exist. I concluded that because I dared to speak out against the mighty and unforgiving NRA I had become *persona non grata*.

TAKING IT TO THE NRA

On June 13, 2001, I attended a meeting of local gun-control activists in Washington, D.C., where I made a luncheon address. I decided that while there I would also make a trip to NRA headquarters to seek an answer to my letter. I announced my intentions at the luncheon, and along with the Brady Campaign issued a press release. A number of participants asked if they could go with me, but I didn't want to distract them from their training sessions and didn't expect them to get caught up in my dispute with the NRA.

Later that afternoon I showed up at NRA headquarters in the suburban community of Fairfax, Virginia. I had with me a copy of my letter to Heston and a sign with Daniel's picture on it. It was a replica of the sign I carried at the NRA protest in 1999. On one side were the words, "My son Daniel died at Columbine. He would expect me to be here today." On the other it read, "Why won't Heston respond to me?"

After arriving at the dark, monolithic structure that housed the NRA, I entered the secured lobby. I couldn't help but notice the words posted in sizeable letters on the wall of the large lobby: "...the right of the people to keep and bear arms shall not be infringed." They're those poignant words from the Second Amendment, but there were those pesky ellipses. There's a good reason for their being there. The NRA, like so many of its minions, doesn't like to acknowledge the opening words of the Second Amendment before the ellipses: "A well regulated militia, being necessary to the security of a free State..."

I thought of how the omitted words were a colossal representation of the schism that exists between many Americans and the NRA. Gun activists didn't like to acknowledge those opening two phrases, probably because they preferred to avoid discussion of our forefathers' inclusion of the words "well regulated" and "for the security of a free State."

I spoke briefly to the security guard in the lobby, handing him a copy of my letter to Heston and a written statement explaining why I was there and why I was requesting a response from the NRA. I asked him to pass it on to the appropriate people, adding that I would be marching outside carrying my sign and awaiting a response.

First I marched along the public sidewalk, where it's legal to do so. I paced back and forth dozens of times. As I marched, one heckler in a car drove up and screamed, "Your son should have had a gun, you stupid motherfucker." A newspaper reporter witnessed it and shook his head in disgust. A few other passersby flipped me the middle finger, while some gave me a "thumbs up."

After about 45 minutes of marching, I discovered that some of the reporters there with me were tired of waiting and contacted the NRA public affairs offices by phone and asked if anyone was going to speak with me. Officials told the reporters they would not do so.

I was furious they were willing to talk to reporters but not to me. Since it was nearing the end of the working day, I decided to demonstrate my anger with a stronger statement: I moved my march from the public sidewalk onto the driveway area, which was private property. For a while I paced back and forth down a driveway traversing under the building, past the entrances to the NRA's offices and a firearms museum.

As I grew weary from the hot, humid weather, and was discouraged that I had failed to stir the beast, I sat down in the driveway in the front of the building, still holding the sign. It made for a terrific and symbolic photograph in newspapers—a father holding a sign with his son's photo, in front of the dark, massive building housing the most powerful lobby in Washington. A father peacefully seeking answers but being ignored.

At one point the NRA sent a man to photograph me. They wouldn't send someone to talk to me, but they saw fit to send someone to photograph me so they would have evidence of my terrible crime. There wasn't much to photograph other than my presence, for I was peaceful and respectful during my picketing.

The Fairfax County police were called by the NRA. The police were pleasant, trying to find a resolution and telling me I could be arrested for trespassing. I said I simply wanted a response to my letter after waiting two years. I told them I realized I might be arrested, but that I had certainly had worse things happen to me.

At about 4:30 an NRA security guard indicated to the police, but not directly to me, that the NRA wanted me off its property. When I refused to leave, I was handcuffed and arrested for misdemeanor trespassing. I was placed in the backseat of a patrol car that must have been well over a hundred humid degrees, cut off from the air conditioning by a plexiglass barrier that separates the police from their backseat passengers. I discovered how awkward it was to sit in the backseat of a car with your hands handcuffed behind your back.

After arriving at the police station, I spent about an hour in a holding cell with more than a dozen unsavory-looking men. I was released after a $250 bond was posted by a friend. I was told I would have to return August 22 to face charges. I was uncertain what the penalty might be when I decided to protest, but I didn't care. I was determined to march.

That summer I hired a Fairfax attorney. She suggested we examine the ways we could respond to the charges, but I told her I was willing to pay the price for what I did, because I realized that my act of civil disobedience came at a cost to the local police who had to deal with me. I only wanted an attorney to ensure my interests were protected and to seek a minimum sentence. I was willing to face my fate in court, but I also wanted to have the NRA face me in court, since they wouldn't acknowledge me in any other way.

I flew back to Virginia in August for the hearing. When my case came before the court, the prosecutor informed my attorney that the arresting police officer had resigned and that summonses had not been issued, so there were no witnesses in the courtroom. The judge dismissed the case. I was disappointed. I had spent a lot of money for the ordeal and did not get the desired face-to-face encounter with the NRA.

After the hearing, since I had plenty of time before my return flight, I went to NRA headquarters and marched for an hour, using the same sign as before, which friends at the Brady Campaign had been storing for me. This time I only marched on the public sidewalk, not on NRA property. But I hoped I kept the NRA guessing.

Not long after I arrived, a man pulled into the NRA parking lot and screamed at me, calling me a "crybaby." Once again, the NRA sent someone out to photograph me. After the photographer surprisingly spoke to me and acknowledged he was with the NRA, I asked him if he knew what it was like to lose a child to a gunshot. He didn't respond. I asked him if I could tell him about my son Daniel. He gave no response and walked away. That was no surprise; the NRA apparently doesn't like to hear stories about gun violence victims.

IN THE BELLY AGAIN

I saw no reason to give up on seeking a response from the NRA, so I returned to NRA headquarters on April 5, 2005, this time wearing

Daniel's Vans shoes. I was in Washington, D.C., to participate in a press conference at the Capitol sponsored by U.S. Senators supporting renewal of the assault weapons ban.

After speaking at the press conference, I mentioned to the media that I would be going to NRA headquarters to march in protest. When I did so, I might have been tipping off the NRA to the protest. The NRA had set up a radio network of sorts to promote itself and had associates with press credentials. I assumed the NRA had a reporter at the press conference because when I arrived at their headquarters a short while later, they seemed to be waiting for me. As I approached the building, I noticed a number of people milling around the outside of the building, watching me and a TV news team that had accompanied me.

I approached the front door of the Darth Vader–like building. In one hand was my sign and in the other was a copy of my 1999 letter to Heston, along with a note requesting a response to the letter. Standing at the front door was a young man in a suit who said not a word when I greeted him. His last name was Welby. When I tried to open the front door, I discovered it was locked. Apparently they were so afraid of me that they decided to lock the doors of the NRA national headquarters building. That must have been one hell of a dangerous letter they thought I was carrying. What power I suddenly had; they feared me so much they felt the need to lock their doors!

I asked Mr. Welby why the doors were locked. He just mumbled something completely unintelligible. I told him why I was there. The young man cluelessly shrugged his shoulders. I felt sorry for him, being asked to deal with this situation and not knowing how to react or how to even speak coherently.

Fittingly, a moment later, as we stood there awkwardly at an impasse, a deliveryman came to the front door. He expressed dismay at the fact that the front door was locked, preventing him from making a delivery. He asked what was going on, and Mr. Welby just stood there, looking confounded. I told the deliveryman I couldn't get in either and that it seemed they didn't want to help us.

Rather than paralyze the helpless young security guard any longer, I picked up my sign, and began to march, allowing him to deal with the

Tom asks NRA security guard why the doors are locked.

Tom, wearing Daniel's shoes, being arrested at NRA headquarters.

baffled deliveryman. But before I walked away I placed my letter in the crack between the two front doors. It made for a great photo opportunity, with my letter suspended in the crack between the two doors that were locked to keep the dangerous Columbine dad from entering the hallways of probably the most powerful lobby in Washington, D.C.

This time I decided I wasn't going to bother walking legally on the public sidewalk, knowing I'd only be ignored. I had come to stir the beast, so I marched right in their driveway, on private property. Again they called the Fairfax County police and told them I was trespassing. Again I was advised by the police that I was on private property and that I could legally march on the public sidewalk. Once again I told police I was aware of that and explained why I was there. And once again I was arrested for trespassing.

The officer took the sign from me, handcuffed me, and took me to police headquarters for booking. On this occasion I didn't have to make bail. I faced a magistrate who was on duty at the courthouse. I told him who I was and why I was protesting at the NRA. He asked questions and seemed sympathetic. He released me on personal recognizance and told me I had to return a few months later to face charges.

FACING THE NRA IN COURT

On August 22, 2005, I returned for a hearing on the charges. I was in Fairfax County General District Court before Judge Stewart Davis to face a misdemeanor charge of violating Va. Code § 18.2-119, "Trespass after having been forbidden to do so."

This time I had a different legal team, one that agreed to use a legal strategy designed to both challenge the charge against me and pressure the NRA to respond to me in some fashion. Not long after I arrived in the courtroom, I noticed the arresting officer was there, and I also saw Gordon Russell, the older NRA security guard who asked the police to arrest me in both cases. He was there with one or two well-dressed men who I assumed to be NRA attorneys or staff members. This clearly was going to be a different experience than my first trip to court.

Early in the proceedings my attorney and I spoke with the district attorney's office. This certainly wasn't a major crime that one would expect to see go to trial. In fact, the courts are accustomed to resolving many such minor cases with a plea bargain deal. They offered me a plea bargain, but frankly, I don't recall the terms of the offer.

Their plea deal didn't really appeal to me. Knowing the NRA was there in the courtroom, I was determined to go ahead with a hearing on the charges. I knew there was a bit of a risk, since the courts aren't fond of proceeding with a hearing on a minor charge. Unless you're clearly innocent, you're usually better off with a plea bargain, for the court prefers to more quickly dispense with cases with plea bargains. I was willing to risk a harsher sentence. The NRA wouldn't acknowledge me, so I felt it was time to force them to at least face me in court and try to get an answer from them as to why they would rather have me arrested than speak to me.

The prosecution introduced two witnesses: Gordon Russell and the arresting police officer. Things got off to a difficult, emotional start for me. Mr. Russell startled me by referring to me as "Daniel Mauser." It was an error that shook me, even more than in everyday instances when someone mistakenly refers to me as Daniel, because I was so emotionally stressed. My initial, gut reaction was to demand that my attorney scream "Objection, Your Honor, the defendant is being badgered!" so that he could correct them. Being called "Daniel" triggered a raw emotion, for it reminded me of the grief associated with losing Daniel.

Moments later, though, I had another reaction: It was satisfyingly ironic that an NRA employee would mention Daniel's name, given that they usually don't like acknowledging gun violence victims.

Mr. Russell acknowledged in his testimony that the NRA had locked the doors when I arrived on the property, and that Mr. Welby did not speak to me, but he wasn't required to explain the reason for either. When asked what I said about my purpose for being there on that day, Russell testified I was "trying to deliver a letter of some sort to our administrators."

Well, I thought, *if they admit that's all I was doing, why in the hell did they need to lock the doors? What kind of threat was I to them? And why couldn't they speak to me as a fellow human being and tell me why they hadn't ever answered my letter?* I daydreamed for a moment, fantasizing how I would have asked them those questions if I were allowed to cross-examine them.

My attorney challenged the trespassing charge on the grounds that neither Russell nor the police officer performed a title search on the property to acknowledge ownership. The judge rejected that argument.

I agreed to testify. I didn't care about the risks of self-incrimination, I wanted to tell my side of the story. In testimony I did not deny carrying a sign and marching on the property, but I did insist I did not recall the NRA representatives ever directly asking me to leave. That's because they simply didn't want to acknowledge or speak to me. I testified about how, on three different occasions, I was told by the NRA that I would get a response to my letter to Mr. Heston but never had.

In his closing argument, my attorney pointed out the ruling in a Virginia case that indicated that a trespass has to be willful, and that if a person goes onto property with a good faith belief he could be on the property, that willfulness element is not satisfied. He asserted that I had a good faith belief I could be on the property, and that if there was something willful and criminal about being on the property, other people who were there with me, like an employee of the Brady Campaign, would have been arrested that day also. Other people there with me in the parking lot were *not* arrested, only me. He emphasized that the NRA had told me in the past that they would respond to me, so I had come to the property because I took them at their word.

In the end, the judge didn't accept our arguments. He just went with the basic facts of the case—I was picketing, I was trespassing, I was asked to leave, and I refused. He didn't address why others who were there with me were not asked to leave or arrested.

PUNISHMENT

Then came sentencing. The judge asked the prosecutor what he sought by way of punishment. The prosecutor said any punishment was up to the court's discretion—a good sign he wasn't seeking something harsh.

The prosecutor also pointed out that representatives of the NRA in the courtroom wanted to make it known they were concerned that my trespass could have resulted in violence if I had stayed on the property. I was appalled! They feared violence? Violence by whom? Violence against whom? What did they know about me that led them to conclude that I could be violent? I have never committed an act of violence nor had I ever threatened any violence against the NRA. How could they make such an outrageous allegation?

I think what they *really* feared was that a gun activist might have committed an act of violence against *me*. That would have been messy and embarrassing for them.

My attorney told the judge I didn't intend to commit a crime and didn't want a criminal record; I just wanted a response to my letter.

The judge didn't address the NRA's concern. He looked at me and said he couldn't imagine what I'd been through, and that he was overwhelmed by the Columbine tragedy. He said he didn't want to give me a criminal record, but that I had to obey the law. He advised me not to get involved with people who believe in the right to bear arms because it was not going to bring my son back and that I was not going to change the minds of my opponents.

He "continued" the case until August 22 of the following year, with the charges to be dismissed if I obeyed the law and didn't trespass again. I stayed out of trouble and the charges were dismissed a year later.

BEYOND HESTON

After Charlton Heston left the NRA presidency my letter was out of date. So I reworked it, addressing it to two subsequent presidents of the NRA, Kayne Robinson and Sandra Froman, during their terms as president. I asked the same basic questions of them that I had asked Heston, adding that I was disappointed the NRA had lied on numerous occasions about responding to me.

I never received an acknowledgment from them either, so I developed a new strategy. In April 2006, I sent a letter to my two U.S. Senators, Democrat Ken Salazar and Republican Wayne Allard, as well as to my House Representative, über conservative Republican Tom Tancredo.

I told them about my quest to get a response from the NRA, and attached the recent letter I had sent to NRA President Froman. I expressed frustration at waiting seven years for a response. "After you read the attached letter," I wrote, "please tell me whether you think I am being unreasonable and whether you think the NRA is justified in being so dismissive towards me. Please tell me if you think the NRA was right to have me arrested when I protested on their property rather than simply respond to me. Please tell me if you think the NRA has shown common courtesy, human decency, and compassion towards a father whose son was murdered....

"Then, if you think the NRA has been unfair or insensitive towards me, I am requesting that you write to them and request that they respond to me. I'm not asking you to demand a response from them, but given that two of you have been good friends of the NRA, I would think you wouldn't be out of line in asking for something in return—for the sake of a constituent."

Much to my surprise, Salazar and Tancredo both responded by sending a request to the NRA, and they cc'd me! Both wrote to Froman, simply saying they were transmitting a letter from their constituent. Neither admonished the NRA in any way or made a special appeal for a response, but I wasn't disappointed. I was surprised they even wrote to the NRA, assuming my request was far too controversial for them to handle.

Allard's office responded much later, after I wrote to him three times and informed him that Salazar and Tancredo had agreed to write to the NRA. His office eventually informed me they sent my letter to Froman with a request for a reply.

Despite this pressure put on the NRA, I never received a response from Froman and the NRA, nor did any of the congressmen tell me they received a response. Not only did the NRA again thumb its nose at me, it also ignored the written requests of two U.S. Senators and a House member. Can you imagine any other lobbying group being so brash and unresponsive? But that's how a powerful organization behaves when it feels untouchable.

ONLY SILENCE

Gun activists have written to me that the NRA should not be expected to respond to someone who has openly criticized and protested against them. I beg to differ. If an organization believes in what it stands for, it ought to be willing to stand up for it in the face of opposition. Most national organizations have a cadre of public relations staff who try to deflect criticism, who try to quell the protests of opponents, who do their best to "kill their opponents with kindness," even when they know they're not likely to win them over. But not the NRA.

How responsible is the NRA if it simply refuses to respond to those who criticize it? If the NRA feels its opposition to gun-control laws is justified and without consequences, it ought to respond to the tough questions put to it. What's there to fear? Sure, it's difficult to respond to grieving victims. But that goes with the territory if you're going to promote unfettered access to weapons. By ignoring those victims, the NRA seems to lack compassion.

I've received many emails from gun activists insisting the NRA has no obligation to respond to me. I have never said the NRA was *obligated* to respond to me. But why not at least acknowledge my letter in some way? Why did they tell me they'd respond and then not do so? What kind of organization so readily dismisses and misleads the victim of a crime?

The NRA could have easily deflected my complaint by simply sending me a letter saying they were sorry for my loss and informing me why they would not respond any further. That's all they'd have to do to at least show a sliver of decency. Nearly any competent public relations expert would confirm that an organization must defuse a situation by acknowledging a complainer's pain and responding without compromising or accelerating the controversy.

But the NRA has refused to do even that. Why? I think it's because doing so would, by their old-fashioned, macho way of thinking, be a sign of weakness. Furthermore, responding to such questions might lead to their having to answer further questions about gun violence in this country. To the NRA it's much better and far safer to just stay quiet and ignore the inquiries of victims.

The refusal of the NRA to respond to me is very *symbolic* its refusal to respond to the many questions that Americans have about gun laws, loopholes, and this epidemic of gun violence. When they diss me, America, they're also dissing *you*.

Chapter 28

Misunderstood

Parents who become advocates for change following the loss of a child often are questioned about their motives and state of mind. Whether they're advocating against drunk driving, drug abuse, suicide, or weak gun laws, people wonder whether their advocacy is intended to mask their grief, or whether they are too upset to take on an emotional issue. If one's advocacy is associated with a controversial social issue such as gun control, there is even tougher scrutiny and criticism.

I was no exception. I heard from people who questioned my motivation, the appropriateness of my going public with my grief, or what they saw as my "exploitation" of Columbine. Some contended I was seeking my "fifteen minutes of fame," others insisted I was being "used" by others to promote gun control. Some asserted my gun-control advocacy grew from my "blaming Columbine all on guns," saying I blamed firearms because the killers were not around to blame or because it was a way to distract myself from the emotional burden of losing Daniel.

Nonsense! What initially motivated me to become a gun-control advocate was the desire to act upon Daniel's question to me about loopholes in our gun laws and my desire to honor Daniel with my advocacy. But what kept me active as an advocate was observing what was happening in my country and abroad. It was based on sound reasoning, not on an emotional overreaction. I want people to understand what motivated me, for I believe it may likewise help motivate them.

MOTIVATION AND DENIAL

My gun-control advocacy was not an attempt to mask my grief, or to deflect blame to guns because Daniel was killed with a gun and his killer was dead. I recognize there is a risk that grieving parents could use advocacy to mask their pain or to strike out against a convenient target. But I believe I overcame those risks. I was able to put aside my grief as well as acknowledge and accept it. I lived the satisfaction of making a difference in the world around me by calling attention to the need for stronger gun laws while also continuing to experience the sense of helplessness and despair of losing Daniel. As I responded to many of my critics, I was capable of grieving and thinking rationally at the same time.

Like many grieving parents, I took on the role of advocate because I believed it honored my son and "made some good out of the bad." Those of us who lose children don't want to see others go through the same pain, so in response we urge caution, awareness, and prevention. We are driven to warn and protect others, telling them we never thought tragedy would strike us.

Some people chastised me for focusing only on the role of guns at Columbine and not on other factors they considered more pertinent, such as bullying, the failure of school and law enforcement officials to predict the killers' violent intentions, poor parenting, and the killers' lack of moral compasses. It's true that most of my time and effort has been directed at gun control, but in large part that's because I came to realize I had limited time. It's true that there were a number of contributing factors that played a role in the Columbine massacre, and I have often acknowledged and addressed those factors. But I could not realistically speak out as an advocate and expert on *all* those factors and expect to be effective.

Many gun activists faulted me for focusing "on the gun, not the shooter" and for irrationally blaming an inanimate object for a shooting.

No, what is irrational is ignoring the role of weak gun laws and easy access to guns as a contributing factor in shootings. That's what gun activists do. They repeatedly cite their weathered cliché, "Guns don't kill people, people kill people," insisting that gun violence is related to "the person and not the gun," seeing little need for more restrictive laws or more preventive steps related to guns. They fail to acknowledge there are two constant elements in America's epidemic of gun violence: people and guns.

There are a number of contributing factors that play a role in most shootings, but it's ridiculous to argue that easy access to guns is not one of the factors related to the problem of gun violence in America. It's simplistic to argue the only problem is the perpetrator.

Consider this: we were rightfully shocked at the tragic loss of nearly 3,000 lives in the 9/11 terrorists attacks. We knew the names of those who were on those airplanes and committed those despicable acts. But did we blame them alone? Did we say the terrorists on the planes alone were responsible? No, we also held the plotters responsible, and we recognized that Muslim extremism was a factor and lax airplane security played a contributing role, even though it didn't "cause" the tragedy. We didn't foolishly conclude that the problem was limited to the terrorists in the airplanes. Likewise, we cannot say that prevention of gun violence is rooted only in the shooter.

Many gun activists were in serious denial about the role of guns at Columbine, downplaying or dismissing their role in email messages to me. Jim Peel from Nebraska wrote, "Be glad they didn't decide to use the bomb built into the basement of the school instead of what they did use…. In the absence of firearms, they might have chosen that option." But, as I responded to him, there were no "bombs built into the basement," and there was no absence of firearms, and there was no question about which option they chose.

Dr. Daniel P. Johnson, a dentist from northern Colorado, wrote that the killers "could just as well have used bombs, knives, poisons, etc." The fact is the Columbine killers had knives with them. They boasted on their "basement tapes" that they would use the knives to attack their victims. But they didn't—probably because they realized it likely would have carried too much of a risk. They likely used guns for the same reason most other murderers select them as their weapon of choice: They are easy to get, easy to use, quick, impersonal, and far more lethal than knives. That's why we rarely hear stories of "mass knifings" and never read about "drive-by knifings."

It's true the Columbine killers intended to kill hundreds with bombs. We can all be thankful their propane bombs didn't detonate. The killers set off dozens of small bombs, but none caused fatalities. The fact remains that when the propane bombs failed, the killers turned to the weapons they knew would be effective for mass murder. Daniel and the other Columbine victims were not stabbed, poisoned, or killed by a bomb—they were all shot. Period.

The gun violence that tragically happened at Columbine was certainly not something rare or isolated. Daniel wasn't simply one of 13 people murdered at Columbine; he was also one of the nearly 11,000 people murdered with guns each year in America. Daniel's death was part of something deeply troubling in America.

EMOTIONLESS ADVOCACY?

Some gun activists thought I was somehow too distraught to be speaking out. John Sovis of Maine wrote to me in 2004, "Mr. Mauser, I think you're a little too emotional at this point to analyze the problem logically."

Kimmy Estrada wrote, "Real men and real women deal with their emotions, they don't blame people for what others have done, they don't throw temper tantrums, they respond logically. It's obvious you can't debate this without resorting to cheap theatrics." David Hendrix, a student at the University of Wyoming, wrote, "You obviously have no control over your emotions, nor does your grasp on reality have any substance.... Emotions will get you nowhere, but facts will."

It was interesting to hear these charges from people who had never met or spoken to me. It was unclear what behavior of mine they were referring to. I doubt these people ever saw me speak in person or read my speeches. If they had, they would know I used facts and logical arguments to make my case and didn't resort to excessive emotional displays in my speaking.

I did speak about the loss of Daniel in my presentations. Would these critics expect me *not* to speak of him? After all, he was my inspiration, my reason for speaking out. I nearly always became choked up when I spoke about Daniel, but usually it was only momentary. Did my opponents think it was inappropriate for me to exhibit any emotion? That's not possible—I'm not a robot. Losing a child is an emotional experience. Still, my emotional displays were natural, not excessive. I did not expect or want people to support my position by making them feel sorry for me. My speeches were mostly focused on solutions.

I recognized early on that emotions are not a substitute for sturdy and substantive debate. Grieving gun-control advocates should not expect people to support them out of pity, nor should they make them feel guilty for opposing their position. Advocacy that relies mostly on an emotional appeal runs the risk of being short-lived and ineffective. While an audience member might be touched by an advocate's emotional appeal in a speech, if that audience member hears someone effectively challenge the advocate's position or begins to question the logic of it, the support for the emotional speaker can quickly fade.

It's hypocritical for gun activists to complain about "emotional appeals," given that they rely so much on emotional appeals to promote *their* cause. They write to me and in letters to the editor using language that clearly suggests they are irritated, perturbed or outraged. Perhaps it never occurred to them that they were reacting emotionally—and that it was natural to do so. Gun activists appeal to their legions with a heavy reliance on emotions, trying to make them *fear* being without a gun in their home, trying to make them *angry* by insisting that their guns are about to be confiscated.

Emotions are natural and not to be avoided. Emotional appeals are only a problem when they are greatly exaggerated, excessive, or unaccompanied by logic, facts, and reasoning. I tried to be like Daniel in his debates, winning people over with strong arguments, logic, and reasoning.

BEING USED?

Critics tried to diminish my gun-control advocacy by insisting I was being "used" by others, including politicians, the media, or those in the gun-control movement. David McRae of suburban Denver wrote in an email, "Whether you want to realize it or not, the anti-gun lobby is using you to try to disarm this country. Why do you think that you are their poster boy?"

There is always the risk that an advocate *could* be used by others, regardless of their good intentions. But I have always taken the integrity of my advocacy seriously, weighing my statements and my associations and making sure I was being true to my own beliefs. I have questioned whether requests for my support were reasonable. There have been some issues, such as certain lawsuits against the gun industry and requests from some people that I oppose certain proposed shooting ranges, where I have had disagreements with colleagues in the gun-control movement.

Seldom did I feel "used" by others. If anything, I was the one who "used" others. I wanted laws changed, so I needed the help of politicians to do so. I had a message I needed to get out to the public regarding gun control, so I "used" the media to get it out for me. The media "uses" people for its news stories all the time, because real people's stories can help audiences better understand a story. That's the way it works in the news business—even for my opponents!

Some people argued that my advocacy "exploited" or "capitalized" on the Columbine tragedy to promote my personal gun control and political beliefs. James Grant from New Castle, Colorado, wrote, "I pity you for the loss of your son. If you would devote your efforts to honoring his memory instead of using his death in a tasteless ploy to further your own political and social objectives, I could sympathize with you. May God someday grant you the courage, strength, and maturity to face the tragedy that has been thrust upon you."

My "social objective" is one that many people support: reducing gun violence. We may disagree on how to achieve that objective, but it's hardly an extreme aspiration. Speaking out for change isn't "capitalizing." Presenting Columbine as an example of tragic gun violence in America hardly qualifies as "exploitation," given that shootings are so commonplace and take such a high toll. It's certainly not unreasonable to remind people that a similar tragedy can hit any community, any child, any parent, any time.

I have an easy response for the charge that I sought the spotlight as a means of getting the proverbial "fifteen minutes of fame." I have had to endure too many reporters' questions, have painfully retold Daniel's story too many times, sacrificed too many vacation days, and faced too many mean-spirited letters and unpleasant encounters with gun activists to think I was in this for anything other than a way to honor Daniel and to prevent the continued loss of so many lives to gun violence.

STRUCK!

While trying to put Daniel's death into perspective, I developed a second motivation for my advocacy: to honor the tens of thousands of other gun violence victims, to speak for those who could not speak out, and to try to prevent more tragic and needless shootings.

Daniel's death was certainly not something rare or isolated. He wasn't simply one of thirteen people murdered at Columbine—he was also one of the nearly 11,000 people killed with guns each year in America. Daniel was born into a "gun nation" and became one of the many innocent victims of its tragic epidemic of gun violence.

He was born into a nation that distinguishes itself from others with its high, unprecedented rate of gun ownership, overabundance of firearms, weak gun laws, and lax social attitude toward guns. It's certainly no coincidence that it's also a nation with the highest rate of gun violence among its peers.

After Columbine I was struck by what I realized I had seen happen in America in my lifetime. When my generation, the Baby Boomers, was growing up, one of the greatest fears most of us had was of "being buried" by the Soviet Union by means of nuclear attack. We were required to practice a protective drill in schools, "duck and cover," which entailed getting under our desks to protect ourselves in case of attack. (As if that would have protected us from a nuclear blast!)

The threat from those "dirty commies" is largely gone now. In its place is the threat of international terrorism. We have demonstrated a willingness, however reluctantly, to undergo invasive security screenings at our airports and public buildings as a means of prevention. However, terrorist attacks on American soil have been rare since the 9/11 attacks.

It struck me that the greater and more frequent threat is that of being shot with a gun, whether it's on the street or in one's own home, workplace, or school. It's this domestic terrorism that greatly eclipses the body count from international terrorism.

So great is the risk of gun violence today that our schools practice a new protective drill: reacting to a school shooting. Today's children are taught about "code red" alerts and know all too well what a "school lockdown" is and what leads to one. Once again the drill involves ducking under one's desk to protect oneself. (As if that's going to protect a child from a student with a semi-automatic firearm and a stockpile of thirty-round magazines!)

METAPHORICALLY SPEAKING

It struck me that America's gun culture is so pervasive it permeates our language, especially our everyday metaphors and idioms. They're not necessarily part of the English language—they're part of America's English language. Among some of the more common ones:

- Dodging a bullet
- "Gunning" for someone or something
- A person who is a "big gun"
- A smoking gun
- Going great guns
- Shot full of holes
- Shot to ribbons
- Shot to hell
- Shot to pieces
- Shot down
- Armed and dangerous
- Quick on the trigger
- Jumping the gun
- Going in with guns blazing
- Having a trigger finger
- Putting someone "in the crosshairs" (of a rifle sight)
- Biting the bullet
- Sweating bullets
- Shoot first and ask questions later
- Shooting off one's mouth
- Give it the gun
- Fire back
- In the line of fire

- Taking a bullet
- A silver bullet
- Taking a shot at it
- Gun shy
- Being a straight shooter
- Under the gun
- Locked and loaded
- Putting a gun to someone's head
- Using a shotgun approach
- Taking aim at someone
- Sticking to one's guns
- Shooting from the hip
- Looking down the barrel
- Being trigger happy
- Being shot in the back
- Then there's the little, round object to the left of this sentence that is not normally referred to as a "dot" or by a special word associated with its word processing usage. It's a "bullet," perhaps because it reminds us of something we commonly hear about— bullet holes

I'm not suggesting these numerous gun metaphors and idioms, in and of themselves, somehow make us more aggressive or violent. Some of the examples above are fairly benign, not even referring directly to firearms, even though their derivation may somehow be related to guns. Others carry a more negative connotation or are more antagonistic in nature. In general they reflect how we relate and apply gun usage to so many aspects of our daily lives. Note how many of them refer to reckless behavior, aggression, danger, or applying power or force to get something from others. They are indicative of a gun culture that has been so shaped by firearms it finds itself frequently using gun metaphors and idioms in its everyday language.

PAINFUL RECURRING HEADLINES

There's a strange obsession I've had since Columbine. I have become a compulsive clipper of newspaper stories about shootings. Perhaps I do so because I'm identifying with others who are likewise going through this terrible pain of losing a loved one to gunfire, or taking some peculiar solace in knowing I'm not the only one who's suffering from the results of gunfire.

I have clippings reporting the death or injury of hundreds and hundreds of people. I have so many I had to separate them into file folders by year—and they're only the articles I happened to catch. They're mostly shooting stories from Colorado, which is certainly not a state with a particularly high crime rate. Colorado has a fairly high median household income and a highly educated populace, yet it also suffers from this epidemic of gun violence.

The overwhelming evidence of America's epidemic of gun violence is right there, day in and day out, observed in some of the words so commonly found in America's newspaper and Web site news headlines: shooting, gunfire, shooter, gunman, gunshots, shootout.

Those words appear so often that perhaps Americans have grown accustomed to them and accept them as unavoidable. Shootings are so common they remain local news stories unless the victim is a notable person, the shooting is particularly tragic, or there are numerous victims. Shooting stories are so common that it's not unusual for ones involving only injuries, or those involving gang members or poor people from the inner city, to be given only three or four column inches of print coverage. I find most local shooting stories in the *Denver Post's* Section B, page 2, in the far left column, which is labeled, "Briefs." How sad, yet fitting, that in this gun nation shooting deaths have become so inconsequential.

ARE WE JUST CRAZY?

I am proud to be an American, but not always.

There are many things to be proud of as Americans: our leadership in the world, our stand on human rights, and our many technological accomplishments. But there are also many things for which I am not proud—particularly our crazed gun culture and our shameful level of gun violence.

Whenever liberals criticize something about America, conservatives routinely accuse us of being anti-American, unpatriotic, hateful, or weak.

Hogwash! Weakness comes from being myopic, from only looking at one's positive attributes and from being unwilling to look inside oneself and acknowledge faults. Weakness comes from not trying to improve oneself. A patriot is someone who acknowledges both the good and the bad in their nation but concentrates on improving the bad rather than only being satisfied with the good.

It struck me that despite all of America's greatness, Daniel's chances of being shot to death would have been far lower if he had grown up in one of our peer nations. One of the greatest lies told by gun activists is that gun control doesn't work. That's simply not true. Our peers—wealthy industrialized nations—have much stricter gun control, and not coincidently, a fraction of America's gun homicide rate. When I have pointed this out in my writings and speeches, it has led gun activists to suggest I should consider moving. "Maybe you should go to Japan if you feel safer there," wrote New Jersey hunter, Bruce Perone, Jr.

I don't want to move. I love my country and was taught I should address problems, not deny them or run away from them. I simply wish we could learn something from our peer nations. I want my children to live in a country where they aren't facing such a high level of danger, rather than one where people become frantic over a few instances of food poisoning but are unwilling to address an *epidemic* of gun violence.

I received hundreds of email messages from people overseas who commented on America's gun culture. David Baird of Melbourne, Australia, wrote in 2004, "We have a gun culture in Australia, but, fortunately, with our 19 million population it is not out of control .... We in Australia cannot understand how America has allowed its crazy, absurd gun culture to get so out of control." Jeremy, an American born in New York City but living in Tokyo, wrote that many Japanese around him remarked after Columbine that "America is so scary." His response to them was that "America is a war zone, only the people that live there don't realize it."

Karl S. from Bonn, Germany, wrote, "It's tragic that America lost 3,000 lives on 9/11, but you lose more people than that to gun violence in just a few months, but you don't seem very shocked or upset that about that. Are you all just crazy in America?"

That's what many people around the civilized world think. They admire many things about America, but they think we're crazy when it comes to our out-of-control gun culture. Can you blame them?

UNRESPONSIVE

There have been more than 140,000 firearm homicides in America since Columbine. That represents more than the number of residents of the city of Savannah, Georgia. Imagine our shock if a city of that size were suddenly wiped off the face of the earth. Perhaps it's less shocking when those losses are spread over 13 years, but is it any less catastrophic?

When you add firearm suicides, accidental deaths and unexplained shootings to the homicides, there have been nearly 390,000 firearm deaths since Columbine. That's more than the number of residents of the city of Minneapolis. And there have been more than 975,000 gunshot injuries not resulting in death, more people than live in the city of San Jose. Imagine the cost of treating or burying those people. It's in the billions, and we are the ones paying for it, through government and private health insurance.

Americans usually respond to these shameful statistics in a predictable manner. Gun-control advocates speak of the needless losses, while gun activists speak of rights and liberties; gun-control advocates call for tougher firearms laws, while gun activists accuse them of overreacting, exploiting tragedy, making a knee-jerk reaction, and attempting to punish law abiding citizens for the acts of criminals. Meanwhile, average Americans in the middle just shake their head, express condolences, remark that it's a terrible shame, and go on with life, feeling helpless to do anything about it, given the power of the gun lobby and the belief that the Second Amendment prevents action.

Conversely, look at how other nations have reacted to gun violence. Following terrible shootings in places like Erfrut, Germany; Port Arthur, Australia; and Dunblane, Scotland, the governments of those nations passed tougher gun laws, and most of the public was supportive.

Our peer nations have strict gun laws. They seemingly show more concern for human life than America, where values are based more on individual freedoms. Despite the claims of religious conservatives that we are a "Christian nation" that values human life, in practice our emphasis is on freedom from government intrusion, with less concern about lives being lost as a result of the danger brought about by so many firearms and weak gun laws. It's not that Americans believe that recklessness and shootings are acceptable—it's that we are far less willing to make sacrifices to prevent them.

Americans are more prone to accept that reckless gun usage and crime will occur, relying primarily on punishment, not prevention. The problem is that punishment means little to the family of a shooting victim. It comes too late.

THERE IS A DIFFERENCE

What's the difference between us and our peer nations? Gun activists and social conservatives often blame our gun violence on an America they see as straying too far from religious and moral teachings, and an America they believe has become too liberal and secular.

In reality, though, America has a higher percentage of people who identify themselves as belonging to a religious denomination, while most other industrialized nations have seen a decline in the number of people associated with religious denominations. Conservatives complain about America's move toward liberalism and socialism, but the reality is that most of our peers are far more liberal on social issues such as universal health care, safety nets, treatment of gays, and social equality. Why is it, then, those "Godless socialists" overseas don't shoot each other in the way we do in this so-called "Christian nation?"

Gun activists and conservatives claim that gun violence in America is exacerbated by broken homes, poverty, unrest, anger, drugs, hatred, mental illness, and bullying. We do suffer from those ills, but it's ridiculous to argue that our peer nations aren't afflicted with the same problems. They have them in differing amounts, but they suffer from them nonetheless.

Because we have far more firearms available, easy access to them via weak gun laws, and lax and irresponsible social attitudes toward firearms, we in essence make it easy for those who cannot *deal* with broken homes, poverty, unrest, anger, drugs, hatred, mental illness, and bullying to deal with them in a definitive, albeit violent, manner. We give distressed and angry people easy access to something that in their minds provides them with power over those social ills.

Whether it's the gang banger who thinks "the world respects me when I've got my 44 Magnum," or the disaffected student wanting violent revenge over those who torment him, or the husband forcing his wife to remain in a torn marriage, the common element is the power they feel in their hands with a firearm. It's true that angst, disrespect, revenge, recklessness, and the lack of a moral compass also are elements in this mix, but the perceived power of the firearm in the hands of these disturbed people is the common element in America that empowers them to take violent action in a way that occurs far less in peer nations. That's what's different.

NO MODEL

Another major difference between us and peer nations is that they have succeeded. Among industrialized nations, our firearm-related death rate is more than twice that of the next highest country, and our rate is *eight* times the average rate of our economic peers.

Most other major industrialized nations have much stricter gun laws than America, yet they are still considered part of the Free World. They have democratic forms of government. Their people live freely despite not having gun rights as permissive as those of America.

Gun activists insist the people in countries with strict gun control are not "truly free," and that they are "tyrannized" by their governments because they do not have a right to bear arms or face many restrictions on gun ownership. If you tell the people of those nations that they are not living freely because they have a limited right to bear arms, most would likely tell you they don't feel the need to own a gun in order to feel free, and that they feel freer than Americans because they live with less fear for their safety. Most would tell you they support their government and insist it is their government and that they use the ballot box to prevent tyranny and anarchy. They'd tell you they don't want gun violence like America's and that they are far less fearful of crime than Americans.

The American gun lobby, feeling threatened by the success of nations that have enacted strict gun laws, has long sought to discredit foreign gun-control efforts. They have tried to argue that crime rates in those countries are rising because citizens are being disarmed. In a sharply worded rebuke, Daryl Williams, the Attorney General of Australia, took the unusual step of writing a letter to the NRA, asking it to stop using misleading statistics to make its case. He wrote to Charlton Heston, "There are many things that Australia can learn from the United States. How to manage firearms ownership is not one of them."

Has it ever occurred to gun activists and conservatives that other nations are not following our lead when it comes to gun laws and widespread gun ownership? Has it ever occurred to them that our gun culture is a monumental failure in the eyes of most of the world—and that it's for good reason?

NRA President Charlton Heston giving his infamous 'From my cold dead hands' exhortation

Chapter 29

Have I Forgiven Them?

It was a question occasionally asked of me in emails by nervy strangers. In most cases, the person asking the question was respectful and well-intentioned. But I often mumbled to myself the same reaction: "It's none of their damned business!" I felt it was insensitive for strangers to ask if I had forgiven the killers, especially within the first few years of the massacre, let alone the first few months. I was experiencing a world of pain, so I didn't appreciate such a personal question. I considered myself a forgiving person but I had never before faced such a difficult question of forgiveness—and I assumed these inquiring strangers never had either. Did they ever bother to ask themselves how they would feel if they found themselves in the same situation?

I felt that many who asked the forgiveness question were either looking for me to condemn the two killers, whom they probably viewed as evil incarnate, or conversely, were hoping I would offer heartfelt forgiveness that would serve as an inspiration to others to also forgive those who had hurt them. I resented having that burden laid on me. I did not see the

Columbine killers as the embodiment of Satan, nor did I want to play spiritual hero to someone by saying I unconditionally and completely forgave the killers. The question of whether I had "forgiven them" was too complicated to address in a short email response with a simple "yes" or "no."

I usually responded that forgiveness is an ongoing process and that it was not a sudden decision I expected to make. I reflected that one's readiness and willingness to express forgiveness was related to the circumstances in which one finds oneself, and that my reaction was made more complex because Daniel's killer died and never asked for my forgiveness. I also reminded them this was about the murder of my son—not exactly an easily forgivable act—and that I assumed Eric Harris found himself asking for God's forgiveness, not mine.

FORGIVEN WHOM?

Often I was tempted to give another response to the forgiveness question: "Forgiven *whom*?" I felt anger toward others who somehow played a role in the events leading up to and following the massacre. What these people did paled in comparison to murder, of course, but nonetheless what they did often was either insensitive, hurtful, disrespectful, deceptive, thoughtless, or contemptible.

With the deaths of Eric Harris and Dylan Klebold, the question of forgiving the killers was not as immediate or imminent. They were gone from this world. I had plenty of time to tackle that question. Instead I found myself nagged by whether I could forgive certain people on earth who failed to react to the signs of danger prior to the massacre. Could I forgive the school teachers and administrators who allegedly failed to respond to the Columbine killers' warning signs?

Within weeks of the tragedy, I came immediately face to face with the question of whether I was willing to forgive one of these people. After Mass one Sunday morning, Linda and I were approached by a priest at our church. He indicated there was a parish member who was a teacher at Columbine who apparently was being accused by some people of not acting on warning signs in the writings or video of the killers. The teacher was upset about the accusation. I was not following every detail of the investigation, so I had not heard the teacher's name nor the details of the accusations.

Much to our surprise, the priest asked if we'd be willing to offer forgiveness to the teacher, saying it would mean a lot to that person. Linda and I can be forgiving people, but this was a very awkward situation since we were unsure of exactly what this teacher had done—or failed to do. To make matters worse, we weren't being asked to come back with a response a week later, we were being asked for an immediate response—the teacher was waiting somewhere in the church sanctuary! When we said we were willing to offer our forgiveness, we were immediately taken to the teacher, to whom we repeated our offer of forgiveness. Ostensibly there was nothing wrong with offering our forgiveness, for I knew the teacher was not responsible for Daniel's death. But, in hindsight, I am resentful for being put on the spot the way we were that Sunday.

I struggled with the question of whether I could forgive people who treated us poorly following the tragedy, such as people who berated Columbine families in the media anytime we spoke out about the massacre or the investigation, telling us we needed to "get on with our lives." And what about members of the media and public who treated Columbine families without sensitivity, as if this tragedy were just some kind of fictional TV drama?

I wondered whether I could forgive the school, which allegedly turned a blind eye to bullying and favoritism toward athletes. What about the bullies and jocks at Columbine who thought nothing of taunting and demeaning the killers and others? Could I forgive them? Could I possibly even think of forgiving the young people who purchased weapons for the killers? Could I ever forgive the parents of the killers for failing to see their children were so angry and disturbed that they wanted to kill hundreds of classmates?

Could I forgive a sheriff's office that failed to act on reports of the killers' activities and treated the Columbine families so poorly? Could I forgive a nation that has done so little to deal with its shameful level of gun violence? What about the gun activists who harassed me and sent insulting, mean-spirited, and hateful mail to me?

I'll stop my list there, since I have probably angered enough people already, either for including someone or for failing to include someone on the list—a classic case of damned if you do, damned if you don't.

A number of people have remarked that I seem to be a relatively calm and forgiving person, especially under the circumstances presented to me following Columbine. Conversely, there are probably others who see me as a sucker for not being angrier at those described above. In truth, I harbored much anger toward many of those mentioned above, along with others. But I also felt it was healthier to channel most of that anger in more positive ways. Sustained and intense anger does not enable one to heal.

I was determined to work to "make something good out of the bad," yet I knew I also couldn't afford to allow myself to pretend I was without anger and let it eat away at me. I knew it would be easier to change hearts and minds, and much easier to find peace and healing, if I could find the right balance of anger, forgiveness and reconciliation. I knew I could not honor Daniel if I were constantly angry and in a poor mental state.

MEASURED FORGIVENESS

I admit I didn't necessarily find it easy to forgive, and some people were easier to forgive than others. One of the factors I weighed was the important distinction between ignorance and knowledge. Some people were easier to forgive because they acted out of ignorance, were oblivious to reality, or were doing what many people would have done in the same situation. Conversely, others were harder to forgive because they acted in ways that were intentional, thoughtless, hurtful, or seemingly without regret.

There were people who thought I should have been angry at Columbine High School administrators and teachers for failing to react properly to the killers' violent writings and videos. Yes, I was disappointed in them, for perhaps they failed us. They should have taken the killers' behavior more seriously. But, as a society, too often we look the other way when there are signs of danger. We all share some responsibility for tolerating and watching media depictions of violence that can desensitize people.

Violent acts have become so commonplace in America that perhaps we take them for granted. We have seen many tragic instances in which people have failed to speak up or act when bullying or signs of potential violence were present. I don't mean to suggest the failure to respond is acceptable, but it does point out how helpless Americans seem to be about dealing with this problem.

People said I should have been angry at administrators and teachers for tolerating bullying and showing favoritism toward jocks. Yes, Columbine had a bullying problem. Sports programs were especially revered at the school, and some jocks likely exploited their celebrity status. But Columbine is certainly not alone in those regards. Bullying remains a serious problem throughout America's schools. Some parents have turned a blind eye to the bullying problem until it hits home, hoping instead that teachers will solve the problem for them, or blaming the bullied child for not speaking up. Some teachers have likewise done too little to address the problem.

This nation is enamored with its athletes. We place undue emphasis on sports competition, often at the expense of academics—then act shocked when other nations perform so much better academically. We have elevated sports figures to hero status, heaping much praise and payroll upon these coddled and overpaid jocks. Then we look away when a treasured athlete breaks the law or the rules, being more interested in what they can do for our beloved sports team than in the poor behavior they model for our children. So it should come as no surprise that some high school athletes are likewise given disproportionate privileges and use their elevated status as a weapon against others. I wish it weren't so. But we shouldn't unfairly single out the jocks at Columbine and collectively blame them for the actions of the killers.

People insisted I should have been angry at the young people who provided the weapons to the killers. I am. I cannot imagine how Robyn Anderson thought nothing of buying three guns for the killers and thought nothing was wrong when they tried to avoid creating a paperwork trail. I cannot imagine how Philip Duran and Mark Manes could watch the killers firing sawed-off shotguns and an assault weapon in the forest and not suspect something might be wrong.

Yet, let's face it; as a nation we have also been negligent. We make it easy for gang members, criminals and the mentally deranged to obtain firearms. We see violent tendencies in some people, yet do little to disarm them until it's too late. We allowed the Assault Weapons Ban to expire. We know criminals and deranged people can easily purchase guns from private sellers at gun shows, yet most of the nation has done nothing to stop it. Are these faults any less forgivable?

FORGIVENESS FOR THE SHERIFF?

The victim of a horrific crime would normally expect to have the support of one's local law enforcement officials. Too often that was sorely missing after Columbine. There was a very public conflict between many of the Columbine parents and the Jefferson County Sheriff, John P. Stone, and his top commanders, particularly John Dunaway and John Kiekbusch.

Stone and his commanders repeatedly displayed a lack of competence, credibility, and sensitivity. A few difficulties or errors could have been forgiven, but these men failed the Columbine families in significant ways and on a number of occasions.

First came the poor response of Stone's commanders on the day of the massacre. I realize that responding to the calamity at Columbine was a challenging undertaking for law enforcement and that hindsight is always 20/20, but it was inexcusable for the sheriff and his commanders to choose to simply "maintain a perimeter" around Columbine High School, rather than react to the situation as it was presented to them.

A few policemen have written to me, urging that I not condemn the sheriff's decision to follow what was standard operating procedure at the time: securing the perimeter, containing the situation, not engaging the shooters and awaiting negotiations. I respectfully disagree. *Knowing* that students were being shot in the school, based on the 911 call from the library, how could the sheriff and his commanders think it was a hostage situation that called for merely maintaining a perimeter? What call for negotiations was signaled to these hapless commanders? There was none.

If the killers had not committed suicide when they did, when *would* Stone and his commanders have changed their tactical approach? How many more lives would have been lost before they decided it was worthwhile to risk the lives of policemen to try to save the lives of children? The tragic consequences of the sheriff's commands were highlighted by the decision to proceed slowly and cautiously in reaching teacher Dave Sanders. They knew he was bleeding to death. They heard no shooting in the school for hours, yet they failed to act quickly and decisively enough to save the life of this heroic teacher. It was totally inexcusable. And totally unforgivable.

TOO LITTLE CONCERN FOR VICTIMS

The lack of competence and integrity of Sheriff Stone and his commanders was demonstrated early in the aftermath of the shootings. A few days after the massacre, Stone suggested that Brooks Brown, a friend of the killers, was under suspicion as a possible accomplice, yet he provided no evidence to back it up. It seemed to be based only on Brooks's relationship with the killers and the fact Eric Harris told Brooks he liked him just before the massacre and he should leave the campus.

It was irresponsible to taint this young man's life so recklessly. Some speculated that Stone was retaliating because Brooks's parents, Randy and Judy Brown, told the media shortly after the massacre that they had spoken to the sheriff's office the previous year about violent Internet threats made by Eric Harris and that the sheriff's office had failed to follow up.

Sheriff Stone assured the Columbine families he would keep us informed of the findings of his investigation and tell us in advance of the release of materials so we were better prepared for the shock and the media onslaught. He failed miserably in that regard a number of times. In particular, Stone enraged the Columbine families late in 1999 when he allowed a *Time* magazine reporter to watch the "basement tapes" taken by the killers, after not giving the Columbine families the opportunity to view them, violating his earlier commitment.

Stone had the nerve to be photographed for the magazine as a valiant, tough-looking cop. He even posed with three of the four firearms used by the killers at Columbine. Most of the families felt blindsided by his egotistical display of bravado, feeling he should have been working with the parents to provide information rather than seeking to enhance his image with magazine readers. At a press conference a number of us called for Stone's resignation but he flippantly brushed aside our suggestion.

DECEPTION

One of the most inexcusable acts directed against the Columbine families and the community occurred just a few days after the massacre. It was an act of deception and a failure of public officials to disclose information—and it happened even before all our loved ones were laid to rest.

Judy and Randy Brown told the sheriff's office in 1998 about threats against their son, Brooks, and about Eric Harris's Web site that made other threats and boasted of building and detonating pipe bombs. Initially, the sheriff's office flatly denied their investigators had ever even met with the Browns to discuss Harris' threats. In an embarrassing turnabout, shortly thereafter they admitted they had indeed met with the Browns, but insisted they found no evidence of action they had taken in response to the reported threats. Their claim was later revealed to be a lie.

In reality, based on the Brown's allegations, bomb investigator Mike Guerra drafted an affidavit for a warrant to search the Harris home. Allegedly Guerra was told by a superior there wasn't sufficient evidence to proceed, so the warrant was never submitted to a judge.

That could have been the end of the story, if the public officials who knew of the affidavit had simply told us about it. But it seems county officials worried that the failed affidavit would make them look bad if the public (rightfully) questioned why the evidence available at the time was not enough to justify a search warrant. So rather than tell us what happened, they chose to lie.

For more than five years we did not know about the deception. It took action by a grand jury summoned by state Attorney General Ken Salazar, and the threat of criminal prosecution, to bring out the truth. The grand jury report in 2004 indicated that several county officials met privately a few days after the massacre and agreed they would suppress key documents related to the 1998 investigation of Harris. They agreed not to reveal them to the parents or to the public. In essence they agreed to a cover-up.

The grand jury report charged that county officials held what later became known infamously as the Open Space meeting, because it was held in the Jefferson County Open Space offices rather elsewhere on the county campus, allegedly because they were trying to lay low and out of sight of a media hungry for information.

At the meeting from the sheriff's office were Stone, Dunaway, Kiekbusch, sheriff's spokesman Steve Davis and deputy Guerra. Others in attendance were county attorney Frank Hutfless and two assistant attorneys, Lily Oeffler and William Tuthill. Even though he was a Democrat in a county where Republicans ruled the commissioner's and sheriff's offices, district attorney Dave Thomas and assistant district attorney Kathy Sasak somehow got word of the meeting and attended.

The sheriff's office already had been forced to admit the Browns had filed a complaint. They released the complaint, but they didn't include the accompanying investigative paperwork. At the Open Space meeting, they essentially agreed they would not disclose the existence of the Guerra affidavit or the investigative paperwork.

Starting at a press conference on April 30, 1999, county officials failed to acknowledge the existence of the failed affidavit and were less than revealing about their investigation of Harris. They contradicted information in Guerra's draft affidavit and failed to acknowledge some of what their investigation had discovered.

Unfortunately, the grand jury did not indict anyone, but its report did raise questions about "suspicious" actions by the Jefferson County Sheriff's Office, including the mysterious disappearance of documents related to the failed warrant. What Stone and the others did may not have been a chargeable crime, but it certainly was a terrible act of deception.

Many people have said everyone failed to "connect the dots" in the Columbine case. That's not really true. Some Jefferson County officials may not have known that they were dealing with two teens who were about to go on a killing spree, but they did see a number of dots that indicated they were dealing with teens who had broken the law, were making threats, and were building and detonating pipe bombs. And they did nothing about it.

It's one thing to make a terrible mistake, but it's far worse to deliberately cover it up. I'm not aware of any of them expressing regret or asking for forgiveness for trying to deceive us. There is little reason to forgive them.

UNREPENTANT

Sheriff Stone and his supporters were largely unrepentant, blameful of others, and insistent that Stone was unfairly targeted and made a scapegoat because Columbine was such an emotional and controversial case. Stone served one term as sheriff and wisely decided not to run for re-election. When he announced that decision, he dodged responsibility for his actions, calling Columbine "a tar baby you can't walk away from once you touch it." He even had the nerve to express confidence he could have won re-election, but complained that he still would have been harassed: "But even if I win it, I don't win because these people won't leave us alone."

How sad that "these people," these reporters seeking answers, and these Columbine parents simply wanting information and respect, were characterized in such a way. John Stone was not being made a "scapegoat." Nobody is suggesting he committed murder. We only sought his help and cooperation. He chose not to keep his commitments to us. He was responsible for the poor command decisions made on April 20, 1999. He failed to stop leaks, he released information at a snail's pace, and he covered up truths. He and other county officials refused to apologize for their actions and failed to earn our support and respect—or my forgiveness.

Chapter 30

Facing the Parents

E ric Harris and Dylan Klebold killed themselves, so the question of how and whether to forgive them was more complicated. It was only natural, then, to wonder about how to treat and view those who were closest to the killers—their parents. I couldn't ignore the question of whether I could forgive these parents for raising these two murderers. I couldn't help but ponder what role their behavior might have played and whether they could have done more to prevent this tragedy. Was it even worth trying to address these questions, given that the parents had chosen not to be forthcoming in the months and years following the massacre?

UNEXPECTED CONTACT

Within a few weeks of the massacre Linda and I, and apparently all the other Columbine parents, received a sympathy card from the parents of Dylan Klebold, who wrote, "It is with indescribable sorrow and humility that we write to wish you comfort." The handwritten card asked that God comfort us and our loved ones. They were comforting words, yet we weren't quite sure how to react to them. It was so soon after the massacre, too early for us to react rationally.

At the time the card seemed to offer little acceptance of responsibility for what had happened, saying Daniel was taken "in a moment of madness" and that they would "never understand why this tragedy happened, or what we might have done to prevent it." We felt as if the words didn't come from the heart, but rather were suggested by an attorney. We were dissatisfied with what we received and chose not to respond to it. The card was tossed onto a pile of Columbine-related papers and forgotten.

While uncovering some Columbine papers recently I discovered that card from the Klebolds. I hadn't seen it for years. I must admit that now, after I've read it again, I'm not quite as cynical about it as I was in 1999. Back then I cringed at the statement, "we never saw anger or hatred in Dylan until the last moments of his life," because I felt the Klebolds were in denial and refused to accept responsibility. But in reading it again, I realized they weren't quite as unresponsive as I had originally thought. "We apologize for the role our son played in your son's death." Their words didn't seem as hurtful, or contrived or unrepentant as they did in 1999.

The Harrises also wrote sympathy cards to the victims' families, but they sent them to the school district for distribution. The cards were intercepted by the sheriff's office and lost. The Harrises were informed of this, and it became public knowledge. Despite knowing they were lost, the Harrises *never* sent replacement cards. For years I loathed them for not doing what I thought was the right response—sending a replacement card.

GETTING IT OFF MY CHEST

For more than seven years I had no contact of any kind with the parents of the killers. I put them out of my mind, assuming I would never hear from them. I made a point of not looking closely at photos of them in the newspaper so I wouldn't remember what they looked like. I didn't want to have an awkward encounter if I happened to see them in a public place.

For years I felt I wasn't mentally or emotionally prepared to face the killers' parents. But with the passage of time, I felt there was a void: how could there not be communication between us? We were part of this tragedy together, yet we were worlds apart.

A few Columbine families communicated with the killers' parents in a different kind of way—they filed suit against them, forcing them to give depositions. They had the limited satisfaction of getting some questions answered by the Harris and Klebold parents. Eventually, though, the Columbine families dropped their suit and none of the testimony given by the Harrises and Klebolds in 2005 was released because the contents of the depositions were sealed by the court for 20 years. Worse yet, the Columbine families who questioned the killers' parents were prohibited from revealing anything they heard in testimony. Linda and I were livid that the documents were sealed and angry with the unwillingness of the Harrises and Klebolds to allow their testimony to be made public.

I became driven to learn whatever I could about the Harrises and Klebolds as parents, about their families, and about their sons. I decided in January 2007 that the time had come to contact Wayne and Kathy Harris. It took me at least three painstaking weeks to write a three-page letter, as I struggled over what to say and how to say it. I debated whether to request a face-to-face meeting with them. I really wanted one, but I realized that asking for one would be difficult if my letter were stern—yet I was unwilling to soften the approach of my letter for that purpose. So I decided not to ask for a meeting.

I sent the letter to their attorney, since I had no idea where they lived after they moved from our neighborhood. My letter opened with an explanation of why I was writing:

> It has now been seven years since the Columbine tragedy, the day your son murdered my son Daniel. Yet we have never met or communicated. I decided it was finally time to write to you. I have thought of writing to you a number of times before, but didn't do so for a variety of reasons: I wanted to allow more time to pass so it would be a less painful experience for me; having more important things to do with my time; and, wondering how I could even begin deciding what to say to the parents of a child who murdered my child.

And, I wanted to wait because I realized that you, too, were grieving and going through your own hell. Yes, I realize that you also lost a child that tragic day, and I am sorry for your loss.

I then went on to say that there were many signs of healing and forgiveness following the school shooting that shocked the Amish community in 2007 and the Oklahoma City bombing case, but I observed that it was disappointing there hadn't been any such signs of reconciliation following Columbine. I mentioned that I had been asked by people if I had ever reached a point of forgiveness toward the killers and their parents, adding, "I wish I could say I had."

I explained to the Harrises that I didn't think of them as the "devil incarnate" and that I didn't spend my time harboring hatred toward them, adding that I probably wouldn't even recognize them if I saw them on the street. Still, I wrote,

I tell people that I believe parents are significantly responsible for the actions of their children, and that it is difficult to even approach any level of reconciliation or understanding when there is not even a single word spoken to you or to anyone by those parents.

So I must ask you, Mr. and Mrs. Harris: why have you never expressed any type of apology or condolences to us?!? Perhaps you'll respond that you did write a letter to us and the other victims' parents but that, as has been reported, they were intercepted by the sheriff's office and lost. But once you knew that was the case, why did you then not follow up with a replacement letter? Did the need to do so end with that convenient excuse? Your son shot my son in the face as he was hunkered helplessly under a table. And for that you don't feel any need to make an expression of sympathy or explanation?!?

After that paragraph, perhaps it was unrealistic to think they would be receptive to reading anything else I wrote. Nonetheless, I went on with what was the most important part of the letter. I wasn't necessarily looking for an apology from them; they had seven years in which to offer one, and we already had hints of their excuses for what happened. I was looking for something else.

I wrote to the Harrises that the nation was being torn apart by school shootings, and was desperately in need of hearing from shooters' parents willing to share what might have gone wrong with their child.

It has always been my feeling that one of the great tragedies of Columbine is the fact that you and the Klebolds shared nothing of your own lessons from Columbine. That is, you've failed to respond to the questions so many parents in the world have: what signs of hatred and despair did you see? What warning signs did you miss? Were you a family that ever spent much time at the dinner table together? What did your son talk about? What would you have done differently in raising Eric?

…Your son was so angry and distressed and hateful and so troubled that he wanted to kill hundreds of his classmates. Hundreds! How in the world could you not have seen that your son was THAT hateful and troubled? Were you so disconnected that you did not see this disposition of his? How could that happen?!?

I think you could do a great service if you were to speak publicly about those lessons. Sure, it would be very difficult for you to do so. Painful, yes. Might people say you were terrible, neglectful parents? Sure. But obviously many say that already. To me what's most important is that the pain you might encounter by being open and speaking publicly could not possibly be worse than the pain you've already experienced in losing your son in such a tragic way.

Sure, it would be very difficult to do. Tell me about it. For the past seven years I have put myself out there in the public eye to try to make something good happen out of this tragedy. And while there are those who admire my advocacy, there are also those who oppose and detest me. My advocacy has come at a cost—hundreds of pieces of hate mail, a death threat, media scrutiny, etc. It is not always the fulfilling advocacy mission that some may think it is. But I do it because the pain is nothing compared to losing Daniel, and I do it for him.

Speaking out is something you could do for your son. True, it's not the same for you, given what your son did. But you could at

least try to address what has happened by doing something posi-
tive—speaking out about what went wrong, how you missed the
signs, etc. Sorry, but I haven't seen a single damned thing you've
done for the community to make up for the pain your son caused.
But you could reach many parents who may have children that are
troubled and prone toward violence—, in a way that few others
could. To not do so is the ultimate tragedy within this tragedy—
that you remain silent and unapologetic. Your silence is deafening.

HEARING BACK

After at least two months passed with no response, I assumed I would never get one, presuming they tossed my letter away. But I was not going to give up easily. I called their attorney's office and asked if my letter had been forwarded to the Harrises. It was not. I was told the attorney represented the Harrises' insurance company and was not their personal attorney, but was assured my letter would now be forwarded to the Harrises' personal attorney.

I received a call from Ben Colkitt, the Harrises' personal attorney, just a week or two later, calling on their behalf. He was a pleasant and engaging man. During our phone conversation, he informed me he was willing to sit down with me and do his best to answer some of the questions I put forth in my letter.

The offer came as a pleasant surprise. He also informed me, though, that the Harrises were not willing to meet with me, given the tone of my letter. I was taken aback by what he said. On one hand, I recognized my letter was harsh, but at the same time, I thought they were overlooking another harsh fact—that their son murdered my son in cold blood. I did not sue them or publicly condemn them, yet they had the nerve to say they were concerned about the harsh tone of my letter? What the hell would they expect to hear from me?

Despite their response, I agreed to meet with the attorney. I knew this was an extremely emotional situation and that I would simply have to take it one step at a time.

A few weeks later I met with Colkitt at his church, a Friends Meeting Hall in south Denver. We spent about two hours together, and it was mostly a relaxed, friendly conversation. He explained that he was not merely legal counsel to the Harrises, but that he also considered them friends.

One thing he said that stood out was that the Harrises did not replace the lost sympathy cards because he, as their attorney, advised against it. I told him I thought it was unfortunate that our society had become so litigious that people would follow the advice of an attorney on such an important personal matter rather than do what was more humane. I told him I would have ignored what my attorney told me and opted to do the compassionate thing—write a replacement sympathy card.

As for what went wrong with Eric, and why he became a murderer, Colkitt insisted the Harrises didn't understand it. I was told about Eric's family and upbringing, as well as his worsening behavior. The Harrises tried to monitor his behavior after he was arrested for breaking into the van and tried for a while to keep him away from Dylan Klebold, but claimed they had no idea he was so seriously disturbed. They took Eric to a psychologist for treatment of his depression, but weren't aware of his deeper troubles, apparently blaming the psychologist for not being more aware of it.

I felt Colkitt did his best to answer my questions. It was certainly not an intense or pointed inquisition, since I knew there were limits to what he, as their attorney, would reveal.

CONTACTING THE KLEBOLDS

A few months later, in September 2007, I wrote a letter to Tom and Sue Klebold. The letter was similar to the Harris letter but not quite as harsh, since their son didn't shoot Daniel. I acknowledged in my letter that Daniel was not shot by their son, but added "it could just as easily have been your son that killed Daniel at that moment, and your son was part of that carnage, so I feel as compelled to write to you as I do to the Harrises."

I received a swift email response from Sue Klebold. She expressed sympathy and said she had been hoping that I would make contact at some point but that she was uncertain when it would have been appropriate for her to contact us. She offered to sit down with me and talk. There were no preconditions. She indicated her husband would not participate. I wrote back and confirmed my willingness to meet and indicated Linda didn't wish to join me.

We sat down one afternoon and talked for about two hours in a meeting room in an office building in downtown Denver. I learned about her son and their family, and about Dylan's temperament leading up to the massacre. The bottom line was somewhat the same as I heard from the Harris' attorney: The Klebolds had no idea what their son was plotting or that he was capable of committing such a heinous crime. What she shared was much the same as what she offered up in an article in Oprah magazine in 2009. She placed much emphasis on her son's suicide, feeling that his depression and suicidal thoughts drove him to capitulate and join Eric Harris.

The meeting was mostly cordial. I didn't get answers to the most troubling aspects of her son's life, but I didn't expect to get them. I was content just to learn whatever I could about Dylan and his family life.

FACE TO FACE

Early in 2009, I requested a second meeting with Ben Colkitt. This meeting was shorter, since I only wanted to ask a few follow-up questions. Not long after that second meeting, Colkitt called and indicated the Harrises were interested in meeting with Linda and me and asked if we were willing to do so. The offer came out of the blue, since I had not asked him for such a meeting, but perhaps was related to the fact my meetings with Colkitt were cordial.

There were no preconditions placed on the meeting. Linda, without hesitation, said she would meet with them, but we wanted to wait until well after the tenth anniversary of Columbine had passed.

Linda and I mentally prepared ourselves for the meeting, wondering how we would approach them and what we would ask. We agreed it should be a conversation among four parents, not anything like an interrogation. After all, the Columbine parents who sued the Harrises and Klebolds already had questioned them. There was no reason to think they would reveal any more to us, particularly when they were not under oath. We didn't plan to be confrontational with them, although that didn't mean we wouldn't ask some probing questions about their son and about their actions leading up to the massacre.

We met the Harrises at 6 p.m. on July 15 at the same Friends Meeting Hall where I had met with Colkitt. First we all gathered outside the church briefly, acknowledged each other with some curt pleasantries, then walked inside. We found ourselves in the church sanctuary, a well-lit, long, narrow room with wooden floors and lots of windows. We quickly agreed to move out of this larger room into a cozy alcove on the west side, where we could sit on wooden benches facing each other. Colkitt then left, saying there was no need for his participation.

Once alone, Wayne Harris smiled and said, "Nice to meet you," and extended his hand. Linda thanked them for coming. Kathy Harris handed Linda a basket of flowers. The Harrises quickly spoke up, expressing condolences and regret for what their son had done to Daniel, saying it was nothing they had ever taught or condoned. We likewise expressed our condolences for their loss and the pain they had to endure, just as I had done in my letter.

Mr. Harris struck us as intelligent and well spoken. He was genial and seemed open to our questions. His precise speech matched our preconceived notions of someone who had been a career military man. (He had been a pilot in the Air Force.) But we both had pictured him as a larger, deeper-voiced, more overbearing, authoritarian man, perhaps because of our preconceptions of the Harris household and of his military background. But he seemed to be none of those things—he seemed a more gentle, softspoken man than expected. Mrs. Harris seemed more shy than he, but like him, was cordial. Nothing about them seemed greatly out of the ordinary, nothing that would lead one to easily and conveniently conclude, "Well, no wonder that kid was messed up."

We spoke about our families. Mr. Harris talked with pride about his elder son, Kevin, about how well he was doing. Naturally I wondered whether Eric felt overshadowed by and inferior to his elder brother. I also reminded myself, though, how many parents show favor toward one child, and it usually doesn't result in the overlooked child becoming a murderer.

The Harrises seemed mystified by what had happened to Eric. They seemed to rather readily accept that perhaps Eric was a psychopath, but indicated they didn't know how he became one. They claimed Eric "fooled them" and fooled the psychologist who was treating him. They felt misled by the psychologist, who they felt had regarded Eric's problems as minor.

In response to a question about whether they were a "dinner table family," they claimed they ate many meals together as a family. They insisted they were never cruel to Eric. Both had jobs, but Mrs. Harris insisted they were always "available" for Eric.

Eric's parents didn't seem to think they missed any red flags. But they did share a few things about their son that seemed to perhaps be signs of something being awry. They admitted that Eric seemed to have intense reactions to being slighted by anyone. They revealed Eric was so mad once that he slammed his fist into a brick wall and scraped his knuckles badly. I wondered to myself whether they considered that abnormal and of concern. I wondered whether outward displays of emotion were discouraged in their household and whether they were tightly wound parents who preferred to shun such outbursts rather than deal with them.

Mr. Harris acknowledged that Eric was probably self-conscious about the fact he had a chest abnormality that made his chest appear slightly caved in. He said Eric was upset that a recent operation on his chest hadn't seemed to help it much, though he didn't think Eric's self-consciousness was something that led to his mental dysfunction.

The Harrises admitted Eric informed them he was not interested in joining any clubs at Columbine. That revelation was particularly disturbing to me. It's not that it would have been an obvious sign of something ominous, but it made me wonder if it should have concerned them more, given his lack of friends and his known depression. I couldn't help but conclude these parents didn't value social interaction very highly. After all, they didn't seem terribly outgoing themselves.

Linda asked Mr. Harris if Eric seemed overly fond of weaponry. He responded that he did not, but admitted that Eric subscribed to a gun magazine, adding that he thought he only did so to help him understand the video game Doom more readily. I wondered how the heck a detailed knowledge of guns would aid one in a computer game involving fantasy.

MISSING SIGNS

Mrs. Harris shared that Eric had made no plans for fall 1999, despite her insistence that he either find a job or be registered for school. She seemed somewhat unclear about whether Eric had taken any college entrance examinations. It seemed odd that she would not remember, but she added she was thinking of community college as an option for him, which would not have required the exams. Still, I felt it was not a good sign to have a depressed yet intelligent teen making no post-graduation plans. The Harrises thought their son might have been manipulating them, holding off their demands for future planning by expressing interest in the Marines.

These accounts may have signaled the Harrises had a troubled teen, but even together they might not have been overwhelming clues that Eric could become a mass murderer. I would not automatically think of a teen who breaks into a car, has an interest in guns and violent video games, and doesn't belong to school clubs, as being a candidate for committing mass murder. If American society thought those traits were evidence of a mass murderer, we'd be warning an awful lot of parents of potential trouble and putting thousands of teens in this country under surveillance.

But there were other signs that should have raised a red flag, such as Eric's depression and his parents' acknowledgment that he had few friends. He cunningly refused to let his parents into his disturbed world, but to me it seemed the Harrises didn't take the time to look more deeply into his life and weren't intrusive enough to become aware of the pipe bombs and guns.

I asked if they would help the world by talking publicly about the signs they missed in Eric, but the Harrises indicated they felt too vulnerable to speak with the media and didn't think they could endure it. I continue to believe it's tragic they have not spoken publicly, but I agree that anyone in their situation would be "eaten alive" by direct media exposure. I don't believe the Harrises' personas could have handled that kind of intense media inquiry.

Anything the Harrises would have said would have been questioned by most people as self-serving and defensive. Many people would not be satisfied unless they capitulated and said they were totally at fault. By not speaking publicly in any way after the massacre, and by not speaking in any helpful way with law enforcement, they had already lost practically any chance of earning the benefit of the public's doubt.

DUPES?

Were Linda and I naïve and too "easy" on the Harrises? Were we simply lied to by them? I'm sure some people will say we were. If that was the case, so be it, but we are not as cynical as those who would insist we were deluded by the Harrises. We are fairly good judges of character and believe we'd know if someone were overtly lying. The Harrises did not strike us as calculating or devious people. If anything, we felt they seemed rather hapless and oblivious. We concluded they likely were not aware enough, engaged enough, or perceptive enough to understand what was going on with their son.

Many other parents could not have easily predicted the viciousness that resided within Eric Harris. But they were negligent for not knowing about Eric's Web site, for not noticing the weaponry stashed in their home, and for not doing more to encourage positive social interaction. At the same time, how many American parents can say they know a lot about their kids' Internet usage? How many closely monitor their teens' rooms? How many do a lot to encourage their teens' social lives? Many do, but many do not.

The Harrises at least seemed to have some minimal level of involvement in their son's life and were getting mental health counseling for him. But their parenting style did not seem to rise to the level of heroic, nor did it seem adequate enough to address his mental illness. They blamed that on Eric's psychologist, but I believe parents also have to take responsibility for comprehending and addressing their child's mental wellness, just as they do their child's physical wellness.

The Harrises did not seem like callous or cruel people, but they also did not seem like overly empathetic or expressive people. We concluded they were not evil or totally disconnected parents, but they also did not strike us as a couple who were highly affectionate or emotionally connected to their child.

At one point I was a bit frustrated by what I thought was a lack of any acknowledgment of failure on the part of the parents, asking the Harrises,

"So there is nothing we can learn from this? Were no mistakes made?" They strongly implied there were none.

One observation that struck Linda was that they did not seem to second-guess themselves to any extent. She believed that if her child had shown signs of concern similar to those shown by Eric, she'd still be questioning herself. That just didn't seem to be the case with the Harrises. They seemed to write it all off as largely unpreventable and the result of Eric's mental illness.

At the end of our meeting, Linda told the Harrises that she forgave their son. That seemed to please them. She later told me she felt uncomfortable extending forgiveness to the parents, because Eric was the one who committed the crime, and because the Harrises didn't ask for her forgiveness. Besides, she felt somewhat ambiguous about them. I felt the same way. That's why I extended no statement offering forgiveness. Nonetheless, at the end of our meeting, Linda wished them peace, and I did the same.

We talked with them for about an hour. I feel better for having met them and looking them in the eye. They did not seem monstrous, maybe just all-too-human. It was yet another part of the healing process. It did not provide an answer to the critical question of "Why?" but I never expected it would. It did provide some clues and a small glimpse into the lives of the people who were closest to Eric.

Chapter 31

The Little Things

To strangers who casually observed my life in the first years after Columbine, it might seem like much of it was taken up by media attention and interviews, lobbying, and Columbine–related events. Sometimes it seemed like it was. But not all my Columbine experiences were necessarily profound, momentous, high profile, or conspicuous. Not all my grief was caused by the loss of Daniel. Not all that comforted me was related to my work in honoring Daniel.

There were many little things that had an impact on my life following Columbine. They may pale in comparison to some of the momentous events I've described, but they are nonetheless part of my story and deserve mention.

BOTHERSOME USE OF WORDS OR STORIES

Something that irritated me at times was the use of certain words. I knew people who used them didn't mean to be insensitive or mean any harm, so I rarely complained to them. For instance, I cringed when people referred to "the Columbine incident." Ashley D. from New Orleans wrote in 2002, "I make sure that I pray especially for those involved in the Columbine incident." Katie from Appleton, Wisconsin wrote, "The Columbine incident touched me greatly, and made me realize what a reality school violence is."

I appreciated their concern but was aggravated when they used such an innocuous word as "incident" to describe a massacre. My dictionary defines incident as "a definite and separate occurrence; a usually minor event or condition that is subordinate to another." While the Columbine massacre may strictly meet the first definition of a mere occurrence, it certainly doesn't meet the second. I also don't think it meets the normal usage to which I am accustomed, which tends to include events like a heightened argument or a minor accident. I don't think the killing of thirteen and the injuring of twenty-five people is befitting of the word "incident."

I usually use the word "massacre" to describe Columbine, but I realize that word may be a bit too strong or disquieting for some people. For those uncomfortable with that word, then "Columbine tragedy" or "Columbine shootings" are suitable alternatives. But I ask that this tragic event not be relegated to a mere "incident."

Sometimes people related to me their experience of Columbine in a way I found insensitive. Again, I'm sure these people didn't *mean* any harm, but it was something that was unsettling to me.

On many occasions I was told by parents, relatives, or friends of a student at Columbine about that student's experience of that tragic day. Invariably they described where that student was when the massacre began, how they managed to escape, and how the student's parents received word they were safe. I'm glad for them and relieved more students weren't injured or killed. I'm sure those who shared these stories were simply trying to relate to me their own Columbine experience by confirming how tragic that day was at the school. But stories about other students' fortuitous escapes were not something in which I usually took solace. Did these people ever stop to think how it made me feel to hear these escape and survival stories, given that Daniel did not escape the carnage?

It was particularly hurtful when the person telling me the story shared how they felt the student's escape was somehow a "miracle" or otherwise a special blessing from God. Again I wondered if they thought about how it made me feel to hear of such a wondrous salvation for that student. Did that mean that Daniel was somehow *not* blessed by God because his life was not spared?

INTENSE SYMPATHIZERS

One unusual aspect of high-profile tragedies like Columbine is that they can attract intense attention from people who are not directly impacted by the tragedy but become so profoundly affected by it that they feel driven to make a connection with the victims. I'm speaking of people who seek more than the exchange of just an email or two. Two or three dozen such people came forward. I found that many of them didn't live near Columbine or even in Colorado, nor were they connected to the victims, yet they found themselves in deep grief, determined to find out more about the tragedy and its victims and to reach out to the families and friends of those victims.

Over the years, dozens of these "intense sympathizers," as I'll call them, made contact with us by mail or email, and continued their contact once they heard back from us. They closely followed the many news stories about Columbine and visited Daniel's Web site frequently. Some stopped their contact within the first few years of Columbine, perhaps because they felt we were healing well, while a few others have continued to this day.

Some are people who, like a young woman from Germany who shares Madeline's first name, faithfully emails us comforting and encouraging messages on the Columbine anniversaries or major holidays. Some are people who write more often, such as Steve from New Jersey, a dedicated Republican who is faithfully pro life but upset with those in the pro-life movement who are uncompromisingly pro gun, which he sees as an inconsistent belief.

Two sympathizers are priests from eastern states who pray for us. One was studying to become a Franciscan priest and says he felt a strong personal connection to the gentleness of Daniel. Later he faced a multitude of life-threatening diseases yet continued to write and call. The other is a priest who feels a connection to us because he was a witness to gun violence. He comes to Colorado almost every year to visit the graves of the

Columbine victims and pay his respects. Some years we have had him at our house for dinner.

Some people might speculate these intense sympathizers are somehow obsessed with Columbine, or perhaps have problems in their own lives from which they seek to be distracted by focusing on the victims of a tragedy, or are trying to connect in some way with people associated with a high-profile news story. Perhaps any one of those could be true, but I think there's a better explanation in most cases: they're simply people who have a lot of empathy and concern to share with others in need. They are people with deep compassion who feel the need to comfort us—people who would do anything in their power to absorb our pain if they could do so.

Just as we saw that some people did not know how to deal with us and became estranged, and just as there were some in the public who said they were "sick and tired of hearing about Columbine," it should come as no surprise that there were others who were the opposite—they were overflowing with concern and love and wanted in some way to relieve our pain. We greatly appreciated their sympathy and took it for the unexpected blessing it was for us.

CRYING HARDER

I have seen a marked change in my reaction to others' pain. Whenever I watch a tragic scene in a movie, or when I view a sad story on the news, I have a much more emotional reaction than I ever had before Columbine. I usually get a lump in my throat, tears well up, and sometimes I sob. It's not that I rarely felt sympathy toward others in the past, but it was never this strong or consistent.

Naturally, news stories portraying death affect me emotionally, but often it's not just stories with a tragic ending that do so. Stories about people who have had to live with some type of disability or have been deprived of something that we all take for granted also impact me emotionally, even when it's a story that supposedly has a happy ending.

It may be uplifting, for instance, to see a news story about a disabled child given a special opportunity to participate for the first time in an activity they would normally be denied. For me, though, it's still sad to think of how tragic it is that they're usually deprived of that activity. I realize disabled children are grateful for these exciting opportunities, but I can't help but still feel sadness, thinking about all the other problems they and their families experience and how they routinely are denied the chance to participate in activities taken for granted by others. Perhaps it's a reflection of my own experience—that although I may feel occasional satisfaction from doing things to honor Daniel, there's still the underlying fact that Daniel is not here.

Most difficult for me are news stories about the death of a child that includes an interview of a family member who relates a sorrowful and tearful story about the loss of the child. While I'm glad to see them able to express their grief, it's heartbreaking to see them go through what I did and it's an upsetting reminder of the pain I lived through.

These new emotional reactions have been difficult to deal with, but they've also been healthy, for through them I have developed more understanding toward others who suffer in this life and have better come to grips with my own emotions.

DREADED ANNIVERSARIES

How could just one day out of 365 cause so much pain and be so reviled? There is such a day for me. It is a date I despised and hearing it mentioned in any context makes me cringe. It was difficult enough living through every June 25 (Daniel's birthday), Father's Day, Mother's Day, Thanksgiving, and Christmas without Daniel. But those days paled in comparison to the stress and pain associated with April 20.

April 20 was the day the rest of the world chose to honor and commemorate those who lost their lives at Columbine. I understood and appreciated that, but that day was such an excruciatingly painful one for my family. At times we felt others wanted to be with us so they could console us, and we felt subtle pressure to attend certain public events on the anniversary. But for us, the anniversary was a day to forget, a day we usually wanted to be alone, a day we just wanted to get through as quickly as possible.

To make matters worse, the days leading up to and following the Columbine anniversary were also awful. Leading up to April 20, I'd often receive requests from the media asking me to reflect on the anniversary or on a recent shooting, or asking me how my family was doing. The news media frequently called me because I was usually accessible to them. While we kept our home phone number unlisted, I made my cell phone number available to members of the media because of my gun-control advocacy.

Many grieving parents in this situation would probably not welcome such calls, and perhaps I was a glutton for punishment, for often I agreed to talk to the media. I felt no obligation to speak, and it wasn't something I looked forward to. Sometimes it was a way for me to get something off my chest, to get my gun-control message out to the public, or to give an update about my family to a community I knew was concerned about us. But mostly I saw my speaking up as an opportunity to honor Daniel, however painful it might be.

I dreaded watching news coverage of Columbine anniversaries, but as someone who regularly watched the news, the coverage was impossible to miss. Inevitably they'd broadcast certain images over and over again—students running from the school, police taking cover behind SWAT vehicles, or Patrick Ireland's limp body dropping from a window of the library. Especially difficult for me were the clips of students crying tears of joy in the arms of their parents, knowing that such a reunion didn't happen with Daniel.

I didn't expect the media not to commemorate the anniversaries. I just wish they could have done so without repeatedly flashing those painful video clips we had all seen so many times before. On the other hand, I realized that might have amounted to a sugar-coating of the Columbine tragedy.

Some earlier anniversaries were made worse by press coverage of whatever was the latest Columbine controversy, whether it was a story related to the release of evidence from an investigation, lawsuits, new accusations, or anything else the media chose to focus on. Even if it weren't a significant news story, it was often made so by a media hungry for some story to accompany the anniversary.

On the other hand, much of the media coverage was respectful and positive. Particularly touching was the kindness and reverence of a simple, silent video clip broadcast each year by Denver's KUSA-TV, which consisted of thirteen candles slowly appearing one by one on the screen, along with the words, "A time to remember. A time to hope." It was simple and solemn, sad yet respectful.

As one might expect, the first anniversary was the most difficult. It was agonizing not just because it was the first, but because there was so much media attention leading up to that day, with helicopters flying over the area (something I have come to despise and fear to this day) and the national news media swarming the community and setting up in tents in Clement Park as they had a year earlier.

We could have gone to the community memorial event or to the commemorative event that took place in front of the state capitol, but we didn't want to have any part of either. While we appreciated the community's concern, we felt we had to get away. We escaped for a short trip to one of our family's favorite spots, the mountain resort town of Glenwood Springs, where we rode bikes through Glenwood Canyon and swam in the world-famous hot springs pool. We took along a friend of Christie's. We tried to erase the pain and enjoy ourselves, but it didn't work. Linda and I were irritable, argumentative, somber, on edge, and in pain during much of the trip.

The ensuing anniversaries followed a pattern. In all but one case I took a vacation day from work in order to be with Linda and away from the office. Christie always went to school except for that first year, because for her it seemed better to be in a familiar setting and away from Linda and me. Linda, Madeline, and I usually hung around the house, went out for lunch, then made a trip to Daniel's grave at Mount Olivet Cemetery. It was often the only trip we made to the cemetery all year, not just because it is more than 20 miles away, but because we find more comfort in remembering Daniel's life in ways other than visiting where his remains lie.

After arriving at the cemetery, we'd always wash off Daniel's headstone with a gallon of water—more an act of reverence than of necessity. We'd put flowers in the permanent metal vase next to the headstone. Then we'd visit the graves of Kelly Fleming and Matt Kechter, which are nearby.

When Madeline was about four years old, we developed a new tradition, one that even Madeline strangely came to enjoy: we'd walk around and visit other graves near Daniel's. In part we were entertained by the messages on the headstones, or by their style, or impressed by the new trend of including photos of the deceased on the headstone.

Linda and I found ourselves looking at the ages of the deceased. The area where Daniel is buried has quite a number of younger people and children. While we certainly felt a sad kinship with those parents who, like us, lost a child, we found a certain solace in knowing we are not alone in losing a child too soon.

Another touching tradition took place over the years. Every year when we arrived at the cemetery there was a solitary rose on the graves of Daniel, Kelly, and Matt. Two wonderful people, Rick and Sue Townsend, father and stepmother of Columbine victim Lauren Townsend, would visit the grave of every Columbine victim, leave a rose, and say a prayer.

Only one year did I go to work on the anniversary of Columbine. It was 2006. The initial meeting of some transportation officials, marking a new program I was managing, was scheduled for April 20. The meeting was scheduled to coincide with another gathering, so the selection of that date was unavoidable. It was a meeting I didn't want to miss.

If I had said I couldn't attend, that would have been acceptable to my supervisor. But I wanted to be there and was convinced I could handle working on that day after seven years had passed. I was wrong. I made it through the meeting, but I sat there quietly and had trouble focusing, and it seemed others at the meeting could tell. When another relatively important work meeting fell on the anniversary in 2011, I didn't hesitate to take a vacation day.

The eighth anniversary was distressing because it fell three days after the Virginia Tech massacre. The twelfth anniversary was disturbing because a pipe bomb and propane tank were placed in a shopping mall less than two miles from Columbine High School. The tenth anniversary was difficult because of all the attention given it by the media. That's the way it is with those round numbers. But I'm guessing that not much attention will be paid to the anniversaries until we reach the twentieth. For us that's a welcome relief.

DREADFUL REMINDERS

I always dreaded it when there was a school shooting somewhere in the nation. To me they were more than just tragic news stories. Inevitably it took no time for someone, often a reporter or coworker, to ask me, "So did this school shooting somehow remind you of the Columbine shootings and bring back painful memories?" What the hell did they think? Of course they did! They all did. I usually had a sinking feeling of helplessness and would return to my own day of darkness. I hated those reminders of April 20, 1999, but those questions inevitably came with the territory.

Two school shootings were especially disturbing to me. The Virginia Tech massacre bothered me immensely because of the horrific body count and because the killer reminded me of the Columbine killers—mentally disturbed, not being treated adequately for his mental illness, disaffected, feeling tormented, unremorseful, and determined to kill as many students as possible.

The shooting at Platte Canyon High School in Bailey also bothered me immensely, though not just because the school was only 40 miles from Columbine. It was disturbing that an adult was determined to do such serious harm to innocent students—and willing to die for it. The worst part for me was watching the news video showing parents crying as they gathered around school buses looking for their children. It reminded me of my wait for a school bus carrying Daniel.

One school shooting demonstrated just how pervasive and widespread is the problem of school violence. About five years after the massacre, the Columbine families gathered to socialize and conduct some HOPE business. We discussed a proposal to replace thirteen wooden crosses on display at a local cemetery with stone crosses, using funds left over from what was raised to replace the library at Columbine High.

As Linda looked at the brochure of the company that would make the crosses, she noticed the address of the company: Cold Spring, Minnesota. She remembered that town was the site of a 2003 school shooting in which a quiet and withdrawn 15-year-old freshman who was teased about his severe acne took a handgun to his high school and fatally shot two students, killing one, before a teacher faced the boy down and took the weapon. We were amazed that of all the places the crosses would come from in the United States, it would be from the site of another school shooting. It demonstrated how we are all so interconnected.

DARK DAYS

Some people have written to compliment me for what they see as my dealing with tragedy in a positive way. I have had some success in being positive and not letting myself become too sullen or glum. There is satisfaction in doing things in Daniel's name and joy associated with adopting Madeline. But that certainly does not mean I was easily able to overcome the painful grief of losing my son or that I did not suffer through some very dark and painful days.

Obviously I had many dark days in the weeks and months following the massacre, and suffered through the Columbine anniversaries and family holidays. That's to be expected. What surprised me was that I still suffered through some other very dark days even years after the tragedy—days when I was depressed, devastated, and paralyzed. Any number of things could trigger those dark days, from news of a school shooting to a bitter argument at home to losing a vote on a gun-related bill to something prompting a sad memory related to Daniel.

They were days I didn't want to get out of bed in the morning. They were days I was unlike my usual self—when I was withdrawn and inconsolable. I would listen to sad, somber music to match my mood, knowing that upbeat music was not going to help. On work days the easy response would have been to call in sick, but I usually felt the day would go by faster at work, where I wouldn't see any reminders of Daniel. But once at work I would avoid people, conversation, and eye contact; I was just there to work my eight hours and get through the day. If I had scheduled a meeting, I would cancel it.

In some cases I felt that I was grieving the feared loss of something. If I had a heated argument with Linda, I feared we were on the verge of divorce and worried about being without my family and friends. If I failed in something I was doing at work, I feared having to resign my job in disgrace. I was irrationally grieving the loss of my marriage and of my job, among other things, even though I had not lost them. I believe it was an unfortunate reaction to trauma—an irrational fear that more tragedy would strike.

Fortunately those dark spells usually only lasted one or two days, and they only happened once every month or two. They were something I learned to live through. By about the ninth anniversary, they greatly decreased in number and intensity.

HOW MANY?

When you're grieving the loss of a child, it can be difficult just to field simple questions from those around you. A tough question for me to handle was one likely experienced by many other parents who have lost a child. It was a dreaded question that occasionally came up in conversations with people who likely didn't know I had lost a child: "How many children do you have?"

I loathed that question. That may seem strange to those who have not lost a child, but it's a question that could be agonizing to answer, depending on the circumstances. If I were casually talking to a stranger who I might never see again, such as someone sitting next to me on an airplane, my answer was a simple one: "I have two girls." There was no point in mentioning my third child, because it might lead to another difficult question such as, "What are their ages?" Then I would have to decide whether to say "My son died when he was fifteen," or "My son would now be twenty-eight." It was easier to not offer something that would prompt those questions in the first place.

If it was someone I met at a party or at a work meeting, it became more complicated to handle. I often paused, wondering if the person already knew I was a Columbine parent and was curious about whether I had other children besides Daniel. It was riskier to respond that I only had two children, since the person with whom I was conversing might later discover I had lost a child at Columbine. He or she might feel awkward about saying anything about my loss, figuring my avoidance was a sign I was trying to avoid the subject. Meanwhile, I'd be ashamed for having denied that I had three children. Why in the world would I deny Daniel?

It might seem that the easy thing to do would be to simply say I had three children and, if the conversation became detailed, acknowledge that one was deceased. But saying you have lost a child or, worse yet, that your child was murdered, will suddenly turn a conversation somber or serious.

People are unsure how to react, especially if you don't provide any idea of how the child died. Yet it was also difficult if I mentioned Daniel was killed at Columbine. It wasn't just the pain of discussing Daniel's death that bothered me; it was the fact that saying I lost a child at Columbine often led the person to struggle with what to say or, worse yet, to reflect in detail about the tragic events at Columbine. It's not as if I didn't already have to deal with those conversations already.

A NEW TIME MEASUREMENT

A new way for my family to measure time came into being after the massacre. We found ourselves dividing our lives into "before Columbine" and "after Columbine." I'm not trying to be overly dramatic or somber about it, that's just the way it is for us. We had one life before Columbine, and another distinct one, without Daniel, afterward.

Our family often speaks of an event in the past in the context of whether it occurred before or after Columbine. We are usually correct about the timing of events, perhaps because it is so vivid to us, and because we think so much in terms of whether Daniel was in the picture when we did a certain thing or went to a certain place. Sometimes we guess right simply because the years following Columbine were so damned different than the years before, with such a different feel to them, and with the element of Madeline being in our lives rather than Daniel.

I'm hoping that as more time passes we will come to develop a third time period. It will be an "after-after Columbine" period. It will be a time not as dark as the years immediately following the massacre. It will not be a time we have forgotten Daniel, or "gotten over" his death, but it will be a time we have experienced much more healing. The only problem is, I don't know if this after-after Columbine period will start five years from now, or ten years from now, or if it is something that has already started. Only time will tell.

Chapter 32

Life in the Epicenter

In the eye of the storm. In the spotlight. At the epicenter of the earthquake. Call it what you wish. It's where I've been for thirteen years, and it's been both blessing and curse, both inspirational and dispiriting, both triumphant and vanquishing, both joyful and sorrowful.

PUBLIC EXPOSURE, PRIVATE GRIEF

I often thought about how *fortunate* we Columbine families were in one respect: we were showered with cards, flowers, and expressions of sympathy from all over the nation and world. Our children's and spouse's life stories were broadcast worldwide. How could one not feel moved by such outpourings of love and compassion, and by admiration for one's child or spouse?

I felt sadness for parents who lost a child in a suicide or a car accident, for they likely would not have experienced as many expressions of love and support from so many people, nor heard so much praise showered upon their loved ones. They might be left to grieve on their own, without the wider support systems available to us.

In many respects we were blessed by the world's attention. But, as one might imagine, it was a two-edged sword. We were not only in the epicenter of a terrible tragedy, we were also thrust onto center stage of a frenzied spectacle.

Many people wanted a front-row seat and the media was more than willing to give it to them. People wanted to see who we were and how we handled this tragedy. Everyone seemed to have an opinion about what went wrong at Columbine. A caring public wanted to know how the Columbine families were doing, but many also wanted to know how we felt about this or that investigation, and who or what we blamed for the massacre. At times there seemed no end to it all.

The outpouring of public sympathy came with the loss of privacy. One could not easily hide from the spotlight suddenly pointed at us. The outpouring of public sympathy came with exposure to a media-crazed public that was just as quick to condemn as it was to console. Some people were irritated with the Columbine families who filed lawsuits, or irate that some Columbine families criticized the police or school for failing to prevent the massacre, or upset about the removal of the crosses on Rebel Hill.

It didn't seem to matter whether we were among the families who did or said any of those things; we still were painted with the same brush and pushed by the media and by people on both sides to declare a position on these issues. In this no-win situation we inevitably would upset some people just by speaking out on either side. If we were critical of the school, teachers, or law enforcement, we risked angering those who were supportive of them. Why couldn't people give us some leeway and understanding? After all, we did not ask to be in this tragic play.

The Columbine families could have remained quiet and not reacted to the news stories, and indeed some family members chose that course. Perhaps it would have been better if we all had stayed quiet. The problem was that the public and the media weren't staying quiet, and sometimes what they said was wrong, misguided, or hurtful, so what they said often *deserved* a response. Furthermore, in this age of widespread cynicism, if one doesn't respond to an outrageous statement it can be seen as an indication of one's concurrence with that statement. Once you go down that path and speak out, it's difficult to turn back.

HIGH-PROFILE EXPOSURE

It was difficult to grieve privately in such a high-profile case. Being in the camera lens certainly didn't end after our loved ones were laid to rest. One of my first memorable media intrusions occurred May 20, 1999, one month after the massacre, when President Clinton and the first lady came to Littleton to console the Columbine victims' families.

It was supposed to be a private event at Light of the World Catholic Church. The media was not invited but knew where and when it would take place. The press was kept at a distance, but photographers with telephoto lenses were taking pictures of the parents as they walked from the parking lot to the church.

A photo of Linda, Christie, and me appeared in a Denver newspaper the next day. I felt violated by it. That might seem strange to say, given that I had already thrown myself into the public spotlight at the NRA protest, on *The Today Show*, and at the White House in the prior weeks. But those exposures were by *my* choice. This was my family, and we weren't welcoming the exposure at the time. To us it was a private moment, yet there we were, being photographed from a distance. After having been shielded from the media at Daniel's funeral and the Bowles Crossing memorial service, I was taken aback by this invasion. It oddly felt as if we were being shadowed by the paparazzi for some tabloid.

My experiences as an advocate included meeting a number of high-profile state and national political leaders and news correspondents. As a political science major and news junkie, it was exciting to find myself conversing with these people, yet I was not particularly impressed by it all. I was rarely star struck or intimidated by these people. It wasn't that I thought poorly of them, it's just that my encounters with them were different than if they had been the result of a chance or fortuitous encounter. I knew all too well there was nothing chance or fortuitous about it. I was encountering these people only because my son was one of the victims of a high-profile shooting and because I had spoken out about it publicly and provocatively.

It was never easy for me to be in these high-profile encounters. It was comforting to know they gave me an opportunity to honor Daniel and to do things in his name, but it was never something to which I looked forward. They brought Daniel's death to the forefront even more than everyday situations. Rather than grieving quietly, I was acknowledging my loss in a very public way.

The exposure was also difficult for Linda, who is more private than I am. She rarely joined me in any of my gun-control appearances or activities, in part because she was caring for Christie and Madeline, but also because she preferred not to be in the public eye. (A few times, though, she spoke to the media and did a terrific job.) Sometimes the privacy issue became source of conflict between us. She was supportive of my efforts but not of the intrusions and the loss of privacy. She did not like having to field calls from the media—which was part of the reason we got an unlisted number. She also grew uncomfortable with media interviews taking place in our home, so I stopped them.

NOTORIETY

There were times I sensed I was being recognized in the community because of my media appearances. It was rare for strangers to actually stop me and say, "Aren't you the father of one of the Columbine victims?" Instead it was usually a certain look, an awkward glance that lingered a bit longer than normal—the kind that ended abruptly if I looked back at them. I wasn't fond of getting "that look." I appreciated that people felt sympathy for me and perhaps theirs was a natural curiosity to some extent, but I didn't want to be gawked at or seen as "that poor Columbine dad." I wanted to be another face in the crowd. I wanted to be a "normal person" again—whatever that was.

There have been situations in which I have met strangers at a work or social gathering and had them ask me with a puzzled look after being introduced, "Tom Mauser? Where have I heard that name before?" Or, "You look familiar. Have we met before? Where have I seen you before?"

I hated having to deal with those situations. I had to assume that in many cases they knew my name or face because of Columbine but it wasn't readily apparent because they were seeing me somewhere other than on TV or in the newspaper. But how could I react? It was too awkward and painful to simply tell them I might look familiar because they had seen me in the media as a result of my son being one of the victims at Columbine. Likewise, if I told them who I was, it would be awkward if that turned out not to be the reason I looked familiar to them.

Explaining who I was made me uncomfortable because it might lead people to apologize for questioning me in the first place, and because it usually led to them offering their condolences. I don't have a problem accepting others' condolences, but I'd rather not put either of us in that situation in the first place if I can avoid it. After all, most people don't hear of the loss of a child and simply move onto another subject. It usually leads to a long conversation about the Columbine massacre, sharing where they were when "it" happened, who they knew who escaped the massacre, how terrible it must be to be the parent of a victim, or why they think it happened. It's difficult to simply shift the conversation to something less serious. I find myself in these situations often enough as it is, so I don't really want to encourage more of them.

Consequently, when asked, I often pretended not to know why they might be familiar with my face or name. I'd often change the subject. Only if the person persisted, or if I knew I'd encounter this person often in the future, would I share the likely reason my face or name seemed familiar.

In the first few years after the massacre, if we went to a restaurant and had to put our name on a waiting list, we would rarely provide our last name because we didn't want to have it announced over the intercom. My last name is fairly uncommon, so I feared people would peer at us with "that look" when it was announced. We would instead provide either our first names or a fictitious last name.

When shoppers use their customer discount card at Safeway grocery stores, cashiers are trained to look at the customer's last name printed on the receipt and speak it as they return the card and thank the customer. I usually stand there hoping they'll forget to read the name, or be unsure how to pronounce it, or speak it lightly, because I don't want that cashier or others in line to hear my name and glance at me with "that look."

Again, some people might find my discomfort difficult to understand. Why did I put myself in the public eye if I was uncomfortable with it? The answer is simple: when I spoke at a public event, I didn't mind being recognized as "that Columbine father" because I was there to speak as a

Columbine father and I was prepared for the attention and recognition. When I gave media interviews, it was somewhat impersonal, businesslike, and aimed at delivering a message to an audience.

In both cases I was in control, whereas in public I was not. In everyday situations I was vulnerable; I was being observed; I was alone in my grieving. I had an expectation, however terribly unrealistic, that I could somehow separate the public speaking and private life.

BEING FOLLOWED

It was a strange feeling being seen and read about in the media. It was exhilarating to be quoted and have people reading my opinions and following my reasoning. But it also was a great burden, because I'm a person who takes his work seriously, worries about how others view him, and is very self-critical. I knew that just as I could influence others with my words, I could also hurt my cause with a misstatement of facts, or a wayward comment, or any number of other mistakes that might be assailed by my opponents or exploited by an opportunistic reporter seeking to sensationalize a story.

I often saved newspaper clippings and television videos that featured me in some way. I did so only in part because of vanity. I mostly did so to critique my choice of words and find ways to improve my arguments and presentations. I'd often second-guess myself for not saying something in a different way, or I'd be mad at the media for the particular quote they chose. I was self-conscious about my appearance, particularly my idiosyncrasies, such as my tendency to open my eyes widely and raise my eyebrows excessively when speaking.

I tried not to let myself be overly impressed with the media attention and notoriety I received. When I was interviewed for a television news story, I seldom told friends or coworkers to "watch me on TV tonight." I didn't want to call unnecessary attention to myself, especially since I was not easily pleased with my work. Often I didn't even tell Linda I was going to be on TV; I knew she'd be concerned about how I would feel emotionally after giving an interview about Daniel or a pro-gun bill I was opposing. It wasn't unusual for her to find out about my interviews afterward from a friend and say something like, "Marlene said she saw you on TV last night. What was that all about?"

Even when I was going to appear on a national news program I rarely informed many family members or friends. I didn't think of those media appearances as anything special. For me, what I did wasn't "being on TV," it was painful and demanding work. I wouldn't invite my family or friends to a speech I was giving at work, so why would I do so for these interviews?

I tried not to let the media attention and notoriety make me big-headed. One way I did so was by downplaying the exposure I was getting. If I were quoted in the *Denver Post* or appeared in a local television news story, I told myself it was no big deal because we had two daily newspapers in Denver and five television news outlets, so I was missing much of the potential audience. If I were on a morning news program, I told myself most people were either asleep, preparing for work, or already on their way there.

For me, satisfaction came from knowing I was fighting for Daniel and changing minds, not from being in the public eye.

ADVOCACY'S HEARTACHES

It was difficult enough being the parent of a victim in a high-profile massacre. Becoming an advocate for a cause brought with it an additional glut of emotional highs and lows to deal with—joys and heartaches, thrilling victories and crushing defeats.

People often have said to me about my advocacy work, "It must give you lots of satisfaction to do things in your son's name." In most respects it does. I feel I am doing what Daniel would want me to do. I feel he is proud of what I am doing. There also is solace in knowing that one's work is appreciated by others. I'm proud of the awards I received for my advocacy. Being called someone's "hero" is both gratifying and humbling.

But there have also been many down sides to being a parent advocate. The toughest aspect was simply the fact that exposing myself to others usually meant repeatedly fielding those common, heartrending questions about Columbine: "How did you get the news about your son? Where were you? How did you feel? Is the pain still great after all these years?" I'm reminded of that tragedy every day, yet relating that story in front of strangers or a camera is still upsetting, regardless of how many times I do it.

One of the most difficult things for me to do, when speaking to a group, is simply saying those painful words: "I'm the father of Daniel Mauser, who was killed at Columbine High School...." They are words I speak in most public presentations, in front of church or school groups, press conferences, gun-control rallies, and civic club meetings. I usually cannot do so without getting choked up. You can see it in my appearance in Michael Moore's documentary, *Bowling For Columbine*.

In particular, I have trouble saying the words "Daniel" and "killed." Usually my head drops and the difficult words are muffled. I will generally regain my composure and continue without a significant problem, but then I am usually emotionally upset the rest of the day.

I never have gotten over it. It's as if it is fresh news when I speak those difficult words, and as if I don't want to acknowledge it.

HUMANITY'S UGLIER SIDE

Prior to Columbine, I led a rather uneventful private life. I am a bit shy but friendly and upbeat once I'm comfortable in my surroundings. I kept conversations polite, usually steering away from controversial issues with strangers or people I assumed might not share my personal, religious, or political beliefs. I tried not to hold grudges against those with whom I had disagreements. I usually avoided conflict rather than take it on, or at least sought an understanding middle ground.

I made few enemies in my lifetime. I spent most of my career as a manager and supervisor. Although I had disagreements with my employees or work colleagues, seldom do I think I was ever scorned or hated by them. Disagreements were civil, professional, and respectful.

That changed after Columbine. While I mostly encountered outpourings of love and the best of humanity, I also was thrust into a public arena where I found myself facing anger and belligerence.

It was something for which I was not well prepared. As a mild-mannered, likable person it was difficult for me to deal with suddenly being confronted by upset, strident, and even malicious people. Intuitively I knew that angry opposition simply went with the territory when dealing with an emotional event like Columbine and a divisive issue like gun control. But intuition didn't take away my uneasiness and anxiety.

I didn't have much choice but to try to develop a thicker skin and reluctantly learn to deal with it as best I could, telling myself I would not cower to people who thought nothing of treating me this way. But taking on adversity also came at a cost: even today my heart races and my muscles tense up when I face opposition.

COLUMBINE HEALING

I was often asked by the media and email writers how the Columbine community was healing. People wanted to know, for example, whether Columbine High School had returned to "normal" and whether the students who were in the library, cafeteria, or elsewhere in the school during the massacre were doing okay.

I was not the best person to answer such questions, since I was in the epicenter of this tragedy. It was hard for me to see through my own painful experience and have a clear and unbiased perspective of how the rest of the community was doing. In general, though, it seems the Columbine community in the middle and outer "rings" of the earthquake has returned to some degree of normalcy, if for no other reason than it had to.

The school largely healed with the passage of time, the turnover of teachers (some of whom left because it was just too painful to remain), and the arrival of a new generation of students who were too young at the time of the massacre to have been burdened with as many horrific memories. Still, today's students are all well aware of their school's dark and tragic past. It's impossible to escape.

There have been many efforts to honor the victims and take pride in the resiliency of the Columbine community, as evidenced by the many "We Are Columbine" bumper stickers once displayed on cars in the area. But there also has been concern that the Columbine community remains tainted by this tragedy. There are still parents who refuse to send their children to Columbine High School.

There still remain hard feelings and controversies. My elected state representatives, all pro-gun Republicans, seldom return my phone calls to their offices. The local newspaper continues to publish letters to the editor written by Randy and Judy Brown. The letters mostly remind people of the need to learn lessons from the many wrongs of the school and police and other public officials, but some in the community have responded with their own letters to complain about the Browns, saying it is time to "get over it" and not have to be reminded of the massacre.

But the Columbine community has also come together in some wonderful ways, including its effort to build a memorial to Columbine. Some observers lamented that it took so long after the tragedy to build a memorial. But one must consider the circumstances to understand why it took so long to do so.

Shortly after the massacre, people began making contributions for the construction of a memorial to the victims, even though no formal group had been established to build one. No formal memorial effort proceeded because the Columbine families and community concentrated on fundraising to replace the school's library—to us that was more important than a memorial.

Once the library was finished, plans to build a permanent memorial largely remained on hold because the Columbine families were exhausted from the library project and reluctant to ask the community for money for yet another project. Eventually, though, leaders in the Columbine community established a committee to work toward construction of a permanent memorial and raising the funds for it. Their efforts were bolstered by President Clinton, who contributed money to the project and twice came to Colorado to help with fundraising.

Plans were made to build the memorial in Clement Park, incorporating it into Rebel Hill, the small knoll a short distance from the school that became noted for the crosses erected at its top shortly after the massacre. A touching groundbreaking ceremony was held on June 16, 2006. President Clinton was in attendance. Columbine parent Dawn Anna Beck opened the ceremony with moving words that brought tears to many eyes. "They're here. Can you feel them? Our angels? Kyle, Kelly…"

Within a short while, strong winds rolled in. Thunder could be heard and lightning bolts could be seen not too far away, and both moved closer. A light rain began to fall. We were on a high point in the park and there were trees next to the stage. Danger was imminent, yet the ceremony forged ahead. Speeches were finished and ground was broken. The circumstances were eerily symbolic of the difficult time experienced by the

Columbine families and those community members who fought to build the memorial.

Ground was broken but all the funds were not yet raised. The project had to be scaled back, as it became clear it would be difficult to raise enough for the ambitious initial design. Thanks to dedicated people in the community, enough money was raised for the revised project. The memorial was dedicated in a wonderful ceremony on September 21, 2007.

The memorial serves to honor the victims but also to provide a historic record of the tragedy and deliver a message of hope for future generations. It's in a beautiful setting, at the high point of Clement Park. A sidewalk rises from the memorial and nearly encircles it, rising to the top of Rebel Hill where an overlook provides a panoramic view of the memorial and of the majestic foothills of the Rocky Mountains.

The memorial includes an outer Ring of Healing and an inner Ring of Remembrance. The outer ring contains the etched words of injured victims and those of other Columbine students, teachers, and staff as well as community members. Among my favorites were ones attributed to students:

- "I would be misleading you if I said I understand this. I don't."
- "My friend was laughing, and then it turned into crying, and I thought my God, why is this happening to us."
- "When my mom finally found me, she just couldn't seem to let go of me the rest of the day."

The inner Ring of Remembrance has thirteen stations, one for each of those killed, with engraved messages written by their families. The inspiring words on Daniel's station were beautifully penned by Linda.

The memorial is a wonderful gift to all who lost something that awful day. It was also a special gift to Columbine High School. For years people were coming to the high school to pay their respects. I heard stories of curious tourists and busloads of people driving around for a look at the school where the massacre took place. Some people even came onto the school grounds to gawk; some asked if they could walk through the school, while others did so without even bothering to ask.

It's difficult to return to any semblance of normalcy when such gawking distracts students. But then, what other single place could people go to see Columbine and pay their respects? The Columbine Memorial now provides such a place.

YES, BUT...

There are many people who prayed that those who were impacted by the Columbine massacre would be able to recover and heal. Their hope was that the students who were at Columbine that fateful day would be able to lead normal lives. Their hope was that the students who were in the library that day and survived could live without recurring images of the unspeakable carnage they witnessed. Their hope was that the physically and mentally injured would heal from their deep wounds. Their hope was that those who lost loved ones would find healing and peace.

Their prayers were heard and appreciated. Many were answered. There has been much healing, and there are many inspiring success stories arising from this tragedy. The Columbine community has shown its great strength, resilience, and big heart. The families of the victims have honored their children in countless ways and been a model for others suffering losses.

But this community should not be expected to achieve the impossible. No tragedy should be sugarcoated so others can feel relief. At times I felt there were people who only wanted to talk about signs of healing, as if they wanted to return to their lives feeling that everything was fine in Columbine and had returned to normal. That was true even here within the Columbine community, as demonstrated by people who didn't want to fully acknowledge the horror that occurred here, who didn't want to use the words "shootings," "guns," or "murders," or who only wanted to focus on the uplifting stories. But unless we acknowledge the pain, there can be no real healing.

Like millions of others before them who have lost a child, a spouse, a friend, or their innocence, the people of this community have suffered through unthinkable pain. There are still signs of post traumatic stress disorder in the community. In particular, I have heard that some students who survived the carnage in the library have struggled with PTSD.

The Columbine families and the Columbine community have each handled this tragedy differently. Some have seemingly coped well. Some have had a harder time doing so. Some have been greatly damaged. Some had a hard time at their job, in their marriages, or in their relationships. Some have found themselves going back and forth between healing and heartache, between hopelessness and hopefulness, between happiness and depression, and between resurrection and relapse. None of this should come as a surprise, for we in the Columbine community are no different than any other people who experience such a horrific event. We are all Columbine, after all.

Chapter 33

Thirteen Years On

I struggled with how to end this book. It's not as if there has been any clear "ending" to this story. I continue to grieve my loss, continue to advocate and continue to celebrate Daniel's life.

Perhaps I should simply end by answering the most basic questions that many of you have: How am I doing and how have I managed to make it through this tragedy? Why did "it" happen? Have I forgiven Eric Harris and Dylan Klebold? And, is there some greater lesson or meaning to it all?

BETTER

I know they're overused phrases, but they hold so true for me: The loss of a child is something you never get over. It's something you have to deal with every day the rest of your life. You learn to live with it. It gets a little better each day.

Hearing those observations coming from other parents who have lost children has helped me understand and get through this tragedy and heartache. Trying to live them has helped even more.

I have learned, as have many parents whose children have died, that the pain lessens over time but does not go away. It shouldn't. Only those who don't love their children could ever experience the complete loss of pain. But in honor of our children, and in recognition of the fact they would want our lives to be happy, we learn to survive without them.

Cindy Bullens's album had a fitting final track, titled, "Better Than I've Ever Been," where she sings with much emotion about how she was doing.

> *I laugh louder*
> *Cry harder*
> *I take less time to make up my mind and I*
> *Think smarter*
> *Go slower*
> *I know what I want*
> *And what I don't*
> *'n I'll be better than I've ever been*
> *Maybe I'll be better than I've ever been.*

They're powerful lyrics that reflect feelings I likewise have experienced. I find that I'm not as upset by some of the small hassles in life, for they pale in comparison to what I've lived through. Sometimes, for example, I get impatient with other people's everyday complaints and squabbling, believing that much of what preoccupies and bothers people is rather petty in the scheme of things.

When I am under stress at work, or when I am experiencing physical pain, I'm not as bothered as I was before Columbine, perhaps because I have come to realize that stress and pain are nothing compared to what I suffered through in 1999. I no longer find myself getting as caught up in the rat race. Seldom will you find me driving fast or aggressively to get somewhere or putting myself into debt buying things to "keep up with the Joneses."

I have learned to develop a thicker skin when criticized by others and am more inclined to take responsibility if I screw something up rather than be defensive or try to blame someone else. I have become more assertive and often am more straight-forward and blunt with people. Perhaps my frankness has been seen as careless or thoughtless at times, but for me it's a matter of deciding that life is too short to waste on "beating around the bush" or hiding one's feelings about something.

Life has settled down for us. Thirteen years on, we still live in our same house; we spoke of moving, but perhaps that was just an entertaining distraction. Linda has continued as a stay at home mom. I still work for the same agency. I received a promotion in 2001, though I suspect I was being rewarded for past performance more than performance at that time. Since then two other promotional opportunities have come along that would have been natural progressions for me, though that's certainly not to say I would have been selected. But I never even applied for the positions. While I enjoy my job and do well at it, getting more money and authority just doesn't hold great appeal to me now.

I have increasingly learned to deal better with what life has dealt me. I allow myself to be angry about what happened to Daniel, but not so much that it clouds my view of the world around me.

FAMILY STRONG

Much of the credit for being able to return to something closer to normalcy goes to my family. I discovered how much their support helped me based on something I knew about myself: that I am not someone who responds well to crises. If you are in a car accident or have a heart attack, I would probably be the last person you would want to show up on the scene to rescue you. While I can deal with everyday problems, I usually become flustered, anxious, disorganized and unable to be counted on to deal with major crises. Yet to some extent I was able to deal coherently with the Columbine crisis. It was largely because of the steady support of my family. We were able to come together and support each other, despite our difficult individual struggles.

There is no greater salve for pain than the love and support of one's family. Linda kept our family together and grounded while I was struggling to return to a routine at work and stressing myself out as a gun-control advocate. She challenged me along the way, questioning me as to whether I was taking on too much, though I often ignored her advice. And like many wives and mothers, she focused more on caring for the rest of us rather than on herself.

Christie was an inspiration for Linda and me, showing how one could keep one's head above water while swimming in an ocean of tears. Christie lost her brother, playmate and best friend. She was present when her friend next door was struck by a car and seriously injured, watched as she struggled out of a coma, then mourned that friend's death a year later. Not a lot of young people have to face so much tragedy.

Christie had to deal with thoughtless middle school students who didn't know how to treat her with empathy. She was given some counseling by the school system, and we had her meet with our grief counselor a few times, but what she probably needed was more time, understanding and support from Linda and me. We did at times, but too often we were incapacitated, dealing with our own pain. I regret not providing her more support in the weeks, months and years following her troubles.

Years after the massacre she told us she often felt unlike her middle-schoolmates, showing little interest in boys, video games or other pursuits common among her peers. Christie showed some interest in acting prior to the massacre, and she had some genuine talent, but troubles and tragedies put a damper on any hope of fully following through on her ambition. One summer after Columbine she participated in an acting workshop, but we didn't demonstrate enough support for her interest, and our adoption of Madeline distracted us. Christie's interest in acting died on the vine as a result.

Christie easily could have lost her positive outlook on life after what she had been through. She did not. She worked in a bagel shop during her high school years. After dropping Madeline off at a Chinese cultural class on Saturday mornings, I would often drop in to the shop on busy Saturday mornings without her noticing me. I was proud as I observed how pleasant, friendly, upbeat and conscientious she was with her customers.

Christie weathered the Columbine storm, graduating from Fort Lewis College in 2008 with a bachelor's degree in sociology—and she did it in four years! After college her first job was as a counselor for troubled teen girls in a residential facility. It was a grueling job, dealing with girls who were suicidal, emotionally unstable, and prone to harming themselves physically. It was challenging to be in such a thankless and negative environment for a young woman who was so upbeat and had such a positive view of the world around her, but she handled it well for her two years there. I'm sure there were young women she helped in unseen ways.

In 2011 Christie moved to the San Francisco bay area, where a good friend lived. Like me when I moved from Pittsburgh to Denver, she had no job prospects when she moved, only a strong desire to make the move work for her. As a parent I obviously was disappointed to see her move so far away. But it occurred to me that her move was like her father's. She wanted to embark on a new life and put behind her some painful memories. I think she wanted to make her own identity and not be known primarily as the sister of a Columbine victim.

Madeline has been our spark plug, full of energy and wit. She is growing up and becoming a charming and intelligent girl. Like Linda and me, she is shy around strangers, but more talkative around those with whom she's comfortable. She has done well at nearly everything she's been exposed to—including piano, art, gymnastics, soccer, swimming, cross country skiing, and ice skating. She's an excellent student, having earned her way into the gifted and talented program in middle school. She likes animals, YouTube, computer and video games, and, like her mom, is a voracious reader.

We started telling Madeline about her brother Daniel from an early age, sharing that he had died. After all, she was bound to ask who the boy was in the pictures around the house. We were not going to hide his sad story from her, though we presented information to her thoughtfully and progressively, sparing her the darker details of his death.

There are people who claim that having a young child at an older age somehow helps keep you feeling young. It's true! I'm losing my hair and my hearing, and I have more aches and pains to deal with, yet I believe that in other respects I have maintained a younger outlook on life than many others in my age group—thanks to Madeline. Because of my desire to keep up with Madeline and be able to play with her, I work to keep myself in better physical shape. I still ride my bike, jog, toss a mean Frisbee, and hike 14,000-foot mountain peaks. I certainly feel odd and old when I go to a school function and see parents of Madeline's classmates who are in their 30s and 40s. But, so what? I may be older but I have an appreciation and understanding of parenthood and life that some of them could only dream of having.

ALL FOR A REASON?

Some people insist that God "allowed" Columbine to happen in order to awaken America to the need for more spirituality or to prevent other school shootings. If that's the case, it was a miserable failure, for we continue to have school shootings and we continue to be more spiritually polarized in this country, not more united. We continue to have a bullying problem in our schools and we still see religion used to justify attacks on people who are different or have differing beliefs.

Some people believe all things happen for a reason, that there is a greater good that comes from tragedies, and that God's hand is directly on those things. I don't profess to know why God does what He does, but I don't believe that a loving God would "allow" tragedies to happen as a means of teaching us a lesson. After all, we already should know those lessons. We should all know that parents must pay more attention to their children, that bullying is wrong, and that we are in need of more spirituality. Do we really need to continually experience tragedies to learn these lessons? Should we not act to correct the things we know to be wrong rather than need to be tragically "reminded" by God?

Let's not blame tragedies on God. Too often it is we who fail to prevent these human tragedies, perhaps because we're careless, ignorant, or uncaring. Too often we experience violence like Columbine's because there are lost souls who feel they are tortured and unloved by the world around them. *We* are the world around them. Often this type of violence happens because we live in an impersonal, individualistic society where too few people are willing or able to intervene in troubled lives. It happens because not enough people are tuned in to the lives and the cries for help of disaffected, tormented, disillusioned, or mentally disturbed people. It happens because we have become a society too tolerant of violence, too accepting of social injustices, and too awash with the means for committing violence. It happens because we live in a society that has tolerated too many expressions of unbridled anger and rage.

Violent tragedies too often occur in America because we are more concerned with our material wealth than with our spiritual wealth; more concerned with moving up and not enough with moving closer together; more concerned with power than cooperation; more focused on what makes us different than in what makes us the same; more intent on making others like us than in being more accepting of others' differences; more consumed with confrontation than with compassion; and more attracted to achieving personal success than on building caring relationships.

WHY?

They are the questions that linger to this day: why did two teenage boys plot for more than a year to kill hundreds of their classmates? And why did one of them look right at Daniel and purposely choose to shoot him? *Why?*

Some will say this book is incomplete if I don't answer those burning questions. How can I make sense of Daniel's death if I don't try to explain why I think he was murdered?

Being the father of a victim doesn't endow me with special powers to ascertain those answers. Only God knows. But since He hasn't clued me in, and since I've obviously studied this tragedy, I'll offer my thoughts.

I agree with those who argue that Eric Harris was a psychopath. From all I've seen and read, he detested much of the world around him and blamed the world for what he saw as the injustices done to him. I suspect his mental illness greatly poisoned his perception of what he considered injustices. That is, although I don't doubt that bullying greatly increased Harris's anger toward the world, I think it was something that also was heightened by his contempt for the world and his belief the world was responsible for his woes. After all, many kids are bullied but few become murderers as a result.

What Eric Harris really wanted was what all of us really want—to be loved, included, and accepted. But if you are mentally ill, make yourself socially and behaviorally different from others (and are uncomfortable with those differences), shut the world out, and develop contempt for the world around you, there will likely be serious discord and conflict.

Harris apparently believed he was far superior to the world around him, but down deep inside I believe he hated himself. That's why he was determined to commit suicide. But like other angry people in this disgruntled and violent nation, he wasn't going to do it without showing his contempt by taking others with him.

As for Dylan Klebold, I believe he also was mentally ill, suffering from severe depression and a poor self-image. He was mostly a follower, feeding off the rage of Harris. I don't think he would have become a mass murderer on his own, without the prodding of someone like Harris. But in saying that, I do not mean to imply that Klebold is somehow less responsible than Harris for what happened at Columbine. For more than a year, the two of them plotted to murder hundreds of classmates, so there was plenty of time for Klebold to remove himself from their devious plot. More important, it should never be forgotten that Klebold chose to pull a trigger repeatedly that fateful day.

There are those who argue that blaming the massacre on mental illness is a cop-out designed to ignore the other factors at play. While placing much responsibility on mental illness, I also recognize there were many other factors at play: students teased, taunted, humiliated, and bullied the killers; students, friends, teachers, and the killers' parents failed to see the rage that was building in the killers; and the police failed to act in response to Harris's threats. But none of those things directly caused the mental illness at the core of those two troubled teens. Mental illness, exacerbated by bullying, was at the heart of the question "why?"

NOT DEFEATED

Eric Harris and Dylan Klebold got the world's attention—too much of it, in fact. Their actions will, unfortunately, not be forgotten because people are fascinated with the criminal mind and captivated by this catastrophic story of young people committing such carnage. But the attention and notoriety the Columbine killers have received is not an indication they ultimately "succeeded." Their actions and deaths were tragic and criminal, not triumphant, heroic, or sacrificial. The killers succeeded only in murdering, in garnering pity and scorn, and in shaming and failing their parents.

The killers did not destroy the Columbine families' spirits. It is the victims' families who have triumphed. The Columbine families replaced the library where much of the carnage took place. We established countless memorial funds that promote good in the world. Three families adopted children. Some brought about changes in gun laws. Some helped establish programs addressing bullying, peacemaking, and spiritual reflection. We inspired others by telling the stories of our loved ones' lives.

The Columbine families ensured that the world will remember the victims, even if they're not easily recognized by their names. Sadly, for years to come, many more people will remember the names of the killers and not those of the victims. That's because it is easier to remember two names rather than thirteen, but also because the media and public too often focus more on the perpetrators of crime than on its innocent victims. What's more important, though, is that people will remember that there were many special, positive stories behind the victims of this tragedy, even if they don't remember their names.

Yes, the killers managed, albeit in a dreadful way, to bring attention to some serious problems and injustices afflicting our youth. But they should not be thanked for that, for they demonstrated they had absolutely no courage or tenacity to deal with the problems and injustices they encountered. They surrendered to their rage rather than deal with it. They were disturbed kids, not martyrs who had no choice. They still had some sense of right and wrong.

There will continue to be bullied young people who admire these two wretched losers, but they will remain only a sliver of the population. It will continue to be up to the rest of us to lovingly reach out to those few if we hope to avoid such tragedies in the future.

A NEW NORMAL

While I was in a grocery store a few weeks after the tenth anniversary, I ran into a woman from my former church. I knew her before Columbine but hadn't seen her for at least eight years. She told me she had seen me on the news recently and was glad to see that I looked so much better and happier than she had seen me since the tragedy.

At first I was upset and perplexed by what she said. But then it occurred to me that for years she only saw me on TV, not in person. It was probably difficult for people who didn't see me in everyday life to understand how my life was progressing. People who only saw me on TV news stories probably saw me as an intense, serious, and often sad person. No doubt that's how I came across, since I was usually speaking about a gun bill or was reflecting on a school shooting somewhere. Those appearances were serious ones, not ones intended to be upbeat. Some people just didn't realize they were only seeing one aspect of my life.

I admire the tagline used by a group called Murder Victims' Families for Reconciliation, an organization of families whose loved ones were murdered but who oppose the death penalty. The group's mailings post the banner, "Reconciliation means accepting you cannot undo the murder but you can decide how to live afterwards." That's what's most important here for me. I decided to be reconciled to it and to live on afterward and not let Eric Harris and Dylan Klebold destroy my life.

Few would want to have their entire life gauged, driven, or destroyed by one singular event, but the loss of a child is certainly one event that has the power to do so. It is a tremendous test of one's spirit and will. The Columbine massacre was such a test for me—something like no other event I had ever experienced.

If Eric Harris and Dylan Klebold had had their way, it would have destroyed me. I didn't let it do so. I am not exactly the same person I was before Columbine, but I have survived and have grown emotionally. I have settled on my "new normal," living in a new world without Daniel. I still have a serious, quiet side, but my carefree and humorous side has returned. I still make people laugh with my humorous slide shows, play practical jokes, and use my dry wit to entertain. It's the way I'm sure Daniel would want it to be.

Recently someone I knew professionally asked a puzzling question: "So, do you feel you've been able to return to the normalcy there was in your life before Columbine?" I was thrown by that for it implied some larger questions, including, "What is normalcy after the death of your child?" and "Is that what I should be expecting—to feel like I did before the massacre, to somehow live life like I did back then?"

"No," I told him, "life is just what it is now." I can't go back to my life before April 20, 1999, and I shouldn't be expected to do so. The measurement of success in my dealing with grief is not how well I turn back the clock. I can't do that. But what I can do is develop a new sense of "normal."

This new normal is based on keeping Daniel in my thoughts, honoring him, and keeping his loss in perspective. It's based on accepting new things in my life, including Madeline, wonderful new friends, and an inspiring new church.

It's not a case of the 15 years before Columbine being "better" years and the years since then being abnormal or horrific. Those 15 years when Daniel was in my life were wonderful, but I cannot hope to return to those years. What I can hope for is not to be sad because of that. There's no reason to be. My hope lies in trying to make the best out of this new normal.

FORGIVENESS FOR THE KILLERS?

I still haven't answered the lingering question of whether I have forgiven Eric Harris and Dylan Klebold for the Columbine massacre and for murdering Daniel. Unfortunately, we live in a world where many people expect you to provide a simple, yes-or-no response to questions—yet in the next breath might chastise you for not taking into account the gray in between. I resent those demands for a black-or-white response to the question of forgiveness, for this world is indeed filled with much gray.

What's most important for me is that my anger toward the killers is not something that consumes me. In the months following the massacre, I was obviously angry at the killers. How the hell could I not be? How could I even entertain the thought of forgiveness in those early months and years?

As time went on, though, my thoughts shifted, largely because of my spiritual beliefs related to forgiveness. It is my belief people who are not willing to forgive, or who seek revenge or carry lingering anger, are in essence questioning God. Christians are taught that God will pass His judgment on us. Then who are we to instead pass that judgment or to not allow that person to redeem themselves? Too often, especially in America, people seek relentless revenge when they should instead seek measured and appropriate punishment. Those who seek overly harsh punishment, or are unwilling to offer forgiveness, are essentially not trusting that God will pass a just judgment on those people in the hereafter, deciding they must instead seek revenge here on earth.

I trust God to pass judgment, whether it's judgment on the person who steals, assaults, shows no compassion toward those who are less fortunate, kills a person while driving drunk, knowingly harms the environment, bullies others, is materialistic, or murders students at their school. Would God send any or all of these sinners to the depths of hell? Damned if I know. None of us knows, and it's none of our business. I leave that to God, for it's something I can't control. I simply trust that God's punishment will be just and believe that our punishment in this world should be likewise.

I am reconciled to my belief that Eric Harris and Dylan Klebold were mentally disturbed young men who so hated themselves and those who mistreated them, and so blamed the world around them for their misery, that they felt the need to end their lives and those of others around them.

I am reconciled to my belief that the killers did not kill Daniel because of who he was or what he had done to them. They killed Daniel because they could, because he was there, because they had the power to do so, and because they wanted to exercise power over life and death. In particular, though, I believe Eric Harris killed Daniel because he dared to challenge that power by fighting back when he defiantly and bravely pushed a chair toward Harris.

Still, I admit I cannot yet bring myself to forgive Eric Harris and Dylan Klebold for the act of murdering Daniel and the other twelve, for injuring twenty-five others, and for doing such deep and unending harm to an entire community. I fear that offering full forgiveness at this time sends the message to other troubled people that murder is somehow "the only way out" and can easily be forgiven and forgotten. They cannot.

But I can and do forgive Eric Harris and Dylan Klebold for being two tragic, hopeless characters who were mentally ill. I can forgive them for that because, after all, the world collectively bears a shred of responsibility for not reaching out and doing more to save poor, lonely, disturbed souls like theirs.

PROUD FATHER

As I wrote earlier, I didn't have a good relationship with my father. It wasn't much of a relationship at all, unless you consider fear, disregard, and apathy the basis for a father-son relationship. I have almost no memories of my father, let alone positive ones. There was no bond between us.

For years I feared the lack of a relationship with my father meant it would have a negative impact on my life, predisposing me to being a poor or clueless father. In my 20s I wondered if I had the makings for being a good father and never dreamed of having children of my own. That was the last thing on my mind.

But in my 30s I came to understand my negative experience with my father instead had a profoundly positive impact on me. I decided I *wanted* to have kids, because I was determined to *never* be the kind of father mine was with me, just as I had decided I wanted a better education than my dad, just as I did not want to be abusive of those close to me, and just as I never wanted to constantly hang out at a tavern the way he did. I was determined that my kids and I would play together, eat out together, travel together, have fun together, and be a family together.

One way to deal with a painful tragedy is to think of how much worse life could have been for you. The Columbine tragedy would have been far worse for me if Daniel had died and I was burdened with guilt about not having been close to him, or not having spend enough time with him, or not having given him enough of my love. I can't say I couldn't have spent more time with him, or that I couldn't have been closer to him. But that's probably true of many loving fathers. When Daniel died, though, I wasn't left with any major regrets regarding my relationship with him. I could say I was satisfied that we had a good relationship and that we truly loved each other.

I learned to make up for my father's poor modeling. I gave Daniel what my father failed to give me. I gave Daniel a good life for his 15 years and ten months on this earth. And now I'm so pleased I've been able to continue with a new kind of relationship with him, doing things to honor him and sharing his story with so many new people. I'm thrilled that so many strangers have learned about Daniel through my works and through his Web site.

I don't expect others to think of Daniel as some kind of hero or saint. If he is, he is one among many on this earth. I want him to be remembered as a great kid, a lovable child who didn't have a hateful bone in his body. And someone who was so undeserving of being murdered.

Daniel was a kid who didn't blame the world for his problems or weaknesses. He was instead a kid who took them on.

Not a day has passed in all these years that I haven't thought in some way of Daniel. He is my hero. He is my guardian angel. I am proud to walk in his shoes.

Acknowledgments

My deepest appreciation goes to Linda, Christie and Madeline, who were so understanding over the last three years as I wrote this book and often was so unavailable, distracted, or cranky.

Thanks to my best friend Steve Wewer and others for encouraging me to not give up on this book.

Thanks to the many people in the gun control movement who have inspired and educated me, especially Jim and Sarah Brady and others who became active after experiencing tragedy.

Thanks to my friend Rolland Douglas for the cover photo, taken at the Columbine Memorial Garden at Chapel Hill Cemetery, where there are thirteen crosses for those slain at Columbine.

Thanks to Arnie Grossman, John Head, and other leaders of SAFE Colorado for giving me the opportunity to act on Daniel's message.

Thanks to Cynthia Pasquale and Sue Collier for their excellent editing. At work I considered myself a good proofreader and editor, but that kind of writing is far different. I learned that writing a book was far more challenging. Additional thanks to Sue for taking on the self-publishing tasks with such a short deadline.

Thanks to "4-20: A Columbine Site by Cyn Shepard," *www.acolumbinesite.com*, which helped as I put together the chronology.

Thanks to David Henry Sterry for his advice and assistance.

Thanks to God for giving me the tools to deal with this tragedy.

And, of course, the greatest acknowledgment goes to Daniel, for inspiring me and serving as my hero.

A Chronology

June 25, 1983—Daniel Conner Mauser is born

September 11, 1983—Daniel baptized at St. Elizabeth Church in Denver

April 21, 1991—Daniel receives first Holy Communion at St. Frances Cabrini Church in Littleton

April 20, 1999—The massacre at Columbine High School

April 21, 1999—Police officially confirm Daniel's death

April 23, 1999—Wake for Daniel, Kelly Fleming, and Matt Kechter at St. Frances Cabrini Church.

April 25, 1999—Public memorial service for Columbine victims at Bowles Crossing shopping center

April 25, 1999—Funerals for Kelly Fleming and Daniel Mauser held jointly at St. Frances Cabrini Church.

April 26, 1999—Private burial service for Daniel at Mt. Olivet Cemetery

May 1, 1999—Rally protesting NRA Convention in Denver is held on west steps of Colorado State Capitol; Tom addresses crowd

May 4, 1999—Tom gives his first national television interview, on the NBC Today show

May 8, 1999—Tom makes presentation on gun violence prevention at White House event hosted by First Lady Hillary Clinton

May 11, 1999—Tom sends letter to NRA President Charlton Heston

May 20, 1999—President Bill Clinton and First Lady Hillary Clinton meet with the Columbine families at Light of the World Catholic Church

June 1999—Daniel Mauser memorial website goes online

Fall 1999—Columbine families form HOPE

November 22, 1999 (est.)—Liu Hai Xing is born in Liuzhou, China and abandoned approximately two weeks later

January 3, 2000—Tom's first day of as lobbyist for SAFE Colorado

January 20, 2000—Jefferson County school board approves HOPE's plans to demolish the old library at Columbine and build an atrium in its place.

January 27, 2000—Daniel and Tom are honored during President Clinton's State of the Union address

February 11, 2000—House Bill 1242, which would have closed the gun show loophole in Colorado, was defeated in the House Appropriations Committee

March 2000—Mausers travel to Guatemala to visit facilities built with funds raised in Daniel's name

April 12, 2000—President Clinton attends a SAFE Colorado rally in Denver to promote the closing of the so-called Gun Show Loophole

May 2, 2000—HOPE reaches its goal of $3.1 million needed to replace the old library with an atrium and build a new library

May 3, 2000—First petition signatures were collected on the steps of the State Capitol for Amendment 22

August 2, 2000—SAFE Colorado turns in 110,000 petition signatures to the Colorado Secretary of State to place Amendment 22 on the Colorado ballot in November

August 19, 2000—Atrium dedicated at Columbine High School

October 16, 2000—Liu Hai Xing is handed over to Tom and Linda for adoption in Nanning, China

November 7, 2000—Amendment 22 is passed by the voters of Colorado by a margin of 70% to 30%

December 1, 2000—Tom leaves job at SAFE Colorado and returns to job at the Colorado DOT

February 10, 2001—Neighbor Ali Meyer is struck by car while crossing S. Pierce St. with Christie

June 9, 2001—New library at Columbine High School is dedicated

June 13, 2001—Tom arrested for trespassing in parking lot of NRA headquarters

September 2001—Tom is interviewed by Michael Moore for inclusion in an upcoming documentary film

December 14, 2001—Members of the Tyranny Response Team protest in front of the Mauser home

October 18, 2002—Tom and Linda attend a private showing of Moore's documentary, Bowling for Columbine; Denver premier follows the next evening

November 22, 2002—Ali Meyer passes away

February 24, 2004—Jefferson County holds a private exhibition for the

Columbine families, displaying all the evidence related to the Columbine massacre; exhibition is opened to the public the following day

Fall, 2004—Jefferson County Sheriff's Office releases final personal belongings of the Columbine victims; Tom obtains shoes wore by Daniel on April 20, 1999

April 5, 2005—Tom arrested for second time while trespassing in parking lot of NRA headquarters

June 16, 2006—Ground is broken for the Columbine Memorial

January 2007—Tom writes a letter to the parents of Eric Harris; that summer he meets with Harris' attorney

June 1, 2007—Gun activist Darren Morrison is sentenced to five days in jail for threatening Tom

September 2007—Tom writes a letter to the Klebolds, followed shortly thereafter by a meeting with Sue Klebold

September 21, 2007—The Columbine Memorial is dedicated

July 15, 2009—Tom and Linda meet with Wayne and Kathy Harris

Spring 2009—Tom begins writing of book

January 2012—Tom finishes final text of book

April 20, 2012—Completion of book is announced

Links and Resources

To make this book more resourceful and alive, links are being provided so readers can view referenced documents in detail and can view video of Daniel and his family. To spare the reader having to write down these links, they have been placed on Daniel's website exclusively for book purchasers at **www.danielmauser.com/booklinks.html**. Below is a sampling of what can be found there.

YouTube video of Daniel at various times of his life, and things done in his name by his father. "A Tribute to Columbine Victim Daniel Mauser," at **http://www.youtube.com/watch?v=SIz0ixdLFA0**

Tom's Amendment 22 victory speech. **http://www.youtube.com/watch?v=w_1pJavyjXU**

Tom's video response to Harris and Klebold admirers. **http://www.youtube.com/watch?v=8kBuLYYdn1w&feature=youtube_gdata**

Photos found in this book and many more. **www.danielmauser.com/bookphotos.html**

Photos from the spontaneous memorial in Clement Park at **www.danielmauser.com/Spontaneous.html**.

Tom's letter to Charlton Heston, dated May 11, 1999. **www.danielmauser.com/HestonLetter.html**

To those interested in getting involved in the struggle for stronger gun laws, you are encouraged to examine the following websites and to join both the Brady Campaign as well as your state gun control organization.

Brady Center to Prevent Gun Violence: **http://www.bradycenter.org/**

Brady Campaign to Prevent Gun Violence: **http://www.bradycampaign.org/**

Note: The Brady Center is the advocacy organization and the Brady Campaign is the lobbying arm; the NRA is also set up with a membership arm and a lobbying arm.

Violence Policy Center: **http://www.vpc.org/**

States United Against Gun Violence: **http://www.supgv.org/**

Note: Here you can find names of affiliated state organizations. If your state isn't listed, Google gun control + your state's name; if you find nothing—well, what are you waiting for! Start one!

Mayors Against Illegal Guns: **http://www.mayorsagainstillegal-guns.org/**

Note: See if YOUR mayor is listed as a member; if not—what are you waiting for?

Legal Community Against Violence: **http://www.lcav.org/**

And one other important address—that of the NRA headquarters. I ask all readers to flood the NRA with letters asking why they haven't responded to my letter.

President

National Rifle Association

11250 Waples Mill Road

Fairfax, Virginia 22030